MINDING THE BUDDHA'S BUSINESS

Studies in Indian and Tibetan Buddhism

This series was conceived to provide a forum for publishing outstanding new contributions to scholarship on Indian and Tibetan Buddhism and also to make accessible seminal research not widely known outside a narrow specialist audience, including translations of appropriate monographs and collections of articles from other languages. The series strives to shed light on the Indic Buddhist traditions by exposing them to historical-critical inquiry, illuminating through contextualization and analysis these traditions' unique heritage and the significance of their contribution to the world's religious and philosophical achievements.

Members of the Editorial Board

Tom Tillemans (co-chair), Emeritus, University of Lausanne
Leonard van der Kuijp (co-chair), Harvard University
Shrikant Bahulkar, Bhandarkar Oriental Research Institute
José Cabezón, University of California, Santa Barbara
Georges Dreyfus, Williams College, Massachusetts
Vincent Eltschinger, École Pratique des Hautes Études
Janet Gyatso, Harvard University
Paul Harrison, Stanford University
Toni Huber, Humboldt University, Berlin
Pascale Hugon, Austrian Academy of the Sciences
Shoryu Katsura, Ryukoku University, Kyoto
Kataoka Kei, Kyushu University, Fukuoka
Thupten Jinpa Langri, Institute of Tibetan Classics, Montreal
Chenkuo Lin, National Chengchi University, Taipei
Hong Luo, Peking University
Cristina Scherrer-Schaub, University of Lausanne
Ernst Steinkellner, Emeritus, University of Vienna
Jan Westerhoff, Oxford University
Jeson Woo, Dongguk University, Seoul
Shaoyong Ye, Peking University
Chizuko Yoshimizu, Tsukuba University

STUDIES IN INDIAN AND TIBETAN BUDDHISM

Minding the Buddha's Business

Essays in Honor of Gregory Schopen

Edited by Daniel Boucher and Shayne Clarke

Wisdom

Wisdom Publications, Inc.
132 Perry Street
New York, NY 10014 USA
wisdom.org

Library of Congress Cataloging-in-Publication Data
Names: Schopen, Gregory, honoree. | Boucher, Daniel, editor. | Clarke, Shayne, editor.
Title: Minding the Buddha's business: essays in honor of Gregory Schopen / edited by Daniel Boucher and Shayne Clarke.
Description: First edition. | New York, NY, USA: Wisdom, [2025] | Series: Studies in Indian and Tibetan Buddhism | Includes bibliographical references.
Identifiers: LCCN 2024042778 (print) | LCCN 2024042779 (ebook) | ISBN 9781614297482 (hardcover) | ISBN 9781614297635 (ebook)
Subjects: LCSH: Mahayana Buddhism—India—History. | Monastic and religious life (Buddhism)—India—History. | Buddhist monasticism and religious orders—India—Rules. | Buddhist art—India—History. | Buddhist literature, Sanskrit—India—History and criticism.
Classification: LCC BQ300 .M563 2025 (print) | LCC BQ300 (ebook) | DDC 294.3/920954—dc23/eng/20241209
LC record available at https://lccn.loc.gov/2024042778
LC ebook record available at https://lccn.loc.gov/2024042779

ISBN 978-1-61429-748-2 ebook ISBN 978-1-61429-763-5

29 28 27 26 25 5 4 3 2 1

Cover image: Buddha giving safety to mariners (minding his and their business?). Illustrated palm-leaf manuscript dated to ca. 1090 CE from India (Bengal) or Bangladesh. Courtesy of The Metropolitan Museum of Art, New York.
Cover and interior design by Gopa & Ted 2, Inc..
Typeset by Tony Lulek.

Printed on acid-free paper that meets the guidelines for permanence and durability of the Production Guidelines for Book Longevity of the Council on Library Resources.

Printed in the United States of America.

Publisher's Acknowledgment

The publisher gratefully acknowledges the generous help of the Hershey Family Foundation in sponsoring the production of this book.

Contents

Preface ix

Introduction 1
Daniel Boucher and Shayne Clarke

PART 1. MAHĀYĀNA AND TANTRA STUDIES

The Visualization Stage (*utpattikrama*) and Its Workings 27
Yael Bentor

Orality, Literacy, and the Cult of the Book in Early Mahāyāna Revisited 45
Daniel Boucher

Practice in Text: Words and Wordplay in a Mahāyāna Sūtra 95
Jason McCombs

Writing the Word of the Buddha: An Instance of Redaction Practice in a "Middle Period" Mahāyāna Sūtra 117
Andrew Skilton

PART 2. MONASTICISM AND VINAYA STUDIES

A Preliminary Survey of Viśākha(deva)'s *Bhikṣuvinayakārikākusumasraj* 155
Shayne Clarke

Buddhist Monks, Outdated Technology, and Meditation 201
Kate Crosby

Forms of Intertextuality and Lost Sanskrit Verses of the *Buddhacarita*: The *Tridaṇḍaka* and the *Tridaṇḍamālā* 225
Jens-Uwe Hartmann

The Double Life of *Gahapati* 255
Stephanie W. Jamison

A Preliminary Report on the *Vinayasaṃgraha*: *Viśeṣamitra's Discussion Following *Pāyantikā* 72 279
Ryōji Kishino

Marginalia to an Endnote: More on the *Tridaṇḍaka* 321
Diego Loukota Sanclemente†

Saṅghabheda: Monastic and Political 349
Patrick Olivelle

The Evolution of the First *Nissaggiya-pācittiya* and the *Bodhisattvabhūmi* 365
Shizuka Sasaki

PART 3. EPIGRAPHICAL AND ART-HISTORICAL STUDIES

King Pūrṇavarman's Fiery Feet 389
Robert L. Brown

Making Room for the Buddha: The Rise of the Buddhist Image Cult at the Kānherī Caves 399
Robert DeCaroli

Sambhoga-grāma in the Jetavanārāma Sanskrit Inscription 423
Petra Kieffer-Pülz

Art and Practice in a Fifth-Century Indian Buddhist Cave Temple: A New Identification of an Old Mahāyāna Painting at Ajaṇṭā 441
Nicolas Morrissey

The Visuality of Sukhāvatī, Chinese Depictions, and Early Indian Images 479
Juhyung Rhi

Schism and Sectarian Conflicts as Revealed—and Concealed—in Indian Buddhist Inscriptions 513
Richard Salomon

About the Contributors 539

Preface

THE GENESIS of this volume is a bit hazy. A few of Gregory Schopen's former students had been raising the topic of a Festschrift from time to time when we'd see each other at various academic gatherings. It's a familiar academic dance, each side hoping the other would take the initiative to get the thing going. One thing we could all agree on: Gregory certainly deserved to be honored. Finally Daniel sent an email to Shayne in the spring of 2017 to inquire if anyone was seriously contemplating such a project. Shayne agreed that it was time and noted that he was indeed contemplating such an endeavor himself (he had started initial planning of a clandestine volume with prompting and advice from Diego Loukota Sanclemente, Stephanie Jamison, and Alice Fleming). After a few back-and-forths, we agreed to undertake the project together. It was a fitting pairing, with Daniel having worked with Gregory near the very beginning of his teaching career at Indiana University and Shayne coming along later at the University of California, Los Angeles (UCLA). Topically too, we nicely encapsulated some of Schopen's range. Gregory's early interest in Mahāyāna literature had rubbed off on Daniel and precipitated his own academic journey through the problems and promises of that field. And Shayne would go on to extend Gregory's deep engagement in Sanskrit, Pāli, and Tibetan Vinaya materials into the rich array of available Chinese and Japanese sources.

The timing of these conversations was also fortunate, as the 18th Congress of the International Association of Buddhist Studies was to convene that August in Toronto, where conversations with both contributors and presses could take place in person. We found many scholars supportive of this project, well beyond the number who could commit to a contribution. We were especially fortunate to have received very enthusiastic interest from David Kittelstrom of Wisdom Publications, who immediately committed to the publication of the Festschrift at a time when many presses shy away from them. David has since remained as supportive as he has been patient in seeing this to fruition.

This volume has brought together both former students of Gregory's as well as long-term admirers of his work. Additionally, the contributions to this volume have largely mirrored the range of Schopen's primary interests: Mahāyāna literature, monasticism and Vinaya studies, and epigraphical and art-historical sources for the study of Buddhism. None of us could imagine our work in Buddhist studies today without the legacy of Gregory Schopen's trailblazing articles over almost a half century. Serving early in his career as Vice-President (1996–2002) of the International Association of Buddhist Studies, Schopen published no fewer than nine articles in the association's official organ, the *Journal of the International Association of Buddhist Studies*, for which he also served as co-editor (1986–1989). Schopen's earliest articles appeared in the *Indo-Iranian Journal*, and several more were published in the *Journal of the American Oriental Society*, *East and West*, *History of Religions*, and the *Journal of Indian Philosophy*. Still more of Schopen's articles have appeared in volumes dedicated to other scholars of Buddhism, both living and deceased, and in monographs on topics as diverse as specific Buddhist sacred sites and devotional objects in global perspective. Indeed so diffuse have been the venues for Schopen's articles that it has only been with the publication of four volumes of his collected papers by the University of Hawai'i Press that many scholars have discovered anew the range of his scholarly contributions.

The editors would like to note that all of the contributions to this volume have been anonymously peer reviewed. We would like to extend our gratitude to the many scholars who offered their help, sometimes more than once and in multiple rounds, to produce the best possible tribute we could for Gregory. The editors also wish to acknowledge the generous publication subventions from Cornell University and McMaster University's Centre for Buddhist Studies.

Introduction

Daniel Boucher and Shayne Clarke

BORN AND RAISED in Deadwood, South Dakota, Gregory Schopen first discovered Buddhism when he read a translation of the *Laṅkāvatāra-sūtra* in high school. As he would later advise his undergraduate students, "Be very careful what you read, because you never know where it's going to lead you." Unlike a number of his contemporaries (and future colleagues), Schopen did not run off to a Zen monastery to seek enlightenment. Instead he would major in American literature at Black Hills State College in Spearfish, South Dakota. His undergraduate experience, however, would include a detour to the University of Washington because he was pursuing a particular girl. There he would make a fateful acquaintance with both the inimitable Edward Conze and Luis Gómez and receive his first formal introduction to Sanskrit and the academic study of Buddhism. Schopen continued his forays in Buddhist studies at McMaster University in Ontario, Canada, where he would study with Jan Yün-hua and train in Sanskrit under Ronald Morton Smith and in classical Tibetan with Shōryū Katsura (both of the University of Toronto), completing his master's degree in 1975. It was at McMaster that several of Schopen's lasting interests were forged, most especially in the study of Mahāyāna sūtra literature. His master's thesis included a chapter on the cult of the book in the early Mahāyāna, a study that would become his first publication and one that radically transformed the scholarly conversation concerning the sociological origins of this movement. It was also at McMaster that he first took an interest in the Gilgit corpus and in particular the *Bhaiṣajyaguru-sūtra*, a "middle period" text that would become the focus of his PhD thesis. Jan Willem de Jong invited Schopen to pursue his doctoral studies at the Australian National University in Canberra, where he wrote a thesis entitled, "The *Bhaiṣajyaguru-sūtra* and the Buddhism of Gilgit." Both the thesis and the critical edition of the text it contains remain unpublished, but as discussed below, Gregory is revisiting the text in light of the find of additional manuscripts of the *Bhaiṣajyaguru* in the Schøyen Collection.

Gregory completed his PhD in 1979, at which time he accepted an invitation from fellow ANU alumnus Akira Yuyama to be a research fellow at the Reiyūkai Library in Tokyo, enjoying for a year one of the finest Buddhological libraries in the world. Subsequently returning to the United States after a ten-year absence, his first job was as a night watchman in a sawmill in Wyoming, which he has described as a near perfect setting for getting reading done uninterruptedly. Luis Gómez would offer him his first academic appointment at the University of Michigan in 1981, and this was soon followed by his first tenure-track job at Indiana University in 1984. Within a year of his arrival at Indiana, Schopen was awarded a MacArthur Fellowship, a prestigious five-year grant that afforded him large blocks of uninterrupted research and writing time. This period of heightened productivity saw the publication of several articles on epigraphical sources for the study of Indian Buddhism, along with a burgeoning interest in monastic law codes.

Gregory joined Patrick Olivelle in moving from Indiana to the University of Texas at Austin in 1991, creating a concentration of talent in classical South Asia that was, and still is, altogether rare in the U.S. The influence of having two colleagues specializing in Indian legal literature in Austin clearly had an impact on Gregory, as evidenced by the numerous studies he produced on the *Mūlasarvāstivāda-vinaya*. In 1999 Schopen moved to UCLA, where he would spend the last twenty years of his career, with brief stints at both Stanford University and Brown University, retiring in 2019. It was at UCLA that Schopen was able to attract and train a talented coterie of graduate students, several of whom have gone on to productive careers of their own in Buddhist studies. Additionally, Gregory was elected to the American Academy of Arts and Sciences in 2015, a tribute to his profound contributions to Buddhist studies specifically and the humanistic study of religion more broadly.

Gregory Schopen's Contributions to Buddhist Studies

We hope here to briefly survey Gregory Schopen's contributions to Buddhist studies in three primary areas: Mahāyāna studies, Buddhist monasticism and Vinaya, and archeological, art-historical, and epigraphical data for the study of Buddhism. We of course cannot do justice to the full range and depth of his many publications here. But we hope to orient the reader in the principal arenas that are the focus of the various contributions to this volume.

Mahāyāna Studies

It is fitting to begin with Schopen's contributions to the study of the Mahāyāna since this is where he began his own journey into Buddhist studies in graduate school. And it is noteworthy that his very first publication, drawn from his master's thesis at McMaster University, has become one of his best known and most influential. This article on the cult of the book in the Mahāyāna took as its departure two previously overlooked passages from the *Vajracchedikā* featuring the phrase *sa pṛthivīpradeśaś caityabhūto bhavet*. When read next to a number of like passages in other texts, Schopen observed a noticeable pattern emerging in which the authors of a significant strand of Mahāyāna literature appeared to be advocating a move away from traditional devotional centers and toward alternative sites where their books or the Dharma preachers who recited their books were located for congregation and practice (1975). This argument made a huge splash in the field, since it flew in the face of a previously popular hypothesis advanced by Akira Hirakawa that located early Mahāyāna adherents among lay practitioners who were engaged in cult activities specifically at stūpas. Schopen's article on the cult of the book has since been coopted for a wide range of applications, often well beyond the scope of Schopen's original argument and at times with none too few misunderstandings. Schopen himself has qualified his thinking on the matter in subsequent publications (2004c, 2005b, 2010c). Daniel Boucher's contribution to this volume takes up the cult of the book again, responding to some of Schopen's critics and advancing a somewhat revised version of how we might continue reflections on literacy and the book in the early Mahāyāna.

Soon after his cult of the book paper, Schopen published an article in the same journal arguing that the goal of rebirth in Sukhāvatī appears in a wide swath of Mahāyāna sūtras of all periods, including the earliest. The context of these passages suggests a widely generalized promise rather than a cult dedicated to Amitābha. This observation also aligns rather well with the seeming lack of archeological or art-historical evidence for such devotion, in sharp contrast with evidence from East Asia, where devotion to Amitābha became conspicuous rather early. Juhyung Rhi takes up the textual depictions of Sukhāvatī in relation to the Chinese evidence again in this volume. In another early publication, Schopen also took note of another generalized goal within certain strands of Mahāyāna literature, namely *jātismara*, "the recollection of former births" (1983). Whereas in earlier Mainstream texts *jātismara* was viewed as an extraordinary attainment by the religious virtuoso, in a significant number of Mahāyāna texts, this same attainment could be achieved by quite a number of nonmeditational activities, including worship directed at images, the copying

Gregory Schopen, circa late 1980s, combining three of his passions: duckies, colorful neckties, and Buddhist studies. (Photo kindly provided by Alice Fleming.)

or reciting of texts, and activities tied to the use of *dhāraṇīs*, and by virtually anyone, regardless of their lay or monastic status. And this recollection, the texts suggest, could restructure an individual's behavior in a way that leads to a release from future unfortunate rebirths, thus abating, Schopen speculates, at least one of the central anxieties fueled by the doctrine of karma.

By the late 1990s, Schopen's interests in the Mahāyāna had become increasingly informed by his intensive investigation of the *Mūlasarvāstivāda-vinaya*. One of his first forays in this direction was to examine conservative monastic values embedded in the *Maitreyamahāsiṃhanāda-sūtra* (1999). More specifically, the *Maitreyasiṃhanāda* seems particularly concerned about widespread monastic involvement with cult practice, particularly the worship of images or stūpas, so as to generate revenue. As such, it sought to reform monastic behavior rather than to argue for a particular sectarian position related to adherence to the Great Vehicle. And in this regard, much of the polemic of its author would appear to overlap with similar pronouncements found in the *Mūlasarvāstivāda-vinaya*, suggesting that this Mahāyāna author had some familiarity with this code or one very much like it. Schopen continued these reflections in a paper published a year later, "The Mahāyāna and the Middle Period in Indian Buddhism: Through a Chinese Looking-Glass" (2000b). Here Schopen argues that scholars of the early Mahāyāna, especially those who actively consult early Chinese sources, have not always sufficiently appreciated the degree to which developments in India and those in China did not keep pace with one another. Texts and practices that were early successes in China did not necessarily enjoy similar notoriety in the Indian context. Again, Schopen makes the important observation that the public emergence of the Mahāyāna in art and inscriptions appears to be quite late, in contrast to a rather early gentrification of Mahāyāna Buddhism in China. Many of the earliest Indian Mahāyāna texts recommend instead a more ascetic vision, enjoining their coreligionists to retreat to the wilderness and embrace the *dhutaguṇas*. Several studies since have reinforced this important early strand of the Mahāyāna. Schopen returned to the conservative themes in early Mahāyāna literature in his 2005b article "On Sending the Monks Back to Their Books: Cult and Conservatism in Early Mahāyāna Buddhism," appearing for the first time in the third volume of his collected papers. Here he revisits the ambivalence, if not at times hostility, toward Buddhist cult practices connected with stūpas and images. The textual, epigraphical, and archeological evidence all points toward these cults being under the stewardship of monks and the traditional *nikāya*s to which they belonged. And this remains true even when one looks for a cult of bodhisattvas, presumed by many Buddhologists and art historians to be an early interest of the Mahāyāna but with little material evidence to support the supposition (2005b, 127–128).

It is not only in the realm of its literature that Schopen has had an impact on Mahāyāna studies. Early in his career he surveyed the extant references to Mahāyāna adherents, monastic and lay, in the epigraphical record (1979a). A few patterns emerged from this survey. Schopen noted the widespread use of the votive formula *sarvasattvānām anuttarajñānāvāptaye* ("for the obtaining of supreme knowledge for all beings"), often found in conjunction with specific titles of donors: *śākyabhikṣu/-bhikṣuṇī* or *paramopāsaka/-opāsikā*. These titles in turn are associated in several inscriptions with those described as *mahāyānayāyin* or *mahāyānika*, thus connecting both the votive formula and the donor epithet to this movement. What stands out from this data is how late it all occurs, with such titles and formulae only appearing hesitantly from the fourth century, and most of it even later. And as Schopen notes elsewhere, the emergence of such designations appears to coincide with the gradual disappearance of inscriptions dedicated to monks and nuns of named *nikāya*s (2000b, 18–19).

We do have one earlier inscription from near Mathurā related to the Mahāyāna dated during the reign of the Kuṣāṇa king Huviṣka (late second century CE) and containing an unambiguous reference to the buddha Amitābha. Schopen, who re-edited and retranslated this important epigraph (1987b),

Gregory Schopen, 2019, at his retirement party. (Photo courtesy of UCLA.)

however, notes that this seemingly unique early record, contrary to initial scholarly reactions, appears to confirm the marginal status of the Mahāyāna in north India of the early first millennium. Not only does Amitābha not occur again in inscriptions until the seventh century, but the majority of the extant data points toward Śākyamuni as the cult figure of choice for Kuṣāṇa Buddhists in the Mathurā area and beyond. Moreover, attempts to see references to both Amitābha and Avalokiteśvara in an early Kharoṣṭhī inscription have also proven highly doubtful (Salomon and Schopen 2002b). Thus nothing from our earliest data would suggest a widespread, active cult of Amitābha, or any other Mahāyāna buddha or bodhisattva, once again demonstrating the dangers of drawing assumptions about actual religious praxis solely on the basis of literary sources.

Besides drawing from textual and epigraphical sources for the study of the Mahāyāna, Schopen has also ventured into the art-historical realm, identifying a painted scene from Cave 10 at Ajaṇṭā as likely depicting the bodhisattva Avalokiteśvara (2005c). He makes a compelling case for seeing this scene as drawn from an episode in chapter 24 of the *Saddharmapuṇḍarīka-sūtra*. If this identification holds up, and Nicolas Morrissey's contribution to this volume concerning Cave 9 at Ajaṇṭā would seem to buttress it, then this would be our earliest data for the actual use or application of a Mahāyāna sūtra at any Buddhist site in India.

More recently, Schopen has returned to the study of a text with which he began his forays into Buddhist studies, the *Bhaiṣajyaguru-sūtra* found at Gilgit. Noting the proclivity of scholars to seek out urtexts of early Mahāyāna sūtras, often through the lens of early Chinese translations, Schopen reminds us that different versions of relatively early Sanskrit manuscripts of some of these texts circulated simultaneously in approximately the same geographical zone, as in the case of both the *Kāśyapaparivarta* and the *Saddharmapuṇḍarīka* in the vicinity of Khotan/Kashgar (2009a). Determining the historical priority of one version over the others may not get us very far toward understanding what these differences meant to the communities that used them—if they meant anything at all. This is all the more complicated when we come to the case of a text like the *Bhaiṣajyaguru-sūtra*, which circulated in four, or perhaps even five, exemplars at Gilgit with significant variations among them. Since these variants circulated simultaneously at Gilgit, in all probability not very far removed from the time of their composition, Schopen suggests that no version of this text may ever have been fixed or standard. Our quest to realize some hypothetical urtext then says more about our philological preoccupations than it does about the communities that drew from these texts for their own ritual agendas. These questions will likely be revisited since additional manuscripts of the *Bhaiṣajyaguru-sūtra* have surfaced from the area of Bāmiyān in the Schøyen Collection, at least one of which Schopen will edit and situate in relationship to the Gilgit finds in a forthcoming publication (see also 2017b).

Monasticism and Vinaya Studies

The Buddhist monk Gregory Schopen encountered as a graduate student in the 1970s was an aloof, avowed ascetic almsman professing perpetual poverty, and a member of a community of like-minded spiritual wayfarers committed to complete renunciation of all ties—familial, parental, marital, and property—and intent to "wander alone like the rhinoceros." Much like the rhinoceros itself, this view of the ideal Buddhist monk roamed rampant and generally unchallenged in the writings of earlier generations of scholars, even if it may now face extinction. To be sure, some scholars prior to Schopen had occasionally noted, discussed, and even translated particular passages that presented a view of the Buddhist bhikṣu that stood in stark contrast to the hopelessly romanticized view prevalent in both the popular imagination and, as he has often pointed out, our textbooks (1995a, 473; 1996b, 124; 2004b, 25). But it is Schopen to whom we owe a substantial and substantiated reimagining of the Indian Buddhist monk and his female counterpart, and a comprehensive and coherent overview of the financial framework, legal and ritual obligations, and

Gregory Schopen, 2010. (Photo by Alice Fleming, with minor digital enhancement.)

economic activities that preoccupied the minds of their jurists, the authors/redactors of the *Mūlasarvāstivāda-vinaya*.

Perhaps the first misconception about the Indian Buddhist monk that Schopen shattered was the notion that Indian bhikṣus did not participate in acts of religious giving and filial piety, unlike their later Chinese counterparts. On the basis of Indian inscriptional evidence, Schopen demonstrated that the making of religious gifts for the benefit of one's parents was not a specifically or even largely lay activity, to say nothing of a Chinese adaptation or transformation of Indian Buddhism (1984a). Rather, Indian Buddhist monks and nuns were as—if not more—concerned about the welfare of their parents as the laity, as evidenced by the large proportion of monastic donors in the extant corpus of Indian donative inscriptions. But how could monks and nuns, those who supposedly had taken vows of poverty, sponsor significant objects of worship such as images or stūpas?

The simple answer is that unlike their Benedictine brethren in medieval European monasteries (1995b, 101), Indian Buddhist monks and nuns—terms used only for convenience given their baggage (2004e)—did not in fact renounce all personal property and wealth. This is not to say that monks and nuns ignored or disobeyed monastic injunctions to do so; rather, what have been interpreted as rules prohibiting the possession of individual wealth or property by ordained monks and nuns are not so straightforward, as Schopen makes clear in most everything he has published in the last four decades. Moreover, the extant Buddhist monastic law codes abound with stories and instructions that attest to the fact that Indian Buddhist monks and nuns—or at least the authors/redactors of the law codes who envisioned these monks and nuns—were entrepreneurially and financially astute ascetics.

Schopen addresses the Indian Buddhist monk's ongoing rights to retain personal property and wealth in several articles in his collection of essays entitled *Buddhist Monks and Business Matters* (2004a). This volume opens with an article titled, appropriately, "The Good Monk and His Money in a Buddhist Monasticism of 'The Mahāyāna Period'" (2000a), in which Schopen notes that the ordination formulary from the *Mūlasarvāstivāda-vinaya* includes a question about whether ordinands have any debts. A debtor is allowed to be ordained as a monk only if he has the ability to repay his debts post ordination. In other words, the ritual formula for making a man into a monk (translated in 2004g) assumes and requires that a newly ordained monk can and will continue to possess personal property or wealth (2000a, 88). That this rule is by no means an aberration but very much characteristic of the vision of the Buddhist bhikṣu found throughout the *Mūlasarvāstivāda-vinaya* is demonstrated by Schopen in the numerous examples he marshals. These monks, Schopen tells us, are required to pay taxes and tolls for their own personal possessions from their private wealth as opposed to "corporately owned" goods belonging to the Buddha, Dharma, or Saṅgha, for which the duties must be paid from the appropriate corporate fund (2000a, 88–89); own and are financially responsible for their furniture and damage to that belonging to other monks; pay for their own medicine and health care; possess personal seals; charge interest on loans; borrow money; inherit property; sell off estates of deceased coreligionists; and tend to dying laymen in a transaction that sees the monastic institution inherit the layman's estate (2000a, 103–104), what Schopen tells us was known as *captatio* or "legacy hunting" or "inheritance hunting" in Roman law (2008b, 635–636; 2014b, 102). This is a savvy monk operating in a fully developed, sophisticated monasticism in a world rife with religious competition. The wandering beggar content to meditate at the foot of a tree is but a distant memory of a bygone time.

The Buddhist monk is not the only one to have undergone a complete image makeover at the hands of Schopen. The Indian Buddhist nun has also become quite unrecognizable from her portrayal in the nineteenth and twentieth centuries. Noting the existence of rules in the *Mūlasarvāstivāda-vinaya* that state that nuns must not live in the forest and that nunneries must be built in cities, Schopen discusses the existence of "votive tanks" (*devacchan-*

das) found in the archeological record only at urban Buddhist sites and rules that seem to make it an offense for nuns to use such objects in protective rites for children (2009b). With this evidence, Schopen begins to build a partial picture of the urban Buddhist nun, one that he fleshes out with a series of studies on the legal and economic activities and rights of Indian Buddhist nuns. He establishes that despite their hierarchical and ritual subservience to and dependence on bhikṣus, the Buddhist bhikṣuṇī enjoyed both legal independence and the right to inherit the property of a deceased coreligionist or "sister-in-the-Dharma," a position that would have been unique in classical India (2008b). Placing the archeological data in conversation with the textual, Schopen digs deep into the narrative of a seemingly run-of-the-mill rule about the nun Sthūlanandā tossing the contents of a chamber pot over a wall to uncover additional evidence for the urban location of nunneries (2008a). As he argues, a narrative in which a nun carelessly empties a pisspot over a wall in the nunnery on an unsuspecting brahmin officer heading toward the royal palace makes sense only if the nunnery is physically located within the city.

Schopen explores narratives and associated rules in which Buddhist nuns are envisioned as having not only the legal rights to own property but also the business acumen to rent out the nunnery (*varṣaka*) and residential and commercial property for a profit, run taverns, and finance brothels (2012a). Rules, of course, are promulgated to prevent just such events, but the promulgation of said rules suggests, as Schopen often reminds us, that the male jurists who composed or redacted the *Mūlasarvāstivāda-vinaya* "either thought or assumed that Buddhist nuns could do all these things, and worried that they would. And although male anxieties are probably not the best indicators of reality, only the densest among such men would have made rules against what they knew could not possibly happen" (2012a, 607).

In artful translations that capture the *rasa* of the original, a flavor that may be a little too intense for some, especially those accustomed to the bland offerings of other genres and the texts of other schools, Schopen brings to life complex and often larger-than-life characters such as the Group-of-Six monks and the nun Sthūlanandā and their intricately woven web of dastardly devious deeds designed to test the Buddha's patience and bring about new and revised legislation. By focusing on the stories that monks told other monks, Schopen shines light on not only the anxieties of the canonical authors/redactors but also the literary genius of the *Mūlasarvāstivāda-vinaya*, a text that, as Schopen notes in several places with almost audible approbation, Sylvain Lévi long ago characterized as a masterpiece of Sanskrit literature (see 2007a, 203–204; 2008b, 625; 2010e, 885). More than just regaling us with tales of antics and (mis)adventures in what may sometimes seem like the weird and wacky world of Mūlasarvāstivādin monasticism, Schopen has opened up new ways of looking at Buddhist monasticism with his unmatched ability to bring together disparate bodies of evidence—archeological, art-historical, epigraphical, legal (dharmaśāstra), and textual.

As Schopen points out, the position that posits the extant monastic law codes as early—dating back to anywhere near the time of the Buddha—denies Buddhist monasticism both a history and a subsequent development. Such a position does not accord with the early archeological record, one in which we find no trace of the fully fledged, settled, and even sedentary monasticism of the extant Vinayas. The earliest extant monasteries in the archeological record are, Schopen tells us, nothing but rudimentary remains that could not have possibly housed, for instance, steam rooms, and thus the inhabitants of these monastic communities could not have possibly compiled the elaborate rules surrounding such complex and fundamentally foreign architectural additions that are completely at home in monasticisms of what Schopen calls the "early medieval period" or "the Mahāyāna period" (2000a, 85–86). Not making an argument for the early date of any particular Vinaya, Schopen tells us that all Vinayas are late and thus, by implication, far removed from the initial inspiration of the founding fathers of Indian Buddhist monasticism. The fact that most developments cannot be traced back to the historical Buddha is precisely why Indian Buddhist monasticism warrants investigation. Schopen tells us not what Buddhist monasticism might have looked like in some semi-mythical haze but rather what it had become by the time we can actually locate it in both time and space, both in and out of texts.

At first blush, it may appear that the Buddhist monk and nun have not fared particularly well in their skirmishes with Schopen. The solitary ascetic renouncer has turned out to be a shrewd businessman, his sister a multitalented, urbane, no-nonsense, religious entrepreneur. This is quite the makeover, and no doubt some will disapprove. In seeking to deepen our understanding of fundamental questions about the who, what, why, and how of Indian Buddhist monasticism(s) in concrete terms, the incomparable artist has taken a fine brush (some might say "sledgehammer") to the stick-figure sketches of yore to better express more fulsome and rounded features of not only the inhabitants of Buddhist monasteries in India but their vision of the monastic and religious life, what it meant to be Buddhist, non-Buddhist, and even human in India in the first few centuries of the Common Era and beyond.

Archeology and Epigraphy in the Study of Indian Buddhism

Animating Schopen's work from the beginning was a quest to know what it might have been like to be a Buddhist monk in the ancient Indian context. Generations of scholars have long known what the concerns and obligations of monks should have been. But what most motivated Gregory's curiosity was to investigate how we might discern the actual lifestyles and practices of monks, practices that none too infrequently seemed at odds with some canonical prescriptions. This reorientation from the normative to the lived realities of religious behaviors "on the ground" had significant implications for how we use our sources. Indeed, Schopen directly challenged his students and colleagues, both in print and in person, to wrestle with the unacknowledged preference for canonical texts to discern the values of Indian Buddhist monks at the expense of archeological and epigraphical sources, data that "records or reflects at least a part of what Buddhists—both laypeople and monks—actually practiced and believed" (1991a, 2).

The larger irony of this preference is that archeological and epigraphical data have been available to scholars for as long as textual sources, which is to say from roughly the middle of the nineteenth century. Nevertheless, even as scholars sometimes noted the value of Buddhist art, inscriptions, and coin legends for Buddhist history, these material artifacts were always read through the lens of the texts. In short, archeology was to be the handmaiden of history. However, it is precisely in this relationship between texts and material culture that Schopen could begin to ask some uncomfortable questions of his colleagues. For example, archeologists have long noted the presence of substantial hoards of coins and other valuables in the ruins of ancient Buddhist monasteries, seemingly at odds with the austere lifestyle recommended in some readings of monastic law. But, as Schopen notes, the evidence is often even more troubling for received portraits of Buddhist "ascetics." At Nāgārjunakoṇḍa, in the ruins of a monastery gifted by a lay sister (*upāsikā*) to Theravādin teachers from Sri Lanka, we find not only stashes of coins but also earthenware dies for the manufacture of coins. As Schopen remarks, researchers of the site appear not to have fully grasped the fact that either the monks were empowered by the state to mint coins, or else they were engaged in what could only be called counterfeiting (1991a, 9). Either way, none of this accords very well with what many literary sources suggest as proper occupations for Buddhist monastics.

It is not only with regard to possessions that actual monastic practice departed from literary expectations. To judge from the archeological and epigraphical record, as Schopen has noted across several publications, Indian

Buddhist monastics appear to have been preoccupied with the dead, not only the Buddha but also fellow monks and prominent lay donors to whom they owed mortuary rites. While ancient Buddhist scholastics spilled more than a little ink debating the precise nature of the Buddha's parinirvāṇa, few of them would claim that the Buddha was in some sense still present to the Buddhist community. But this is precisely what our epigraphical records suggest (1988). As Schopen has demonstrated, no small number of the Buddhist faithful took the remnants of the Buddha's cremated body as an ongoing living presence. These relic shrines were often surrounded by mortuary shrines of deceased monks, who sought postmortem proximity to the Buddha or a Buddhist saint in a kind of burial *ad sanctos*, paralleling a similar practice at Christian shrines from Late Antique times (1987a). In fact, one of the particularly edifying contributions of Schopen's work on the inscriptional evidence of these practices is his demonstration of a broad pattern across geographically diffuse sites—from Mathurā and Sāñcī in the north, Bedsā, Bhājā, and Kānherī in the western Deccan, to Nāgārjunakoṇḍa and Amarāvatī in the south—for enshrining the local monastic dead at Buddhist monastic and cultic centers (1991d). The fact that a number of monasteries and stūpas appear to have also been situated on sites occupied by the proto-historical dead would only have reinforced the impression to the local Indian populations that Buddhist monks were indeed to be regarded—whether they wanted this role or not—as caretakers of the dead (1996e). The vast majority of this data points toward practices on which canonical sources are either ambivalent or utterly silent.

While Schopen has never regarded himself as a proper art historian, he certainly has not ignored the role of cult images in the history of Indian Buddhism. Taking on the two-tiered model of religious innovation in which changes are presumed to begin always from lay influence, Schopen demonstrated that our earliest extant inscribed images show a very substantial involvement of Buddhist monastics—both monks and nuns—in this cult practice (1988–1989). In fact fully two-thirds of the donors of images dated during the Kuṣāṇa period were monks or nuns, some of whom are described as *trepiṭaka*s ("knowers of the Three Baskets"), which is to say, very learned individuals. But Schopen has noticed another pattern among these epigraphs that may be even more remarkable. Among the earliest donative inscriptions of cult images, we find that women—both lay and monastic—played an active role, except in the far northwest and Nāgārjunakoṇḍa regions. But by the Gupta period (ca. fourth century CE), this participation drops off markedly, and at the same time we see the epigraphical appearance of a new monastic title, the *śākyabhikṣu*. This title is almost certainly to be linked with monks affiliated with the Mahāyāna, again conflicting with the oft-cited hypothesis that it was the Mahāyāna that embraced a broadening of religious options for the laity and women (1988–1989, 164–165).

Schopen has also argued that medieval Indian Buddhists also understood the Buddha represented by such images to be a permanent, living resident at their monasteries, owning property and occupying their own dedicated "perfume chamber" (*gandhakuṭī*) (1990). The confluence of epigraphical, architectural, and archeological evidence—not to mention support from the *Mūlasarvāstivāda-vinaya*—of such a concrete, localized presence of the Buddha may well be related to the contemporary philosophical development of an increasingly abstract, etherealized conception of his personhood. Exactly what this relationship might have been has still to be worked out. But it is clear that such highly intellectualized conceptions will now have to be read against the evidence of the material culture (1990, 204–205). Additionally, the *Mūlasarvāstivāda-vinaya* contains many narratives and injunctions related to the cult of the bodhisattva image, in every case clearly referring to the historical Buddha prior to his enlightenment. This practice involved taking the image on procession into towns and appears to have been a source of considerable revenue for monastic communities, requiring detailed rules for negotiating its distribution (2005e and 2005b, 128–137).

*Publications of Gregory Schopen**

1975 "The Phrase '*sa pṛthivīpradeśaś caityabhūto bhavet*' in the *Vajracchedikā*: Notes on the Cult of the Book in Mahāyāna." *Indo-Iranian Journal* 17.3–4: 147–181.

1977a Review of *The Large Sutra on Perfect Wisdom with the Divisions of the Abhisamayālaṅkāra*, translated by Edward Conze. *Indo-Iranian Journal* 19.1–2: 133–152.

1977b "Sukhāvatī as a Generalized Religious Goal in Sanskrit Mahāyāna Sūtra Literature." *Indo-Iranian Journal* 19.3–4: 177–210.

1978a Review of *Prajñā-pāramitā-ratna-guṇa-saṃcaya-gāthā (Sanskrit Recension A)*, edited by Akira Yuyama. *Indo-Iranian Journal* 20.1–2: 110–124.

1978b "The Five Leaves of the *Buddhabalādhānaprātihāryavikurvāṇanirdeśa-sūtra* Found at Gilgit." *Journal of Indian Philosophy* 5.4: 319–336.

1979a "Mahāyāna in Indian Inscriptions." *Indo-Iranian Journal* 21.1: 1–19.

1979b *Buddhist Studies by J. W. de Jong*, edited by Gregory Schopen. Berkeley: Asian Humanities Press.

* What follows is a revised, rearranged, supplemented, and updated list of publications found in Professor Schopen's professional curriculum vitae, successively—but perhaps not successfully—maintained and mangled by hordes of research assistants over several decades, including the present editors.

1982a “Hīnayāna Texts in a 14th Century Persian Chronicle: Notes on Some of Rashīd al-Dīn's Sources.” *Central Asiatic Journal* 26.3–4: 225–235.

1982b “The Text on the ‘Dhāraṇī Stones from Abhayagiriya’: A Minor Contribution to the Study of Mahāyāna Literature in Ceylon.” *Journal of the International Association of Buddhist Studies* 5.1: 100–108.

1983 “The Generalization of an Old Yogic Attainment in Medieval Mahāyāna Sūtra Literature: Some Notes on *Jātismara*.” *Journal of the International Association of Buddhist Studies* 6.1: 109–147.

1984a “Filial Piety and the Monk in the Practice of Indian Buddhism: A Question of ‘Sinicization’ Viewed from the Other Side.” *T'oung Pao*, 2nd ser., 70.1–3: 110–126.

1984b “The Indravarman (Avaca) Casket Inscription Reconsidered: Further Evidence for Canonical Passages in Buddhist Inscriptions.” Coauthored with Richard Salomon. *Journal of the International Association of Buddhist Studies* 7.1: 107–123.

1985a “The Bodhigarbhālaṅkāralakṣa and Vimaloṣṇīṣa Dhāraṇīs in Indian Inscriptions: Two Sources for the Practice of Buddhism in Medieval India.” *Wiener Zeitschrift für die Kunde Südasiens* 29: 119–149.

1985b “Two Problems in the History of Indian Buddhism: The Layman/Monk Distinction and the Doctrines of the Transference of Merit.” *Studien zur Indologie und Iranistik* 10: 9–47.

1987a “Burial *‘Ad Sanctos’* and the Physical Presence of the Buddha in Early Indian Buddhism: A Study in the Archeology of Religions.” *Religion* 17.3: 193–225.

1987b “The Inscription on the Kuṣān Image of Amitābha and the Character of the Early Mahāyāna in India.” *Journal of the International Association of Buddhist Studies* 10.2: 99–134.

1988 “On the Buddha and His Bones: The Conception of a Relic in the Inscriptions of Nāgārjunikoṇḍa.” *Journal of the American Oriental Society* 108.4: 527–537.

1988–1989 “On Monks, Nuns and ‘Vulgar’ Practices: The Introduction of the Image Cult into Indian Buddhism.” *Artibus Asiae* 49.1–2: 153–168.

1989a “The Manuscript of the Vajracchedikā Found at Gilgit: An Annotated Transcription and Translation.” In *Studies in the Literature of the Great Vehicle: Three Mahāyāna Buddhist Texts*, edited by Luis O. Gómez and Jonathan A. Silk, 89–139. Michigan Series in Buddhist Literature 1. Ann Arbor: Collegiate Institute for the Study of Buddhist Literature and Center for South and Southeast Asian Studies, The University of Michigan. [Text reprinted in B. Oguibénine, *Initiation pratique à l'étude du sanskrit bouddhique*. Paris: Picard, 1996, 252–265; translation reprinted in Donald S. Lopez Jr. ed., *Buddhist Scriptures*. London: Penguin Books, 2004, 450–463.]

1989b “A Verse from the *Bhadracarīpraṇidhāna* in a 10th Century Inscription Found at Nālandā.” *Journal of the International Association of Buddhist Studies* 12.1: 149–157.

1989c “The Stūpa Cult and the Extant Pāli Vinaya.” *Journal of the Pali Text Society* 13: 83–100.

1990 "The Buddha as an Owner of Property and Permanent Resident in Medieval Indian Monasteries." *Journal of Indian Philosophy* 18.3: 181–217.

1991a "Archaeology and Protestant Presuppositions in the Study of Indian Buddhism." *History of Religions* 31.1: 1–23.

1991b *From Benares to Beijing: Essays on Buddhism and Chinese Religion in Honour of Jan Yün-Hua*, edited by Koichi Shinohara and Gregory Schopen. Oakville, Ontario: Mosaic Press.

1991c "Monks and the Relic Cult in the *Mahāparinibbānasutta*: An Old Misunderstanding in Regard to Monastic Buddhism." In *From Benares to Beijing: Essays on Buddhism and Chinese Religion in Honour of Jan Yün-Hua*, edited by Koichi Shinohara and Gregory Schopen, 187–201. Oakville, Ontario: Mosaic Press.

1991d "An Old Inscription from Amarāvatī and the Cult of the Local Monastic Dead in Indian Buddhist Monasteries." *Journal of the International Association of Buddhist Studies* 14.2: 281–329.

1992a "On Avoiding Ghosts and Social Censure: Monastic Funerals in the *Mūlasarvāstivāda-vinaya*." *Journal of Indian Philosophy* 20.1: 1–39.

1992b "The Ritual Obligations and Donor Roles of Monks in the Pāli Vinaya." *Journal of the Pali Text Society* 16: 87–107.

1992c "Yindu shike mingwen zhong de dasheng fojiao" 印度石刻銘文中的大乘佛教. *Diguan* 諦觀 (*Satya-darśana: A Buddhist Studies Quarterly*) 68: 1–36. [A Chinese translation of Schopen 1979a by Chou Pokan 周伯戡.]

1993 "Tracking Religion." *Discovery: Research and Scholarship at the University of Texas at Austin* 13.2: 13–19.

1994a "Ritual Rights and Bones of Contention: More on Monastic Funerals and Relics in the *Mūlasarvāstivāda-vinaya*." *Journal of Indian Philosophy* 22.1: 31–80.

1994b "*Stūpa* and *Tīrtha*: Tibetan Mortuary Practices and an Unrecognized Form of Burial Ad Sanctos at Buddhist Sites in India." In *The Buddhist Forum*, vol. 3: *1991–1993: Papers In Honour and Appreciation of Professor David Seyfort Ruegg's Contribution to Indological, Buddhist and Tibetan Studies*, edited by Tadeusz Skorupski and Ulrich Pagel, 273–293. London: School of Oriental and African Studies.

1994c "The Monastic Ownership of Servants or Slaves: Local and Legal Factors in the Redactional Histories of Two *Vinayas*." *Journal of the International Association of Buddhist Studies* 17.2: 145–173.

1994d "Doing Business for the Lord: Lending on Interest and Written Loan Contracts in the *Mūlasarvāstivāda-vinaya*." *Journal of the American Oriental Society* 114.4: 527–554.

1995a "Deaths, Funerals, and the Division of Property in a Monastic Code." In *Buddhism in Practice*, edited by Donald S. Lopez Jr., 473–502. Princeton: Princeton University Press.

1995b "Monastic Law Meets the Real World: A Monk's Continuing Right to Inherit Family Property in Classical India." *History of Religions* 35.2: 101–123.

1996a "What's in a Name: The Religious Function of the Early Donative Inscriptions." In *Unseen Presence: The Buddha and Sanchi*, edited by Vidya Dehejia, 58–73. Bombay: Marg Publications.

1996b "The Lay Ownership of Monasteries and the Role of the Monk in Mūlasarvāstivādin Monasticism." *Journal of the International Association of Buddhist Studies* 19.1: 81–126.

1996c "*Daihatsu nehan-gyō* ni okeru biku to ikotsu ni kansuru girei: shukke bukkyō ni kansuru furuku kara no gokai" 『大般涅槃経』における比丘と遺骨に関する儀礼：出家仏教に関する古くからの誤解. *Ōtani gakuhō* 大谷学報 (*Journal of Buddhist Studies and Humanities, Otani University*) 76.1: 1–20. [A Japanese translation of Schopen 1991c by Hiraoka Satoshi 平岡聡.]

1996d "The Suppression of Nuns and the Ritual Murder of Their Special Dead in Two Buddhist Monastic Texts." *Journal of Indian Philosophy* 24.6: 563–592.

1996e "Immigrant Monks and the Proto-Historical Dead: The Buddhist Occupation of Early Burial Sites in India." In *Festschrift Dieter Schlingloff zur Vollendung des 65. Lebensjahres dargebracht von Schülern, Freunden und Kollegen*, edited by Friedrich Wilhelm, 215–238. Reinbek: Dr. Inge Wezler: Verlag für Orientalistische Fachpublikationen.

1997a *Bones, Stones, and Buddhist Monks: Collected Papers on the Archaeology, Epigraphy, and Texts of Monastic Buddhism in India*. Studies in the Buddhist Traditions. Honolulu: University of Hawai'i Press.

1997b "If You Can't Remember, How to Make it Up: Some Monastic Rules for Redacting Canonical Texts." In *Bauddhavidyāsudhākaraḥ: Studies in Honour of Heinz Bechert on the Occasion of His 65th Birthday*, edited by Petra Kieffer-Pülz and Jens-Uwe Hartmann, 571–582. Indica et Tibetica 30. Swisttal-Odendorf: Indica et Tibetica Verlag.

1998a "Relic." In *Critical Terms for Religious Studies*, edited by Mark C. Taylor, 256–268. Chicago: The University of Chicago Press.

1998b *Sūryacandrāya: Essays in Honour of Akira Yuyama On the Occasion of His 65th Birthday*, edited by Paul Harrison and Gregory Schopen. Indica et Tibetica 35. Swisttal-Odendorf: Indica et Tibetica Verlag.

1998c "Marking Time in Buddhist Monasteries: On Calendars, Clocks, and Some Liturgical Practices." In *Sūryacandrāya: Essays in Honour of Akira Yuyama On the Occasion of His 65th Birthday*, edited by Paul Harrison and Gregory Schopen, 157–179. Indica et Tibetica 35. Swisttal-Odendorf: Indica et Tibetica Verlag.

1999 "The Bones of a Buddha and the Business of a Monk: Conservative Monastic Values in an Early Mahāyāna Polemical Tract." *Journal of Indian Philosophy* 27.4: 279–324.

2000a "The Good Monk and His Money in a Buddhist Monasticism of 'The Mahāyāna Period.'" *The Eastern Buddhist*, n.s., 32.1: 85–105.

2000b "The Mahāyāna and the Middle Period in Indian Buddhism: Through a Chinese Looking-Glass." *The Eastern Buddhist*, n.s., 32.2: 1–25.

2000c *Daijō bukkyō kōki jidai: Indo no sōin seikatsu* 大乗仏教興起時代：インドの

僧院生活 (*Indian Monastic Life: The Period of the Origins of the Mahāyāna*). Translated by Odani Nobuchiyo 小谷信千代. Tokyo: Shunjūsha 春秋社.

2000d "Hierarchy and Housing in a Buddhist Monastic Code: A Translation of the Sanskrit Text of the *Śayanāsanavastu* of the *Mūlasarvāstivāda-vinaya*. Part One." *Buddhist Literature* 2: 92–196.

2001 "Dead Monks and Bad Debts: Some Provisions of a Buddhist Monastic Inheritance Law." *Indo-Iranian Journal* 44.2: 99–148.

2002a "Counting the Buddha and the Local Spirits In: A Monastic Ritual of Inclusion for the Rain Retreat." *Journal of Indian Philosophy* 30.4: 359–388.

2002b "On an Alleged Reference to Amitābha in a Kharoṣṭhī Inscription on a Gandhāran Relief." Coauthored with Richard Salomon. *Journal of the International Association of Buddhist Studies* 25.1–2: 3–31.

2003 "The Suppression of Nuns and the Ritual Murder of Their Special Dead in Two Buddhist Monastic Texts." In *The Living and the Dead: Social Dimensions of Death in South Asian Religions*, edited by Liz Wilson, 127–158. Albany: State University of New York Press. [A reprint of Schopen 1996d.]

2004a *Buddhist Monks and Business Matters: Still More Papers on Monastic Buddhism in India*. Studies in the Buddhist Traditions. Honolulu: University of Hawai'i Press.

2004b "Art, Beauty, and the Business of Running a Buddhist Monastery in Early Northwest India." In Schopen 2004a, 19–44.

2004c "Mahāyāna." In *Encyclopedia of Buddhism*, edited by Robert E. Buswell, 2:492–499. New York: Macmillan Reference USA.

2004d "*Mūlasarvāstivāda-vinaya*." In *Encyclopedia of Buddhism*, edited by Robert E. Buswell, 2:572–573. New York: Macmillan Reference USA.

2004e "Vinaya." In *Encyclopedia of Buddhism*, edited by Robert E. Buswell, 2:885–889. New York: Macmillan Reference USA.

2004f "On Buddhist Monks and Dreadful Deities: Some Monastic Devices for Updating the Dharma." In *Gedenkschrift J.W. de Jong*, edited by H. W. Bodewitz and Minoru Hara, 161–184. Studia Philologica Buddhica, Monograph Series 17. Tokyo: The International Institute for Buddhist Studies of the International College for Advanced Buddhist Studies.

2004g "Making Men into Monks." In *Buddhist Scriptures*, edited by Donald S. Lopez Jr., 230–251. London: Penguin Books.

2005a *Figments and Fragments of Mahāyāna Buddhism in India: More Collected Papers*. Studies in the Buddhist Traditions. Honolulu: University of Hawai'i Press.

2005b "On Sending the Monks Back to Their Books: Cult and Conservatism in Early Mahāyāna Buddhism." In Schopen 2005a, 108–153.

2005c "The Ambiguity of Avalokiteśvara and the Tentative Identification of a Painted Scene from a Mahāyāna Sūtra at Ajaṇṭā." In Schopen 2005a, 278–298.

2005d "A Note on the 'Technology of Prayer' and a Reference to a 'Revolving Bookcase' in an Eleventh-Century Indian Inscription." In Schopen 2005a, 345–349.

2005e "Taking the Bodhisattva into Town: More Texts on the Image of 'the Bodhisattva' and Image Processions in the *Mūlasarvāstivāda-vinaya*." *East and West* 55.1–4: 299–311.

2006a "On Monks and Menial Laborers: Some Monastic Accounts of Building Buddhist Monasteries." In *Architetti, Capomastri, Artigiani: L'Organizzazione dei Cantieri e della Produzione Artistica nell'Asia Ellenistica. Studi Offerti a Domenico Faccenna nel suo Ottantesimo Compleanno*, edited by Pierfrancesco Callieri, 225–245. Serie Orientale Roma 100. Rome: Istituto Italiano per l'Africa e l'Oriente.

2006b "A Well-Sanitized Shroud: Asceticism and Institutional Values in the Middle Period of Buddhist Monasticism." In *Between the Empires: Society in India 300 BCE–400 CE*, edited by Patrick Olivelle, 315–347. New York: Oxford University Press.

2006c "The Buddhist 'Monastery' and the Indian Garden: Aesthetics, Assimilations, and the Siting of Monastic Establishments." *Journal of the American Oriental Society* 126.4: 487–505.

2007a "The Learned Monk as a Comic Figure: On Reading a Buddhist Vinaya as Indian Literature." *Journal of Indian Philosophy* 35.3: 201–226.

2007b "The Buddhist *Bhikṣu*'s Obligation to Support His Parents in Two Vinaya Traditions." *Journal of the Pali Text Society* 29 [Festschrift in Honour of the 80th Birthday of K. R. Norman in 2005 and the 125th Anniversary in 2006 of the Founding of the Pali Text Society, edited by O. von Hinüber, R. M. L. Gethin, and Mark Allon]: 107–136.

2007c "Art, Beauty, and the Business of Running a Buddhist Monastery in Early Northwest India." In *On the Cusp of an Era: Art in the Pre-Kuṣāṇa World*, edited by Doris Meth Srinivasan, 287–317. Brill's Inner Asian Library 18. Leiden: Brill. [A reprint of Schopen 2004b.]

2007d "Cross-Dressing with the Dead: Asceticism, Ambivalence, and Institutional Values in an Indian Monastic Code." In *The Buddhist Dead: Practices, Discourses, Representations*, edited by Bryan J. Cuevas and Jacqueline I. Stone, 60–104. Honolulu: University of Hawai'i Press. [A reprint, in a slightly different version and under a new title, of Schopen 2006b.]

2007e "Archaeology and Protestant Presuppositions in the Study of Indian Buddhism." In *Defining Buddhism(s): A Reader*, edited by Karen Derris and Natalie Gummer, 24–43. Critical Categories in the Study of Religion. London: Equinox Publishing. [A reprint of Schopen 1991a.]

2008a "On Emptying Chamber Pots without Looking and the Urban Location of Buddhist Nunneries in Early India Again." *Journal asiatique* 296.2: 229–256.

2008b "Separate but Equal: Property Rights and the Legal Independence of Buddhist Nuns and Monks in Early North India." *Journal of the American Oriental Society* 128.4: 625–640.

2009a "On the Absence of Urtexts and Otiose Ācāryas: Buildings, Books, and Lay Buddhist Ritual at Gilgit." In *Écrire et transmettre en Inde classique*, edited by Gérard Colas and Gerdi Gerschheimer, 189–219. Études thématiques 23. Paris: École française d'Extrême-Orient.

2009b "The Urban Buddhist Nun and a Protective Rite for Children in Early North India." In *Pāsādikadānaṁ: Festschrift für Bhikkhu Pāsādika*, edited by Martin Straube, Roland Steiner, Jayandra Soni, Michael Hahn, and Mitsuyo Demoto, 359–380. Indica et Tibetica 52. Marburg: Indica et Tibetica Verlag.

2009c "Regional Languages and the Law in Some Early North Indian Buddhist Monasteries and Convents." *Bulletin of the Asia Institute*, n.s., 23 [Evo ṣuyadi: Essays in Honor of Richard Salomon's 65th Birthday, edited by Carol Altman Bromberg, Timothy J. Lenz, and Jason Neelis]: 171–178. Actually published 2013.

2010a "Une belle vie de moine..." *Le Point*, hors-série: *Les maîtres penseurs* 5 (février–mars) [Bouddha]: 58–61.

2010b "Trois morceaux en forme de poire: Réflexions sur la possibilité d'un monachisme comparatif." *Religions & Histoire*, hors-série 3 (mars) [Être moine]: 14–21.

2010c "The Book as a Sacred Object in Private Homes in Early or Medieval India." In *Medieval and Early Modern Devotional Objects in Global Perspective: Translations of the Sacred*, edited by Elizabeth Robertson and Jennifer Jahner, 37–60. New York: Palgrave Macmillan.

2010d "On Incompetent Monks and Able Urbane Nuns in a Buddhist Monastic Code." *Journal of Indian Philosophy* 38.2: 107–131.

2010e "On the Underside of a Sacred Space: Some Less Appreciated Functions of the Temple in Classical India." In *From Turfan to Ajanta: Festschrift for Dieter Schlingloff on the Occasion of His Eightieth Birthday*, edited by Eli Franco and Monika Zin, 2:883–895. Bhairahawa, Nepal: Lumbini International Research Institute.

2010f "On Some Who Are Not Allowed to Become Buddhist Monks or Nuns: An Old List of Types of Slaves or Unfree Laborers." *Journal of the American Oriental Society* 130.2: 225–234.

2010g *Indian Monastic Buddhism: Collected Papers on Textual, Inscriptional and Archaeological Evidence*. Delhi: Motilal Banarsidass. [An Indian reprint of Schopen 1997a and 2004a in one volume.]

2012a "The Buddhist Nun as an Urban Landlord and a 'Legal Person' in Early India." In *Devadattīyam: Johannes Bronkhorst Felicitation Volume*, edited by François Voegeli, Vincent Eltschinger, Danielle Feller, Maria Piera Candotti, Bogdan Diaconescu, and Malhar Kulkarni, 595–609. Worlds of South and Inner Asia 5. Bern/New York: Peter Lang.

2012b "Redeeming Bugs, Birds, and Really Bad Sinners in Some Medieval Mahāyāna Sūtras and *Dhāraṇīs*." In *Sins and Sinners: Perspectives from Asian Religions*, edited by Phyllis Granoff and Koichi Shinohara, 276–294. Leiden: Brill.

2013a "A New Hat for Hārītī: On 'Giving' Children for Their Protection to Buddhist Monks and Nuns in Early India." In *Little Buddhas: Children and*

Childhoods in Buddhist Texts and Traditions, edited by Vanessa R. Sasson, 17–42. New York: Oxford University Press.

2013b "Bukkyō bunkengaku kara bukkyō kōkogaku e: Indo bukkyō ni okeru seija no katawara e no maizō to budda no gensonsei" 仏教文献学から仏教考古学へ：インド仏教における聖者の傍らへの埋葬とブッダの現存性. In *Daijō bukkyō no ajia* 大乗仏教のアジア (*Mahāyāna Buddhism's Asia*), edited by Katsura Shōryū 桂紹隆, Saitō Akira 斉藤明, Shimoda Masahiro 下田正弘, and Sueki Fumihiko 末木文美士, 4–43. Shirīzu daijō bukkyō シリーズ大乗仏教 (Series Mahāyāna Buddhism) 10. Translated by Katsura Shōryū 桂紹隆. Tokyo: Shunjūsha 春秋社. [A Japanese translation of Schopen 1987a.]

2013c "Indo pulgyosa e issŏsŏ ŭi tu kaji munje: sŭng・sok ŭi kubun'gwa pok ŭi hoehyang e kwanhan kyoŭi" 인도 불교사에 있어서의 두 가지 문제: 승・속의 구분과 복의 회향에 관한 교의. *Pulgyohak ribyu* 불교학리뷰 (*Critical Review for Buddhist Studies*) 13: 193–244. [A Korean translation of Schopen 1985b by Han Daesŏng 한대성.]

2014a *Buddhist Nuns, Monks, and Other Worldly Matters: Recent Papers on Monastic Buddhism in India*. Studies in the Buddhist Traditions. Honolulu: University of Hawai'i Press.

2014b "On the Legal and Economic Activities of Buddhist Nuns: Two Examples from Early India." In Schopen 2014a, 95–118.

2014c "Celebrating Odd Moments: The Biography of the Buddha in Some Mūlasarvāstivādin Cycles of Religious Festivals." In Schopen 2014a, 361–389.

2014d "Liberation Is Only for Those Already Free: Reflections on Debts to Slavery and Enslavement to Debt in an Early Indian Buddhist Monasticism." *Journal of the American Academy of Religion* 82.3: 606–635.

2014e "On the Legal and Economic Activities of Buddhist Nuns: Two Examples from Early India." In *Buddhism and Law: An Introduction*, edited by Rebecca Redwood French and Mark A. Nathan, 91–114. Cambridge: Cambridge University Press. [A reprint of Schopen 2014b.]

2015a "The Fragrance of the Buddha, the Scent of Monuments, and the Odor of Images in Early India." *Bulletin de l'École française d'Extrême-Orient* 101: 11–30.

2015b "*Kŭmgang gyŏng* (*Vajracchedikā*) ŭi chŏnghyŏng gu '*sa pṛthivīpradeśaś caityabhūto bhavet*': taesŭng bulgyo (Mahāyāna) esŏ kyŏngjŏn sungbae e kwanhan saenggak" 『금강경』 (*Vajracchedikā*) 의 정형구 '*sa pṛthivīpradeśaś caityabhūto bhavet*': 대승불교 (Mahāyāna) 에서 경전 숭배에 관한 생각. *Pulgyohak ribyu* 불교학리뷰 (*Critical Review for Buddhist Studies*) 17: 111–169. [A Korean translation of Schopen 1975 by Ryu Hyŏnjŏng 류현정.]

2016 "A Tough-Talking Nun and Women's Language in a Buddhist Monastic Code." In *Sahasram Ati Srajas: Indo-Iranian and Indo-European Studies in Honor of Stephanie W. Jamison*, edited by Dieter Gunkel, Joshua T. Katz,

Brent Vine, and Michael Weiss, 385–398. Ann Arbor/New York: Beech Stave Press.
2017a "The Training and Treatments of an Indian Doctor in a Buddhist Text: A Sanskrit Biography of Jīvaka." In *Buddhism and Medicine: An Anthology of Premodern Sources*, edited by C. Pierce Salguero, 184–204. New York: Columbia University Press.
2017b "Help for the Sick, the Dying, and the Misbegotten: A Sanskrit Version of the *Sūtra of Bhaiṣajyaguru*." In *Buddhism and Medicine: An Anthology of Premodern Sources*, edited by C. Pierce Salguero, 235–251. New York: Columbia University Press.
2018a "On the Legality of Copying Texts: A Buddhist Discussion of Copyright in Early Medieval India." In *Saddharmāmṛtam: Festschrift für Jens-Uwe Hartmann zum 65. Geburtstag*, edited by Oliver von Criegern, Gudrun Melzer, and Johannes Schneider, 399–409. Vienna: Arbeitskreis für Tibetische und Buddhistische Studien Universität Wien.
2018b "A Buddhist Monastic Code as a Source for Indian Law." In *Hindu Law: A New History of Dharmaśāstra*, edited by Patrick Olivelle and Donald R. Davis Jr., 383–401. The Oxford History of Hinduism. Oxford: Oxford University Press.
2018c "On Monks and Emergencies: The Brahmanical Principle of *Āpad* in a Buddhist Monastic Code." In *Reading Slowly: A Festschrift for Jens E. Braarvig*, edited by Lutz Edzard, Jens W. Borgland, and Ute Hüsken, 375–391. Wiesbaden: Harrassowitz Verlag.
2019 "The Business Model of a Buddhist Monasticism: Acquiring Productive Assets." *Hualin International Journal of Buddhist Studies* 2.2: 217–249.
2020 "Biku to bikuni to 'teizoku na' jissen to ni tsuite: Indo bukkyō ni okeru butsuzō sūhai no dōnyū" 比丘と比丘尼と「低俗な」実践とについて：インド仏教における仏像崇拝の導入. In *Minami ajia 1: mauriya-chō ~ guputa-chō* 南アジアI：マウリヤ朝～グプタ朝 (*South Asia 1: Maurya Dynasty to Gupta Dynasty*), edited by Miyaji Akira 宮治昭 and Fukuyama Yasuko 福山泰子, 195–224. Translated by Kishino Ryōji 岸野亮示. Ajia bukkyō bijutsu ronshū アジア仏教美術論集 (Collected Essays on Asian Buddhist Art). Tokyo: Chūō kōron bijutsu shuppan 中央公論美術出版. [A Japanese translation of Schopen 1988–1989.]
2021 *Taesŭng pulgyo hŭnggi sidae Indo ŭi sawŏn saenghwal* 대승불교 흥기시대 인도의 사원 생활. Translated by Im Ŭnjŏng 임은정. Seoul: Unjusa 운주사. [A Korean translation of Schopen 2000c.]
2022a "Attitudes Toward the Wealth and Comfort of Monks and Monasteries in a Buddhist Monastic Code." In *Connecting the Art, Literature, and Religion of South and Central Asia: Studies in Honour of Monika Zin*, edited by Ines Konczak-Nagel, Satomi Hiyama, and Astrid Klein, 353–363. New Delhi: Dev Publishers and Distributors.
2022b "The Monk Mūlaphalguna and the Nuns: Biography as Criticism." *Hualin International Journal of Buddhist Studies* 5.1: 313–333. Also published in *From Jetavana to Jerusalem: Sacred Biography in Asian Perspectives and*

Beyond. Essays in Honour of Professor Phyllis Granoff, edited by Jinhua Chen, 2:811–831. Singapore: World Scholastic Publishers, 2022.

2022c "On Buddhist Image Processions and Monastic Fund Drives in Early and Medieval India." In *A Forest of Knowledge: A Collection of Essays on Texts and Images in Celebration of Professor Koichi Shinohara's Eightieth Birthday*, edited by Jinhua Chen, 102–133. Singapore: World Scholastic Publishers.

2022d *Indo daijō bukkyō no kyozō to danpen* インド大乗仏教の虚像と断片. Translated under the supervision of Watanabe Shōgo 渡辺章悟 by Ueda Noboru 上田昇, Kanō Kazuo 加納和雄, Keira Ryūsei 計良龍成, Choi Jinkyoung 崔珍景, Matsumura Junko 松村淳子, and Yonezawa Yoshiyasu 米澤嘉康. Tokyo: Kokusho kankōkai 国書刊行会. [A Japanese translation of Schopen 2005a.]

2023a "Selling Space at the Monastery and Making Economic Sense of the 'Intrusive' at Monastic Sites in Gandhāra." In *Gandhāran Art in Its Buddhist Context: Papers from the Fifth International Workshop of the Gandhāra Connections Project, University of Oxford, 21st–23rd March, 2022*, edited by Wannaporn Rienjang and Peter Stewart, 1–11. Oxford: Archaeopress Archaeology.

2023b "The Business Side of a Buddhist Monastery." In *Tree and Serpent: Early Buddhist Art in India*, edited by John Guy, 118–122 with notes on 298. New York: The Metropolitan Museum of Art.

2023c "On the Loss of Legal Documents and Business Records from Indian Buddhist Monasteries." In *Rethinking Buddhism: Text, Context, Contestation*, edited by Anand Singh, 227–249. Delhi: Primus Books.

2024 "On Pious Ladies and Merchants Making Money for Buddhist Monks: An Inscription and a Rule." In *Transcending Boundaries: Premodern Cultural Transactions across Asia: Essays in Honour of Osmund Bopearachchi*, edited by Susmita Basu Majumdar, 471–480. Delhi: Primus Books.

2025 *Property and Privilege in a Buddhist Monastic Code: A Sanskrit Text and Translation of Two Books of the Mūlasarvāstivādavinaya*. Rocher Indology Series. New York: Oxford University Press.

Forth. a "Everyday Life and Ordinary Activities in Kushan Buddhist Monasteries and Convents." In preparation.

Forth. b "Making a Monastery Beautiful: Two Versions of a Vinaya Text on Paintings and Their Placement." In a volume for Juhyung Rhi. In preparation.

Forth. c *Making Ends Meet in an Indian Buddhist Monastery: The Convergence of Lay and Monastic Goals*. In progress.

Forth. d *One Version of a* Bhaiṣajyaguru-sūtra *from Bāmiyān and Gilgit*. In progress.

Part 1
Mahāyāna and Tantra Studies

The Visualization Stage (*utpattikrama*) and Its Workings*

Yael Bentor

To Gregory, with endless gratitude from your very first PhD student

Introduction

In the visualization stage (*utpattikrama, bskyed rim*) known also as the generation, development, or creation stage, aspirants visualize themselves as a buddha (*iṣṭadevatā, deva; yi dam, lha*)[1] according to the specifications set forth in a sādhana manual. But what distinguishes yogis who meditate on themselves as a buddha from a beggar boasting to be a king? Why, according to Indian and Tibetan authors, can aspirants who visualize themselves as buddhas eventually become buddhas? What, if anything, makes tantric visualization capable of achieving a soteriological transformation? In numerous tantric texts this potential of the practice is taken for granted, as long as all necessary conditions are met. Other explanations hinge on the powers the guru transmits to the disciples during the initiation or the blessing bestowed by the enlightened being the yogis aspire to become. There are even certain techniques to "arouse the heart" of this *devatā*.[2] However, more rationally inclined Indian and Tibetan scholars of tantra seek less miraculous and more philosophical explanations for the working of the visualization stage. It is the latter approach that will be the focus of my paper. As we will see, these scholars resort to some rather unexpected authorities.

* This research was supported by the Israel Science Foundation, grant no. 401/13. I would like to thank Eli Franco for his valuable comments on a draft of this paper.

1. Akṣobhya in the *Guhyasamāja-tantra*. See chapter 1 of this tantra, Matsunaga 1978, 4 and 6.

2. "You should arouse the heart" *hṛdayaṃ pracodayet* or *codanaṃ hṛdaye proktam, thugs ni bskul bar bya* or *snying kha ru bskul bar bya*. See, for example, the *Guhyasamāja-tantra* 10.5–14, Matsunaga 1978, 30–31; Stog 408, Rgyud, vol. *ca*, 24a–b.

Relinquishing Conceptual Thoughts and Achieving Nondual Profundity and Sublimity[3]

A major goal suggested for the visualization stage is relinquishing conceptual thoughts that create the aspirant's ordinary world and, instead, developing the special vision of the maṇḍala and the deities residing therein. Nāgārjuna, "the founder" of the Ārya school of the Guhyasamāja,[4] opens his manual of the visualization stage, the *Piṇḍīkramasādhana*, by stating that the goal of the visualization stage is to purify the mind of conceptualizations (*vikalpa, rnam rtog*), as these are the source of delusion of all beings in the world.[5]

Crucially, though, the visualization stage is essentially conceptualization. The usual question arises: how can a visualization of manifold details of an embellished celestial mansion, with dozens of different buddhas and bodhisattvas dwelling in it, bring the meditator to overcome conceptualizations and advance toward the goal of enlightenment? In addressing this difficulty, we will explore traditional explanations about the workings of maṇḍala visualization and about the role of visualization in advancing aspirants toward the soteriological goal of averting saṃsāric existence.

Jñānapāda (active ca. 770–820),[6] "the founder" of the Guhyasamāja school named for him, explains the working of the visualization stage by drawing upon the notion of the pair "profound and sublime" vis-à-vis conceptualization. This pair, profound (*gambhīra, zab*) and sublime (*udāra, rgya che ba*), is found also in nontantric works, such as Asaṅga's *Mahāyānasūtrālaṅkāra*[7] and Dharmakīrti's *Pramāṇavārttika*.[8] In these works, this pair stands as antithet-

3. Or the yoga of nondual profundity and manifestation; see below.

4. On the dates and chronology of the Ārya Nāgārjuna and Jñānapāda schools of the *Guhyasamāja-tantra*, see Tomabechi 2008.

5. According to Nāgārjuna: "The wise should observe the three worlds, which are deluded as a result of faulty imprints for conceptualization and purify them with yoga tantra." *Piṇḍīkramasādhana*, La Vallée Poussin 1896, verse 3: *vikalpa-vāsanā-doṣān jagat-traya-vimohakān samabhivīkṣya tān dhīmān yoga-tantreṇa śodhayet*. Sde dge 1796, Rgyud, vol. *ngi*, 1b.

6. Jñānapāda was not only one of the earliest tantric theoreticians but also a highly influential scholar. For more on the life and thought of Jñānapāda, see Dalton and Szántó 2019.

7. According to *Mahāyānasūtrālaṅkāra* 1.13, the sublime and the profound bring about nonconceptuality: "From the sublime and the profound arise ripening and nonconceptuality. Thus both have been taught. This method is [found] in this supreme [pair]." Lévi 1907–1911, 1:5: *audāryād api gāmbhīryāt paripāko 'vikalpanā, deśanāto dvayasyāsmin sa copāyo niruttare*.

8. In *Pramāṇavārttika, Pramāṇasiddhi* 1, the pair of profound and the sublime is associated with the relinquishing of conceptualization: "Homage to him who is universally good, whose manifestations are divested of the snares of conceptualizing and are profound and lofty [sublime]

ical to conceptual thoughts. No doubt Jñānapāda was aware that his terminological choice alludes to the *Mahāyānasūtrālaṅkāra*,[9] and to Dharmakīrti as well, as we will see.

Jñānapāda uses "profound and sublime" at the end of his *Guhyasamāja* sādhana, titled *Samantabhadra*, where he points out certain general observations about the visualization stage as a whole. Jñānapāda associates ordinary conceptual thoughts (*prākṛtavikalpa, tha mal rnam rtog*) with saṃsāric suffering (*bhavaduḥkha, srid pa'i sdug bsngal*) and states that the antidote to both is a mind endowed with a profound and sublime nature.[10] Jñānapāda then continues: "Conceptual thoughts will not appear to [the mind] endowed with a profound and sublime nature."[11] Here too, conceptual thoughts stand in contrast to the profound and sublime. It is the mind endowed with a profound and sublime nature that dispels conceptual thoughts. In this context, the mind endowed with a profound and sublime nature is the mind that visualizes the maṇḍala with its celestial mansion and deities.[12]

Then Jñānapāda discusses how such a mind is capable of overcoming conceptual thoughts.[13] What Jñānapāda seems to be saying[14] is that when an antidote occurs once, it will advance and increase through practice and finally totally block its opposite. In other words, when a mind endowed with a profound and sublime nature is cultivated to its fullest, it will be able to wholly

. . ."; translated in Hayes and Gillon 1991, 2. Miyasaka 1971–1972, 2: *vidhūta-kalpanā-jāla-gambhīrodāra-mūrtaye, namaḥ samanta-bhadrāya samanta-spharaṇatviṣe.* Sde dge 4210, Tshad ma, vol. *ce*, 94b.

9. Jñānapāda cites the *Mahāyānasūtrālaṅkāra* in his *Ātmasādhanāvatāra*, Sde dge 1860, Rgyud, vol. *di*, 54a, a treatise on the visualization stage.

10. See Jñānapāda, *Samantabhadrasādhana*, v. 158, Sde dge 1855, Rgyud, vol. *di*, 35b. The Sanskrit terms can be found in Szántó, in progress. Furthermore, Szántó points out that this verse is quoted in the *Abhayapaddhati*, which has been preserved in Sanskrit. For an edition of the Sanskrit and an English translation, see Luo 2010, 5.

11. *Samantabhadrasādhana*, Sde dge 1855, Rgyud, vol. *di*, 35b6–7: *zab cing rgya che ba yi bdag nyid can, gang yin der ni kun rtog snang mi 'gyur.*

12. See Thagana, *Samantabhadrasādhanavṛtti*, Sde dge 1868, Rgyud, vol. *di*, 229b, and Vaidyapāda, *Caturaṅgasādhanasamantabhadrīṭīkā*, Sde dge 1872, Rgyud, vol. *ni*, 176b–177a.

13. *Samantabhadrasādhana*, Sde dge 1855, Rgyud, vol. *di*, 35b–36a: *gang zhig gang dang mi mthun pa dag tu, lan cig gyur pa'ang de bgrod rgyas gyur pa, mthong ba'i bslab pa rnam par 'phel ba yis, rang gi mi mthun shin tu 'gag par byed.*

14. The Tibetan translation of this verse is unclear, and unfortunately, we do not have access to the Sanskrit of this verse, though the manuscript is kept in Lhasa. I rely here on the kind explanation of Harunaga Isaacson in Vienna on May 16, 2019, about Samantabhadra's commentary (available in Sanskrit) on this verse. The commentator Samantabhadra should not be confused with the work he commented on, the *Samantabhadrasādhana*.

eradicate ordinary conceptualizations. But why would it be that a mind endowed with a profound and sublime nature that visualizes the maṇḍala circle is guaranteed to transcend ordinary conceptualization and liberate practitioners from saṃsāric suffering? We will now turn to this question.

The Jñānapāda School's Reliance on the Thought of Dharmakīrti

All the Indian commentaries on Jñānapāda's *Samantabhadrasādhana* turn to the *Pramāṇasiddhi* chapter in Dharmakīrti's *Pramāṇavārttika* (vv. 205–216)[15] to explain these lines.[16] In these works, ordinary conceptual thoughts that typify saṃsāric suffering are identified with grasping at I and mine,[17] while the mind visualizing the maṇḍala circle is equated with the wisdom that realizes no-self. For Dharmakīrti, by engaging in selflessness, the mind prevents the opposite of selflessness, thus uprooting the basis for self-grasping. As Cristina Pecchia explains: "For the contrary of the view of selflessness can no longer maintain its grip on a mind whose epistemic condition is defined by selflessness."[18]

Likewise, the commentaries on Jñānapāda's *Samantabhadrasādhana* explain that the mind engaged in the maṇḍala circle—endowed with inconceivable nature[19]—is capable of bringing about the irreversible cessation of

15. These verses are edited and translated into English in Pecchia 2015.

16. Vaidyapāda, *Caturaṅgasādhanasamantabhadrīṭīkā*, Sde dge 1872, Rgyud, vol. *ni*, 177a, alludes to *Pramāṇavārttika*, *Pramāṇasiddhi* 212cd–213ab in Miyasaka 1971–1972; Phalavajra, *Samantabhadrasādhanavṛtti*, Sde dge 1867, Rgyud, vol. *di*, 185b3–4, cites *Pramāṇavārttika*, *Pramāṇasiddhi* 208cd–211ab in Miyasaka 1971–1972; Samantabhadra, *Sāramañjarī*, Sde dge 1869, Rgyud, vol. *ni*, 44b, cites *Pramāṇavārttika*, *Pramāṇasiddhi* 211cd–213ab in Miyasaka 1971–1972; and Ratnākaraśānti, *Guhyasamājamaṇḍalavidhiṭīkā*, Sde dge 1871, Rgyud, vol. *ni*, 127b2, cites *Pramāṇavārttika*, *Pramāṇasiddhi* 210cd–211ab = *Svārthānumāna*, v. 221, in Miyasaka 1971–1972.

17. Sanskrit *ātmātmīya*, Tibetan *bdag dang bdag gi*. See Samantabhadra, *Sāramañjarī*, Sde dge 1869, Rgyud, vol. *ni*, 43b; Vaidyapāda, *Caturaṅgasādhanasamantabhadrīṭīkā*, Sde dge 1872, Rgyud, vol. *ni*, 176b; Phalavajra, *Samantabhadrasādhanavṛtti*, Sde dge 1867, Rgyud, vol. *di*, 185b; Thagana, *Samantabhadrasādhanavṛtti*, Sde dge 1868, Rgyud, vol. *di*, 229b; and Ratnākaraśānti, *Guhyasamājamaṇḍalavidhiṭīkā*, Sde dge 1871, Rgyud, vol. *ni*, 127a.

18. Pecchia 2015, 240. Here she explains Dharmakīrti's lines in *Pramāṇavārttika*, *Pramāṇasiddhi* 210cd–211ab in Miyasaka 1971–1972; v. 210 in Pecchia 2015, 240, and in Franco 2017b, 341. The latter paraphrases the verse in the following words: "The nature of the mind which is truthful and free from afflictions is not sublated by the opposites (i.e., by errors and defilements) even if one makes an effort, because the mind takes sides with them (i.e., with truth and purity)." Translated also by Dunne 2004, 369–370, and Yaita 1988, 436.

19. See, respectively, Samantabhadra, *Sāramañjarī*, Sde dge 1869, Rgyud, vol. *ni*, 43b (*acintya*),

conceptual thoughts and saṃsāric suffering. The example Dharmakīrti uses to explain why grasping at the self will not recur is the false perception of a rope as a snake.[20] Vaidyapāda or Vitapāda,[21] one of the earlier commentators on the *Samantabhadrasādhana*, offers this very simile in order to illustrate how the mind visualizing the maṇḍala circle entirely blocks saṃsāric suffering.

These commentators also follow Dharmakīrti's view of the unique nature of the antidote.[22] In the *Pramāṇasiddhi* chapter, Dharmakīrti contrasts the antidote that can achieve an irreversible transformation with antidotes such as benevolent love (*maitrī, byams pa*), taken to be an antidote to aversion (*dveṣa, zhe sdang*).[23] The latter type of antidotes cannot completely eliminate afflictions such as aversion, because they still have at their root the notion of an existing self.[24] The mind endowed with the inconceivable nature of the maṇḍala circle, by contrast, is distinguished as capable of completely stopping conceptual thoughts and saṃsāric suffering thanks to its nondual profound and sublime essence.

Thus, in accordance with Dharmakīrti, Jñānapāda and his commentators hold that the mind visualizing the maṇḍala is capable of achieving a soteriological transformation, such as putting an end to saṃsāric suffering, because it is characterized by nondual profundity and sublimity.[25]

---

and Vaidyapāda, *Caturaṅgasādhanasamantabhadrīṭīkā*, Sde dge 1872, Rgyud, vol. *ni*, 176b (*bsam gyis mi khyab pa*); and Phalavajra, *Samantabhadrasādhanavṛtti*, Sde dge 1867, Rgyud, vol. *di*, 185b (*kun tu bzang po*).

20. *Pramāṇavārttika, Pramāṇasiddhi* 208 in Miyasaka 1971–1972; v. 207 in Pecchia 2015, 230, and Franco 2017b, 341. Yet this metaphor is found in texts that precede Dharmakīrti, including *Laṅkāvatāra-sūtra, Sagāthaka*, v. 498; Asaṅga, *Mahāyānasaṃgraha* 3.8; and Vasubandhu, *Abhidharmakośa*, autocommentary on 6.58.

21. Vaidyapāda, *Caturaṅgasādhanasamantabhadrīṭīkā*, Sde dge 1872, Rgyud, vol. *ni*, 177b.

22. Vaidyapāda, *Caturaṅgasādhanasamantabhadrīṭīkā*, Sde dge 1872, Rgyud, vol. *ni*, 177a: "This is unlike kindness and so forth" (*byams pa la sogs pa de lta bu min no*); Samantabhadra, *Sāramañjarī*, Sde dge 1869, Rgyud, vol. *ni*, 44a–b; Ratnākaraśānti, *Guhyasamājamaṇḍalavidhiṭīkā*, Sde dge 1871, Rgyud, vol. *ni*, 127b: "It totally eliminates" (*shin tu ldog pa nyid yin pa'i phyir ro*).

23. *Pramāṇavārttika, Pramāṇasiddhi* 212cd–213ab in Miyasaka 1971–1972; v. 212 in Pecchia 2015, 245, and Franco 2017b, 342.

24. These antidotes are classified as *sattvālambana, sems can la dmigs pa*, while a bodhisattva reaches the level of *nirālambana*. See Pecchia 2008, 169–170.

25. As we would expect, the commentators on the *Samantabhadrasādhana* associate the two poles indivisibly united in this mind with emptiness (*śūnyatā*) and compassion (*karuṇā*), wisdom (*jñāna*) and method (*upāya*), as well as profound (*zab mo*) and manifest (*gsal ba*). See, respectively, Vaidyapāda, *Caturaṅgasādhanasamantabhadrīṭīkā*, Sde dge 1872, Rgyud, vol. *ni*, 176b, and Samantabhadra, *Sāramañjarī*, Sde dge 1869, Rgyud, vol. *ni*, 44a; Thagana,

The Importance of the Mind Endowed with a Profound and Sublime Nature in the Mantra Vehicle

The Jñānapāda school takes the mind endowed with the nondual profound and sublime nature as one of the features that makes the Mantra Vehicle superior to the Pāramitā Vehicle.[26] In his *Ātmasādhanāvatāra*,[27] Jñānapāda explains that a mind endowed with a profound and sublime nature can attain its fruit because it is granted the same nature as the fruit, or it cultivates causes that accord with the result. In fifteenth-century Tibet, Tsong kha pa considered this point to be of utmost importance, elaborating on it at the beginning of his *Sngags rim chen mo*.[28] For Tsong kha pa, a profound and sublime nature accords with the fruit of the path, the two *kāya*s of the Buddha. The profound nature of the mind brings about the *dharmakāya* and wisdom, while the sublime brings about the *rūpakāya*, which is the method aspect that can act for the sake of others. In this way, aspirants on the Mantra Vehicle engage in causes that are compatible with the goal and are therefore efficacious. On the other hand, in the Pāramitā Vehicle meditations on emptiness accord with the *dharmakāya*; but since this vehicle offers no meditations that are similar to a *rūpakāya*, it lacks causes that accord with one of the goals of the path. In other words, both the Pāramitā and the Mantra vehicles specify that the path of wisdom is meditation on emptiness. However, the path of method described in the Pāramitā Vehicle—the other five *pāramitā*s—lacks a feature that can lead directly to the *rūpakāya*. Therefore, only in the Mantra Vehicle the methods—meditation on the deity during the visualization stage and the practice of the illusory body during the completion stage—accord in their nature with the fruit and are thus effective. Tsong kha pa sees this very characteristic of the mantric path as its advantage over the path of the *pāramitā*s.

Samantabhadrasādhanavṛtti, Sde dge 1868, Rgyud, vol. *di*, 229b; and Vaidyapāda, *Caturaṅgasādhanasamantabhadrīṭīkā*, Sde dge 1872, Rgyud, vol. *ni*, 177a, *zab mo dang gsal ba.*

26. See Jñānapāda, *Samantabhadrasādhana*, Sde dge 1855, Rgyud, vol. *di*, 36a (v. 161); as well as the commentaries by Vaidyapāda, *Caturaṅgasādhanasamantabhadrīṭīkā*, Sde dge 1872, Rgyud, vol. *ni*, 177b, and by Thagana, *Samantabhadrasādhanavṛtti*, Sde dge 1868, Rgyud, vol. *di*, 230a.

27. Jñānapāda, *Ātmasādhanāvatāra*, Sde dge 1860, Rgyud, vol. *di*, 54b.

28. Tsong kha pa, *Sngags rim chen mo*, 20–42; translated in Hopkins 1977, 115–150.

The Efficacy of a Mind Endowed with a Profound and Sublime Nature According to Ratnākaraśānti

Ratnākaraśānti (ca. 970–1045)[29] disagrees with some of the earlier commentators on Jñānapāda's *Samantabhadrasādhana* with regard to the term "once." As we saw, Jñānapāda speaks about a contradictory event or an antidote that occurs *once*, after which, through gradual practice, aspirants intensify their experience of the mind endowed with the profound and sublime until they are finally able to totally block its opposite: conceptual thoughts. This is not the only case where the sudden and gradual are thus taken together,[30] but certain commentators understood *lan cig* as *lhan cig*, that is, "simultaneously."[31] According to Samantabhadra, the Sanskrit here is *sakṛt*: *sa* + *kṛt* which is equally ambiguous; it means either "once" or "simultaneously."

Ratnākaraśānti, by contrast, emphasizes that it is not the case that ordinary appearances do not arise in the aspirant's mind simply because this mind is submerged in maṇḍala visualization. He says: "Conceptual thoughts do not appear since the mind endowed with the aspect of the maṇḍala engages in dispelling all false conceptualizations, and not because they do not appear simultaneously."[32] "They" here refers to conceptual thoughts and the visualization of the maṇḍala. In other words, it is not that when the maṇḍala appears, false conceptualizations cannot appear. Rather, Ratnākaraśānti emphasizes, a mind absorbed in maṇḍala visualization cannot but dispel false conceptualizations, because it is "endowed with a profound and sublime nature" that is capable of eliminating conceptual thoughts that bring about saṃsāric suffering.

Ratnākaraśānti supports his argument by comparing the mind endowed with the form of the maṇḍala to the meditative absorption on infinite space (*ākāśānantyāyatana*, *nam mkha' mtha' yas skye mched*).[33] He concludes that while the latter meditation cannot avert saṃsāric suffering, the visualization stage can do so because there the mind is endowed with "a profound and sublime nature."

This brings us to a fundamental difference between the visualization stage

29. Seton 2018, 366.

30. See, for example, Paṇ chen Blo bzang chos kyi rgyal mtshan (1570–1662), *Dngos grub rgya mtsho'i snying po*, 37b: "You should visualize instantaneously and develop the clarity of the visualization step by step." Translated in Bentor and Dorjee 2019, 118.

31. Including Vaidyapāda, *Caturaṅgasādhanasamantabhadrīṭikā*, Sde dge 1872, Rgyud, vol. *ni*, 177a, and Phalavajra, *Samantabhadrasādhanavṛtti*, Sde dge 1867, Rgyud, vol. *di*, 185b.

32. Ratnākaraśānti, *Guhyasamājamaṇḍalavidhiṭikā*, Sde dge 1871, Rgyud, vol. *ni*, 127a7–b1.

33. Ratnākaraśānti, *Guhyasamājamaṇḍalavidhiṭikā*, Sde dge 1871, Rgyud, vol. *ni*, 127a5–b5.

and the meditative absorption on infinite space. While the latter meditation reduces the mental content to a bare minimum, the visualization stage inflates it with incredible elaborations. This very difference pertains also to the closely related *kṛtsna* (*zad par*, Pāli *kasiṇa*) meditation, the single-pointed concentration of *śamatha* practice, and absorptions (*samāpatti*, *snyoms par 'jug pa*) on the formless realm (*ārūpya*). For our author, then, mental overload is more effective than mental deprivation. Hence, in comparison with a mind emptied of any mental content, the mind meditating on an embellished maṇḍala—where numerous ornamented deities holding varied emblems reside—can better achieve a transformation of soteriological significance. In a famous verse of the *Hevajra-tantra*, the role of the elaborate mental contents is stressed as well. We will return to this point below, but first let us briefly revisit Dharmakīrti.

For Dharmakīrti, meditations on *kṛtsna* and the loathsome (*aśubha*, *mi gtsang*) are nonconceptual because they are created through the power of meditation.[34] This is despite the fact that, in these meditations, the objects are unreal (*abhūta*). At the same time, in his *Pramāṇaviniścaya*,[35] Dharmakīrti defines direct perception (*pratyakṣa*, *mngon sum*) as nonconceptual and nonerroneous (*abhrānta*, *ma 'khrul pa*).[36] As Vincent Eltschinger notes, cognitions meditating on the *kasiṇa* and the loathsome meet the first defining condition of a direct perception but not the second.[37] Although nonconceptual, these cognitions are erroneous because their objects are imaginary and not real; hence, they are not reliable or valid (*pramāṇa*, *tshad ma*).

As we saw above, the mind endowed with a profound and sublime nature that visualizes the maṇḍala circle is free of conceptualization. Can this mind, however, be taken as nonerroneous or valid and therefore qualify for Dharmakīrti's definition of direct perception? Dharmakīrti's concern in the aforementioned discussions of the meditations on *kasiṇa* and direct perception is the nonconceptual and direct perception of the four noble truths. Yet Samantabhadra, in his commentary on Jñānapāda's *Samantabhadrasādhana*, writes about a nonconceptual and valid mind in relation to the mind endowed with a profound and sublime nature that visualizes the maṇḍala circle. Samantabhadra concludes his explanation of Jñānapāda's verse cited above—

34. *Pramāṇavārttika*, *Pratyakṣa* 284 in Miyasaka 1971–1972. Translated by Dunne 2006, 516, and Eltschinger 2009, 194.

35. As Eli Franco (2017a, 119–121) points out, Dharmakīrti does so only in the *Pramāṇaviniścaya*, while in the *Pramāṇavārttika*, he still keeps Dignāga's definition as nonconceptual alone.

36. *Pramāṇaviniścaya*, Steinkellner 2007, 7.7. See Eltschinger 2009, 192.

37. Eltschinger 2009, 195–196.

"conceptual thoughts will not appear to [the mind] endowed with a profound and sublime nature"—by saying: "That experience itself is valid (*pramāṇa*)."[38] The context of this statement is unclear, if not outright obscure. Can we entertain the possibility that what Samantabhadra has in mind is Dharmakīrti's definition of direct perception as nonconceptual and valid? In other words, does Samantabhadra explain that the mind endowed with a profound and sublime nature that visualizes the maṇḍala circle is a direct perception as defined by Dharmakīrti? I suggest he does.

The Efficacy of a Mind Endowed with a Profound and Sublime Nature According to Tsong kha pa

In the chapter on the visualization stage in his *Sngags rim chen mo*, Tsong kha pa expands on Jñānapāda's notion of the mind endowed with the inconceivable nature of the maṇḍala circle.[39] Tsong kha pa stresses that this mind meditates simultaneously on emptiness and appearances (*zab gsal*). The notion of nondual form and emptiness is, of course, not unique to the present case. We may mention Ratnarakṣita, who in his *Padminī* commentary on the *Saṃvarodaya-tantra*,[40] in the context of the visualization stage, emphasizes that yogis should not meditate exclusively on the form of the deities but on the form of the deities that are inseparable from *dharmatā*. Jñānapāda and Tsong kha pa, however, speak about nonduality specifically in relation to the meditating mind. Form and emptiness are united indivisibly in a single cognition (*shes pa gcig*).

Tsong kha pa explains how a single mind can be absorbed in both meditation on the absence of intrinsic nature and the visualization of the maṇḍala wheel. One aspect of the mind realizing emptiness arises as a special appearance of the celestial mansion and the deities therein. In other words, while the subjective aspect of the mind that understands the absence of intrinsic nature is absorbed in emptiness, the objective aspect of this mind arises as the maṇḍala, with its celestial mansion and deities. Hence, this mind, endowed with nondual profundity and sublimity, engages here in the visualization as nondual and therefore is capable of achieving a soteriological goal:

38. Samantabhadra, *Sāramañjarī*, Sde dge 1869, Rgyud, vol. *ni*, 44a: *nyams su myong ba nyid tshad ma yin*; Szántó, in progress, 159.1: *anubhava eva pramāṇam*.

39. Tsong kha pa, *Sngags rim chen mo*, 493.

40. Ratnarakṣita, *Saṃvarodayapadminīpañjikā*, *Sdom pa 'byung ba'i dka' 'grel padma can*, Sde dge 1420, Rgyud, vol. *wa*, 1b1–101b3. For the Sanskrit *na khalv akāra-mātraṃ bhāvyate, dharmatā-mātraṃ cākāracakram apāsya taṭasthaṃ na saṃbhavati*, see Tanemura, Kanō, and Kuranishi 2017, 9.

> Once you have meditated on the wheel of deities, take the deities as the focus of your visualization and allow the subjective aspect of your mind—in its mode of apprehension that understands the meaning of appearances without intrinsic nature—to absorb in emptiness, while the objective aspect of your mind arises as the maṇḍala with its celestial mansion and deities. In this way you meditate on the yoga of nondual profundity and manifestation.[41]

Followers of the Dge lugs school consider this a unique feature of their tradition. Still, members of other schools, including A myes zhabs (1597–1662),[42] follow this meditative method as well.

Proliferation of Mental Constructs

The *Hevajra-tantra* advocates the tantric technique known as "employing one's enemy" for overcoming that "enemy": "By passion sentient beings are bound and by that very passion they are released."[43] The same chapter of the *Hevajra-tantra* provides an explanation of how conceptual visualization is employed in order to overcome conceptualization: "By means of the yoga of the visualization stage, *vratin*s should meditate on the proliferations of mental constructs (*prapañca*, *spros pa*). Once they have made the proliferations dream-like, they should use this very proliferation to de-proliferate (*niḥprapañcayet*, *spros med bya*)."[44] Aspirants of the visualization stage first meditate on mental proliferation, visualizing themselves as the maṇḍala and the awakened beings who reside in it. Then, coming to understand that this mental visualization is a dream-like illusion, they comprehend the nature of all mental elaborations. In this way, de-proliferation is accomplished by means of proliferation.

41. Tsong kha pa, *Sngags rim chen mo*, 493, my translation. For another English translation, see Yarnall 2013, 195.

42. A myes zhabs Ngag dbang kun dga' bsod nams, *Rgyu dang 'bras bu'i theg pa'i spyi don*, 139a.

43. Snellgrove 1959. *Hevajra-tantra*, II.ii.51 (English in vol. 1, Sanskrit and Tibetan in vol. 2); Sde dge 418, Rgyud 'bum, vol. *nga*, 16a4–5, my translation. A similar notion is found in the *Saṃdhinirmocana-sūtra*, where a *nimitta* (Tibetan *mtshan ma*) is removed by another *nimitta*, as a large wedge is removed by means of a small wedge; chapter 8, Sde dge 106, Mdo sde, vol. *ca*, 36b5–6. Yamabe, personal communication, Sept. 9, 2018.

44. Snellgrove 1959. *Hevajra-tantra*, II.ii.29 (English in vol. 1, Sanskrit and Tibetan in vol. 2); Sde dge 418, Rgyud 'bum, vol. *nga*, 15a7, my translation. Sanskrit *utpatti-krama-yogena prapañcaṃ bhāvayet vratī, prapañcaṃ svapnavat kṛtvā prapañcair niḥprapañcayet*. See also Isaacson 2001, 470n95.

In his commentary on the verses of the *Hevajra-tantra*, the *Muktāvalī*,[45] Ratnākaraśānti glosses "proliferations of mental constructs" with a multitude of different forms, explaining that "once they have made [them] dream-like" means that the aspirants should examine these forms until they understand their nature to be just like appearances produced by a dreaming mind. Ratnākaraśānti then conflates "should de-proliferate" with *should not conceptualize*, thus aligning the terminology of the *Hevajra-tantra* with that of the literature we have seen above.[46] He urges meditators in the visualization stage to investigate the ways that the myriad appearances they visualize come into being.

The *Hevajra-tantra* uses the example of dreams to illustrate its point. Just as upon awakening from sleep, dreams are realized as products of the mind, meditators in the visualization stage should grasp the nature of their visualizations. By dissolving their ordinary world and recreating it as a maṇḍala inhabited by awakened beings, aspirants begin to grasp the workings of their ordinary mind and the illusory nature of all appearances. They come to recognize conceptualization as conceptualization and understand how their ordinary world came into being, why it appears to them in the way it does, and why they perceive things as they do. They come to know how their minds work and how these insights apply not only to their ordinary world but to their visualized maṇḍalic world as well.

Although they are initially created by proliferations of mental constructs, visions seen during the visualization stage are in a sense "more than real"—that is, more real than any other saṃsāric appearance. These are, after all, the buddhas and other awakened beings who dwell in the maṇḍala. On the one hand, aspirants know precisely how these visions appeared, since they themselves created them. On the other hand, these visions are considered "reality" as it appears to the awakened eye, and they constitute the transformed reality that is a central goal of tantric practice.

It is perhaps in order to authenticate the reality of the maṇḍala that Samantabhadra points to a mind visualizing the maṇḍala circle as being not

45. Tripathi and Negi 2001, 141; Sde dge 1189, Rgyud, vol. *ga*, 274b1–3. See also the similar comments in Kāṇha, *Yogaratnamālā*, Snellgrove 1959, 2:138 (Sanskrit); Sde dge 1183, Rgyud vol. *kha*, 38a.

46. The step of de-proliferation is taken by certain tantric commentators as aiming at abandoning attachment to the appearances created by the visualization itself. It is often termed "completion stage," but it refers not to the completion stage that relies on yogic practices but to the nonconceptual phase at the end of the visualization stage.

only nonconceptual but also valid (*pramāṇa*).[47] In this way, Samantabhadra sanctions "reality" as it appears to the awakened eye through Buddhist philosophical terminology.

As Luis Gómez has pointed out,[48] there is an important difference between ordinary magicians and wonder-worker bodhisattvas. While the former seek to deceive their audience, the latter aim to alert their disciples to the fact that they are constantly deceived by ordinary perceptions. Accomplished tantric yogis are considered to realize, on their own, how their visualizations work, and how their ordinary and maṇḍalic worlds alike are illusionary.

The Position of the Visualization Stage within Tantric Paths to Enlightenment

The tantric visualization stage has been presented here thus far as a tantric practice that can bring its practitioners to the ultimate goal of complete buddhahood. This view is supported, for example, by the *Tārāsādhana* by Anupamarakṣita, which according to Luis Gómez, "is one of the longest and most detailed in the *Sādhanamālā*."[49] This sādhana closes with an explanation of the benefits of the visualization beginning with the eight siddhis up until: "In the very palm of the hand of such a person [who has completed the sādhana] the Blessed Tārā will place even the state of a buddha, so hard to win."[50] Hence, this *Tārāsādhana*, much like other sādhanas included in the *Sādhanamālā* as well as in the Tibetan Bstan 'gyur, is an independent undertaking in its own right. No doubt, one finds in all scriptures—and even practice manuals—claims regarding the potential benefits of reading or practicing that particular scripture or practice. It is nonetheless possible that, under certain circumstances, the visualization stage has been considered as capable of inducing buddhahood, and Anupamarakṣita's *Tārāsādhana* is not unique in this regard.

Yet, for the vast majority of Indian and Tibetan scholars of tantra, the visualization stage is but the first step in the tantric path toward awakening. It is followed by the completion stage (*niṣpannakrama* or *utpannakrama*, *rdzogs rim*), which is thus called the "second stage" (*rim pa gnyis pa*). According to

47. Obviously Samantabhadra could not have seen the aforementioned *Hevajra-tantra* and Ratnākaraśānti's *Muktāvalī*, dated to perhaps the eleventh century.

48. Gómez 1977, 229.

49. Gómez 1995, 319.

50. Anupamarakṣita, *Sādhanamālā*, Bhattacharyya 1925, 1:206; Sde dge 3491, Rgyud, vol. *mu*, 147b5.

Tanemura, the earliest witness to the integration of the two stages is found in a work by *none other than* Jñānapāda—on whom we relied in our discussion on the working of the visualization stage.[51] Visualizations are still important in the completion stage, yet goals are achieved through practices that draw from Indian yogic exercises, such as the yoga of the winds (*prāṇa, lung*), the penetration of key points in the body (*lus la gnad du bsnun pa*), the power of bliss, and so forth.

Thus, while the visualization stage has become a preparatory practice, the completion stage is regarded as capable of achieving a true transformation. When all the winds and minds of the so-called subtle body dissolve into the heart cakra, a true realization of nonduality can be attained. Though the vast majority of tantric scholars accept this, Jñānapāda and Tsong kha pa, among others, do at times describe the visualization stage in terms of a mind that apprehends nonduality. In doing so, they momentarily set aside the restraints they themselves imposed on the visualization stage.

Conclusions

One of the tantric methods for overcoming conceptualization involves meditating on the proliferations of mental constructs, thus revealing how these constructs operate. In contrast to meditations that aim to reduce mental content, the techniques of the visualization stage do the opposite. Yet, not only do aspirants grasp the nature of their visualizations, they also realize that their vision is more real than anything else.

Jñānapāda, one of the early tantric theoreticians, maintains that since the mind visualizing the maṇḍala circle is endowed with a nondual profundity and sublimity, it is capable of dispelling ordinary conceptual thoughts. In other words, this mind can act as an antidote that leads to an irreversible soteriological transformation—putting an end to saṃsāric suffering. In this regard this antidote differs from "saṃsāric" antidotes, such as benevolent love, and is therefore superior to methods of the Pāramitā Vehicle.

Another reason the mind endowed with a profound and sublime nature is efficacious according to Jñānapāda is that its two aspects joined together are consonant with the fruit of the practice. Tsong kha pa develops this notion, maintaining that such a mind is potent, because in meditating on emptiness and visualizations of the maṇḍala circle, the mind's two aspects correspond to the *dharmakāya* and *rūpakāya* at the fruition of the practice. The crucial point

51. Tanemura 2015, 329. Another early source for the division of the practice into the two stages is *Guhyasamāja-tantra* 18.84, Matsunaga 1978, 119.

for Tsong kha pa, however, is the nonduality of the mind endowed with a profound and sublime nature. In his view, the subjective aspect of this mind is immersed in emptiness, while its objective aspect arises as the maṇḍala circle. Though the manifold details of the celestial mansion and the deities therein do arise, these are now not ordinary conceptualizations but special appearances.[52]

Finally, it is worth bearing in mind that tantric authors writing on the visualization stage, especially members of Jñānapāda school and its followers, resorted to the theoretical approach of Dharmakīrti. We still need to explore if and when the views of these tantric scholars diverge from those of Dharmakīrti. In any case, a better understanding of tantric theories on the visualization stage requires that we take into account the great Buddhist treatises on logic.

Works Cited

Abbreviations

Sde dge *The Sde-dge Mtshal-par Bka'-'gyur: A Facsimile Edition of the 18th Century Redaction of Si-tu Chos-kyi-'byuṅ-gnas Prepared under the Direction of H.H. the 16th Rgyal-dbaṅ Karma-pa.* 103 vols. Delhi: Delhi Karmapae Chodhey Gyalwae Sungrab Partun Khang, 1976–1979.

Sde-dge Bstan-'gyur Series, Published as Part of the Dgoṅs-rdzogs of H.H. the Sixteenth Rgyal-dbaṅ Karma-pa. 213 vols. New Delhi: Delhi Karmapae Chodhey, 1982–1986.

Stog *The Tog Palace Manuscript of the Tibetan Kanjur.* 109 vols. Leh, Ladakh: Smanrtsis Shesrig Dpemzod, 1975–1980.

Canonical Texts

Guhyasamāja-tantra. Stog 408, Rgyud 'bum, vol. *ca,* 1b1–82a5. For an edition of the Sanskrit, see Matsunaga 1978.

Hevajra-tantra. Sde dge 417 and 418, Rgyud 'bum, vol. *nga,* 1b1–13b5 and 13b5–30a3. For an edition of the Sanskrit and Tibetan as well as an English translation, see Snellgrove 1959.

52. Tibetan *khyad par can gyi snang ba* or *snang ba khyad par can.* See Tsong kha pa, *Sngags rim chen mo,* 462–464.

Indic Texts

Abhayākaragupta. *Buddhakapālamahātantrarājaṭīkābhayapaddhati. Sangs rgyas thod pa'i rgyud kyi rgyal po chen po'i rgya cher 'grel pa 'jigs pa med pa'i gzhung 'grel.* Sde dge 1654, Rgyud, vol. *ra*, 166b1–225b3. For a partial Sanskrit edition and English translation, see Luo 2010.

Anupamarakṣita. *Tārāsādhana. Sgrol ma'i sgrub thabs.* Sde dge 3491, Rgyud, vol. *mu*, 144b6–147b7. For a Sanskrit edition, see Bhattacharyya 1925, 1:200–206. For an English translation, see Gómez 1995.

Asaṅga. *Mahāyānasūtrālaṅkāra. Theg pa chen po mdo sde'i rgyan.* Sde dge 4020, Sems tsam, vol. *bi*, 1b1–39a4. For a Sanskrit edition and French translation, see Lévi 1907–1911.

Dharmakīrti. *Pramāṇavārttikakārikā. Tshad ma rnam 'grel gyi tshig le'ur byas pa.* Sde dge 4210, Tshad ma, vol. *ce*, 94b1–151a7. Sanskrit and Tibetan edited in Miyasaka 1971–1972.

———. *Pramāṇaviniścaya. Tshad ma rnam par nges pa.* Sde dge 4211, Tshad ma, vol. *ce*, 152b1–230a7. For a Sanskrit edition of chapters 1 and 2, see Steinkellner 2007.

Jñānapāda or Buddhaśrījñāna. *Ātmasādhanāvatāra. Bdag sgrub pa la 'jug pa.* Sde dge 1860, Rgyud, vol. *di*, 52a7–62a7. According to Kawasaki 2004, 51–52, a Sanskrit manuscript is kept in Lhasa.

———. *Samantabhadrasādhana. Kun tu bzang po'i sgrub pa'i thabs.* Sde dge 1855, Rgyud, vol. *di*, 28b6–36a5. For a partial Sanskrit edition, see Tanaka 1996 and Kanō 2014. According to Kawasaki 2004, 51, a Sanskrit manuscript is kept in Lhasa.

Kāṇha. *Yogaratnamālāhevajrapañjikā. Dgyes pa rdo rje'i dka' 'grel rnal 'byor rin po che'i phreng ba.* Sde dge 1183, Rgyud, vol. *kha*, 1b1–61a3. For a Sanskrit edition, see Snellgrove 1959, 2:103–159.

Nāgārjuna. *Piṇḍīkramasādhana. Sgrub pa'i thabs mdor byas pa.* Sde dge 1796, Rgyud, vol. *ngi*, 1b1–11a2. For a Sanskrit edition, see La Vallée Poussin 1896, 1–14.

Phalavajra. *Samantabhadrasādhanavṛtti. Kun tu bzang po'i sgrub pa'i thabs kyi 'grel pa.* Sde dge 1867, Rgyud, vol. *di*, 139b3–187b4.

Ratnākaraśānti, Śāntipa. *Guhyasamājamaṇḍalavidhiṭīkā. Dpal gsang ba 'dus pa'i dkyil 'khor gyi cho ga'i 'grel pa.* Sde dge 1871, Rgyud, vol. *ni*, 59a7–130a7.

———. *Hevajrapañjikā Muktikāvalī. Dpal dgyes pa'i rdo rje'i dka' 'grel mu tig phreng ba.* Sde dge 1189, Rgyud, vol. *ga*, 221a1–297a7. For a Sanskrit edition, see Tripathi and Negi 2001.

Ratnarakṣita. *Saṃvarodayapadminīpañjikā. Sdom pa 'byung ba'i dka' 'grel padma can.* Sde dge 1420, Rgyud, vol. *wa*, 1b1–101b3.

Samantabhadra. *Sāramañjarī = Caturaṅgasādhanaṭīkāsāramañjarī. Yan lag bzhi pa'i sgrub thabs kyi rgya cher bshad pa snying po snye ma.* Sde dge 1869, Rgyud, vol. *ni*, 1b1–45b4. For a Sanskrit edition, see Szántó, in progress.

Thagana. *Samantabhadrasādhanavṛtti. Kun tu bzang po'i sgrub pa'i thabs kyi 'grel pa.* Sde dge 1868, Rgyud, vol. *di*, 187b4–231a7.

Vaidyapāda or Vitapāda. *Caturaṅgasādhanasamantabhadrīṭīkā. Yan lag bzhi pa'i sgrub thabs kun tu bzang mo'i rnam par bshad pa*. Sde dge 1872, Rgyud, vol. *ni*, 130b1–178b7.

Tibetan Texts

A myes zhabs Ngag dbang kun dga' bsod nams (1597–1662). *Rgyu dang 'bras bu'i theg pa'i spyi don legs par bshad pa mdo sngags bstan pa rgya mtsho'i sgo 'byed*. In *Collected Works*, 7:359–846. Kathmandu: Sa skya rgyal yongs gsung rab slob gnyer khang, 2000.

Paṇ chen Blo bzang chos kyi rgyal mtshan (1570–1662). *Dngos grub rgya mtsho'i snying po = Rgyud thams cad kyi rgyal po gsang ba 'dus pa'i bskyed rim gyi rnam bshad dngos grub kyi rgya mtsho'i snying po*. In *Collected Works*, 2:299–452. New Delhi: Gurudeva, 1973.

Tsong kha pa Blo bzang grags pa (1357–1419). *Sngags rim chen mo = Rgyal ba khyab bdag rdo rje 'chang chen po'i lam gyi rim pa gsang ba kun gyi gnad rnam par phye ba*. Xining: Mtsho sngon mi rigs dpe skrun khang, 1995.

Secondary Sources

Bentor, Yael, with Penpa Dorjee. 2019. *The Essence of the Ocean of Attainments: The Creation Stage of the Guhyasamāja Tantra according to Paṇchen Losang Chökyi Gyaltsen*. Studies in Indian and Tibetan Buddhism. Somerville, MA: Wisdom Publications.

Bhattacharyya, Benoytosh. 1925. *Sādhanamālā*, vol. 1. Gaekwad's Oriental Series. Baroda: Central Library.

Dalton, Catherine, and Péter-Dániel Szántó. 2019. "Jñānapāda." In *Brill's Encyclopedia of Buddhism*, vol. 2: *Lives*, edited by Jonathan A. Silk, Richard Bowring, Vincent Eltschinger, and Michael Radich, 264–268. Leiden and Boston: Brill.

Dunne, John D. 2004. *Foundations of Dharmakīrti's Philosophy*. Studies in Indian and Tibetan Buddhism. Boston: Wisdom Publications.

———. 2006. "Realizing the Unreal: Dharmakīrti's Theory of Yogic Perception." *Journal of Indian Philosophy* 34.6: 497–519.

Eltschinger, Vincent. 2009. "On the Career and the Cognition of Yogins." In *Yogic Perception, Meditation and Altered States of Consciousness*, edited by Eli Franco, 169–213. Vienna: Verlag der Österreichischen Akademie der Wissenschaften.

Franco, Eli. 2017a. "Introduction, Dharmakīrti." In *Encyclopedia of Indian Philosophies*, vol. 21: *Buddhist Philosophy from 600 to 750 A.D.*, edited by K. H. Potter, 51–136. Delhi: Motilal Banarsidass.

———. 2017b. "10.1.2 *Pramāṇasiddhi*, Summary by Eli Franco." In *Encyclopedia of Indian Philosophies*, vol. 21: *Buddhist Philosophy from 600 to 750 A.D.*, edited by K. H. Potter, 297–354. Delhi: Motilal Banarsidass.

Gómez, Luis O. 1977. "The Bodhisattva as Wonder-Worker." In *Prajñāpāramitā and Related Systems: Studies in Honor of Edward Conze*, edited by Lewis Lancaster, 221–261. Berkeley Buddhist Studies Series. Berkeley: University of California Press.

———. 1995. "Two Tantric Meditations: Visualizing the Deity." In *Buddhism in Practice*, edited by Donald S. Lopez Jr., 318–327. Princeton: Princeton University Press.

Hayes, Richard P., and Brendan S. Gillon. 1991. "Introduction to Dharmakīrti's Theory of Inference as Presented in *Pramāṇavārttika Svopajñavṛtti* 1–10." *Journal of Indian Philosophy* 19.1: 1–73.

Hopkins, Jeffrey. 1977. *Tantra in Tibet: Volume 1 of The Great Exposition of Secret Mantra, by Tsong-kha-pa*. London: George Allen & Unwin.

Isaacson, Harunaga. 2001. "Ratnākaraśānti's *Hevajrasahajasadyoga* (Studies in Ratnākaraśānti's Tantric Works I)." In *Le Parole e i Marmi: Studi in onore di Raniero Gnoli nel suo 70° compleanno*, edited by Raffaele Torella, 1:457–487. Serie Orientale Roma 92. Rome: Istituto Italiano per l'Africa e l'Oriente.

Kanō Kazuo 加納和雄. 2014. "*Fugen jōjuhō* no shinshutsu bonbun shiryō ni tsuite" 『普賢成就法』の新出梵文資料について (Newly Available Sanskrit Materials of Jñānapāda's *Samantabhadrasādhana*). *Mikkyōgaku kenkyū* 密教学研究 (*Journal of Esoteric Buddhist Studies*) 46: 61–73.

Kawasaki, Kazuhiro. 2004. "On a Birch-Bark Sanskrit Manuscript Preserved in the Tibet Museum." *Indogaku bukkyōgaku kenkyū* 印度學佛教學研究 (*Journal of Indian and Buddhist Studies*) 52.2: 905–903 (reverse pagination).

La Vallée Poussin, Louis de. 1896. *Études et textes tantriques: Pañcakrama*. Ghent: Université de Gand.

Lévi, Sylvain. 1907–1911. *Mahāyāna-Sūtrālaṃkāra: Exposé de la doctrine du Grand véhicule selon le système Yogācāra*. 2 vols. Paris: Librairie Honoré Champion.

Luo, Hong. 2010. *Abhayākaragupta's Abhayapaddhati: Chapters 9 to 14, Critically Edited and Translated*. Beijing and Hamburg: China Tibetology Publishing House and Centre for Tantric Studies.

Matsunaga Yūkei 松長有慶. 1978. *The Guhyasamāja Tantra: A New Critical Edition*. Osaka: Tōhō shuppan 東方出版.

Miyasaka Yūsho 宮坂宥勝. 1971–1972. "*Pramāṇavārttika-kārikā* (Sanskrit and Tibetan)." *Indo koten kenkyū* インド古典研究 (*Acta Indologica*) 2: 1–206.

Pecchia, Cristina. 2008. "Is the Buddha Like 'a Man in the Street'? Dharmakīrti's Answer." *Wiener Zeitschrift für die Kunde Südasiens* 51: 163–192.

———. 2015. *Dharmakīrti on the Cessation of Suffering: A Critical Edition with Translation and Comments of Manorathanandin's* Vṛtti *and Vibhūticandra's Glosses on* Pramāṇavārttika II.190–216. With the assistance of Philip Pierce. Brill's Indological Library 47. Leiden: Brill.

Seton, Gregory. 2018. "Ratnākaraśānti." In *Brill's Encyclopedia of Buddhism*, vol. 2: *Lives*, edited by Jonathan A. Silk, Richard Bowring, Vincent Eltschinger, and Michael Radich, 366–370. Leiden and Boston: Brill.

Snellgrove, David L. 1959. *Hevajra Tantra: A Critical Study*. 2 vols. London: Oxford University Press.

Steinkellner, Ernst. 2007. *Dharmakīrti's Pramāṇaviniścaya: Chapters 1 and 2*. Beijing and Vienna: China Tibetology Publishing House and Austrian Academy of Sciences Press.

Szántó, Péter-Dániel. In progress. "The *Sāramañjarī* of Samantabhadra, a Commentary to the *Samantabhadrasādhana* of Jñānapāda: Critical Edition of the 'Pāla Recension.'"

Tanaka Kimiaki 田中公明. 1996. *Indo, Chibetto mandara no kenkyū* インド・チベット曼荼羅の研究 (*Studies in the Indo-Tibetan Maṇḍala*). Kyoto: Hōzōkan 法蔵館.

Tanemura, Ryugen. 2015. "Guhyasamāja." In *Brill's Encyclopedia of Buddhism*, vol. 1: *Literature and Languages*, edited by Jonathan A. Silk, Oskar von Hinüber, and Vincent Eltschinger, 326–333. Leiden and Boston: Brill.

Tanemura Ryūgen 種村隆元, Kanō Kazuo 加納和雄, and Kuranishi Ken'ichi 倉西憲一. 2017. "Ratnarakṣita cho *Padminī* dai 13 shō bōron zenhan: Preliminary Edition oyobi chū" Ratnarakṣita 著 *Padminī* 第13章傍論前半：Preliminary Edition および註 (Ratnarakṣita's *Padminī*: A Preliminary Edition of the Excursuses in Chapter 13, Part 1). *Kawasaki Daishi kyōgaku kenkyūsho kiyō* 川崎大師教学研究所紀要 (*Journal of Kawasaki Daishi Institute for Buddhist Studies*) 2: 1–34.

Tomabechi, Tōru. 2008. "Vitapāda, Śākyamitra, and Āryadeva: On a Transitional Stage in the History of *Guhyasamāja* Exegesis." In *Esoteric Buddhist Studies: Identity in Diversity. Proceedings of the International Conference of Esoteric Buddhist Studies, Koyasan University, 2006*, edited by the Editorial Board of the ICEBS, 171–177. Kōyasan: Kōyasan University.

Tripathi, Ram Shankar, and Thakur Sain Negi. 2001. *Hevajratantram with Muktāvalī Pañjikā of Mahāpaṇḍitācārya Ratnākaraśānti*. Sarnath: Central Institute of Higher Tibetan Studies.

Yarnall, Thomas F. 2013. *Great Stages of Mantra (Sngags rim chen mo): Chapters 11–12, The Creation Stage*. New York: The American Institute of Buddhist Studies at Columbia University in New York with Columbia University's Center for Buddhist Studies and Tibet House U.S.

Yaita, Hideomi. 1988. "Dharmakīrti on the Person Free from Faults: Annotated Translation of the *Pramāṇavārttikasvavṛttiḥ* ad v. 218–223." *Naritasan bukkyō kenkyūsho kiyō* 成田山仏教研究所紀要 (*Journal of Naritasan Institute for Buddhist Studies*) 11.2: 433–445.

Orality, Literacy, and the Cult of the Book in Early Mahāyāna Revisited

Daniel Boucher

ONE WOULD BE HARD pressed to find a contribution to the social history of the early Mahāyāna that has had a greater impact than Gregory Schopen's "The Phrase '*sa pṛthivīpradeśaś caityabhūto bhavet*' in the *Vajracchedikā*: Notes on the Cult of the Book in Mahāyāna." Few articles have been more widely cited, more frequently misunderstood, or more often put to unintended applications than this seminal piece. But perhaps more troubling, the implications of this article have not spurred the kinds of follow-ups Schopen might have hoped for and all of us in Mahāyāna studies should want: how is writing itself implicated in the genre-specific characteristics of Mahāyāna sūtras, particularly their self-reflexivity as texts? How is the cult of the book related to other Buddhist cult practice, such as the relic cult, with which it was sometimes in tension? Why are some Mahāyāna sūtras seemingly preoccupied with the localized sacrality of their books whereas others display nary a hint of concern? To what degree were orality and literacy maintained in creative tension with one another in the wake of the newly embraced technology of writing? My goal here is to reflect on the legacy of this important contribution to early Mahāyāna studies, especially in light of some of the more recent critiques of its argument. In addition, I would like to situate my re-evaluation of this cult in light of its role in what must have been a most audacious development in the history of Indian Buddhism: the materialization of new scriptures in book form.

The Cult of the Book in the Early Mahāyāna

The first thing to note about the cult of the book is that it is not necessarily about books at all. This has been a source of confusion among some who have attempted to re-evaluate Schopen's findings or apply them to other contexts. Schopen opens his discussion by focusing on a formula that occurs in two places in the *Vajracchedikā*: *sa pṛthivīpradeśaś caityabhūto bhavet*. The occurrences of this formula in the *Vajracchedikā* represent in his view "the least fully articulated form of the phrase and its supportive context, and, as a consequence, are most open to misunderstanding if confronted in isolation" (Schopen 1975, 147). The fundamental problem of this formula is how to understand the expression *caityabhūta*, as varied explanations for it have been offered, from medieval Indian scholiasts and early Tibetan translators down to modern interpreters. At the heart of the matter is this: does the participle *bhūta* here suggest a simile, such that this spot of ground becomes "like a shrine," as some commentators and translators, ancient and modern, have suggested, or, as Schopen prefers, that it instead designates an emphatic? That is to say, Mahāyāna authors, in Schopen's view, want to argue that the spot of ground where their texts are preached or where they are set up as a book would become equivalent to competing shrines, most especially relic stūpas, controlled by Mainstream Buddhists. And this cultic attitude toward the localized presence of the Dharma is expressed in many other texts, both those demonstrably early as well as those arguably later, with similar if not almost identical phrasing.

Schopen also attempts to expose two patterns with regard to the development of the cult of the book that may have chronological implications. First, he sees a development from an essentially oral tradition represented in the *Vajracchedikā* to a written tradition represented by the *Aṣṭasāhasrikā*, where the emphasis is more squarely on the book as sacred object. That is to say, in Schopen's view, the *Aṣṭasāhasrikā* remodels this pericope from a focus on the spot where the text is recited, studied, or taught to one where the physical book is established and venerated with incense, perfumes, banners, lamps, and so on. Such a chronological relationship between these two texts is at odds with what is usually assumed, since we know that the *Aṣṭasāhasrikā* was translated into Chinese by Lokakṣema already in 179 CE, and recently, Gāndhārī fragments of a Perfection of Wisdom text have come to light that correspond to parts of chapters 1 and 5 of the *Aṣṭasāhasrikā*. These fragments have been tentatively dated to the first century CE.[1] The *Vajracchedikā* was not translated into Chinese until the early fifth century, and our earliest Sanskrit manuscripts cannot be any earlier. Of course, the dates of their Chinese translations alone should not be thought to close the discussion of the dates of their respective compositions.

There is another early text, also translated by Lokakṣema in the late second century, that seemingly spans the oral/written divide. Schopen calls our attention to the end of the *Kāśyapaparivarta*, where the Buddha contrasts the

1. On these fragments and their dating, see Falk 2011, esp. 20–23, and Falk and Strauch 2014 on the Split Collection in which these fragments are found.

merit derived from giving uncountable gifts to buddhas versus the far superior merit that would accrue from upholding even a single verse from this *Mahāratnakūṭa*, as the text calls itself. The text then iterates a version of this same pericope. It is sufficiently interesting to quote in full, especially since we now have a better edition than was available to Schopen in 1975, along with access to plates of the original manuscript:

> On which spot of ground this discourse on Dharma, the *Ratnakūṭa*, is recited or taught or is written or, being written, would be set up as a book, that spot of ground becomes a shrine for the world together with its gods. And should one hear, take up, write, or master this discourse on Dharma from a certain preacher of the Dharma, he should generate respect toward this preacher of the Dharma of such a kind, Kāśyapa, as he would toward the Tathāgata. Which son or daughter of good family will honor, respect, esteem, and venerate the Dharma preacher, that one I prophesy to unexcelled, complete and perfect awakening.[2] And at the moment of his death, he will see the Tathāgata.[3]

This passage from the *Kāśyapaparivarta* makes use of some of the same verbs used in the related passages from the *Vajracchedikā* and the *Aṣṭasāhasrikā*, fusing both the emphasis on the oral performance of the text and its localization in book form.[4] Additionally, we see that the text can be localized not only by establishing it as a book but also by the presence of a Dharma preacher (*dharmabhāṇaka*) who, having internalized the text or reading a manuscript aloud, makes it known to others. It is the spot of ground where either are found that becomes a genuine shrine (*caityabhūta*) for the whole world because either can serve as a stand-in for the Buddha himself.

The second pattern Schopen observes is the development of a functional equivalence between the book cult and the relic/stūpa cult as it figures

2. The text of this last clause is damaged in the extant Sanskrit manuscript and so is translated from the Tibetan.

3. Vorobyova-Desyatovskaya 2002, 57 (§ 160). All translations are mine unless otherwise indicated.

4. What is less clear in this section is Schopen's claim (1975, 159) that the *Kāśyapaparivarta* represents a contrast between the book cult and the relic/stūpa cult akin to the *Aṣṭasāhasrikā*. Paragraphs 158–160 of the *Kāśyapaparivarta* contrast service to the tathāgatas (extensive gifts, building monasteries, serving his śrāvakas, and so on) with upholding even a single verse of this *dharmaparyāya*. It is difficult to see in any of the three texts a reminiscence of one from another in a strict sense.

prominently in the *Saddharmapuṇḍarīka-sūtra* (the *Lotus Sūtra*). In this case the historically novel book cult doesn't merely co-opt the formal practices associated with the well-established stūpa cult (worship with flowers, incense, unguents, and so on). It instead declares that a tathāgata shrine is to be made (*tathāgatacaityaṃ kārayitavyaṃ*) at the spot of ground where its text is recited, taught, or written down and established as a book.[5] Such a site has no need of a relic, the author of the *Saddharmapuṇḍarīka* declares, because it is sacralized by the presence of the sūtra itself and worthy of worship in all the same ways. Schopen notes that rather than declaring the site where its *dharmaparyāya* is preached or located in a book to be a "true shrine" (*caityabhūta*), in contrast with the historically prior relic cult, the *Saddharmapuṇḍarīka* attempts to synthesize the two cults: "And where, Ajita, the son or daughter of good family (who preserves this discourse on Dharma) would stand or sit or stroll, there, Ajita, a *caitya* is to be made for the Tathāgata. And it should be declared by the world together with its gods: 'This is a stūpa of the Tathāgata.'"[6]

Both the *Saddharmapuṇḍarīka* and the *Aṣṭasāhasrikā* buttress their cultic innovations by linking the sites where their texts are preached or set up as books with the well-known cultic centers connected with the spiritual career of the historical Buddha, most notably the site of his awakening at Bodh Gayā. The *Aṣṭasāhasrikā* declares that beings who go to the seat of awakening (*bodhimaṇḍa*) cannot be harmed there by men or ghosts, except as a result of the fruition of former deeds, because that site is sacralized by the power of the signature event of the whole Buddhist tradition, the Buddha's conquest over death and his promotion of fearlessness and nonenmity in all beings. In the same way, the site where this Perfection of Wisdom text is taken up, preserved, taught, and recited, there too beings cannot be harmed because, by the presence of this Perfection of Wisdom, that spot of ground is made a true shrine (*caityabhūta*), worthy of honor and worship in the same way as the more famous and historically prior shrine at Bodh Gayā.[7] The *Saddharmapuṇḍarīka*, for its part, expands the association between its sūtra and well-known pilgrimage sites where the Buddha preached his first sermon and entered parinirvāṇa:

> And sons of good family, on which spot of ground this discourse on Dharma would be spoken or revealed or taught or written or

5. See for example Kern and Nanjio [1908–1912] 1970, 231.7–232.5, translated and discussed in Schopen 1975, 163–164, and again later in this paper.

6. Kern and Nanjio [1908–1912] 1970, 340.6–8. See also Schopen 1975, 165.

7. See Wogihara [1932] 1973, 205–207, for this passage from the *Aṣṭasāhasrikā* and the discussion in Schopen 1975, 153–156.

> reflected upon or declared or recited to oneself or would be established as a book, whether in a park or in a monastery or in a house or in a forest or in a city or at the foot of a tree or on a lofty terrace or at a place of rest or in a cave, at that spot of ground a *caitya* for the Tathāgata should be made. Why? Because this spot of ground is to be known as the seat of awakening (*bodhimaṇḍa*) of all tathāgatas. And it is to be known that all tathāgatas, arhats, completely and perfectly awakened ones have awakened to unexcelled, complete and perfect awakening at this spot of ground. And it is to be known that on this spot of ground the wheel of the Dharma has been turned by all tathāgatas and on this spot of ground all tathāgatas have entered parinirvāṇa.[8]

Clearly then, early Mahāyāna authors attempted to legitimate their cultic innovation by tying the sites where their texts were recited, copied, or set up as books with the pilgrimage centers that had in all likelihood enjoyed centuries of established cultic practice. Schopen argued that these efforts would come with specific implications:

> However, the early architects of the cult of the book, by adopting the structure of the established cult which surrounded them, committed themselves to a pattern which required at least one very important thing for continued organizational development: localization. This again presented problems of legitimation.[9]

Thus, insofar as Mahāyāna authors regarded their texts as both the source and the manifestation of the Buddha's awakening experience, they could legitimate their cultic innovation by linking it with the very sites on which the Buddha's salvific career took place. It is this that makes the spot of ground where their texts are preached or set up as a book a "true shrine" (*caityabhūta*), matching the undisputed sacrality of the *bodhimaṇḍa* at Bodh Gayā, along with other famous sites in the Buddha's life. And it is worth emphasizing here that in all instances of this formula, it is the spot of ground (*pṛthivīpradeśa*) that is sacralized, not the book or the preacher or any formal structure that

8. Kern and Nanjio [1908–1912] 1970, 391.6–13; compare slight variations in language in the Kashgar manuscript, Toda 1981, 185–186 (folios 378a–b). See also Schopen 1975, 166, on this passage.

9. Schopen 1975, 170–171.

would enshrine either. This has been a frequently misunderstood feature of this formula and one to which I will return below.

These two patterns observed by Schopen, the shift from an oral to a written orientation in the literature and the subsequent equivalence of the cults of the stūpa and the book in at least the *Saddharmapuṇḍarīka*, coalesced in his view to create centers "which would have a more permanent character and which would, by that fact, make possible the development of a cult in a more truly sociological sense of the term" (Schopen 1975, 179). If this were the case, these new cultic centers would, of course, be in some competition with the well-established relic/stūpa cult, a cult overwhelmingly controlled by Mainstream monastics, as attested by the plethora of donative inscriptions from these sites. This tension, Schopen concludes, also renders very unlikely the hypothesis proposed by Akira Hirakawa with regard to the sociological origins of the Mahāyāna—namely, that those drawn to the bodhisattva orientation were initially lay men and women who congregated at stūpas and organized themselves around the worship of them. Hirakawa's thesis has been responded to many times since Schopen's study on the cult of the book, and the overwhelming majority of these responses concur with Schopen in rejecting his argument.[10]

Before we assess both the applications and criticisms of Schopen's argument, it may be worth pausing to consider what is and is not essential to his hypothesis. First, Schopen would like to see in the texts he surveys a development from a fundamentally oral phase governed by a tradition of *bhāṇaka*s to a written tradition in which the physical book becomes the locus of cult activity. We might want to ask in what meaningful sense one can talk about an "oral phase" of a cult of the book. What is striking about the early Mahāyāna is the degree to which it may have participated in a fundamental shift toward literature and literariness that was infiltrating learning and textual transmission broadly in India from the turn of the Common Era. In all likelihood, preachers of these new sūtras remained central to the emerging tradition, and the texts confirm as much. But the materialization of their teachings in book form changed the ways in which the Dharma was conceptualized, encountered, and circulated. Thus one does not have to see here a chronological development in our texts in order to recognize the degree to which so many of our early witnesses display new modes of narrativity that are at once self-reflexive and deeply insecure.

Second, we may also want to ask what it would mean for emerging bodhi-

10. See, in this regard, especially Harrison 1995, Sasaki 1997, Nattier 2003, 89–93, and Boucher 2008a, 40–43.

sattva fraternities to have permanently located cultic centers. The very instability that Schopen speculates would have governed a wandering *bhāṇaka* tradition may not have been ameliorated by the circulation of manuscripts. That our authors repeatedly expressed a desire to fix their teachings firmly in time and space does not mean that they achieved their ends. On the contrary, the very proliferation of such polemic—efforts that took forms beyond what Schopen has himself suggested—points to a tradition sorely lacking in institutional self-confidence. I will return to both of these issues below.

Rewriting Tradition

Responses to Schopen's cult of the book argument, both appreciative and critical, have been numerous. I deal with the most significant criticisms in the next section of this paper. Here I take up an implication of Schopen's thesis that has attracted some attention, albeit still not nearly as much as it deserves. If, as Schopen has argued, the spot of ground on which their books were set up, read aloud, and perhaps even venerated formed the institutional basis for early Mahāyāna fraternities, whether permanent or portable, then this set of movements must have attributed far greater prestige to writing and the written word than we have reason to believe was the case for the preceding half millennium within the Buddhist tradition. Obvious as this seems, this shift has far-reaching implications that have not been adequately addressed in the scholarship on the Mahāyāna.

One of the first to address theories on the origins of the Mahāyāna vis-à-vis writing was Richard Gombrich in his article "How the Mahāyāna Began." Ignoring and in some ways misunderstanding Schopen's core argument, Gombrich argued that the Mahāyāna survived as a new movement within Buddhism because it embraced writing at the outset.[11] Gombrich accepts the majority opinion that writing appears not to have figured prominently in the earliest Buddhist schools, as evidenced primarily from the Pāli canon. He argues that since the monastic establishment would have been responsible for memorizing, preserving, and transmitting the canon from one generation to the next, those texts that fell outside such transmission lineages would not have been passed on unless they were preserved through an alternative means,

11. The problems with Gombrich's understanding of Schopen's argument come toward the end of his article, where he declares, "It is well known that the *Lotus Sūtra* commends the enshrinement of written scriptures in *stūpa*s as the equivalent of corporeal relics" (Gombrich [1988] 1990, 29). It is quite clear that the *Saddharmapuṇḍarīka* is not different from other Mahāyāna texts in sacralizing the spot of ground where the text is preached or located in book form as a shrine. I will return to the *Saddharmapuṇḍarīka* on this question below.

which, he contends, the relatively new technology of writing afforded. This argument, Gombrich is quick to add, is neutral with regard to other theories about the institutional basis of the early Mahāyāna, though he notes that claims for a lay origin of the kind espoused by Hirakawa are all the more implausible under his proposed hypothesis.

Many scholars of the early Mahāyāna have either accepted or assumed that the authors of these new works made use of writing and circulated their productions as written texts. Some have gone so far as to define "a Mahāyāna community as one constituted by the authors of these texts," authors presumed to be monks in complex relationships with their śrāvaka confrères (Silk 2002, 378). But others have not been persuaded, and more recently there has been some pushback against the centrality of writing as a technology of preservation and the book as a locus of cult activity.

David Drewes has been the sharpest and most persistent critic of Schopen's cult of the book argument. I deal with his specific criticisms in detail in the next section. Here I would like to consider Drewes's 2015 article "Oral Texts in Indian Mahāyāna," since it speaks to the more fundamental nature of Mahāyāna textuality vis-à-vis writing. Drewes discusses at length three Sanskrit verbs that often occur together in Mahāyāna sūtras as prescribed practices with regard to their use: *ud-√grah* ("to grasp"), *√dhṛ* ("to hold, preserve"), and *pari-ava-√āp* ("to master, comprehend"). Drewes rehearses the most common translations of these verbs by scholars since the nineteenth century, their parallels in Pāli suttas, and their appearance in commentarial literature and Mahāyāna sūtras and śāstras. Not surprisingly, Drewes concludes his survey by highlighting the importance both non-Mahāyāna and Mahāyāna traditions place on oral and mnemonic practices. But his survey paints a portrait of a huge range of literature spanning more than a millennium with a very broad brush. It should repay our efforts to attend to discontinuities of textual practices as much as the continuities.

We might begin, then, near where Drewes leaves off, with a charge to think about what effect writing might have had on textual production in the Mahāyāna:

> Even if all Mahāyāna sūtras were composed in writing, however, and we could somehow know this, since the effect of writing on consciousness, especially in India, is really no less mysterious than Mahāyāna thought itself, it would be difficult to link Mahāyāna thought or imagery to it in any more than a vague, speculative manner. To link specific Mahāyāna ideas or tendencies to writing in a meaningful way, one would like, for example, to be able to specify

> what additional factors led writing to cause the tendencies in question to develop in the Mahāyāna, but not in other "written" Buddhist traditions—and questions like this would take us back to the proverbial square one.[12]

Indeed it may be worth going back to square one, since many of the issues raised by Drewes, particularly with regard to the relationship between orality and literacy, have received careful attention in recent years by scholars outside Buddhist studies.

In what is surely one of the most ambitious and thought-provoking reflections on premodern South Asian literature and literariness, Sheldon Pollock describes the birth of *kāvya* and the emerging use of Sanskrit for both literary and political ends as a new aesthetics of power articulated through the written word:

> The written differs from the oral in a variety of ways. For one thing, even in cultures like those of premodern South Asia that hypervalue orality—an attitude possible only given the presence of literacy, by the way—writing claims an authority the oral cannot. . . . For another, writing enables textual features far in excess of the oral; for literature it renders the discourse itself a subject for discourse for the first time, language itself an object of aestheticized awareness, the text itself an artifact to be decoded and a pretext for deciphering.[13]

One of the most prominent features by which Mahāyāna sūtras differ so markedly from those of the earlier tradition is the way they often present themselves not merely as teachings of the Buddha but as narratives about themselves as texts.[14] Even more to the point, as Alan Cole has poignantly noted, many Mahāyāna sūtras presume omniscient narrators who are fundamentally impossible:

> In many sūtras, the story is told from a point of view that no one in the story could occupy and in fact bounces between geographic and

12. Drewes 2015, 133.

13. Pollock 2006, 4.

14. I am not the first to make this point. Cf. Lopez 1995, 41: "The Mahāyāna sūtras differ from the earlier works, however, in their self-consciousness and often exaltation of their own status as texts, as physical objects, with many works being devoted almost entirely to descriptions of benefits to be gained by reciting, copying, and worshipping them."

> temporal time zones that no one person could be privy to. Similarly, there is no attempt to explain how actual action and discourse were observed and then compiled into one narrative sequence. Consequently, one has the distinct impression that the narrative sequence has broken free of a simpler form of narration and now is the product of literary genius that chose to re-create the world as need be.[15]

As Cole argues, rightly I think, there is a new level of narrative sophistication evinced in Mahāyāna sūtras. This manifests above all else as "a very different style of presenting the voice of the Buddha . . . and suggests that the shift from orality to textuality was not simply effected by writing down oral discourse and then lightly embellishing it by tacking on simple statements about the value of rewriting the literary version of the previous oral teaching or worshiping it as a sublime Thing" (Cole 2005, 14).

When we think about the literariness of Mahāyāna scriptures, it is impossible not to be struck by the sharp contrast with the earlier sūtras contained in the Pāli canon or preserved in the Chinese Āgamas. There is of course widespread scholarly agreement that the earliest Buddhist scriptures were composed, preserved, and circulated orally and that writing in all likelihood was either unknown or functionally unavailable before Aśoka.[16] Mnemonic techniques that made use of standardized lists, fixed pericopes, and frequent repetition have long been recognized as hallmarks of orality, as well shown by the now classic study of Yugoslavian folklore and Homeric epics by Albert B. Lord ([1960] 1974).[17] One of the principal debates among scholars, particularly those working with the Pāli tradition, is whether composition and transmission was improvisational, with texts constructed in an ad hoc manner from a large corpus of textual building blocks, or verbatim, given concerns expressed within the tradition for standards by which to evaluate accuracy of transmission.[18]

15. Cole 2005, 15.

16. For a review of the best scholarship to date on the origins of writing in India, with perspicacious reflections of his own, see Salomon 1995.

17. The recently discovered Gāndhārī texts of Mainstream genres are a rare window into early Buddhist manuscript culture that show, both in their variations from other received traditions and in their formulae of abbreviations, traits of an ongoing oral transmission. See, for example, the discussions in Salomon 2000, 45–48, on the *Rhinoceros Sūtra* and Lenz 2003, 85–91, on the Gāndhārī *pūrvayoga* genre.

18. This debate can be seen in the contrast between Cousins 1983 and Wynne 2004, among others. See also most recently McGovern 2019 for an attempt to revive the improvisational element of oral discourse theory and Allon 2021 for a comprehensive overview of all of these debates.

The most detailed study on this problem to date is Mark Allon's analysis of the repetitions that occur in the unabbreviated version of the *Udumbarikasīhanāda-sutta* in the Dīgha Nikāya (Allon 1997, 273–363). Allon shows that 87 percent of this sutta involves quantifiable repetition, including verbatim repetition, repetitions with various degrees of modification, and structural repetitions (Allon 1997, 359). The remaining 13 percent consists mostly of the opening and closing sections, which themselves contain formulaic elements often found in other suttas. Thus Allon sees in this scale of repetition a strong indication of verbatim transmission, one that does not parallel the improvisational techniques studied by Lord for the Yugoslav epics or in contemporary Indian oral epic tales (Allon 1997, 357–358).[19]

By contrast, the very narrative complexity of Mahāyāna sūtras, with stories nested within stories, with temporal shifts in which a mythical past is subsumed within the narrative present, points to a literate, not oral, composition.[20] And the Mahāyāna is not alone in its literary ambitions, in its desire to entice its readers/auditors into a new, textually constructed Buddhist world in which identity is reformulated and realigned with a proper community. We see these developments in Pāli *vaṃsa* literature as well—which is to say, what is probably the first juncture at which Pāli becomes literary, at least in Sri Lanka. Starting around the fourth century CE with the *Dīpavaṃsa*, we see an attempt to rework the history of the Buddhist orders in Sri Lanka so as to secure a place for the Mahāvihāran lineage, long marginalized by the dominant, royally supported Abhayagiri fraternity.[21] The *Dīpavaṃsa* is written in what would have by then become an archaic idiom, Pāli, composed clumsily, with many grammatical errors, but representing the language of the canon,

19. Gethin 2007 has reconsidered this debate by looking at structural repetitions across the whole of the Saṃyutta Nikāya, noting the possibility that reciters of this collection may have resorted to a style of repetition that was to some extent open-ended, utilizing both abbreviation so as to establish a framework for memorization, and fully elaborated recitations in performed religious contexts. Clearly there are still open questions surrounding these matters.

20. There have been a handful of studies on the narrativity of Mahāyāna sūtras. For example, a particularly detailed study of the chiasmic structure of the *Aṣṭasāhasrikā*, which has the potential to force a reconsideration of the integrity of the whole text vis-à-vis scholarly hypotheses about its composition, can now be found in Shi Huifeng 2017. Similar arguments can be made easily for the *Vimalakīrtinirdeśa-sūtra*, the quintessential philosophical narrative of the early Mahāyāna tradition. By merging complex verbal repartees about doctrine with stunning visual displays that undermine realist views of the phenomenal world, the *Vimalakīrti* foregrounds its poetics as it destabilizes traditional Buddhist ontology in dramatic fashion. See the insightful remarks on its literary strategies in Hamlin 1988 and an even more innovative reading of its plot in Cole 2005, 236–325.

21. See Walters 1999 and 2000, esp. 111–118, for situating this chronicle historically.

thereby signaling the Mahāvihārans as its proper heirs.[22] The *Mahāvaṃsa*, written one or perhaps two centuries later in more elegant śloka meter, continues the *Dīpavaṃsa*'s defense of the Mahāvihārans as the legitimate heirs to the Buddhist *sāsana*. Both chronicles assume "the existence of a consciously objectified tradition of transmittable, prestige discourse (of which literacy and books are a subcategory)" whose sources can be traced to historically identifiable moments.[23]

What stands out most for our purposes from these two chronicles is that they contain the earliest mention of the writing down of the Tripiṭaka together with the commentaries.[24] Both date the first writing down of the canon to the reign of the Sri Lankan king Vaṭṭagāmaṇī in the first century BCE. Most scholars have taken these reports as documenting a historical event, but this ignores the context in which the claim occurs. Canons are generally fixed in times of religious rivalry and dispute, and the Sri Lankan case is no exception. King Mahāsena's support of the Abhayagiri fraternity in the late third century CE is almost certainly the historical backdrop for the writing of the *Dīpavaṃsa*, what Jonathan Walters has called a "plea for survival" by the Mahāvihāran faction, which precipitated the transition from orality to inscription.[25] What is ironic in the context of our discussion here is that this anxiety on the part of the Mahāvihāran fraternity was due to the dominance of a lineage, the Abhayagiri, who are frequently said to have sympathies for, if not outright alliances with, Mahāyāna traditions.[26] So whereas the Mahāyāna in India may have emerged as writing and literariness came to overtake textual

22. Walters 2000, 114–115, has suggested that it might have been composed by Mahāvihāran nuns after the monks of their fraternity were sent away in exile.

23. The quoted remarks are taken from Collins 1998, 277, and occur in the context of a longer reflection on how *vaṃsa* literature treats narrative and temporality more broadly; see Collins 1998, esp. 254–281.

24. On the textual problems surrounding these claims, see Bechert 1992.

25. Walters 1999, 331–337, and 2000, 111. For a thorough recent treatment of the *vaṃsa*s from a literary-critical perspective, see Scheible 2016. See too the insightful comments in Collins 2003, esp. 652–657, on *vaṃsa* literature, but also the article as a whole for ways in which Pāli may have achieved literariness in other genres, particularly in relationship to the Sanskrit *kāvya* tradition exemplified by the *Rāmāyaṇa*.

26. Walters 1997 argues that Theravāda as a self-identity is very likely quite late, not before the third or fourth century CE, and that it may have emerged in Sri Lanka as a school primarily tied to Mahāyāna traditions, which came to be explicitly resisted by the Mahāvihārans (this latter point, and the evidence Walters marshals for it, will likely need some qualifications). More recently, Cousins 2012 has argued compellingly that the split between the Abhayagiri and Mahāvihāra fraternities does not predate the third century CE, with almost no plausible evidence for separate factions before that.

production, the literary turn in Sri Lanka may well have been a tool of defense against the encroachment of the Mahāyāna in Theravādin circles.[27]

To come back to Pollock's argument on the birth of an aestheticized language in Sanskrit, we must note the radical departure in many ways from old models:

> To argue that the specific and differential language we call *kāvya* at some point in time *began* is to claim the first occurrence of a confluence of conceptual and material factors that were themselves altogether new. These include new specific norms, both formal and substantive, of expressive, workly discourse; a new reflexive awareness of textuality; a production of new genre categories; and the application of a new storage technology, namely writing. . . . Indeed, however legitimate it may be to stress the changeableness of the idea of "literature" transhistorically and transculturally, the factors of normativity, reflexive textuality, genre, and inscription may be taken to constitute a large part of what we mean by "literary culture" everywhere.[28]

Thus there may be ways in which it is appropriate to conceive of Mahāyāna sūtras as participating in the beginning of Buddhist literature, or at least Buddhist literariness. They were not alone in this transformation to be sure. But they certainly distinguished themselves by a deep textual reflexivity, both in the ways in which they talk about themselves as objects—books to be circulated, copied, and venerated—and in the manner in which they treat oral recitation normatively in novel terms.

Pollock illustrates this new oral normativity by reference to the prologue

27. And the similarities do not end there. Even as the *Mahāvaṃsa* enjoins orality, telling its readers to listen to its account so as to generate serene joy (*pasāda*) and emotional resonance (*saṃvega*), the text simultaneously objectifies textuality within itself, as when in chapter 27, for example, it describes the inscribed gold plates kept in a chest predicting the pious constructions of the future king Duṭṭhagāmaṇī, or in chapter 32, when King Duṭṭhagāmaṇī has his book of meritorious deeds read aloud on his deathbed. Veidlinger 2006 has argued that Mahāyāna influence later in Sri Lanka and later still in much of Southeast Asia (apart from northern Thailand) led to a positive valuation of writing absent in early Theravāda sources and eventually to the replication of a cult of the book with Pāli texts. I find myself unable to follow the chain of evidence he offers, however, since by the period from which his sources derive (generally 9th–15th centuries), writing had surely become divorced from any specific religious ideology, as it already had much earlier in South Asia. See also Berkwitz 2009 on Sri Lankan manuscript culture and the cultic use of books.

28. Pollock 2006, 77.

of the *Rāmāyaṇa*, universally hailed in the Sanskritic literary tradition as the "first poem" (*ādikāvya*), wherein the invention of *kāvya* itself is shown to begin with Vālmīki. The sage Vālmīki, we are told, retired to the forest with his disciple and, upon seeing a hunter kill a *krauñca* bird, produced a verse (*śloka*) in fixed metrical quarters out of grief (*śoka*). Soon after, the great god Brahmā appeared to him, and Vālmīki, still lost in grief, sang his verse before Brahmā. Brahmā replied:

> "Brahman, it was by my will alone that you produced this elegant speech. Greatest of seers, you must now compose the entire history of Rāma.
>
> "You must tell the world the story of the righteous, virtuous, wise, and steadfast Rāma, just as you heard it from Nārada, the full story, public and private, of that wise man. For all that befell wise Rāma, Saumitri, the *rākṣasas*, and Vaidehī, whether in public or private, will be revealed to you, even those events of which you are ignorant.
>
> "No utterance of yours in this poem shall be false. Now compose the holy story of Rāma fashioned into *ślokas* to delight the heart.
>
> "As long as the mountains and rivers shall endure upon the earth, so long will the story of the *Rāmāyaṇa* be told among men.
>
> "And as long as the story of Rāma you compose is told, so long will you live on in my worlds above and below."

Vālmīki's disciples chanted his śloka again, thus inaugurating poetry.

> Then the contemplative Vālmīki conceived this idea: "Let me compose an entire poem, called the *Rāmāyaṇa*, in verses such as these." And thus did the renowned sage with enormous insight compose this poem that adds to the glory of the glorious Rāma, with hundreds of *ślokas* equal in syllables, their words noble in sound and meaning, delighting the heart.[29]

Mahāyāna authors also routinely enacted the trope of the oral reception of their "new Dharma" from long-lived deities who heard these discourses under previous buddhas, teachings long since lost to the contemporary world. As in the *Rāmāyaṇa*, these teachings are often conveyed to sages and heroes meditating alone in the forest. Many such examples from well-known texts could be marshaled here. Let me offer one from a lesser-known text in the *Ratnakūṭa*

29. Goldman [1984] 1990, 129.

collection called the *Pūrṇaparipṛcchā* to illustrate the pervasiveness of this topos. This text, available only in a Chinese translation by Kumārajīva (early fifth century) and a Tibetan translation thought to have been translated from this Chinese version, includes several episodes that speak to its own etiology as a text.[30] Here I would like to focus on just one of these narratives, part of an extended myth nested within chapter 4 of the sūtra that deals with the dispensation of the former buddha *Merugandha (*miloujiantuo* 彌樓揵馱).[31] This buddha lived for six thousand years incalculable eons ago, and his Dharma remained for five hundred years after his parinirvāṇa. After the death of this buddha and his principal disciples, many individuals shaved their heads and put on religious robes, but these new monks routinely consorted with householders, abandoned the Buddha's profound sūtras on morality and the *dhutaguṇa*s, and pursued the five kinds of desire.

At that time the local king had an only son named *Damaśrī (*tuomoshili* 陀摩尸利). The prince was moved to renounce the household in light of a revelation by a deity concerning the Dharma of the buddha Merugandha. His parents questioned this course of action, given the degeneracy of the contemporary Buddhist saṅgha, but Damaśrī, undeterred, left home to practice the *dhutaguṇa*s deep in the forest. Damaśrī found a monastic assembly in which he took the precepts and inquired about Merugandha's Dharma, to which the monks replied, "We have not heard the Dharma taught by this buddha. We only follow what is practiced by our preceptors and teachers. You should also now practice according to this Dharma." Dejected, Damaśrī went to another monastery, questioned the monks in the same way, and got the same response. Finding no satisfaction among his brethren, he left the monks to live alone in the forest.

Previously among the disciples of the buddha Merugandha there was a great arhat named *Dṛḍha (*jianlao* 堅牢) who spiritually cultivated himself in the wilderness. On the wall in the cave where he lived deep in the mountains, Dṛḍha wrote four verses summarizing the Dharma. When Damaśrī was passing by, he saw these four verses on the wall of the cave. He recited them and reflected upon their meaning, obtaining the five supernormal powers, and arrived at the place where the buddha Merugandha had formerly been

30. On Tibetan scriptures derived from Chinese translations, see most recently Silk 2019, esp. 233, on the *Pūrṇaparipṛcchā* specifically.

31. The asterisk indicates that I am reconstructing the Indic name here and below on the basis of the Chinese translation or transcription with varying degrees of certainty. I will only use it in the first instance of each name.

cremated. Sitting down with legs crossed, he made this vow: "I will not rise from here until I see the Buddha and hear the rest of his Dharma."

The god Śakra perceived Damaśrī's deep commitment and descended from the Trāyastriṃśa heaven in order to teach him a sūtra taught by the buddha Merugandha called the *Eight Hundred Thousand Entrances*, which Śakra had long ago memorized. Additional profound sūtras concerning emptiness and detachment came to Damaśrī's mind spontaneously. The buddha Merugandha appeared to him in bodily form, as did his monastic assembly and hosts of supernatural beings. Damaśrī rose from his seat and subsequently returned to his home kingdom in order to teach his parents these newly revealed sūtras, after which he journeyed from one village to another, broadly disseminating and explaining the Dharma of the buddha Merugandha.[32]

We see in this brief episode of what is a much more complex narrative a seeming celebration of the oral transmission of new sūtras to, and then by, a young monk desperate to recover the lost teaching of a former buddha. Sensing his frustration, the god Śakra appears to him and transmits a text he had long ago "recited and preserved" (*songchi* 誦持) while the buddha Merugandha was in the world. The young monk then traveled throughout his home kingdom, teaching multitudes of people who all revered him. The text goes on to describe that after Damaśrī died, he was repeatedly reborn in Jambudvīpa, left the household in each of his subsequent lives, during which he spontaneously obtained texts "previously never before heard" and was again and again rejected by contemporary monks who refused to accept sūtras that "have not been heard by us from our preceptors and teachers."

We would do well to recognize that orality does not function here at face value. The *Pūrṇaparipṛcchā* is at pains to explain its very own textual existence by positing the existence of a "shadow sūtra," a "never before heard" teaching by a former buddha. The author in effect provides a model for how an ideal reader can situate himself within a rewritten tradition—to see within the narrative what it looks like to accept a newly revealed text as he is asked to do for the very text he is reading.[33] To accomplish this, genealogy comes strongly to the fore, since contemporary controversies regarding textual legitimacy must be shown to be the residue of previous rejections by dimwitted monks, some of whom have made the same mistake across many lifetimes. All of this narrative complexity, of which my summary above is but a snippet, with stories

32. Taishō 310.17.11.445c12–447a25.

33. In this analysis I have benefited from Cole 2005, esp. 59–61, where he discusses a similar "shadow sūtra," the *Sūtra of Limitless Meaning*, in the *Saddharmapuṇḍarīka* and the function of this narrative ploy to stabilize textual authority for the *Saddharmapuṇḍarīka* itself.

about the past collapsed into the narrative present, necessitates that textuality be objectified in a way we almost never see in early scriptures. Put another way, while early sūtras—as found in the Pāli Nikāyas, Chinese Āgamas, and now, the growing body of early manuscripts of Gāndhārī texts of many genres—purport to be discourses of the Buddha, many Mahāyāna sūtras are in effect discourses about discourses. The textual anxiety that dominates Mahāyāna literature generates a nostalgia for orality and the authenticity born of being "present" before buddhas who guarantee it.

This deep-seated textual insecurity, one that seeks to recover a "lost" orality, can only take place in a context in which literacy and writing have come to dominate textual production. Returning to the prologue of the *Rāmāyaṇa*, which likewise imagines an oral transmission from the divine and its oral dissemination among poets, Pollock insightfully observes:

> The carefully constructed image of a purely oral culture in the prelude—a text unquestionably dated later than the main body of the work—cannot mean what it literally says. When Vālmīki is shown to compose his poem after meditating and to transmit it orally to two young singers, who learn and perform it exactly as he taught it to them, we are being given not a realist depiction but a sentimental "fiction of written culture." . . . For it clearly cognizes orality as such from outside of orality, so to speak, and in a way impossible to do in a world ignorant of any alternative—ignorant, that is, of writing. Nostalgia for the oral and a desire to continue to share in its authenticity and authority, with the same lingering effects of remembered oral poetry, mark other first moments of literary invention across Eurasia.[34]

It is very probably not merely coincidental that the emergence of an aestheticized use of Sanskrit, signaled by the composition of the *Rāmāyaṇa* in the very last centuries BCE, coincided temporally with the composition of the first Mahāyāna sūtras.[35] None of this is to suggest that these developments

34. Pollock 2006, 78. Cf. also 305: "The prelude to the *Rāmāyaṇa*, the first poem, could foreground the work's oral origins and transmission only because the new mode of literacy made it possible to conceptually grasp orality as such in the first place. In its structure and complexity the *kāvya* of the post-*Rāmāyaṇa* period is unthinkable without literacy, and it was without a doubt always preserved through literate and not oral transmission. Orality undoubtedly remained central to the performance of *kāvya*, but it was oral performance of a written text, read out from the script when not memorized outright."

35. On the dating of the *Rāmāyaṇa*, I follow Pollock rather than Goldman, who, in the

undermined the persistent bias toward the oral that had long dominated Indian textual culture. But again, as Pollock reminds us, "Orality in India sometimes seems as much an ideology as a fact of practice, for the oral ideal persisted long after writing had become fundamental to the Sanskrit tradition itself" (Pollock 2006, 83). We have no reason to believe that everyone who encountered these texts did so via the written word. Drewes is not wrong to suppose that literacy was not common in ancient India, which makes it ironic that he seems to have largely glossed over the prevalent use of the verb √*vac* in the causative in connection with the other three verbs he discusses. *Vācayati*, as Pollock points out, "literally means to make [a text] speak," which is to say, to read it aloud (Pollock 2006, 85). Thus there is no shortage of stock phrases, character names in the vocative to signpost dialogue, and parallel narrative structuring to aid aural comprehension.

The anxious normativity about oral transmission exhibited in Mahāyāna sūtras is less a reflection of real practice and more a call to arms. These authors needed to conceal their roles in the construction of the or a buddha's oral pronouncement of a "new" Dharma within a literate tradition by transporting their audiences back to the originating event, one that places them within a lineage of oral transmission in mythic time so as to provide a proper etiology for the very text that literally reinscribes their identity. But it is also the case that these authors rather often reveal their hand and cognize a textuality that bursts through the seams of orality. And here I must come back to a text that Drewes discusses explicitly and that has had a prominent place, for good reason, in arguments for and against the cult of the book in the early Mahāyāna.

If the *Pūrṇaparipṛcchā* is rather little known among scholars of the Mahāyāna and has little to say about writing and books specifically, the same cannot be said of the *Aṣṭasāhasrikā*. In the passage from chapter 3 described at the beginning of this paper, we saw that the spot of ground where the written text of the Perfection of Wisdom is established is likened to the *bodhimaṇḍa*, the seat of the Buddha's awakening and a cultic center of great prestige. Sons and daughters of good family cannot be harmed at such a site because the Perfection of Wisdom in book form has made it a true shrine worthy of worship. The cult of the book is then compared favorably to the cult of the relics, since, our author tells us, the Tathāgata acquired his name not from his physical body (*ātmabhāvaśarīra*) but from his acquisition of omniscience born of and manifest in this Perfection of Wisdom. The *Aṣṭasāhasrikā* is not hostile to the relic cult, since the very contrast it attempts to make with the book cult

introduction to his translation of the *Bālakāṇḍa* book, would place the core of the epic contemporaneously with the Buddha, if not somewhat before. See Goldman [1984] 1990, 14–23.

depends on a recognition of the widespread appeal of the stūpa as cultic center: "For the relics of the Tathāgata are the genuine support (*āśrayabhūta*) of the gnosis of omniscience, and this gnosis of omniscience is born of the Perfection of Wisdom" (Wogihara [1932] 1973, 273). But our author could not be clearer that it is the book, and the teachings it contains, that should be the focus of attention for his bodhisattva faction.

Chapter 5 of the *Aṣṭasāhasrikā* opens with another comparison, this time between a person who would trust in and venerate the Perfection of Wisdom versus another who, having venerated the text, would give a copy away to someone eager for it (Wogihara [1932] 1973, 285–289). It is the latter who would beget the greater merit. And this is true even when compared to persons who have attained mastery of the four states of meditative absorption, the four unbounded mental states, the four formless attainments, and the five supernormal powers. This focus in chapter 5 on copying and circulating the Perfection of Wisdom as a book is noteworthy in light of recent finds. Fragments of a Kharoṣṭhī manuscript written in the Gāndhārī language that correspond to chapter 5 of the *Aṣṭasāhasrikā* have recently come to light, along with fragments corresponding to chapter 1.[36] These fragments, like the much later Sanskrit manuscripts, repeatedly refer to the Perfection of Wisdom as a book (Gāndhārī *postao*). In addition, a colophon found with these fragments describes the scroll on which these two chapters were written as "the first book of the Prajñāpāramitā" (*paṭhamage postage prañaparamidae*).[37] Significantly, these fragments have been dated approximately to the first century CE, a century or more before the earliest Chinese translation by Lokakṣema (dated to 179 CE). This data is further corroborated by Chinese records describing the transmission of the *Aṣṭasāhasrikā* to China by the Indian śramaṇa Zhu Shuofo, who brought the Kharoṣṭhī text with him to the capital at Luoyang.[38] Additionally, we also have an even larger number of fragments of the *Aṣṭasāhasrikā* in a Kuṣāṇa-period Brāhmī script, dated on paleographic grounds to the third

36. For an edition and translation of these fragments, see Falk and Karashima 2012 on chapter 1 and Falk and Karashima 2013 on chapter 5. For a discussion and translation of these two chapters from the Gāndhārī manuscript, see also Salomon 2018, 335–358.

37. It should be mentioned that the writer of the colophon is not the same as the scribe of the sūtra text and the birch bark on which the colophon is written is not physically connected to the text. See also the remarks in Schopen 2018, esp. 407–408n22, on this colophon and the starkly positive valuation of copying manuscripts in Mahāyāna sources, contrasted with a certain ambivalence in some Buddhist legal literatures.

38. *Chu sanzang ji ji* 出三藏記集 (*A Collection of Records on the Translation of the Tripiṭaka*) Taishō 2145.55.6b8–9. On *huben* 胡本 as Kharoṣṭhī text, see Boucher 2000.

century, that may have originated in the area around Bāmiyān.[39] Thus there can be no doubt that at an early date, and even as a minority movement on the periphery of the Indianized world, Gandhāran Mahāyānists copied, circulated, and used the *Aṣṭasāhasrikā* as a book.[40]

References to books and writing don't end at chapter 5. In chapter 10, our author warns that Māra will be eager to cause difficulties for those who take up, preserve, read aloud, study, circulate, teach, explain, instruct in, recite, and write this Perfection of Wisdom: "Therefore this Perfection of Wisdom should be copied by writing it down quickly, be it over a month, or two months, or three months—so it should be copied. Or for more than that, for a year it should be copied by a son or daughter of good family" (Wogihara [1932] 1973, 480). Chapter 11 continues this theme, warning that, among the deeds of Māra, bodhisattvas will copy the Perfection of Wisdom while yawning, laughing, or sneering. They will copy the text while ridiculing one another or become demoralized that the book does not mention their home town or clan name or family and thus take their leave (Wogihara [1932] 1973, 500–501). In chapter 14 the bodhisattva is advised not to abandon or mock the Dharma preacher so long as he has not yet internalized this Perfection of Wisdom or obtained it as a book (Wogihara [1932] 1973, 582).

By far the most detailed descriptions of cultic activities dedicated to the book come in chapter 30, in the famous description of the quest of the bodhisattva Sadāprarudita to obtain this teaching. A voice in the sky tells him to head east to hear this Perfection of Wisdom and to abide in the conviction that all dharmas are empty, without signs, and without aim: "When you practice like this, noble son, you will before long hear the Perfection of Wisdom, either from a book or from a monastic Dharma preacher who has internalized it" (*pustakagatāṃ vā dharmabhāṇakasya bhikṣoḥ kāyagatāṃ*).[41] In a scene reminiscent of the *Pūrṇaparipṛcchā*, Sadāprarudita has a vision of a tathāgata standing before him who reveals to him that five hundred *yojana*s to the east there is a city called Gandhavatī, where the bodhisattva Dharmodgata preaches the Perfection of Wisdom. "Then the bodhisattva mahāsattva Sadāprarudita, standing on that very spot of ground (*pṛthivīpradeśe*), heard the bodhisattva mahāsattva preaching the Perfection of Wisdom" (Wogihara

39. On these fragments see Sander 2000 and 2002.

40. I am not claiming, on the basis of this data, that the *Aṣṭasāhasrikā* was necessarily composed in Gandhāra, though this has been often proposed and is certainly possible. For recent reassertions of this thesis, see Bronkhorst 2012 and Karashima 2013.

41. Wogihara [1932] 1973, 930. For *kāyagataṃ* as "internalize" I follow Zimmermann 2002, 147n253, where he cites also this passage from the *Aṣṭasāhasrikā*.

[1932] 1973, 940). Sadāprarudita then enters into a series of samādhi states in which he sees innumerable buddhas in the ten directions teaching the Perfection of Wisdom. It is also during these states of meditative concentration that Sadāprarudita learns that long ago he was trained by the bodhisattva Dharmodgata, and it is for that reason that he now seeks his instruction again. Thinking that it would be unseemly to approach Dharmodgata without a gift, Sadāprarudita attempts to sell himself in order to secure an appropriate offering. Śakra, the lord of the gods, disguises himself as a man in order to test the bodhisattva's resolve. He requests his heart, blood, and marrow, and Sadāprarudita obliges in a gruesome display of self-sacrifice. A merchant's daughter sees these events unfold and intervenes on Sadāprarudita's behalf, offering to provide him the means to make a generous offering to Dharmodgata. They travel east together to Gandhavatī along with the daughter's parents and retinue. Alighting from their carriages, Sadāprarudita and company approach the place where the bodhisattva Dharmodgata has enshrined the Perfection of Wisdom:

> Then the bodhisattva mahāsattva Sadāprarudita went to where the bodhisattva mahāsattva Dharmodgata was, surrounded and accompanied by the five hundred young women led by the merchant's daughter, amid a marvelous display of worship without measure. At that time the bodhisattva mahāsattva Dharmodgata had constructed for the Perfection of Wisdom a *kūṭāgāra*[42] made of the seven precious substances, adorned with red sandalwood, and overspread with a net of pearls. In the four corners of the *kūṭāgāra* were placed gems that functioned as lamps. Four jars of incense made of silver were suspended on its four sides, inside which pure, black aloe burned so as to worship the Perfection of Wisdom. In the middle of this *kūṭāgāra* a couch was set up and a box of four precious substances was made, into which was inserted the Perfection of Wisdom written with melted *vaiḍūrya* inscribed on gold plates. And this *kūṭāgāra* was adorned with variegated strips of cloth and garlands hanging down from it.[43]

Sadāprarudita and his entourage then see thousands of gods led by Śakra perform worship of this *kūṭāgāra*, for, as Śakra says, "This is the Perfection of

42. A *kūṭāgāra* is typically a hall, pavilion, or temple surmounted by an ornamental and gabled roof. No single English equivalent adequately captures its meaning.

43. Wogihara [1932] 1973, 955.

Wisdom, the mother and guide of bodhisattvas mahāsattvas; bodhisattvas mahāsattvas who train in it quickly obtain all buddha qualities that follow from the perfection of all virtues and also knowledge of all perspectives (*sarvākārajñatāṃ*)" (Wogihara [1932] 1973, 955–956). Learning from Śakra that the Perfection of Wisdom was located inside the *kūṭāgāra* of Dharmodgata, he and his entourage all pay homage to it, each depositing their portion of the offerings they brought, with an aim to also honor the bodhisattva Dharmodgata. The offered flowers rise up in the air to form another *kūṭāgāra*, and robes, garments, and jewels form a pavilion in midair. When Sadāprarudita and his entourage see this miraculous display of supernormal power, they think to themselves:

> As marvelous the great supernormal power possessed by the bodhisattva mahāsattva Dharmodgata, as great his charismatic authority (*anubhāva*), as great his power, so too is his bodhisattva career while this noble son is practicing. Such is his miracle of supernormal power. How much more will it be when he has awakened to unexcelled, complete and perfect awakening.[44]

In response to this marvel, the merchant's daughter and her retinue all make the aspiration to awakening so as to acquire the very qualities possessed by the bodhisattva Dharmodgata.

Clearly the cult of the book described here is heavily mythologized and thus cannot provide us specifics of actual practice. But what we can discern here is a particular orientation toward the text, which is the object of an arduous quest. In this narrative, unlike the *Pūrṇaparipṛcchā*, a visionary experience does not reveal the text directly to the bodhisattva Sadāprarudita but instead tells him where to find it, either as a book or as embodied in a Dharma preacher. He learns by entering a series of trance states that that person is the bodhisattva Dharmodgata, presented clearly as a layman who lives in a grand mansion and sports in parks with his retinue for pleasure. Despite appearances, Sadāprarudita finds that the bodhisattva possesses the Perfection of Wisdom in both senses: he preaches in the marketplace from his own internalized understanding of the text, and he has enshrined a physical copy, elaborately written on gold plates, within a magnificently adorned shrine-tower.

It is patently obvious that the author of *Aṣṭasāhasrikā* could not have intended his fellow bodhisattvas to take the extravagant worship of the book

44. Wogihara [1932] 1973, 957.

presented here as a model for their own behavior. Instead, as Cole has argued, we are witnessing here, as elsewhere, a sophisticated literary seduction:

> In short, one is reading over Ever Wailing's [i.e., Sadāprarudita's] shoulder as he seeks out the text one is reading, with the important difference that Ever Wailing's implacable longing for the text will deliver him to the land of Gandhavati with all its splashy pleasures, whereas the reader of the text will only arrive at a *description of Gandhavati*. Thus, with his or her pleasures deferred, the reader is left to find satisfaction in worshipping the text in the standard form detailed above in the case of the *Lotus Sūtra*: one is expected to read, recite, copy, and explain the text. In brief, the text has sought to generate desire for itself by demonstrating just how strong that desire for the text ought to be—as demonstrated by the indefatigable Ever Wailing—and, correspondingly, just how pleasurable the completion of the journey/narrative will be when one really gets "to" the text.[45]

Sadāprarudita's arduous journey to find Dharmodgata, his willingness to sacrifice his own flesh and blood as an offering, and his elaborate homage to both the text and to the Dharma preacher are all intended to reorient the central focus of this textual community—some of whom our author clearly feared were prone to backsliding to lesser aims—amid competing alternatives as to where and in whom the true Dharma is to be found.

Having concluded the story of Sadāprarudita by describing his vision of manifold buddhas and bodhisattvas in the ten directions all teaching this Perfection of Wisdom to multitudes of monks, the Buddha entrusts this sūtra to Ānanda:

> Then the Blessed One addressed the venerable Ānanda: "By this means, Ānanda, it should be known that this Perfection of Wisdom brings the bodhisattva mahāsattva near to the gnosis of

45. Cole 2015, 153. I part ways with Cole, however, who sees the key to this literary seduction to be the promise that the reader too will win access to the pleasures of the city of Gandhavatī, "provided that he reads devotedly about that city and the rules to get there" (153). The pleasures of Gandhavatī are indeed elaborately detailed, with its jeweled gardens, fragrant flowers, tinkling bells, and cooing birds. But presuming that the ideal reader is being invited to assume the subject position of Sadāprarudita in the story, the orientation of the narrative is always toward access to the text, not the city, and that orientation is thoroughly devotional, both to the physical text and the *dharmabhāṇaka* who has embodied it.

> omniscience. Therefore, Ānanda, the bodhisattva mahāsattva who wishes to obtain the gnosis of omniscience should practice in this Perfection of Wisdom. This Perfection of Wisdom should be heard, taken up, preserved, read aloud, mastered, taught, explained, declared, recited, and written down. When it has been carefully written with distinct letters in a large book by the supernatural power (*adhiṣṭhāna*) of the Tathāgata, it should be honored, venerated, revered, worshipped, treated with respect, and esteemed with flowers, incense, fragrances, wreaths, unguents, aromatic powders, robes, instrumental music, garments, parasols, banners, bells, flags, and with rows of lamps all around and with many forms of worship. This is our admonition to you, Ānanda. For in this Perfection of Wisdom will the gnosis of omniscience be fully developed.[46]

The text concludes thus with a veritable epitome of the cult of the book, a book worthy of worship because it embodies the very cognition that defines a buddha and thereby provides the bodhisattva with a means toward that end.

Criticisms of the Cult of the Book Hypothesis

It is perhaps fitting even if a bit ironic that it is Schopen himself who has been among the first to call some of his earlier hypotheses concerning the cult of the book into question. In a pair of articles on the Mahāyāna in 2004 and 2005, Schopen argued that much of early Mahāyāna rhetoric is reformist in a conservative sense: rather than embracing or innovating in cult practice, many among our early bodhisattva authors sought to disentangle themselves from the very rituals that tied monks to donors and the mutual obligations such relationships entailed:

> Here too it is important to note that Gregory Schopen was almost certainly wrong—and his theory too must go the way of Hirakawa's—in seeing in these passages only an attempt by the "new" movement to substitute one similar cult (the cult of the book) for another similar cult (the cult of relics). That such a substitution occurred—and perhaps rather quickly—is likely, but it now appears that it is very unlikely that this was the original or fundamental intention. That intention—however precarious, unpopular, or successful—was almost certainly to shift the religious focus from cult and giving to

46. Wogihara [1932] 1973, 989–990.

> doctrine, to send monks, nuns, and even laymen quite literally back to their books. That in this attempt the book itself was—again, it seems, rather early—fetishized may only be a testament to the strong pressures toward cult and ritual that seem to have been in force in Indian Buddhism from the beginning.[47]

Fleshing out this argument in more detail, Schopen wonders aloud how anyone could have come to believe that the stūpa/relic cult could have been the institutional center of the emerging bodhisattva movement when all of our archeological and epigraphical evidence points strongly toward Mainstream monastic control, even as a number of early Mahāyāna texts express a certain ambivalence toward the stūpa cult that starkly undermines any attempt to see it as providing a basis for innovation (Schopen 2005b, 108–113). The cultic innovation that does appear most visibly in the archeological record nearly contemporaneously with the composition of new Mahāyāna sūtras is the buddha image, mostly notably the image of the bodhisattva Siddhārtha. Where epigraphical records indicate a specific affiliation for the monks who received or sometimes commissioned these cult images, these affiliations are always to named *nikāyas* (Schopen 2005b, 113–117). This fact does not preclude participation in the image cult by members of various bodhisattva factions, but apart from a single image of Amitābha from Mathurā, there is nothing in our extant finds that points to a specific interest in cultic images by those aligned with the Mahāyāna.[48] Attempts to see art-historical expressions of early Mahāyāna image cult activity have generally been unconvincing.[49] Here again Schopen notes that many of our early Mahāyāna authors appear to have been more interested in fostering particular kinds of inward experiences and cognitive transformations than in engaging in the kinds of ritualized exchange that embedded monks and their donors in a complex socioreligious network.[50]

47. Schopen 2004, 497.

48. On this Mathurā image, see Schopen 1987.

49. On this problem, see Boucher 2008b and now Rhi 2018. Mahāyāna textual interest in cult images is more ambiguous. They are seemingly embraced in some texts, such as the *Pratyutpannasamādhi-sūtra*, but primarily as a means for obtaining this samādhi, understood both as a particular meditative state and as the very text itself. Other texts, such as the *Vimaladattāparipṛcchā-sūtra*, enjoin bodhisattvas to make buddha images seated on lotus blossoms and to pay homage to them; on this and other such references, see Rhi 2003, 168–170. More work will be necessary to coordinate these textual injunctions with the evidence of the plastic media.

50. The move away from ritualized exchange is a common element of religious reform movements. The shift to an internalized or "spiritualized" goal focused upon individual self effort

As Paul Harrison noted long ago, and Schopen reiterated, the overwhelming majority of our Mahāyāna texts call upon their adherents to become bodhisattvas (and eventually buddhas), not worship them.[51]

How does this affect our understanding of the book and cult practice dedicated to it? Schopen argues that the cult of the book must be revisited, since he deems his 1975 article, which he termed "a piece of juvenilia," to be

> especially weak on the oral character of much of the activity that the *sūtras* say should be undertaken in regard to a given text, and it pays too little attention to the exhortations not only to preserve the Dharma, but also to put it into practice, and to the embodiment of the text in oneself rather than in the book. There is as well the related fact that in a number of the texts more recently recommended as early . . . there is very little reference to writing, and even less to books, although an emphasis on the value of the Dharma, even a single verse of it, is strong.[52]

If my observations above about the literariness of Mahāyāna sūtras, their self-reflexivity about themselves as texts, and their tropes of a nostalgic orality projected back to the originating revelation merit further consideration, then it appears I may be in the unexpected—and certainly amusing—position of defending Schopen 1975 against Schopen 2005b. But there are more issues to consider and other critics to account for before we draw even tentative conclusions.

Without a doubt the most vociferous critic of Schopen's argument has been David Drewes (2007). Drewes has called into question several points in Schopen's thesis: the understanding of the term *caityabhūta* within the standard

---

and intention is precisely the language we would expect from a movement critiquing the social mechanisms that reproduce and sustain the status-quo relationship between monks and the laity. But this move away from cult ritual is not a critique of devotion per se. One would be hard pressed to find many Mahāyāna sūtras of any period that were not interested in pūjā as a means for generating the merit that will result in unexcelled, complete and perfect awakening. This pūjā, however, is almost always directed toward buddhas who inhabit alternative world systems. Bodhisattvas generate merit from repeatedly offering flowers, unguents, and so on to manifold buddhas, who have attained their goal and established their own buddhafields precisely so as to make this kind of goal-directed behavior possible for others. But this is a devotion that could not have manifested the usual relationships of exchange. It had to be projected onto another time and place, idealized and therefore outside the usual means for generating spiritual commodities.

51. Harrison 1987, 80; Schopen 2005b, 138.

52. Schopen 2005b, 153n118.

pericopes in which it occurs in texts like the *Vajracchedikā*, the shift from orality to writing as reflected in passages focusing upon recitation at specific sites versus more permanently situated book cults, the institutional status of bodhisattva sodalities and their localization at specific cultic centers, and finally the presumed frictions between this cultic innovation and the preexisting stūpa/relic cult. These points are mutually implicated in some ways and can only be partially disentangled.

Leading off with long citations from Schopen's 1975 article, Drewes declares:

> What is perhaps most notable about Schopen's argument in support of these theses is that the only evidence that he cites for the existence of Mahāyāna book shrines is his *caityabhūta* passages and their variants. A key question, then, is whether or not these passages actually make reference to shrines.[53]

That Schopen's evidence is exclusively textual is not surprising since almost all of the evidence we have for the early Mahāyāna is entirely textual. But what Drewes identifies as a "key question" is indeed the focus of his entire paper: are these early Mahāyāna sūtras referring to what he calls "actual shrines," or "institutional book shrines," or "semi-permanent public *caitya*"? Insofar as "actual" and "institutional" for Drewes implies the existence of physical structures akin to the shrines depicted on bas reliefs at famous Buddhist sites such as Sāñcī, Bhārhut, or Amarāvatī, two points should be made. First, this is not Schopen's argument, and this confusion is rife throughout Drewes's article. As noted in the first section above, it is the spot of ground (*pṛthivīpradeśa*) that is sacralized by the presence of the written text or the Dharma preacher who reads it aloud there. No elaborate structures need be present for this sacralization to have been so situated, even if some Mahāyānists, such as the author of the *Aṣṭasāhasrikā*, could imagine what such a shrine might look like under ideal conditions. Second, it is unclear, to say the least, how early Mahāyānists might have commandeered the resources to establish elaborate competing structures to house and venerate their books. Indeed, that is the point of this particular polemic. These early bodhisattva sodalities are claiming discursive space precisely because real space was likely denied them. "Spots of ground" could be designated as alternative loci around which bodhisattva fraternities could gather because the usual cultic centers were beyond their control for their own agendas, most notably reading, copying, reciting, and preaching their new textual productions.

53. Drewes 2007, 105.

There could be only one Bodh Gayā, a site tied to a very specific event within the well-known biography of the Buddha and highly revered as a cultic center seemingly from very early in the Buddhist tradition. Mahāyāna practices related to books, by contrast, were arbitrarily situated. These spots of ground where the text is located or where the *dharmabhāṇaka* recites them aloud merely need be deemed as suitable for cultic activities to be the focus of a complex, self-referential system of legitimation.[54] Thus when Mahāyāna texts declare that a *pṛthivīpradeśa* where a manuscript is physically located or read aloud is a *caityabhūta*, they are indeed making an implicit comparison to other shrines, generally the stūpa or *bodhimaṇḍa*, both of which are explicitly referred to in a variety of texts. But this comparison works precisely by *not* being similetic. To declare such spots to be "true shrines" (more literally, to "really be *caitya*") our authors are not presuming the construction of actual edifices for their books—even when they all too hopefully imagined them—but instead are attempting to rally their supporters around alternative foci for congregation by playing off the positive valorization of well-known shrines whose legitimacy was undisputed. In other words, Mahāyāna authors were all too well aware that their textual innovations pushed against the reigning Buddhist orthopraxis. Such spots of ground must be presented as genuine shrines, equivalent if not superior to the *bodhimaṇḍa* or stūpa. A simile cannot convey this force, since it presents as optional what our authors are desperately trying to prescribe from a likely position of limited influence. This is all too typical of how religious rhetoric works in small-sect movements.

For this reason, I must reject Paul Harrison's suggestion, picked up also by Drewes, that the *caityabhūta* passages in the *Vajracchedikā*, rather than referring to a cult of the book, instead are "of the same order as English expressions like 'He worships the ground on which she walks.'"[55] Such passages, Harrison contends, provide "about as much evidence for the cult of the book as a physical object, or of the particular places in which it is kept, recited, and so on, as the aforementioned English locution furnishes proof of ground worship." This dismissal takes a mandate to extend the significance of an already dominant cult practice to an innovation within a minority movement as equivalent to a cliché designed to be humorous precisely because its literal sense is so outland-

54. My thinking here is very much indebted to the well-known and influential study of ritual in Smith 1987, particularly chapters 4 and 5, where Smith contrasts the arbitrariness of the temple in Jerusalem with the generation of Christian pilgrimage sites in fourth-century Palestine specifically tied to biblical events.

55. This occurs in a note to Harrison's translation of the *Vajracchedikā*; see Harrison 2006, 148n57, and Drewes 2007, 114 and n18, on this passage.

ish. To treat both kinds of statements as mere hyperbole of the same order is to ignore the force of our authors' narrative programs as they sought to claim space for themselves and their confrères within Buddhist communities. We should be able to avoid reducing our explanatory options to either literal readings of polemical texts or dismissals of their injunctions as hyperbolic throwaways and instead should aim to understand how our authors might artfully entice sympathetic Buddhists to enter their elaborated discursive arenas with an aim to redefine or reinforce a contested religious affiliation.

This flatfooted understanding of how religious narrative works unfortunately mars Drewes's critique throughout. In referring to several passages from both non-Mahāyāna and Mahāyāna texts, Drewes notes the use of the recurring phrase "becomes a *caitya* for the whole world," which besides its use for spots of ground where Mahāyāna sūtras are revealed, is also applied to people rather than places: "Since it seems fairly clear that none of these other passages are referring to actual shrines. . . . The idea that *caitya*s are to be worshipped, or that they are 'for' certain beings, seems simply to be a stock element of passages of this sort" (Drewes 2007, 116). It seems not to have occurred to Drewes that stock clichés with potent associations can take on different meanings in different contexts precisely because the phrasing was immediately recognizable, allowing the author to transfer one set of affinities to another. Since early Mahāyāna authors were advocating new forms of textuality that appear to have required alternative loci for use, they clearly wanted to couch their efforts in well-known pericopes that would mask any appearance of innovation.

In an extended discussion of the famous passage in chapter 3 of the *Aṣṭasāhasrikā*, where the spot of ground at which a written copy of this text is located is declared to be a genuine shrine, equivalent to the seat of awakening, an already well-established cultic center, Drewes notes: "On Schopen's reading, this passage, like the two passages from the *Vajracchedikā*, serves as evidence that shrines dedicated to particular sūtras served as early Mahāyāna cult centers" (Drewes 2007, 119). Again, it is important to pay attention to the rhetorical function of this passage and others like it. Our author here is attempting to relocate where those drawn to his bodhisattva faction should congregate—in this case, around the text that is responsible for the Buddha's attainment of omniscience, which literally embodies his awakening and fixes it in space in the same way the *bodhimaṇḍa* was widely perceived to do.[56] None of this presupposes or requires what Drewes repeatedly refers to as "actual

56. Lamotte long ago drew attention to the multivalence of the term *bodhimaṇḍa*, which can indicate both the "seat of awakening" at Bodh Gayā and the "essence of awakening," the epitome of the Buddha's experience at this site. See Lamotte [1965] 1998, 195–196n242.

shrines," though the *Aṣṭasāhasrikā* is more explicit than many texts in describing idealized cultic centers, as we saw above in the description of the *kūṭāgāra* constructed by the bodhisattva Dharmodgata.[57] Again, at the risk of beating a dead horse, the apotropaic claims of this passage in chapter 3 function not ostensively but as polemic. The *Aṣṭasāhasrikā* is not a manual for ritual practice. It is a complex manifesto for aspiring *bodhisattvayānika*s occupying the margins of Buddhist authority designed to reinforce their ranks and draw others into the fold. Both objectives required sophisticated literary strategies for seducing the author's intended audience to share in his understanding of where tradition should be relocated, all the while disguising his own role in the process. To lay bare these strategies and expose these roles is the task of critical historical analysis. To accept our author's rhetoric at face value is to do something else altogether.

Thus the *Aṣṭasāhasrikā* furnishes little reason for us to worry about "actual shrines." But the *Saddharmapuṇḍarīka*, to which Drewes turns next, overtly identifies the spot of ground where its book is recited or copied or taught to be a *tathāgatacaitya*—to be, in fact, a stūpa. A passage referred to above in the first section of this paper is worth translating here in full:

> Furthermore, Bhaiṣajyarāja, on which spot of ground this discourse on Dharma would be declared, or taught, or copied, or written down as a book, or recited, or chanted in chorus, at that spot of ground, Bhaiṣajyarāja, a *tathāgatacaitya*, grand, made of precious substances, high, and lofty, is to be made, and relics of the Tathāgata need not be established therein. For the entirety of the Tathāgata's body is deposited in it. On which spot of ground this discourse on Dharma would be declared, or taught, or read aloud, or chanted in chorus, or copied, or, having been written down, would be set up in a book—at that stūpa veneration, honor, respect, worship, and

57. I am perplexed by Drewes's repeated assertion that the various benefits promised by the author of the *Aṣṭasāhasrikā* are most often directed to those who keep and preserve the text in their home (see esp. Drewes 2007, 121–122). Schopen 2010, esp. 49–50, moves in this direction as well. While it is true that there are a few passages that include the *gṛha* as one of the places where a son or daughter of good family might be protected from harm by possession of the text, it is also clear that this is one of several possible sites, including a monastic cell or palatial mansion (depending on the precise significance of *prāsāda* here). We certainly cannot discount the possibility that Mahāyānists may have envisioned a wide range of sites at which to locate their scriptures for storage and dissemination. This seems especially true of later, medieval sources, such as the cache found at Gilgit, where lay involvement in textual practice is specifically detailed. The more essential point is that wherever the book is located, that site becomes a veritable shrine.

> homage are to be done with all flowers, incense, and so on, and with all manner of song, music, dancing, and so on should worship be done. Furthermore, Bhaiṣajyarāja, those sentient beings who would get the opportunity to praise or worship or see this *tathāgatacaitya* should all be known as having come near to the unexcelled, complete and perfect awakening.[58]

Drewes concedes here that this passage, which Schopen cited in his 1975 article, enjoins the construction of sūtra shrines (Drewes 2007, 124). And other scholars have taken this injunction to suppose that the *Saddharmapuṇḍarīka* is recommending that manuscripts be placed inside stūpas as an act of consecration, equal in every way to the relics of the Buddha. But the text in fact says nothing of the sort. Instead, it makes the same kind of rhetorical move here that the authors of the *Aṣṭasāhasrikā* did: to associate the sacrality and authority of a well-known cultic center (the stūpa or the *bodhimaṇḍa*) with sites tied to a Mahāyāna innovation, the very places where textual practice of manifold kinds would take place. Drewes's concern to find "actual stūpas" tied to books in the *Saddharmapuṇḍarīka* is just as misplaced as his search for "actual shrines" elsewhere. The ostensible injunction to build a lofty *tathāgatacaitya* made of precious substances here cannot be taken any more literally than Dharmodgata's "construction" of a *kūṭāgāra* in the *Aṣṭasāhasrikā*. Once again, as Schopen made clear long ago, it is the spot of ground where textual practices related to this Dharma discourse (*yasmin pṛthivīpradeśe 'yaṃ dharmaparyāyo . . .*) are conducted that makes such a spot a shrine of the Tathāgata in no need of relics because the entirety of the Buddha's body is there located. At that stūpa (*tasmiṃś ca stūpe . . .*) veneration, honor, and worship are called for in the usual ways, not because the authors of the *Saddharmapuṇḍarīka* expected their readers to actually build stūpas at such places but because of their insistence that such sites were already made equivalent to stūpas by the very presence of the sūtra that embodies the Buddha's awakening. In other words, stūpas stand here metaphorically for authorized sacred sites, and the rhetoric derives its force precisely by being prescriptive and not similetic. The amalgamation of the cult of the stūpa and the cult of the book represents a shift in strategy from the *Aṣṭasāhasrikā* but not a fundamental shift in polemic.

This realization is important, since Drewes next turns to the possible archeological evidence for a cult of the book in ancient India, notably the possibility that there might be evidence of manuscripts enshrined in stūpas and venerated as "true shrines." This matter can be dealt with quickly: despite the recent

58. Kern and Nanjio [1908–1912] 1970, 231.7–232.5.

discoveries of early manuscripts, there can be no material evidence for the cult of the book as it functioned in the earliest phase of Mahāyāna discourse. Drewes's references to early instances of the interment of inscriptions bearing the *pratītyasamutpāda* formula inside reliquaries or the proliferation of the *ye dharmā* verse throughout the Buddhist world, also often inside stūpas, are not instances of the cult of the book. As I have already discussed elsewhere, the sacralizing effects of these inscriptions are tied to their use as alternative relics, and thus their participation in the stūpa cult has nothing to do with sites where texts are read aloud, copied, or venerated.[59] The cult of the book, by contrast, is fundamentally performative, both in the way it enjoins bodhisattva sodalities to congregate and in the way it treats texts as objects to be copied, circulated, and revered. Nothing in the archeological record could provide evidence of such practices. There is, of course, evidence of textual practice, including homage paid to manuscripts, in the art-historical record, but all of this data is very much later, from a time when Mahāyāna authors and their patrons were no longer vying for cultic space.[60]

Drewes concludes his critique by noting that the accumulated weight of textual and archeological data does not point toward the existence of actual book shrines: "Because it does not seem possible to take Schopen's *caityabhūta* passages and their variants as evidence for the existence of book shrines, and because there does not seem to be any other evidence for their existence, it is difficult to avoid the conclusion that such shrines never existed" (Drewes 2007, 136). Happily, I can agree, as can Schopen, who already in his now classic article of 1975 concluded with regard to the institutional organization of early bodhisattva fraternities:

> As we have discovered above, the *pṛthivīpradeśa*, the spot of earth on which the book stands, is the focal point of the cult of the book—the organizational center around which the cultic activity (flower-pūjā, dancing, etc.) takes place. Further, it is reasonable to assume that the early Mahāyāna texts, being critical of established Buddhist orthodoxy (= the *Śrāvakas*), could not be taught or explained or kept in the usual monastic centers, and would require the develop-

59. See Boucher 1991 for the earlier instances of inscriptions with the full *pratītyasamutpāda* formula interred within stūpas and their replacement by the famous *ye dharmā* verse at sites throughout the Buddhist world from approximately the sixth century.

60. On the later representations of the book as cult object in Buddhism with clear evidence of pūjā carried out for it, see Kinnard 1999, 148–175, and Kinnard 2002, and more recently, the not unproblematic discussions in Kim 2009 and 2013 (on the latter, see the important review in von Hinüber 2016).

> ment of separate centers which would be free of orthodox interference. . . . For the time being, we would like only to suggest that such *pṛthivīpradeśāḥ* may well have formed one of the 'institutional bases' (consciously leaving room for the very likely possibility of there having been more than one) out of which early Mahāyāna arose.[61]

If Drewes has led us down a dead-end path, other scholars have wrestled with Schopen's hypothesis in more productive ways, but still not always without problems. James Apple (2014) has picked up one of the hypotheses Schopen proposed—namely, that early Mahāyāna literature may have begun as oral discourse until gradually being written down and circulated in book form—and he has attempted to demonstrate this with a different kind of data. Schopen suggested that the language of the *Vajracchedikā* recommends an oral performance of its Dharma discourse and that a text like the *Aṣṭasāhasrikā* reveals a transition to writing and books, thus reversing the usual dating of these texts (a position I think is no longer necessary or plausible). Apple for his part attempts to show that we can see a similar transition from the oral to the written when we contrast the earliest Chinese translations of Mahāyāna sūtras with their later Sanskrit recensions or Tibetan translations. In this regard, he zeroes in on a particular trope, *dharmaparyāyo hastagata* ("having the discourse on Dharma in one's hands"), and attempts to show that particularly in the Entrustment chapters of several Mahāyāna sūtras, where injunctions to reproduce, preserve, and circulate the text are often expressed, this phrase is often found in our extant Sanskrit manuscripts and Tibetan translations of the ninth century and may suggest that rather than pointing toward a permanently fixed site for worship, the cult of the book "was comprised of highly mobile and translocal textual communities who carried their object of veneration with them and kept such objects in domestic locations."[62] Certainly this adds an interesting new twist to the discussion, so it may be worth looking more carefully at the evidence Apple marshals.

61. Schopen 1975, 181.

62. Apple 2014, 26. There are passages in a number of Mahāyāna sūtras that indicate that the book was understood to be fully portable. For example, in chapter 16 of the *Saddharmapuṇḍarīka* we find the following: "For that reason he who has made this discourse on Dharma into a book and carries it on his shoulder carries the Tathāgata on his shoulder. Such a noble son or daughter need not make stūpas for me, Ajita, nor monasteries and need not give requisites to cure the sick to the assembly of monks. For such a noble son or daughter has constructed stūpas made of the seven precious substances and has done *śarīra-pūjā* to my relics . . ." (Kern and Nanjio [1908–1912] 1970, 338.4–8).

In one example, Apple cites the "Entrustment" chapter (*Anuparīndanā-parivarta*) of the *Saddharmapuṇḍarīka-sūtra*, which is the twenty-seventh chapter of the Sanskrit and twenty-second chapter of Kumārajīva's early fifth-century Chinese translation. The Sanskrit of the "Entrustment" chapter opens as follows:

> Then the Blessed One Śākyamuni, the arhat, the complete and perfectly awakened one, rose up from his Dharma seat, gathered all the bodhisattvas together, took hold of their right hands with his right hand, which was perfected by the accomplishment of supernatural power, and then said, "I present and entrust, set down and deposit in your hand, noble sons, this unexcelled, complete and perfect awakening that I have acquired over incalculable hundreds of thousands of *nayuta*s of *koṭi*s of eons. Noble sons, see to it that it spreads far and wide."[63]

In Kumārajīva's translation, the concluding section of this citation has the Buddha declare:

> For immeasurable hundreds of thousands of myriads of *koṭi*s of incalculable eons, I practiced this Dharma of unexcelled, complete and perfect awakening, which is difficult to obtain. I now entrust it to you. You should wholeheartedly spread this Dharma so that it will broadly flourish.[64]

As we can see by comparing these two passages, Kumārajīva's translation does not include the trope in which the Buddha deposits the sūtra in the bodhisattvas' hands. We might have more confidence that this could indicate a chronological priority to the Sanskrit text if it weren't for the fact that Dharmarakṣa's translation of 286 appears to know some version of this phrasing. Unfortunately Dharmarakṣa's translation is both confused and confusing at this point, as is not atypical of his earlier translations. The portion parallel to the Kumārajīva translation above has the Buddha say:

63. Kern and Nanjio [1908–1912] 1970, 484.1–7. The Kashgar manuscript is essentially the same with only slight variations in wording; see Toda 1981, 455b7–456a6. The text of the Gilgit manuscript is mostly missing at this point.

64. Taishō 262.9.52c5–8.

> Noble sons, the Buddha, over incalculable, immeasurable hundreds of thousands of *koṭi*s of eons, accumulated and accomplished practices leading to the attainment of unexcelled, complete and perfect awakening and obtained the spiritual perfections (*du wuji* 度無極). Therefore I chose these worthy ones, placing [the text] in their right hands and elevating their hands and lowering them so that they remember it. They should receive this sūtra, uphold, recite, read it aloud, and explicate it in detail for the assembly, causing all sentient beings everywhere to be able to see and hear it.[65]

As one sees immediately, Dharmarakṣa's translation is anything but clear, and we can be fairly sure that his Indic manuscript, which we have good reason to believe was written in the Kharoṣṭhī script with considerable influence from Gāndhārī, did not look like any that have come down to us. But it is also likely that his translation committee, with great difficulty and limited success, was actually trying to render some version of the phrasing we have: *yuṣmākaṃ haste parindāmy anuparindāmi nikṣipāmy upanikṣipāmi* ("I present and entrust, set down and deposit in your hand"). While we can't be certain as to where his committee went wrong, it appears that they may have misunderstood some version of (*upa-*)*ni-√kṣip* ("to set down, deposit") with *ut-√kṣip* ("to raise up, elevate").[66] But there is little doubt that his translation has the Buddha depositing the scripture in his disciples' hands. Given that, it may be safer to assume that Kumārajīva's translation reflects his own trimming of the fuller passage, consistent with a stylistic preference to reduce the prolixity of Indian texts, for which his translations are famous. We have, therefore, little reason to assume a chronological development in the *Saddharmapuṇḍarīka* recensions on this point at least.

In another early text, the *Drumakinnararājaparipṛcchā-sūtra*, translated by Lokakṣema in the late second century, Apple finds another omission of the phrase "ensure that this *dharmaparyāya* will come into the hands of dharma preachers," which does appear in the later Tibetan translation (Apple 2014, 40). The omission of this trope in the earliest Chinese translations led Apple to see in these "snapshots" a development from an oral to a written entrustment. But the immediately following section leaves no doubt that the author enjoined the circulation of a written book:

65. Taishō 263.9.134a22–26.

66. I might also hypothesize that Dharmarakṣa's "worthy ones" (*zhuxian* 諸賢) could be a misreading of *yuṣmākaṃ* ("your," gen. pl.) as if from *āyuṣmat*. Explanations for both mistakes are not obvious, but it is likely that a text in Kharoṣṭhī script with Gāndhārī phonology greatly facilitated the misunderstandings.

> The bodhisattva Maitreya said to the bodhisattva *Devamauli (*diwuli* 提無離): "After the Buddha's parinirvāṇa, we should preserve this Dharma. We should teach and explain it to others and promulgate its purport. In the last age, bodhisattvas who have wholesome roots will obtain this sūtra. We should exhort others to protect it.[67] Those who in the last age obtain this sūtra, who write, recite, or read it aloud, will all become secure. You should know that they are protected by the bodhisattvas Maitreya and Devamauli."[68]

Here again we have clear evidence that this text was conceived of as a book that should be copied and read from aloud already in its earliest, second-century translation.

Apple would also like to see a trend toward what he calls *biblioficaton* in another text translated by Dharmarakṣa, the *Hastikakṣaya-sūtra*.[69] In this example he highlights an antecedent story from the Tibetan version in which the Buddha describes to Mañjuśrī how eons ago a previous buddha named *Siṃhagatigamana explained the *Hastikakṣaya* to the bodhisattva *Vajradhvaja, who then distributed this *dharmaparyāya* throughout the kingdom, thereby healing sentient beings of various maladies (Apple 2014, 41–42). Afterward, the Buddha declares to Ānanda:

> Ānanda, this *dharmaparyāya* will gladden bodhisattvas and will bring forth bodhisattvas. After I have died, it will come into the hands of bodhisattvas. It will come forth as a bodhisattva book (*glegs bam*), and it will come forth as a bodhisattva basket (*sgrom*). It will not come into the hands of outcaste bodhisattvas; it will not come to them as a book, and it will not come to them as a basket.[70]

The parallel passage in Dharmarakṣa's translation occurs not at the end of the text, as it does in the Tibetan, but much closer to the beginning:

67. What I translate as "protect" here is in the Chinese *yonghu* 擁護, literally, "take into one's hands and guard," which may well be a reflex of the very trope Apple claims is missing.

68. Taishō 624.15.367a11–16.

69. Sanskrit fragments of this text have recently been identified and discussed in relation to the early Chinese translation of Dharmarakṣa; see Liu and Chen 2014.

70. Li thang Bka' 'gyur 150, 57: 124a2–5 (etext by ADARSHA, "Resources for Kanjur and Tanjur Studies." Accessed January 30, 2019. https://www.istb.univie.ac.at/kanjur/rktsneu/ekanjur/verif2.php?id=J150&coll=lithang).

> The Buddha explained to Ānanda: "This *dharmaparyāya* (*jingdian-yao* 經典要) will please bodhisattvas. If the assembly of bodhisattvas who are amenable to this sūtra teaching would accept it, their previously acquired wholesome roots will manifest before their eyes. After I have died, this *dharmaparyāya* will be entrusted to bodhisattvas, who will take it up in their hands. With their dispositions serene and their intentions stable, they by this means rely on emptiness, reciting and reflecting upon this *bodhisattvapiṭaka*. It is not entrusted to dull-witted bodhisattvas with meager virtues. It is not entrusted to a person who is a malicious and obsequious counterfeit bodhisattva. It is also not entrusted into the hands of the bodhisattva who has many desires and frivolous thoughts.[71]

Again there are a number of problems in Dharmarakṣa's translation, not all of which we can solve. Dharmarakṣa includes mention of bodhisattvas taking up the book in their hands and also refers to bodhisattvas reflecting upon the *bodhisattvapiṭaka*, which must be related in some way to what in Tibetan is rendered *sgrom*, "basket, chest, container." Dharmarakṣa translates *caṇḍāla-bodhisattva* as "counterfeit bodhisattva" (*wei pusa* 僞菩薩) and in so doing fleshes out the significance of the expression for his Chinese audience beyond what we see in the parallel Tibetan text. So while the early Chinese translation is certainly not an exact match for the later Tibetan, it is very likely that the major pieces of what we see in the Tibetan are already in place, belying the notion that there was a shift toward a greater materialization of the text.

Finally, in the passage from the "Entrustment" chapter of the *Aṣṭasāhasrikā* translated above from the Sanskrit, we see a parallel to it in the earliest Chinese translation by Lokakṣema, albeit with lexical adaptations for a Chinese audience:

> The Buddha said, "Thus, Ānanda, you have affection for the Buddha. For this reason you should repay the Buddha's kindness. Ānanda, you should greatly revere the Perfection of Wisdom, esteem and respect passages (*ju* 句) from within it. The passages reflected upon in your mind should be clearly understood. You should illuminate precisely what you reflect upon. Disregard the rest and concentrate upon those (passages). You should write the entire sūtra, correctly forming the top and corners of the letters (*zitoujiao* 字頭角). When you (wish to) hold or study (this scripture), scrupulously hand it over

71. Taishō 813.17.776a27–b4.

> to the bodhisattva mahāsattva and also give him a long fine silk scroll to carefully copy (the scripture), making the passages of the first part of the sūtra (through?) the last part be in accord. When you copy it, obtain a good brush and write it on fine silk. Put your trust in it, attend upon it, pay homage to it, and worship it with fine flowers, fine incense, mixed incense processed by pounding, unguents, multicolored silk fabrics, flower canopies, banners, flags, sesame (or hemp) oil with all manner of heavenly fragrances put within it, and fine lamp wicks. Putting your trust (in the text), pay obeisance with your head to the ground and afterward light the lamp wicks, respect, pay homage to, and attend upon (the sūtra)."[72]

What all of this suggests then is that Apple's claim that "the chronological 'snapshots' of the Chinese and Tibetan versions demonstrate a transition from predominantly oral transmissions to entrusted transmissions of written texts" (Apple 2014, 43) will likely have to be rethought. Our earliest records of Mahāyāna sūtra literature—that is, the Chinese translations of the second and third centuries, to which we can now add a growing body of manuscripts in Gāndhārī Prākrit—overwhelmingly point to writing as a medium for preserving and circulating these documents. And again, the evidence from Chinese sources lines up with Richard Salomon's observation, based on both textual and archeological data, that the use of writing in the transmission of Buddhist texts generally gathers momentum during the Saka and Kuṣāṇa periods of the first few centuries CE, a portrait that is growing ever more refined with a steady stream of new discoveries.[73]

72. Karashima 2011, 539–540 (= Taishō 224.8.478a28–b9). I have benefited greatly also from Karashima's translation of this passage in his notes 255 and 257, though my rendering differs a bit from his. It is worth reminding the reader too of the fact that this passage is not the first "entrustment" of the text. An entrustment to Ānanda also occurs in chapter 28, and a number of scholars have commented on the implications of this for dating the composition of the various components of the sūtra as a whole. Shi Huifeng 2017 has reexamined these issues via chiasmus theory, and his approach opens exciting new vistas for rethinking the integrity of the text.

73. Salomon 2006, 374–375; 2017; and 2018, 95–99. The majority of these finds of course are of Mainstream genres, which do not exhibit the same literary features that I argue characterize Mahāyāna texts stylistically. In other words, the technology of writing for preserving and circulating Buddhist texts will not alone explain what we see in Mahāyāna sūtras, even if it is a necessary precondition for it.

Conclusion

Where do all these data, arguments, and criticisms leave Schopen's hypothesis on the cult of the book and its relationship to the organizational structure of the early Mahāyāna? If, as I and others before me have argued, Mahāyāna sūtras emerged early on from a literate tradition, there may no longer be any good reason to assume a chronological shift from an oral composition to eventual written transmission of the texts, as Schopen first hypothesized and Apple attempted to buttress. Furthermore, it is also likely that the efforts by our early Mahāyāna authors to create, at least rhetorically, a functional equivalence between the sites where their books were recited, copied, and honored and established cultic centers did not require a cult practice that was permanently fixed and localized in the same way.

In this regard we may need to reconsider the prominent role, often mentioned, of *dharmabhāṇaka*s in Mahāyāna sūtras. It may well have been these highly venerated individuals who copied, circulated, and made written texts aurally available to a wider audience ignorant of letters.[74] Indeed, Mahāyāna texts themselves are known to prescribe gifts to *dharmabhāṇaka*s that include requisites for copying manuscripts. Thus in the "Path of the Requisites" chapter of the *Akṣayamatinirdeśa-sūtra* we see the following:

> These four gifts amass the requisites of gnosis (*jñānasaṃbhāra*). Which four? The gift of birch bark, pens, ink, and books to *dharmabhāṇaka*s; the gift of diverse preacher's seats (*dharmāsana*) to *dharmabhāṇaka*s; the gift of all acquisitions, honor, and praise to *dharmabhāṇaka*s; the gift of stating "Well done!" (*sādhu*) sincerely in order to draw [others to] the Dharma. These four gifts amass the requisites of gnosis.[75]

74. While most of the scholarship on the role of *dharmabhāṇaka*s remains in Japanese, there has been more attention to this topic of late in Euro-American scholarship. MacQueen rightly noted some time ago that "Many of the mysteries of the origins of Mahāyāna are bound up with this figure" (MacQueen 1982, 53–54). He suggests, and I agree, that the *dharmabhāṇaka* is both the bearer and container of scripture. Drewes 2011 has taken up the status of *dharmabhāṇaka*s in early Mahāyāna sūtras but without specific attention to the mechanisms of their transmission of texts. Nance (2008 and 2012, 45–80) has paid due attention to the role of Dharma preachers not merely as preservers and transmitters of texts but as interpreters and analysts as well. For thoughtful reflections on the role of the *dharmabhāṇaka* in the *Suvarṇa(pra)bhāsottama-sūtra*, see Gummer 2012 and note 79 below.

75. Braarvig 1993, 123.6–13 (my translation). I am indebted to Skilling 2014, 506, for this

A nearly identical statement is made in the *Bodhisattvapiṭaka-sūtra*, and a number of other Mahāyāna sūtras prescribe the gift of birch bark, ink, pens, books, seats for preaching, and other necessities required by *dharmabhāṇakas*, as does the author of the *Ratnāvalī*, thought by most specialists to be Nāgārjuna.[76] Moreover, in the colophons to manuscripts preserved at Gilgit, we have references to *dharmabhāṇakas* by name, usually but not always monks, who either participated in the donation of the manuscript or were responsible for copying it (von Hinüber 2012, 61).

Mahāyāna Dharma preachers may, it seems, have functioned differently than their Mainstream predecessors. Preachers of Mahāyāna sūtras may well have memorized large chunks of text or templates from which particular sūtras were elaborated.[77] But it is also likely, as the texts themselves suggest, that a significant portion of their job was to read aloud from a manuscript, to make the text speak (*vācayati*) for those who could not do so themselves.[78]

---

reference. I should note also that this passage is present in Dharmarakṣa's translation, dated, with some uncertainty, to 308; see Taishō 403.13.605c6–11. As is typical of Dharmarakṣa's work, his translation includes both lexical confusions, as when he renders *śloka* ("praise") literally as "verses" (*songjie* 誦偈), and culturally specific interpolations, as when in reference to the gift of the requisites for writing, he says, "He gives paper, bamboo, and silk; he makes a gift of brushes so as to have the sūtra texts written down; he gives fine ink and superior inkstones."

76. See Skilling 2014, 506–510.

77. What we are most lacking and, unfortunately, most in need of is better data on the relationship between early manuscripts and reading practices. The recent discoveries of early manuscripts from the northwest part of the Indian subcontinent are slowly filling out our picture, however incompletely. For example, there are three graphically different forms of the *akṣara sa* in the Gāndhārī manuscript of the *Aṭṭhakavagga*, which Falk suggests resulted from the scribe attempting to differentiate the sounds he uttered as he was reciting the text or as its exemplar was being read to him (Falk 2011, 14). Lenz has argued that the extant fragments of Gāndhārī *pūrvayoga* texts preserve errors in the manuscript, pointing to the likelihood that the scribe was also the author and a specialist in this genre; see Lenz 2003, 102–107. The Bajaur Mahāyāna fragments (Bajaur Collection 4 and 6) show indications of directions to readers rather than auditors, where either explanations for unpacking abbreviations are given or the reader is told to flesh out a given passage in light of a previous parallel; see Schlosser 2022, 22–24. More Kharoṣṭhī fragments are coming to light seemingly every year, and it is hoped that they may provide some insights on book culture in at least one set of regional traditions.

78. It is worth remembering that the level of literacy needed to access much of Mahāyāna literature was not necessarily very high: "Although not usually admitted, much of early medieval Mahāyāna sūtra literature may have been intended for an audience with a limited amount of literary or literacy skills, and certainly would not have required a sophisticated knowledge of Sanskrit. In the Sanskrit of these texts conjugated finite verb forms are not common and appear to have been avoided wherever possible; those of any complexity—aorists, perfects, etc.—are, apart from a small number of almost frozen forms (e.g., *āha*, *abhūt*) rare. There is little beyond the range of presents and futures, the past being overwhelmingly expressed by past participles.

Thus we must use our textual data carefully. Scenes of extemporaneous oral preaching described in the sūtras are a necessary even if sometimes nostalgic fiction designed to transport the reader/auditor back to the mythic originating event—namely, the Buddha's own preaching of this very sūtra, which could only have taken place orally. The text is brought into the present by the *dharmabhāṇaka*, whose authority derives not from argument per se but from "doing things with words," as J. L. Austin would say.[79] These sūtras offer, in other words, a metafiction, a story projected into the plot of another story as an artifact for special attention, allowing the reader to witness the telling of the very story he is reading and must accept so as to participate in its rewards.[80] Any given recipient of these sūtras may have encountered them aurally, but there can be little doubt that the text within a text emerged from a literary milieu.

What is most essentially at stake then in these discussions of the cult of the book in early Mahāyāna discourse is the degree to which the written text had become fetishized.[81] The move in this direction is not unfamiliar. It is well

. . . The vocabulary too is hardly adventuresome, repetitious, simple" (Schopen 2009, 205–206). See the additional remarks on the linguistic shape of medieval Mahāyāna manuscripts in Schopen 2012, esp. 276–278.

79. Gummer 2012 offers a rich meditation on the oral performativity encoded in the *Suvarṇa(pra)bhāsottama-sūtra*. She asks us to imagine what it would be like to listen to the *dharmabhāṇaka* as the sūtra itself envisions his role as "functionally equivalent to the Buddha himself; through a sort of ritual ventriloquism, he makes manifest the voice of the Buddha" (143). Gummer's sensitive reading of the aesthetics by which the sūtra collapses the mythic past with the recitative present shows how the sūtra dismantles "the boundaries between the narrative world within the sūtra and the world in which the sūtra is preached and heard" (147). Granting this, my own take here moves in a somewhat different direction in seeing this oral normativity as itself a literary conjuring of an authoritative relationship between speaker and auditor. The sūtra signals its own materialization repeatedly, as in the story of King Susaṃbhava (chapter 13), which Gummer discusses at length. This king, during the dispensation of the former buddha Ratnaśikhin, has a dream vision of the *dharmabhāṇaka* Ratnoccaya, who was at that very moment in a cave rehearsing the text to himself. Ratnoccaya preaches the sūtra at the request of the king, who, in a profoundly emotional reaction, venerates the *dharmabhāṇaka* and worships the sūtra itself, thereby eliciting a supernatural response in which precious substances rain down upon Jambudvīpa. I agree with Gummer in seeing the *Suvarṇa*'s proclamations of its own narration as "not just about the sūtra: they are the sūtra" (146); but it is precisely this kind of self-reflexivity that is made possible by writing and is largely inconceivable without it.

80. I borrow the notion of metafiction from Waugh 1984.

81. Cole 2015 has a rich discussion on fetishizing tradition, whereby new religious discourses claim to be the appointed successors to the older traditions, which they now subsume and replace by seducing their consumers to accept their place in a newly manufactured lineage. Some kind of strategy like this is clearly at work in a number of Mahāyāna sūtras, as we saw above in the *Pūrṇaparipṛcchā*. Cole, however, has a tendency to overlook the degree to which Mahāyāna

documented in Hindu devotional traditions,[82] in East Asian Buddhisms,[83] and in Tibet[84] and Nepal,[85] to name only a few of the best-studied cases. But it is also clear that much of early Mahāyāna sūtra literature enjoins those on the bodhisattva path to internalize their message, to literally embody it. So the question we must ask is this: what is the relationship between these two trajectories, one that demands a profound cognitive transformation born of the arduous path of the bodhisattva and another that materializes the Dharma, treating it as an object that both sacralizes and protects? Surely not essential, since it is easy to find examples of reformist traditions that are thoroughly uninterested in cult practice. In fact, anti-ritualism tends to be one of the defining traits of critics of tradition, as is readily apparent in any number of early Mahāyāna sūtras, which are often suspicious of the status-quo relationship of exchange between monks and the laity.

But it is not at all unlikely that the more fundamental problem of the early Mahāyāna—namely, explaining how their texts became plausible vehicles for their reformist message—was in part addressed by their composition of complex etiologies of the very texts themselves. These narratives partici-

texts are often directed at insiders more in need of reinforcement than enticement. My own use of the term *fetishize* here is somewhat more prosaic. I am arguing that a fair proportion of early Mahāyāna sūtras are preoccupied with their own objectification, a kind of condensation of the voice of the Buddha into these new productions, and that such a fetishization was only possible in the presence of these new modes of textuality.

82. See Brown 1986 on veneration of the Purāṇas as books and De Simini 2016 for parallel medieval Śaiva developments. Both authors note the Buddhist precedents for these practices.

83. For Chinese Buddhism, see Campany 1991 and Kieschnick 2003, 164–185; for Japan, see most recently Eubanks 2011 for the best discussion of how Mahāyāna sūtras create a particular ontology for themselves that demands a new relationship between reader and text, which she studies in the *setsuwa* genre.

84. Schaeffer 2009, esp. 128–146; Diemberger 2012a and 2012b; and Helman-Ważny 2014, who notes the special attention pious donors give to Buddhist manuscripts; for example, in adorning a Perfection of Wisdom sūtra, they will have the story of Sadāprarudita's lavish offerings to Dharmodgata illustrated on the manuscript itself, with the bodhisattva depicted as a Tibetan lay master, which "seems to conflate personages of the story with wishful representations of the donors, who are shown with lavish offerings while accompanying the main character on his journey to the palace of bodhisattva Dharmodgata" (78).

85. See Emmrich 2009, who, in describing the contemporary restorations of a Newar manuscript of the *Aṣṭasāhasrikā* on the basis of the modern edition by Vaidya, remarks: "The manuscript thus functions as a field of merit for those involved in its maintenance and care, those who ensure that it can be read and worshipped to its greatest effect" (153). Jinah Kim was at the very same temple of Kvābāhāḥ to witness the restoration and worship of this same manuscript of the *Aṣṭasāhasrikā* just a few weeks before Emmrich (summer of 2004); see her discussion in Kim 2013, 271–285.

pated within an emerging literary culture that also served to sharply contrast their textual practices with those of their Mainstream predecessors. As Alan Cole has noted, Mahāyāna sūtras perform their work in the literary space in which one encounters them. Insofar as the reader/auditor confers legitimacy to the text, he receives in turn direct access to legitimacy from the text. This insight helps us understand why some texts—and here one thinks particularly of Cole's principal example, the *Saddharmapuṇḍarīka*—do little more than reinscribe the identities of the interlocutor (the Buddha) in relation to the reader/auditor (sons of the Buddha). The *Saddharmapuṇḍarīka*, it would appear, has little agenda beyond convincing its audience to step onto its stage and engage its dramatis personae. Liberation, in effect, is to be found by placing confidence in stories explaining how liberation is to be achieved.[86] It is the very willingness to do this that in some sense defines one as a *bodhisattvayānika*.

But if we think beyond this self-referential loop in which authoritative narrative is both the medium and the message, we must also ask: What factors initiated this openness to rewritings of tradition that succeed only when one surrenders to a social realignment that enables new forms of identity? In this regard, the book must have often served a pivotal role. On the one hand, it was almost certainly the turn toward literacy and literariness that made it possible for Mahāyāna authors to situate their narratives of origin as plots within texts, texts whose very fabrication recedes back seamlessly—they hoped—into the voice of the Buddha, now channeled through the recitation of the *dharmabhāṇaka*. On the other hand, the book and/or the pulpit (*dharmāsana*) must often have served to locate in space the arena for this encounter. These did not have to be permanent cultic centers, as Apple has reminded us. Devotional behaviors are prescribed for this "spot of ground" because the broader Mahāyāna agenda is to relocate tradition by offering to the physical text or the preacher who embodies the text the same honor one would offer the Buddha, whose voice has been fabricated precisely so as to unseat its traditional locus. Some *bodhisattvayānika*s would come to take these rhetorical moves quite literally, doing pūjā to manuscripts as one would to a shrine or guru. How early in Mahāyāna history this happened is probably impossible to know and quite beside the point. This cultic language can only make sense in a literate culture trafficking in books, and the manifestations of tradition in this new medium had a profound and lasting impact that must have been instrumental to their survival and eventual success.

86. Cole 2015, 127, makes exactly this point in regard to the narrative strategies of the Gospel of Mark.

Works Cited

Abbreviations

Taishō *Taishō shinshū daizōkyō* 大正新脩大藏經 (*The Buddhist Canon in Chinese, Newly Edited in the Taishō Era*). Edited by Takakusu Junjirō 高楠順次郎 and Watanabe Kaikyoku 渡邊海旭. 100 vols. Tokyo: Taishō issaikyō kankōkai 大正一切經刊行會, 1924–1935.

Allon, Mark. 1997. *Style and Function: A Study of the Dominant Stylistic Features of the Prose Portions of Pāli Canonical Sutta Texts and Their Mnemonic Function*. Studia Philologica Buddhica, Monograph Series 12. Tokyo: The International Institute for Buddhist Studies.

———. 2021. *The Composition and Transmission of Early Buddhist Texts with Specific Reference to Sutras*. Hamburg Buddhist Studies Series 17. Bochum and Freiburg: Projekt Verlag.

Apple, James B. 2014. "The Phrase *dharmaparyāyo hastagato* in Mahāyāna Buddhist Literature: Rethinking the Cult of the Book in Middle Period Indian Mahāyāna Buddhism." *Journal of the American Oriental Society* 134.1: 25–50.

Bechert, Heinz. 1992. "The Writing Down of the Tripiṭaka in Pāli." *Wiener Zeitschrift für die Kunde Südasiens* 36: 45–53.

Berkwitz, Stephen C. 2009. "Materiality and Merit in Sri Lankan Buddhist Manuscripts." In *Buddhist Manuscript Cultures: Knowledge, Ritual, and Art*, edited by Stephen C. Berkwitz, Juliane Schober, and Claudia Brown, 35–49. London and New York: Routledge.

Boucher, Daniel. 1991. "The *Pratītyasamutpādagāthā* and Its Role in the Medieval Cult of the Relics." *Journal of the International Association of Buddhist Studies* 14.1: 1–27.

———. 2000. "On *Hu* and *Fan* Again: The Transmission of 'Barbarian' Manuscripts to China." *Journal of the International Association of Buddhist Studies* 23.1: 7–28.

———. 2008a. *Bodhisattvas of the Forest and the Formation of the Mahāyāna: A Study and Translation of the* Rāṣṭrapālaparipṛcchā-sūtra. Studies in the Buddhist Traditions. Honolulu: University of Hawai'i Press.

———. 2008b. "Is There an Early Gandhāran Source for the Cult of Avalokiteśvara?" *Journal asiatique* 296.2: 297–330.

Braarvig, Jens, ed. 1993. *Akṣayamatinirdeśasūtra*, vol. 1: *Edition of Extant Manuscripts with an Index*. Oslo: Solum Forlag.

Bronkhorst, Johannes. 2012. "Reflections on the Origins of Mahāyāna." In *Séptimo Centenario de los Estudios Orientales en Salamanca*, edited by A. Agud, A. Cantera, A. Falero, R. El Hour, M. Á. Manzano, R. Muñoz, and E. Yildiz, 489–502. Estudios Filológicos 337. Salamanca: Ediciones Universidad.

Brown, C. Mackenzie. 1986. "Purāṇa as Scripture: From Sound to Image of the Holy Word in the Hindu Tradition." *History of Religions* 26.1: 68–86.

Campany, Robert F. 1991. "Notes on the Devotional Uses and Symbolic Functions of

Sūtra Texts as Depicted in Early Chinese Buddhist Miracle Tales." *Journal of the International Association of Buddhist Studies* 14.1: 28–72.

Cole, Alan. 2005. *Text as Father: Paternal Seductions in Early Mahāyāna Buddhist Literature*. Berkeley and Los Angeles: University of California Press.

———. 2015. *Fetishizing Tradition: Desire and Reinvention in Buddhist and Christian Narratives*. Albany: State University of New York Press.

Collins, Steven. 1998. *Nirvana and Other Buddhist Felicities: Utopias of the Pali Imaginaire*. Cambridge: Cambridge University Press.

———. 2003. "What Is Literature in Pali?" In *Literary Cultures in History: Reconstructions from South Asia*, edited by Sheldon Pollock, 649–688. Berkeley: University of California Press.

Cousins, Lance S. 1983. "Pali Oral Literature." In *Buddhist Studies: Ancient and Modern*, edited by Philip Denwood and Alexander Piatigorsky, 1–11. London and Dublin: Curzon Press.

———. 2012. "The Teachings of the Abhayagiri School." In *How Theravāda Is Theravāda? Exploring Buddhist Identities*, edited by Peter Skilling, Jason A. Carbine, Claudio Cicuzza, and Santi Pakdeekham, 67–127. Chiang Mai: Silkworm Books.

De Simini, Florinda. 2016. *Of Gods and Books: Ritual and Knowledge Transmission in the Manuscript Cultures of Premodern India*. Berlin and Boston: Walter de Gruyter.

Diemberger, Hildegard. 2012a. "Quand le livre devient relique: Les textes tibétains entre culture bouddhique et transformations technologiques." *Terrain* 59: 18–39.

———. 2012b. "Holy Books as Ritual Objects and Vessels of Teaching in the Era of the 'Further Spread of the Doctrine' (*Bstan pa yang dar*)." In *Revisiting Rituals in a Changing Tibetan World*, edited by Katia Buffetrille, 9–41. Leiden: Brill.

Drewes, David. 2007. "Revisiting the Phrase '*sa pṛthivīpradeśaś caityabhūto bhavet*' and the Mahāyāna Cult of the Book." *Indo-Iranian Journal* 50.2: 101–143.

———. 2011. "Dharmabhāṇakas in Early Mahāyāna." *Indo-Iranian Journal* 54.4: 331–372.

———. 2015. "Oral Texts in Indian Mahāyāna." *Indo-Iranian Journal* 58.2: 117–141.

Emmrich, Christoph. 2009. "Emending Perfection: Prescript, Postscript, and Practice in Newar Buddhist Manuscript Culture." In *Buddhist Manuscript Cultures: Knowledge, Ritual, and Art*, edited by Stephen C. Berkwitz, Juliane Schober, and Claudia Brown, 140–156. London and New York: Routledge.

Eubanks, Charlotte. 2011. *Miracles of Book and Body: Buddhist Textual Culture and Medieval Japan*. Berkeley: University of California Press.

Falk, Harry. 2011. "The 'Split' Collection of Kharoṣṭhī Texts." *Annual Report of the International Research Institute for Advanced Buddhology at Soka University* 14: 13–23.

Falk, Harry, and Seishi Karashima. 2012. "A First-Century *Prajñāpāramitā* Manuscript from Gandhāra—*Parivarta* 1 (Texts from the Split Collection 1)." *Annual Report of the International Research Institute for Advanced Buddhology at Soka University* 15: 19–61.

———. 2013. "A First-Century *Prajñāpāramitā* Manuscript from Gandhāra—*Parivarta* 5 (Texts from the Split Collection 2)." *Annual Report of the International Research Institute for Advanced Buddhology at Soka University* 16: 97–169.

Falk, Harry, and Ingo Strauch. 2014. "The Bajaur and Split Collections of Kharoṣṭhī Manuscripts within the Context of Buddhist Gāndhārī Literature." In *From Birch Bark to Digital Data: Recent Advances in Buddhist Manuscript Research. Papers Presented at the Conference Indic Buddhist Manuscripts: The State of the Field, Stanford, June 15–19 2009*, edited by Paul Harrison and Jens-Uwe Hartmann, 51–78. Vienna: Verlag der Österreichischen Akademie der Wissenschaften.

Gethin, Rupert. 2007. "What's in a Repetition? On Counting the Suttas of the Saṃyutta-nikāya." *Journal of the Pali Text Society* 24: 365–387.

Goldman, Robert P., trans. [1984] 1990. *The Rāmāyaṇa of Vālmīki: An Epic of Ancient India*, vol. 1: *Bālakāṇḍa*. Princeton Library of Asian Translations. 1st paperback ed. Princeton: Princeton University Press.

Gombrich, Richard. [1988] 1990. "How the Mahāyāna Began." *Journal of Pali and Buddhist Studies* 1: 29–46. Reprinted in *The Buddhist Forum*, vol. 1: *Seminar Papers 1987–1988*, edited by T. Skorupski, 21–30. London: School of Oriental and African Studies.

Gummer, Natalie D. 2012. "Listening to the *Dharmabhāṇaka*: The Buddhist Preacher in and of the Sūtra of Utmost Golden Radiance." *Journal of the American Academy of Religion* 80.1: 137–160.

Hamlin, Edward. 1988. "Magical *Upāya* in the *Vimalakīrtinirdeśa-sūtra*." *Journal of the International Association of Buddhist Studies* 11.1: 89–121.

Harrison, Paul. 1987. "Who Gets to Ride in the Great Vehicle? Self-Image and Identity Among the Followers of the Early Mahāyāna." *Journal of the International Association of Buddhist Studies* 10.1: 67–89.

———. 1995. "Searching for the Origins of the Mahāyāna: What Are We Looking For?" *The Eastern Buddhist*, n.s., 28.1: 48–69.

———. 2006. "Vajracchedikā Prajñāpāramitā: A New English Translation of the Sanskrit Text Based on Two Manuscripts from Greater Gandhāra." In *Buddhist Manuscripts*, edited by Jens Braarvig et al., 3:133–159. Manuscripts in the Schøyen Collection. Oslo: Hermes Publishing.

Helman-Ważny, Agnieszka. 2014. *The Archaeology of Tibetan Books*. Leiden: Brill.

von Hinüber, Oskar. 2012. "The Saddharmapuṇḍarīkasūtra at Gilgit: Manuscripts, Worshippers, and Artists." *Journal of Oriental Studies* 22: 52–67.

———. 2016. Review of Kim 2013. *Indo-Iranian Journal* 59.4: 371–382.

Karashima, Seishi. 2011. *A Critical Edition of Lokakṣema's Translation of the Aṣṭasāhasrikā Prajñāpāramitā* 道行般若經校注. Bibliotheca Philologica et Philosophica Buddhica 12. Tokyo: The International Research Institute for Advanced Buddhology, Soka University.

———. 2013. "Was the *Aṣṭasāhasrikā Prajñāpāramitā* Compiled in Gandhāra in Gāndhārī?" *Annual Report of the International Research Institute for Advanced Buddhology at Soka University* 16: 171–188.

Kern, Hendrik, and Bunyiu Nanjio, eds. [1908–1912] 1970. *Saddharmapuṇḍarīka*. Bibliotheca Buddhica 10. Reprint, Osnabrück: Biblio Verlag.

Kieschnick, John. 2003. *The Impact of Buddhism on Chinese Material Culture.* Princeton: Princeton University Press.

Kim, Jinah. 2009. "Iconography and Text: The Visual Narrative of the Buddhist Book-Cult in the Manuscript of the Ashṭasāhasrikā Prajñāpāramitā Sūtra." In *Kalādarpaṇa: The Mirror of Indian Art. Essays in Memory of Shri Krishna Deva,* edited by Devangana Desai and Arundhati Banerji, 255–272. New Delhi: Aryan Books International.

———. 2013. *Receptacle of the Sacred: Illustrated Manuscripts and the Buddhist Book Cult in South Asia.* Berkeley: University of California Press.

Kinnard, Jacob N. 1999. *Imaging Wisdom: Seeing and Knowing in the Art of Indian Buddhism.* Curzon Critical Studies in Buddhism. Richmond, Surrey: Curzon.

———. 2002. "On Buddhist 'Bibliolaters': Representing and Worshiping the Book in Medieval Indian Buddhism." *The Eastern Buddhist,* n.s., 34.2: 94–116.

Lamotte, Étienne. [1965] 1998. *Śūraṃgamasamādhisūtra: The Concentration of Heroic Progress.* Translated by Sara Boin-Webb. Surrey, UK: Curzon Press.

Lenz, Timothy. 2003. *A New Version of the Gāndhārī Dharmapada and a Collection of Previous-Birth Stories: British Library Kharoṣṭhī Fragments 16 + 25.* With contributions by Andrew Glass and Bhikshu Dharmamitra. Seattle: University of Washington Press.

Liu, Zhen, and Huaiyu Chen. 2014. "Some Reflections on an Early Mahāyāna Text *Hastikakṣayasūtra.*" *Bulletin of the School of Oriental and African Studies* 77.2: 293–312.

Lopez, Donald S., Jr. 1995. "Authority and Orality in the Mahāyāna." *Numen* 42.1: 21–47.

Lord, Albert B. [1960] 1974. *The Singer of Tales.* Reprint, New York: Atheneum Press.

MacQueen, Graeme. 1982. "Inspired Speech in Early Mahāyāna Buddhism II." *Religion* 12: 49–65.

McGovern, Nathan. 2019. "Protestant Presuppositions and the Study of the Early Buddhist Oral Tradition." *Journal of the International Association of Buddhist Studies* 42: 449–491.

Nance, Richard F. 2008. "Indian Buddhist Preachers Inside and Outside the Sūtras." *Religion Compass* 2.2: 134–159.

———. 2012. *Speaking for Buddhas: Scriptural Commentary in Indian Buddhism.* New York: Columbia University Press.

Nattier, Jan. 2003. *A Few Good Men: The Bodhisattva Path according to* The Inquiry of Ugra (Ugraparipṛcchā). Studies in the Buddhist Traditions. Honolulu: University of Hawai'i Press.

Pollock, Sheldon. 2006. *The Language of the Gods in the World of Men: Sanskrit, Culture, and Power in Premodern India.* Berkeley: University of California Press.

Rhi, Juhyung. 2003. "Early Mahāyāna and Gandhāran Buddhism: An Assessment of the Visual Evidence." *The Eastern Buddhist,* n.s., 35.1–2: 152–202.

———. 2018. "Looking for Mahāyāna Bodhisattvas: A Reflection on Visual Evidence in Early Indian Buddhism." In *Setting Out on the Great Way: Essays on Early Mahāyāna Buddhism,* edited by Paul Harrison, 243–273. Sheffield, UK: Equinox Publishing.

Salomon, Richard. 1995. "On the Origin of the Early Indian Scripts." *Journal of the American Oriental Society* 115.2: 271–279.

———. 2000. *A Gāndhārī Version of the Rhinoceros Sūtra: British Library Kharoṣṭhī Fragment 5B.* With a contribution by Andrew Glass. Seattle: University of Washington Press.

———. 2006. "Recent Discoveries of Early Buddhist Manuscripts and Their Implications for the History of Buddhist Texts and Canons." In *Between the Empires: Society in India 300 BCE to 400 CE,* edited by Patrick Olivelle, 349–382. New York: Oxford University Press.

———. 2017. "On the Evolution of Written *Āgama* Collections in Northern Buddhist Traditions." In *Research on the* Madhyama-āgama, edited by Dhammadinnā, 239–268. Taipei: Dharma Drum Publishing Corporation.

———. 2018. *The Buddhist Literature of Ancient Gandhāra: An Introduction with Selected Translations.* Classics of Indian Buddhism. Somerville, MA: Wisdom Publications.

Sander, Lore. 2000. "Fragments of an Aṣṭasāhasrikā Manuscript from the Kuṣāṇa Period." In *Buddhist Manuscripts,* edited by Jens Braarvig et al., 1:1–51. Manuscripts in the Schøyen Collection 1. Oslo: Hermes Publishing.

———. 2002. "New Fragments of the Aṣṭasāhasrikā Prajñāpāramitā of the Kuṣāṇa Period." In *Buddhist Manuscripts,* edited by Jens Braarvig et al., 2:37–44. Manuscripts in the Schøyen Collection 3. Oslo: Hermes Publishing.

Sasaki, Shizuka. 1997. "A Study on the Origin of Mahāyāna Buddhism." *The Eastern Buddhist,* n.s., 30.1: 79–113.

Schaeffer, Kurtis R. 2009. *The Culture of the Book in Tibet.* New York: Columbia University Press.

Scheible, Kristin. 2016. *Reading the Mahāvaṃsa: The Literary Aims of a Theravāda Buddhist History.* New York: Columbia University Press.

Schlosser, Andrea. 2022. *Three Early Mahāyāna Treatises from Gandhāra: Bajaur Kharoṣṭhī Fragments 4, 6, and 11.* Gandhāran Buddhist Texts 7. Seattle: University of Washington Press.

Schopen, Gregory. 1975. "The Phrase '*sa pṛthivīpradeśaś caityabhūto bhavet*' in the *Vajracchedikā*: Notes on the Cult of the Book in Mahāyāna." *Indo-Iranian Journal* 17.3–4: 147–181. Reprinted in Schopen 2005a, 25–62.

———. 1987. "The Inscription on the Kuṣān Image of Amitābha and the Character of the Early Mahāyāna in India." *Journal of the International Association of Buddhist Studies* 10.2: 99–134. Reprinted in Schopen 2005a, 247–277.

———. 2004. "Mahāyāna." In *Encyclopedia of Buddhism,* edited by Robert E. Buswell Jr., 2:492–499. New York: Macmillan Reference USA.

———. 2005a. *Figments and Fragments of Mahāyāna Buddhism in India: More Collected Papers.* Studies in the Buddhist Traditions. Honolulu: University of Hawaiʻi Press.

———. 2005b. "On Sending the Monks Back to Their Books: Cult and Conservatism in Early Mahāyāna Buddhism." In Schopen 2005a, 108–153.

———. 2009. "On the Absence of Urtexts and Otiose Ācāryas: Buildings, Books, and Lay Buddhist Ritual at Gilgit." In *Écrire et transmettre en Inde classique,* edited by Gérard Colas and Gerdi Gerschheimer, 189–219. Études thématiques 23. Paris: École française d'Extrême-Orient.

———. 2010. "The Book as a Sacred Object in Private Homes in Early or Medieval India." In *Medieval and Early Modern Devotional Objects in Global Perspective: Translations of the Sacred*, edited by Elizabeth Robertson and Jennifer Jahner, 37–60. New York: Palgrave Macmillan.

———. 2012. "Redeeming Bugs, Birds, and Really Bad Sinners in Some Medieval Mahāyāna Sūtras and *Dhāraṇīs*." In *Sins and Sinners: Perspectives from Asian Religions*, edited by Phyllis Granoff and Koichi Shinohara, 276–294. Leiden: Brill.

———. 2018. "On the Legality of Copying Texts: A Buddhist Discussion of Copyright in Early Medieval India." In *Saddharmāmṛtam: Festschrift für Jens-Uwe Hartmann zum 65. Geburtstag*, edited by Oliver von Criegern, Gudrun Melzer, and Johannes Schneider, 399–409. Vienna: Arbeitskreis für Tibetische und Buddhistische Studien Universität Wien.

Shi Huifeng (= Matthew Osborn). 2017. *The Structure and Interpretation of Early Prajñāpāramitā: An Analysis via Chiasmic Theory*. Hong Kong: Centre of Buddhist Studies, University of Hong Kong.

Silk, Jonathan A. 2002. "What, If Anything, Is Mahāyāna Buddhism? Problems of Definitions and Classifications." *Numen* 49.4: 355–405.

———. 2019. "Chinese Sūtras in Tibetan Translation: A Preliminary Survey." *Annual Report of the International Research Institute for Advanced Buddhology at Soka University* 22: 227–246.

Skilling, Peter. 2014. "Birchbark, Bodhisatvas, and Bhāṇakas: Writing Materials in Buddhist North India." *Eurasian Studies* 12: 499–521.

Smith, Jonathan Z. 1987. *To Take Place: Toward Theory in Ritual*. Chicago: The University of Chicago Press.

Toda, Hirofumi, ed. 1981. *Saddharmapuṇḍarīkasūtra. Central Asian Manuscripts: Romanized Text*. Tokushima: Kyoiku Shuppan Center.

Veidlinger, Daniel. 2006. "When a Word Is Worth a Thousand Pictures: Mahāyāna Influence on Theravāda Attitudes towards Writing." *Numen* 53.4: 405–447.

Vorobyova-Desyatovskaya, M. I. 2002. *The Kāśyapaparivarta: Romanized Text and Facsimiles*. In collaboration with Seishi Karashima and Noriyuki Kudo. Bibliotheca Philologica et Philosophica Buddhica 5. Tokyo: The International Research Institute for Advanced Buddhology, Soka University.

Walters, Jonathan S. 1997. "Mahāyāna Theravāda and the Origins of the Mahāvihāra." *Sri Lanka Journal of the Humanities* 23: 100–119.

———. 1999. "Mahāsena at the Mahāvihāra: On the Interpretation and Politics of History in Pre-colonial Sri Lanka." In *Invoking the Past: The Uses of History in South Asia*, edited by Daud Ali, 322–366. New York: Oxford University Press.

———. 2000. "Buddhist History: The Sri Lankan Pāli Vaṃsas and Their Commentary." In *Querying the Medieval: Texts and the History of Practices in South Asia*, edited by Ronald Inden, Jonathan Walters, and Daud Ali, 99–164. New York: Oxford University Press.

Waugh, Patricia. 1984. *Metafiction: The Theory and Practice of Self-Conscious Fiction*. London and New York: Methuen.

Wogihara, Unrai, ed. [1932] 1973. *Abhisamayālaṃkār'ālokā Prajñāpāramitāvyākhyā: The Work of Haribhadra, Together with the Text Commented On.* Reprint, Tokyo: Sankibo Buddhist Book Store.

Wynne, Alexander. 2004. "The Oral Transmission of Early Buddhist Literature." *Journal of the International Association of Buddhist Studies* 27.1: 97–127.

Zimmermann, Michael. 2002. *A Buddha Within: The Tathāgatagarbhasūtra. The Earliest Exposition of the Buddha-Nature Teaching in India.* Bibliotheca Philologica et Philosophica Buddhica 6. Tokyo: The International Research Institute for Advanced Buddhology, Soka University.

Practice in Text: Words and Wordplay in a Mahāyāna Sūtra

Jason McCombs

THE SCHOLASTIC CAREER of Gregory Schopen has been distinguished by, among other things, his willingness to revisit long-ignored data with fresh eyes. We in Buddhist studies are indebted to Schopen not so much because he explored new sources (though, of course, he did this too) but because he looked anew at data the significance of which others failed to recognize. In Mahāyāna studies in particular, Schopen noticed a telling chronological discrepancy, one that led him to conclude that "what we now call the Mahāyāna did not begin to emerge as a separate and independent group until the 4th century [CE]. . . ."[1] On the one hand, sometime before the beginning of the Common Era, in the first century BCE or perhaps even earlier, we have the start of what would become a flood of Mahāyāna textual production. On the other, the presence of Mahāyāna in the material and epigraphic records is all but absent for many centuries thereafter. In the case of a rare Mahāyāna image, that of the Buddha Amitābha from the "Middle Period" of Indian Buddhism (specifically 153 CE), Schopen offers what I think is his clearest statement on the need to avail ourselves of these two bodies of evidence:

> All of this of course accords badly with the accepted and long current view—based almost exclusively on literary sources—that the movement we call "the Mahāyāna" appeared on the scene somehow fully formed and virtually finished at the beginning of the Common Era. Common sense itself might have suspected such a view, but Indian epigraphy makes it very clear that "the Mahāyāna" as a public movement began—to invert an old line of T.S. Eliot's—"not with a bang, but a whimper." It suggests that, although there was—as we know from Chinese translations—a large and early Mahāyāna

1. Schopen 1979, 15.

> literature, there was no early organized, independent, publicly supported movement that it could have belonged to. It suggests, in fact, that if we are to make any progress in our understanding we may have to finally and fully realize that the history of Mahāyāna *literature* and the history of the religious movement that bears the same name are not necessarily the same thing. This, I would think, should raise some interesting questions.[2]

One of those questions, which he also explores in detail elsewhere, is the degree to which Mahāyāna ideas and practices gained a foothold in India (and if so, when), particularly in relation to their Mainstream Buddhist counterparts.[3]

I do not intend to enter into the maelstrom of the degree of success Mahāyāna Buddhism achieved in India, much less into the equally fraught territory of the characteristics of so-called early Mahāyāna. Instead, I would like to return to this question of the value of texts in posing, if not answering, questions about Buddhist practice. The practice I will focus on here is religious giving. Given the vital role of donations in the subsistence of Buddhist monastics and institutions in India, as well as the function of gift giving as a mechanism for earning spiritual merit, the topic is well worth pursuing. And regarding this critical religious practice, I would like to propose that the way gifts were thought to bring about rewards in at least one Indian Mahāyāna text accords quite well with what we see in donative inscriptions from India.

The text I will turn to, a Mahāyāna sūtra about gift giving, is barely known to modern scholars. It would have been called the **Dānapāramitā-sūtra* (Tibetan *Sbyin pa'i pha rol tu phyin pa'i mdo*) or the *Sūtra on the Perfection of Giving*, but there is no extant version of the text in Sanskrit. To my knowledge, the sūtra was never translated into Chinese. Moreover, the text seems never to have been referenced in another Buddhist work. That is to say, the *Dānapāramitā-sūtra* does not appear anywhere outside of the Mdo section of the Tibetan Bka' 'gyur, whether as a whole text, in quotation, or even in reference to its title. For reasons I cannot delve into at present, I date the current form of this text, as it is preserved in the Bka' 'gyur, to the fifth or sixth century CE, which would make it very late by the standard of Mahāyāna sūtras. I have shown that the *Dānapāramitā-sūtra* has similarities in structure and content with the *Dānānuśaṃsānirdeśa-sūtra*, perhaps better known as chapter 34 of the *Divyāvadāna* under an alternate title, the *Dānādhikaraṇa-sūtra*

2. Schopen 1987, 124–125. His most forceful critique of the preferential treatment of sources in Indian Buddhist studies can be found in Schopen 1991.

3. See especially Schopen 1999, Schopen 2000, and Schopen 2005b.

(= *Dānādhikāra-sūtra*), as well as with parts of the *Akṣayamatinirdeśa* and *Bodhisattvapiṭaka* sūtras.[4]

One of the characteristic features of the *Dānapāramitā-sūtra* is its predilection for wordplay, a suite of literary devices that is prevalent throughout Indian literature and, as has become increasingly clear, relatively common in Buddhist texts as well.[5] My question is what, if anything, this text's fondness for wordplay might suggest about giving in Buddhist India. Admittedly, on the surface it would be difficult to imagine getting further afield from the realities of religious practice than the application of literary devices in a little-known Buddhist text. Before I return to this question, I will need to cast light on the kinds of wordplays present in the *Dānapāramitā-sūtra*, but before that, it is necessary to say a few words about the structure and logic of the text.

The *Dānapāramitā-sūtra* is a fairly short text composed of two chapters. The second chapter of the text formulaically proceeds, in alternating prose and verse, through each type of gift that a bodhisattva should give. (The first chapter, despite the title of the sūtra, doesn't deal with gift giving at all.) It begins with modest quotidian objects like food and drink, works its way up to fine gifts like culinary delicacies and precious ornaments, includes human property like one's slaves and family members, and closes with a series of body parts, beginning with the bodhisattva's feet and ending with his bone marrow. What the *Dānapāramitā-sūtra* has done is to provide a tacit—the reader is never told this explicitly—ranking of gifts. As the text goes on, the gifts become more expensive and/or more difficult to give away.

For much of the *Dānapāramitā-sūtra*, the karmic reward, which likewise becomes more elaborate as the text goes on, is the raison d'être of generosity. The text spells out how the bodhisattva-donor benefits himself and especially other beings for each type of gift. Some of the bodhisattva's gifts result in material or other kinds of mundane rewards. According to the text, giving food brings about, among other things, a long (or healthy) life, a good complexion, and strength, while giving clothing, according to the verse section, causes the donor to acquire a fortune. We might classify the rewards for most of the bodhisattva's gifts as "spiritual," though that term should be understood loosely because the difference between mundane and spiritual rewards in our text is not clear-cut. Usually the reward functions as a kind of spiritual

4. For the most recent scholarship on the *Dānānuśaṃsānirdeśa-sūtra*, including an analysis of a fifth or sixth century CE Sanskrit version in the Schøyen Collection, see Skilling 2021, 171–179. On the approximate date of the *Dānapāramitā-sūtra* and its relationship to other texts, see McCombs 2014, 94–103.

5. See, for example, Visigalli 2016 and Chen 2018.

counterpart to the object given. For instance, when a bodhisattva gives a "gift of medicine, in accordance with an oath (*praṇidhāna*) that was empowered by the Tathāgata, he proclaims the oath: 'On account of this gift of medicine, may I make the ease of the immortal nectar that is without old age and death perfect for all beings.'"[6] Through his gift, the bodhisattva transforms regular medicine into an otherworldly elixir for all beings—the ageless and deathless *amṛta* (Tib. *bdud rtsi*), the nectar of the gods.[7] When he gives lamps in the mundane world, on the other hand, the bodhisattva purifies the divine eye of all beings, which, according to Buddhist thought, will allow them to see the deaths and rebirths of other beings. Similarly, when the bodhisattva gives music, he perfects the divine ear for all beings, which grants them the superhuman ability to hear sounds from different types of beings and at great distances.

In the *Dānapāramitā-sūtra*, the formulaic gift-giving passages equate each gift object with its karmic reward through the Tibetan term *tshig bla dags*, which translates the Sanskrit *adhivacana*.[8] To use the just-cited example of medicine again, the bodhisattva should think the following: "That which is called a 'gift of medicine,' because it is an *adhivacana* for perfecting for all beings the ease of the immortal nectar that is without old age and death, it is certain that I am to give gifts of medicine."[9] In the corresponding portion for the gift of clothing, he should think as follows: "That which is called 'giving clothing,' because it is an *adhivacana* for cleaning up one's modesty, decency, and appearance, it is certain that I am to give gifts of clothing."[10] The term

6. References to the Tibetan will be to the edition of the text found in my dissertation by page(s) and line number(s). For cross-reference I will also cite the Sde dge edition of the Bka' 'gyur in parentheses. See McCombs 2014, 222.10–13: *de sman gyi sbyin pa de sbyin pa na / de bzhin gshegs pas byin gyis brlabs pa'i smon lam bzhin du / sman byin pa 'dis na bdag sems can thams cad kyi rga ba dang / 'chi ba med pa'i bdud rtsi'i bde ba yongs su rdzogs par byed par gyur cig ces smon lam 'debs so //* (= Sde dge 182, Mdo sde, vol. *tsa*, 88a4).

7. The reward for giving medicine in the *Akṣayamatinirdeśa* is exactly the same: *mi rga mi 'chi ba'i bdud rtsi'i bde ba yongs su bskang ba'i phyir na ba dang sman 'dod pa thams cad la sman sbyin pa'o //* (Braarvig 1993, 30.34–35). In the *Dānādhikaraṇa*, a similar reward for giving medicine is promised in the extant Sanskrit versions and the Tibetan translation but not the Chinese; see Ware 1929, 45 (no. 17).

8. Ishihama and Fukuda 1989, no. 6333.

9. McCombs 2014, 222.7–10: *sman gyi sbyin pa zhes bya ba de ni sems can thams cad kyi rga ba dang 'chi ba med pa'i bdud rtsi'i bde ba yongs su rdzogs par 'gyur ba'i tshig bla dags yin gyis / bdag gis sman gyi sbyin pa sbyin par bya gor ma chag snyam mo //* (= Sde dge 182, Mdo sde, vol. *tsa*, 88a3).

10. McCombs 2014, 211.5–7: *gos sbyin pa zhes bya ba de ni ngo tsha shes pa dang / khrel yod pa dang / mdog yongs su dag par byed pa'i tshig bla dags yin gyis / bdag gis gos kyi sbyin pa sbyin par*

adhivacana, according to Monier-Williams, means "an appellation, epithet"; Edgerton similarly defines *adhivacana* as "designation, appellation, name, term."[11] Any of these English equivalents will suffice for our text, but a better rendering of *adhivacana* for the *Dānapāramitā-sūtra* might be "synonym for" or "synonymous with": "That which is called a 'gift of medicine' . . . is a synonym for perfecting for all beings the ease of the immortal nectar that is without old age and death . . ."; and "That which is called 'giving clothing' . . . is synonymous with cleaning up one's modesty, decency, and appearance. . . ." That is to say, the gift formula in the *Dānapāramitā-sūtra* runs like so: because gift X is synonymous with bringing reward Y, the bodhisattva should give gift X. The reader will have noticed that the *adhivacana* inhabits a central place in the *Dānapāramitā-sūtra*'s gift formula. It is precisely *because of* the *adhivacana* (Tib. *tshig bla dags yin gyis*) that the bodhisattva can effect a reward. The *adhivacana* allows the bodhisattva to heal all beings with his gift of medicine and improve the appearance and visible decorum of all beings with his gift of clothing (and the number of such examples from the *Dānapāramitā-sūtra* could be multiplied many times over). The term *adhivacana* is the linguistic bridge through which the author of the *Dānapāramitā-sūtra* can claim homologies between specific rewards and particular gifts.

Beyond the use of the term *adhivacana*, the *Dānapāramitā-sūtra* engages in a series of wordplays. At the outset I should mention briefly that the *Dānapāramitā-sūtra* offers no evidence for elaborate *śleṣa* punning, a favorite technique of the Indian poet in which two (or more) registers are written into the same text simultaneously.[12] Even small Buddhist *śleṣa*s are rare,[13] and I suspect that writing *śleṣa*s was beyond the capabilities of most, if not all, of the composers and redactors of Mahāyāna sūtras.[14] Certainly the

---

bya gor ma chag snyam mo // (= Sde dge 182, Mdo sde, vol. *tsa*, 85a3–4). Cf. Braarvig 1993, 30.14–16: *ngo tsha shes pa dang / khrel yod pa dang / gser gyi kha dog lta bu'i mdog yongs su sbyang ba'i phyir gos 'dod pa rnams la gos sbyin pa'o* //. Compare also a verse from the *Vimalakīrtinirdeśa-sūtra*: *bhūṣaṇā lakṣaṇāny eṣām aśītiś cānuvyañjanāḥ / hrīrapatrāpyavastrās te kalyāṇādhyāśayāḥ śubhāḥ* // (Study Group on Buddhist Sanskrit Literature 2006, 80, verse 8). Here Vimalakīrti explains that bodhisattvas' "clothing is modesty and decency" (*hrīrapatrāpyavastrās*).

11. See Monier-Williams [1899] 2011 and Edgerton [1953] 2004, s.v.

12. See Bronner 2010. A convincing case has recently been made, contra Bronner, that *śleṣa* is as old as the *Ṛg Veda*; see Jamison 2015.

13. On a *śleṣa* in the *Dhammapada*, see Norman 1979; Hara 1992. For a thirteenth-century Pāli *śleṣa* that "shows great Sanskritization," see Collins 2003, 676–677.

14. Locating Mahāyāna sūtras sociolinguistically relative to other forms of Indian literature remains a desideratum. As part of a rosy description of the aesthetic qualities of Mahāyāna sūtras, especially their use of formulas and conventions, Luis Gómez refers to the *Shorter* and

Dānapāramitā-sūtra is a stylistically simple text, displaying a limited vocabulary and replete with formulaic repetition. There is thus no reason to infer that the *śleṣa*s common in Sanskrit *kāvya* ever existed in the Indic text of the *Dānapāramitā-sūtra*, even if we admit that much can be lost upon translation from Sanskrit to Tibetan.

There is at least one oral or sound pun in the *Dānapāramitā-sūtra*.[15] An oral pun occurs when one or more words replace or highlight similar-sounding words for rhetorical or comedic purposes, as in "A Freudian slip is where you think one thing but say a *m*other." In this regard, there is at least one South Asian textual passage, *Manusmṛti* 4.229–232, that has set a precedent for the *Dānapāramitā-sūtra* and other works that deal with gift giving:

> One who gives water obtains satiety; one who gives food, inexhaustible happiness; one who gives sesame seeds, the kind of offspring one desires; one who gives a lamp, the finest eyesight. One who gives land, obtains land; one who gives a house, superb dwellings; one who gives silver (*rūpya*), peerless beauty (*rūpa*); one who gives clothes, residence in the same world as the moon; one who gives a horse (*aśva*), residence in the same world as the Aśvins; one who gives an ox, bounteous prosperity; one who gives a cow, the summit of the sun; one who gives a vehicle or bed, a wife; one who gives secu-

Longer Sukhāvatīvyūha sūtras as "well-wrought, learned works of a well-established literary genre" ([1996] 2002, 51). Based on the extant Sanskrit and Gómez's own translation of these texts, I am not sure how he arrived at this conclusion. The issue merits further study, but for the time being I am much more inclined to agree with the candor of Paul Harrison, who in contrast to Gómez describes the *Longer Sukhāvatīvyūha Sūtra* as "interminably tedious to modern sensibilities, with its endless descriptions of the physical features of Sukhāvatī, its flora, its climatic conditions, and the lifestyle of its inhabitants" (2003, 121). As a point of reference for Mahāyāna sūtras, I think we should not forget the level of aesthetic sophistication that Indian poets were able to achieve—through *śleṣa*, for instance, the simultaneous narration of the *Mahābhārata* and *Rāmāyaṇa*.

15. I have borrowed from the tradition of Sanskrit poetics by differentiating *sound* and *sense* wordplays. India witnessed a long and contentious debate on whether words were defined phonetically or by their meaning, which spilled over into competing understandings and classifications of *śleṣa* or multitextuality. See Bronner 2010, 203–214. Note that sound puns do not translate well between languages, so it would not be surprising if further research reveals additional oral wordplays lurking behind the Tibetan of the *Dānapāramitā-sūtra*. For the erudite discovery of an oral pun traceable to a probable underlying Middle Indic text, see Nattier 2003, 303n641. On a popular Buddhist oral pun between *kaṣāya*, "impurity," and *kāṣāya*, "ochre robe," see Silk 1994, 76–77.

rity, lordship; one who gives grain, eternal happiness; and one who gives the Veda (*brahman*), equality with Brahman.[16]

As we observe in the *Dānapāramitā-sūtra*, the *Manusmṛti* makes logical connections between gifts and rewards—giving away a house, for instance, brings one "superb dwellings," and giving lamps brings good vision.[17] In the *Manusmṛti* and, as we will see, the *Dānapāramitā-sūtra*, we have repetition in the gift and the reward; in the former text, "land" (Skt. *bhūmi*) is repeated in a very terse statement (*Manusmṛti* 4.230, *pāda* a). Both texts play on the multiple meanings of a word; *Manusmṛti* uses *brahman* twice, the first time to refer to the sacred Vedic texts, the second time to the ultimate reality of the cosmos. And here we also see repetitions of similar sounds in the gift and reward—one becomes *rūpa* by giving *rūpya*, and one resides with the Aśvins, the twin chariot-riding gods of the Veda, by giving *aśva*.[18]

Similar wordplays occur in a verse of the *Dānapāramitā-sūtra*:

> With a gift of flavors,
> may all beings perfect
> the practice leading to awakening (*bodhicaryā*) of a complete buddha
> by means of the essence of the flavor of omniscience.[19]

There are a number of sound elements here. There is a repeat of *sarva* (Tib. *kun*) in the Sanskrit compounds *sarvasattva*, "all beings" (Tib. *sems can kun*), and *sarvajña*, "omniscience" (Tib. *kun mkhyen*). We also have a repeat of the Tibetan *ro*, which translates the familiar Sanskrit word *rasa*: the first *rasa* makes up the gift, while the second lies in the "flavor of omniscience" in the gift's reward.[20] The second *ro* actually occurs in the compound *ro yi snying po*,

16. Translation taken from Olivelle 2005, 136 (Skt. on 550–551).

17. In the *Dānapāramitā-sūtra*, giving lamps is also said to bring (good) vision to the donor. See McCombs 2014, 177.

18. These two puns are almost pure repeats because *rūpya* is derived from *rūpa* and *aśvin* from *aśva*. That is, they are very close to the *brahman* example, whereby the text plays on multiple meanings of the same word.

19. McCombs 2014, 217.6–8: *ro yi sbyin pas sems can kun // kun mkhyen ro yi snying po yis // rdzogs sangs rgyas pa'i byang chub kyi // spyod pa yongs su rdzogs gyur cig /* (= Sde dge 182, Mdo sde, vol. *tsa*, 86b6).

20. The prose portion of this section also repeats *rasa*, which I discuss below.

which could only correspond to the Sanskrit *rasasāra*.[21] The syllables of *ra-sa*, when flipped around, make *sā-ra* (allowing for the slight variation in vowel length), so the two Sanskrit words combine to form a kind of mirror-image compound. The author of the *Dānapāramitā-sūtra* therefore created a sound pun by deliberate metathesis.[22] In addition, there is a sense element to the wordplay. Although I translate *rasa* as "flavor" and *sāra* as "essence" because I believe this best captures the meaning of the verse, the two words can be used synonymously. As the author of the *Dānapāramitā-sūtra* no doubt knew, both can mean "essence," "marrow," "best part," and so forth.

What is most abundant in the Tibetan text of the *Dānapāramitā-sūtra* are the multivalent wordplays. One type is the double entendre, in which a single word or set of words has two meanings, one obvious and the other suggested.[23] For example, according to the *Dānapāramitā-sūtra* a bodhisattva should make the following oath when he gives a vehicle: "On account of this gift of a vehicle, may I bring together the ease of all beings and all the foundations of supernatural power."[24] "Ease" here could also be rendered "comfort" or even

21. Skt. *sāra* is the equivalent of Tib. *snying po*. See Ishihama and Fukuda 1989, no. 5160.

22. There may be another oral pun—or at least the residue of one—in the *Dānapāramitā-sūtra*, the possibility of which was pointed out to me by Jonathan Silk. In one passage, giving lamps (Skt. *dīpa*) is said to purify the divine eye (Skt. *divyacakṣus*) of all beings (McCombs 2014, 147). In Middle Indic, Sanskrit *dīpa* would commonly have been written as *dīva* or *diva*. See, e.g., Pischel [1900] 1965, §§ 200 and 243; see also Mehendale [1948] 1997, § 392, and Edgerton [1953] 2004, *Grammar*, § 2.30. And the word *divya-* in the compound could have been written as *divva-* or *diva-*. See the form *divvo-* in Pischel [1900] 1965, § 99; see also Mehendale [1948] 1997, § 409.4. The problem is that I am not certain that any part of the *Dānapāramitā-sūtra* was written in Middle Indic. I believe the "original" *Dānapāramitā-sūtra* was composed much later than most Mahāyāna sūtras, and because of its relatively late date, it may have been written completely (or almost completely) in Sanskrit. If this scenario is true, then the *Dānapāramitā-sūtra* contains an association between a gift and a reward that was first thought of or written down in Middle Indic. But the Middle Indic pun that was central to this association may have been lost in a Sanskritized text, since I am not sure anyone would have recognized an oral wordplay between Sanskrit *dīpa* and *divya*.

23. Double entendres are seen in Buddhist texts with some frequency and were indeed sometimes double-translated into Chinese to preserve both meanings. For good examples of single words carrying multiple meanings in Buddhist texts, see Collins 1993, 332–334; Boucher 1998, 489–493; Nattier 2003, 271n412; Gummer 2014, 1103; Karashima 2015, 174–180. Note that it is possible to consider the double entendre a kind of *śleṣa*, which I will discuss below, but it is rare in Sanskrit literature that "a *śleṣa* is based on exploiting the semantic richness of a single word" (Bronner 2010, 209).

24. McCombs 2014, 210.9–11: . . . *bzhon pa'i sbyin pa 'dis na bdag sems can thams cad kyi bde ba dang / rdzu 'phrul gyi gzhi thams cad sdud par gyur cig ces smon lam 'debs so //* (= Sde dge 182, Mdo sde, vol. *tsa*, 85a1). Cf. Braarvig 1993, 30.13–14: *bde ba dang 'byor pa'i dngos po thams cad bsdu ba'i phyir bzhon pa 'dod pa rnams la bzhon pa sbyin pa'o //*.

"happiness" and translates *bde ba*, the Tibetan equivalent of Sanskrit *sukha*. The second meaning behind *sukha* is not adequately captured by my translation, but it almost certainly would not have been missed by an Indian audience. *Sukha* is derived from the prefix *su*, "good," and the substantive *kha*, "axle-hole," and hence its Vedic meaning was literally "having good axle-holes" (and that of *duḥkha* was "having poor axle-holes"). A vehicle that was *sukha* moved smoothly and reliably. Obviously, the *Dānapāramitā-sūtra*'s association between the gift of a vehicle and *sukha* is not a coincidence, and the same association can be found later in the text[25] as well as in the *Dānapaṭala* of the *Bodhisattvabhūmi*.[26]

As we just saw in the verse about giving *rasa*, the *Dānapāramitā-sūtra* also makes a habit of repeating words in the reward that were already used in the gift. In some instances, the word in question is used in a different context but more or less carries the exact same meaning in the reward as it does in the gift. This is the case for the *Dānapāramitā-sūtra*'s gift of requisites, *requisites* being one English equivalent for the similarly vague Tibetan *yo byad* (Skt. *pariṣkāra*). This term commonly occurs at the end of a *dvandva* compound containing a list of required possessions of a monk or nun[27] but also denotes—as it does, I believe, in the *Dānapāramitā-sūtra*—mundane household items like furniture. Here is the entirety of the prose portion for the gift of requisites:

> Then, how does he [the bodhisattva] make strong efforts with regard to gifts of requisites? Son from a good family, in this case that bodhisattva thinks this: "Since what is called 'giving requisites' is a synonym for perfecting the requisites of awakening, it is certain that I am to give gifts of requisites." When he gives that gift of requisites, in accordance with an oath worthy of the Tathāgata, he proclaims the oath: "On account of this gift of requisites, may I make the requisites of awakening perfect for all beings."[28]

25. McCombs 2014, 245.2–3: *bzhon pa byin pas ni bde ba dang ldan par 'gyur /* (= Sde dge 182, Mdo sde, vol. *tsa*, 93b5). This short sentence occurs at the end of the second chapter of the *Dānapāramitā-sūtra*, where there is a long sequence of mostly terse statements about giving.

26. See the translation of the *Dānapaṭala* at McCombs 2014, 285.

27. Skt. *cīvara-piṇḍapāta-śayanāsana-glānapratyayabhaiṣajya-pariṣkāra*.

28. McCombs 2014, 221.6–222.2: *de la yo byad kyi sbyin pa la ji ltar mngon par brtson par byed ce na / rigs kyi bu 'di la byang chub sems dpa' de 'di snyam du sems te / yo byad sbyin pa zhes bya ba de ni byang chub kyi yo byad yongs su rdzogs par 'gyur ba'i tshig bla dags yin gyis / bdag gis yo byad kyi sbyin pa sbyin par bya gor ma chag snyam mo // de yo byad kyi sbyin pa de sbyin pa na / de bzhin gshegs pa la 'os pa'i smon lam bzhin du yo byad byin pa 'dis na bdag sems can thams cad*

Giving others what they need materially has spiritual currency as well: the bodhisattva is able to help all beings get what they need in order to become awakened.

More commonly, the *Dānapāramitā-sūtra* repeats a word in the reward with a different shade of meaning than it possesses in the gift. The *Dānapāramitā-sūtra* makes use of multivalent wordplay known in linguistics as polysemy. Quite simply, polysemy is the ability of a word to have multiple, related meanings (as opposed to homonymy or sense punning, which occurs when two words have the same pronunciation and spelling but unrelated meanings). The author and/or redactor(s) of the *Dānapāramitā-sūtra* evidently had a penchant for polysemy. The first set of polysemes I will adduce involves a word being used in literal and figurative senses. For example, when a bodhisattva gives ornaments—golden ornaments, pearls, shells, crystal, and so on—the *Dānapāramitā-sūtra* has him make the following oath: "On account of this gift of ornaments, may I see the bodies of all beings ornamented with the marks and secondary characteristics."[29] Here we have the word *ornament* repeated. By giving precious objects that ornament one's body, the bodhisattva will effect all beings' becoming ornamented with the thirty-two major marks and eighty secondary characteristics of a *mahāpuruṣa*. The figurative ornaments are the marks of the superhuman body that are concomitant with awakening, the goal undergirding the generosity of the magnanimous donor of the *Dānapāramitā-sūtra*. When the bodhisattva is rewarded for his gift of literal ornaments, his generosity becomes embodied in all beings.[30]

The *Dānapāramitā-sūtra* also employs wordplay in descriptions of gifts of the bodhisattva's body. As mentioned, the *Dānapāramitā-sūtra* arranges the gifts in one section hierarchically. Gifts of the body come last in this sequence, as they were assumed to be extremely difficult—and painful—to part with.

---

kyi byang chub kyi yo byad yongs su rdzogs par byed par gyur cig ces smon lam 'debs so // (= Sde dge 182, Mdo sde, vol. *tsa*, 87b6–88a1). Cf. Braarvig 1993, 30.32–34: *byang chub kyi yo byad thams cad yongs su bskang ba'i phyir yo byad 'dod pa rnams la yo byad sbyin pa'o //*.

29. McCombs 2014, 212.10–12: *rgyan gyi sbyin pa 'dis na bdag gis sems can thams cad kyi lus mtshan dang dpe byad bzang po dag gis brgyan pa mthong bar gyur cig ces smon lam 'debs so //* (= Sde dge 182, Mdo sde, vol. *tsa*, 85b1).

30. The reward of the superhuman body is felt most strongly with the *Dānapāramitā-sūtra*'s description of eight gifts of the body (Skt. *dehadāna*). See McCombs 2014, 166–175. Several scholars have recently drawn attention to the relationship between the body and moral behavior in Buddhist texts, specifically how moral virtues become embodied in a person's (or Buddha's) physical appearance. See especially Ohnuma 2007, 224–231; Mrozik 2007; Boucher 2008, 3–19.

One such gift is that of the bodhisattva's hands. Here is the relevant prose section of the text:

> Then, how does he [the bodhisattva] make strong efforts with regard to giving the palms of his hands? Son from a good family, in this case that bodhisattva thinks this: "Since what is called 'giving the palms of one's hands' is a synonym for giving the hand of the Dharma to all beings by bodhisattvas, it is certain that I am to give a gift of the palms of my hands." When he gives that gift of the palms of his hands, in accordance with an oath that was understood by the Tathāgata, he proclaims the oath: "On account of this gift of the palms of my hands, may I cause the hand of the Dharma to be given to beings who are inferior, blind, poor, without a master [to look after them], suffering, impoverished, homeless, without refuge, and defenseless, to beings who are born in hell, as animals, or in Yama's world,[31] to those fallen into the unfavorable destinies and unfavorable states, and to those born at the inopportune times."[32]

"Palms of the hands" is almost certainly an example of synecdoche, referring to the entire hand. It translates Tibetan *lag mthil*, which probably corresponds to Sanskrit *hastatala* or *karatala*.[33] Evidently, by removing the palms of his hands—or his entire hands, assuming synecdoche is at work—and giving them away, the bodhisattva causes the hand of the Dharma (Tib. *chos kyi lag pa*; probably Skt. *dharmahasta* or *dharmakara*) to be given to those who need

31. Being reborn in hell, as an animal, or in Yama's Realm (Skt. *yamaloka*) is a standard triad in Mahāyāna texts for the three worst possible fates. The three lower destinies in Buddhist cosmology are those of hell-beings, hungry ghosts, and animals—Yama was regarded as the king of the hungry ghosts (Skt. *preta*), so Yama's world is equivalent to the realm of hungry ghosts.

32. Pāli and Sanskrit Buddhist texts enumerate different lists of eight inopportune times when one could be reborn. See Edgerton [1953] 2004, s.v. *akṣaṇa*. The Tibetan text can be found at McCombs 2014, 236.5–237.4: *de la lag mthil sbyin pa la ji ltar mngon par brtson par byed ce na / rigs kyi bu 'di la byang chub sems dpa' de 'di snyam du sems te / lag mthil sbyin pa zhes bya ba de ni byang chub sems dpa' rnams kyis sems can thams cad la chos kyi lag pa sbyin pa'i tshig bla dags yin gyis / bdag gis lag mthil sbyin pa sbyin par bya gor ma chag snyam mo // de lag mthil gyi sbyin pa de sbyin pa na / de bzhin gshegs pas rnam par mkhyen pa'i smon lam bzhin du lag mthil sbyin pa 'dis na / bdag sems can dman pa dang / long ba dang / bkren pa dang / mgon med pa dang / sdug bsngal ba dang / dbul po dang / gnas med pa dang / skyabs med pa dang / dpung gnyen med pa rnams dang / sems can dmyal ba dang / dud 'gro'i skye gnas dang / gshin rje'i 'jig rten dang / ngan song ngan 'gro log par ltung ba dang / mi khom par skyes pa rnams la chos kyi lag pa sbyin par byed par gyur cig ces smon lam 'debs so //* (= Sde dge 182, Mdo sde, vol. *tsa*, 91b4–7).

33. See Ishihama and Fukuda 1989, nos. 3987 and 6878, respectively.

it most.[34] By the machinations of karma, the gift of the hands brings Dharmic assistance to the downtrodden—the blind, the poor, the homeless, and the like in the human realm, as well as those suffering in the three lowest Buddhist *gatis*. The *Dānapāramitā-sūtra* does not spell out exactly the manner by which this would occur, but somehow the hand of the Dharma appears to be able to lift up such creatures from their miserable fates. The bodhisattva, then, gives a helping hand: his literal hand is transformed through the gift into the figurative hand of the Buddhist Dharma.

Aside from words with literal and figurative meanings, the *Dānapāramitā-sūtra* plays with the specialized meanings of polysemes in other ways. Among the *Dānapāramitā-sūtra*'s gifts of the body, feet are discussed first since they are the lowest point on the body. The gift of the feet begins thus:

> Then, how does he [the bodhisattva] make strong efforts with regard to giving his feet? Son from a good family, in this case that bodhisattva thinks this: "Since what is called 'giving one's feet' is a synonym for going to the terrace of awakening (*bodhimaṇḍa*) that is the base of the Dharma by bodhisattvas, it is certain that I am to give a gift of my feet."[35]

The polysemic wordplay lies in the Sanskrit word *pāda* (Tib. *rkang pa*), which means "bottom" or "base" in addition to "foot," the bottom or base of the body. According to the *Dānapāramitā-sūtra*, the bodhisattva's giving away his own *pāda* is equivalent to allowing other bodhisattvas the opportunity to go to the *dharmapāda* (Tib. *chos kyi rkang pa*), the base of the Doctrine. The *Dānapāramitā-sūtra* implies that because of the gift of the foot, bodhisattvas will be able to repeat the actions of the Buddha Śākyamuni, who of course defeated Māra and discovered the Dharma at the *bodhimaṇḍa*, and become awakened themselves. I suspect that there is also a double entendre intended for *dharmapāda*, with it meaning the actual spot—at the base of a

34. The *Akṣayamatinirdeśa* speaks of the "hand of the True Dharma [*saddharma*]" as the result of giving away the palms of one's hands: *sems can thams cad la dam pa'i chos kyi lag pa sbyin pa'i phyir byang chub sems dpa' rnams kyi lag mthil sbyin pa'o //* (Braarvig 1993, 31.19–21). Cf. Bendall [1897–1902] 1992, 24.4–6: *bodhisatvo hastapādān parityajan yācanakebhyaḥ śraddhāhasta-prayuktenānugrahacāritreṇa bodhisatvasiṃhavikrama-tyāgapratatapāṇinā. . . .*

35. McCombs 2014, 234.2–6: *de la rkang pa sbyin pa la ji ltar mngon par brtson par byed ce na / rigs kyi bu 'di la byang chub sems dpa' de 'di snyam du sems te / rkang pa sbyin pa zhes bya ba de ni byang chub sems dpa' rnams kyi chos kyi rkang pa byang chub kyi snying por 'gro ba'i tshig bla dags yin gyis / bdag gis rkang pa sbyin pa sbyin par bya gor ma chag snyam mo //* (= Sde dge 182, Mdo sde, vol. *tsa*, 91a4–5).

tree—where bodhisattvas will discover the Dharma in the future, as well as the figurative base or foundation of that Doctrine.

Yet another polysemic wordplay comes from an additional instance of the gift of a vehicle, the second of three occasions when the *Dānapāramitā-sūtra* mentions this type of gift. The *Dānapāramitā-sūtra* describes this gift as follows:

> That which is called the "gift that totally surrenders a vehicle, such as that of horses, elephants, and wagons" . . . is a synonym for assembling the Great Vehicle (*mahāyāna*), the best vehicle, the vehicle equal to the unequalled, and the unsurpassed, chief, ultimate, most excellent vehicle of an Awakened One. . . .[36]

And when the bodhisattva gives this gift, he should proclaim the following:

> On account of this gift that totally surrenders a vehicle, such as that of horses, elephants, and wagons, may I cause all beings to be brought into the Great Vehicle, the best vehicle, the vehicle equal to the unequalled, and the unsurpassed, chief, ultimate, most excellent vehicle of an Awakened One.[37]

The term for "assembling" and "brought into" is the same—Tibetan *sdud pa*, Sanskrit *saṃgraha* or something very close to it. The wordplay thus lies in the *Dānapāramitā-sūtra*'s repeat of *saṃgraha* and its application of the word's two different but closely related meanings. The first use of *saṃgraha* is the putting together of a vehicle, piece by piece. By giving vehicles in this life the bodhisattva can put together the best vehicle—the *mahāyāna*, the *buddhayāna*—that leads beings on the highest religious path. This usage of *saṃgraha* is juxtaposed with and intimately connected to its second meaning as a Buddhist technical term for bringing people into the religious life. Giving a vehicle hence attracts people to Mahāyāna, the great spiritual vehicle that ferries its riders to salvation.

36. McCombs 2014, 226.6–9: *rta dang / glang po che dang / shing rta'i bzhon pa yongs su gtong ba'i sbyin pa zhes bya ba de ni byang chub sems dpa' rnams kyi theg pa chen po dang / theg pa mchog dang / theg pa mi mnyam pa dang mnyam pa dang / sangs rgyas kyi theg pa bla na med pa / gtso bo dam pa rab mchog sdud pa'i tshig bla dags yin* . . . (= Sde dge 182, Mdo sde, vol. *tsa*, 89a5–6).

37. McCombs 2014, 227.4–8: . . . *rta dang / glang po che dang / shing rta'i bzhon pa yongs su gtong ba'i sbyin pa 'dis na bdag gis sems can thams cad theg pa chen po dang / theg pa mchog dang / theg pa mi mnyam pa dang mnyam pa dang / sangs rgyas kyi theg pa bla na med pa / gtso bo dam pa / rab mchog gis sdud par byed par gyur cig* . . . (= Sde dge 182, Mdo sde, vol. *tsa*, 89a7–89b1).

My last example of wordplay in the *Dānapāramitā-sūtra* is difficult to categorize.[38] Like the passages about giving one's hands, this wordplay also works in both English and the original Sanskrit. The wordplay comes from the bodhisattva's gift of fine foods, which I translate as "delicacies":

> Then, how does he [the bodhisattva] make strong efforts with regard to gifts of delicacies? Son from a good family, in this case that bodhisattva thinks this: "Since what is called 'giving delicacies' is a synonym for the mark of a great man (*mahāpuruṣa*) that is [called] the height of taste, it is certain that I am to give gifts of delicacies, [such as those that have] the flavor of grapes, the flavor of sugarcane, the flavor of honey, the flavor of butter, the flavor of oil, or the flavor of salt." When he gives that gift of delicacies, in accordance with an oath that was commended by the Buddha, he proclaims the oath: "On account of this gift of flavors, may I totally perfect the mark of a great man that is [called] the height of taste for all beings."[39]

"Delicacies" is my translation for the Tibetan *ro bro ba*; "flavor" is my translation for *ro*. As I mentioned above, *ro* corresponds to the Sanskrit *rasa*,[40] while *ro bro ba* is likely the equivalent of the reduplicated *rasarasa* or something very close to it. If *rasa* here means "tasty" or "flavorful" or "fine food," then consequently *rasarasa* must be "very tasty" or "extremely flavorful" or "exquisite food"—hence "delicacy." Now just as in English, the Sanskrit word for "taste," *rasa*, can be applied either to the flavor of food and drink or to the aesthetic sensibilities—including for the erotic—of a human being. This passage plays with the double meaning of *rasa*: by giving something that tastes very good, one acquires very good taste.[41] The bodhisattva, in effect, gives all

38. Several other (certain or suspected) wordplays in the *Dānapāramitā-sūtra* and related texts are not discussed here. The interested reader should consult the notes to the full translation of the *Dānapāramitā-sūtra* at McCombs 2014, 120–183.

39. McCombs 2014, 216.8–217.6: *de la ro bro ba'i sbyin pa la ji ltar mngon par brtson par byed ce na / rigs kyi bu 'di la byang chub sems dpa' de 'di snyam du sems te / ro bro ba sbyin pa zhes bya ba de ni ro bro ba'i mchog tu 'gyur ba'i skyes bu chen po'i mtshan du 'gyur ba'i tshig bla dags yin gyis / bdag gis ro bro ba'i sbyin pa rgun gyi ro 'am / bu ram shing gi ro 'am / sbrang rtsi'i ro 'am / mar gyi ro 'am / 'bru mar gyi ro 'am / lan tshva'i ro sbyin par bya gor ma chag snyam mo // de ro bro ba'i sbyin pa de sbyin pa na / sangs rgyas kyis bsngags pa'i smon lam bzhin du / ro'i sbyin pa 'dis na / bdag gis sems can thams cad la ro bro ba'i mchog tu 'gyur ba'i skyes bu chen po'i mtshan yongs su rdzogs par byed par gyur cig ces smon lam 'debs so //* (= Sde dge 182, Mdo sde, vol. *tsa*, 86b3–5).

40. Ishihama and Fukuda 1989, no. 1862.

41. The *Akṣayamatinirdeśa* also connects this gift to *rasa*: *skyes bu chen po'i mtshan ro bro ba'i*

beings the finest sense of taste by which to judge all things. All beings gain *ro bro ba'i mchog*—they have acquired (in Sanskrit) *rasarasāgra* or *rasarasāgratā* or become *rasarasāgrin*.[42] In this case we have another instance in the *Dānapāramitā-sūtra* of a bodhisattva's leading beings to buddhahood: being endowed with the "height of taste" is one of the thirty-two physical marks of the *mahāpuruṣa* or superhuman that one gains en route to awakening. The play on words in this passage, which includes both sense and sound elements,[43] resists neat categorization. It is a polyseme because of the multiple meanings of *rasa* that are called into use, but it also involves the mere repetition of *rasa* with *rasarasa*, *rasarasāgra*, and so on.

Such wordplays, I hope by now is clear, are peppered throughout the *Dānapāramitā-sūtra*. For the author they seem to have been integral in creating for the bodhisattva donor a kind of idealized guidebook to generosity, which in the world of the *Dānapāramitā-sūtra* makes up a vital part of the bodhisattva's quest to bring awakening to all beings, the *summum bonum* of Mahāyāna soteriologies. The wordplays help describe what the bodhisattva should give, what he should think and say when he gives, and, critically, the logic underpinning the karmic reward. But I want to suggest that they do more than that. In so doing I would like to return to this question of the relationship between text and practice or, put another way, the relationship between the imagined universe within a Buddhist text and the lived reality outside of that text.

To borrow terms from semiotics, words are signifiers that relay concepts, the signified. But in the *Dānapāramitā-sūtra* the opposite appears to be occurring simultaneously. The language employed by the text's author seems to determine reality instead of—or in addition to—the other way around. Thus the logic of the gift transaction in the *Dānapāramitā-sūtra* is contingent not just on *what* words are used but also *how* they are used: their use as puns, double entendres, and so on make a gift's reward possible. To return to the last example of giving delicacies, when the bodhisattva gives his gift he should proclaim, "On account of this gift of flavors (*rasa*), may I totally perfect the

---

mchog yongs su rdzogs par bya ba'i phyir bro thams cad 'dod pa rnams la bro thams cad sbyin pa'o // (Braarvig 1993, 30.24–26).

42. According to Ishihama and Fukuda 1989, no. 245, *rasarasāgratā* is the equivalent of *ro bro ba'i mchog dang ldan pa*. See also Edgerton [1953] 2004, s.v. *rasāgra*.

43. I would stop short of identifying an oral or sound pun here because *rasa* is just repeated, by itself or in clearly related words. This differentiates it, for example, from the *rūpya/rūpa* pun of the *Manusmṛti* passage cited above, since *rūpya* and *rūpa* are distinct words with separate meanings, even if they are etymologically related.

mark of a great man that is [called] the height of taste (again, *rasa*) for all beings."[44] In this example, it is only because of the polysemy of the word *rasa* that the homology between gift and reward can work; without it, the logic of the exchange falls apart, and the bodhisattva cannot therefore endow all beings with one of the marks of a superhuman being.

The inverted relationship I am suggesting between the signifier and signified in the *Dānapāramitā-sūtra* is difficult to prove. This Mahāyāna text leaves no record of commentary, and of course we are not privy to the thought processes—where the signifier and signified are given meaning—of its author or putative readers. I would therefore like to leave this reading open as a possibility and draw from a culture of an entirely different time and place to reinforce how wordplay in the *Dānapāramitā-sūtra* might have functioned. In modern Japan, it is common for petitioners to request favors from the pantheon of Japanese deities. Not infrequently, these requests come in the form of or are expressed with puns. Prayers for academic success, for instance, are often written on pentagonal tablets because "the word for pentagon (*gokaku*) sounds almost the same as that for scholastic success (*gōkaku*)."[45] Similarly, at a Zen monastic center in Saijōji, Japan, those looking to increase their wealth can purchase a "tree that becomes money" (Japanese *kane no naru ki*), which is shaped like a small pine tree with brass bells attached: "There are multiple puns implied and intended here: the word '*kane*' is a homonym that can mean either bell or money depending on the ideogram with which it is written; the word '*naru*' (to become) can also mean, with a different ideogram, to cry or sing. Hence the tree that becomes money can also be the tree that rings the bell."[46] These two Japanese examples involve requests to gods, not gifts, and they have a visual element that the gift formulas in the *Dānapāramitā-sūtra*, as far as I know, do not have. I believe that the logic in each case, however, is the same. The linguistic homologies allow for the homologies between the input, the gift in the *Dānapāramitā-sūtra* or the request for benefits by the Japanese petitioners, and the output, the karmic reward or the divine granting of benefits.

Regarding the relationship between the signifier and signified, it is also important to note that in the *Dānapāramitā-sūtra* gifts are couched in the bodhisattva's *praṇidhāna*s, his "oaths" or "vows," which the text claims are sanctioned in various ways (e.g., the oath for the gift of delicacies is said to be "commended by the Buddha"). In his oaths the bodhisattva of the

44. See note 39 above for the full passage.

45. Reader and Tanabe 1998, 197.

46. Reader and Tanabe 1998, 119. See also 158–161, 217, 237, 247, 249, and 251.

Dānapāramitā-sūtra declares his intention to bring about the rewards of his various gifts. Such oaths are common in Indian Buddhist literature, including Mahāyāna sūtras, in which they essentially operate as written analogs to oral, performative "speech acts."[47] It is not sufficient for the bodhisattva to want particular rewards to ensue from his gifts. He must formulaically express his resolve that his gifts bring about specific karmic effects. In this way, the bodhisattva's oaths will his intentions into existence. His words, instead of merely describing reality, also seem to allow reality to take shape.

This illocutionary structure of the language in the *Dānapāramitā-sūtra* is present in another body of evidence from Buddhist India—inscriptions. There are thousands of extant inscriptions recording gifts by or to Buddhists in India. They are among the earliest records we have indicating the presence of Buddhist activity in India, and they continued to be produced until Buddhism all but disappeared from India around the thirteenth century. Many surviving Indian Buddhist inscriptions record the intentions behind the gift of the donor.[48] Among the Indian inscriptions that Gregory Schopen has associated with Mahāyāna, for example, there is a donative formula that reads, in its most basic form: *yad atra puṇyaṃ tad bhavatu sarvvasatvānām anuttarajñānāvāptaye* ("May the merit here be for the attainment of unsurpassed knowledge for all beings.").[49] This is not a Buddhist *praṇidhāna*. However, as in the oaths from the *Dānapāramitā-sūtra*, with this epigraphic formula donors expressed their wishes with an optative verb. It does not appear that the donors who used some variation of this inscriptional formula felt comfortable merely hoping for the desired karmic effects of the gift to come true. On the contrary, it seems that writing the intention of the gift—writing it in stone, in many cases—was thought necessary to bring about what was desired. In my reading, the written words of this epigraphic formula, along with those of hundreds of other Buddhist inscriptions that record the intentions of donors, were thought to will the goals of the donors' gifts into existence.

Long ago the Indian epigrapher Sten Konow proposed that inscriptions "were more or less considered as a kind of charm."[50] I would like to suggest

47. There is extensive discussion on speech acts in literature related to linguistics, the philosophy of language, sociology, and anthropology. See especially the discussion on the illocutionary act of the promise in Searle 1969.

48. Many, though, don't. Frequently, Indian Buddhist inscriptions, especially early inscriptions, have little more than the names of the donors. See the discussion on the presence of names in the Indian Buddhist epigraphic record in Schopen 1996.

49. Schopen 1979, 4–15. Also see McCombs 2014, 311–348.

50. Konow 1929, cxviii. With regard to the inscriptions on the images recovered from the

that much of the language used in the *Dānapāramitā-sūtra* to describe the gifts of the Mahāyāna bodhisattva—the *adhivacana*s, the *praṇidhāna*s, and the assortment of wordplays—were also thought to work as a kind of charm. In this limited but critical sense, the way that giving was thought to work in an Indian Buddhist text seems to parallel how real Buddhist donors from India conceived of the gifts that they recorded in inscriptions.[51]

Words have power, and not just the power to relate ideas. They can work, in short, as magic. And they can work in magical ways within and outside of a religious text. When Indian Buddhist texts are read not just as discursive products that convey ideas that their authors wanted to disseminate but also (depending on the particular text) as repositories of illocutionary acts that were believed capable of fulfilling desires, then the dichotomy between text and practice can become artificial.[52]

Works Cited

Abbreviations

Sde dge — *The Sde-dge Mtshal-par Bka'-'gyur: A Facsimile Edition of the 18th Century Redaction of Si-tu Chos-kyi-'byuṅ-gnas Prepared under the Direction of H.H. the 16th Rgyal-dbaṅ Karma-pa*. 103 vols. Delhi: Delhi Karmapae Chodhey Gyalwae Sungrab Partun Khang, 1976–1979.

---

monastic site at Jauliān, Konow (1929, 93) says much the same thing: "[T]he aim of the votive inscriptions was not, perhaps, that they should be read and understood, but to ensure religious merit through the mystic power of the aksharas."

51. It is beyond the scope of this essay, but I believe parallels can be drawn here with a variety of Indian religious practices, including non-Buddhist practices. For instance, Axel Michaels describes the *saṃkalpa* or "declaration of purpose" of Brahmanical rituals as an utterance that intentionally marks off the sacred space, time, and actor of a ritual, without which a ritual becomes merely a sequence of actions that do not produce the desired effects: "It seems, then, that everyday behaviour has to be intentionally directed towards religious aims in order to be ritually acceptable. Unknowingly, unconsciously and unwillingly performed rituals have no religious result (*phala, puṇya*)" (2005, 49).

52. This has been said before but bears repeating (see, e.g., Nattier 2003, 103–105). It is helpful to remember that producing religious texts is also a type of practice. Regarding so-called early Mahāyāna, if we were to interpret the composition, redaction, and interaction with texts—reading them, copying them, worshipping them—as a or as *the* dominant form of religious practice, then Mahāyāna starts to look much more significant as a historical movement in India despite the paucity of material and epigraphic records during the Middle Period.

Apple, James B. 2009. "'Wordplay': Emergent Ideology through Semantic Elucidation: A Rhetorical Technique in Mahāyāna Buddhist formations." *Bulletin of the Institute of Oriental Philosophy* 25: 161–173.

Bendall, Cecil, ed. [1897–1902] 1992. *Çikshāsamuccaya: A Compendium of Buddhistic Teaching Compiled by Çāntideva Chiefly from Earlier Mahāyāna-Sūtras*. Bibliotheca Buddhica 1. Reprint, Delhi: Motilal Banarsidass.

Boucher, Daniel. 1998. "Gāndhārī and the Early Chinese Buddhist Translations Reconsidered: The Case of the *Saddharmapuṇḍarīkasūtra*." *Journal of the American Oriental Society* 118.4: 471–506.

———. 2008. *Bodhisattvas of the Forest and the Formation of the Mahāyāna: A Study and Translation of the* Rāṣṭrapālaparipṛcchā-sūtra. Studies in the Buddhist Traditions. Honolulu: University of Hawai'i Press.

Braarvig, Jens, ed. 1993. *Akṣayamatinirdeśasūtra*, vol. 1: *Edition of Extant Manuscripts with an Index*. Oslo: Solum Forlag.

Bronkhorst, Johannes. 2001. "Etymology and Magic: Yāska's Nirukta, Plato's Cratylus, and the Riddle of Semantic Etymologies." *Numen* 48.2: 147–203.

Bronner, Yigal. 2010. *Extreme Poetry: The South Asian Movement of Simultaneous Narration*. New York: Columbia University Press.

Chen, Ruixuan. 2018. "An Opaque Pun: Tentative Notes on *Kāśyapaparivarta* § 68." *Indo-Iranian Journal* 61.4: 369–395.

Collins, Steven. 1993. "The Discourse on What Is Primary (Aggañña-Sutta): An Annotated Translation." *Journal of Indian Philosophy* 21.4: 301–393.

———. 2003. "What Is Literature in Pali?" In *Literary Cultures in History: Reconstructions from South Asia*, edited by Sheldon Pollock, 649–688. Berkeley: University of California Press.

Edgerton, Franklin. [1953] 2004. *Buddhist Hybrid Sanskrit Grammar and Dictionary*. 2 vols. Reprint, Delhi: Motilal Banarsidass.

Gómez, Luis O., trans. [1996] 2002. *The Land of Bliss: The Paradise of the Buddha of Measureless Light*. Reprint, Delhi: Motilal Banarsidass.

Gummer, Natalie D. 2014. "Sacrificial Sūtras: Mahāyāna Literature and the South Asian Ritual Cosmos." *Journal of the American Academy of Religion* 82.4: 1091–1126.

Hara, Minoru. 1992. "A Note on Dhammapada 97." *Indo-Iranian Journal* 35.2–3: 179–191.

Harrison, Paul. 2003. "Mediums and Messages: Reflections on the Production of Mahāyāna Sūtras." *The Eastern Buddhist*, n.s., 35.1–2: 115–151.

Ishihama, Yumiko, and Yōichi Fukuda, eds. 1989. *A New Critical Edition of the* Mahāvyutpatti: *Sanskrit-Tibetan-Mongolian Dictionary of Buddhist Terminology*. Studia Tibetica 16. Materials for Tibetan-Mongolian Dictionaries 1. Tokyo: The Toyo Bunko.

Jamison, Stephanie W. 2015. "*Śleṣa* in the *Ṛg Veda*?: Poetic Effects in *Ṛg Veda* X.29.1." *International Journal of Hindu Studies* 19.1–2: 157–170.

Karashima, Seishi. 2015. "Vehicle (*yāna*) and Wisdom (*jñāna*) in the Lotus Sutra—The Origin of the Notion of *yāna* in Mahāyāna Buddhism." *Annual Report of the*

International Research Institute for Advanced Buddhology at Soka University 18: 163–196.

Konow, Sten. 1929. *Kharoshṭhī Inscriptions with the Exception of Those of Aśoka*. Corpus Inscriptionum Indicarum 2.1. Calcutta: Government of India Central Publication Branch.

Lopez, Donald S., Jr. 1996. *Elaborations on Emptiness: Uses of the Heart Sūtra*. Princeton: Princeton University Press.

McCombs, Jason. 2014. "Mahāyāna and the Gift: Theories and Practices." PhD thesis, University of California, Los Angeles.

Mehendale, Madhukar Anant. [1948] 1997. *Historical Grammar of Inscriptional Prakrits*. Reprint, Pune: Deccan College Postgraduate and Research Institute.

Michaels, Axel. 2005. "*Saṃkalpa*: The Beginnings of a Ritual." In *Words and Deeds: Hindu and Buddhist Rituals in South Asia*, edited by Jörg Gengnagel, Ute Hüsken, and Srilata Raman, 45–63. Wiesbaden: Harrassowitz Verlag.

Monier-Williams, Monier. [1899] 2011. *A Sanskrit-English Dictionary: Etymologically and Philologically Arranged with Special Reference to Cognate Indo-European Languages*. Reprint, Delhi: Motilal Banarsidass.

Mrozik, Susanne. 2007. *Virtuous Bodies: The Physical Dimensions of Morality in Buddhist Ethics*. New York: Oxford University Press.

Nattier, Jan. 2003. *A Few Good Men: The Bodhisattva Path according to* The Inquiry of Ugra (Ugraparipṛcchā). Studies in the Buddhist Traditions. Honolulu: University of Hawai'i Press.

Norman, K. R. 1979. "Dhammapada 97: A Misunderstood Paradox." *Indologica Taurinensia* 7: 325–331.

Ohnuma, Reiko. 2007. *Head, Eyes, Flesh, and Blood: Giving Away the Body in Indian Buddhist Literature*. New York: Columbia University Press.

Olivelle, Patrick. 2005. *Manu's Code of Law: A Critical Edition and Translation of the Mānava-Dharmaśāstra*. South Asia Research. New York: Oxford University Press.

Pischel, R. [1900] 1965. *Comparative Grammar of the Prākrit Languages*. Translated by Subhadra Jhā. Reprint, Delhi: Motilal Banarsidass.

Reader, Ian, and George J. Tanabe Jr. 1998. *Practically Religious: Worldly Benefits and the Common Religion of Japan*. Honolulu: University of Hawai'i Press.

Schopen, Gregory. 1979. "Mahāyāna in Indian Inscriptions." *Indo-Iranian Journal* 21.1: 1–19. Reprinted in Schopen 2005a, 223–246.

———. 1987. "The Inscription on the Kuṣān Image of Amitābha and the Character of the Early Mahāyāna in India." *Journal of the International Association of Buddhist Studies* 10.2: 99–134. Reprinted in Schopen 2005a, 247–277.

———. 1991. "Archaeology and Protestant Presuppositions in the Study of Indian Buddhism." *History of Religions* 31.1: 1–23. Reprinted in Schopen 1997, 1–22.

———. 1996. "What's in a Name: The Religious Function of the Early Donative Inscriptions." In *Unseen Presence: The Buddha and Sanchi*, edited by Vidya Dehejia, 58–73. Bombay: Marg Publications. Reprinted in Schopen 2004, 382–394.

———. 1997. *Bones, Stones, and Buddhist Monks: Collected Papers on the Archaeology,*

Epigraphy, and Texts of Monastic Buddhism in India. Studies in the Buddhist Traditions. Honolulu: University of Hawai'i Press.

———. 1999. "The Bones of a Buddha and the Business of a Monk: Conservative Monastic Values in an Early Mahāyāna Polemical Tract." *Journal of Indian Philosophy* 27.4: 279–324. Reprinted in Schopen 2005a, 63–107.

———. 2000. "The Mahāyāna and the Middle Period in Indian Buddhism: Through a Chinese Looking-Glass." *The Eastern Buddhist*, n.s., 32.2: 1–25. Reprinted in Schopen 2005a, 3–24.

———. 2004. *Buddhist Monks and Business Matters: Still More Papers on Monastic Buddhism in India*. Studies in the Buddhist Traditions. Honolulu: University of Hawai'i Press.

———. 2005a. *Figments and Fragments of Mahāyāna Buddhism in India: More Collected Papers*. Studies in the Buddhist Traditions. Honolulu: University of Hawai'i Press.

———. 2005b. "On Sending the Monks Back to Their Books: Cult and Conservatism in Early Mahāyāna Buddhism." In Schopen 2005a, 108–153.

Searle, John R. 1969. *Speech Acts: An Essay in the Philosophy of Language*. Cambridge: Cambridge University Press.

Silk, Jonathan Alan. 1994. "The Origins and Early History of the Mahāratnakūṭa Tradition of Mahāyāna Buddhism with a Study of the *Ratnarāśisūtra* and Related Materials." PhD thesis, University of Michigan.

Skilling, Peter. 2021. *Questioning the Buddha: A Selection of Twenty-Five Sutras*. Classics of Indian Buddhism. Somerville, MA: Wisdom Publications.

Study Group on Buddhist Sanskrit Literature at the Institute for Comprehensive Studies of Buddhism, Taisho University, ed. 2006. *Vimalakīrtinirdeśa: A Sanskrit Edition Based upon the Manuscript Newly Found at the Potala Palace*. Tokyo: Taisho University Press.

Visigalli, Paolo. 2016. "The Buddha's Wordplays: The Rhetorical Function and Efficacy of Puns and Etymologizing in the Pali Canon." *Journal of Indian Philosophy* 44.4: 809–832.

Ware, James R. 1929. "Studies in the Divyāvadāna: II. *Dānādhikāramahāyānasūtra*." *Journal of the American Oriental Society* 49: 40–51.

Writing the Word of the Buddha: An Instance of Redaction Practice in a "Middle Period" Mahāyāna Sūtra*

Andrew Skilton

Introduction

It is accepted that the composition and transmission of the early Buddhist canon was an oral process. This is, after all, a part of the Buddhist self-narrative but also seems to be borne out by internal features of the canonical texts—repetition, pericope, waxing syllables, and so on—that are inferred to indicate orality.[1] Unfortunately, while the fact of textual recitation per se is not in doubt, explicit emic accounts of any Buddhist mnemonic technique—that is, the method(s) of composition and of subsequent acquisition of the memorized text—are missing for any period except for contemporary practice, and

* The original research that produced the core data of this paper was undertaken in a previous century. I recall that Professor Schopen saw a version of it at the time and that it made him laugh—no reason was forthcoming. My understanding of this data has evolved in the meantime and, once reformulated as the subject of a paper some ten years ago, has undergone various revisions, benefiting here and there from feedback from a variety of people (not all of whom liked its tiresome detail or its multiple trajectories). I am grateful to everyone who has commented on its contents, including the editors and reviewers of this volume, while reserving ownership of all its faults and errors.

1. Allon's 1997 study of the style of the prose in Pāli suttas is the most detailed, scientific, and convincing study of oral features in that literature. Allon 2021 offers a broader discussion of composition and transmission and reviews recent scholarship on oral composition in the final chapter. Anālayo 2022 offers a recent and easily accessible summary survey of these characteristics. We should note that some of these features in the early canon would be regarded by others as incompatible with the features of orality attested in other literatures. See Ong [1982] 1988, 37–57, although the relevance of Ong's theories to the Indian context has been disputed. The debate regarding orality in the Indian context is rightly affected by the nature of the transmission of the Vedas, but the relevance of Vedic chant to Buddhist orality is moot. This is not the place to review that debate.

indeed I would even suggest that insufficient attention has been paid to the difference between these two processes, with a number of discussions seeming to blur the distinction between composition and transmission.[2] It is also accepted that at some point in the history of Buddhist sacred literature on the Indian subcontinent, writing came to play a role in the composition and transmission of this same literature. It is unlikely that memorization practice(s) simply stopped at that point, to be replaced globally by writing. However, the details of the interplay of Buddhist mnemonic and literary technologies is also poorly understood and until recently has not attracted the attention that the subject deserves. Discussions only seem to postulate the replacement of oral recitation by writing. It is my hope that the following discussion will make a solid contribution to the debate on orality and writing in relation to Buddhist scripture, by demonstrating unambiguously that one text at least was in part composed in writing.

A subset of the mnemonic and literacy debate is found in Mahāyāna studies, where it takes on colors that reflect ongoing interests in that field. Notably, writing has been linked with the origins of Mahāyāna Buddhism: by Gregory Schopen[3] through the postulation of written texts as religious foci for the emergent tradition, based on statements within the texts, and by Richard Gombrich (1988) through the inductive proposition that the technology of writing allowed the preservation of peripheral religious experiences and attitudes outside the mainstream of saṅgha-based oral transmission. Schopen's thesis has been challenged by a number of scholars, despite the evidence adduced from several Mahāyāna sūtras, while Gombrich's theory seems to have accumulated support despite the lack of any evidence.[4] More recently both positions have been challenged by David Drewes, drawing on his work on the role of the *dharmabhāṇaka* in the transmission of Mahāyāna scriptures.

2. For an account of contemporary memorization of canonical material, especially Abhidhamma in Myanmar, see Kyaw 2015; for Tibet, see Dreyfus 2003. I would further complicate the issue of orality by differentiating not just composition and transmission but also performance as aspects of oral culture that need to be considered in ascribing orality to any Buddhist text.

3. This is of course the highly influential Schopen 1975. I am very pleased to reference this publication of Professor Schopen's on the occasion of celebrating his work, since it also happened to be a major stimulus to my personal research interests from my very first reading of it when an undergraduate student in 1986.

4. Some thirty years after the deed, Schopen himself has proposed a more moderated position from that early work on book cults in Mahāyāna Buddhism—one that addresses physical embodiment as books and could thus be seen as a contribution relating to transmission—and suggested that more attention needed to be given to orality in early Mahāyāna sūtras. See Schopen 2005b, 153n118. Attention has been given in Drewes 2011 and 2015.

He makes a strong case that in the early centuries of their existence these texts specified an oral transmission.[5] He remains skeptical that there is or that *there can be* any evidence for composition in writing, although he acknowledges that "[t]hough most Mahāyāna sūtras undoubtedly would eventually have been lost without writing, this is a separate issue, and something that is also true of *nikāya/āgama* sūtras" and goes on to conclude, "[w]riting was not necessary for the Mahāyāna to emerge." In other words, he takes the early transmission of Mahāyāna texts to be oral but that this mnemonic technology was subsequently replaced by a chirographic one. He also infers that "[s]ince oral and mnemic practices seem to have remained central in Mahāyāna, there is a significant likelihood that Mahāyāna sūtras were typically composed orally" (Drewes 2015, 133). It is certainly the case that, if only for rhetorical purposes, Mahāyāna sūtras explicitly identify themselves as the products of oral composition by their opening phrases, *evaṃ mayā śrutaṃ*, a point usefully discussed by Lopez in his article on orality and authority in Mahāyāna.[6]

The picture of transition between oral and written technologies of preservation offered by Drewes seems to be neatly affirmed by a work of James Apple in which the author traces a transition from oral to book-based preservation (= transmission) of texts, a process he dubs *bibliofication*. This is evidenced particularly by textual formulae for entrustment—that is, *parīndanā*—in which the Buddha is depicted as entrusting the future transmission of his freshly delivered discourse to an individual or group. Typically this change, evidenced most decisively between recensions of a single text from different centuries, shows through the change from injunctions to memorize the text to undertakings to place the text "in the hand(s)" of the recipients; that is, the text is by that point considered as a physical object, a book. Apple concludes that "[t]his evidence also indicates that the use of the book develops and becomes more predominant after the fourth century, a time period that falls in line with developments of worshipping the book in the Gupta era (300–600 C.E.) . . ." (Apple 2014, 43). Alongside that conclusion, however, we should also remember that recent carbon-14 analysis of Buddhist manuscripts from Gandhāra has demonstrated that several Mahāyāna sūtras were preserved in writing in the early first to second and early third to fifth centuries CE, thus placing physical rather than textual evidence for the role of writing in transmission at

5. There is always the possibility that such claims could just be intentionally archaizing motifs employed by literate composers, although at the moment I do not claim this suggestion to be the case. Cole 2015 does.

6. See Lopez 1995 for a discussion of this dimension of their self-identity.

a rather earlier date[7]—once again, practice "on the ground" trumps what we are told by books themselves.

Thus, while it cannot be denied that Mahāyāna sūtra literature eventually came to be transmitted by writing, the relevance of writing for the origination of the Mahāyāna may be less certain, and its role in transmitting texts falls within a rather large window: between the first century CE and roughly the middle of the first millennium. However, just as for oral composition, there is also a dearth of direct evidence for the written composition of these texts. This study, which focuses on a short piece of text "borrowed" from one sūtra by the redactor of another, contributes to the data available for broader theorization. It shows how this particular redaction of a new text involved copying from a source text making use of a single, small format *poṭhi*-style manuscript some time prior to the mid-seventh century CE. In other words, it discusses both direct and inferential evidence for the composition of a Mahāyāna sūtra as a piece of written text. The following discussion will look very closely at the details of a list of terms contained in this borrowed material, examining its order and omissions, before reaching broader conclusions about the process of its redaction and what this may tell us about sūtra composition.

We can start this investigation by introducing the source text for the loan. The Mahāyāna *Samādhirāja-sūtra* (SRS) survives more or less complete in three Sanskrit-language recensions,[8] a Tibetan translation by Śīlendrabodhi and Dharmatāśīla of the ninth century, and a Chinese translation made in the sixth century by Narendrayaśas.[9] Until recently the earliest attested date for any part of the text may have been the translation of what appears to be a single chapter of the SRS by Zhi Qian (ca. 222–252 CE; Taishō 169; see Nattier 2008, 142), and there are two sections of a fifth-century translation (Taishō 640 and 641), but a fragment of a first- to second-century Gāndhārī manuscript of the

7. Falk (2011, 20) discusses the carbon-14 dating of a *Prajñāpāramitā* manuscript to the earlier period, and Allon (2006, 290) discusses a *Bhadrakalpika-sūtra* manuscript carbon-dated to the later date. We must not forget, however, that carbon-14 dating tells us only about the date of harvesting of the base material, the fabric, of the manuscript but not the year in which it was utilized in creating a manuscript. Salomon 2018, 88–90, discusses seven Mahāyāna texts in Gāndhārī finds.

8. There is very fragmentary evidence for a fourth Sanskrit recension, which is related to that of the Chinese translation of Narendrayaśas. See Skilton 1999.

9. *'Phags pa chos thams cad kyi rang bzhin mnyam pa nyid rnam par spros pa ting nge 'dzin gyi rgyal po zhes bya ba theg pa chen po'i mdo*; Peking 795, Mdo sna tshogs, vol. *thu*, 1b1–185a8 (vols. 31, 271.1.2–312.4.8 and 32, 1.1.4–34.4.8 in the Tokyo reprint, 1955–1958). *Yuedeng sanmei jing* 月燈三昧經, Taishō 639.15.549a–620a made by Narendrayaśas, completed in 557 CE. See Skilton 1999.

first chapter of the *Samādhirāja-sūtra* has recently been discovered and thus seems to anchor at least the core chapter of the text at this early date.[10] As a literary composition it is characterized by the repeated exposition in three different chapters of a samādhi-list—that is, a list of approximately 330 terms that is described by the text itself as a samādhi.[11] This samādhi-list first appears in chapter 1, is then repeated in verse form in chapter 17, and finally as prose again but with glosses in chapter 39; there the list items are restated as *lemmata*, followed by a short phrase or sentence by way of explanation.[12] It is also possible to see this samādhi-list as having its own internal structure, as falling into two sections, with the division between the two occurring somewhere between items 220–240 depending on the recension. It seems that the first part was the "samādhi-list proper" and the second part a list of "names" or attributes of the former, and this division turns out to be significant for our discussion later on.[13] In all recensions, the full list—that is, both parts just mentioned—is concluded by a statement of identification: *iti sarvadharmasvabhāvasamatā vipañcito nāma samādhiḥ* (Dutt 1941, 23) "This is the samādhi known as that elaborated as the sameness in their essence of all phenomena."

The precise function of the samādhi here is not fully clear, although there is evidence that it was understood to be connected with the extempore composition of teachings. Despite being referred to as a samādhi, it is not connected

10. This fragmentary text, identified by Mark Allon, contains the very word list that is the subject of this present discussion. It is as yet unpublished, although it has been read by an international group of Gāndhārī specialists and the full contents established.

11. "Approximately 330" because different editions arrive at lists with different totals, although none, other than Skilton and Murakami, bother to number them. Thus Skilton 1997 arrives at 329, Matsunami 1975 at 324, Murakami 1966 at 330, and Dutt 1941 at 326. Exceptionally for the manuscripts of this text, the Sāṅkṛtyāyana manuscript of the SRS (Bandurski 1994, 68–69) provides in numerals a final total of "333," although it is not clear if this is the actual number transmitted in that manuscript. Other manuscripts—among which I include the Gilgit manuscript, all the Nepalese manuscripts, and even the Tibetan editions that I have consulted—offer no total number. Leaving aside the vagaries of scribal fidelity and all the accidents that occasionally affect manuscript copies, the calculation of the number of items in a list like this depends in large part on the construal of nominal compounds and the grammar of nominal phrases, both of which are radically compromised by the endless variants of the manuscripts. Without some kind of privileged access to the original redactor's intention, we are unlikely ever to be able to establish the list in its original form and thus arrive at a definitive number. Throughout this discussion I will refer to the numbering as established in Skilton 1997, since this is the only critical edition of the text that tries to establish the text of a single recension. In all other editions the list is a conflation of redactions, and unnumbered.

12. Murakami 1966, Skilton 2002a.

13. There is internal (grammatical) and external (Chinese translation) evidence to support this interpretation. See Skilton 1997, 109–110.

directly with meditation, or at least with instructions for meditation practice. But we do not need to understand its function for the purposes of this study, just that it is a passage of text that consists of a long and stable list of words and phrases. Crucial to this study is that a part of this samādhi-list is borrowed by the later Mahāyāna text known as the *Praśāntaviniścayaprātihāryasamādhi-sūtra* (PVPS). The main work of this article is to supply more detail of this redaction than is currently available and to draw out inferentially details of the redaction process, while assessing in passing the value of the PVPS as a witness to the text of the SRS. The reader should understand that the following discussion does not bear on the content or meaning of this list in either source but seeks only to track the details of its transposition between the two sūtras—noting just the numbers of items moved and the order of their movement—and to extrapolate cautiously from the picture that emerges from that process.

The Samādhi-List of the Praśāntaviniścayaprātihāryasamādhi-sūtra

It has already been observed by Murakami Shinkan that the *Samādhirāja-sūtra*'s samādhi-list is "borrowed" in another text, the *Praśāntaviniścayaprātihāryasamādhi-sūtra*, which is known to us through the Chinese translation by Xuanzang in 663/4 CE and a ninth-century Tibetan translation by Jinamitra, Dānaśīla, and Ye shes sde.[14] This is a composite sūtra, of which the core is a lengthy samādhi-list compiled by the redactor from at least two preexisting samādhi-lists, that of the SRS and one taken from the *Śūraṃgamasamādhi-sūtra* (Taishō 642).[15] Murakami has performed an initial analysis of the redaction of the SRS samādhi in the PVPS, indicating with the line numbers of Dutt's edition the extent of the borrowed material (1970).

My own study of this passage suggests that it is possible to augment Murakami's work, and I would like to give more precision and detail to his analysis

14. *Jizhao shenbian sanmodi jing* 寂照神變三摩地經 (Taishō 648.15.723a–727b); *'Phags pa rab tu shi ba rnam par nges pa'i cho 'phrul gyi ting nge 'dzin shes bya ba theg pa chen po'i mdo* (Peking 797, Mdo sna tshogs, vol. *thu*, 189b–228a).

15. See Skilton 2002a, 73–76. Note that Cüppers (1990, xxivn2) queries the dependence of the PVPS on SRS and raises the possibility of the borrowing in fact running in the other direction, although I do not understand how one could sustain this claim given the chronology of the two texts. His speculation is effectively disproved by the discovery of the samādhi-list predating the PVPS by several centuries, and by irrefutable evidence that PVPS borrows from at least two earlier Mahāyāna sūtras. The idea is also refuted by the evidence of dependence explored in this article—namely, that the SRS material was the source for the PVPS and that there could be no viable explanation of the distribution of the borrowed material if the borrowing ran the other way.

in order to add some refinements to our understanding of the process of redaction that took place.[16] While this is not the place for a full examination of the SRS and other borrowed material in the PVPS per se, the following description is also offered to clarify the nature of the PVPS as a witness to the SRS samādhi (and *vice versa*).[17]

The PVPS uses in total 217 items from the 330 of the full SRS samādhi-list. These 217 are drawn from the first two-thirds of the SRS list, covering items from the start up to 239. However, the PVPS does not quote them in the same order as they are found in their source. Instead, the material can be divided into sections, which run as follows in column A of table 1 (see next page).

Correcting Murakami

One might conclude from Murakami (1970) that the sections of the list are transposed faithfully into the PVPS, whereas in fact this transposition is imperfect in several respects. Several items are omitted from the SRS list, mainly at the junctions to the sections described below (column J), but also within the sections copied, plus several passages wholesale, none of which is tabulated by Murakami. The items omitted from the SRS list between the sections in the PVPS are terms numbered 1–3; 60–76; 106; 140; 171; plus the whole of the final third of the list, terms 240–329. In due course I will argue that these gaps are due to several causes: intentional omission, recensional variation, and accidental damage to the material source.

It so happens that the SRS also contains a second, much shorter but similar, terminological list (also identified with the label *samādhi*) in its fourth chapter.[18] This one consists of forty-three items in Dutt's edition and runs from

16. Murakami's pioneering work of 1966 correlates primarily the Chinese text of the full SRS list as found in the three chapters of the SRS, although he also references the Sanskrit and occasionally the Tibetan text, usually in footnotes. His 1970 article on the *Praśāntaviniścayaprātihārya-sūtra* draws attention to parallels to its text in the SRS and quotations of it in the *Śikṣāsamuccaya* and *Sūtrasamuccaya*. His treatment of the SRS parallels consists of a table, which lists the page references for the nine sections of the PVPS list from three editions of the PVPS text, arranged alongside the page references in Dutt's edition for the items in the three SRS chapters in which the samādhi is rehearsed: 1, 39, and 17. This information equates to columns F, G, and H in table 1, although the page/lines of Dutt have been adjusted according to my understanding of the text, particularly of PVPS (5).

17. A critical edition of PVPS is lacking, and the comparison here has to be based on the text as conserved in traditional editions.

18. Once again, we need not be detained here by the function of the list in chapter 4 as its significance for the present discussion is just that it is a list of words copied from SRS by the redactor of PVPS. See Skilton 2002a for a discussion of the lists in chapters 1 and 4.

Table 1

A	B	C	D	E	F	G	H	I	J
PVPS	SRS chap. 1	SRS chap. 4	Skilton (1997) #	Murakami (1966)	Dutt	Chinese	Tibetan	Items present	Items not present
1	(2)		77–105	77–106	17.2–17.11	726b10–18	198a6–b2	28	1
2	(1)		4–59	4–59	15.11–16.12	726b18–c1	198b2–8	55	17
3		(9)			45.11–46.8	726c1–9	198b8–199a4	28	0
4	(7)		207–239	208–239	20.5–20.12	726c9–14	199a4–8	32	0
5		(8)			45.4–45.10	726c15–18	199a8–b2	16	0
6	(6)		191–206	192–207	19.11–20.4	726c19–24	199b2–5	15	0
7	(5)		172–190	173–191	19.5–19.11	726c24–727a1	199b5–7	18	0
8	(4)		141–170	143–170	18.6–19.4	727a1–8	199b7–200a3	29	1
9	(3)		107–139	108–141	17.12–18.6	727a8–18	200a3–7	32	1

Key to Columns

A the sequence of items in the samādhi-list in the PVPS

B the sequence in the SRS, chapter 1, in which identifiable passages of items from the PVPS samādhi-list occur

C the sequence in the SRS, chapter 4, in which identifiable passages of items from the PVPS list occur

D item numbers within those sections, as established in the critical edition of Skilton 1997

E item numbers within chapter 1 sections, as cited in Murakami 1966[19]

F page and line references in Dutt's edition of the Sanskrit text

G page, section, and line references in the Taishō Tripiṭaka edition

H page and line references in the Peking edition of the Tibetan translation

I the total number of items that are redacted from each sequence in the PVPS

J the number of items missing between the redacted sequences, as established in Skilton 1997

19. In this article Murakami assigns numbers to all the items in the list but does not specify the sections of material borrowed in PVPS.

page 45, line 4 to page 46, line 8 therein. The redactor of the PVPS took material from this list as well and incorporated it into the passage borrowed from SRS chapter 1 when creating the new text. Murakami, in turn, is aware of some intermixing of material from chapter 4. He identifies one extract of this chapter 4 list embedded in the midst of the other material from chapter 1 in the PVPS (i.e., PVPS 3 in the table above). However, he does not mention the transposition of another section of sixteen items from chapter 4 (i.e., PVPS 5 in the table above).

Instead, at this point in the PVPS he misidentifies three items of the sixteen taken from chapter 4 as having been taken from a much later point in the chapter 1 list.[20] Where I understand a sequence of borrowed material in sections PVPS 4–6 that moves from SRS chapter 1 to SRS chapter 4 and then back to SRS chapter 1, he understands a movement solely within SRS chapter 1. Moreover, by his analysis, this middle section (1B in fig. 1 below) is just three terms in length, not sixteen. In other words, he does not see what is actually a sixteen-term passage taken from chapter 4 and instead only notes three of those items as if they came from another, later place in chapter 1.

In his article Murakami identifies these three items from chapter 4 as corresponding to page 22, line 9 of Dutt's edition of chapter 1, *anāgamo rāgasya, vigamo dveṣasya, abhūmir mohasya*—that is, terms 302–304 of the list (as numbered in Skilton 1997; terms 305–307 in Murakami 1966). These terms should be contrasted with the following terms from the corresponding place in the list in chapter 4: *rāgacikitsā, doṣavyupaśamaḥ, mohasya prahāṇam*, which correspond to Dutt page 45, line 7. The chapter 4 terms correspond well to the items in PVPS: *'dod chags spong ba dang | zhe sdang dang bral ba dang gti mug spong ba dang* (see table 2).

Correcting this misidentification reveals that section PVPS 5 is actually a continuous transcription of material from SRS chapter 4 and in fact corresponds to the first sixteen items of its list. Murakami seemingly did not notice this. His identification of terms 302–304 from chapter 1 is therefore misleading. Were he correct, this passage from chapter 4 would be suddenly interrupted with a sequence of just three terms extracted from a completely different location in the source text—but this is not the case. See figure 1.

20. In Skilton 1997 I followed Murakami's lead and accepted his identification as accurate.

FIGURE 1

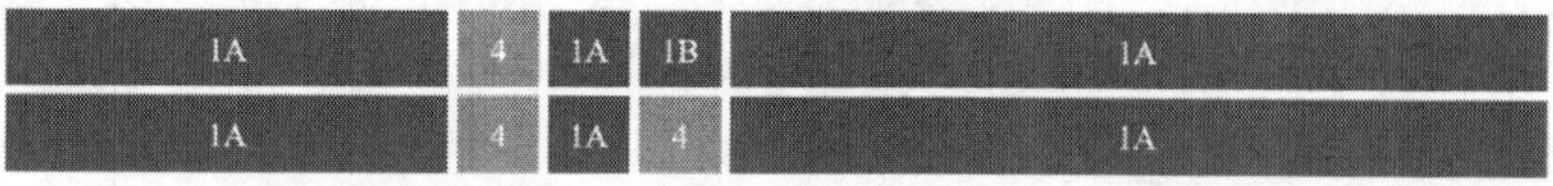

In the figure above, the top line represents the analysis of this material in Murakami. The lower line represents the corrected analysis that recognizes all the material from SRS chapter 4; 1A represents continuous material taken from the first section of the chapter 1 list; and 1B represents material taken out of sequence from the second section of the chapter 1 list—that is, material from chapter 4 that is mistaken by Murakami as coming from chapter 1.

In table 2, the items erroneously identified in Murakami 1970 are extracted from PVPS with contextual material on either side. The disputed terms themselves are underlined. The PVPS material occupies the middle row. The equivalent passage from SRS chapter 4 is provided in the top row. The sequence in SRS chapter 1 with which Murakami mistakenly identifies this material is in the bottom row (= 1B in fig. 1).

TABLE 2

<table>
<tr><td>**SRS CHAP. 4**</td><td>*pratisandhijñānam, apahṛtabhāratā, tathāgatajñānam, buddhavṛṣabhitā, rāgacikitsā, doṣavyupaśamaḥ, mohasya prahāṇam, yuktayogitā, ayuktavivarjanatā* (Dutt 1941, 45.5–8)</td></tr>
<tr><td>**PVPS 5**</td><td>無滯著智、不運重擔、如來妙智、療治貪欲、除去瞋恚、永斷愚癡、和合正理、遠離非理 (Taishō 648.15.726c15–17) *nying mtshams mi sbyor ba shes pa dang khur bor ba dang | de bzhin gshegs pa'i ye shes dang 'dod chags spong ba dang | zhe sdang dang bral ba dang gti mug spong ba dang rnal 'byor la brtson pa dang | mi rigs pa dang bral ba dang |* (Peking 797, Mdo sna tshogs, vol. *thu*, 199a8–b1)</td></tr>
<tr><td>**SRS CHAP. 1**</td><td>*pariśuddhiḥ kāyasya, pariniṣpattir mokṣamukhānām, asaṃkleśo buddhajñānasya, anāgamo rāgasya, vigamo dveṣasya, abhūmir mohasya, āgamo jñānasya, utpādo vidyāyāḥ* (Dutt 1941, 22.7–10)</td></tr>
</table>

Discussion of the Redacted Text

The granular textual details of this analysis reveal a number of interesting features of the redacted PVPS material that deserve further clarification.

Firstly, the material taken from chapter 4 of the SRS is the complete samādhi-list from that chapter and is copied over in its entirety, but for some reason it is split in two and separated by another passage from chapter 1. The item *buddhavṛṣabhitā* in Dutt's edition of SRS chapter 4 might be queried as it is not supported by the combined witness of the Chinese and Tibetan translations of PVPS, but it is rightly included in both Dutt's and Matsunami's editions of the Sanskrit text of SRS as it was in all manuscript witnesses used by these editors.[21] We must conjecture that *buddhavṛṣabhitā* was absent in or dropped from the source for PVPS. However, we cannot determine whether this omission was an artifact of the redaction of PVPS itself or was a feature of its source.

Secondly, it is also a striking feature that the PVPS version of the SRS material only starts at item 4 of the chapter 1 list. While this could have been an accidental omission of the first three items, we also need to consider other evidence from inside the SRS concerning these three items. The omission of terms 1–3 of the list from SRS chapter 1 could be seen as suggesting that the PVPS list had been redacted from the list items in SRS chapter 39 rather than chapter 1, where the *lemmata* of the commentary also begin at item 4 in the list.[22] However, closer inspection shows that characteristic features of the *lemmata* of chapter 39's glossary of the list (diagnostic omissions, and so on, elsewhere in its version of the list) are not present in PVPS, and we are justified in assuming for the meantime that the PVPS is quoting a version of the list as found in chapter 1, not chapter 39, of the SRS. Differences in its account of that list are due to the process of redaction itself. In fact, it is also possible to explain the absence of these three items as due to folio damage in a manuscript (see below).

Thirdly, we can now see that the redactor quotes exclusively from the first part of the SRS chapter 1 samādhi-list (= 1A in fig. 1). This may suggest that he did not regard the second part of the list—that is, the "names" (240–329 in Skilton 1997; 242–330 in Murakami 1966)—as suitable for redaction, possibly because he saw it as not a part of the samādhi-list proper (Skilton 1997, 109ff.). This view of the internal structure of the SRS text is circumstantially

21. Although the text is damaged in the Gilgit manuscript, the term is clearly visible in photographs of this source as "[ddha]vṛṣabhitā" (folio 3, line 4 in Kudo, Fukita, and Tanaka 2018, 17). It is also present in the ca. eleventh-century Sāṅkṛtyāyana manuscript text of chapter 4.

22. This possibility is briefly mentioned by Cüppers (1990, xxivn2) in justification of his speculation that the SRS is textually dependent on the PVPS. However, in SRS the first three items are expounded at length in full-chapter treatments immediately prior to chapter 39.

confirmed by the Chinese translation of the SRS, which makes a division in the chapter 1 list at the point corresponding to item 218 (in Skilton 1997; 220 in Murakami 1966) between items up to that point, and those coming after. Items before this point are the samādhi-list proper, while those that follow it are identified as "names" of the samādhi-list as a whole.[23]

Even more significant is that while the redactor only used the first part of the chapter 1 list in creating PVPS, he nevertheless included the statement of identification for the full list at the end of his total extract from the *Samādhirāja-sūtra* consisting of material from both chapters 1 and 4. His extract ends: *iti sarvadharmasvabhāvasamatāvipañcito nāma samādhiḥ*.[24]

Looking in detail at diagnostic omissions that have been shown elsewhere to differentiate the recensions of the *Samādhirāja-sūtra*, we can also begin to locate the recensional affiliation of PVPS's borrowings.[25] Inclusion of item 166, *mārdavatā*, shows that the PVPS was redacting from a source close to the recension SRS 1 rather than SRS 2 of the *Samādhirāja-sūtra*.[26] The omission of *priyavāditā* (between items 35 and 36), *pravrajyacittam* (between items 93 and 94), *jñānaprativedhajñānam* (between items 125 and 126), and *upāyakau* ... (between items 193 and 194) shows that it is not quoting the Gilgit recension of the text. On the other hand, the PVPS list omits 167 *mandamantraṇatā* and 212 *ātmajñatā* in common with the Gilgit text, which may demonstrate that the source for the PVPS either predates the redaction of SRS 1 and 2 or is not in a direct ancestry to them. It is also possible that item 212 was lost at the transition between folios in the source manuscript for the redaction of PVPS. Otherwise, the most significant omission of items from SRS consists of seventeen items between PVPS 1 and 2 (= SRS 60–76), although, as I will argue shortly, this does not reflect recensional variation.

More useful information about the redaction process can be extracted from table 1 by reassembling its main elements to show the original order in SRS, as in table 3, where we can then see how the PVPS text rearranges the sources in the SRS.

23. This observation also circumstantially supports my present revision of Murakami's analysis of the PVPS list, disproving his claim that items 302–304 (= 1B in fig. 1) are inserted in the midst of PVPS 5.

24. Any attempt to speculate that the second component of the SRS chapter 1 list, the "names" section, was a pre-sixth-century interpolation to the text (its *terminus ad quem* demonstrated by the Chinese SRS translation of that date) but that the source of the PVPS preserved a pre-interpolated form of the list must reconcile this speculation with the evidence of the first- to second-century Gāndhārī fragment, which shows the "names" section already in place.

25. On the SRS recensions, see Skilton 1999.

26. For these recensional variants, see Skilton 1997, 128–175.

TABLE 3

P	Q	R	S
SRS SEQUENCE	PVPS ARRANGEMENT OF SRS MATERIAL	TOTAL OF ITEMS REDACTED	ITEMS MISSING
			(3)
1	2	55	
			17
2	1	28	
			1
3	9	32	
			1
4	7	29	
			1
5	8	16	
			0
6	6	15	
			0
7	5	32	
			(90)
8	4	16	
9	3	28	

Key to Columns

P the sequence of sections of the samādhi-list as they occur in the SRS
Q the overall position of column P sections within PVPS
R the number of list items in each of the sections redacted in PVPS
S items missing in PVPS that are present in SRS

Shaded rows mark the contents of column S. The value (3) denotes the missing first three items of the SRS samādhi. The PVPS also omits the last ninety items of the SRS chapter 1 samādhi-list—that is, the section of "names." The situation regarding chapter 4, sections 8 and 9, is less easy to document. There is not yet a fully definitive edition of this chapter: Dutt lists a total of forty-three items; Matsunami's edition, forty-two. It is not possible at this stage to assert with confidence whether there are any losses from the chapter 4 material due to the redaction process, other than the term *buddhavṛṣabhitā*.

Discussion of the Redaction Process

This rearrangement of sections in table 3 allows us to explore the redactional process involved in creating this part of the PVPS. We can begin with some simple observations:

> There are nine segments of material redacted from SRS: seven segments from SRS chapter 1 and two segments from SRS chapter 4.
>
> The items redacted from chapter 4 come from a list in that chapter—one very similar to the samādhi-list of chapter 1—which is itself offered as part of an explicit explanation of samādhi as understood in the SRS. The redactor was therefore concerned to extract two samādhi-lists from the SRS as part of creating the PVPS.
>
> Assigning consecutive numbers to the sections from chapters 1 and 4 to reflect their original occurrence in the SRS—that is, their source—we find that they are distributed in PVPS in the sequence: 2, 1, 9, 7, 8, 6, 5, 4, 3 (column Q). This shows that material from the SRS source had been moved around when finally redacted into PVPS. Apart from sections 1 and 2, it appears that the remainder was integrated in a kind of reverse order, although 7 and 8 are in the correct sequence.
>
> The internal integrity of the units in which the SRS text was available to the redactor is preserved, and it seems likely that the minor losses can be assigned to error or manuscript damage—a matter of the loss of a single term between three sections: items 106, 140, and 171.

With these observations made we can move to more substantive conclusions to be drawn from the data assembled and to explain some of its features. Perhaps most significantly, we can note that three units of redaction contain fifteen or sixteen items. Furthermore, the remaining sections are all multiples of between fourteen and sixteen items. Allowing for differences in word length to explain this small variation, this is surprisingly uniform and suggests that the text of the SRS was available to the redactor in stable units of roughly equal length—that is, fourteen to sixteen items each. The most obvious candidate for these units would be the manuscript folio. If so, this inference obviously places the composition of the PVPS samādhi-list in a literary rather than an oral context. There is no theory of oral transmission that would explain such a feature. This inference is supported by the precise accuracy of the borrowing. Verbatim quotation is incompatible with the variations to be expected from oral transmission (see Ong [1982] 1988; Cousins 1983).

These folios, if such they were, clearly must have come from a physically small manuscript, since an average of fifteen terms, such as those already quoted above, takes up little physical space. This in turn suggests a small working manuscript of a type one finds only occasionally in monastic libraries, rather than a presentation manuscript on large, high-quality, and expensive folios commissioned by donors.[27] One is further tempted to conjecture that this may have been a personal manuscript (the equivalent of a notebook) used to collate the desired material from another source of the SRS. Otherwise, if we want to assume that this source was a complete text of the SRS, we should understand that the samādhi-list material cited here in PVPS constitutes under 1 percent of the volume of the total SRS, so that, if this original had been a complete SRS manuscript in such a small format, it would have had to contain a total of circa one thousand folios.[28]

Having come this far, we can move on to deduce that, if we accept that the folios of the source text could each contain around fifteen samādhi-list items, then this had to be fifteen items per folio side, since one side of a folio is the smallest physical unit size available in a manuscript. Moreover, all the sections of the PVPS redaction contain sequences of items in rough multiples of this number. This allows us to better understand the insertions from chapter 4. The first insertion, PVPS 3, was the equivalent of a complete folio—that is,

27. I have in mind as an example of the type Bodleian Library manuscript Sansk e 20 (R), a late twelfth-century Nepalese manuscript recently identified by the present author as containing the *Sūryaśataka* of Mayūra Bhaṭṭa. Folios are 155 x 37 mm (7.5 x 1.5 in.) and contain roughly two Śragdharā verses per side—that is, eighty-four syllables of text—a total roughly equal to the syllable count for fifteen of the items under consideration here.

28. This calculation is extrapolated using an e-text of Dutt's *editio princeps* of the SRS. From my survey of all known manuscripts of SRS, I can state that all examples of this text in which folio numbers are known are copied on large-format paper or palm-leaf folios. The invariably later paper manuscripts from Nepal contain 200–250 folios, while three rather earlier manuscripts had considerably fewer: the birch bark Gilgit manuscript had 176 folios (the full number is known through reliable calculation); the palm-leaf Sāṅkṛtyāyana manuscript had 107 folios (excluding the last four chapters); and a twelfth-century palm-leaf manuscript now divided between Tokyo and NGMPP had 120 folios (excluding the last two chapters). See Skilton 1997 for further details.

two sides—from the chapter 4 list, in which items from that chapter, numbering twenty-eight in total, filled the two sides. The second segment, PVPS 5, is just one more side of material from the same source—chapter 4—containing the final sixteen items.

Having suggested that our redactor was working from a small manuscript, we must also consider the arrangement of the redacted folios. The general disorder of the material as redacted in PVPS leads us to conclude that either the manuscript in front of the redactor lacked folio numbers, possibly through damage, or the redactor did not understand the numbering system in use in his exemplar, a consideration that does not seem so likely. In a similar vein, we should probably understand that this was a *poṭhi*-type manuscript consisting of loose leaves probably of palm-leaf (or possibly birch bark). These folios had not been bound effectively (i.e., they were not strung) in the correct order, and thus some, but not all, had come to be arranged not just in reverse order but in a couple of instances had been inverted individually so that the back side (b, or verso) was read before the front side (a, or recto). This suggests that no numbering device was visible. Again, this may support the inference that this was an unnumbered personal, working manuscript—a notebook—rather than a formally copied and numbered presentation manuscript. It might also be seen as an argument for the manuscript having been made of birch bark or even of paper, since the well-known tendency for palm-leaf manuscripts to "cup" unless kept pressed between board covers could easily signal to the reader any folio that had been inverted. However, this consideration is too circumstantial to be useful here.

Since the source folios used in the redaction contained circa fifteen items per side, we can calculate that the redactor copied a total of seventeen sides of samādhi-list from the SRS.[29] This is the equivalent of eight full folios plus one side. It is reasonable to suppose that this source document began as a record of the SRS chapter 1 samādhi-list, supplemented by 1.5 folios (i.e., three sides) of similar material from chapter 4.

The absence in PVPS of the seventeen items between PVPS 1 and 2 (items 60–76) suggests that the redactor omitted one side of a folio. It is not physically possible to lose one side of a folio, and the simplest explanation of this omission is that this material was lost through the well-attested scribal error of accidental omission—that is, the redactor copied the first side (recto) of the folio but forgot to turn it over before moving on to the first side of the next one. This means that the gap here arose through the failure to copy the rear

29. That is, by dividing the total number of items in the PVPS material derived from SRS (255) by the average folio size (fifteen).

side (verso) of a folio. One usually does not forget to copy the first side of a folio, only the second side. In any case, the material is continuous with what precedes it rather than what follows, confirming that it was the verso that was omitted. If we add in this lost material, we can conclude that the source manuscript originally covered eighteen sides.

Four sides of material precede the gap created by this omission, which means that the source text began on the verso of the first folio. This is consistent with the known practice of manuscript usage that leaves the recto of the first folio blank, except perhaps for a title, and suggests that the source manuscript may have begun with the SRS samādhi-list alone, again indicating perhaps a notebook arrangement that contained an extract from the full sūtra. There could hardly be a reason to create such a sectional division at this point in a complete copy of the SRS chapter 1.

Turning again to the minor losses mentioned above, I am inclined to speculate that these, which include the first three items of the list, are due to damage that affected the upper left-hand corner of the versos of a manuscript. This was worst on the first folio affected, leading to a loss of the opening three items, but less for the other three folios. Such damage can even lose data on one side of the folio but not on the other.[30] Unboarded notebook manuscripts can be vulnerable to edge damage of this sort. While damage can occur sporadically to the folios of a poorly protected manuscript, the damage here may be consistent with the disordered rearrangement of the folios prior to redaction into the PVPS—that is, that the damaged folios were, at the time of damage, adjacent to each other—thus explaining why the losses come from folios out of their true numerical sequence.[31]

We can conclude therefore that, at this point in the process of redaction, the redactor had in front of him a source manuscript that consisted of ten folios. The manuscript began on the verso of the first folio and finished on the recto of the last. The two outer sides, 1a and 10b, were blank—except perhaps for a title. The accidentally omitted side was 3b. The layout of this source manuscript is shown in table 4.

30. MacDonald describes similar losses in the Bodleian manuscript of the *Prasannapadā*, where she observes damage to the bottom line of the rectos but not to the top line of the versos (MacDonald 2015, 37).

31. We can see from table 4 below that they did lie adjacent to one another.

TABLE 4

ORIGINAL FOLIOS	ITEMS PRESENT	SKILTON (1997) #	PVPS	SRS CHAP. 1	SRS CHAP. 4
1a	0				
1b, 2ab, 3a	55	4–59	2	(1)	
3b	17	60–76			
4ab	28	77–105	1	(2)	
5ab	32	107–139	9	(3)	
6ab	29	141–170	8	(4)	
7a	18	172–190	7	(5)	
7b	15	191–206	6	(6)	
8ab	32	207–239	4	(7)	
9a	16	from chap. 4	5		(8)
9b, 10a	28	from chap. 4	3		(9)
10b	0				

The sequence of folios 9ab and 10a is here determined by the sequence of the contents from chapter 4. At the point of copying the contents of this manuscript into the new text of the PVPS, its folios had become shuffled and the sequence of copying was:

As before, the lighter shaded sections indicate the material from chapter 4. Even if the folios of the source manuscript lacked visible numbers, this looks like slovenly or incompetent scribal practice: both the first and last folios, each with only one side covered and therefore clearly identifiable as first and last folios, were incorporated within the body of the passage redacted. Folio 9 had its reverse side copied, was put down, but was then taken up later to copy the front side out of its proper sequence. It is worth reflecting on the oddness of this pattern. The treatment of folio 9 suggests an active mishandling rather than the passive copying of misordered folios.

How Do We Understand the Borrowing?

Are we justified in taking this feature of the text to be the result of the redaction process rather than just an accident in the transmission of the PVPS post-redaction? One could, after all, speculate that a confusion of folios just in this section while the PVPS itself was being copied *in toto* could account for the structure of the SRS borrowing in PVPS as we now know it. This would involve the speculation that a complete manuscript of the PVPS was copied intact except for an unfortunate jumbling of folios that affected our passage alone. I think this unlikely insofar as the skills required to copy a complete manuscript include paying close attention to pagination, and moreover, the lengthy manuscript of the full PVPS would surely have been numbered and thus easily ordered.[32] The jumbling of the folios for this passage is only credibly explained by an absence of folio numbering, as in a notebook rather than a full copy. Explaining an accidental loss of numbers within the body of the complete manuscript would be more problematic. We have already considered that the units of redaction are probably too small to reflect a complete manuscript of the lengthy SRS itself, and the same argument can be applied to a complete copy of the PVPS even though it is somewhat shorter than the SRS.

That folio 1a was not copied, implying that it was blank, is further, if circumstantial, evidence that the source was not a complete manuscript of PVPS but a separate record employed in the process of its composition. The text of PVPS has no gap indicating loss of text from this folio but has continuous text: "Furthermore, Bhadrapāla, [that] called the *praśāntaviniścayaprātihāryasamādhi* is the knowledge of the sameness in their essential nature of all dharmas . . . ," whereafter it starts its extract of the SRS list.[33] The fact that there is no gap in PVPS indicating a lost folio (= 1a) and that the start of the list as borrowed from SRS begins at the start of a folio also confirm that this was a separate text, in which the start of the material we are considering was on its first folio.

There are two further considerations. The same formulation of the PVPS list is transmitted in both the Chinese and Tibetan translations. It is probably

32. I am well aware that late scribal practice in Nepal sometimes produced copies in which leaves are occasionally jumbled, but this in my experience is rare, in itself a feature of a craft in decline and not perpetuated by further copying.

33. *Bzang skyong ga nan yang rab tu zhi ba rnam par nges pa'i cho 'phrul gyi ting nge 'dzin ces bya ba ni 'di lta ste / chos thams cad mnyam pa nyid du shes pa dang . . .* (Peking 797, Mdo sna tshogs, vol. *thu*, 198a).

justified to invoke Occam here and in the absence of any evidence to the contrary, to assume the simplest explanation—that is, that jumbling of the folios relating to the SRS material reflects the redaction of the PVPS as a whole. The most likely source of the error was the process of composition rather than transmission. PVPS was transmitted within Tibetan and Chinese traditions in relatively close association with the sūtra from which its samādhi-lists were borrowed, and the identity of the SRS section within PVPS is explicit (see above in "Discussion of the Redacted Text"). Yet this new order of the SRS list as now redacted in PVPS was considered authentic and viable. It is now a new text, and the proximity of a "correct" exemplar (the SRS itself) in canonical collections is irrelevant.

So we have now reviewed a short passage of material redacted from one Mahāyāna sūtra to another. We have been able to make deductions and propose inferences that construct a picture of both the recensional source of the redaction but also of the physical medium of this process. We can now take stock of what this picture might tell us in relation to the text itself. We can begin by thinking about intention and by differentiating the creation of the source manuscript—that is, the small palm-leaf manuscript containing the samādhi-lists—from the redaction of that material as part of the creation of the PVPS.

The source manuscript for the PVPS redaction contained two word lists copied scrupulously from the *Samādhirāja-sūtra*. They were copied faithfully and conscientiously, unlike the process later used with this source manuscript to create the PVPS. As far as we can discern, this notebook manuscript was an accurate record of the two lists. They are both concerned with samādhi and show that the copyist of this source manuscript intentionally extracted these passages from the SRS to create a record of them that was independent of the didactic and narrative context(s) of the *Samādhirāja-sūtra* proper in which they are embedded. The copyist of this source manuscript presumably valued these samādhi-lists in their own right, over and above the SRS as a whole—a view not inconsistent with the SRS itself, which repeatedly treats the chapter 1 list as the core of the sūtra, augmented by the additional supporting didactic material and stories that make up the bulk of the sūtra. It is also reasonable to infer that this scribe saw the two lists, from chapters 1 and 4, as of similar value, worth extracting and recording together, seemingly without distinction.

These observations leave us with a conundrum. How do we reconcile the apparently scrupulous making of the initial notebook record of the material from the SRS with the apparent sloppiness of its redaction as part of the PVPS? How is the intentional seeking out of this material consistent with the seemingly careless disorder of its subsequent use? Even ignoring the fact that similar material is borrowed by the PVPS from the *Śūraṃgamasamādhi-sūtra* and possibly another as yet unidentified source, we cannot ignore that it required some considerable knowledge and application to locate and extract the samādhi-lists of the SRS. But if we take into account those other sources, then we can see that the copyist was obviously intent on locating and copying this type of material from at least two substantial sūtra texts. The effort and skill required for this is not insignificant. Even the copying of the two lists from the SRS also shows an effort to record samādhi-list material and a detailed knowledge of the SRS itself. These two lists in chapters 1 and 4 of the SRS are embedded within narrative material. The original copyist must have been quite familiar with the internal structure of the *Samādhirāja-sūtra* and also have known the *Śūraṃgamasamādhi-sūtra* as a similar source of such list material.[34]

Countering some of these reflections, it is certainly relevant to note that a significant number of manuscripts from Nepal, plus two early witnesses (the Gilgit and the Sāṅkṛtyāyana manuscripts), punctuate the end of the chapter 1 samādhi-list with decorative section markers that indicate the conclusion of a section. In other words, punctuation is employed to signpost internal division within the chapter proper—there is a separate chapter 1 colophon (or punctuation) provided at a later point in both manuscripts.[35] If this marking of the end of the list was a widespread practice—a significant group of Nepalese manuscripts do not do it—then we could argue that the process of locating the list material, at least in chapter 1 of the SRS, was maybe easier than my comments above suggest. But, to counter this counter, it is also the case that these punctuation marks come at the very end of the list in SRS itself, whereas the PVPS redactor seems to have had in mind a clear internal division within the list, between samādhi-list proper and the following "names" section, as discussed above. Our redactor did not use this "names" section. The copy he made was therefore not a mechanical extraction but a careful selection.

One way of explaining this seeming contradiction between evidence of care in collection contrasted with lack of care in reuse might be to extrapolate two separate hands in this process—that is, one party, presumably a *paṇḍit*,

34. These considerations also confirm the existence of a genre of samādhi-list sūtra, an argument I have made elsewhere (Skilton 2002a).

35. We must also recall that comparing the recensions of SRS indicates fluidity in chapter divisions, and it may well be the case that the present chapters (and hence, of course, chapter titles) reflect an editorial intervention that considerably postdates the composition of the SRS (see Skilton 2000).

who scrupulously made the first copy, and then another party who took that record and used it sloppily to make the PVPS. This model simplifies the problem by assigning what at first glance appear to be contradictory behaviors—scrupulosity versus sloppiness—to separate people. It is more challenging, but on balance equally relevant, to contemplate another scenario in which the contrasted outputs (an accurate source record but a disorganized application) are manifest by a single individual. This might involve two speculative strategies: first, that we should drop my pejorative language used above, and, second, instead of positing a binary and unreconcilable opposition between (laudable) precision and (culpable) sloppiness exhibited in two separate phases of action, we might imagine a mindset that encompassed scrupulous capture of the list content as a whole but indifference to the internal organization of the copied list. From the mindset of a modern textual editor the latter looks like a culpable error, but from the religious point of view that same phenomenon could be explained by emphasizing that what is important is the content in general but not its internal sequence. As a textual scholar I assume that it would be normal for a copyist to care to copy the source text in its correct order—but one might reasonably query whether the same concern might apply to an unstructured list, such as we have here. A rationale for the contents and order of the SRS samādhi-list as we know it is not yet apparent, and for all we know there may never have been one. A single copyist might thus have demonstrated fidelity to the substance rather than the internal sequence of his source and thus had an undisturbed conscience. This requires that the redactor saw the sequence of the items in the list as insignificant. This in turn is perhaps easily reconcilable with the fact that the redactor of the PVPS has drawn together material from at least two independent sources to create his text and thereby demonstrates a similar lack of concern with preserving the exact textual contexts of the new text's precursors.

On balance, my slight preference at the moment is to differentiate two hands in the process I have been trying to discern here: the hand of "the copyist" who made the original record—that is, created our little notebook manuscript—and the hand of "the redactor," who utilized that record in creating the PVPS. This allows that the two processes could well have been separated by sufficient time for the notebook both to sustain edge damage and for its folios to have become shuffled. Of course, looking around my study at my own books and papers, piled or strewn, many on the floor where they too can sustain minor edge damage from the passage of my feet or my dog (who took to using the *Tattvasaṃgraha* as a head pillow for several weeks as I worked on a revision of this paper), it is entirely possible that these two hands were one and the same, and that the primary factor differentiating them is just the passage of time between the record being made—the extract—and that record later being used in the redaction of the PVPS. After all, Xuanzang had had his manuscript of the PVPS in hand for twenty years before he got around to translating it—literary projects take time. (I extracted the data for this article in the mid-90s of the last century, but only started thinking about it analytically some twenty-plus years later.) What these reflections might show about the PVPS is hard to say and is probably only discernible when placed in a rather broader context. This broader context might include both a study of the PVPS itself as a complete text, and also of evidence for the processes of redaction in other Mahāyāna sūtras. The latter might usefully include a study of the variety of evidence for redaction of composite texts as a route to understanding better the literary and editorial practices—as distinct from the religious motives, doctrinal positions, or historical circumstances—that were employed by the individuals or communities that compiled Mahāyāna sūtra texts.

Reflections on Changing Perspectives

Toward the end of his article on orality in the Mahāyāna, David Drewes comments on his evidence that shows that a number of Mahāyāna sūtras appear to advocate oral transmission. He writes, "The various attempts that have been made to link aspects of Mahāyāna thought or textual imagery to the use of writing are too numerous to discuss individually, but they too now seem dubious, *mainly because it is no longer clear that Mahāyāna sūtras were written compositions in the first place*" (Drewes 2015, 133; my italics). We can now respond that at least one Mahāyāna sūtra was—at least in part—a written composition, and I do not think it would be controversial to suggest that some others also probably were.[36] I would find it hard to believe that in the PVPS we have the only sūtra text that is (or contains) a written composition. However, Drewes's article addresses a strand of western academic discourse that flourished across the final decades of the last century and was concerned with the origins of Mahāyāna Buddhism. That the PVPS is possibly a late sūtra text composed in Schopen's "middle period" therefore places it in a different chronological frame from that on which Drewes is focused and concerning which he drew this conclusion. In that sense the PVPS might never have been considered by him as relevant to the category of material he is addressing.

36. I am aware that I am making a simplistic distinction between oral and textual composition, a distinction that might not survive under certain lights, particularly those shone by scholars who have worked in depth in the area of oral literature and the verbal arts.

We have already noted that the PVPS appears in its Chinese translation in 663 CE. The formal dependence of the PVPS on those texts from which it borrows certainly places it later than them, but—there being no rule for determining how long it takes to borrow something—my only thought is that, in a culture allegedly unconcerned with plagiarism, it makes most sense to borrow from something that is well known and popular. To take the case of the SRS, empirical evidence now demonstrates that it existed as early as the first or second centuries CE, although it only came to be translated into Chinese in the early fifth century CE (if we ignore Zhi Qian's text). On the other hand, the *Śūraṃgamasamādhi-sūtra* was translated by Lokakṣema in the late second century. These dates therefore delimit the window of composition for the PVPS, which borrows material from both, between the second through to early seventh centuries CE—again, only half a millennium! This tells us nothing very useful about its year of composition, although I am inclined toward seeing it as a relatively late composition in the sūtra genre, and one that at least took place in a period when writing was used as the medium for composition. Quite what this parameter might have been is altogether unclear unless we were to rely on the evidence from Apple's study, which would place it, as a written text, in a post-fourth-century frame (2014, 43). But Apple's evidence concerns the manner of transmission of texts rather than the manner of composition, and this also ignores the carbon-14 evidence for several Mahāyāna sūtras from Gandhāra, including now the SRS, which locates written transmission a couple of centuries earlier.

In what I read as an ironic voice, Drewes goes on to comment: "Even if all Mahāyāna sūtras were composed in writing, however, *and we could somehow know this*, since the effect of writing on consciousness, especially in India, is really no less mysterious than Mahāyāna thought itself, it would be difficult to link Mahāyāna thought or imagery to it in any more than a vague, speculative manner" (Drewes 2015, 133; my italics). The PVPS shows us that it is possible to know that a Mahāyāna sūtra was composed as a written text, although the indicators for this provenance lie not in any figments of a Mahāyāna consciousness but in the fragmented literary form of the text. It is perhaps there that we might conduct a more fruitful search for evidence of writing than, as has been hitherto assumed, among religious doctrines and practices.

Drewes continues, "To link specific Mahāyāna ideas or tendencies to writing in a meaningful way, one would like, for example, to be able to specify what additional factors led writing to cause the tendencies in question to develop in the Mahāyāna, but not in other 'written' Buddhist traditions—and questions like this would take us back to the proverbial square one"

(2015, 133). While I remain unclear what "proverbial square one" he has in mind here (querying what makes Mahāyāna mahayanist?), he makes a reasonable case that if writing is to be associated decisively with the origins (rather than the transmission) of Mahāyāna, then we must be able to identify specific characteristics of Mahāyāna that reflect written composition. Specifically, he seeks links between writing and distinctive Mahāyāna doctrines or imagery and suggests that since, as he argues, non-Mahāyāna texts were also probably being written in the same period as Mahāyāna texts would have been, we need to identify what else it was about writing or in conjunction with writing that produced distinctive Mahāyāna positions in the one and not in the other.[37]

Drewes does not mention that something very like this had been attempted some ten years before he wrote this challenge. In an important, exciting, and I suspect undervalued study of early Mahāyāna, *Text as Father* (2005), Alan Cole performs an illuminating close reading of four texts that demonstrates a religious agenda that is quintessentially literary in its formulation.[38] Cole's argument is that these early Mahāyāna texts articulate a repositioning of authority away from the śrāvaka tradition and toward the texts themselves as expressions of Mahāyāna and that this repositioning is achieved through narrative means. He goes even further in suggesting that certain characteristic early Mahāyāna doctrines—emptiness, compassion, universal buddhahood, and expedient means—are favored in these texts because they serve the narrative drive of the text! Since Drewes does not deal with Cole's work, the reader must judge the success of Cole's analysis and decide whether it answers Drewes's challenge.[39] Nevertheless, Drewes's point is not unreasonable, and by

37. Gombrich's theory looks away from the content in detail and proposes that an incidental technological development (writing) allowed the preservation of the ongoing and universal peripheral religious phenomenon of innovation. We could say that his theory addresses the material cause. Schopen's thesis in his 1975 publication could be seen as addressing the teleological cause.

38. The texts are the *Saddharmapuṇḍarīka-sūtra*, *Vajracchedikā*, *Tathāgatagarbha-sūtra*, and *Vimalakīrtinirdeśa*.

39. Cole conducts a close reading of the texts, as one might give to a novel. This approach assumes that a text is a complete and finished literary construct offered up to an astute readership, so that each phrase can be validly scrutinized for nuanced meanings. His method is essentially a literary one. Cole comments, "Apparently, there is a stable resistance to thinking about these texts as literary constructions, designed for readers who are to move through the narrative and absorb information on several layers of symbolic communication. This lack of enthusiasm for reading narratives as narratives is even more limiting when it becomes clear that many Mahāyāna sūtras are quite aware of themselves as plots lodged in physical texts and thus seem to be functioning at a fairly sophisticated level of symbolic exchange. Consequently, I

way of addressing it myself, albeit once again from an angle he does not have in mind, it is illuminating to consider what our scholarly counterparts among the Buddhist intelligentsia of the day thought about the production of scripture. This looks not so much at "the effect of writing on consciousness," as he puts it, but at *the effect of consciousness on writing*. In doing this, we will discover that Buddhist thinkers not too far removed from the time of our translated text had zero interest in the issue of orality versus writing, argued for a highly impersonal relationship between "awakened mind" and scripture, and avoided reliance on issues pertaining to transmission because of its inherent vulnerability to corruption.

By the year of the translation of the PVPS into Chinese, which is the only objectively ascertained date that we have for this text, the Buddhist intellectual world was complex and diverse. The text's translator was none other than Xuanzang, and we might infer that he personally collected the text on his travels in India. Certainly, he translated it after he returned from his travels there in 645, although it was among the very last he translated and thus obviously rather low on his list of priorities. In this narrow sense we can claim that the PVPS was popular enough to have been collected by an intellectual outlander pilgrim by the year 645 CE and subsequently translated into another language by that collector, but only twenty years later. Xuanzang's interests seemingly lay in the area of Vijñānavāda doctrine, and it is therefore of note that within less than a century of Xuanzang's translation, the eighth-century Buddhist author Śāntarakṣita (d. 788 CE) makes some telling observations on the authorship of Buddhist scripture in his *Tattvasaṃgraha*. While Śāntarakṣita postdates the composition and trans-

would argue that reading these texts without considering how the plots work rather skews how we appreciate their content and intent" (Cole 2005, 4). This synchronic literary approach goes against the instincts of scholars steeped in diachronic methods of textual analysis, which engage with texts almost exclusively as historical products, often fragmented and composite—methods that moreover assume a position of historical objectivity, rather than subjective reader response. Even after putting aside the specialist vocabulary and concepts of literary theory, which can be a formidable barrier for the outsider, synchronic methods tend to carry little weight with diachronic practitioners, and it is these latter who have, for obvious reasons, dominated the discussion of the history of Buddhism to date. Diachronically oriented practitioners run shy of symbolic exchanges, and so on, and may well tend to see synchronic analyses as running roughshod over un-ignorable diachronic warning signs, such as evidence of a text being composite, having multiple recensions, or of clear expansion over time. When Buddhist studies matures to a stage at which synchronic and diachronic analyses of texts can be utilized in a harmonious and complementary fashion for the exploration of text-based discussions of Buddhist literature, we might consider a "second turning of the wheel" of Buddhist studies scholarship to have taken place. (I am indebted to the long-matured discipline of Biblical studies for the terminology of diachronic and synchronic exegesis.)

lation of the PVPS, I suggest that the views he expresses would have applied and been known at the time of Xuanzang and can be taken as representing a synthesized Vijñānavāda-Madhyamaka viewpoint. Donald Lopez summarizes Śāntarakṣita's position as saying that Buddhist scriptures "are not the product of human authorship."[40] Śāntarakṣita maintains that, having reached a state of nonconceptual awareness (*nirvikalpa*), the Buddha did not, indeed could not, formulate his scripture through a conceptual process but that the word of the teaching (*deśanā*) "rolls on" as if with the momentum of a potter's wheel that has been vigorously turned (*Tattvasaṃgraha* [TS] 3368).[41] Moreover, the Buddha did not personally formulate his teaching, because it is an impersonal articulation of the truth based on direct knowledge of things as they are, and as such even "when the Buddha is settled in meditative concentration, teachings spontaneously issue forth even from the walls, and so on (*kuṭyādibhyo 'pi*)" (TS 3241, a point repeated at 3608 and 3611).[42] In this sense the Buddha is not an author but just the "supervisor" (*adhipati*) of the production of scripture, and it is this sense in which he should be understood as its originator (*praṇetṛ*). As a result of this it is not necessary to authorize scripture by relying on the Buddha's personal speakership (*vaktṛtvam*) of its specific content (TS 3608–9).[43] In his commentary on this passage Kamalaśīla adds that from a Vijñānavāda point of view, everything experienced is just the reflection of one's own mind, and "ultimately there is no speaker" (*paramārthato na kasya cid vaktṛtvam asti*).[44]

To summarize this position from a slightly different perspective from that offered by Lopez, Śāntarakṣita understands the conceptual content of scripture to express the awakened insight of the Buddha's mind, even if the articulation of that in conceptual form (in words) is an activity separate, one way or another, from the concept-free Buddha mind itself. Śāntarakṣita prefers a model of momentum to explain scriptural production, a metaphor

40. Lopez 1995, 36. I am indebted to this article for bringing Śāntarakṣita's material to my attention.

41. The Buddha's speech is the product of the momentum of his former accumulations (*sambhāra*) of merit and wisdom (*pūrvapuṇyajñānasambhāravegavaśāt*), according to Kamalaśīla in his commentary on this verse (Krishnamacharya 1926, 884).

42. The term is given as *kuḍya* in Apte's and Monier-Williams's dictionaries. I resist the temptation to interpret *kuṭyādibhyo* as *kuṭi* + *ādibhyo*, "from the [monks'] huts, and so on," even though this would form a delightful excursion.

43. Kamalaśīla's commentary (Krishnamacharya 1926, 926).

44. Kamalaśīla's commentary (Krishnamacharya 1926, 884).

consonant with successive turnings of the wheel of the Dharma, and of course from our current perspective this separation of supervision from personal authorship in conventional senses sits easily with the post-Buddha production of scripture.

These assertions have an implicit significance for the origins or production of Mahāyāna scripture. Śāntarakṣita's assertions invoke an implicit model for scriptural production that allows for the specific content to be produced apparently under the supervision of the Buddha but not necessarily through his personal articulation. It is surely intentional that Śāntarakṣita uses the expression "rolls on" (*saṃpravartate*) in this discussion, evoking the universal Buddhist metaphor of scriptural production, the turning of the wheel of the Dharma (*dharmacakrapravartana*). A quintessentially diachronic metaphor such as this is highly compatible with the continued production of scripture not personally spoken by the Buddha, as is the case, in the eyes of analytic scholarship at least, with Mahāyāna sūtras. If the Dharma still exudes from the walls even while the Buddha meditates, it is surely possible that the Dharma can be legitimately organized one way or another by his human followers under the supervision of the Buddha mind. After all, the historical Buddha, as we know him, was just a magical creation anyway, *nirmitas tv iha budhyate* (TS 3551). While the nonconceptual mind of a Buddha could not compose fallible discourses, there remains the possibility that the unawakened minds of his followers under his supervision could.

What is missing from Śāntarakṣita's extended discussion is any concern for the arrangement of the redaction and transmission of scripture. The crucial characteristic of the Buddha as supervisor of the teaching is that he knows the difference between *dharma* and *adharma*. Reference to the medium rather than the message only occurs in a passage where Śāntarakṣita critiques pointless debates about omniscience that involve people exerting themselves in books and debates (*granthavāda*) on the topic—although here he is seemingly referencing the composing of treatises (śāstra) rather than sūtra (TS 3140–1). While Śāntarakṣita repeatedly discusses the Buddha's speakership of his teachings, his is not a discussion of orality. None of his considerations directly address the issue of writing versus orality in either composition or transmission of the Dharma, although interestingly they could have done so. We may have to conclude from this silence that our concerns here were of no significance to the Buddhist community itself by the time of our sūtra. Śāntarakṣita's discussion of these issues comes after a lengthy argument concerning the fallibility of the Veda and the infallibility of *buddhavacana*. He clearly states, contrary I think to Buddhist practice elsewhere, that the only criteria for valid knowledge (*pramāṇa*) of what is right and what is wrong—that is, the entire basis of the religious life—are direct perception and inference. In maintaining this he excludes scripture (*āgama*) as a valid source of knowledge, perhaps because the vagaries of transmission per se might adversely affect the Buddhist position as much as they do that of the Veda. Scripture is itself validated not on its transmission but on the basis of the same criteria for valid knowledge: direct perception and inference (TS 2775).[45] For Śāntarakṣita, Buddhism is a watertight system, the truth of which is demonstrable by direct perception and inference alone. It is not therefore subject to the vagaries of textual composition and transmission, real as they are, and the origin of the text as such is apparently not to be attributed personally to the Buddha but to those he has supervised.[46]

Some Conclusions

Articulating a mainstream syncretic doctrinal perspective, Śāntarakṣita probably wrote his *Tattvasaṃgraha* near the middle of the eighth century, at a point at which the production of written compositions had been a part of the Buddhist milieu for several centuries.[47] It is quite possible that he expected pupils to be able to recite his text from memory and similarly that he not only knew his own composition by heart but drew on materials committed to his own memory in its composition. In other words, he worked in a milieu where oral and literary skills complemented one another.[48] The use of writing and of memory in parallel is in these senses well known from some modern Buddhist cultures. Neither should we be surprised were we to dis-

45. Mahāyāna Buddhists, or more accurately, the composers of what we know as Mahāyāna sūtras, seem to have been aware from the earliest period that their scripture was vulnerable to the accusation of being the work of clever or inspired people, *kavikṛtam*, rather than *buddhavacana* in any historical sense, e.g., the accusation placed in Māra's mouth in the early *Aṣṭasāhasrikā* (Vaidya 1960, 163) but echoed elsewhere in the early Mahāyāna canon.

46. Śāntarakṣita's discussion is about validity, something not affected by the medium of the Buddha's message, but this is a matter distinct from the ritual role of text. His pupil Haribhadra glosses the injunction to recite a sūtra as a matter of reading it in full from a manuscript, rather than from memory: *samādānena pustaka-vācanād vācayitavyā* (Wogihara [1932] 1973, 42).

47. Nakamura asserts "it is a certain fact" that this text was written "before Śāntarakṣita entered Tibet" (Nakamura 1983, 84). Seyfort Ruegg suggests that his first visit to Tibet took place in 763CE (Seyfort Ruegg 1982, 508).

48. Mary Carruthers's evocation of the working methods of Aquinas and others is a useful model here (Carruthers 1990).

cover that the PVPS, despite being composed as a literary text, nevertheless was also at times memorized. While the oral composition of Buddhist texts from the earliest period is universally accepted by tradition and by scholarship, the documentation of the features of orality and the transition to written composition and transmission is still in its early stages. All of these reflections suggest to me that the discussion of the interaction of orality and writing in the history of Buddhist literature needs to proceed by making as clear a distinction as possible between evidence concerning composition versus transmission on the one hand and between mnemonic techniques and writing techniques on the other.

Our discussion has another methodological lesson to offer regarding where we look for evidence concerning the creation of Buddhist sūtra texts. Over the last 150 years of interest in Buddhist literature in the West, we and our predecessors have often looked to doctrinal statements and stated or implied religious motives in accounting for the composition of Buddhist texts, but it may be that we could mine new seams of insight if we displace our attention to alternative features of a text. Here, examining a piece of borrowed text, without any reference to its actual meaning or function in religious, doctrinal, or sectarian terms, seems to have shed some interesting light on the creation of a Mahāyāna sūtra as a literary—that is, written—text. Textual borrowing has always been in the toolkit of topics considered by textual historians, and so it is worth emphasizing that the significance of the borrowing examined here is not its content but just its physical format.[49] This suggests that we might find it fruitful to focus on issues of embodiment, macro- and micro-structural features of a text, and observed mnemonic technique and performance as ways forward in this discussion.

Turning to the text under discussion here, for textual editors working on the SRS, the *Praśāntaviniścayaprātihārya-sūtra* offers us an incomplete, but nevertheless interesting, witness to an important passage in the *Samādhirāja-sūtra*: its samādhi-list. That this witness is of such early date—seventh century in the case of the Chinese translation and early ninth century in that of the Tibetan—means that the Chinese translation of the PVPS is the earliest witness of all for the recension SRS 1 of the *Samādhirāja-sūtra*, which is otherwise only concretely attested from the eleventh century (Skilton 1999).[50] The

49. Another example of such an approach is Paul Harrison's analysis of the physical format of An Shigao's translation of the *Ekottarikāgama* (Harrison 1997).

50. SRS 1 is distinct from but closely related to the Gilgit recension, for which we have earlier physical witnesses in the Gilgit manuscript itself and in the Schøyen manuscript. See Skilton 2002b.

PVPS's selection of material from chapter 1 prior to item 240 suggests that the division of this list into two parts was known in the Indic Buddhist environment and is not just an artifact of the Chinese translation. This internal structural feature of the list should therefore be borne in mind when reading it in its other recensions and languages.

The redactor of the PVPS was concerned to insert relevant material from the SRS but did not do so with the greatest of attention to the folio sequence of his source, a *poṭhi* manuscript, which may imply that the value of the content did not reside in its specific sequence or its perfect fidelity to the source text. We might infer that its presence was more important to the redactor than its sequence, and I am inclined to interpret this as representing a view in the redacting community of the PVPS that saw samādhi-lists as powerful language rather than conceptual statements available for extempore composition and preaching. This interpretation is consistent with the fact that the PVPS redacts without attribution similar material from at least two further independent sources, each containing a samādhi-list, in order to compile its own.

Moving on to physical specifics, the PVPS also offers us an unprecedented window into the process of redaction by which, sometime prior to the mid-seventh century (the date of its earliest translation), a new sūtra—the PVPS—was created by borrowing material from several others. A notebook-type small manuscript had been compiled by reliably copying specific, coherent sections of SRS. The folios of this notebook then became disordered and slightly damaged and were recopied without this being rectified and while also making errors such as omitting a side of one folio and copying the two sides of another separated from one another by two other disordered folios. The weight of the evidence gathered here does not support the theory that writing accounts for the origin of Mahāyāna sūtra literature, not least because the window through which we are looking here postdates the likely origins of Mahāyāna by half a millennium. Nevertheless, through this window we can see the redactor of the PVPS consulting a written source consisting of ten leaves of a *poṭhi*-style notebook that had been shuffled and had thereby lost their proper order. The redactor was himself working from a reliable manuscript but did not copy it with the same reliability. Whatever the case, for perhaps the first time we are able to witness directly the use of writing in the composition of a Buddhist sūtra.

Works Cited

Abbreviations

NGMPP	Nepal-German Manuscript Preservation Project
Peking	*Eiin Pekin-ban chibetto daizōkyō: Ōtani daigaku toshokan-zō* 影印北京版西蔵大蔵経：大谷大学図書館蔵 (*The Tibetan Tripitaka: Peking Edition. Kept in the Library of the Otani University, Kyoto*). Edited by Chibetto Daizōkyō Kenkyūkai 西蔵大蔵経研究会. 168 vols. Tokyo: Chibetto daizōkyō kenkyūkai 西蔵大蔵経研究会, 1955–1961.
PVPS	*Praśāntaviniścayaprātihāryasamādhi-sūtra*
SRS	*Samādhirāja-sūtra*
Taishō	*Taishō shinshū daizōkyō* 大正新脩大藏經 (*The Buddhist Canon in Chinese, Newly Edited in the Taishō Era*). Edited by Takakusu Junjirō 高楠順次郎 and Watanabe Kaikyoku 渡邊海旭. 100 vols. Tokyo: Taishō issaikyō kankōkai 大正一切經刊行會, 1924–1935.
TS	*Tattvasaṃgraha*

Allon, Mark. 1997. *Style and Function: A Study of the Dominant Stylistic Features of the Prose Portions of Pāli Canonical Sutta Texts and Their Mnemonic Function*. Studia Philologica Buddhica, Monograph Series 12. Tokyo: The International Institute for Buddhist Studies.

———. 2021. *The Composition and Transmission of Early Buddhist Texts with Specific Reference to Sutras*. Hamburg Buddhist Studies Series 17. Bochum and Freiburg: Projekt Verlag.

Allon, Mark, Richard Salomon, Geraldine Jacobsen, and Ugo Zoppi. 2006. "Radiocarbon Dating of Kharoṣṭhī Fragments from the Schøyen and Senior Manuscript Collections." In *Buddhist Manuscripts*, edited by Jens Braarvig et al., 3:279–291. Manuscripts in the Schøyen Collection. Oslo: Hermes Publishing.

Anālayo, Bhikkhu. 2022. *Early Buddhist Oral Tradition: Textual Formation and Transmission*. Somerville, MA: Wisdom Publications.

Apple, James B. 2014. "The Phrase *dharmaparyāyo hastagato* in Mahāyāna Buddhist Literature: Rethinking the Cult of the Book in Middle Period Indian Mahāyāna Buddhism." *Journal of the American Oriental Society* 134.1: 25–50.

Bandurski, Frank. 1994. "Übersicht über die Göttinger Sammlungen der von Rāhula Sāṅkṛtyāyana in Tibet aufgefundenen buddhistischen Sanskrit-Texte (Funde buddhistischer Sanskrit-Handschriften, III)." In *Untersuchungen zur buddhistischen Literatur*, 9–126. Sanskrit-Wörterbuch der buddhistischen Texte aus den Turfan-Funden, Beiheft 5. Göttingen: Vandenhoeck & Ruprecht.

Carruthers, Mary J. 1990. *The Book of Memory: A Study of Memory in Medieval Culture*. Cambridge: Cambridge University Press.

Cole, Alan. 2005. *Text as Father: Paternal Seductions in Early Mahāyāna Buddhist Literature*. Berkeley and Los Angeles: University of California Press.

Cousins, Lance S. 1983. "Pali Oral Literature." In *Buddhist Studies: Ancient and Modern*, edited by Philip Denwood and Alexander Piatigorsky, 1–11. London and Dublin: Curzon Press.

Cüppers, Christoph. 1990. *The IXth Chapter of the Samādhirājasūtra*. Stuttgart: Franz Steiner Verlag.

Drewes, David. 2011. "Dharmabhāṇakas in Early Mahāyāna." *Indo-Iranian Journal* 54.4: 331–372.

———. 2015. "Oral Texts in Indian Mahāyāna." *Indo-Iranian Journal* 58.2: 117–141.

Dreyfus, Georges B. J. 2003. *The Sound of Two Hands Clapping: The Education of a Tibetan Buddhist Monk*. Berkeley: University of California Press.

Dutt, Nalinaksha. 1941. *Gilgit Manuscripts*, vol. 2, part 1. Edited with the assistance of V. S. N. Sharma. Srinagar: Calcutta Oriental Press.

Falk, Harry. 2011. "The 'Split' Collection of Kharoṣṭhī Texts." *Annual Report of the International Research Institute for Advanced Buddhology at Soka University* 14: 13–23.

Gombrich, Richard. [1988] 1990. "How the Mahāyāna Began." *Journal of Pali and Buddhist Studies* 1: 29–46. Reprinted in *The Buddhist Forum*, vol. 1: *Seminar Papers 1987–1988*, edited by T. Skorupski, 21–30. London: School of Oriental and African Studies.

Harrison, Paul. 1997. "The *Ekottarikāgama* Translations of An Shigao." In *Bauddhavidyāsudhākaraḥ: Studies in Honour of Heinz Bechert on the Occasion of His 65th Birthday*, edited by Petra Kieffer-Pülz and Jens-Uwe Hartmann, 261–283. Indica et Tibetica 30. Swisttal-Odendorf: Indica et Tibetica Verlag.

Krishnamacharya, Embar. 1926. *Tattvasaṅgraha of Śāntarakṣita With the Commentary of Kamalaśīla*, vol. 2. Baroda: Oriental Institute.

Kudo, Noriyuki, Takanori Fukita, and Hironori Tanaka. 2018. *Samādhirājasūtra*. Gilgit Manuscripts in the National Archives of India: Facsimile Edition II.3. New Delhi and Tokyo: The National Archives of India and The International Research Institute for Advanced Buddhology, Soka University.

Kyaw, Pyi Phyo. 2015. "Foundations of Criticality: Applications of Traditional Monastic Pedagogy in Myanmar." *Contemporary Buddhism* 16.2: 401–427.

Lopez, Donald S., Jr. 1995. "Authority and Orality in the Mahāyāna." *Numen* 42.1: 21–47.

MacDonald, Anne. 2015. *In Clear Words: The* Prasannapadā, *Chapter One*, vol. 1: *Introduction, Manuscript Description, Sanskrit Text*. Vienna: Verlag der Österreichischen Akademie der Wissenschaften.

Matsunami Seiren 松濤誠廉. 1975. "Bonbun *Gattō zanmai-kyō*" 梵文月燈三昧経 (Sanskrit Text of the *Yuedeng sanmei jing* [*Samādhirāja-sūtra*]). *Taishō daigaku kenkyū kiyō* 大正大学研究紀要 (*Memoirs of Taisho University*) 60: 244–188; 61: 796–761 (reverse pagination).

Murakami Shinkan 村上眞完. 1966. "*Samādhirājasūtra* kenkyū: 1, 17, 38–39 shō no hikaku taishō" Samādhirājasūtra 研究：1, 17, 38~39 章の比較對照 (Research on the *Samādhirājasūtra*: Comparative and Contrastive [Study] of Chapters 1, 17,

38–39). *Hachinohe kōgyō kōtō senmon gakkō kiyō* 八戸工業高等専門学校紀要 (*Research Reports: Hachinohe Technical College*) 1: 65–80.

———. 1970. "*Praśāntaviniścayaprātihāryasūtra* ni tsuite" Praśāntaviniścayaprātihāryasūtra について (On the *Praśāntaviniścayaprātihāryasūtra*). *Indogaku bukkyōgaku kenkyū* 印度學佛教學研究 (*Journal of Indian and Buddhist Studies*) 18.2: 867–871.

Nakamura, Hajime. 1983. *A History of Early Vedānta Philosophy*. Delhi: Motilal Banarsidass.

Nattier, Jan. 2008. *A Guide to the Earliest Chinese Buddhist Translations: Texts from the Eastern Han* 東漢 *and Three Kingdoms* 三國 *Periods*. Bibliotheca Philologica et Philosophica Buddhica 10. Tokyo: The International Research Institute for Advanced Buddhology, Soka University.

Ong, Walter J. [1982] 1988. *Orality and Literacy: The Technologizing of the Word*. Reprint, London: Routledge.

Salomon, Richard. 2018. *The Buddhist Literature of Ancient Gandhāra: An Introduction with Selected Translations*. Classics of Indian Buddhism. Somerville, MA: Wisdom Publications.

Schopen, Gregory. 1975. "The Phrase '*sa pṛthivīpradeśaś caityabhūto bhavet*' in the *Vajracchedikā*: Notes on the Cult of the Book in Mahāyāna." *Indo-Iranian Journal* 17.3–4: 147–181. Reprinted in Schopen 2005a, 25–62.

———. 2005a. *Figments and Fragments of Mahāyāna Buddhism in India: More Collected Papers*. Studies in the Buddhist Traditions. Honolulu: University of Hawai'i Press.

———. 2005b. "On Sending the Monks Back to Their Books: Cult and Conservatism in Early Mahāyāna Buddhism." In Schopen 2005a, 108–153.

Seyfort Ruegg, David. 1982. "Towards a Chronology of the Madhayamaka School." In *Indological and Buddhist Studies: Volume in Honour of Professor J. W. de Jong on His Sixtieth Birthday*, edited by L. A. Hercus, F. B. J. Kuiper, T. Rajapatirana, and E. R. Skrzypczak, 505–530. Canberra: Faculty of Asian Studies, Australian National University.

Skilton, Andrew. 1997. "The *Samādhirāja Sūtra*: A Study Incorporating a Critical Edition and Translation of Chapter 17." PhD thesis, University of Oxford.

———. 1999. "Four Recensions of the *Samādhirāja Sūtra*." *Indo-Iranian Journal* 42.4: 335–356.

———. 2000. "The Gilgit Manuscript of the *Samādhirāja Sūtra*." *Central Asiatic Journal* 44: 67–86.

———. 2002a. "State or Statement? *Samādhi* in Some Early Mahāyāna Sutras." *The Eastern Buddhist*, n.s., 34.2: 51–93.

———. 2002b. "Samādhirājasūtra." In *Buddhist Manuscripts*, edited by Jens Braarvig et al., 2:97–177. Manuscripts in the Schøyen Collection 3. Oslo: Hermes Publishing.

Vaidya, Paraśurāma L. 1960. *Aṣṭasāhasrikā Prajñāpāramitā*. Buddhist Sanskrit Texts 4. Darbhanga: The Mithila Institute of Post-Graduate Studies and Research in Sanskrit Learning.

Wogihara, Unrai, ed. [1932] 1973. *Abhisamayālaṃkār'ālokā Prajñāpāramitāvyākhyā: The Work of Haribhadra, Together with the Text Commented On*. Reprint, Tokyo: Sankibo Buddhist Book Store.

Part 2
Monasticism and Vinaya Studies

A Preliminary Survey of Viśākha(deva)'s *Bhikṣuvinayakārikākusumasraj**

Shayne Clarke

Introduction

The Vinaya of the Mūlasarvāstivādins has received considerable attention in recent decades, and no one has contributed more to its study and understanding than Gregory Schopen. This sprawling Buddhist monastic law code, which in its Tibetan translation consists of some thirteen large volumes,[1] was described by Sylvain Lévi (1863–1935), the great French Indologist, as "monstrueux" in terms of its size and as a masterpiece of Sanskrit literature.[2] This colossal compilation is traditionally divided into four smaller, albeit still massive, sections: *Vibhaṅgas*, *Vastus*, *Kṣudrakavastu*, and *Uttaragrantha*.[3]

Of the four sections that constitute the *Mūlasarvāstivāda-vinaya*, the lion's share of scholarly activity has centered on the seventeen thematic chapters or *Vastus* that deal chiefly with the corporate concerns of the cenobitic

* For the last few years, I have read the Sanskrit manuscript and Tibetan and Chinese translations of the *Vinayakārikā* with graduate and postdoctoral students at McMaster University. I am especially indebted to Gerjan Altenburg, Jens Borgland, Chris Emms, Annie Heckman, Joe LaRose, Anna Phipps-Burton, Kazuho Yamasaki, and Fumi Yao for many informative discussions and helpful suggestions. I thank Chris Emms, Jens-Uwe Hartmann, Annie Heckman, Petra Kieffer-Pülz, Ryōji Kishino, Bob Miller, Pema Sherpa, and Fumi Yao for offering valuable comments and corrections on this paper while it languished in an *antarābhava*. All errors, inconsistencies, and misunderstandings remain the sole responsibility of the present author.

I wish to thank Prof. Francesco Sferra for kindly providing PDFs of printouts of the relevant folios in the Tucci Collection, and the Niedersächsische Staats- und Universitätsbibliothek Göttingen for providing images from the Sāṅkṛtyāyana Collection. This paper draws on research supported by the Social Sciences and Humanities Research Council of Canada (file number: 435-2017-0363).

1. Sde dge 1–7, 'Dul ba, vols. *ka–pa* (= 1–13); see Ui et al. 1934a, 1–2.

2. Lévi 1909, 113.

3. Eimer 1986 and 1987.

community, all of which are extant, some imperfectly, in a single Sanskrit manuscript from Gilgit.[4] Most of the *Vastu*s have been or soon will be re-edited in new editions that improve upon the pioneering work of Nalinaksha Dutt (1893–1973) and Count Raniero Gnoli (b. 1930).[5] Many have also been or are currently in the process of being translated into modern languages, often not from the incomplete Sanskrit texts but from the more complete early ninth-century translation into classical Tibetan.[6] Three of the ten substantial texts that comprise the *Uttaragrantha*, extant primarily only in Tibetan albeit with several important exceptions,[7] have been edited and translated.[8] The two *Vibhaṅga*s[9] and the *Kṣudrakavastu*,[10] on the other hand, which, unlike the *Vastu*s or *Uttaragrantha*, cannot be simply split into manageable yet meaningful sections,[11] have not formally seen a competent editor or translator[12]

4. On a newly identified Sanskrit manuscript of the *Bhaiṣajyavastu*, see Yao 2013, 2015a, 2018, and 2019.

5. For a diplomatic edition and complete translation of the *Cīvaravastu* and *Śayanāsanavastu*, see Schopen 2025.

6. For facsimiles of the Gilgit Vinaya manuscripts preserved in the National Archives of India, information on the folios preserved elsewhere, and a bibliographical survey of editions and translations with detailed concordances to the Sanskrit, Tibetan, and Chinese, see Clarke 2014a.

7. For references to Sanskrit remains, see Clarke 2015, 76. See now also Shōno 2020a. On an early (435 CE) Chinese translation of significant sections of an *Uttaragrantha*, see Clarke 2016.

8. There are two *Uttaragrantha*s preserved in Tibetan: one incomplete, one seemingly complete. See Kishino 2006 for the incomplete *Upāliparipṛcchā* in the incomplete *Uttaragrantha* and Kishino 2013 for the *Nidāna*, preserved only in the complete *Uttaragrantha*. For the *Māṇavikā*, see Lee 2024a and 2024b.

9. On the Sanskrit fragments of the *Vinayavibhaṅga*, see Hartmann and Wille 2014, 148–149; Shōno 2012, 2016, 2018, 2020b, and 2021a.

10. For references to Sanskrit quotations and paraphrases of the *Kṣudrakavastu*, see Clarke 2015, 76. In addition to the sources mentioned there, we should add Guṇaprabha's *Autocommentary*, in which numerous quotations and paraphrases are found; we might also include the paraphrases in the extant Sanskrit folios of the *Vinayakārikā*. As far as I know, no Sanskrit manuscript or fragments of the *Kṣudrakavastu* have been published. The so-called *Bhikṣuṇīkarmavācanā* is perhaps an extract from this text; see Chung 1998. Note, however, that Sāṅkṛtyāyana (1937, 57 [text no. 350]) reports a significant manuscript find of a text that he terms *Vinayakṣudraka* ("complete," three thousand ślokas, either photographed or copied, from Ṣha-lu [*sic*]). This text is not reported in Bandurski 1994, Sferra 2008a, or Harrison 2014.

11. For brief comments on the size of the *Bhikṣuvibhaṅga*, see Clarke 2021, 63.

12. My comments above refer only to the lack of progress made since the 1930s and in no way are intended as a criticism or even comment on the eagerly awaited "in progress" translations of both the *Kṣudrakavastu* and the two *Vibhaṅga*s listed on the website of the 84000 translation project: "The Collection / The Kangyur / Discipline." 84000:

since the 1930s, when their Chinese translations were rendered into the artificial scholarly language (*kakikudashi* 書き下し or *yomikudashi* 読み下し) that is used by Japanese scholars for reading off Chinese.[13] Almost all of Yijing's Vinaya translations were not only thus translated from the Chinese but carefully checked against the Tibetan translations by the largely forgotten and under-appreciated Vinaya scholar Nishimoto Ryūzan 西本龍山 (1888–1976).[14]

This flurry of scholarly activity centering on editing Sanskrit texts and translating Tibetan translations thereof has not yet caught up with the commentarial tradition on the *Mūlasarvāstivāda-vinaya*.[15] Of the thirty-four or so texts preserved in the Vinaya section of the Bstan 'gyur,[16] only one short text has been translated fully—twice into English, in fact[17]—and not a single one has

Translating the Words of the Buddha. Accessed January 1, 2025. https://84000.co/canon-sections/discipline. On the section on ordination for nuns in the *Kṣudrakavastu*, see now the excellent work by Roloff 2020.

13. I use the terms *kakikudashi* 書き下し and *yomikudashi* 読み下し interchangeably, taking them to be synonyms referring to the same style of writing or reading; one emphasizes the writing (*kaki* 書き), the other the reading (*yomi* 読み). A related Japanese form of reading Chinese (*sodoku* 素読) was criticized already by the great Confucian scholar Ogyū Sorai 荻生徂徠 (1666–1728); see Wakabayashi 2005, 135, synthesizing the work of R. P. Dore. Dore (1965, 134; quoted in Wakabayashi 2005, 128 [correcting her 143 to 134]) colorfully refers to this practice as "'reading off' Chinese texts in bastard Japanese." As discussed by Wakabayashi, there is considerable debate as to whether *yomikudashi* or *kundoku* is translation. This situation and its deleterious impact on Buddhist studies has been discussed most recently by Kishino 2018, 88.

14. For the *Kṣudrakavastu*, see Nishimoto 1933–1938, vols. 25–26; for the *Vibhaṅga*s, see vols. 19–22; for the *Vastu*s, vols. 22–24. On the life and contributions of Nishimoto, see Kishino 2019.

15. Under the term "commentarial" or "commentaries," used here very loosely, I include handbooks and digests.

16. Here I refer to the first thirty-four texts in the Bstan 'gyur of the Sde dge edition (4104–4137) and leave aside, for the time being, the otherwise-important schism accounts and *avadāna*s, etc., also included therein.

17. Dagpa et al. 1975; Mullin and Rabgay 1978. Although this handbook (*'Phags pa gzhi thams cad yod par smra ba'i dge tshul gyi tshig le'ur byas pa*, Sde dge 4127; Peking 5629) is often attributed to Nāgārjuna (hence its prestige and two English translations), both Rong ston and Bu ston suggest a different authorship. Rong ston gives Saṅghabhadra (Dge 'dun bzang po). Rong ston, *'Dul ba me tog phreng rgyud kyi rnam 'grel tshig don rab tu gsal ba'i nyi 'od*, 258b5–6: *dge 'dun bzang pos mdzad pa'i kā ri kā lnga bcu pa dang* /. Bu ston's comments require some clarification. Bu ston states that some attribute this text to Nāgārjuna (Klu sgrub), some to 'Dus pa bzang po, and some to Vinītadeva (Dul ba lha); Bu ston, *'Dul ba spyi'i rnam par gzhag pa*, CWB, vol. 21 (*zha*), 58a4–5 (= 115): *dge tshul gyi kā ri kā lnga bcu pa ye shes sde'i 'gyur / 'di la kha cig / 'dus pa bzang pos mdzad zer / kha cig / klu sgrub kyis mdzad zer / kha cig dul ba lhas mdzad zer te* /. On the basis of his writings elsewhere, it is possible that Bu ston intended Saṅghabhadra here.

been critically edited. Three Mūlasarvāstivādin commentarial texts are preserved in Chinese translations by the pilgrim-monk Yijing 義淨 (635–713 CE; travel dates 671–695).[18] Chinese translations of two Tibetan commentaries by 'Gro mgon Chos rgyal 'Phags pa Bla ma Blo gros rgyal mtshan (1235–1280), fifth leader of the Sa skya pas and the first Imperial Preceptor (1270–1274)[19] appointed by Qubilai Khan (1215–1294) around the dawn of Mongol rule (Yuan dynasty 1271–1368), are also extant,[20] as are, it seems, the Tibetan originals.[21] There is, moreover, at least one unidentified Mūlasarvāstivādin Vinaya commentary preserved in Chinese in the Dunhuang manuscripts[22] and a number of fragmentary commentaries preserved there in the cache of Tibetan manuscripts collected by Sir Aurel Stein (1862–1943) and Paul Pelliot (1878–1945),[23] most of which have no counterpart in the Bstan 'gyur.[24]

The Vinaya commentaries that have attracted the most scholarly attention to date are, perhaps not surprisingly, those preserved in Sanskrit. Here Guṇaprabha's *Vinayasūtra* and *Autocommentary* (*Vinayasūtravṛttyabhidhāna-*

In his *History of Buddhism* (*Bde bar gshegs pa'i bstan pa'i gsal byed chos kyi 'byung gnas gsung rab rin po che'i mdzod*), CWB, vol. 24 (*ya*), 155a7 (= 941), Bu ston does not mention the author. Cf. Nishioka 1981, 48 (468). Note, however, that the *Abhidharmakośaśāstrakārikābhāṣya* attributed to 'Dus bzang by Bu ston (Nishioka 1981, 49 [491]) is attributed in the Peking Catalog (Suzuki [1961] 1985, no. 5592) to 'Dul bzang (Vinītabhadra) and in the Sde dge Catalog (Ui et al. 1934a, no. 4091) to 'Dus bzang (衆賢), which I take as Saṅghabhadra.

18. Taishō 1453 (*Ekottarakarmaśataka*), 1458 (*Vinayasaṃgraha*), and 1459 (*Vinayakārikā*).

19. Petech 1990; Densapa 1977.

20. Taishō 1904 (*Genben shuoyiqieyou bu chujia shou jinyuan jiemo yifan* 根本說一切有部出家授近圓羯磨儀範) and 1905 (*Genben shuoyiqieyou bu bichu xixue lüefa* 根本說一切有部苾芻習學略法); see Kishino 2013, 6–7n4. See Qindamuni 2008 for a comparative study of Taishō 1905 with Yijing's translation of the *Bhikṣuvibhaṅga*; Qindamuni notices important differences between the two texts, especially in the section on *śaikṣa* rules (some eighteen discrepancies are reported). Qindamuni states that the Tibetan original has not survived; this appears to be incorrect (see note 21 below). See Qindamuni 2014 for a comparison of Taishō 1904 with the *Ekottarakarmaśataka*s (on which see note 29 below).

21. The two texts have almost identical Tibetan titles. See Blo gros rgyal mtshan, *Dge bsnyen dang dge tshul dang dge slong du nye bar sgrub pa'i cho ga'i gsal byed bsdus pa* and *Dge bsnyen dang dge tshul dang dge slong du nye bar sgrub pa'i cho ga'i gsal byed*. A comparative study of these two texts and their purported Chinese counterparts is a desideratum.

22. *Genben shuoyiqieyou bu jietuo jiejing shu bu* 根本說一切有部別解脱戒經疏部. Noted in Chen 2015, 13; International College for Postgraduate Buddhist Studies Library 2015, 282.

23. The extant catalogs of the Tibetan Dunhuang material are unreliable in their coverage of Vinaya texts. For a brief description of some of the problems, see Clarke 2015, 75.

24. On Tibetan Dunhuang manuscripts that transmit not the received Tibetan translation but Yijing's Chinese version, see Meng 2021 and Li 2022.

svavyākhyāna) hold pride of place, with a number of editions, re-editions, and translations already published and ongoing.[25] Given the understandable scholarly preference for texts that are preserved in Sanskrit, it is curious that one commentary in particular seems to have avoided almost all academic attention: the *Bhikṣuvinayakārikākusumasraj* (hereafter *Vinayakārikā*). It is rarely cited by anyone other than Gregory Schopen, who cites the Tibetan since the Sanskrit has remained unedited and unpublished.[26] Indeed, in the case of the *Vinayakārikā*, fourteen folios of a Sanskrit manuscript have languished in relative obscurity since their discovery was first reported in 1937 by Rāhula Sāṅkṛtyāyana (1893–1963).[27]

The lack of attention afforded the *Vinayakārikā* is unfortunate given its position among the corpus of extant Mūlasarvāstivādin Vinaya commentaries. This text is unique in at least three respects.

First, the *Vinayakārikā* is one of only two Vinaya commentaries extant in both Tibetan translation and Yijing's corpus of Chinese translations,[28] the other being Viśeṣamitra's (Khyad par bshes gnyen; Shengyou 勝友; ca. seventh century) *Vinayasaṃgraha*.[29] Moreover, it is the only one of these two for which a Sanskrit text, partial or otherwise, is preserved.

25. For details on re-editions and Japanese translations of this corpus by the study group at Taishō University, see, for convenience, Yonezawa and Nagashima 2014. Note also the important work by Luo Hong; see, inter alia, Luo 2019 (on which see Clarke 2021, 86–87n185), 2020, 2021a, and 2021b. See also Yonezawa 2020 and Shōno 2021b.

26. For select references to this text in Schopen's works, see the entries in the index of texts in Schopen 2014. See also Ende 2016, 89. For a draft edition of the Sanskrit, Tibetan, and Chinese, see Clarke, in progress.

27. On the Sanskrit manuscript, see below.

28. Note also Taishō 1473 (*Foshuo shami shijie yize jing* 佛説沙彌十戒儀則經), which appears to be a translation of the text for novices attributed to Nāgārjuna; see Liu 2017, 125; Clarke 2021, 87–88n196. A close comparison is a desideratum.

29. The author's name is sometimes reconstructed as Jinamitra. For further information on Viśeṣamitra, see Kishino's contribution in the present volume. Tibetan: *'Phags pa gzhi thams cad yod par smra ba'i 'dul ba bsdus pa* (Sde dge 4105; Peking 5606); Chinese: *Genben sapoduo bu lüshe* 根本薩婆多部律攝 (Taishō 1458). Although there is an *Ekottarakarmaśataka* extant in both Chinese (Taishō 1453) and Tibetan (Sde dge 4118; Peking 5620), I exclude these since they seem to be separate texts, with different organizational principles, that cannot easily be compared. The Chinese text is presented as if it were canonical (The text begins "At that time, the Bhagavān was . . ." [爾時薄伽梵]), whereas the Tibetan text is attributed to Guṇaprabha. A comparative study of both texts is a desideratum. According to Maeda (2001, 2), Bu ston remarks that the Tibetan text follows the structure of the *Vinayasūtra*, which it does, although I have not been able to locate the exact passage in Bu ston's *'Dul ba spyi'i rnam par gzhag pa* that Maeda states he is summarizing. In his *History of Buddhism*, Bu ston mentions that some attribute the *Ekottarakarmaśataka* to Vinītadeva (*Bde bar gshegs pa'i bstan pa'i gsal byed chos kyi*

Second, unlike the *Vinayasaṃgraha* and Guṇaprabha's *Vinayasūtra*, the *Vinayakārikā* is composed entirely in verse. Although we have a number of Mūlasarvāstivādin verse compilations for novice monks preserved in Tibetan[30] and a commentary on a verse compilation for novices preserved in Sanskrit perhaps from the Mahāsāṅghika tradition,[31] the *Vinayakārikā* is the only extant Sanskrit text transmitting an abridged, versified version of the Vinaya.

Third, according to the colophon, the Chinese translation was made while Yijing was still in Nālandā (675–685) and then revised after his return to China[32] and issued in the year 710 CE.[33] Along with Mātṛceta's *Śatapañcāśatka*, this verse text was one of only two texts translated already by Yijing in Nālandā.[34] It is notable that the first Vinaya text translated by Yijing is not a canonical Vinaya text but a digest or handbook. Of course, one should not discount the possibility that our text was translated simply because it is comparatively short in relation to the canonical Vinaya.[35] Yijing's choice, however, is perhaps suggestive of an attitude in India analogous to the situation in Tibet, where Guṇaprabha's *Vinayasūtra* and related commentaries are read and studied in

'byung gnas gsung rab rin po che'i mdzod), CWB, vol. 24 (*ya*), 113a4 (= 857): *kha cig / las brgya rtsa gcig dul ba lhas byas par 'dod do //*; Obermiller 1931, 160, in the biography of Guṇaprabha; cf. Stein and Zangpo 2013, 256. Bu ston mentions a commentary by Kalyāṇamitra on the *Ekottarakarmaśataka* that was not translated into Tibetan. *'Dul ba spyi'i rnam par gzhag pa*, CWB, vol. 21 (*zha*), 58a6–7 (= 115): *slob dpon dge legs bshes gnyen gyis mdzad pa dpal brtsegs kyi 'gyur / des mdzad pa'i las brgya rtsa gcig gi bshad pa yod de / bod du ma 'gyur /*. Note also that the distribution of *karmans* into the three classes—*jñapti*, *jñaptidvitīya*, and *jñapticaturtha*—differs between the two texts, suggesting an important institutional difference between these two separate Mūlasarvāstivādin traditions; see Clarke 2015, 81.

30. See Liu 2017 for a preliminary survey.

31. For Jayarakṣita's *Sphuṭārthā Śrīghanācārasaṅgrahaṭīkā*, see Singh 1983. For identification of the missing folio (Singh's x+95a), see Clarke 2016–2017, 205n14, and now Clarke, forthcoming a, note 68.

32. Taishō 1459.24.657b20–21: 在那爛陀已翻此頌還至都下重勘疎條.

33. Taishō 2154.55.568a14: 尊者毘舍佉造景龍四年大鳫福寺翻經院譯先在西域那爛陀寺譯出還都刪正景龍奏行.

34. Chen 2015, 2; Miyabayashi and Katō 2004, 446.

35. See the comments by Rong ston below on the voluminous nature of the canonical *Mūlasarvāstivāda-vinaya* and hence the need for handbooks. Yijing also comments on the size of the Vinaya and the comparative utility of the much shorter *Ekottarakarmaśataka*; see Taishō 1453.24.500b7–12: 右此羯磨言百一者。蓋是舉其大數。於大律中撿有多少不同。乃是以類相收無違妨也。又復聖許爲單白成。爲白二白四成。據理相應通融可足。比由羯磨本中與大律二百餘卷相勘。爲此尋撿極費功夫。後人勿致遲疑也。See also note 156 below.

monastic curricula over the canonical law code itself.[36] Since Yijing mentions Guṇaprabha (Deguang 德光) and his renown as a Vinaya master in both his travel record and account of eminent monks,[37] it is perhaps curious that Yijing did not translate the *Vinayasūtra*, the most important Mūlasarvāstivādin text on monastic discipline in Tibet even up to the present day. Yijing's early translation of the *Vinayakārikā*, however, points to its importance within the Mūlasarvāstivādin tradition known to him at Nālandā, a tradition that seems to differ from the Mūlasarvāstivādin exegetical lineage known to Guṇaprabha in Mathurā,[38] and this and many other documented differences suggest the need to understand our Mūlasarvāstivādin sources as representing not a single, unified tradition but multiple Mūlasarvāstivādin monasticisms.[39]

In sum, the *Vinayakārikā* is the only example of a Mūlasarvāstivādin verse "commentary" even partially preserved in Sanskrit, one which was chosen by Yijing as the first Vinaya text of the new wave of monastic literature to be translated and transmitted to China over the famous Guṇaprabha's (infamously difficult) *Vinayasūtra*, and one of only two Indian Vinaya commentaries translated into both Chinese and Tibetan.[40] Although the *Vinayakārikā* is clearly a text that deserves our attention, to date hardly any systematic information has been published on it.[41]

36. See Dreyfus 2003, 116–117; Jansen 2018, 18.

37. Taishō 2125.54.229b17 and b20–21. Translated in Takakusu 1896, 181–182; Li 2000, 152; Miyabayashi and Katō 2004, 358–359. Taishō 2066.51.9a12, translated in Lahiri 1986, 89, albeit erroneously giving Guṇaprabha as "Puṇyaprabha."

38. On the relationship between Guṇaprabha and Mathurā, see Clarke 2015, 73–74. As I have previously noted (2016, 53n10), explicit mention of Mathurā is found in the colophon to Guṇaprabha's *Autocommentary*; see Study Group of the *Pravrajyāvastu* in the *Vinayasūtra* 2012, 37 (omitted in Bapat and Gokhale 1982, 59). See Yonezawa 2016, 1149.

39. On multiple Mūlasarvāstivādin monasticisms, see, inter alia, Clarke 2014b, 201n45; 2015, 73; 2016, 58–59n26, 94–95; 2016–2017, 215–216n47, 268–269.

40. Both the *Vinayakārikā* and *Vinayasaṃgraha* are reported in the Dunhuang Chinese finds; see International College for Postgraduate Buddhist Studies Library 2015, 218. To my knowledge, of these two texts, only the *Vinayasaṃgraha* is found in Tibetan at Dunhuang; see Yang 2012. Note that a partially annotated manuscript of the *Vinayasaṃgraha* is available at Matho, as is an important manuscript witness to the *Vinayakārikā* (see further references in note 46 below). For an overview of Yijing's Vinaya texts found at Dunhuang, see Chen 2015, 34–40 (table 4).

41. The most detailed description to date in any European language (ten lines, mostly romanized titles) is found in Banerjee 1957, 46; although the above was correct when this paper was first written, see now Liu 2023. In Japanese, see the five lines in Maeda 2001, 2, and the useful summary, primarily on the basis of the Chinese translation, by Nishimoto Ryūzan in BKDJ 3:535.

Below, in a series of labeled sections, I discuss various problems related to the title of the text and the name of the author. I then survey the extant Sanskrit folios and the Chinese and Tibetan translations. After brief notes on the total number of verses and the various poetic meters employed, I outline the extant Tibetan commentarial tradition on the *Vinayakārikā*. I end with a discussion of a number of scholarly misunderstandings related to the *Vinayakārikā*'s composition and its relationship to the extant commentarial corpus.

Title

The Sanskrit title *Vinayakārikā* is confirmed in Tibetan phonetic transcription (*bi na ya kā ri kā*) at the head of the Tibetan translation.[42] The *Vinayakārikā* is popularly known in Tibetan sources by the alternative title *Me tog gi phreng rgyud*, which is given in the colophon.[43] This Tibetan title is usually rendered into Sanskrit as *Puṣpamālā* ("Flower Garland"), but as is often the case with such renderings this is probably little more than a good, albeit incorrect, guess.[44] Indeed, in two verses preserved almost immediately prior to the colophon (extant Sanskrit verses 346–347),[45] wherein the author dedicates the merit of his composition, we find the Sanskrit title *Kusumasraj*, corresponding to Tibetan *Me tog phreng rgyud*, but with no correspondence in the Chinese translation:

> granthanād bhikṣuvinayakārikākusumasrajaḥ |
> yad avāpi mayā puṇyaṃ tenāhaṃ saha dehibhiḥ |
> kāmajambālavimukhaḥ śraddhādibhir alaṃkṛtaḥ |
> bhūyāsam bhikṣur anyeṣu janmasv ā parinirvṛteḥ |
> (Anuṣṭubh meter)

> dge slong chos 'dul thig ler (read: tshig le'ur) byas mdzes me tog
> phreng rgyud legs brgyus las //

42. Sde dge 4123, 'Dul ba, vol. *shu*, 1b1; Peking 5625, 'Dul ba'i 'grel pa, vol. *hu*, 1a1: *bi na yā* (*sic*) *kā ri kā*.

43. Sde dge 4123, 'Dul ba, vol. *shu*, 63a4; Peking 5625, 'Dul ba'i 'grel pa, vol. *hu*, 67a6.

44. We also find *Mālākāra*; see Liu 2023.

45. Verse numbers given throughout refer to my own tentative numbering of the partial and complete verses preserved in the extant Sanskrit folios with reference to the Tibetan and Chinese translations from my draft edition in Clarke, in progress. See also note 115 below.

gang thob bsod nams dpal des 'khor ba'i lus can rnams dang lhan cig bdag /
'dod pa'i 'dam las rnam par brgal nas dad sogs yon tan kun gyis brgyan //
mya ngan 'das par tshe rabs gzhan du'ang bsnyen par rdzogs pa byed par shog /[46]

我於苾芻調伏教　略爲少頌收廣文　願得普共諸群生　因此能成福智業
五欲淤泥生厭背　恒持淨信作莊嚴　生生常得苾芻身　堅持佛語窮眞際[47]

Through what merit is sown by me,
on account of stringing together the *Flower Garland of Verses of the Vinaya for Monks*,
may I, together with [all] living creatures, in other births until final liberation, become a monk,
disinclined toward the mud of desire, adorned with faith and so on.

Author

The name of the author is usually given in secondary sources either as Viśākhadeva or the rather improbable Sagadeva.[48] The latter probably results

46. Here and in notes 51 and 160 below, I present the readings from the Matho manuscript (on which see note 113), which exhibits significant variation from the received text, initially prepared by Pema Sherpa (McMaster). The readings are presented here with only minor modifications/corrections. [61]a4–5: *dge slong 'dul ba tshig ler byas pa'i me tog 'phreng ni brgyus pa las // bsod nams gang thob de yis 'khor ba'i lus can rnams dang lhad cig dag // 'dod pa'i 'dam las rnam par rgal nas dad pa la sogs rnams kyis brgyan // mya ngan 'das par skye ba g[zha]n dag tu'ang bsnyen par rdzogs par shog /*.

47. Folio 62v4–5; Sde dge 4123, 'Dul ba, vol. *shu*, 63a1–3; Peking 5625, 'Dul ba'i 'grel pa, vol. *hu*, 67a2–4; Golden 3628, Mdo 'grel ('Dul ba), vol. *hu*, 93a4–5; Snar thang 4414, 'Dul ba'i 'grel pa, vol. *hu*, 70b3–4; Comp. Ed., vol. 93, p. 152, lines 12–16; Taishō 1459.24.657b12–15. Note that *daṇḍa*s have been presented as they appear in the Sanskrit manuscript. In certain places, the scribe uses single and double *daṇḍa*s as one would expect. In some places, such as here, we find only single *daṇḍa*s. In some places, the *daṇḍa*s have been rewritten (changing single to double, and double to single, e.g., in this verse, after *alaṃkṛtaḥ*, where a double *daṇḍa* has been changed to a single) in the manuscript. Note that in the last *pāda*, the Chinese gives "strictly upholding the Buddha's words" (堅持佛語), a phrase for which no parallel is found in the Sanskrit.

48. Teramoto 1928, 217, 218nn4–5: Sagadeva (noting that s.f.'s [= Anton Schiefner 1869, 146: Viçâkhadeva] Viçabhadeva is mistaken); Chimpa and Chattopadhyaya [1970] 2004, 197 and nn10–11: *Sagadeva or Viśākhadeva; Maeda 2001, 2: Sagadeva; Schaeffer and van der Kuijp 2009, 3n1: Sagadeva or Viśākhadeva; Sopa 2009, 221: Śakadeva; note 926: "Neither the author nor a Vinaya commentary by this name is listed in the Tōhoku catalogue."

from a misunderstanding of the Tibetan translation of the name (*sa ga'i lha*) found in the colophon as being a combination of transcription (*sa ga* for *saga*, which is well attested as a translation for Sanskrit Viśākha[49]) and translation (*lha* for *deva*), as opposed to a straight translation. In Yijing's Chinese translation, the author's name is recorded phonetically as Pishequ 毘舍佉, suggesting Viśākha and perhaps precluding Viśākhadeva.

In connection with the name of the author, we should consider the following verse (no. 344), again extant in all three languages but with enough differences and ambiguity among them to make a felicitous translation frustratingly trying.[50] In this stanza declaring the superiority of the words of men when harnessed to the word of the Well-Gone One, and even a minute poem when composed yoked to the Dharma, the author clearly identifies himself as Viśākha.

vāco nṛṇāṃ sugatavāci varaṃ prayuktāḥ
kāvyaṃ varaṃ racitam aṇv api dharmayuktaṃ |
cintābhyupāyavidhir eṣa ca me 'navadya
ity etad anyakṛtam apy akarod viśākhaḥ |
(Vasantatilakā meter)

bder gshegs bka' ni mi rnams tshig las khyad 'phags phyir //
chos gang cung zad spros kyang snyan dngags mchog gyur te //
bsam pa'i thabs kyis bsgrub 'bras kha na ma tho med //
'di de las gzhan be sha kas kyang byas pa la //[51]

言論佛教言中勝　頌陳正法頌中尊　我毘舍佉罄微心　結頌令生易方便[52]

49. Yao 2015b, 222n20; 2017, 113n17.

50. How best to understand the referent of *anya* "other" in *etad anyakṛtam* (or *etadanyakṛtam*? Cf. SWTF, s.v. *tadanya*) is unclear to me. I am unsure of what exactly our poet is contrasting here, whether it be his own poetical prowess or lack thereof (cf. the next verse; given on p. 185 below), his views on religious versus secular poetry, or his position in a commentarial lineage. This phrase is notably absent from the Chinese translation. The term *cintābhyupāyavidhi* has also proved to be anything but a method (*vidhi*) for the remedy (*abhyupāya*) of anxiety (*cintā*). I thank Jens-Uwe Hartmann for constructive comments and an enlightening exchange on this verse—for helping me understand just how little I understand—at the eleventh hour.

51. Matho [61]a2–3: *myi rnams tshig las bde' gshegs bka' ni khyad 'phags ldan // nyung zad chos ldan rnam par spras kyang snyan sngags mchog // bsaṁ pa'i thabs kyis bsgrub kyang kha na ma tho myed // 'di de las gzhan be sha kas kyang byas pa la //.*

52. Folio 62v3; Sde dge 4123, 'Dul ba, vol. *shu*, 62b7–63a1; Peking 5625, 'Dul ba'i 'grel pa, vol. *hu*, 66b8–67a1; Golden 3628, Mdo 'grel ('Dul ba), vol. *hu*, 93a2–3; Snar thang 4414, 'Dul ba'i 'grel pa, vol. *hu*, 70b1; Comp. Ed., vol. 93, p. 152, lines 6–9; Taishō 1459.24.657b8–9.

Here we see no mention of the suffix *deva* in any version of this verse. In Sanskrit the author is clearly identified as Viśākha, as is also the case in both the Tibetan and Chinese translations wherein the name is transcribed (Be sha ka; Pishequ 毘舍佉). Of course, it is possible that the author here mentions not his full name but only the first part, perhaps for metrical considerations; it might be worth noting that this verse appears almost at the end of the composition, where—or close to where—we might expect a signature.[53] As far as I know, evidence for the suffix *deva* (*lha*) as part of our author's name is found only in the colophon to the Tibetan translation and other Tibetan works that mention the author.[54]

The colophon of the Tibetan translation records our author, Śrī Ārya *Viśākha(deva) (Dpal 'Phags pa Sa ga'i lha), as being a pupil of the Mahāvinayadhara Ārya *Saṅghadāsa (*'dul ba 'dzin pa chen po 'phags pa dge 'dun 'bangs kyi slob ma*), whom the Tibetan historian Tāranātha (Kun dga' snying po, 1575–1634) lists as a contemporary of Sthiramati (ca. 475–555), Dignāga (ca. 480–540), and Guṇaprabha (ca. fifth century).[55] According to Tāranātha's *History* (completed in 1608), Saṅghadāsa was a student of Vasubandhu (fl. fourth or fifth cents.).[56] Tāranātha places Viśākha chronologically along with Guṇaprabha's disciple, *Candramaṇi (dates unknown), Candrakīrti (550–650 CE),[57] the early stages of the lives of Dharmapāla (530–561), and, perhaps problematically if we follow Akira Saitō's suggested dates,[58] Śāntideva (690–750).[59] Elsewhere, Viśākha is referred to as an arhat,[60] a designation that perhaps stands in meaningful contradistinction to Guṇaprabha's title

53. On "signed verses" in Sanskrit, see Emeneau 1955; the convention seems to be not to include the full name in these "cleverly constructed" verses. For a Buddhist example, see Harrison's argument (2007, 228–229) that *mati* is used as a double entendre for Akṣayamati, a name by which Śāntideva appears also to have been known, in the last verse of the *Bodhicaryāvatāra*.

54. On *deva* as one of the most common suffixes for Indian Buddhist poets, see Sternbach 1978–1980, 1:21 (§ 42.1). It is also possible that this suffix indicates an ordination lineage similar to the usage described in van der Kuijp 2013, 185. Note also that the colophon to the Matho manuscript (on which see note 113 below) gives the author as Vaiśākha: [61]a7: b+hai sha ka. See now also Almogi 2022, 323n84, for Bi shā khā de wa.

55. Teramoto 1928, 192; Chimpa and Chattopadhyaya [1970] 2004, 177. On references to Guṇaprabha in Chinese sources, see Taki 2001.

56. Teramoto 1928, 203; Chimpa and Chattopadhyaya [1970] 2004, 185.

57. Lang 2003, 7, and references in 210n6.

58. Saito 2018, 164.

59. Teramoto 1928, 217; Chimpa and Chattopadhyaya [1970] 2004, 197.

60. See, for instance, Bu ston, *History of Buddhism* (*Bde bar gshegs pa'i bstan pa'i gsal byed chos kyi 'byung gnas gsung rab rin po che'i mdzod*), CWB, vol. 24 (*ya*), 155a4 (= 941): *dgra bcom pa*

"bodhisattva."[61] No other works are attributed to Sa ga'i lha (Viśākha[deva]) in the Bstan 'gyur.[62] Until further evidence in support of the name Viśākhadeva appears, I am inclined to take the author at his word and call him Viśākha or Viśākha(deva).

As we have seen, very little is known about Viśākha(deva) from Buddhist sources. According to Ludwik Sternbach (1909–1981), in the various Sanskrit *subhāṣita* anthologies that have come down to us, only one verse is ascribed to Bhadanta Viśākhadeva, whom Sternbach identifies—probably justifiably—as a Buddhist monk.[63] The verse in question, in Vasantatilakā—a meter used by our author—appears in Jalhaṇa's *Sūktimuktāvalī* of 1258 CE, hence Sternbach's *terminus ad quem* of the "middle of the 13th century . . . but probably earlier." The evidence cited for an earlier date is the fact that the same verse is quoted in the *Subhāṣitaratnakaraṇḍakakathā*, a compilation traditionally "attributed to Āryaśūra from the 4th century." Michael Hahn, however, suggested that the compiler of the *Subhāṣitaratnakaraṇḍakakathā* was not the famous Āryaśūra, author of the *Jātakamālā*, but another later poet also by the name of Śūra—actually the third Āryaśūra, accepting the author of the *Pāramitāsamāsa* as the second—probably the tenth-century Kashmiri teacher Śūra mentioned by Tāranātha.[64]

Although there is some slight variation in the verse between the *Sūktimuktāvalī*[65] and the earlier *Subhāṣitaratnakaraṇḍakakathā* (chapter 5: *Puṇyakathā*),[66] the version cited in the latter is also quoted in the *Dvāviṃ-*

sa ga lhas mdzad pa 'dul ba me tog phreng brgyud bam po drug byams pa'i dpal gyi 'gyur /. Cf. Nishioka 1981, 48 (460).

61. See, for instance, his *Autocommentary*: *saṃgrahāyākarod yāni bodhisatvo guṇaprabhaḥ* / . . . (Study Group of the *Pravrajyāvastu* in the *Vinayasūtra* 2003, 52, 60).

62. Ui et al. 1934b, 99; Suzuki [1961] 1985, Index (172).

63. Sternbach 1978–1980, 2:461–462 (entry 1509).

64. Hahn 1983, 322–324; Yamasaki 2018. On the three Āryaśūras, see Hahn 1993, 36–40. Note also the recent observations by Péter-Dániel Szántó (2021, 300–301, esp. n18) with regard to the numerous quotations of works traditionally ascribed to Āryaśūra in the **Saddharmaparikathā*: "I am not of course suggesting that the work per se is by Āryaśūra after all, rather that it contains more verses of this author than was previously thought."

65. Krishnamacharya 1938, 436, lines 1–5; Sternbach 1974, 118–119 (entry 694); and Sternbach 1978–1980, 2:461–462 (entry 1509).

66. In Hahn's edition (1983, 335, verse 5.35), the verse reads: *atyucchritonnatasitadhvajapaṅkticitrair nāgāśvapattirathasaṃkṣubhitair balaughaiḥ / uddhūtacāmaravirājitagātraśobhāḥ puṇyādhikāḥ kṣitibhujo bhuvi saṃcaranti* / /; cf. Zimmermann 1975, 70–71. Hahn describes the Tibetan of the *Subhāṣitaratnakaraṇḍakakathā* as "the poorest Tibetan translation of an Indian work that I have seen in more than forty years of reading Tibetan canonical texts" (2007, 124).

śatyavadānakathā (chapter 5: *Puṇyakāmakathā*).[67] The verse,[68] whether from the *Subhāṣitaratnakaraṇḍakakathā* and *Dvāviṃśatyavadānakathā* or the *Sūktimuktāvalī*, is vaguely reminiscent of—although certainly considerably different from—our own Viśākha(deva)'s description of a monarch's military maneuvers, preserved only in Tibetan and Chinese.[69] It is unclear whether the poet Bhadanta Viśākhadeva who is quoted by name in the *Sūktimuktāvalī* and whose verse appears to have been quoted anonymously in the *Subhāṣitaratnakaraṇḍakakathā* and *Dvāviṃśatyavadānakathā* is our author.

Sanskrit Manuscript

In 1936 an incomplete Sanskrit palm-leaf manuscript was discovered by Rāhula Sāṅkṛtyāyana in the "Library-Temple" built by 'Phags pa at Sa skya monastery in Tibet.[70] Sāṅkṛtyāyana reports the existence of fourteen folios measuring 22 by 1⅝ inches, with "3, 5" lines of text on each folio side.[71] In fact, each folio has either four or five lines of text per side. Sāṅkṛtyāyana's reporting of fewer lines of text than actually exist can perhaps be explained by the

Note that this Sanskrit verse is also found in the *Mahajjātakamālā*; see Hahn and Bühnemann 1985, chapter 6 (*Cakravartijanmasugatabhajanāvadāna*), verse 57.

67. Okada 1993, 18, lines 5–8.

68. The version in the *Sūktimuktāvalī*, in which *puṇyādhikāḥ kṣitibhujo* has been replaced with *puṇyena bhūmipatayo*, was translated by A. A. Ramanathan as follows: "Kings move about in their kingdom happily, as a result of meritorious deeds done in previous births, with their bodily splendour shining by the waving chowries, accompanied by armies shaking the earth with forces of elephants, horses, chariots and foot-soldiers and rendered colourful with rows of extremely high and white fluttering banners" (Sternbach 1974, 118–119 [entry 694]).

69. Sde dge 4123, 'Dul ba, vol. *shu*, 36a6–b1; Peking 5625, 'Dul ba'i 'grel pa, vol. *hu*, 39a1–3: *rgyal po 'am ni blon po sogs // mdza' bshes tshig gis kyang rung ste // gnas pa na yang cho ga ni // rta dang glang sogs ched mi lta // dmag tshogs rnams kyi bkod pa dang // dpung dang rgyal mtshan mchog gi yang // rgyal po dang ni blon po yis // bshams pa dkrug par mi bya'o // de la dpung mchog gang du dpung // de yi bkod pa spras la bya // gang du gnas pa'i rgyal mtshan mchog // de ni rgyal mtshan mchog ces bya //*; Taishō 1459.24.640a11–16: 軍旅象馬眾 旗王及兵力 國主及大臣 見時便得罪 軍旅謂整裝 兵力謂驍勇 若立標旗處 於此號旗王 人主大臣請 有障難及怖 假使住多時 斯亦非成犯.

70. Sāṅkṛtyāyana 1937, 4 and 21: Chhag-pe-lha-khang (*phyag dpe* [Pecchia 2015, 112–113]) of Lha-khang-chhenmo. Sāṅkṛtyāyana's name is spelled Sāṅkṛityāyana in his 1935 and 1937 articles but Sāṅkṛtyāyana in 1938. I have standardized all to Sāṅkṛtyāyana.

71. Sāṅkṛtyāyana 1937, 23. The denominator is slightly unclear.

layout of the folios, which each contain two string holes placed roughly at one third and two thirds of the length of the folios. A glance at the left-hand side of certain folios might give the impression that some contain only three lines of text since the last line of text occasionally (e.g., folio 52) begins not at the left margin but close to the space created for the first string hole.[72]

Sāṅkṛtyāyana reported the following folios as extant: 41, 44, 47, 50–54, 56–59, 60, and 62. This is slightly incorrect. Folio numbers are wholly or partially[73] preserved for all extant folios bar Sāṅkṛtyāyana's 60, which is in fact folio number 46 (and photographed in the reverse order [verso, recto]).[74] Thus, the extant folios are: 41, 44, 46–47, 50–54, 56–59, and 62. Folio numbers are written on the versos of the folios.

The manuscript was photographed at least twice, once by Sāṅkṛtyāyana (or his photographer) and once by the team led by Giuseppe Tucci (1894–1984).[75] Glass negatives and photographs from the Sāṅkṛtyāyana Collection are held in the Bihar Research Society in Patna, and printed photographs are available at Göttingen State and University Library (Niedersächsische Staats- und Universitätsbibliothek Göttingen) (Shelf Number Xc 14/63). For the present study I used high-resolution digital images of the printed photographs in Göttingen. The quality of the photographs taken by Tucci is significantly inferior to those in the Sāṅkṛtyāyana Collection. In general, the left-hand sides of the folios in the Tucci Collection are blurred (as one can see in many of the reproductions in Sferra 2008b).[76] The photographs by Sāṅkṛtyāyana, on the other hand, at least of this manuscript, are crisp and very legible. The only utility to the Tucci photographs for this manuscript is that they allow one to read *akṣaras* otherwise covered up by tacks where the palm-leaf folios had been pinned to a door by Sāṅkṛtyāyana's team for the sake of photographic practicalities. Each of the four photographs taken by Sāṅkṛtyāyana records the recto

72. The string holes are approximately the height of one line of text. Around the first string hole is a well-defined space, spanning the entire height of the folios. The second string hole has not been afforded such generous spacing; in most cases, blank space around the second string hole is limited to only one or two lines.

73. Folio numbers 41 and 57 are partially covered by tacks in Sāṅkṛtyāyana's photographs. Folio number [5]3 is only partially preserved. Folio number 46 is not preserved.

74. Sāṅkṛtyāyana's 60r is in fact 46v, and 60v is 46r.

75. See Sāṅkṛtyāyana 1937, 14–15, on the insufficient "photographic knowledge of our photographer friend." On Tucci's lack of familiarity with photographic equipment, see Sferra 2008a, 15n1.

76. On photographs of this text, see Sferra 2008a, 49. The line numbers (4–5) have been corrected in Sferra, but the folio numbers remain incorrect (and in fact more incorrect: Sferra lists 60, as does Sāṅkṛtyāyana, but also 45 for 47).

or verso of seven folios. The intention seems to have been to photograph all of the rectos and versos separately. However, where folio numbers were missing and the text did not continue from one folio to the next, it was impossible to determine whether a specific folio side was either recto or verso.[77]

The script is listed by Sāṅkṛtyāyana as "Kuṭilā."[78] Francesco Sferra gives "Hooked Nepalese."[79] It is similar to the script of the *Śrāvakabhūmi*, also labeled Kuṭilā by Sāṅkṛtyāyana[80] but which Alex Wayman (1921–2004) referred to as "a popular form of Vartula"[81] and dated to the twelfth century.[82] Florin Deleanu rejects some of Wayman's observations, dating the *Śrāvakabhūmi* manuscript to the first half of the eleventh century.[83] The script of the *Vinayakārikā* manuscript also shares similarities with the Proto-Bengali-cum-Proto-Maithili script (also labeled Kuṭilā by Sāṅkṛtyāyana[84]) of the *Abhisamācārikadharma*,[85] which is the same script—written by the same scribe[86]—as that used in the *Bhikṣuṇīvinaya*, which Gustav Roth (1916–2008) dates to "the 11th (or lastest [*sic*]) 12th century."[87] Certain *akṣaras* seem to be closer to the "Nepalese hooked script" of the *Saddharmapuṇḍarīka-sūtra* manuscript dated to 1082 CE than to the Proto-Bengali-cum-Proto-Maithili script.[88]

I can offer no detailed paleographical analysis here. Needless to say, an eleventh- or twelfth-century dating of the script would put the manuscript roughly in the same ballpark as the Tibetan translation, which Leonard W. J.

77. Of course, this could have been figured out with reference to the Tibetan translation, but time was not on their side *in situ*, and Sāṅkṛtyāyana seems to have concluded that no Tibetan translation was known (see pp. 172–173 below).

78. Sāṅkṛtyāyana 1937, 23. See also Pecchia 2015, 104–106, and references therein, on the script of Manorathanandin's *Pramāṇavārttikavṛtti* copied by Vibhūticandra (on whom see Stearns 1996). The script of this manuscript (thus, Vibhūticandra's handwriting) is also described by Sāṅkṛtyāyana (1937, 33 [text no. 237]) as Kuṭilā. On Vibhūticandra's handwriting, see Sāṅkṛtyāyana 1937, 11, and the photograph between pages 10 and 11.

79. Sferra 2008a, 49.

80. Sāṅkṛtyāyana 1938, 144 (text no. 350).

81. Wayman 1961, 18.

82. Wayman 1961, 17. The script of the *Śrāvakabhūmi* has been documented in Suzuki 1995.

83. Deleanu 2006, 55.

84. Sāṅkṛtyāyana 1935, 28 (text no. 12: *Bhikṣuprakīrṇakavinaya*).

85. On the script of the *Abhisamācārikadharma*, see Matsunami 1998.

86. Roth 1970, xxi.

87. Roth 1970, xxiv.

88. Ye 2005.

van der Kuijp places "in, most likely, the eleventh century at the behest of Lha bla ma Zhi ba 'od (1016–1111)."[89] Given the fact that the extant Sanskrit manuscript also preserves Tibetan interlinear glosses (in *dbu med* script), it is not impossible that the manuscript discovered by Sāṅkṛtyāyana was used either in the process of the initial translation into Tibetan or in its subsequent revision (on which see below).[90] In this connection, it may be useful to investigate the Tibetan glosses alongside the commentary by Rong ston, the later reviser of the translation, in which, as noted by van der Kuijp, reference is made to a previous translation in various places.[91]

Chinese Translation and Content

Of the three extant texts—Sanskrit, Tibetan, and Chinese—the Chinese is, as will be explained below, the most navigable. Accordingly, it makes some sense to provide a brief overview of the content on the basis of the Chinese translation.

Yijing's Chinese translation, *Genben shuoyiqieyou bu pinaiye song* 根本說一切有部毘奈耶頌, is preserved in three fascicles (Taishō 1459.24.617b–657b).[92] The first two fascicles of the Chinese translation cover chiefly the *Bhikṣuprātimokṣa*;[93] the final fascicle digests the seventeen *Vastus*.[94] After 141

89. Van der Kuijp 2013, 186n156.

90. There are a number of texts in the Sāṅkṛtyāyana Collection for which we may possess "original" manuscripts. See note 78 above on Vibhūticandra's autograph. On Śīlākara or Steng lo tsā ba Tshul khrims 'byung gnas (1107–1190), co-translator of the *Vinayasūtravṛttyabhidhānasvavyākhyāna*, as scribe and manuscript transporter, see Yonezawa 2016.

91. Van der Kuijp 2013, 188n156, refers to the phrase *sngon 'gyur*, which I am unable to locate in the text. Note, however, that Rong ston mentions an "earlier translation" (*snga 'gyur*) approximately fifty-six times, "old translation" (*'gyur rnying*) at least four times, and "new translation" (*'gyur gsar*) some seven or so times. I assume that van der Kuijp is referring to the first two terms, all of which warrant further investigation, collectively as "*sngon 'gyur*." See also note 113 below.

92. Listed as five *juan* in the *Catalog of Buddhist Teachings [Compiled in the] Kaiyuan Period* (*Kaiyuan shijiao lü* 開元釋教録; 730 CE), Taishō 2154.55.568a14: 根本說一切有部毘奈耶頌五卷. A five-fascicle version is available in several collections in Japan, including Shōgozō 聖語蔵, Kongōji 金剛寺, Nanatsudera 七寺, Ishiyamadera 石山寺, and Kōshōji 興聖寺; see Kokusai Bukkyōgaku Daigakuin Daigaku Gakujutsu Furontia Jikkō Iinkai 国際仏教学大学院大学学術フロンティア実行委員会 2021, 225.

93. At the end of the second fascicle we read: "Both fascicles above elucidated the *Prātimokṣasūtra*. Next, the one fascicle below elucidates the *Vastus*" (Taishō 1459.24.646a15–16: 已上兩卷明波羅底木叉戒本了次下一卷明跋窣覩等也).

94. Taishō 1459.24.646a21–22: 下明於十七跋窣覩等中述其要事(跋窣覩是事).

introductory verses,[95] the text moves on to the *Prātimokṣa* rules. Navigation in the first two fascicles of the Chinese is simple since the rules are presented in their order of appearance in the *Bhikṣuprātimokṣa*. The *Prātimokṣa* rules are introduced with headings indicating groups of rules (four *pārājika*s, thirteen *saṅghāvaśeṣa*s, two *aniyata*s, thirty *naiḥsargika*s, ninety *pāyantikā*s, four *pratideśanīya*s, *śaikṣa*s, and seven *adhikaraṇaśamatha* procedures) and, in all but the last two groups, subheadings delineating individual rules within their respective groups. Although the Tibetan translation follows this order, these individual headings are not found in the Tibetan version, and the Sanskrit text for this part is mostly lost.[96]

Unfortunately, the aforementioned headings are not found in the third fascicle of the Chinese, in which Yijing tells us the *Vastu*s are digested. Thus, for the verses from the *Vastu* section, there is no clear indication in any language of which sections of the massive *Mūlasarvāstivāda-vinaya* our poet is drawing from. Moreover, the author does not limit himself to only the *Vastu*s; he—like Guṇaprabha and Viśeṣamitra—draws freely on several sections of the *Uttaragrantha* and also on the *Kṣudrakavastu*. Chapter or *Vastu* breaks are not explicitly identified in the Tibetan or the Sanskrit, although specific punctuation (a circle or dot bookended with double *daṇḍa*s, *viz*., || ∘ || or || • ||) in the Sanskrit manuscript often coincides with what appear to be thematic shifts, perhaps corresponding to *Vastu* breaks, in the text.

Unlike most other Vinaya texts translated by Yijing, the *Vinayakārikā* was not rendered into Japanese in the 1930s in the project that saw the translation of the Chinese Buddhist canon in some 257 volumes (1930–1988).[97] The only other

95. The verses are introduced with the following statement or heading: "[Here] begins elucidation of the matters of receiving ordination (*upasaṃpadā*) and of rules for essential conduct of *bhikṣu*s, etc." (Taishō 1459.24.617b7: 創明受近圓事及苾芻等要行軌式). This is most likely not meant as a direct reference to the *Pravrajyāvastu*. Yijing does not use the terms *shou jinyuan* 受近圓 or *jinyuan* 近圓 for initiation (*pravrajyā*; *chujia* 出家). The first twenty stanzas in this section discuss the motivation for distilling the entire Vinaya into a verse compilation and the benefits of equipping oneself with knowledge of Vinaya. Around verse 21 (凡欲出家者), the topic changes to the so-called impediments to ordination and other topics discussed in the *Pravrajyāvastu*. In any case, even a direct reference to the *Pravrajyāvastu* here in the final fascicle cannot be taken as evidence of a similar or identical organizational principle to that employed by Guṇaprabha in his *Vinayasūtra*, which indeed begins with the *Pravrajyāvastu*.

96. Judging from the extant Tibetan and Chinese texts, only approximately half of the section dealing with the *adhikaraṇaśamatha* procedures has survived on folio 41 (twenty-three verses, mostly in Āryā meter with one in Gīti; two of the twenty-three verses are fragmentary).

97. On Daitō Shuppansha's 大東出版社 *Kokuyaku issaikyō* 國譯一切經 (*Translation into the National Language, or Japanese, of the Entire Canon*) project, see BKDJ 12:234–239. Indian texts (Indo senjutsu-bu 印度撰述部) are contained in the first section, comprising 155

texts in Yijing's Vinaya corpus not thus rendered are the *Ekottarakarmaśataka* (Taishō 1453), the *Nidāna-Muktaka*[98] (Taishō 1452) and its *Uddāna* collection (Taishō 1456), the *Uddāna* collection of the *Kṣudrakavastu* (Taishō 1457),[99] and the two *Prātimokṣas* (Taishō 1454 and 1455).[100] Accordingly, the *Vinayakārikā* is one of the few Vinaya texts preserved in Chinese for which we lack any kind of published interpretative attempt by modern Japanese scholars of Buddhism.

Tibetan Translation

Sāṅkṛtyāyana marks his catalog entry with "T" in the fourth column,[101] indicating that the text of the Sanskrit manuscript is "Preserved in Tibetan Translation."[102] However, at the end of the single note in his catalog in which he introduces this manuscript, he writes "Here and there the translation of some sentences is found in the MS. It shows that the book was translated into Tibetan, though it is not found in the Tibetan Stangyaur (*sic*) by the

volumes (published 1930–1936); Chinese and Japanese texts (Wakan senjutsu-bu 和漢撰述部) are contained in the second section, comprising 102 volumes (published 1936–1988). The number of volumes cited here includes the index volume. By comparison, Daizō Shuppan's 大蔵出版 *Shin kokuyaku daizōkyō* 新国訳大蔵経 (*New Translation of the Tripiṭaka into the National Language*) project (1993–) has only published approximately sixty-five volumes to date (fifty-three vols. in the section on Indian texts and twelve in the section on Chinese and Japanese texts). Unfortunately, only two Vinaya volumes have been published: Satō Tatsugen's 佐藤達玄 (1924–) masterful annotated translation of the Dharmaguptaka *Prātimokṣas* (2008) and Mitomo Ryōjun's 三友量順 (1946–) annotated translation of the *Vinayamātṛkā-sūtra* (or: *-śāstra*) (*Pinimu jing* 毘尼母経) (2005), which should be consulted with considerable caution. On the *Vinayamātṛkā-sūtra/śāstra* and its relationship to the Merv Vinaya manuscript, see Clarke, forthcoming a.

98. The title of the second of these texts (*Muktaka*) has often been rendered erroneously as *Mātṛkā*. This confusion goes back at least to Nanjō Bun'yū's *Catalog* (Nanjio 1883, 250, s.v. 1134). The *Mātṛkā* is a separate text, one neither related stylistically to the *Nidāna* nor translated by Yijing. On the *Muktaka*, see Clarke 2001 and Kishino 2016.

99. On the two *Uddāna* collections or *Uddānagāthās*, see Clarke 2002, 49–51.

100. Daizō Shuppan's (2007) handy catalog to the Taishō edition provides quick references to the *Kokuyaku issaikyō* 國譯一切經 volumes (including section and volume number), indicated with the abbreviation *koku* 国 "National" after each entry, as appropriate. Unfortunately, as I recently found out, this must be used with caution; it erroneously lists no "*kokuyaku*" for Taishō 411 (大乘大集地藏十輪經), the *Daśacakrakṣitigarbha-sūtra*, but this was translated by none other than Yabuki Keiki 矢吹慶輝 (1879–1939).

101. Sāṅkṛtyāyana 1937, 23 (text no. 195).

102. See Sāṅkṛtyāyana 1935, 27.

name of Viśākha."[103] How exactly to understand this statement is somewhat unclear, but I take it to mean that Sāṅkṛtyāyana was unaware of the existence of the Tibetan translation in the Bstan 'gyur, whether attributed to Viśākha or Viśākha(deva). In any case, the Tibetan translation of the *Vinayakārikā* is found in the Bstan 'gyur as *'Dul ba tshig le'ur byas pa* (Sde dge 4123; Peking 5625; 6 *bam po*).

The details concerning the transmission of the text in Tibet are complicated.[104] According to the colophon of the extant Tibetan translation, the translation was made and revised by the Nepalese paṇḍita Jayākara, said to be a disciple of Nāropa[105] (d. 1040; fl. mid-eleventh century),[106] and the Tibetan translator Bhikṣu Prajñākīrti (Snyel cor Shes rab grags; dates unknown; fl. mid- to late eleventh century).[107] This tradition is also recorded in Gzhon nu dpal's (1392–1481) *Blue Annals* (*Deb ther sngon po*; composed 1476–1478), as discussed below.[108] Again according to the colophon, the translation was later revised by Rong ston Shes bya kun rig (Shākya rgyal mtshan) (1367–1449/51)[109] and the East Indian (Bengali) paṇḍita Vanaratna (1384–1468) from Sadnagara.[110] Bu ston rin chen grub (1290–1364), on the other hand, states that the translation was made by Byams pa'i dpal (1172–1236),[111]

---

103. Sāṅkṛtyāyana 1937, 23–24n1. It is unclear to me which catalog of the Bstan 'gyur Sāṅkṛtyāyana consulted. However, his citation of "Stan-gyur. Mdo. XLIV" (*sic*) (1935, 41n3) in relation to the "*Madhyāntavibhaṃga ṭikā*" (*viz.*, *Madhyāntavibhāgabhāṣya*) corresponds to Cordier 1915, 375 (XLV).

104. For a Tibetan transmission lineage of the *Vinayakārikā*, see the fifth Dalai Lama's (1617–1682) *Gsan yig*; see Ngag dbang blo bzang rgya mtsho, *Zab pa dang rgya che ba'i dam pa'i chos kyi thob yig gaṅgā'i chu rgyun las glegs bam dang po*, 1:13.12–14.3. See now also Liu 2023, 381–382. The lineages associated with the Vinaya works of Guṇaprabha, Śākyaprabha, and Bu ston are given on pages 14–15. On the transmission lineages (*gsan yig*) of the fifth Dalai Lama in general, see Ehrhard 2012.

105. Templeman 1983, 49, translating Tāranātha's *Bka' babs bdun ldan* "The Seven Instruction Lineages." See also Roerich [1949] 1996, 87. Here and throughout, I have benefited from the references compiled in Dan Martin's *TibSkrit Philology* [2006] 2021.

106. Lo Bue 1997, 635.

107. On Shes rab grags/Prajñākīrti, see Kragh 2010, esp. 210; Dimitrov 2000, 22n41, gives his birthdate as 1017 CE. See now Almogi 2022, 347, for the identification of Prajñākīrti (Snyel cor Shes rab grags) as Pu rangs lo chung.

108. Roerich [1949] 1996, 87.

109. On the life and works of Rong ston, founder of the Sa skya pa monastery Nalendra, see Jackson 1988, i–xxii.

110. On Vanaratna, see Niyogi 1988, 30; Ehrhard 2004; Parajuli 2014; Damron 2021. See also Almogi 2022, 323, who gives "*Sadhagara."

111. See note 60 above.

interpreter to Śākyaśrībhadra (1127/40s–1225).[112] The commentary on the text produced by Rong ston, discussed below, mentions the Indian *upādhyāya* Mūlasarvāstivādin bhikṣu paṇḍita Jayākaragupta (who is presumably the Jayākara mentioned above) along with Prajñākīrti as the translators.[113]

112. Stearns 1996, 130. Note that Liu 2023, 370, asserts—but does not demonstrate—the existence of "an alternative translation produced in the thirteenth century but now lost and little known." Liu states that this "little-known alternative translation came from Śākyaśrībhadra and his Tibetan assistant," *viz.*, Byams pa'i dpal (2023, 372). It is unclear to me whether a separate translation by Śākyaśrībhadra (or Byams pa'i dpal) was made or whether what Liu is seeing is simply confusion over the name of the translator(s), of which there is plenty. Note, however, the comments about previous translations in Rong ston's commentary mentioned in note 91 above.

113. Rong ston, *'Dul ba me tog phreng rgyud kyi rnam 'grel tshig don rab tu gsal ba'i nyi 'od*, 257b5: *rgya gar gyi mkhan po 'phags pa gzhi thams cad yod par smra ba'i dge slong paṇḍita dza yā a ka ra gup ta'i zhal snga nas dang*; see van der Kuijp 2013, 188, and now Almogi 2022, 344–347; cf. 322–323. Note that this colophon will now need to be restudied in light of the colophon from the Matho manuscript collection (W1BL9-v105); see [61]a6–b. The manuscripts are available at "Mang spro dgon pa'i mchod rten nas thob pa'i dpe rnying dum bu." Buddhist Digital Resource Center. Accessed December 30, 2023. http://purl.bdrc.io/resource/W1BL9. The verse in the Matho colophon is fuller than that preserved in Rong ston's commentary. The Matho colophon seems to name those by whom the translation was requested (underlined text found only in Matho; [61]b3): . . . *mkhas pa dza ya a kara la // sa bdag dang mtshungs blon po'i rigs // dge slong dri myed rgyal mtshan dang // rngegs phrug bsod nams tshul khrims kyis // gsol ba btab nas bdag gis bsgyurd //*. Almogi 2022, 345n164, interprets "*bdag* ('I') to be referring to Rong ston, who apparently claims to have actually translated the text anew rather than having only revised it, as suggested by the canonical colophons." In cautiously advancing this interpretation, Almogi states that it is premised on the verse not being a citation: "unless of course one understands the verse to be a citation—as implied by van der Kuijp's translation—but there is no linguistic evidence for this." The fact that a fuller verse appears in the Matho manuscript of the *Vinayakārikā* suggests that the version in Rong ston's commentary is a paraphrase, and this in turn would mean that Rong ston did not retranslate the text but merely revised the existing translation. Almogi further notes (2022, 346) that "whereas in the verse the translators are named as Prajñākīrti in collaboration with Jayākara, in the prose Rong ston records two translations—namely, one by the Indian Jayākaragupta and bsNyel 'or Prajñākīrti and a second by the Nepalese Jayākara and Prajñākīrti. This seems very unlikely for two main reasons: firstly, no other source records such two translations, and secondly, it is hard to believe that the members of the two teams had nearly identical names." The Matho manuscript makes no mention of this "second translation" by the Nepalese Jayākara and Prajñākīrti. Since the Matho manuscript does not mention a Nepalese Jayākara, I take Jayākara in the verse to be the Indian Jayākaragupta mentioned in prose, his name shortened in verse for metrical considerations. The text of the *Vinayakārikā* as preserved in the Matho collection is significantly different from the received text as it has come down to us. A full comparison of the Matho recension is a desideratum, especially with reference to Rong ston's comments about previous translations (see note 91 above).

Verse Count and Numbering

The exact number of verses contained in the complete text is unclear and of course would depend on how one divides up the verses. One not particularly careful modern paperback edition of the Tibetan text gives 1,689 verses.[114] The extant fourteen Sanskrit folios contain, by my count, approximately 348 verses;[115] averaged out over sixty-two folios, this yields 1,532 verses. In his *'Dul ba spyi'i rnam par gzhag pa*, Bu ston states that the text consists of 1,800 ślokas in six *bam po*, but this nice, round number is likely simply a calculation based on the standard ratio of three hundred ślokas per *bam po* and not reflective of a systematic count.[116]

In his catalog of the Göttingen collection of Sanskrit Buddhist texts collected by Sāṅkṛtyāyana in Tibet, Frank Bandurski refers to the notes of Gustav Roth, which apparently state that an edition was being prepared by R. N. Pandey (presumably Raghunātha Pāṇḍeya [b. 1931]).[117] To my knowledge, this has never appeared.

In a footnote to his catalog entry, Sāṅkṛtyāyana transcribes two verses from folio 41r (verses 2–3), ten verses from 62r (328–337), and eight verses from 62v (341–348). As far as I know, these twenty verses, buried in a footnote to a catalog published in 1937, are all that has ever been published of the Sanskrit text until recently.[118]

114. Tshe ring Shar pa 2005. The verses in each of the six *bam po* are numbered in this edition. Problems include the following: the verse directly after 212 (p. 170) is numbered 223 (p. 171) but should be 213; the last verse on p. 175 is unnumbered; there is no verse number 111 on p. 188.

115. This number includes partial and whole verses. At the beginning or end of a folio, occasionally we have only a few *akṣaras* remaining. See also note 45 above.

116. Bu ston, *'Dul ba spyi'i rnam par gzhag pa*, CWB, vol. 21 (*zha*), 57a1–2 (= 113): *'phags pa sa ga'i lhas / 'dul ba tshig le'ur byas pa me tog phreng rgyud / shlo ka stong brgyad brgya / bam po drug / 'dis 'dul ba'i dge slong gi bya ba gtso che rnams bsdus nas bstan pa ste / yongs su rdzogs pa bsdus pa ma yin no //*. Maeda 2001, 2, states that there are eight hundred verses, but this is probably a typo or misreading of the Tibetan. Given the late translation date, no entry is found in the two extant early (ninth century) imperial catalogs, the *Lhan kar ma* (812 CE; Herrmann-Pfandt 2008) and *'Phang thang ma* (842 CE as "the earliest possible date" of compilation [Dotson 2007, 4]; for the text, Kawagoe 2005; for a study, Halkias 2004). Likewise, it is not listed in Bcom ldan ral gri's (1227–1305) *Bstan pa rgyas pa rgyan gyi nyi 'od* (Schaeffer and van der Kuijp 2009, 163–165, "Vinaya" Section, including commentaries).

117. Bandurski 1994, 100.

118. Sāṅkṛtyāyana 1937, 23n1. For a translation and edition of verses 176–192 of the extant manuscript, see Clarke 2024. An edition and translation of verses 308–317 on oral hygiene and dental decorum was initially included in this paper, but it was cut due to the publisher's

Recently, five verses from the *Vinayakārikā* were discovered at the beginning of a second Sanskrit manuscript of the *Śikṣāsamuccaya* found in Tibet and edited by Olivier Brasseur (Lausanne) as part of his doctoral thesis.[119] The five verses consist of three stanzas of praise to the Three Jewels from the beginning of the *Vinayakārikā* and two verses from toward the end of the text. The first three verses were previously unknown in Sanskrit; the final two verses are found also in Sāṅkṛtyāyana's manuscript (verses 342–343). Péter-Dániel Szántó transcribed the verses and identified the last two as coming from the *Vinayakārikā*. Knowing I was working on the *Vinayakārikā*, Jens-Uwe Hartmann kindly sent me Szántó's transcription of the verses, from which I was able to identify the first three with the beginning of the *Vinayakārikā* and also—somewhat surprisingly—the opening of the Tibetan translation of the *Abhiniṣkramaṇa-sūtra*.[120]

Meters

Although different meters are employed throughout the text, the predominant meter in the Sanskrit manuscript is Anuṣṭubh (śloka), the work-horse of Indian poets. More sophisticated meters, including Āryā, Gīti, Praharṣiṇī, Upajāti, Upendravajrā, Vaṃśastha, and Vasantatilakā, are also used. Occasionally the Sanskrit text is metrically deficient. The Chinese translation presents most verses in quatrains of five characters, with some, usually translating the more complicated Sanskrit meters, employing seven or nine characters per

concerns about the overall length of the volume. This is unfortunate since these verses seemed like a fitting tribute for our honoree as he approaches an age at which he might be considered by some—not me—to be long in the tooth. These verses will now be published elsewhere; see Clarke, forthcoming b.

119. Brasseur 2024, 165–170.

120. For the opening verses of praise, see Sde dge 4123, 'Dul ba, vol. *shu*, 1b2–2a1; Peking 5625, 'Dul ba'i 'grel pa, vol. *hu*, 1b4–2b1; there are no corresponding verses in Yijing's Chinese translation; for the *Abhiniṣkramaṇa-sūtra* in Tibetan, see Sde dge 301, Mdo sde, vol. *sa*, 1b1–5. For the two final verses, see Sde dge 4123, 'Dul ba, vol. *shu*, 62b6–7; Peking 5625, 'Dul ba'i 'grel pa, vol. *hu*, 66b7–8; Taishō 1459.24.657b4–7. There are significant differences between the Tibetan translations of the verses in the *Vinayakārikā* and the *Abhiniṣkramaṇa-sūtra*. A detailed study of the sources of the Tibetan translation of the *Abhiniṣkramaṇa-sūtra* (*Mngon par 'byung ba'i mdo*) is a desideratum. For an overview of the structure of the *Mngon par 'byung ba'i mdo*, see Matsuda 1990. In relation to his study of the *Bimbisārapratyudgamana-sūtra*, Peter Skilling notes that the translation of the *Abhiniṣkramaṇa-sūtra* is "*identical* with the corresponding sections of the *Saṅghabhedavastu* of the Mūlasarvāstivādin *Vinaya*" (1997, 131; emphasis in original).

line. The Tibetan generally has quatrains of seven syllables, with occasional verses in four equal lines of nine, eleven, or fifteen syllables.

Tibetan Commentaries

In the *Blue Annals* (*Deb ther sngon po*; composed 1476–1478),[121] we read of commentaries made by Seng ge zil gnon (chief teacher of one of Bu ston's "five main teachers,"[122] Bsod nams mgon) and Shangs pa Jo gdan[123] after they heard the *Vinayakārikā* being taught by Śākyaśrībhadra (1127/40s–1225; in Tibet from 1204–1214) during the summer retreat at Snar blas mo che sometime between 1204 and 1213. This account is attributed to Bu ston, who, incidentally, is said to be a reincarnation of Śākyaśrībhadra.[124] Byang chub dpal (1183–1264), ordained in 1204 under Śākyaśrībhadra with Shangs pa Jo gdan as Karmācārya,[125] is also said to have composed a commentary on the *Vinayakārikā*.[126] These commentaries appear not to have survived.

At least three premodern Tibetan commentaries have come down to us,[127] and determining the exact nature of the relationship between them remains an important desideratum. Arguably the most important extant commentary is the one written by the reviser of the Tibetan translation, Rong ston (1367–1449/51): *'Dul ba me tog phreng rgyud kyi rnam 'grel tshig don rab tu gsal ba'i nyi 'od* (259 folios).[128] Although no date is available for the commentary, van der Kuijp tells us that sources put it at the end of his life, perhaps between 1448 and 1451.[129]

121. Gzhon nu dpal (1392–1481), the author of the *Blue Annals*, is said to have been a student of Vanaratna (1384–1468), one of the purported revisers of the Tibetan translation of the *Kusumasraj* (Niyogi 1988, 30; Roerich [1949] 1996, 380). On the transmission of the *Flower Garland* in Tibet, see Liu 2023.

122. Van der Kuijp 2016, 294, and 296.

123. Shangs pa Jo gdan (= Byang ston Rin chen grags); see Heimbel 2013, 194. Variant spellings of Jo gdan include Jo stan and Jo ston.

124. Hadano [1957] 1986, 243 (with variant: Snar klas mo che); Roerich [1949] 1996, 82. See also Hadano [1968] 1987, 105; Liu 2023, 373–374 (with variant: Snar glas mo che).

125. Heimbel 2013, 193–194.

126. Heimbel 2013, 194.

127. See Liu 2023, 373–376.

128. For a translation and discussion of the verse at the end of this text, in which the history of translation is mentioned, see van der Kuijp 2013, 186–189n156, esp. 187–188.

129. Van der Kuijp 2013, 188–189n156, and Liu 2023, 375.

Dka' bzhi pa Shes rab seng ge (1383–1445),[130] a student of Tsong kha pa (1357–1419) and founder of the Lower Tantric College (*rgyud smad*),[131] composed a topical outline (*'Dul ba me tog phreng rgyud kyi sa bcad*, thirty folios) and a commentary on the *Vinayakārikā* (*'Dul ba me tog phreng rgyud kyi ṭi ka legs bshad rgya mtsho*, 179 folios). Shes rab seng ge seems to have received a transmission or teachings from Rong ston.[132] The topical outline and commentary are available in two editions, one from Nepal in *dbu med* script and one in *dbu can*.[133] Both texts appear to have been written at Snar thang, and the topical outline is said to be based on an earlier work by Mchims Thams cad mkhyen pa Nam mkha' grags (1210–1285), the seventh abbot of Snar thang.[134] Shes rab seng ge's commentary has been dated by some to 1333 based on a reference in the text to a "water-female-hen" year, but this appears to be a red herring.[135] If we accept that Rong ston's commentary was written in his twilight

130. But see note 135 below.

131. Buswell and Lopez 2014, 712, s.v. Rgyud smad.

132. "Sherab Sengge." The Treasury of Lives. Accessed August 21, 2022. https://treasuryoflives.org/biographies/view/Sherab-Sengge/3762.

133. For the *dbu med* text, see Shes rab seng ge, *Commentaries on Viśakhadeva's* (*sic*) *Vinayakārikā mālākāra*, 1977. For the *dbu can* text, see Shes rab seng ge, *'Dul ba me tog phreng rgyud kyi sa bcad bka' bzhi pa shes rab seng ges mdzad pa*, and Shes rab seng ge, *'Dul ba me tog phreng rgyud kyi ṭi ka legs bshad rgya mtsho*.

134. Shes rab seng ge, *Commentaries on Viśakhadeva's Vinayakārikā mālākāra by Dka'-bźi-pa Śes-rab-seṅge of Snar-thaṅ*, English table of contents. On Mchims Thams cad mkhyen pa Nam mkha' grags and his dates, see Fushimi 2010.

135. Van der Kuijp is careful to note that the commentary itself is "undated." He writes: "The 'all-knowing lama' to whom Bsam gtan bzang po on occasion makes reference is a certain Dka' bzhi pa She rab seng ge. This Snar thang master's own undated summary and a commentary on the *Vinayakārikā*, which was petitioned by a certain Shes rab bzang po, . . . is subtitled *Legs bshad rgya mtsho*. The Dka' bzhi pa . . . does note at one point, on p. 241, that three thousand four hundred and thirty-four years had elapsed from the Buddha's passing to a water-female-hen year. Given that the Bka' gdams pa communities at Snar thang generally held that the Buddha passed away ca. 2133 B.C., this can only mean that the water-female-hen year in question is 1333" (2013, 187n156). Liu 2023, 374, referring to van der Kuijp's note, takes this as the date of composition, but later on in the same paper (382) accepts She rab seng ge's dates as 1383–1445. If we accept these dates, how She rab seng ge could have composed a commentary in 1333 is beyond me. Although discussion of a "water-female-hen" year (*chu mo bya lo*) can be located in the manuscript on the page (241) given in van der Kuijp 2013, 187n156, the number of years mentioned is 3,468 (*sum stong bzhi brgya drug bcu rtsa brgyad*) not 3,434. The text mentions that there are 1,532 years remaining, and these two numbers must total five thousand since this is a discussion of how long the Dharma will last after the Buddha's passing. See Shes rab seng ge, *Commentaries on Viśakhadeva's* (*sic*) *Vinayakārikā mālākāra* (*dbu med*), 106a7–b1 (= 241–242), and *'Dul ba me tog phreng rgyud kyi ṭi ka legs bshad rgya mtsho* (*dbu can*), 177a5–b1 (= 413–414): *lnga stong gi lugs la yang 'dod tshul du ma yod mod kyi bal po'i rgyal po 'od zer go cha*

years, between 1448 and 1451, and if we accept Shes rab seng ge's dates as 1383–1445, then we are still obliged to conclude that Shes rab seng ge's commentary precedes that by Rong ston even if we must reject the 1333 date.

The last extant premodern commentary of which I am aware is Bsam gtan bzang po's handwritten *dbu med* commentary written at Snar thang: *Me tog phreng rgyud kyi ṭīkka legs bshad rgya mtsho* (102 folios).[136] The author, whose dates appear to be unknown, is said to have been a student of Bcom ldan ral gri (1227–1305)[137] but also, perhaps confusingly, of Shes rab seng ge (1383–1445).[138] His commentary has been dated by some to 1356 but this too seems improbable, especially if we accept that he was a disciple of Shes rab seng ge.[139]

---

dang bdag nyid chen po blo ldan shes rab kyi bzhed pas chu mo bya lo yan chad la sum stong bzhi brgya drug [b]cu rtsa brgyad 'das shing da ste lo stong dang lnga brgya sum bcu rtsa gnyis nas nub par 'gyur bas . . .). My guess is that van der Kuijp's 3,434 is merely a typographical error for 3,468 (note that the *dbu med* manuscript occasionally uses numerals instead of writing out the numbers in dates). This passage is mentioned also in Rong ston's commentary (*'Dul ba me tog phreng rgyud kyi rnam 'grel tshig don rab tu gsal ba'i nyi 'od*, 256b3: *chu mo bya lo phan chad la sum stong bzhi brgya dang drug cu rtsa brgyad 'das shing*), but this is to be expected since the passage is a commentary on one of the final verses in the *Vinayakārikā* itself. Note also that Rong ston's commentary is almost verbatim identical to She rab seng ge's here, although the latter's is much fuller and the former's mentions Sakya Paṇḍita (1182–1251). Although more work is required, it seems to me that She rab seng ge's dates are more secure than 1333 as a date of composition for his commentary, especially given that the same passage appears also in Rong ston's commentary.

136. Schaeffer and van der Kuijp 2009, 3n1; van der Kuijp 2013, 187n156. See Bsam gtan bzang po, *Me tog phreng rgyud kyi ṭīkka legs bshad rgya mtsho*.

137. Schaeffer and van der Kuijp 2009, 3n1.

138. Van der Kuijp 2013, 187n156, refers to him as a "fourteenth century Bka' gdams pa scholar." Elsewhere he is given as fifteenth century; see "Snar thang pa bsam gtan bzang po." Buddhist Digital Resource Center. Accessed August 21, 2022. http://purl.bdrc.io/resource/P3JT13451.

139. Van der Kuijp 2013, 187n156; Liu 2023, 374–375. The colophon to the text itself, however, gives the date only as the ugly-face/fire-monkey year some 3,493 years after the Buddha's parinirvāṇa, which van der Kuijp argues is 1356. But if we accept 1383–1445 as the dates for Shes rab seng ge, then Bsam gtan bzang po's commentary could not have been composed in 1356 (fire-monkey in the sixth *rab byung* cycle) since the colophon also mentions the author's indebtedness to Shes rab seng ge. In the introduction to his commentary, moreover, Bsam gtan bzang po pays homage to the feet of the incomparable She rab seng ge; see Bsam gtan bzang po, *Me tog phreng rgyud kyi ṭīkka legs bshad rgya mtsho*, 1b3 (= 178): *mtshungs med shes rab seng ge'i zhabs la 'dud* /. Rather, we would need to look for a later fire-monkey year such as 1416 or 1476, being the fire-monkey years in the seventh and eighth *rab byung* cycles. Note that the modern Tibetan editor paraphrases the colophon and suggests the eighth cycle (*bod rab byung brgyad pa'i me sprel*; 1476) in the concise introduction to the author (*rtsom pa po'i ngo sprod mdor bsdus*) on p. 171. For the manuscript itself, see Bsam gtan bzang po, *Me tog phreng rgyud kyi ṭīkka legs bshad rgya mtsho*, 102a4–5 (= 381): *bla ma thaṃd (= thams cad) mkhyen pa dka' bzhi pa shes rab seng ge'i gsung la rten nas mang du thos pa bsaṃ gtan bzang pos rnam g.yengs spangs te ston pa mya*

Additionally, a recent printing of a modern edition is available: *'Dul ba me tog phreng rgyud kyi 'grel chung legs bshad kun btus.*[140]

Missteps

At least in part, the lack of reliable information on the *Vinayakārikā* may have led some astray. Priya Singh, for instance, in an astonishingly short article on the *Vinayasūtra* that curiously makes no mention of the Sanskrit edition by Sāṅkṛtyāyana (1981) or the partial edition of the *Autocommentary* by Bapat and Gokhale (1982), lists the *Vinayakārikā* as the last of six texts that "are either translations of the text [i.e., *Vinayasūtra*] into Tibetan or are the adaptation of the very text."[141] Paul Nietupski, citing Singh, refers to the *Vinayakārikā* as "[t]he last known commentarial text on the *Vinayasūtra*,"[142] and states that the *Vinayakārikā* "is included in the list of commentaries on the *Vinayasūtra*, but is in fact not a commentary but a *kārikā* summary of the contents of the *Vinayasūtra*."[143] Nietupski does not specify to which "list of commen-

ngan las 'das nas lo sum gtong bzhi brgya dgu bcu rtsa gsum pa'i dus su / gdong ngan gyi lo sa ga'i dkar phyogs tshes brgyad la dpal snar gi gtsug lag khang chen por rdzogs par sbyar ba'o.

140. Tshe ring 2011. The modern edition is helpful insofar as it embeds the root verses, unlike the aforementioned premodern commentaries. Otherwise, it seems simply to be a slightly expanded version of Rong ston's commentary, one which often provides further lexical clarity. It also stipulates the number of feet of verse per commentarial subunit (e.g., *so shing zhes pa la sogs rkang pa bzhi bcu ste* "The forty feet [of verse] starting with 'Tooth-stick,' etc., . . ." [2:394, line 5]), something which is not found in Rong ston's commentary but seems to be drawing on and abridging Shes rab seng ge's commentary (e.g., . . . *so shing bcas shing zhes pa rkang pa bzhi bcu ste*; note that the underlined first four words of this verse are also underlined—actually marked with small circles under each word—in the Tibetan xylograph [167b1]). Shes rab seng ge's text preserves the reading *so shing bcas shing* not *so shing byas shing*; whether or not such variants are meaningful requires further investigation, especially in light of the recent discovery of a significantly different version from Matho (see note 113 above) and the fact that Rong ston sometimes quotes a previous translation. Unfortunately, however, the modern edition occasionally excises discussions of the previous translation (see note 91 above) and other canonical quotations found in the manuscript version of Rong ston's commentary. Shes rab seng ge seems to indicate most if not all words, not just the first few, from the root text with circles underneath, thus enabling navigation between the root text and commentary. In his topical outline, moreover, Shes rab seng ge records the first two syllables of each verse, usually in the line below and in a smaller hand, and connects them to the relevant part of the topical outline with a dotted line.

141. Singh 1986, 106; square brackets are mine. The same article is reproduced in Singh 1994 with the addition of little more than a single paragraph and two notes (the original article had no notes).

142. Nietupski 2009, 10.

143. Nietupski 2009, 10.

taries" he is referring; it seems that he is simply accepting Singh's uncritical list, uncritically. No basis for the claim that the *Vinayakārikā* summarizes the *Vinayasūtra* is presented, and neither Singh nor Nietupski offers any evidence of a relationship between these two texts.[144] Both are probably referring to the earlier statement by Bapat and Gokhale that the Sanskrit text of the *Vinayasūtra* "along with its commentaries has been translated into Tibetan,"[145] immediately after which they provide a list of six "Tibetan works directly concerned with [the *Vinayasūtra*]," the last of which is the *Vinayakārikā*.[146] Needless to say, Bapat and Gokhale also offer no evidence of a connection between the *Vinayakārikā* and the *Vinayasūtra*.[147] Nietupski states that "Though useful in its own right as an independent treatise, the *Puṣpamālā* is of little use for understanding the *Vinayasūtra* texts and commentaries."[148] I suspect that the reason why the "*Puṣpamālā* is of little use for understanding the *Vinayasūtra* texts and commentaries" is precisely because it is "an independent treatise" and is entirely unrelated to the *Vinayasūtra* (other than insofar as they both digest the same Vinaya).

In fact, there is evidence—very old evidence—suggesting exactly the opposite of the unsubstantiated claims made by both Singh and Nietupski, and even earlier by Bapat and Gokhale, although this too seems to have been overlooked. First, in his *History of Buddhism* (*Bde bar gshegs pa'i bstan pa'i gsal byed chos kyi 'byung gnas gsung rab rin po che'i mdzod*, completed 1322), available in English since 1931, Bu ston contrasts the *Vinayakārikā* with the *Vinayasūtra* and correctly notes that the organization of the former is based primarily on the *Vibhaṅga*.[149] This is clearly different from the *Vinayasūtra*,

144. Singh's three-page article is neither particularly reliable nor authoritative. Half of the text numbers cited for the Peking edition (1986, 106), for instance, are incorrect: for 5023 read 5623; for 2624 read 5624; for 5651 read 5625 (this last error is copied over from Bapat and Gokhale 1982, xviii).

145. Bapat and Gokhale 1982, xvii.

146. Bapat and Gokhale 1982, xviii.

147. Perhaps the only thing that could be considered a connection is the fact that all six texts are contained in volumes 123–127 of the Suzuki reprint of the Peking edition.

148. Nietupski 2009, 10.

149. Bu ston, *History of Buddhism* (*Bde bar gshegs pa'i bstan pa'i gsal byed chos kyi 'byung gnas gsung rab rin po che'i mdzod*, CWB, vol. 24 (*ya*), 19b1–2 (= 670): *lung gzhi bcu bdun gyi rab byung gi gzhi dang por bstan / de nas rnam 'byed gnyis dang gzhi bcu drug bstan pa gzhir byas pa la gzhung dam pa'i zhu ba 'dul byed la sogs dag phran tshegs kyi skabs nas 'byung ba rnams ji ltar rigs par sbyar nas 'chad pa mdo rtsa dang / rnam 'byed gzhir byas nas gzhan ji ltar rigs par sbyar nas 'chad pa me tog phreng rgyud dam sum brgya pa lta bu'o //*; Obermiller 1931, 50, translates this as: "(The practical side of Early Scripture) is exposed in the *Vinaya-sūtra*, which first of all

which starts with the *Pravrajyāvastu* and digests the entire *Mūlasarvāstivāda-vinaya* based on a sequence that corresponds closely, but not exactly,[150] with the *Vastu* sequence of the *Mūlasarvāstivāda-vinaya* itself.[151]

A second piece of evidence may be found in Rong ston's commentary, wherein he discusses five distinctive features of the *Vinayakārikā* that distinguish it from the *Vinayasūtra* (*'dul ba mdo rtsa ba las khyad chos lngas khyad par du 'phags te*),[152] a claim made with considerable authority given that Rong ston is said to have lectured on the *Vinayasūtra* (and Śākyaprabha's *Prabhāvatī*).[153] In other words, for Rong ston the relationship between the *Vinayakārikā* and the *Vinayasūtra* was one of equals or even rivals but not one of subcommentarial subordination. Rong ston claims that the author of the *Vinayakārikā* was

---

demonstrates the tenets of monkhood the first of the 17 subjects of Vinaya, then, having for its principal subject-matter (the contents of) the two *Vinayavibhanga*, and the (remaining) 16 subjects, — it explains (all these points), referring to passages from the *Uttara-grantha* — the chapter of questions and that of instructions, — and the divisions of the *Vinaya-kṣudraka*, when necessary. (Other works) as the *Puṣpamālā* or the *Triçata-kārikā* expound (Vinaya) on the basis of the *Vinaya-vibhanga*, with references, when needed, to the other (canonical works on Vinaya)." Cf. Stein and Zangpo 2013, 48–49.

150. It would be wrong to conclude that the Vinaya used by Guṇaprabha contained *Vastus* with the same titles that he uses for convenience in the organization of his *Vinayasūtra*. That he knows the same *Vastu* titles as have come down to us is clear from his comments on sūtras 1 and 98 in his *Autocommentary*; see Study Group of the *Pravrajyāvastu* in the *Vinayasūtra* 2003 and 2007 for a re-edition and translation; for a revised edition and translation of parts of sūtra 98, see Yonezawa 2017.

151. Of course, the *Vibhaṅga* is dealt with in the *Vinayasūtra*; it is contained within the section on the *Poṣadhavastu*.

152. Rong ston, *'Dul ba me tog phreng rgyud kyi rnam 'grel tshig don rab tu gsal ba'i nyi 'od*, 2b1–2. Three of the five claims are repeated in a statement found in the *Par skrun gsal bshad* (= *Publication Clarification* or *Preface*) to, as it is known in its shorter title, *'Dul ba'i las chog mthong bas don 'grub* (Bkra shis phun tshogs 2012, ix): *bod kyi lo tsā ba cog ro klu'i rgyal mtshan gyis rgya gar nas bod skad du bar nas 'chad nyan gyi rgyun shin tu dar rgyas che ste / rgyal ba'i dbang po karma pa mi bskyod rdo rjes mdzad pa'i las brgya rtsa gcig pa'i 'grel pa las / slob dpon yon tan 'od kyis bshad pa rnams go rims dang bcas ste phyogs gcig tu mdzad pa 'di dag dar che zhing / zhes dang / dba' bo gtsug lag phreng bas chos 'byung mkhas pa'i dga' ston las kyang / 'dul ba me tog phreng rgyud 'di la phyis kun mkhyen rong po sogs kyis dgra bcom pas brtsams pa dang / tshigs bcad bzang por yod pa dang / gleng gzhi rtsa bas zin pa ste khyad chos gsum yod ces rtsal du bton yang dgra bcom pa las byang chub sems dpa' bsam pa rgya che ba'i rten 'brel gyis da dung mdo rtsa kho nar dar ro // zhes gsungs pa'i phyir /.*

153. Jackson 1988, v. Quite inexplicably, Liu 2023, 372–373, seems to understand Śākyaprabha's *Prabhāvatī* (*'od ldan*) to be a commentary on the *Vinayasūtra*. It is, of course, an autocommentary to his *Śrāmaṇerakārikā*.

an arhat (*rtsom pa po dgra bcom pa yin zhing*) and, if I understand Rong ston's Tibetan correctly, that the canonical Vinaya narratives (*nidāna*s) are taken up by the root text of the *Vinayakārikā* (*gleng gzhi rtsa bas zin pa dang*), that Viśākha achieved extensive meaning with an economy of words (*tshig nyung zhing don rgya che ba dang*), that its poetical composition is elegant (*tshig gi sdeb sbyor legs shing*), and that it is easily comprehended (*don go sla ba'o*).[154] As is well known, Guṇaprabha achieved unparalleled economy of expression but at the cost of comprehensibility to the degree that he had to pen an autocommentary. Of course, incomprehensibility should not be taken immediately as an indication of an unsuccessful enterprise; this is exactly what one expects of an Indian sūtra (not a Buddhist sūtra), which is to be expanded or amplified in other commentarial formats.[155]

In addition, consider the following introductory verses (preserved only in Tibetan and Chinese) in which Viśākha himself states his reasons for compiling the *Vinayakārikā*: in order to train or discipline (**vi-√nī*; *gdul ba'i phyir*) those who are to be trained he has uttered a short composition from or on the basis of the Vinaya (*'dul ba las*; 略攝毘奈耶). The goal is to make those who are lazy, of little intelligence, and frightened by the voluminous nature of the canonical Vinaya,[156] enter the ocean that is the Well-Proclaimed Vinaya without fatigue using the *Vinayakārikā* as a staircase. Below I tentatively translate the verse from the Chinese, but a translation from Tibetan would not come out too differently:

敬禮如是師　法及於聖眾　我今隨所解　略攝毘奈耶
嬾惰少慧者　於廣文生怖　雖勤亦不樂　入斯調伏海
欲令彼趣入　不起大疲勞　結頌作階梯　勝人見津路[157]

chos dang 'phags pa'i tshogs bcas kyi //
ston pa de la phyag 'tshal nas //

154. Rong ston, *'Dul ba me tog phreng rgyud kyi rnam 'grel tshig don rab tu gsal ba'i nyi 'od*, 2b2: *rtsom pa po dgra bcom pa yin zhing / gleng gzhi rtsa bas zin pa dang / tshig nyung zhing don rgya che ba dang / tshig gi sdeb sbyor legs shing don go sla ba'o //*.

155. Westerhoff 2018, 15.

156. A similar justification is cited by Dharmamitra with regard to Guṇaprabha's *Vinayasūtra*; see Peking 5622, 'Dul ba'i 'grel pa, vol. *ru*, 3a6–b1. I thank Bob Miller for bringing this passage to my attention.

157. This could also mean, I think, "[just as] a ford is seen by Victor[s]." Sde dge 4123, 'Dul ba, vol. *shu*, 2a2–4; Peking 5625, 'Dul ba'i 'grel pa, vol. *hu*, 2b2–4; Golden 3628, Mdo 'grel ('Dul ba), vol. *hu*, 2b4–3a2; Snar thang 4414, 'Dul ba'i 'grel pa, vol. *hu*, 2b2–5; Comp. Ed., vol. 93, p. 4, lines 5–11; Taishō 1459.24.617b8–13.

gdul bya rnams ni gdul ba'i phyir //
'dul ba las brtsams cung zad brjod //
le lo can dang blo dman dag /
gzhung mangs rnams kyis 'jigs pa ni (ste) //
legs gsungs 'dul ba'i rgya mtsho la //
yon tan ldan yang 'dod mi byed //
de phyir de dag gzhug don du //
skyo med 'gro ba'i che ba yi //
tshig ler (read: le'ur) byas pa'i them skas kyis //
rtag tu mu stegs ston byed bzhin //[158]

Having paid homage to this kind of Teacher, Dharma, and Noble Assembly,[159] I now, in accordance with that which has been understood (by me), summarize the Vinaya so that those who are lazy and of little wisdom, who produce fear with regard to the voluminous text, who although they strive [to understand it] still do not take pleasure in it, [may] enter this ocean of discipline.

Wishing to make them cross over and enter without causing great fatigue, I have joined verses to make a staircase [just as] a path is forded by Victor[s].

158. Rong ston, *'Dul ba me tog phreng rgyud kyi rnam 'grel tshig don rab tu gsal ba'i nyi 'od*, 4b2–5a3: *gnyis pa rtsom par dam bca' ba ni / cung zad brjod par bya'o // gang las brtsams te zhe na / 'dul ba ston pa las brtsams te'o // dgos pa gang gi don du zhe na / gdul bya rnams kyi nyon mongs pa ni 'dul bar bya ba'i phyir du'o // dus gang gi tshe na / mchod brjod kyi rjes thog nas so // 'o na lung las / mngon pa dang mdo sde ni lha dang mi gnyis la bzhag la / mdo sde ni klu la bzhag go / 'dul ba ni zab cing rtogs par dka' ba'i phyir de dag la ma bzhag ces gsungs pa ma yin nam zhe na / de ni 'dul ba'i gdul byar ma gyur pa la dgongs pas skyon med do // ci'i phyir 'dul ba las brtsams te brjod par mdzad ce na / 'dul ba ston pa ni ston pa yang dag par rdzogs pa'i sangs rgyas la mchod pa yin te / 'dul ba rnam 'byed las / dge slong ma 'gags pa 'di de bzhin gshegs pa la skyes dang bcas nas 'ongs pa yin te / de bzhin gshegs pa'i skyes ni 'di ltar 'dul ba las gzhan pa de lta bu ni med do zhes so // gsum pa dgos 'brel bshad pa gnyis te / rjod byed tshig gi dgos pa dang / brjod bya don gyi dgos pa'o // dang po ni / gdul bya le lo can dang blo shes rab dman pa mi gsal ba dag ni thub pas legs par gsungs pa 'dul ba'i rgya mtsho la gnas skabs dang mthar thug gi yon tan du ma dang ldan yang 'jug par 'dod par mi byed do // de ci'i phyir zhe na / gzhung tshig mang po dag gis 'jigs pas so // mi byed pa de'i phyir 'dul ba tshig le'ur byas pa'i gzhung gis 'dul ba'i lung gi don ston par byed do // dgos pa gang gi don du zhe na / gdul bya de dag gzhung mang bas 'jigs pa'i skyo ba med par 'dul ba'i gzhung lugs kyi rgya mtsho la gzhug pa'i don du'o // 'di las ji ltar 'dul ba la 'jug par 'gyur zhe na / chu klung gi mu'i 'bab stegs las chu ngogs su 'jug pa de bzhin du 'dul ba'i gzhung lugs la 'jug pa'i them skas lta bur gyur pa nyid kyis so // 'dul ba la zhugs nas bslab pa la dgos pa ci yod ce na / rtag tu 'gro ba'i che ba'i yon tan dang ldan pa myang 'das kyi rten mtho ris su skye bar 'gyur ba'o //.*

159. The three verses almost directly preceding this stanza, which is the fifth, sing the praises of the Three Jewels.

A similar sentiment is espoused in the following verse, found directly after the verse discussed above (no. 344; pp. 164–165). Here our poet begs the reader's indulgence, offering what is in effect an apology for any infelicities in his composition. He ends with an excuse used by all scholars of the *Mūlasarvāstivāda-vinaya* apart from Gregory Schopen: that working through the Vinaya is hard yakka, a term no doubt familiar to our honorand having completed his PhD "down under." Verse 345 reads:

> yan nyūnaṃ samadhikam anyathākṛ[ta]m vā
> pūrvoktād abhihitam ākulākulam vā |
> tat santaḥ prakṛtiśivāśayāḥ kṣamantāṃ
> kin nāndhāḥ pathi viṣame pariskhalanti ||
> (Praharṣiṇī meter)
>
> gang zhig ma tshang lhag gam yang na gzhan du byas //
> sngar bshad rnams las go rims 'chol bar bshad kyang rung //
> de kun rang bzhin zhi ba'i bsam pas bzod par mdzod //
> nyam nga'i lam du long ba rdeg 'chos min nam ci //[160]
>
> 若於聖說有增減　前後參差乖次第
> 願弘見者共相容　無目循途[161]能不失[162]
>
> May the wise, having gracious dispositions by nature, forgive that which is deficient, superfluous, or erroneously rendered or stated completely confused [in order] from what has been previously spoken.
> Do the blind not stumble on a rugged path?

In short, we have compelling statements from three reliable witnesses, all suggesting that the *Vinayakārikā* is not related to the *Vinayasūtra* in any meaningful manner. Bu ston discerns a key difference between the *Vinayakārikā* and

160. Matho [61]a3–4: *gang zhig ma tshang lhag gam yang na gzhan du byas // sngar bshad rnams las go rims chol par bshad kyang rung // de kun rang bzhin zhi ba'i bsam bas bzod par mdzod // nyam nga'i lam du long ba rdeg 'chos myin nam ci // //.*

161. Or *tu* 塗; above I have accepted the variant listed in the Taishō's apparatus over the Taishō's preferred reading.

162. Folio 62v3–4; Sde dge 4123, 'Dul ba, vol. *shu*, 63a1; Peking 5625, 'Dul ba'i 'grel pa, vol. *hu*, 67a1–2; Golden 3628, Mdo 'grel ('Dul ba), vol. *hu*, 93a3–4; Snar thang 4414, 'Dul ba'i 'grel pa, vol. *hu*, 70b1–2; Comp. Ed., vol. 93, p. 152, lines 9–12; Taishō 1459.24.657b10–11.

Vinayasūtra in terms of the core organizational principles. Rong ston enumerates five characteristics that distinguish the *Vinayakārikā* from the *Vinayasūtra*. Finally, Viśākha(deva), author of the *Vinayakārikā*, states that he has compiled the text from or on the basis of the Vinaya (*'dul ba las*; 略攝毘奈耶) for those who find the canonical Vinaya itself to be overwhelming. It seems clear, then, that the *Vinayakārikā*—more fully, the *Bhikṣuvinayakārikākusumasraj*—is a poetical composition digesting the *Mūlasarvāstivāda-vinaya*, particularly the *Bhikṣuvinaya*. Other than that it may have been conceived of as a comprehensive, comprehensible, and competing composition, it would seem to have little, if anything, to do with Guṇaprabha's *Vinayasūtra*. It is perhaps understandable, then, why this text, intended for those who are lazy and of little intelligence, who produce fear with regard to "ce Vinaya monstrueux," has been of only limited interest to the intellectually fearless Gregory Schopen.

Works Cited

Abbreviations

BDRC — Buddhist Digital Resource Center. https://www.bdrc.io.

BKDJ — *Bussho kaisetsu daijiten* 佛書解說大辭典 (*Great Dictionary Explaining Buddhist Writings*). Edited by Ono Genmyō 小野玄妙. 11 vols. (1930–1932), with supplements (vols. 12–13) edited by Maruyama Takao 丸山孝雄 (1974–1977), an additional volume 別巻 (vol. 14) entitled *Bukkyō kyōten sōron* 佛教經典總論 (*General Theory on Buddhist Scriptures*) by Ono Genmyō (1936), and an author-title index *Choshabetsu shomei mokuroku* 著者別書名目録 (1988). Tokyo: Daitō shuppan 大東出版, 1930–1988.

Comp. Ed. — Comparative Edition. See Zhongguo zangxue yanjiu zhongxin «*Dazangjing*» duikanju 2002.

CWB — *The Collected Works of Bu-ston*. Edited by Lokesh Chandra. 28 vols. Śata-piṭaka Series. Indo Asian Literatures 41–68. New Delhi: International Academy of Indian Culture, 1965–1971.

SWTF — *Sanskrit-Wörterbuch der buddhistischen Texte aus den Turfan-Funden und der kanonischen Literatur der Sarvāstivāda-Schule*. Edited by Heinz Bechert, Klaus Röhrborn, and Jens-Uwe Hartmann. 4 vols. Göttingen: Vandenhoeck & Ruprecht, 1973–2017.

Taishō — *Taishō shinshū daizōkyō* 大正新脩大藏經 (*The Buddhist Canon in Chinese, Newly Edited in the Taishō Era*). Edited by Takakusu Junjirō

高楠順次郎 and Watanabe Kaikyoku 渡邊海旭. 100 vols. Tokyo: Taishō issaikyō kankōkai 大正一切經刊行會, 1924–1935.

Tibetan Texts

Bkra shis phun tshogs, ed. and comp. *'Dul ba'i las chog mthong bas don 'grub*. Or: *Dge 'dun gyi las dang / dge 'dun dang 'brel ba'i gang zag gi las dang / gang zag gi las kyi rnam par bzhag pa go don lag len cho ga mthong bas don 'grub pa*. By Karma pa Mi bskyod rdo rje. Varanasi: Vajra Vidya Institute Library, 2012.

Blo gros rgyal mtshan. "*Dge bsnyen dang dge tshul dang dge slong du nye bar sgrub pa'i cho ga'i gsal byed* [*bsdus pa*]." In *Sa skya bka' 'bum dpe bsdur ma las 'gro mgon chos rgyal 'phags pa'i gsung 'bum*, 4:447–454. Peking: Krung go'i bod rig pa dpe skrun khang / Zhongguo zangxue chubanshe 中国藏学出版社, 2007. BDRC: W2DB4571.

———. "*Dge bsnyen dang dge tshul dang dge slong du nye bar sgrub pa'i cho ga'i gsal byed*." In *Sa skya bka' 'bum dpe bsdur ma las 'gro mgon chos rgyal 'phags pa'i gsung 'bum*, 4:455–503. Peking: Krung go'i bod rig pa dpe skrun khang / Zhongguo zangxue chubanshe 中国藏学出版社, 2007. BDRC: W2DB4571.

Bsam gtan bzang po. "*Me tog phreng rgyud kyi ṭikka legs bshad rgya mtsho*." In *Bka' gdams gsung 'bum phyogs bsgrigs*, edited by Dpal brtsegs bod yig dpe rnying zhib 'jug khang, 38 (= vol. 8 of 2nd ser.): 177–381. For the outline (*dkar chag*), see 173–176; for the modern editor's paraphrase of the colophon, see the concise introduction to the author (*rtsom pa po'i ngo sprod mdor bsdus*) on 171. Chengdu: Si khron dpe skrun tshogs pa, Si khron mi rigs dpe skrun khang / Sichuan chuban jituan, Sichuan minzu chubanshe 四川出版集团 四川民族出版社, 2007. BDRC: W1PD89084.

Ngag dbang blo bzang rgya mtsho. "*Zab pa dang rgya che ba'i dam pa'i chos kyi thob yig gaṅgā'i chu rgyun las glegs bam dang po*." In *Rgyal dbang lnga pa ngag dbang blo bzang rgya mtsho'i gsung 'bum* (五世达赖阿旺洛桑嘉措文集), vols. 1–4 (*ka–nga*). Peking: Krung go'i bod rig pa dpe skrun khang / Zhongguo zangxue chubanshe 中国藏学出版社, 2009. BDRC: W1PD107937.

Rong ston Shes bya kun rig. *'Dul ba me tog phreng rgyud kyi rnam 'grel tshig don rab tu gsal ba'i nyi 'od. A Commentary on the Vinayakārikā of Viśākhadeva by Roṅ-ston Śes-bya-kun-rig. Reproduced from Clear Prints from the Sde-dge Dgon-chen Blocks*. Manduwala: Pal Ewam Chodan Ngorpa Centre, 1985. BDRC: W8469.

Shes rab seng ge. *Commentaries on Viśakhadeva's Vinayakārikā Mālākāra by Dka'-bźi-pa Śes-rab-seṅge of Snar-thaṅ and the First Chapter of the Guhyasamāja Tantra by 'Jam-dbyaṅs Grags-pa-rgyal-mtshan: Reproduced from a Collection of Rare Manuscripts from Nepal at the Order of Mkhan-po Rin-chen*. Delhi: Trayang and Jamyang Samten, Manjutila Camp, 1977. BDRC: W1KG9604.

———. *'Dul ba me tog phreng rgyud kyi sa bcad bka' bzhi pa shes rab seng ges mdzad pa*. Thim-phu: Kunsang Topygel and Mani Dorji, 1979. BDRC: W26074.

———. *'Dul ba me tog phreng rgyud kyi ṭi ka legs bshad rgya mtsho*. Thim-phu: Kunsang Topygel and Mani Dorji, 1979. BDRC: W26074.

Tshe ring Shar pa (Dge slong), ed. and comp. *'Dul ba me tog phreng rgyud dang / dge tshul kā ri kā sum brgya pa dang / lnga bcu pa bcas*. Varanasi: Vajra Vidya Institute Library, 2005.

———, ed. and comp. *'Dul ba me tog phreng rgyud kyi 'grel chung legs bshad kun btus*. 2 vols. Varanasi: Vajra Vidya Institute Library, 2011.

Zhongguo zangxue yanjiu zhongxin «*Dazangjing*» duikanju 中国藏学研究中心《大藏经》对勘局, ed. *Zhonghua dazangjing* «Danzhuer» *(duikanben) (zangwen)* 中华大藏经《丹珠尔》（对勘本）（藏文） (*Buddhist Canon of China: Tanjur [Collated Edition] [Tibetan Text]*). Beijing: Zhongguo zangxue chubanshe 中国藏学出版社, 2002.

Secondary Sources

Almogi, Orna. 2022. "The Translation Endeavours of Shes rab grags Revisited: An Investigation of Translations Done by Pu rang lo chung Shes rab grags and 'Bro lo tsā ba Shes rab grags." *Revue d'Etudes Tibétaines* 63: 289–400.

Bandurski, Frank. 1994. "Übersicht über die Göttinger Sammlungen der von Rāhula Sāṅkṛtyāyana in Tibet aufgefundenen buddhistischen Sanskrit-Texte (Funde buddhistischer Sanskrit-Handschriften, III)." In *Untersuchungen zur buddhistischen Literatur*, 9–126. Sanskrit-Wörterbuch der buddhistischen Texte aus den Turfan-Funden, Beiheft 5. Göttingen: Vandenhoeck & Ruprecht.

Banerjee, Anukul Chandra. 1957. *Sarvāstivāda Literature*. Calcutta: D. Banerjee.

Bapat, P. V., and V. V. Gokhale, eds. 1982. *Vinaya-sūtra and Auto-Commentary on the Same by Guṇaprabha: Chapter I—Pravrajyā-vastu*. Tibetan Sanskrit Works Series 22. Patna: Kashi Prasad Jayaswal Research Institute.

Brasseur, Olivier. 2024. "Le Don chez Śāntideva: Considérations à partir d'une traduction commentée du premier chapitre du Śikṣāsamuccaya." PhD thesis, Université de Lausanne.

Buswell, Robert E., Jr., and Donald S. Lopez Jr., eds. 2014. *The Princeton Dictionary of Buddhism*. Princeton and Oxford: Princeton University Press.

Chen, Ming. 2015. "Vinaya Works Translated by Yijing and Their Circulation: Manuscripts Excavated at Dunhuang and Central Asia." Translated by Jeffrey Kotyk. *Studies in Chinese Religions* 1.3: 1–40.

Chimpa, Lama, and Alaka Chattopadhyaya, trans. [1970] 2004. *Tāranātha's History of Buddhism in India*. Edited by Debiprasad Chattopadhyaya. Reprint, Delhi: Motilal Banarsidass.

Chung, Jin-il. 1998. "'Bhikṣuṇī-Karmavācanā' of the Mūlasarvāstivādins." In *Facets of Indian Culture: Gustav Roth Felicitation Volume. Published on the Occasion of His 82nd Birthday*, edited by C. P. Sinha, 420–423. Patna: Bihar Puravid Parishad.

Clarke, Shayne. 2001. "The *Mūlasarvāstivāda Vinaya Muktaka* 根本説一切有部目得迦." *Bukkyō kenkyū* 仏教研究 (*Buddhist Studies*) 30: 81–107.

———. 2002. "The *Mūlasarvāstivādin Vinaya*: A Brief Reconnaissance Report." In *Sakurabe Hajime hakushi kiju kinen ronshū: shoki bukkyō kara abidaruma e* 櫻部建博士喜寿記念論集：初期仏教からアビダルマへ (*Early Buddhism and Abhidharma Thought: In Honor of Doctor Hajime Sakurabe on His Seventy-Seventh*

Birthday), edited by Sakurabe Hajime Hakushi Kiju Kinen Ronshū Kankōkai 櫻部建博士喜寿記念論集刊行会, 45–63. Kyoto: Heirakuji shoten 平樂寺書店.

———. 2014a. *Vinaya Texts*. Gilgit Manuscripts in the National Archives of India: Facsimile Edition 1. New Delhi and Tokyo: The National Archives of India and The International Research Institute for Advanced Buddhology, Soka University.

———. 2014b. *Family Matters in Indian Buddhist Monasticisms*. Honolulu: University of Hawai'i Press.

———. 2015. "Vinayas." In *Brill's Encyclopedia of Buddhism*, vol. 1: *Literature and Languages*, edited by Jonathan A. Silk, Oskar von Hinüber, and Vincent Eltschinger, 60–87. Leiden and Boston: Brill.

———. 2016. "The *'Dul bar byed pa* (*Vinītaka*) Case-Law Section of the Mūlasarvāstivādin *Uttaragrantha*: Sources for Guṇaprabha's *Vinayasūtra* and Indian Buddhist Attitudes towards Sex and Sexuality." *Journal of the International College for Postgraduate Buddhist Studies* 20: 49–196.

———. 2016–2017. "Lost in Tibet, Found in Bhutan: The Unique Nature of the Mūlasarvāstivādin Law Code for Nuns." *Buddhism, Law & Society* 2: 199–292.

———. 2021. "On Some Curious Cases Where the Buddha Did *Not* Make a Rule: Palliative Care, Assisted Suicide, and Abortion in an Indian Buddhist Monastic Law Code." *International Journal of Buddhist Thought & Culture* 31.1: 13–113.

———. 2024. "A Short Sermon on Impermanence Preserved in Viśākha(deva)'s *Bhikṣu-vinaya-kārikā-kusuma-sraj*. In *Buddhakṣetrapariśodhana: A Festschrift for Paul Harrison*, edited by Charles DiSimone and Nicholas Witkowski, 123–157. Marburg: Indica et Tibetica Verlag.

———. Forthcoming a. "Searching for Authority in Vinaya Matters: On the Sanskrit Merv Manuscript and Its Parallels in the *Vinaya in Ten Recitations* (十誦律) and the **Vinaya-mātṛkā-śāstra* (毘尼母經)." *Indo-Iranian Journal*.

———. Forthcoming b. "Digesting the Dharma: Viśākha(deva)'s Vinaya Verses on Dental Decorum."

———. In progress. "A Preliminary Edition of the Sanskrit, Tibetan, and Chinese text of Viśākha(deva)'s *Bhikṣuvinayakārikākusumasraj*."

Cordier, P. 1915. *Catalogue du fonds tibétain de la Bibliothèque nationale: Troisième partie, Index du Bstan-ḥgyur (Tibétain 180–332.)*. Paris: Imprimerie Nationale, Ernest Leroux.

Dagpa, Lobsang, Migmar Tsering, and Ngawang Samten Chophel, trans. 1975. *The Discipline of the Novice Monk Including: Ācārya Nāgārjuna's* The (Discipline) of the Novice Monk of the Āryamūlasarvāstivādīn (*sic*) in Verse *and Vajradhara Ngorchen Kunga Zangpo's* Word Explanation of the Abridged Ten Vows, the Concise Novice Monks' Training. Mussoorie: Sakya College.

Daizō Shuppan Henshū-bu 大蔵出版編集部, ed. 2007. *Taishō shinshū daizōkyō sōmokuroku* 大正新脩大蔵経総目録 (*Complete Catalog of the Buddhist Canon in Chinese, Newly Edited in the Taishō Era*). Tokyo: Daizō shuppansha 大蔵出版社.

Damron, Ryan C. 2021. "Deyadharma—A Gift of the Dharma: The Life and Works of Vanaratna (1384–1468)." PhD thesis, University of California, Berkeley.

Deleanu, Florin. 2006. *The Chapter on the Mundane Path* (Laukikamārga) *in the* Śrāvakabhūmi: *A Trilingual Edition (Sanskrit, Tibetan, Chinese), Annotated*

Translation, and Introductory Study, vol. 1: *Introductory Study, Sanskrit Diplomatic Edition, Sanskrit Critical Edition*. Studia Philologica Buddhica, Monograph Series 20a. Tokyo: The International Institute for Buddhist Studies of the International College for Postgraduate Buddhist Studies.

Densapa, Tashi. 1977. "A Short Biography of 'Gro-mgon Chos-rgyal 'Phags-pa." *Bulletin of Tibetology* 13.3: 5–14.

Dimitrov, Dragomir. 2000. "Lakṣmī°—On the Identity of Some Indo-Tibetan Scholars of the 9th–13th Centuries." *Zentralasiatische Studien* 30: 9–26.

Dore, R. P. 1965. *Education in Tokugawa Japan*. Berkeley and Los Angeles: University of California Press.

Dotson, Brandon. 2007. "'Emperor' Mu rug btsan and the *'Phang thang ma Catalogue*." *Journal of the International Association of Tibetan Studies* 3: 1–25.

Dreyfus, Georges B. J. 2003. *The Sound of Two Hands Clapping: The Education of a Tibetan Buddhist Monk*. Berkeley: University of California Press.

Ehrhard, Franz-Karl. 2004. "Spiritual Relationships Between Rulers and Preceptors: The Three Journeys of Vanaratna (1384–1468) to Tibet." In *The Relationship Between Religion and State* (chos srid zung 'brel) *in Traditional Tibet: Proceedings of a Seminar Held in Lumbini, Nepal, March 2000*, edited by Christoph Cüppers, 245–265. LIRI Seminar Proceedings Series 1. Lumbini: Lumbini International Research Institute.

———. 2012. "'Flow of the River Gaṅgā': The gSan-yig of the Fifth Dalai Bla-ma and Its Literary Sources." In *Studies on the History and Literature of Tibet and the Himalaya*, edited by Roberto Vitali, 79–96. Kathmandu: Vajra Publications.

Eimer, Helmut (ヘルムート・アイマー). 1986. "Chibetto daizōkyō kanjuru no kairitsubu ni okeru tekisuto no hairetsu junjo" 西蔵大蔵経甘殊爾の戒律部におけるテキストの配列順序 (The Order of Arrangement of Texts in the Vinaya Section of the Kanjur of the Tibetan Tripiṭaka). Translated by Okada Yukihiro 岡田行弘. *Bukkyōgaku* 佛教學 (*Journal of Buddhist Studies*) 20: 1–10.

———. 1987. "Zur Reihenfolge der Texte in der Abteilung Vinaya des tibetischen Kanjur." *Zentralasiatische Studien* 20: 219–227.

Emeneau, M. B. 1955. "Signed Verses by Sanskrit Poets." *Indian Linguistics* 16: 41–52.

Ende, Rein. 2016. "The *Mūlasarvāstivāda Vinaya*: An Attempt at an *Index Locorum* with a Focus on the Works of Gregory Schopen." MA project, McMaster University.

Fushimi Hidetoshi 伏見英俊. 2010. "mChims Nam-mkha'-grags to sNar-thang-ji no gakukei ni tsuite" mChims Nam-mkha'-grags と sNar-thang 寺の学系について (mChims Nam-mkha'-grags and the sNar-thang-pa Tradition). *Kansai daigaku tōzai gakujutsu kenkyūsho kiyō* 関西大学東西学術研究所紀要 (*Bulletin of the Institute of Oriental and Occidental Studies, Kansai University*) 43: 21–33.

Hadano Hakuyū 羽田野伯猷. [1957] 1986. "Kāśmīra-mahāpaṇḍita 'Śākyaśrībhadra': chibetto kinsei bukkyōshi: josetsu" Kāśmīra-mahāpaṇḍita 'Śākyaśrībhadra': チベット近世仏教史・序説 (The Kāśmīra-mahāpaṇḍita 'Śākyaśrībhadra': Early-Modern Buddhist History of Tibet: An Introduction). Reprinted in Hadano Hakuyū 羽田野伯猷, *Chibetto, indogaku shūsei* チベット・インド学集成 (*Col-*

lected Studies on Tibet and India), vol. 1: *Chibetto hen* I チベット篇 I (*Tibet Section I*), 239–258. Kyoto: Hōzōkan 法蔵館.

———. [1968] 1987. "Chibetto no bukkyō juyō no jōken to hen'yō no genri no ichisokumen" チベットの仏教受容の条件と変容の原理の一側面 (One Aspect of the Receptive Conditions and the Principles of Change of Buddhism in Tibet). Reprinted in Hadano Hakuyū 羽田野伯猷, *Chibetto, indogaku shūsei* チベット・インド学集成 (*Collected Studies on Tibet and India*), vol. 2: *Chibetto hen* II チベット篇 II (*Tibet Section II*), 3–195. Kyoto: Hōzōkan 法蔵館.

Hahn, Michael. 1983. *Die Subhāṣitaratnakaraṇḍakakathā: Ein spätbuddhistischer Text zur Verdienstlehre*. Göttingen: Vandenhoeck & Ruprecht.

———. 1993. "Notes on Buddhist Sanskrit Literature: Chronology and Related Topics." In *Studies in Original Buddhism and Mahāyāna Buddhism in Commemoration of Late Professor Dr. Fumimaro Watanabe*, edited by Egaku Mayeda, 31–58. Kyoto: Nagata Bunshodo.

———. 2007. "Striving for Perfection: On the Various Ways of Translating Sanskrit into Tibetan." *Pacific World: Journal of the Institute of Buddhist Studies*, 3rd ser., 9: 123–149.

Hahn, Michael, and Gudrun Bühnemann. 1985. *Der grosse Legendenkranz (Mahajjātakamālā). Eine mittelalterliche buddhistische Legendensammlung aus Nepal*. Asiatische Forschungen 88. Wiesbaden: Otto Harrassowitz.

Halkias, Georgios T. 2004. "Tibetan Buddhism Registered: A Catalogue from the Imperial Court of 'Phang Thang." *The Eastern Buddhist*, n.s., 36.1–2: 46–105.

Harrison, Paul. 2007. "The Case of the Vanishing Poet: New Light on Śāntideva and the *Śikṣā-samuccaya*." In *Indica et Tibetica: Festschrift für Michael Hahn. Zum 65. Geburtstag von Freunden und Schülern überreicht*, edited by Konrad Klaus and Jens-Uwe Hartmann, 215–248. Vienna: Arbeitskreis für Tibetische und Buddhistische Studien Universität Wien.

———. 2014. "Earlier Inventories of Sanskrit Manuscripts in Tibet: A Synoptic List of Titles." In *From Birch Bark to Digital Data: Recent Advances in Buddhist Manuscript Research. Papers Presented at the Conference Indic Buddhist Manuscripts: The State of the Field, Stanford, June 15–19 2009*, edited by Paul Harrison and Jens-Uwe Hartmann, 279–290. Vienna: Verlag der Österreichischen Akademie der Wissenschaften.

Hartmann, Jens-Uwe, and Klaus Wille. 2014. "The Manuscript of the Dīrghāgama and the Private Collection in Virginia." In *From Birch Bark to Digital Data: Recent Advances in Buddhist Manuscript Research. Papers Presented at the Conference Indic Buddhist Manuscripts: The State of the Field, Stanford, June 15–19 2009*, edited by Paul Harrison and Jens-Uwe Hartmann, 137–155. Vienna: Verlag der Österreichischen Akademie der Wissenschaften.

Heimbel, Jörg. 2013. "The Jo gdan tshogs sde bzhi: An Investigation into the History of the Four Monastic Communities in Śākyaśrībhadra's Vinaya Tradition." In *Nepalica-Tibetica: Festgabe for Christoph Cüppers*, edited by Franz-Karl Ehrhard and Petra Maurer, 1:187–241. Beiträge zur Zentralasienforschung 28. Andiast: International Institute for Tibetan and Buddhist Studies GmbH.

Herrmann-Pfandt, Adelheid. 2008. *Die lHan kar ma: Ein früher Katalog der ins Tibe-*

tische übersetzten buddhistischen Texte. Kritische Neuausgabe mit Einleitung und Materialien. Vienna: Verlag der Österreichischen Akademie der Wissenschaften.

International College for Postgraduate Buddhist Studies Library, comp. 2015. *A Concordance to the Taishō Canon and Dunhuang Buddhist Manuscripts*. 3rd (provisional) ed. The Taishō Canon Concordance Series 2. Tokyo: International College for Postgraduate Buddhist Studies Library.

Jackson, David P., ed. 1988. *Rong-ston on the Prajñāpāramitā Philosophy of the Abhisamayālaṃkāra: His Sub-Commentary on Haribhadra's 'Sphuṭārthā.' A Facsimile Reproduction of the Earliest Known Blockprint Edition, from an Exemplar Preserved in the Tibet House Library, New Delhi*. Edited in collaboration with Shunzo Onoda. Kyoto: Nagata Bunshodo.

Jansen, Berthe. 2018. *The Monastery Rules: Buddhist Monastic Organization in Pre-Modern Tibet*. Oakland: University of California Press.

Kawagoe Eishin 川越英真. 2005. *dKar chag 'Phang thang ma*. Tohoku Society for Indo-Tibetan Studies, Monograph Series 3. Sendai: Tōhoku indo-chibetto kenkyūkai 東北インド・チベット研究会.

Kishino Ryōji 岸野亮示. 2006. "Futatsu no *Uttaraguranta*: '*Upāri mondō*' no kōsatsu" 2つの『ウッタラグランタ』:「ウパーリ問答」の考察 (The Two *Uttaragranthas*: A Study of the *Questions of Upāli*). MA thesis, Kyoto University.

———. 2013. "A Study of the *Nidāna*: An Underrated *Canonical* Text of the *Mūlasarvāstivāda-vinaya*." PhD thesis, University of California, Los Angeles.

———. 2016. "A Further Study of the *Muktaka* of the *Mūlasarvāstivāda-vinaya*: A Table of Contents and Parallels." *Bukkyō daigaku bukkyō gakkai kiyō* 佛教大学仏教学会紀要 (*Bulletin of the Association of Buddhist Studies, Bukkyo University*) 21: 227–283.

———. 2018. "From Gyōnen 凝然 to Hirakawa Akira 平川彰: A Cursory Survey of the History of Japanese *Vinaya* Studies with a Focus on the Term *Kōritsu* 広律." *Bukkyō daigaku bukkyō gakkai kiyō* 佛教大学仏教学会紀要 (*Bulletin of the Association of Buddhist Studies, Bukkyo University*) 23: 85–118.

———. 2019. "Ritsu sonja Nishimoto Ryūzan: Ōtani daigaku to '*Konpon-setsuissaiubu ritsu*' kenkyū" 律尊者 西本龍山:大谷大学と「根本説一切有部律」研究 (Vinayadhara Nishimoto Ryūzan [1888–1976]: Studies of the *Mūlasarvāstivāda-vinaya* at Otani University). *Bukkyōgaku seminā* 佛教學セミナー (*Buddhist Seminar, Otani University*) 109: 27–66.

Kokusai Bukkyōgaku Daigakuin Daigaku Gakujutsu Furontia Jikkō Iinkai 国際仏教学大学院大学学術フロンティア実行委員会, ed. 2021. *Nihon genson hasshu issaikyō taishō mokuroku* 日本現存八種一切経対照目録 (*A Concordance to Eight Buddhist Canons Extant in Japan*). Tokyo: Kokusai bukkyōgaku daigakuin daigaku 国際仏教学大学院大学.

Kragh, Ulrich Timme. 2010. "On the Making of the Tibetan Translation of Lakṣmī's **Sahajasiddhipaddhati*: 'Bro Lotsā ba Shes rab Grags and His Translation Endeavors. (Materials for the Study of the Female Tantric Master Lakṣmī of Uḍḍiyāna, Part I)." *Indo-Iranian Journal* 53.3: 195–232.

Krishnamacharya, Embar. 1938. *The Sūktimuktāvalī of Bhagadatta Jalhana*. Baroda: Oriental Institute.

van der Kuijp, Leonard W. J. 2013. "Some Remarks on the Textual Transmission and Text of Bu ston Rin chen grub's *Chos 'byung*, a Chronicle of Buddhism in India and Tibet." *Revue d'Etudes Tibétaines* 25: 115–193.

———. 2016. "The Lives of Bu ston Rin chen grub and the Date and Sources of His *Chos 'byung*, a Chronicle of Buddhism in India and Tibet." *Revue d'Etudes Tibétaines* 35: 203–308.

Lahiri, Latika, trans. 1986. *Chinese Monks in India: Biography of Eminent Monks Who Went to the Western World in Search of the Law during the Great T'ang Dynasty*. Buddhist Traditions Series 3. Delhi: Motilal Banarsidass.

Lang, Karen C., trans. and intro. 2003. *Four Illusions: Candrakīrti's Advice for Travelers on the Bodhisattva Path*. New York: Oxford University Press.

Lee, Hyebin. 2024a. "A Preliminary Report on the Sanskrit Manuscript of the *Uttaragrantha* of the Mūlasarvāstivāda *Vinaya*." *Religions* 15.6: 669. https://doi.org/10.3390/rel15060669.

———. 2024b. "A Study of the Māṇavikā Chapter in the Uttaragrantha with Newly Identified Sanskrit Fragments." PhD thesis, University of Oslo.

Lévi, Sylvain. 1909. "Les saintes écritures du bouddhisme: Comment s'est constitué le Canon sacré." In *Conférences faites au Musée Guimet*, edited by T. Homolle, Salomon Reinach et al., 105–129. Paris: Ernest Leroux.

Li, Channa. 2022. "By No Means Doodles or Scraps: Reading Manuscripts IOL Tib J 3 and 218 as Bilingual Dunhuang Vinaya Works." *Bulletin of the School of Oriental and African Studies* 85.2: 265–305.

Li, Rongxi, trans. 2000. *Buddhist Monastic Traditions of Southern Asia: A Record of the Inner Law Sent Home from the South Seas*. BDK English Tripiṭaka 93-I. Berkeley: Numata Center for Buddhist Translation and Research.

Liu, Cuilan. 2017. "A Survey of Vinaya Texts on Novice Precepts Preserved in Tibetan." In *Rules of Engagement: Medieval Traditions of Buddhist Regulation*, edited by Susan Andrews, Jinhua Chen, and Cuilan Liu, 111–133. Hamburg Buddhist Studies Series 9. Bochum and Freiburg: Projekt Verlag.

———. 2023. "*Flower Garland*: The Transmission of the *Vinayakārikā Mālākāra* in Tibet." In *Histories of Tibet: Essays in Honor of Leonard W. J. van der Kuijp*, edited by Kurtis R. Schaeffer, Jue Liang, and William A. McGrath, 367–386. Somerville, MA: Wisdom Publications.

Lo Bue, Erberto F. 1997. "The Role of Newar Scholars in Transmitting the Indian Buddhist Heritage to Tibet (c. 750–c. 1200)." In *Les habitants du toit du monde: Études recueillies en hommage à Alexander W. Macdonald*, edited by Samten Karmay and Philippe Sagant, 629–658. Nanterre: Société d'ethnologie.

Luo, Hong. 2019. "Guṇaprabha." In *Brill's Encyclopedia of Buddhism*, vol. 2: *Lives*, edited by Jonathan A. Silk, Richard Bowring, Vincent Eltschinger, and Michael Radich, 198–203. Leiden and Boston: Brill.

———. 2020. "The Cakrabhedavastu of Guṇaprabha's *Vinayasūtra*." *Journal of Indian and Tibetan Studies* 24: 49–56.

———. 2021a. "The Parikarmavastu of Guṇaprabha's *Vinayasūtra*." *Journal of Indian and Tibetan Studies* 25: 174–211.

———. 2021b. "The Karmabhedavastu of Guṇaprabha's *Vinayasūtra*." *Acta Asiatica Varsoviensia* 34: 97–143.

Maeda Takashi 前田崇. 2001. "Chibetto ni okeru kairitsu-kan (1)" チベットにおける戒律観 (1)(Vinaya and Śīlasaṃvara in Tibetan Buddhism [1]). *Tendai gakuhō* 天台学報 (*Journal of Tendai Buddhist Studies*) 43: 1–8.

Martin, Dan, comp. [2006] 2021. "Tibskrit Philology: A Bio-Bibliographical Reference Work." Edited by Alexander Cherniak. https://tibeto-logic.blogspot.com.

Matsuda Yūko 松田祐子. 1990. "Zōyaku Abhiniṣkramaṇa-sūtra kenkyū (jo)" 蔵訳 Abhiniṣkramaṇa-sūtra 研究 (序) (The Tibetan Translation of the *Abhiniṣkramaṇa-sūtra*: Introduction). *Nippon bukkyō gakkai nenpō* 日本仏教学会年報 (*Journal of the Nippon Buddhist Research Association*) 55: 5–25.

Matsunami, Yasuo. 1998. "The Script of the *Abhisamācārika-Dharma* Palm-Leaf Manuscript." In *A Guide to the Facsimile Edition of the Abhisamācārika-Dharma of the Mahāsāṃghika-Lokottaravādin*, edited by Abhisamācārika-Dharma Study Group, 131–154. Tokyo: The Institute for Comprehensive Studies of Buddhism, Taisho University.

Meng, Xiaoqiang. 2021. "A Preliminary Study of the Dunhuang Tibetan Fragments of the *Mūlasarvāstivāda-Ekottarakarmaśataka* (I): *Tarjanīyakarman*." *Acta Asiatica Varsoviensia* 34: 205–241.

Mitomo Ryōjun 三友量順. 2005. *Binimo-kyō* 毘尼母経 (*Vinayamātṛkā-sūtra*). Shin kokuyaku daizōkyō: Ritsu-bu 新国訳大蔵経：律部 (New Translation of the Tripiṭaka into the National Language: Vinaya Section) 10. Tokyo: Daizō shuppan 大蔵出版.

Miyabayashi Shōgen 宮林昭彦 and Katō Eiji 加藤栄司. 2004. *Gendaigo-yaku* Nankai kiki naihōden*: nana seiki indo bukkyō sōgya no nichijō seikatsu* 現代語訳 南海寄帰内法伝：七世紀インド仏教僧伽の日常生活 (*A Modern Translation of* A Record of the Inner Law Sent Home from the South Seas: *The Daily Life of the Seventh-Century Indian Buddhist Saṅgha*). Kyoto: Hōzōkan 法蔵館.

Mullin, Glenn H., and Lobsang Rabgay (also spelt Rapgay), trans. 1978. *Lama Mipam's Commentary to Nagarjuna's Stanzas For a Novice Monk together with Tsong Khapa's Essence of the Ocean of Vinaya*. Dharamsala: Library of Tibetan Works and Archives.

Nanjio, Bunyiu. 1883. *A Catalogue of the Chinese Translation of the Buddhist Tripiṭaka: The Sacred Canon of the Buddhists in China and Japan*. Oxford: The Clarendon Press.

Nietupski, Paul K. 2009. "Guṇaprabha's *Vinayasūtra* Corpus: Texts and Contexts." *Journal of the International Association of Tibetan Studies* 5: 1–19.

Nishimoto Ryūzan 西本龍山, trans. 1933–1938. *Ritsu-bu* 律部 (*Vinaya Section*) 19–26. In *Kokuyaku issaikyō* 國譯一切經 (*Translation into the National Language, or Japanese, of the Entire Canon*). Tokyo: Daitō shuppansha 大東出版社.

Nishioka Soshū 西岡祖秀. 1981. "*Pu tun bukkyōshi* mokuroku-bu sakuin II" 『プトゥン仏教史』目録部索引 II (Index to the Catalogue Section of Bu-ston's "History of Buddhism" [II]). *Tōkyō daigaku bungakubu bunka kōryū kenkyū shisetsu kenkyū kiyō* 東京大学文学部文化交流研究施設研究紀要 (*Annual Report of the Institute for the Study of Cultural Exchange*) 5: 43–94.

Niyogi, Puspa. 1988. "Buddhist Scholars of Ancient Bengal: Part Two." *Annali dell'Università degli studi di Napoli "L'Orientale." Rivista del Dipartimento di Studi Asiatici e del Dipartimento di Studi e Ricerche su Africa e Paesi Arabi* 48.1: 11–34.

Obermiller, E. 1931. *History of Buddhism (Chos-ḥbyung) by Bu-ston*. Part I: *The Jewelry of Scripture*. Translated from Tibetan by E. Obermiller with an Introduction by Prof. Th. Stcherbatsky. Heidelberg: In Kommission bei O. Harrassowitz, Leipzig.

Okada, Mamiko. 1993. *Dvāviṃśatyavadānakathā: Ein mittelalterlicher buddhistischer Text zur Spendenfrömmigkeit. Nach zweiundzwanzig nepalesischen Handschriften kritisch herausgegeben*. Indica et Tibetica 24. Bonn: Indica et Tibetica Verlag.

Parajuli, Punya Prasad. 2014. "Vanaratna and His Activities in Fifteenth-Century Nepal." In *Himalayan Passages: Tibetan and Newar Studies in Honor of Hubert Decleer*, edited by Benjamin Bogin and Andrew Quintman, 289–300. Studies in Indian and Tibetan Buddhism. Somerville, MA: Wisdom Publications.

Pecchia, Cristina. 2015. *Dharmakīrti on the Cessation of Suffering: A Critical Edition with Translation and Comments of Manorathanandin's* Vṛtti *and Vibhūticandra's Glosses on* Pramāṇavārttika II.190–216. With the assistance of Philip Pierce. Brill's Indological Library 47. Leiden: Brill.

Petech, Luciano. 1990. *Central Tibet and the Mongols: The Yüan - Sa-skya Period of Tibetan History*. Serie Orientale Roma 65. Rome: Istituto Italiano per il Medio ed Estremo Oriente.

Qindamuni 欽達木尼. 2008. "*Genben shuoyiqieyou bu bichu xixue lüefa* ni tsuite" 『根本説一切有部苾芻習学略法』について (On 'Phags-pa's *Summary Teachings on the [Moral] Training of Mūlasarvāstivādin Monks*). *Sengokuyama ronshū* 仙石山論集 (*Sengokuyama Journal of Buddhist Studies*) 4: 196–174 (reverse pagination).

———. 2014. "*Genben shuoyiqieyou bu chujia shou jinyuan jiemo yifan* (*Bichu xixue lüefa fu*) ni tsuite" 『根本説一切有部出家授近圓羯磨儀範（苾芻習學略法附）』について (On the *Genben shuoyiqieyou bu chujia shou jinyuan jiemo yifan*). *Sengokuyama bukkyōgaku ronshū* 仙石山仏教学論集 (*Sengokuyama Journal of Buddhist Studies*) 7: 166–116 (reverse pagination).

Roerich, George N., trans. [1949] 1996. *The Blue Annals*. 2nd ed. Reprint, Delhi: Motilal Banarsidass.

Roloff, Carola. 2020. *The Buddhist Nuns' Ordination in the Tibetan Canon*. Hamburg Buddhist Studies Series 15. Bochum and Freiburg: Projekt Verlag.

Roth, Gustav, ed. 1970. Bhikṣuṇī-Vinaya: *Including* Bhikṣuṇī-Prakīrṇaka *and a Summary of the* Bhikṣu-Prakīrṇaka *of the Ārya-Mahāsāṃghika-Lokottaravādin*. Tibetan Sanskrit Works Series 12. Patna: Kashi Prasad Jayaswal Research Institute.

Saito, Akira. 2018. "Facts or Fictions: Reconsidering Śāntideva's Names, Life, and Works." *Journal of the International College for Postgraduate Buddhist Studies* 22: 1–20.

Sāṅkṛtyāyana, Rāhula. 1935. "Sanskrit Palm-Leaf Mss. in Tibet." *Journal of the Bihar and Orissa Research Society* 21.1: 21–43.

———. 1937. "Second Search of Sanskrit Palm-Leaf Mss. in Tibet." *Journal of the Bihar and Orissa Research Society* 23.1: 1–57.

———. 1938. "Search for Sanskrit Mss. in Tibet." *Journal of the Bihar and Orissa Research Society* 24.4: 137–163.

———. 1981. *Vinayasūtra of Bhadanta Guṇaprabha*. Singhi Jain Śāstra Śiksāpītha Singhi Jain Series 74. Bombay: Bharatiya Vidya Bhavan.

Satō Tatsugen 佐藤達玄. 2008. *Shibun ritsu biku kaihon, Shibun ritsu bikuni kaihon* 四分律比丘戒本・四分律比丘尼戒本 (The *Four-Part Vinaya Bhikṣuprātimokṣa* and the *Four-Part Vinaya Bhikṣuṇīprātimokṣa*). Shin kokuyaku daizōkyō: Ritsubu 新国訳大蔵経：律部 (New Translation of the Tripiṭaka into the National Language: Vinaya Section) 7. Tokyo: Daizō shuppan 大蔵出版.

Schaeffer, Kurtis R., and Leonard W. J. van der Kuijp. 2009. *An Early Tibetan Survey of Buddhist Literature: The* Bstan pa rgyas pa rgyan gyi nyi 'od *of Bcom ldan ral gri*. Harvard Oriental Series 64. Cambridge, MA: The Department of Sanskrit and Indian Studies, Harvard University.

Schiefner, Anton, trans. 1869. *Târanâtha's Geschichte des Buddhismus in Indien*. St. Petersburg: Commissionäre der Kaiserlichen Akademie der Wissenschaften.

Schopen, Gregory. 2004. *Buddhist Monks and Business Matters: Still More Papers on Monastic Buddhism in India*. Studies in the Buddhist Traditions. Honolulu: University of Hawai'i Press.

———. 2014. *Buddhist Nuns, Monks, and Other Worldly Matters: Recent Papers on Monastic Buddhism in India*. Studies in the Buddhist Traditions. Honolulu: University of Hawai'i Press.

———. 2025. *Property and Privilege in a Buddhist Monastic Code: A Sanskrit Text and Translation of Two Books of the Mūlasarvāstivādavinaya*. Rocher Indology Series. New York: Oxford University Press.

Sferra, Francesco. 2008a. "Sanskrit Manuscripts and Photographs of Sanskrit Manuscripts in Giuseppe Tucci's Collection." In *Sanskrit Texts from Giuseppe Tucci's Collection: Part I*, edited by Francesco Sferra, 15–78. Manuscripta Buddhica 1. Serie Orientale Roma 104. Rome: Istituto Italiano per l'Africa e l'Oriente.

———. 2008b. *Sanskrit Texts from Giuseppe Tucci's Collection: Part I*. Manuscripta Buddhica 1. Serie Orientale Roma 104. Rome: Istituto Italiano per l'Africa e l'Oriente.

Shōno Masanori 生野昌範. 2012. "Vinayavibhaṅga no shinshutsu bonbun shahon dankan" Vinayavibhaṅga の新出梵文写本断簡 (A Newly Identified Sanskrit Fragment of the Vinayavibhaṅga in the Private Collection, Virginia). *Indogaku bukkyōgaku kenkyū* 印度學佛教學研究 (*Journal of Indian and Buddhist Studies*) 61.1: 328–324 (reverse pagination).

———. 2016. "Vinayavibhaṅga no bonbun shahon dankan ni okeru mondaiten" Vinayavibhaṅga の梵文写本断簡における問題点 (On Sanskrit Fragments of the Vinayavibhaṅga in the Private Collection, Virginia). *Indogaku bukkyōgaku kenkyū* 印度學佛教學研究 (*Journal of Indian and Buddhist Studies*) 64.2: 830–825 (reverse pagination).

———. 2018. "Amerika gasshūkoku Vājinia-shū no puraibēto korekushon ni okeru shinshutsu sansukuritto-go shahon dankanshū" アメリカ合衆国ヴァージニア州のプライベート・コレクションにおける新出サンスクリット語写本断簡集

(Newly Identified Fragments in a Private Collection in Virginia, USA). *Bulletin of the International Institute for Buddhist Studies* 1: 61–75.

———. 2020a. "*Vinaya-uttaragrantha* no *Upāliparipṛcchā*, Prātideśanikā dai 2–4 jō ni sōtō suru sansukuritto-go dankan" *Vinaya-uttaragrantha* の *Upāliparipṛcchā*, Prātideśanikā 第2–4条に相当するサンスクリット語断簡 (Sanskrit Fragments from Prātideśanikā 2–4 of the *Upāliparipṛcchā* in the *Vinaya-uttaragrantha*). *Bulletin of the International Institute for Buddhist Studies* 3: 91–120.

———. 2020b. "*Konpon-setsuissaiu-bu ritsu* ni zoku suru *Vinayavibhaṅga*, Pāyattikā dai 6 jō no sansukuritto-go dankan" 『根本説一切有部律』に属する *Vinayavibhaṅga*, Pāyattikā 第6条のサンスクリット語断簡 (Sanskrit Fragments of Pāyattikā 6 of the *Vinayavibhaṅga* Belonging to the *Mūlasarvāstivāda-vinaya*). *Journal of the International College for Postgraduate Buddhist Studies* 24: 166–123.

———. 2021a. "*Konpon-setsuissaiu-bu ritsu* ni zoku suru *Vinayavibhaṅga* no Naissargikā Pāyattikā dainijō ni sōtō suru sansukuritto-go dankan" 根本説一切有部律に属する *Vinayavibhaṅga* の Naissargikā Pāyattikā 第二条に相当するサンスクリット語断簡 (Sanskrit Fragments from Naissargikā Pāyattikā 2 of the *Vinayavibhaṅga* Belonging to the *Mūlasarvāstivādavinaya*). *Bulletin of the International Institute for Buddhist Studies* 4: 33–70.

———. 2021b. "*Vinayasūtravṛttyabhidhānasvavyākhyāna* no furukute atarashii sansukuritto-go shahon" *Vinayasūtravṛttyabhidhānasvavyākhyāna* の古くて新しいサンスクリット語写本 (More Folios Belonging to the *Vinayasūtravṛttyabhidhānasvavyākhyāna*). *Journal of the International College for Postgraduate Buddhist Studies* 25: 63–92.

Singh, Priya Sen. 1986. "The Vinaya Sūtra of Guṇaprabha: A Historical Note." *Buddhist Studies: The Journal of the Department of Buddhist Studies, University of Delhi* 10: 105–107.

———. 1994. "The Vinaya-Sūtra of Guṇaprabha: An Appraisal." In *Sarvāstivāda and Its Traditions*, edited by Sanghasen Singh, 168–172. Delhi: Department of Buddhist Studies, Delhi University.

Singh, Sanghasen. 1983. *A Study of the Sphuṭārthā Śrīghanācārasaṅgraha-ṭīkā*. 2nd ed. Tibetan Sanskrit Works Series 24. Patna: Kashi Prasad Jayaswal Research Institute.

Skilling, Peter. 1997. *Mahāsūtras: Great Discourses of the Buddha*, vol. 2: *Parts 1 and 2*. Sacred Books of the Buddhists 46. Oxford: The Pali Text Society.

Sopa, Geshé Lhundub, trans. 2009. *The Crystal Mirror of Philosophical Systems: A Tibetan Study of Asian Religious Thought. Grub mtha' shel gyi me long.* With E. Ann Chávez and Roger R. Jackson. By Thuken Losang Chökyi Nyima (Thu'u bkwan Blo bzang cho kyi nyi ma; 1737–1802). Edited by Roger R. Jackson. The Library of Tibetan Classics 25. Somerville, MA: Wisdom Publications.

Stearns, Cyrus. 1996. "The Life and Tibetan Legacy of the Indian *Mahāpaṇḍita* Vibhūticandra." *Journal of the International Association of Buddhist Studies* 19.1: 127–171.

Stein, Lisa, and Ngawang Zangpo. 2013. *Butön's History of Buddhism in India and Its Spread to Tibet: A Treasury of Priceless Scripture*. The Tsadra Foundation Series. Boston and London: Snow Lion.

Sternbach, Ludwik. 1974. *Mahā-subhāṣita-saṁgraha: Being an Extensive Collection of Wise Sayings in Sanskrit Critically Edited with Introduction, English Translation, Critical Notes, etc.*, vol. 1: *Subhāṣitas* nos. 1–1873. Hoshiarpur: Vishveshvaranand Vedic Research Institute.

———. 1978–1980. *A Descriptive Catalogue of Poets Quoted in Sanskrit Anthologies and Inscriptions*. 2 vols. Wiesbaden: Otto Harrassowitz.

Study Group of the *Pravrajyāvastu* in the *Vinayasūtra* [*Ritsukyō 'Shukkeji'* Kenkyūkai 『律経』「出家事」研究会]. 2003. "*Ritsukyō 'Shukkeji'* no kenkyū (1)" 『律経』「出家事」の研究 (1) (The *Pravrajyāvastu* in the *Vinayasūtra* [1]). *Taishō daigaku sōgō bukkyō kenkyūsho nenpō* 大正大学綜合佛教研究所年報 (*Annual of the Institute for Comprehensive Studies of Buddhism, Taisho University*) 25: 44–93.

———. 2007. "*Ritsukyō 'Shukkeji'* no kenkyū (4)" 『律経』「出家事」の研究 (4) (The *Pravrajyāvastu* in the *Vinayasūtra* [4]). *Taishō daigaku sōgō bukkyō kenkyūsho nenpō* 大正大学綜合佛教研究所年報 (*Annual of the Institute for Comprehensive Studies of Buddhism, Taisho University*) 29: 26–65.

———. 2012. "*Ritsukyō 'Shukkeji'* no kenkyū (8)" 『律経』「出家事」の研究 (8) (The *Pravrajyāvastu* in the *Vinayasūtra* [8]). *Taishō daigaku sōgō bukkyō kenkyūsho nenpō* 大正大学綜合佛教研究所年報 (*Annual of the Institute for Comprehensive Studies of Buddhism, Taisho University*) 32: 29–44.

Suzuki, Daisetz T. [1961] 1985. *The Tibetan Tripitaka: Peking Edition: Catalogue & Index*. Reduced-size ed. Kyoto: Rinsen Book Co.

Suzuki, Kōshin. 1995. "The Script of the Śrāvakabhūmi Manuscript." In *Studies on the Buddhist Sanskrit Literature*, edited by the Śrāvakabhūmi Study Group and the Buddhist Tantric Texts Study Group: The Institute for Comprehensive Studies of Buddhism, Taisho University, 21–38. Tokyo: The Sankibo Press.

Szántó, Péter-Dániel. 2021. "Buddhist Homiletics on Grief (*Saddharmaparikathā, *ch. 11*)." *Indo-Iranian Journal* 64.4: 291–347.

Takakusu, J. 1896. *A Record of the Buddhist Religion as Practised in India and the Malay Archipelago (A.D. 671–695) by I-tsing*. Oxford: The Clarendon Press.

Taki Eikan 瀧英寛. 2001. "Chūgoku bukkyō bunken shiryō ni mirareru Tokkō Guṇaprabha ni tsuite" 中国仏教文献資料に見られる徳光 Guṇaprabha について (Guṇaprabha in Chinese Buddhist Sources). *Bukkyō bunka gakkai kiyō* 仏教文化学会紀要 (*Journal of Research Society of Buddhism and Cultural Heritage*) 10: 21–36.

Templeman, David, trans. and ed. 1983. *Tāranātha's Bka'.babs.bdun.ldan: The Seven Instruction Lineages by Jo.nang. Tāranātha*. Dharamsala: Library of Tibetan Works and Archives.

Teramoto Enga 寺本婉雅, trans. 1928. *Tāranātha* Indo bukkyōshi ターラナータ印度佛教史 (Tāranātha's *History of Buddhism in India*). Tokyo: Heigo shuppansha 丙午出版社.

Ui Hakuju 宇井伯壽, Suzuki Munetada 鈴木宗忠, Kanakura Yenshō 金倉圓照, and Tada Tōkan 多田等觀, eds. 1934a. *Chibetto daizōkyō sōmokuroku* 西藏大藏經總目錄 (*A Complete Catalogue of the Tibetan Buddhist Canons [Bkaḥ-ḥgyur and Bstan-ḥgyur]*). Sendai: Tōhoku teikoku daigaku 東北帝國大學.

———. 1934b. *Chibetto daizōkyō sōmokuroku sakuin* 西藏大藏經總目錄索引 (*A Cat-*

alogue-Index of the Tibetan Buddhist Canons [Bkaḥ-ḥgyur and Bstan-ḥgyur]). Sendai: Tōhoku teikoku daigaku 東北帝國大學.

Wakabayashi, Judy. 2005. "The Reconceptualization of Translation from Chinese in 18th-Century Japan." In *Translation and Cultural Change: Studies in History, Norms and Image Projection*, edited by Eva Hung, 121–145. Benjamins Translation Library 61. Amsterdam and Philadelphia: John Benjamins Publishing Co.

Wayman, Alex. 1961. *Analysis of the Śrāvakabhūmi Manuscript*. University of California Publications in Classical Philology 17. Berkeley and Los Angeles: University of California Press.

Westerhoff, Jan. 2018. *The Golden Age of Indian Buddhist Philosophy*. Oxford: Oxford University Press.

Yamasaki, Kazuho. 2018. "On the Author of the *Subhāṣitaratnakaraṇḍakakathā*." *Indogaku bukkyōgaku kenkyū* 印度學佛教學研究 (*Journal of Indian and Buddhist Studies*) 66.3: 1056–1062.

Yang Benjia 杨本加. 2012. Genben sapoduo bu lüshe *yanjiu* 《根本萨婆多部律摄》研究 (*Research on the* Mūlasarvāstivādin Vinayasaṃgraha). Beijing: Minzu chubanshe 民族出版社.

Yao, Fumi. 2013. "A Brief Note on the Newly Found Sanskrit Fragments of the *Bhaiṣajyavastu* of the *Mūlasarvāstivāda-vinaya*." *Indogaku bukkyōgaku kenkyū* 印度學佛教學研究 (*Journal of Indian and Buddhist Studies*) 61.3: 72–77.

———. 2015a. "A Preliminary Report on the Newly Found Sanskrit Manuscript Fragments of the *Bhaiṣajyavastu* of the Mūlasarvāstivāda *Vinaya*." *Indo ronrigaku kenkyū* インド論理学研究 (*Indian Logic*) 8: 289–303.

———. 2015b. "The Story of Dharmadinnā: Ordination by Messenger in the Mūlasarvāstivāda *Vinaya*." *Indo-Iranian Journal* 58.3: 216–253.

———. 2017. "Dharmadinnā Becomes a Nun: A Story of Ordination by Messenger from the Mūlasarvāstivāda *Vinaya*. Translated from the Tibetan Version." *Asian Literature and Translation* 4.1: 105–148.

———. 2018. "Two Sanskrit Manuscripts of the Mūlasarvāstivādin *Bhaiṣajyavastu* from Gilgit." *Waseda Institute for Advanced Study: Research Bulletin* 10: 91–102.

———. 2019. "*Konpon-setsuissaiu-bu ritsu yakuji* no shinshutsu shahon: genson jōkyō, kōsei no mondai, girugitto shahon to no kankei" 根本説一切有部律薬事の新出写本：現存状況、構成の問題、ギルギット写本との関係 (The Newly Identified Manuscript of the *Bhaiṣajyavastu* of the Mūlasarvāstivāda *Vinaya*: Its Present Status, Structure, and Relationship with the Gilgit Manuscript). *Bukkyōgaku* 佛教學 (*Journal of Buddhist Studies*) 60: 1–19.

Ye, Shaoyong. 2005. *Akṣara List of the Manuscript of the Saddharmapuṇḍarīkasūtra (1082 CE, Collection of Sanskrit Mss. Formerly Preserved in the China Ethnic Library)*. Research Institute of Sanskrit Manuscripts & Buddhist Literature, Peking University. http://www.fanfoyan.com/resour/pale/saddharma.pdf.

Yonezawa, Yoshiyasu. 2016. "sTeng lo tsā ba Tshul khrims 'byung gnas: Tibetan Translator of the *Vinayasūtravṛtty-abhidhāna-svavyākhyāna*." *Indogaku bukkyōgaku kenkyū* 印度學佛教學研究 (*Journal of Indian and Buddhist Studies*) 64.3: 1147–1154.

———. 2017. "The *Vinayasūtra* and the *Mūlasarvāstivāda-Vinaya*." *Indogaku bukkyōgaku kenkyū* 印度學佛教學研究 (*Journal of Indian and Buddhist Studies*) 65.3: 1171–1178.

———. 2020. "Sanskrit Manuscripts of the *Vinayasūtravṛtti-abhidhāna-svavyākhyāna*." In *Sanskrit Manuscripts in China III: Proceedings of a Panel at the 2016 Beijing International Seminar on Tibetan Studies, August 1 to 4*, edited by Birgit Kellner, Xuezhu Li, and Jowita Kramer, 445–456. Beijing: China Tibetology Publishing House.

Yonezawa, Yoshiyasu, and Jundō Nagashima. 2014. "The Sanskrit Manuscript Research Project at Taisho University." In *From Birch Bark to Digital Data: Recent Advances in Buddhist Manuscript Research. Papers Presented at the Conference Indic Buddhist Manuscripts: The State of the Field, Stanford, June 15–19 2009*, edited by Paul Harrison and Jens-Uwe Hartmann, 323–332. Vienna: Verlag der Österreichischen Akademie der Wissenschaften.

Zimmermann, Heinz. 1975. *Die Subhāṣita-ratna-karaṇḍaka-kathā (dem Āryaśūra zugeschrieben) und ihre tibetische Übersetzungen: Ein Vergleich zur Darlegung der Irrtumsrisiken bei der Auswertung tibetischer Übersetzungen*. Wiesbaden: Otto Harrassowitz.

Buddhist Monks, Outdated Technology, and Meditation

Kate Crosby

Introduction

As I write from my home in southern England gazing out over my small orchard, I am reminded that it is a bumper harvest for wasps this year. While newspaper reports have focused on those currently enjoying the windfalls, the rowdy, cider-swilling social variety, of which there are just eight different kinds in the UK, my attention has been drawn to those that avoid the limelight, the solitary wasps, of which the UK alone has over seven thousand species. It is not the shy wasps themselves that catch my eye but the spectacular evidence that they leave behind: galls on trees and other plants at the periphery of my garden, particularly the oaks. Silk button, spangle, knopper, marble, and oak apple—their colorful, resonant names capture the variegated, textured outcrops, distortions of budding acorns induced by a range of oak gall wasps to house their young through their incubation and early life.[1] These names have disappeared from everyday parlance, but once they were just that, everyday, for the solitary wasp's technique of fashioning the oak gall was crucial for medieval monastics of the northern hemisphere to produce ink for writing manuscripts. The pulverized, tannin-rich galls combined with iron sulfates to produce indelible purple and red-brown inks that adhered to vellum and paper, darkening after application. From the fifth to nineteenth centuries, monks throughout Europe would have been rejoicing at such a bumper harvest of galls and restocking the stationery cupboard for the cold months of manuscript copying ahead.

Although this technology was in use for at least two thousand years, from Pliny the Elder in the first century CE through to Leonardo da Vinci and

1. On the seventy-nine varieties of British oak galls and the creatures that cause them, see Williams 2006.

even the American Postal Service—which had its own special recipe—it could have been forgotten as easily as the names, but for the iron compounds. Still required in the ink of legal documents in Germany and the UK because of its permanence, the iron shows up using spectrometry, allowing us to date medieval European manuscripts, detect the ghosts lurking in palimpsests, and even read fragments of texts without opening them.[2] The traces allow us to read the lines and between them, opening up a vista not just to a now-peripheral technology that long pervaded and determined the everyday life of both lay persons and monastics in Europe but also to the thoughts and lives of entire cultures and communities.

Gregory Schopen is widely recognized as having opened up new vistas onto the day-to-day lives and worldviews of monks of South Asia, those of ancient Buddhist communities, and sites long uninhabited. He has transformed Buddhist studies and scholarship in other fields, as eloquently conveyed by the tributes at an event held in his honor in May 2019 to mark his retirement.[3] By reading the lines and between them, he has shifted our gaze from what was, and for some still is, regarded as center-stage in the study of Buddhism—meditation, renunciation, doctrine, and the preservation of texts—to monks' involvement in a varied range of religious, business, financial, familial, and practical activities. With his first ground-breaking and oft-cited work appearing in 1975, nearly half a century ago, he has inspired several generations of scholars to both emulation and reaction, with both responses furthering the field. Using the combined resources of archeology, texts, humor, and a whodunnit writing style, he has shown us how to take the everyday lives of early Buddhist monks seriously, and their spiritual lives not so seriously.

This approach by Schopen has revolutionized our subject, and here I want to push for the further turning of the wheel—or rather the cogs—of one area of Buddhist studies that this has illuminated: the early and ongoing Buddhist monastic involvement in technology. Like the wasp galls and related technology of European monasticism, some of this involvement may be barely visible now, hidden by time and change as well as by essentializing through reform and political change of assumptions and practical expectations of what being a monk should entail. Nonetheless, as Schopen has shown, traces remain. What has sparked my interest is that some of these traces are to be found in a rather unexpected place: meditation. I propose to show here that the practice

2. Nesměrák and Němcová 2012.

3. "Fellow Scholars Deliver Affectionate Tribute to Gregory Schopen." UCLA International Institute. Accessed September 1, 2019. https://www.international.ucla.edu/Institute/article/205229.

of meditation was also shaped by the practical technologies of monastic life that have been uncovered in the writings of Schopen and those he inspired. While those writings take delight in the social monks, the rowdier the better, evidence suggests that meditation monks, like the oak gall wasps, were also busy constructing complex means to enhance the effectiveness of their practice. This contribution suggests that meditation was itself understood as a practical technology in far more literal a sense than has previously been realized, and as such was influenced by close connections to the pragmatic world of its context. The structures I shall examine, evidenced in manuals generated by meditators at some period between the fifth to nineteenth centuries CE, reveal some of these connections and suggest further avenues to pursue in developing the historiography of Buddhism. Before turning to look at the influence of practical technologies on premodern Buddhist meditation, I shall first review some of the ways in which monks and monasteries were involved in, and even led the way in developing, practical technologies.

The Involvement of Buddhist Monastics in Technology

The association between Buddhist monks and technology—that is, the practical application of knowledge or science, is most well recognized in relation to the technology of writing, used—albeit without the ingredient of oak galls—to preserve texts of different kinds through manuscript production, inscriptions, and, in East Asia, print. The study and preservation of texts is one of the two occupations the Buddha assigns to monks in a number of canonical passages—the other being meditation—and it is this technological expertise that has provided us with such rich evidence for their lives and concerns.

As Schopen has shown, the claim that religious texts and meditation are the only permitted occupations for monks was a widely repeated form of polemical rhetoric from at least the Kuṣāṇa period by those reacting against what they perceived as a broadening out of the business of monks.[4] Among the other occupations for monks widely recognized in scholarship is the early association with medicine. This pertains even in areas of medicine that might seem surprising for a celibate monastic order, such as obstetrics, the care of the mother-to-be and the unborn child in the womb. The monastic familiarity with obstetrics is reflected in the advanced understanding of the development of the embryo found in the *Sāratthapakāsinī*, the commentary on the Saṃyutta Nikāya, including the recognition of the role of the umbilical cord in providing nutrition to the developing fetus, as demonstrated by Leslie

4. Schopen 1999.

(R. A. H. L.) Gunawardana, whose important work demonstrating extensive monastic involvement in practical matters such as the economy, medicine, and agriculture complements Schopen's own.[5]

Schopen has pointed to further types of technology in which monks were involved. Some seem to be natural extensions of a monastic schedule, such as horology to provide the means for measuring time, while others, such as minting coins, have overturned our understanding of what monastic life might entail.[6] Potential avenues for further research include brewing, even if only in relation to medicine, and textiles, since the using and mending of cloth was an important component of monastic life, with concerns that the saṅgha might be running a fabric business occasionally turning up in narratives.[7]

Another technology in which monks were involved was monumental architecture, often in relation to stūpas and sites for relics. Reaction against such involvement found in some "proto-Mahāyāna" sūtras, whose compilers reassert the importance of texts and meditation for monks and glorify the forest as the place to pursue them, has contributed to Schopen's reassessment of the earlier scholarly understanding of early Mahāyāna as a lay-oriented movement, demonstrating that at least some strands of early Mahāyāna were concerned with reasserting forest-living and strict monasticism.[8] Schopen has shown that the role of monks in construction could nonetheless be substantial, entailing not just receiving the gift of the building but contributing to the donations, overseeing the works, and even engaging in the construction itself, a role monks still find themselves in to this day. This activity has left behind the other main source of evidence for Buddhist history—namely, the spectacular archeological remains that grace the South Asian peninsula.

Monastic Hydrology

Among the types of monumental architecture in which monks were involved, again highlighted by Gunawardana, was the management of irrigation and water storage. Gunawardana was working on Sri Lanka, where the monumental reservoirs were sponsored by a variety of donors, including successive

5. Gunawardana 1984–1985, 18–20.

6. On clocks, see Schopen 1998; on minting coins, see Schopen 1991, 8–9.

7. See, for example, the Pāli canonical-commentarial *Jātaka* 157 (Rouse 1895, 18). I have noticed terminology relating to fabric and sewing, as well as methods for spoiling the taste of alcohol intended only for medicinal use while reading Pāli Vinaya commentaries in the past, but unfortunately I have not retained relevant notes.

8. Schopen 1999, 284–285, 298–299.

kings famous also for their patronage of Buddhism. To this day these tanks continue to enable rice cultivation in Sri Lanka's inland dry zone. Drawing on inscriptions and texts, including the Pāli commentaries and chronicles, Gunawardana shows very direct monastic involvement in the management of the irrigation systems based around these reservoirs. Particularly revealing is the following passage he cites from the *Samantapāsādikā*, one of the two commentaries on the Pāli *Vinaya* attributed to Buddhaghosa.[9] It offers guidance on how to use the monastery's control over the irrigation system to persuade—we might say coerce—new farmers who have taken over a particular stretch of land to make offerings to the monks. If they fail to do so:

> [I]t is permissible to stop the supply of water; but this should be done in the ploughing season and not in the crop season. And if the people were to say, "Reverend sirs, even in the past people raised crops with water from this reservoir," then they should be told, "They helped the *saṅgha* in such and such manner, and provided the *saṅgha* with such and such articles." And if they say, "We, too, shall do so," it is permissible to accept what they offer.[10]

Here the reservoir has been built for the monks on land they own, but they in turn control it in order to ensure further support from those in the surrounding region whose farming is reliant on the irrigation system supplied by that reservoir. Archeological investigations by Coningham et al. in the Anurādhapura region, with its large, sophisticated reservoirs and irrigation system, indicate that Buddhist monasteries were key in administering these sites and home to other forms of technology such as metalwork and lapidary.[11] The review of inscriptional evidence of irrigation management in the region by Abeywardana et al., while complicating the picture in revealing a diversity of agents, still confirms Coningham's findings, with 50 percent of references linking irrigation to Buddhist monks and institutions.[12]

9. See Norman, Kieffer-Pülz, and Pruitt 2018, xvi–xxi and xlv–vi, for a summary of discussions and refutations of this attribution.

10. Gunawardana 1979, 58, citing *Samantapāsādikā* III 679.

11. Coningham et al. 2007, 714.

12. Abeywardana et al. 2018, responding in part to Coningham et al. 2007; and Coningham and Gunawardhana 2013. A caveat here is that Buddhism's recognized role in encouraging the use of inscriptions to record donations and other events of legal significance, also pointed out in Abeywardana et al. 2018, means that Buddhism might be disproportionately represented in inscriptions.

Even though their management was disrupted by colonial administration and required some rediscovery, the association of Buddhist monasteries with water technology is still best documented in Sri Lanka, where the dramatic scale and continued use of the irrigation systems act as a visible and practical reminder.[13] Increasingly, however, we can piece together research from across Asia that paints a picture of this technology as a key factor in the success of Buddhism. It facilitated the propagation of Buddhism and supported those monumental monastic and stūpa complexes with which Buddhism is more usually associated. In the early 1970s, Kenneth Ch'en had already observed the expertise of monastics in relation to water mills in China and Central Asia, his evidence including manuscripts found in the Dunhuang library cave.[14]

Also beginning in the 1970s, the late Janice Stargardt (1934–2020) made numerous discoveries of extensive, advanced irrigation and canal works throughout mainland Southeast Asia, again often in association with Buddhist temples and monumental architecture. The construction of these systems required a sophisticated analysis of the water flow and capacity in relation to local knowledge both of terrain and of very varied soil types and ground water levels. This is highlighted in her recent comparison of irrigation works in India, Sri Lanka, and mainland Southeast Asia, which shows how construction was designed to achieve maximum water capture for minimal effort. Her analysis also reveals that these sites could be maintained for generations by local collective work, her point being that the previous assumption that such substantial sites were always the result of top-down control and imposition of labor can be overturned.[15] This is reminiscent of the collective contribution of multiple donors to the construction and maintenance of Buddhist monumental architecture analyzed by Schopen in his work on Sāñcī donative inscriptions.[16]

It is from the Sāñcī area that we find some of the most detailed evidence for early Buddhist monastic involvement in monumental hydrology. Julia Shaw's work over the past two decades reveals a close association between Buddhist

13. A further disruption has come recently in the form of cheap rice imports undermining the profitability of maintaining traditional irrigation systems in Sri Lanka.

14. Ch'en 1973, 152–155.

15. Stargardt 2018, 262–266. Not all the sites examined by Stargardt are Buddhist. However, see the location of Buddhist temples (*wat*) in her map of the canal system of the Satinpra peninsula of Thailand (2018, 263).

16. See, for example, Schopen 1991, 9, and 1985. While Schopen's focus in these writings is the role of monastics in making donations, they also reveal the composite patronage of Buddhist monumental architecture.

sites and irrigation works, including mechanisms for controlling flow and flooding, going back to the third to second centuries BCE. She demonstrates the use of reservoirs for upland irrigation in areas that already had a Buddhist presence, with the new irrigation systems enabling a transition to rice-growing. The far higher yields offered by rice in comparison to wheat meant that these areas could support more dense populations, which in turn provided patronage and labor for the associated monumental Buddhist architecture for which Sāñcī is famous.

Shaw's calculations of monsoon rain runoff from the hills supplying the water basins that were dammed to form these reservoirs indicate that the designers of the dams made very accurate assessments of the complex topography in relation to the volume of rainfall. That these calculations were made ahead of construction, rather than by trial and error or generational development, is indicated by the single-phase construction of dams revealed through core sampling.[17] This suggests both familiarity with the local terrain and advanced trigonometry, a branch of mathematics known to have developed early in India in relation to astronomy. Particularly associated with the fifth- to sixth-century CE astronomer Āryabhaṭa, it also has a longer history, important for the correct construction and positioning of Brahmanical sacrificial altars.[18] The sophistication of the water irrigation systems presented by Shaw suggests that such mathematics may also have been used for theoretical modeling of reservoirs in advance of construction. She writes that "the relationship between reservoir volume, local catchments and run-off volumes suggests that they were built by a professional engineering class following a considerable period of local water balance observation."[19] Shaw proposes that this technological know-how, with the huge advantages for food production, "formed part of a cultural package that accompanied the spread of new religio-cultural traditions from the Gangetic valley."[20]

17. Shaw 2007, 237.

18. On Āryabhaṭa, see Ansari 1977, 11, 15. On the link between Vedic altar construction and trigonometry, see Hayashi 2005.

19. Shaw 2018, 246.

20. Shaw 2018, 245. This analysis allows Shaw (2018, 233) to propose that the representation of water in monastic decoration is a direct demonstration of this ability, contra Schopen 2006, 498–505.

Technology and Religious Values

Just as the Buddhist association with medicine, which made monks useful to new societies, may have been a mechanism for its spread, so water technology may also have been a hitherto-unrecognized aspect of its attractiveness. While Schopen's work draws a contrast between a focus on doctrine and the practicalities of monastic life that are revealed through his reading of Vinaya texts, Shaw's work suggests that some practical engagement might be the natural expression of underlying Buddhist doctrine or worldview. Shaw links the use of irrigation with the Buddhist quest of intervening in suffering: "Water shortage is a primary cause of human suffering, especially in regions where 90 per cent of the annual rainfall occurs in two to three months, and the *saṅgha*'s ability to alleviate this suffering was made explicit through outward symbols of its engagement with environmental control,"[21] a similar argument being possible in relation to the association between Buddhism and medicine. In part inspired by Schopen's and Gunawardana's work on the engagement of monks in society, Shaw uses this association between water irrigation and Buddhist monasticism to propose a model for Buddhist environmentalism that eschews the extremes of world-renouncer and engaged Buddhism that currently hinder the development of that subject.

One might at first regard this association between the practical and the doctrinal as a romantic or aspirational interpretation motivated by the quest for inspiration for—in Shaw's case—modern environmental approaches in Buddhist regions. The need is great: one of the biggest threats to biodiversity in Asia is the modern use of oversized reservoirs that do not consider the effect for the entire water basin. However, once sensitized to this issue, one notices not only the discussions of reservoir construction and control found in inscriptions and commentarial texts, as drawn on by Gunawardana, but also references to water as a source of conflict. A story found in the *Dhammapada-aṭṭhakathā* and *Jātaka* tells of the Buddha intervening to prevent a full-scale war between the Sākiyas and Koliyas, which began as a conflict over water for crop irrigation after a shortage had resulted from a significant drop in the water level in a reservoir across a shared water basin.[22] The *Mahāparinibbāna-sutta* (Dīgha Nikāya 16) opens with the Buddha's attempt to persuade King Ajātasattu's minister Vassakāra ("Rain-Maker") of the positive values of the Vajjī confederacy, an attempt that, far from dissuading the king from war, inspires Vassakāra to engage in a cold war of disinformation ahead of a hot war. The background

21. Shaw 2018, 233.

22. Deegalle 2014, 567–569.

to the war is the location of the king's new capital, Pāṭaliputra, modern-day Patna, on the confluence of a number of rivers in the Ganges basin and thus a highly strategic position for controlling trade and irrigation.[23]

Why have I digressed into talking about such matters as irrigation when what I want to talk about is meditation? Three aspects interest me here, and I shall explain their connection with meditation below. The first is the association of Buddhist monasteries not just with day-to-day practical life but with advanced technology. The second is the relevance of mathematics to this and other technologies. The third is how utterly transformative this technology is. Through the carefully regulated suffusion of the substrate (earth) with another catalyzing element (water), for example, an entirely new landscape is generated, in which particularly wholesome seeds can germinate. The resulting surplus of rice can nourish and contribute to the health of increased populations, and by extension, support large monasteries. Now I want to consider whether theories of how to bring about radical transformation are shared between practical and spiritual technologies. This brings me to examine meditation as a technology, in other words as the application of knowledge about causality to bring about a practical, reproducible end-product or result and to compare the methods directed at spiritual transformation for transcending this life with those used for more immediate, this-life, practical ends. This is not to deny the this-worldly aspects of spiritual and religious practice or to assume that meditation does not also have this-worldly aims, as will be seen below. However, I am interested in the application of pragmatic technology for the purpose of transcendence precisely because the latter is often treated in scholarship as something undefinable and even unreal, and at worst, to be ignored—reflecting the *physis-psyche* divide that has influenced religion and scholarship from the European Enlightenment period onward. As my exploration below indicates, for practitioners, the path to transcending *saṃsāra* has been neither undefinable nor unreal, but subject to the same logic, causal processes, and treatment as more practical activities, and so rested on a spectrum that joined the two spheres of engagement.

Premodern Theravāda Meditation Manuals

To examine this, I turn to my own area of specialization, premodern Theravāda meditation. Rather than use the canonical and commentarial sources most frequently drawn on by both scholars and modern revivalists for understanding Theravāda meditation—namely, the *Mahāsatipaṭṭhāna-*

23. Crosby 2014, 264.

sutta and its commentary along with Buddhaghosa's *Visuddhimagga*—I want to discuss meditation as found in practitioner manuals. "Secret" texts that passed from teacher to student are mentioned in the fifth-century treatise, the *Visuddhimagga*, and other commentarial works attributed to Buddhaghosa, though their content—naturally—is not. As Lance Cousins has shown, this indicates that esotericism was present in Pāli-oriented Buddhism, what we now term Theravāda, by this time. A few centuries later, Dhammapāla, commenting on the *Visuddhimagga*, interprets this as referring to secret meditation texts.[24] In other words, Dhammapāla regards the *Visuddhimagga* as an exoteric presentation and is aware of a related esoteric presentation of meditation. The practitioner manuals I shall examine were composed within esoteric practice lineages, finding their way into library collections only as they fell out of use.[25] Scores of such manuscripts have survived from Cambodia, Laos, Sri Lanka, and Thailand, with the most extensive stemming from mid-eighteenth-century Sri Lanka. Their content is closely related to available commentarial-period, exoteric sources on meditation such as the *Visuddhimagga* in terms of topic, but is more geared to the practicalities of individual practice. As such these manuals reveal something about what the practitioner was doing when meditating and about the understanding of how meditation was believed to bring about change.

We do not know whether these manuscripts represent the type of esoteric meditation texts mentioned by Dhammapāla. The physical evidence, in the form of the above-mentioned manuscripts, printed texts from the early to mid-twentieth century and a few inscriptions, comes from much later, only datable with certainty to the period from the sixteenth to early twentieth centuries.[26] If we try to assess the date in relation to content and terminology, we observe that this form of meditation relates to Abhidhamma of the commentarial period—that is, the fifth century onward—and so presumes the same stage of doctrinal and terminological development as the *Visuddhimagga*.

I shall refer to this type of meditation as *boran* (Pāli *purāṇa*) "old/traditional" meditation, a designation found in Cambodia and Thailand. It appears to have first acquired this name in early twentieth-century Thailand to dis-

24. Cousins 1997, 193.

25. On the evidence for this type of meditation and the ways it made its way into collections and publications, see Crosby 2020, chapter 3.

26. For a detailed chronology of the evidence, see Crosby 2020, 101–102, and Choompolpaisal 2019. For a more detailed account of the Sri Lankan manuscripts that provide the most detailed accounts of the higher stages of these practices, see Crosby 2019. For an example of their presence in art, see Terwiel 2019.

tinguish it from the new methods of meditation that began to emerge from the late nineteenth century onward. The latter looked back to the canon and *Visuddhimagga* directly and in turn contributed to the emergence of global mindfulness. *Boran* practice has also been referred to as *yogāvacara*, literally "practitioner of meditation," a term that recurs in its manuals, including the first manual to be published from this tradition by the Pali Text Society in 1896.[27]

Boran meditation is recognizably standard Theravāda practice in that it develops *jhāna* experience and the different types of pliability and responsiveness of mind usually identified as *samatha* ("calming") outcomes of meditation as well as the *vipassanā* outcomes associated with increasingly higher levels of insight into the three characteristics of impermanence, suffering, and no-self.[28] A strikingly distinctive feature of *boran* meditation, however, is the way in which it seeks to incorporate such meditative experience into the body. It does this through *nimitta* "signs." These are sensory experiences, often in the form of lights or physical sensations, that practitioners experience in many types of meditation. In *boran* practice, they are induced in various ways according to the particular lineage. For the most part, they appear in response to meditations that use breath and a repeated phrase or term such as *a ra haṃ* as the anchor of the meditator's focus, while allowing the *nimitta* to arise spontaneously, or while seeking answers to questions, in the form of Pāli or vernacular phrases, the meaning of which is often not understood by the meditator. Some *boran* traditions teach active visualizations of the *nimitta*. In *boran* practice, these *nimitta* are seen as diagnostic of changes in mental state resulting from the meditation, and the ability to generate these signs for most of the stages of the practice is emphasized. The *nimitta* experiences, once attained, are drawn into the body along pathways beginning from the tip of the nose and nasal cavity, through certain centers in the body, such as the throat and heart, and eventually incorporating them into the body close to the navel. In the higher stages, meditation attainments that are *animitta*, signless, are treated in the same way.

The use of energy pathways and centers in the body is reminiscent of the *nāḍī*, energy channels, as well as the cakra and *marma*, energy or treatment points, of tantra, yoga, and Indic medical practice. This has led to speculation that Tibetan or other non-Theravāda sources have either influenced the development of *boran* practice or, more likely, shared an understanding of the

27. Rhys Davids [1896] 1981.

28. For a discussion of the different Theravāda meditation systems and the place of *samatha* and *vipassanā* within them, see Crosby 2020, chapter 2.

mind-body relationship and related medical systems. Nonetheless, all the terminology found in *boran* practice, as well as the stages of the path it promotes, clearly situate it within a Pāli Abhidhamma framework. The *nimitta* represent the neutral, skillful, resultant, and functional aspects of consciousness (*cetasika*) that are developed in meditation as attributes of the positive or beautiful (*sobhana*) states of consciousness (*citta*). These lead to the increasingly elevated spiritual states of the practitioner, culminating in the supramundane (*lokuttara*) states from stream entrant to arhat, which constitute the highest spiritual attainments within Theravāda soteriology. Such progress from ordinary to supramundane is tracked in the Abhidhamma, which looks carefully at the complex causality that makes such transformation possible.

If we were to pursue this entirely from an Abhidhamma perspective, we would need to look at the Abhidhamma understanding of the relationship between consciousness (*citta* and *cetasika*) and the body or form (*rūpa*). Elsewhere I have done this, showing that this system of meditation seeks to actualize the Abhidhamma path by progressively substituting less refined aspects of consciousness and physicality with higher ones, until the types of consciousness that pertain in the supramundane states are reached.[29] What I want to look at here is not the intricacies of these stages identified in Abhidhamma but how this process of progressive substitution reflects the broader scientific culture of premodern South-Southeast Asia. To do this I shall examine techniques applied to bring about change found in such disciplines as medicine, grammar, hydrology, and chemistry.

Correlation between Boran Meditation and Ayurvedic Obstetrics

The first parallel discipline I would like to examine is obstetrics, the treatment of the pregnant mother and the unborn child. The development of the unborn child as a metaphor for spiritual development is familiar from a range of religious traditions. The most familiar in Buddhism is probably the Mahāyāna concept of *tathāgatagarbha*, the presence of an embryonic Buddha awaiting development within all sentient beings.[30] In the *boran* meditation of Theravāda, the model of developing the unborn spiritual potential—that is, potential Buddhahood—within the practitioner is taken quite literally. The practitioner's internalization of the *nimitta* through the intranasal cav-

29. Crosby 2019.

30. For examples of the use of embryology in different Buddhist traditions, see Dolce 2015, Garrett 2008, and Sanford 1997.

ity down delivery pathways and energy centers shows clear parallels with how medicine is applied to the embryo/fetus in traditional Indic obstetrics.

The use of the intranasal cavity for delivery of medicines for a range of treatments is recognized in seminal Ayurvedic works such as the pre-second-century CE *Carakasaṃhitā*, with the types of such treatment summarized circa sixth century CE by Vāgbhaṭa in his *Aṣṭāṅgahṛdayasaṃhitā*.[31] It was used in obstetrics to treat the fetus for any suspected humor (*doṣa*) imbalances and resulting symptoms, to ensure a safer and more comfortable stay in the womb, and to inculcate the desired attributes, such as male or female, warrior, learned scholar, and so on. A correlation was made between the character of the embryo and the equivalent cosmological realm, just as with meditative attainments. A male embryo, or an embryo that is to be made male, should be provided with medication through the right-hand nasal cavity and a female, or female-to-be embryo, treated through the left-hand nostril. This right hand–left hand correlation is found in *boran* meditation: a male practitioner should use the right-hand nostril, the female practitioner the left-hand nostril to begin the movement of *nimitta* from the tip of the nose to the "womb" of the practitioner. Gradually the practitioner inculcates into the embryonic Buddha in their womb the qualities required to progress on the path to enlightenment. One of several ways to ensure the birth of a male child in traditional Indic medicine was to wear a small metal figure of a male slightly to the right of the navel. Another, simpler *boran* practice was to visualize the *nimitta* of a small Buddha near the navel.[32]

In more complex *boran* practice, the meditation attainments drawn down to the practitioner's womb are implanted in combinations. After one quality is brought down, another is added, until the full set of desirable mental attributes of the given stage are implanted in combination. The mathematics of this parallels the formulation of Ayurvedic pharmaceuticals: the medical substances—that is, herbs, minerals, and so on—are selected for properties designed to counteract imbalances in the three humors, their relative proportion related to the diagnosed imbalance. Similarly, the combination of meditative attainments is used to counteract the imbalances in the practitioner that are rooted in the three fires of greed, hatred, and delusion. For example, the second stage of the full sequence of *boran* practice is the inculcation of six pairs of positive attributes of body and mind to ensure physical and mental pliability, steadiness, and rigor.[33] These attributes of consciousness, *cetasika*, act

31. Meulenbeld 1999–2002, vol. 1A, 13 and 404.

32. Choompolpaisal 2019, 166.

33. The full list of the six *yugala* is *kāya-* (body) and *citta-* (mind) *-passaddhi* ("calmness"),

as antidotes to the five hindrances that block progress in meditation: desire, ill will, sloth and torpor, restlessness, and worry and doubt. These pharmaceutical substances—whether medicinal or meditational—are then combined with the elements that make up the physicality, *rūpa*, of the individual: earth, water, wind, heat, and space. Thus we have pharmaceuticals to address imbalances arising from three humors in one context and the three unskillful root causes in the other, both in combination with the elements that make up our physical body, both administered through delivery routes starting at the intranasal cavity and ending in the womb.[34]

Using aspects of mentality to change physicality rather goes against the modern conception of Buddhist meditation as mind science, an approach to meditation that developed in the modern period and informs the extensive expansion of the study of this subject within psychology and cognitive science. However, it does fit the Abhidhamma understanding of the individual as made up of an interdependent and constantly changing configuration of *citta*, *cetasika*, and *rūpa* and, more specifically, the creation of *rūpa* from *citta*: *cittaja-rūpa*.[35] To seek to change the practitioner's body by incorporating desired states of consciousness and their concomitants is not, therefore, as tantric, unorthodox, or "magic"-oriented as it might at first seem, and thus an anomaly within a Theravāda context. Rather it combines Abhidhamma with techniques for inducing change also found in medicine, especially obstetrics, one of the practical fields identified above as familiar to at least some monastics.

Correlation between Boran Meditation and Generative Grammar

The interrelationship between consciousness and physicality finds interesting parallels with language. Language is a physical manifestation of consciousness that also alters consciousness: a person has a thought, speaks to convey that thought, and the listener understands.[36] Philosophy of language and

---

-lahutā ("lightness"), *-mudutā* ("softness"), *-kāmaññatā* ("malleability"), *-pāguññatā* ("skillfulness"), and *-ujuggatā* ("straightness"). Phibul Choompolpaisal describes how the *nimitta* for these are bi-colored (2019, 163).

34. For a more detailed explanation of the correlations between *boran* meditation and Ayurvedic obstetrics, see Crosby 2020, chapter 5.

35. For my suggestions as to why we have an emphasis on mind science in the meditation of the revivals of the nineteenth to early twentieth centuries, see Crosby 2020, chapter 1. For the relationship between *boran* meditation and Abhidhamma, see Crosby 2019.

36. For differing developments in the understanding of this process within Abhidhamma, in relation to *paññatti* "making known" or "concept," see Gornall 2020, 99–106.

generative grammar were important features of Buddhist monastic training throughout its institutional history in South Asia, as might be expected given the association between Buddhism and writing technology noted above. This preoccupation remained important in Theravāda even after the thirteenth century when the scholarly traditions on the Indian subcontinent ceased to be hegemonic in the shaping of Pāli culture.

Generative grammar is the distinctive science, or technology, developed in the most widely recognized system for Sanskrit today by Pāṇini in around the fourth century BCE. His grammar, the *Aṣṭādhyāyī*, provides a system for developing almost all Sanskrit language forms from a basic set of roots, using codes and algorithms or rules. In the Theravāda world, simplified versions of the Sanskritic grammatical traditions were adapted to Pāli. The most influential Pāli grammarian is Kaccāyana, whose work remains a core part of the curriculum of traditional monastic education to this day. Kaccāyana's grammar is explicitly referred to in *boran* practice and the Buddhist culture that surrounds it. Cosmogonic myths drawing on Kaccāyana identify language as the source of all creation, the entirety of the Buddhist teaching, and of the human body.[37] The potential of language to generate meaning beyond itself and to transfer between physicality and consciousness and *vice versa* is thus taken to its logical extreme, a development we might find surprising in Buddhism given its early rejection of parallel Brahmanical preoccupations with creative, sacred language.

In *boran* meditation, the potency of language is harnessed in several ways. The *nimitta* of the meditation attainments may be marked or represented by potent Pāli syllables. These usually constitute phrases with a recognizable exoteric meaning, such as *a ra haṃ* "worthy one" or *na mo bu ddhā ya*, "homage to the Buddha," that here have an esoteric correlation (or often multiple esoteric correlations) such as the three breaths or the five *pīti*, the "delights" which are *cetasika* attained in the first *jhāna*. These states of consciousness—namely, the *cetasika*s and *citta* that arise as meditative attainments—therefore generate syllables in the practitioner's consciousness. The syllables, implanted in the body, facilitate the transformation of the psychophysical being. In this system of meditation, language is used as a medium between consciousness and the practitioner's psychophysical substance, generating change in the latter, just as in the cosmogonic myths surrounding the origins of generative grammar. As I have explored in more detail elsewhere, the understanding of how Pāli syllables can have this effect is an extension of the processes of substitution and

37. See Bizot 1980 for both the importance of embryology in *boran* practice and the *boran* theory of language as the source of all creation.

change used within generative grammar to develop all the complete words of the Pāli language from verbal roots.[38]

We find these applications of potent language extended in *boran* meditational culture to protective practices, with specific rules of grammar being recited in the preparation of the powder used in the creation of *yantra* and *yantra*-tattoos. In preparing the powder the practitioner writes and recites sequences of Pāli syllables, repeatedly erasing them and substituting them with a new set of Pāli syllables. The rules quoted in *boran* manuals specifically relate to Kaccāyana's rules for the substitution of syllables.[39]

Contemporary readers and even contemporary practitioners would mostly make a distinction here between modes of technology that are acceptable to a modern materialist worldview—that is, material technologies—and "technologies" that are nonmaterial and by virtue of being "non-scientific" might be judged as belonging only to the sphere of religion or labelled "magic." But in premodern times practitioners considered the latter technologies to be efficient in the same way as the material technologies of the day, as demonstrated by the explicit use of the same techniques between these different spheres of application.

Correlation between Boran Meditation and Techniques of Suffusion

As with the syllables in the protective practices, so too in *boran* meditation exercises, the desired states of consciousness are brought into the body not just once but multiple times. While the energy centers and the area between the heart and the womb (reflecting early understandings of the transmission of nutrients to the fetus) are the primary focus of this incorporation, the practice involves the movement of these transformative elements around the body.[40] The way these transformative qualities are made to pervade the body in order to transform it suggests a parallel with the hydrology that was associated with Buddhist monasticism above: the radical transformation of the substratum of the ground with the transformative agent of water that allows the seed,

38. Crosby 2020, chapter 4. See also Javier Schnake's discussion of the extensive sixteenth-century *Vajirasāratthasaṅgaha* on Pāli syllables used for protection, the proposition in the late fifteenth-century *Saddabinduvinicchaya* that Pāli syllables may contain multiple meanings, and the significance of number in Pāli protective phrases and *yantra* (2018).

39. Bizot and von Hinüber 1994, 39, discussed in Crosby 2000, chapter 4.

40. For the movements around the body found in one *boran* lineage, that at Wat Ratchasittharam in Thonburi, Bangkok, see Skilton and Choompolpaisal 2014, 103–106, and Skilton and Choompolpaisal 2015, 223. Movements around the body are far more extensive in the eighteenth-century manuals from Sri Lanka discussed in Crosby 2019.

the potential, to grow, to provide something greater than the original components. The compounding of two or more components creating something greater than the component parts is a concept familiar from grammar.

In the form of *boran* meditation attested in manuscripts from Sri Lanka, noted above as the most detailed handed down to us, the flooding of the body with transformative qualities of consciousness is repeated with qualities being first implanted then withdrawn. This practice of repeated impregnation and withdrawal has been noted in other Indic religious practices such as Śaiva tantra, where the parallels between both embryology and traditional chemistry have been highlighted by David Gordon White. The purification of the practitioner's body by repeatedly retracting the essence of his semen from the female body is based on the process used to purify mercury (seen as male) using sulfur (seen as female).[41] The process requires that the mercury first suffuses the sulfur and is then withdrawn out of the sulfur again, with this process repeated until the mercury is pure.[42] While Theravāda practice does not include the sexual rites parallel to this that are found in Śaiva and Vajrayāna tantra, the repeated suffusion and withdrawal of the transformative aspects of *boran* meditation practice into and out of the body shows clear parallels with the mercury purification described here. Again, evidence for the working of metal within monastic compounds of ancient India and Sri Lanka was noted above.

Changes to Theravāda Meditation in the Modern Period

The *boran* path found in the premodern meditation manuals of Theravāda Buddhism discussed above is based on an understanding of the potential for progressive transformation outlined in Abhidhamma. Moreover, it takes the Abhidhamma path as being about actual transformation in our current embodiment. This leads to the use in this meditation system of techniques for bringing about physical or material transformation employed in other technologies familiar to the monastics who developed these forms of meditation. These different technologies share a number of underlying principles and features, such as substitution, antidotes, delivery pathways, and repetitive suffusion.[43]

41. White 1984, 51–52.

42. White 1984, 66.

43. As I have explored in more detail elsewhere, these disciplines have in common various types of mathematics, especially group theory, which deals with sequencing and combinations. See Crosby 2020, chapter 4.

The resulting methods for internalizing the meditation experiences in the body are unrecognized in modern Theravāda. Even *boran* lineages that have survived do not perform the full range of techniques identified in premodern manuals, particularly those from Sri Lanka that detail advanced practice. The lack of recognition began in the late colonial period, which saw the suppression of the technologies with which they resonated. In their respective dominions, British and French colonial powers and Thailand's increasingly centralized and modernizing government of the period took control of chemistry, suppressed local medicine, increasingly bio-medicalized pregnancy, disrupted monastic control of water irrigation, and brought in new models of language and language learning. The reforms of Buddhism that took place at this time used early exoteric textual sources as their authority. In Cambodia and Thailand reformists also largely avoided Abhidhamma or increasingly came to regard it as a form of scholasticism rather than as a framework for practice. This attitude to texts contributed to an active rejection of the meditation practices themselves as uncanonical. The lack of recognition of these practices as effective techniques for change, then, largely relates to changes in hegemonic technology during the European colonial period and the nature of Buddhist reform based on canonical texts that took place in response to colonialism and modernization.[44] Meanwhile, meditation practices that did not address physical transformation, either eschewing it or leaving it implicit, fared better in a world where material technology had been transformed and come under the control of colonial and increasingly centralized political powers.[45] These more successful practices include Vipassanā and other text-derived meditations that developed during this period and went on to influence global Buddhist and Buddhist-derived practices such as mindfulness.[46]

44. Crosby 2020, chapter 6.

45. Crosby 2013, 2017, and 2020, chapters 5 and 7.

46. See Sharf 1995 on the modern development of Zen and Vipassanā practice in response to encounters with the West and the danger of imposing a Cartesian divide retrospectively onto Buddhist meditation in seeing it entirely concerned with internalized psychological states. It is in part through the imposition of this Cartesian divide retrospectively that the relevance of material technologies was rendered invisible. The complexity of meditation practices in the manuals and practice traditions that I work on extends the correlation he points out between meditation stages and a prescribed path regardless of which side of the prescriptive-descriptive divide one stands on in relation to meditation. However, that same complexity indicates that we need to revise Sharf's characterization of premodern Theravāda meditation as consisting "largely of the recitation of Pāli texts pertaining to meditation (such as the *Satipaṭṭhāna-sutta* and the *Mettā-sutta*), chanting verses enumerating the qualities of the Buddha, reciting formulaic lists of the thirty-two parts of the body, and so on" (1995, 242).

Implications of Meditation as Technology

The above discussion summarizes the correlation between premodern meditation and technologies used to bring about change in other spheres within the broader culture that supported Buddhism. Such correlation indicates that meditation monks were influenced by the practical world that surrounded them, adapting aspects of practical technologies to spiritual transformation, including the quest to reach the supramundane states believed to lead to liberation from *saṃsāra*. We may never know whether this relationship was the result of direct causation, with meditators applying techniques seen elsewhere, or whether the means of bringing about change found across the practical-spiritual spectrum developed in tandem, as mathematics and understandings of processes of change developed across different technologies.

In opening our eyes to the practical engagement of Buddhist monastics, Schopen has brought life to the archeology and texts that they left behind, overturning much unrealistic romanticization that previously obscured the field. We appreciate the degree of ingenuity demonstrated by the Buddhist monks that form the focus of Schopen's writings in their acquisition of favor, fame, and fortune, their concerns to ensure a good rebirth, or simply to get away with as much unsaintly conduct as possible. What we see in the premodern meditation manuals discussed here is that meditation monks were also applying developing technologies to their endeavors, seeking ways to guarantee their transformative effects. When we treat meditation as a radically different activity from more practical religious and other activities, we risk imposing an anachronistic post-Cartesian bifurcation on premodern Asia.

The consideration of monastic familiarity with a range of systems of complex causality, applied in practices I here describe as technologies, offers other potential advances in the study of Buddhist history. Reading texts afresh with an eye to technological engagement and enhancement makes sense of, for example, the collocation of monasteries and advanced water technology. Examining references to other technologies not as metaphor but as practice might not only reveal more about the scope of monastic life but also allow us to relate Buddhist texts to the textual lineages of mathematical and scientific schools, which often offer firmer chronologies, and to the archeology of the material culture of such sciences.

Developing the subject in this way will be challenging, since each technology has its own vocabulary, a vocabulary that may well have slipped into obscurity or entailed the transposition of existing Sanskrit and Pāli terms to new purposes undetected and unexpected. An example of such repurposing can be found in the *boran* meditation manuals themselves. There, the terms used for the five *pīti*, the types of delight experienced in the first *jhāna*, are also used to refer to the five main physical locations in the body to which the first type of *pīti* and other *cetasika*s must be moved.[47] The instruction to place the *pīti* in the *pīti* had long flummoxed me and prompted others to dismiss the intelligence of the manuals' authors. Finally, it makes sense! If we saw in a medieval European manuscript the words *silk button*, *spangle*, *knopper*, *marble*, and *oak apple*, would we instantly recognize that a chemical formulation for iron sulfate compounds was in the offing? Only by reading the lines with technology in mind, as exemplified by Gregory Schopen's work illuminating monastic engagement in such practical matters.

Works Cited

Abeywardana, Nuwan, Wiebke Bebermeier, and Brigitta Schütt. 2018. "Ancient Water Management and Governance in the Dry Zone of Sri Lanka Until Abandonment, and the Influence of Colonial Politics during Reclamation." *Water* 10.12: 1746. https://doi.org/10.3390/w10121746.

Ansari, S. M. Razaullah. 1977. "Āryabhaṭa I, His Life and His Contributions." *Bulletin of the Astronomical Society of India* 5: 10–18.

Bizot, François. 1980. "La grotte de la naissance: Recherches sur le bouddhisme khmer, II." *Bulletin de l'École française d'Extrême-Orient* 67: 222–273.

Bizot, François, and Oskar von Hinüber. 1994. *La guirlande de Joyaux*. Textes bouddhiques du Cambodge 2. Paris: École française d'Extrême-Orient.

Ch'en, Kenneth K. S. 1973. *The Chinese Transformation of Buddhism*. Princeton: Princeton University Press.

Choompolpaisal, Phibul. 2019. "*Nimitta* and Visual Methods in Siamese and Lao Meditation Traditions from the 17th Century to the Present Day." *Contemporary Buddhism* 20.1–2: 152–183.

Coningham, Robin, and Prishanta Gunawardhana. 2013. *Anuradhapura*, vol. 3: *The Hinterland*. British Archaeological Reports International Series. Oxford: Archaeopress.

Coningham, Robin, Prishanta Gunawardhana, Mark Manuel, Gamini Adikari, Mangala Katugampola, Ruth Young, Armin Schmidt, K. Krishnan, Ian Simpson, Gerry McDonnell, and Cathy Batt. 2007. "The State of Theocracy: Defining an Early Medieval Hinterland in Sri Lanka." *Antiquity* 81: 699–719.

47. This repurposing was decoded by Skilton and Choompolpaisal (2014, 104), working in collaboration with Ven. Veera Thanaveero of Wat Ratchasittharam, Thonburi, head of one of the few living lineages of *boran* practice.

Cousins, L. S. 1997. "Aspects of Esoteric Southern Buddhism." In *Indian Insights: Buddhism, Brahmanism and Bhakti*, edited by S. Hamilton and P. Connolly, 185–207. London: Luzac Oriental.

Crosby, Kate. 2013. *Traditional Theravada Meditation and Its Modern-Era Suppression*. Hong Kong: Buddha-Dharma Centre of Hong Kong.

———. 2014. *Theravada Buddhism: Continuity, Diversity, Identity*. Oxford: Blackwell-Wiley.

———. 2019. "Abhidhamma and *Nimitta* in 18th-Century Meditation Manuscripts from Sri Lanka: A Consideration of Orthodoxy and Heteropraxy in *Boran Kammaṭṭhāna*." *Contemporary Buddhism* 20.1–2: 111–151.

———. 2020. *Esoteric Theravada: The Story of the Forgotten Meditation Tradition of Southeast Asia*. Boulder, CO: Shambala Publications.

Deegalle, Mahinda. 2014. "The Buddhist Traditions of South and Southeast Asia." In *Religion, War, and Ethics: A Sourcebook of Textual Traditions*, edited by Gregory M. Reichberg, Henrik Syse, and Nicole M. Hartwell, 544–596. New York and Cambridge: Cambridge University Press.

Dolce, Lucia. 2015. "The Embryonic Generation of the Perfect Body: Ritual Embryology from Japanese Tantric Sources." In *Transforming the Void: Embryological Discourse and Reproductive Imagery in East Asian Religious*, edited by Anna Andreeva and Dominic Steavu, 253–310. Leiden and New York: Brill.

Garrett, Frances. 2008. *Religion, Medicine and the Human Embryo in Tibet*. London and New York: Routledge.

Gornall, Alastair. 2020. *Rewriting Buddhism: Pali Literature and Monastic Reform in Sri Lanka, 1157–1270*. London: UCL Press.

Gunawardana, R. A. L. H. 1971. "Irrigation and Hydraulic Society in Early Medieval Ceylon." *Past and Present* 53: 3–27.

———. 1979. *Robe and Plough: Monasticism and Economic Interest in Early Medieval Sri Lanka*. The Association for Asian Studies: Monographs and Papers 35. Tucson: The Association for Asian Studies by the University of Arizona Press.

———. 1984–1985. "Obstetrics and Theories of Reproduction in Ancient and Early Medieval Sri Lanka." *Kalyāṇī: Journal of Humanities and Social Sciences of the University of Kelaniya* 3–4: 1–22.

Hayashi, Takao. 2005. "Indian Mathematics." In *The Blackwell Companion to Hinduism*, edited by Gavin Flood, 360–375. Oxford: Basil Blackwell.

Meulenbeld, Gerrit Jan. 1999–2002. *A History of Indian Medical Literature*. 3 vols. Groningen: Egbert Forsten.

Nesměrák, Karel, and Irena Němcová. 2012. "Dating of Historical Manuscripts Using Spectrometric Methods: A Mini-Review." *Analytical Letters* 45.4: 330–344.

Norman, K. R., Petra Kieffer-Pülz, and William Pruitt. 2018. *Overcoming Doubts (Kaṅkhāvitaraṇī): The Bhikkhu-Pātimokkha Commentary*, vol. 1. Bristol: The Pali Text Society.

Rhys Davids, T. W. [1896] 1981. *The Yogāvacara's Manual*. Reprint, London: Pali Text Society.

Rouse, W. H. D. 1895. *The Jātaka or Stories of the Buddha's Former Births: Translated from the Pāli by Various Hands under the Editorship of Professor E. B. Cowell*, vol. 2. Cambridge: The Cambridge University Press.

Sanford, James H. 1997. "Wind, Waters, Stupas, Mandalas: Fetal Buddhahood in Shingon." *Japanese Journal of Religious Studies* 24.1–2: 1–38.

Schnake, Javier. 2018. "Letters and Numbers: Protective Aspects in the *Vajirasāratthasaṅgaha*." In *Katā me rakkhā, kata me parittā: Protecting the Protective Texts and Manuscripts. Proceedings of the Second International Pali Studies Week, Paris 2016*, edited by Claudio Cicuzza, 157–195. Bangkok and Lumbini: Fragile Palm Leaves Foundation, Lumbini International Research Institute.

Schopen, Gregory. 1985. "Two Problems in the History of Indian Buddhism: The Layman/Monk Distinction and the Doctrines of the Transference of Merit." *Studien zur Indologie und Iranistik* 10: 9–47. Reprinted in Schopen 1997, 23–55.

———. 1991. "Archaeology and Protestant Presuppositions in the Study of Indian Buddhism." *History of Religions* 31.1: 1–23. Reprinted in Schopen 1997, 1–22.

———. 1997. *Bones, Stones, and Buddhist Monks: Collected Papers on the Archaeology, Epigraphy, and Texts of Monastic Buddhism in India*. Studies in the Buddhist Traditions. Honolulu: University of Hawai'i Press.

———. 1998. "Marking Time in Buddhist Monasteries: On Calendars, Clocks, and Some Liturgical Practices." In *Sūryacandrāya: Essays in Honour of Akira Yuyama On the Occasion of His 65th Birthday*, edited by Paul Harrison and Gregory Schopen, 157–179. Indica et Tibetica 35. Swisttal-Odendorf: Indica et Tibetica Verlag. Reprinted in Schopen 2004, 260–284.

———. 1999. "The Bones of a Buddha and the Business of a Monk: Conservative Monastic Values in an Early Mahāyāna Polemical Tract." *Journal of Indian Philosophy* 27.4: 279–324. Reprinted in Schopen 2005, 63–107.

———. 2004. *Buddhist Monks and Business Matters: Still More Papers on Monastic Buddhism in India*. Studies in the Buddhist Traditions. Honolulu: University of Hawai'i Press.

———. 2005. *Figments and Fragments of Mahāyāna Buddhism in India: More Collected Papers*. Studies in the Buddhist Traditions. Honolulu: University of Hawai'i Press.

———. 2006. "The Buddhist 'Monastery' and the Indian Garden: Aesthetics, Assimilations, and the Siting of Monastic Establishments." *Journal of the American Oriental Society* 126.4: 487–505. Reprinted in Schopen 2014, 224–250.

———. 2014. *Buddhist Nuns, Monks, and Other Worldly Matters: Recent Papers on Monastic Buddhism in India*. Studies in the Buddhist Traditions. Honolulu: University of Hawai'i Press.

Sharf, Robert H. 1995. "Buddhist Modernism and the Rhetoric of Meditative Experience." *Numen* 42.3: 228–283.

Shaw, Julia. 2007. *Buddhist Landscapes in Central India: Sanchi Hill and Archaeologies of Religious and Social Change, c. Third Century BC to Fifth Century AD*. London: The British Academy.

———. 2018. "Early Indian Buddhism, Water and Rice. Collective Responses to Socio-Ecological Stress: Relevance for Global Environmental Discourse." In *Water Societies and Technologies from the Past and Present*, edited by Yijie Zhuang and Mark Altaweel, 233–255. London: UCL Press.

Skilton, Andrew, and Phibul Choompolpaisal. 2014. "The Old Meditation (*boran kammatthan*), a Pre-Reform Theravāda Meditation System from Wat Ratchasittharam: The *piti* Section of the *kammatthan matchima baep lamdap*." *Aséanie* 33: 83–116.

———. 2015. "The Ancient Theravāda Meditation System, *Borān Kammaṭṭhāna*: *Ānāpānasati* or 'Mindfulness of The Breath' in Kammatthan Majjima Baeb Lamdub." *Buddhist Studies Review* 32.2: 207–229.

Stargardt, Janice. 2018. "Water for the State or Water for the People? Wittfogel in South and South East Asia in the First Millennium." In *Water Societies and Technologies from the Past and Present*, edited by Yijie Zhuang and Mark Altaweel, 256–268. London: UCL Press.

Terwiel, Barend Jan. 2019. "The City of Nibbāna in Thai Picture Books of the Three Worlds." *Contemporary Buddhism* 20.1–2: 184–199.

White, David Gordon. 1984. "Why Gurus Are Heavy." *Numen* 31.1: 40–73.

Williams, Robin. 2006. *Oak-Galls in Britain*, vol. 1. Somerset: Kyntons Mead.

Forms of Intertextuality and Lost Sanskrit Verses of the *Buddhacarita*: The *Tridaṇḍaka* and the *Tridaṇḍamālā**

Jens-Uwe Hartmann

IT WAS NOTED long ago that the *Anityatā-sūtra*, a short discourse on impermanence, must have had a ritual function in certain traditions of Indian Buddhism and, moreover, that there must have been some kind of relationship between this sūtra and a work with a rather strange title, the *Tridaṇḍaka*. This text, again, seemed connected with the *Tridaṇḍamālā*, which tradition ascribes to the famous poet Aśvaghoṣa. The last to comment on the three texts was Gregory Schopen in his paper on monastic funerals in the *Mūlasarvāstivāda-vinaya*. In one of his famous footnotes—often enough short papers in themselves—he presented the state of knowledge regarding the texts and their relationship. He also indicated that there were still a number of open questions and ended his footnote with the statement: "All of this will, of course, require further research to settle; so too will the attribution of the formulary to Aśvaghoṣa."[1] As I attempt here to add further bits of information on the *Tridaṇḍamālā* and its relationship with the *Tridaṇḍaka*, I do this with a feeling of deep gratitude for the progress achieved by Gregory in Buddhist studies. But I am no less grateful for the combination of fun and scholarship characteristic of him that I enjoyed and profited personally from in all our discussions, most notably in Paris and Los Angeles.

In August 2018, Kazunobu Matsuda invited me to join his project of editing the *Tridaṇḍamālā*, and the following remarks are a first result of this joint endeavor.[2] Here it will be helpful to build on Schopen's footnote in order to

* It is my pleasant duty to thank two anonymous reviewers for excellent comments leading to valuable improvements, Grace Ramswick and Sophie Florence for correcting my English, Vincent Eltschinger for his observations, and Shayne Clarke for countless improvements in both form and content.

1. Schopen 1992, 32–34n62; see also the additional footnote in Schopen 2010a, 118n35.

2. I am very grateful to my friend Kazunobu Matsuda for allowing me to make use of the material prepared by him, which directed me to the *Tridaṇḍaka* and initiated this paper.

present the—rather limited—history of research on this text. In his third report on Sanskrit manuscripts in Tibet, published in 1938, Rāhula Sāṅkṛtyāyana drew attention to a work with the title *Tridaṇḍamālā* he had found in the library of Spos khang monastery.[3] Sāṅkṛtyāyana noted that the first page carried the title in not only Sanskrit but also Tibetan—namely, "Rgyud-3-gyi-phreṅ-ba" and "Rgyud-phyag-3-paḥi-phreṅ-ba," where the numeral 3 evidently stands for the word *gsum*. He quoted from the beginning and the end of the manuscript, and the colophon left no doubt as to the author: *samāptā ceyaṃ tridaṇḍamālā kṛtir ācāryasthavirāśvaghoṣa*(115r4)*sya śākyabhikṣoḥ sarvvāstivādino* <*mahā*>*vādinaḥ*, "and finished is this *Tridaṇḍamālā*, a work of the teacher (*ācārya*) and elder member of the order (*sthavira*) Aśvaghoṣa, the Buddhist monk (*śākyabhikṣu*), follower of the Sarvāstivāda, the eloquent."[4] Sāṅkṛtyāyana's quotation revealed that the text consisted of a mixture of stanzas and prose. His excerpts reached up to folio 3r of the manuscript, and they indicated that the text contained at least one sūtra quotation from one of the Āgamas, since folio 2r, line 3, preserved the standard opening formula of a sūtra, *evam mayā śrutam ekasmin samaye bhagavān cchrāvastyāṃ* (r4) *viharati sma jetavane 'nāthapiṇḍadasyārāme | tatra bhagavān bhikṣūn āmantrayate sma*, followed by a passage on the four *avetyaprasāda*s, the four forms of "trust founded in knowledge."[5]

However, it did not raise tremendous curiosity among scholars, and the strange title of the text most likely contributed to this indifference, as did the apparent absence of photographs.[6] The only one to comment on Sāṅkṛtyāyana's

3. Sāṅkṛtyāyana 1938, 157–160; it came together with a second text, a *parikathā*, presently being studied by Péter-Dániel Szántó, who provisionally names it **Saddharmaparikathā* and considers it a preacher's manual on how to provide sermons for the laity (Szántó 2021). Such manuscripts are notoriously difficult to date, but a date around the twelfth century seems likely.

4. The word *mahā* is inserted below the line; for the translation "eloquent" see Johnston 1928, 117. Neither the exact meaning of *mahāvādin* nor the precise reference of the term *śākyabhikṣu* is fully determined. Tzohar 2019, 188, translates *mahāvādin* as "Buddhist preacher," but without giving a reference. For *śākyabhikṣu*, see Schopen 1979, but also Cousins 2003 and Seyfort Ruegg 2004, 13–14n17.

5. Cf. SWTF, s.v. *avetya-prasāda*.

6. From the list prepared by Frank Bandurski it would appear that Sāṅkṛtyāyana took photographs of the manuscript (Bandurski 1994, 79–80). However, Giuseppe Tucci visited Spos khang monastery a year later in 1939 and took photographs of the same manuscript (Sferra 2008, 48 and 71–72). When Matsuda compared them with Sāṅkṛtyāyana's photographs he found to his surprise that they were identical. This riddle is solved in a lecture given by Tucci in Kyoto in 1955. There he reported on his stay at Spos khang and mentioned that he was able to photograph the *Tridaṇḍamālā*. He also disclosed that Sāṅkṛtyāyana had been in a rather bad condition when he visited Spos khang and that it had been difficult for him to

quotations was E. H. Johnston, whose interest in the text understandably focused on the question of authorship. In 1939, only a year after the publication of Sāṅkṛtyāyana's report, he published a short note in which he reached the conclusion that Aśvaghoṣa had to be ruled out as the author of the text. He deduced this from a comparison between "the three certain works of Aśvaghoṣa, whose Sanskrit texts are wholly or partly preserved,"[7] and the extracts from the *Tridaṇḍamālā* presented by Sāṅkṛtyāyana, where he found none of the characteristics of Aśvaghoṣa's "highly individual style which is easily recognizable."[8] He saw his conclusion to be "reinforced by a consideration of the various colophons," since the epithets *ācāryasthavira*, *śākyabhikṣu*, and *sarvāstivādin* were not found in the colophons of the genuine works, where other epithets appeared instead. The characterization as *sarvāstivādin* yielded particular cause for distrust, since Johnston had suggested in his translation of the *Buddhacarita* "that the evidence, so far as it went, indicated that he [i.e., Aśvaghoṣa] was an adherent of one of the Mahāsaṅghika [*sic*] sects."[9] For him the obvious solution, as in practically all such cases, lay in the assumption of two Aśvaghoṣas.

In one regard Johnston was right, but in another he couldn't have been more wrong, as will soon be demonstrated. Moreover, despite his firm conviction, his three arguments are rather weak. Poets are known to change their style, if only to adapt to the requirements of different genres; colophons depend on time, place, and the predilections of their authors (or scribes), who most likely are not the authors of the texts themselves; the school affiliation of Aśvaghoṣa

take photographs. Finally, Tucci announced an edition of the *Tridaṇḍamālā* after his return from Japan (Tucci 1956, 14–15). Although he never found time to realize this project, he must have put copies of at least some of his photographs at Sāṅkṛtyāyana's disposal. It appears that Sāṅkṛtyāyana himself took only two photographs (Xc 14/42 in Bandurski 1994, 79) and copied the beginning and end of the manuscript by hand. We are grateful to Francesco Sferra, Napoli, for permission to use Tucci's photographs. Regrettably, in some places they are rather blurred and therefore extremely difficult, if not impossible, to read. Tucci used the same technique as Sāṅkṛtyāyana, fixing the lengthy palm-leaf folios with pins on a wooden board (cf. Bandurski 1994, 16). Usually this leads to a part of the photograph being out of focus, often to the degree that up to one third of a folio becomes blurred and the *akṣara*s remain illegible. According to information received by Kazuo Kano when he visited the monastery in 2004, all the ancient manuscripts have been burned; see Kanō 2020, 196.

7. Johnston 1939, 11; the three works he refers to must be the *Buddhacarita*, the *Saundarananda*, and the *Śāriputraprakaraṇa*.

8. Johnston 1939, 11. But cf. Diego Loukota Sanclemente's paper in this volume, where he shows that a stanza quoted by Sāṅkṛtyāyana must be identical with a stanza in the Chinese translation of a *Tridaṇḍaka* that Yijing attributes to Aśvaghoṣa (see also below).

9. Johnston 1939, 13.

continues to be disputed, and Eltschinger's recent work on the sources of certain passages in the *Buddhacarita* indicates with welcome unambiguousness that Aśvaghoṣa based (at least some of) his accounts on the textual transmission generally connected with the (Mūla)Sarvāstivādins,[10] whatever his dogmatic position may have been.[11] These deliberations are not arguing for the identity of the authors of the *Buddhacarita* and the *Tridaṇḍamālā*, but quite the contrary: within the Indian tradition it is such a common phenomenon to ascribe a text to a famous figure that in most cases it is simply not worth speculating who the original author may have been, at least when no authoritative evidence is available.[12]

Although for Johnston the *Tridaṇḍamālā* was not by Aśvaghoṣa, he hoped for a publication of the text in due course, since Sāṅkṛtyāyana's excerpts showed "that it contained a number of valuable quotations of sūtras from the Sarvāstivādin canon."[13] He concluded his paper with thoughts on the title. It seemed that *tridaṇḍa* could not mean the staff of a non-Buddhist ascetic; he saw a possible connection with Pāli *tidaṇḍa* (Skt. *triveṇu*), the pole on a chariot to which the flag was attached, and he considered a reference "to the control of thought, word and deed, as in *Manu*, XII, 10,"[14] but conceded that the extracts from the text itself provided no hint at an explanation.

Schopen's concern was with the *Tridaṇḍaka* as something to be recited during the rites for a deceased monk. A specific presentation of the *Anityatā-sūtra* appeared to be a likely candidate since the Chinese Tripiṭaka contains a short sūtra (Taishō 801; cf. Taishō 2912), translated by Yijing 義淨 around 700 CE,[15] with the title *Wuchang jing* 無常經 and the alternative title *Sanqi jing* 三啓經, the former being a likely rendering of *Anityatā-sūtra* and the latter of *Tridaṇḍa(ka)-sūtra*;[16] in Taishō 2912 both titles are combined into *Wuchang sanqi jing* 無常三啓經. Moreover, Yijing reported in his travel record that a sūtra on impermanence is recited while the corpse of a monk is cremated.[17] Here Yijing made no connection with the *Tridaṇḍaka*, but in another passage

10. Eltschinger 2012, 2013, 2018, and 2020.

11. Cf. Yamabe 2003.

12. Cf. Hartmann 2023 for a telling example.

13. Johnston 1939, 13.

14. Johnston 1939, 13–14.

15. October 28, 701 CE, according to Willemen 2019, 67.

16. Willemen understands *sanqi* 三啓 as "tripartite statement" (2019, 67).

17. Taishō 2125.54.216c9–10; for a thorough discussion of the relevant passages in Yijing's travel record, see Loukota Sanclemente's paper in this volume.

he described a ritual of sūtra recitation after the circumambulation of *caityas* and stated that generally the *Tridaṇḍaka* 三啓 was used for this purpose. He also mentioned that it was a work of Aśvaghoṣa and explained that the three parts consisted of: (1) ten verses for the veneration of the Three Jewels, (2) a sacred text spoken by the Buddha himself, and (3) another set of verses for the dedication of the merit (*pariṇāmanā*) and the generation of the firm resolve (*praṇidhāna*). Obviously the *Tridaṇḍaka* described by Yijing is "not a specific text, but a set form of recitation consisting of three parts," and the sūtra in the middle "is unspecified and can apparently be any text suitable to the occasion of the recitation."[18]

In an appendix to his work on the *Saddharmasmṛtyupasthāna-sūtra*, Lin Li-Kouang showed that the *Wuchang jing* 無常經 or *Sanqi jing* 三啓經 (Taishō 801) consisted of a section of seventeen verses, the first seven of them venerating the Three Jewels, then the sūtra itself, and finally a third section of another sixteen verses.[19] Lin succeeded in identifying one of the verses in the *Buddhacarita* and tried to establish parallels in the *Saundarananda* or in other works ascribed to Aśvaghoṣa, such as the *Sūtrālaṃkāra* and the *Nairātmyaparipṛcchā* (Taishō 1643). He also drew attention to a Chinese Dunhuang fragment of the *Wuchang sanqi jing* 無常三啓經 in the British Library collection.[20] It contained an additional note that accorded with the information given by Yijing in his travel record and said, in Lin's translation: "Les éloges et les exhortations au début et à la fin de cet ouvrage ont été compilés (*tsi*) et composés (*tsao*) par le vénérable Aśvaghoṣa sur la base des idées du *Sūtra*. Au milieu de l'ouvrage, c'est le texte propre du *Sūtra* prononcé par la bouche d'or. Cet ouvrage comporte trois divisions : c'est pourquoi il est appelé *Sūtra Tripartite*."[21]

A closer look at the manuscript of the *Tridaṇḍamālā* reveals that its structure corresponds perfectly well with Yijing's description of the *Tridaṇḍaka*. With all the necessary caution—we are still at the beginning of the editorial work—the following can be said about the text. It consists of forty chapters and contains forty canonical sūtras that form the core of each chapter. These sūtras are quoted in full length. The remainder of the text appears to consist

18. Schopen 1992, 33.

19. Lin 1949, 303–305.

20. In fact there are more: Or.8210/S.274, Or.8210/S.3887, and Or.8210/S.153; see Loukota Sanclemente's paper in this volume.

21. Lin 1949, 304; cf. Taishō 2912.85.1459a8–9 (初後讚歎乃是尊者馬鳴取經意而集造。中是正經。金口所說。事有三開，故云三啓也。) and its possible source, Yijing's travel record, Taishō 2125.54.227a13–17. Again, see the discussion in Loukota Sanclemente's paper and his translation of Taishō 801; for another translation of this text, see Willemen 2019.

exclusively of verses. Each chapter begins with verses of homage to the Three Jewels, often followed by another set of verses, and it concludes with one or more sets of verses. These sets before and after the canonical text are related to the main doctrinal contents of the embedded sūtra. Whether they were composed "sur la base des idées du *Sūtra*," as the note to the *Anityatā-sūtra* tells us, or selected from fitting passages in other works, remains to be seen and will be discussed below. Each chapter ends with two or three verses that wish for the duration of the Buddha's teaching, or its protection, and exhort others to practice it. Some of them are taken from the canonical literature, while for others a source has yet to be found; as well, they may have been composed by the compiler(s) of the text for this purpose. There is no set form, but some verses are repeatedly quoted, sometimes, but not consistently, abbreviated by *iti yāvat*, *iti vācyam*, and so on:[22]

yānīha bhūtāni samāgatāni
sthitāni bhūmāv athavāntarīkṣe |
kurvantu maitrīṃ satataṃ prajāsu
divā ca rātrau ca carantu dharmam ||

May those beings assembled here,
on the ground or in the air,
always act with love for others
and practice the Dharma day and night.[23]

ye 'bhyāgatā iha surāsuranāgayakṣa-
gandharvakinnaranarāḥ śravaṇāya dharmam |
rakṣantu te jagad idaṃ jinaśāsanaṃ ca
dharmaṃ munīndrakathitaṃ ca carantu nityam ||

May those gods, titans, snake gods, spirits,
heavenly musicians, kinnaras, and men who have come here to listen to the Dharma,
protect this world and the teaching of the conqueror

22. For instance, at the end of chapter 7, folio 14v3–4; for the first one, an Upajāti, see *Divyāvadāna* (Cowell and Neil 1886, 340), *Pravrajyāvastu* (Vogel and Wille 1996, 261), *Mahāmantrānusāriṇī* (Skilling 1994, 620), and *Mahāsāhasrapramardanī* (Iwamoto 1937, 26); at the end of chapter 8 it is repeated but abbreviated as *yānīha bhūtānīti vācyam* (16v5). The second one, a Vasantatilakā verse, seems to be unique to the *Tridaṇḍamālā*. Both stanzas are contained in Taishō 801; see III.14–15 on p. 342 in Loukota Sanclemente's translation.

23. Translation from Rotman 2017, 149.

and always practice the Dharma spoken by the chief among sages.

The sūtras are a very welcome addition, since in many cases their Sanskrit original was lost or known only from fragments. More sensational, perhaps, are some of the verse passages, which bring us back to Aśvaghoṣa and the question of authorship. When Johnston gave his verdict regarding the author, he could not have foreseen the singular chance he was missing. Had he considered the ascription in a more open-minded way and taken it seriously, at least in the sense that there may have been a reason for selecting Aśvaghoṣa among the many illustrious figures of Indian Buddhism, he would have been in for a big surprise once he started to read the manuscript. When we began to study the single chapters, we quickly noticed that they contain verses from the *Buddhacarita* and the *Saundarananda*. It is well known that only the first half of the *Buddhacarita* has survived in its Sanskrit original (up to stanza 31 of chapter 14), while the full text including the latter part (chapter 14.32–108 and chapters 15–28) is preserved only in a Chinese and a Tibetan translation. Therefore, the location of verses from the second half of the *Buddhacarita* will be especially welcome. The following list shows the verses identified so far.

Buddhacarita:
6.46–49 in chapter 30.3 (*Pañcasthāna-sūtra*)
7.21 in chapter 35.1 (last sūtra in the *Itivṛttaka*, Taishō 765)
11.9–33 in chapter 19.1 (SĀ 592)
12.70–81 in chapter 8.1 (*Paramārthaśūnyatā-sūtra*)
14.36–45 in chapter 35.1 (last sūtra in the *Itivṛttaka*, Taishō 765)
15.1–58 (full canto) in chapter 34.1 (*Dharmacakrapravartana-sūtra*)
16.76, 80–89 in chapter 8.1 and 16.90–93 in 8.3 (*Paramārthaśūnyatā-sūtra*)
18.62–78 in chapter 16.1 (**Sumanārājakumārī-sūtra*, cf. AN III 32)[24]

24. The passage comprises most of the Buddha's speech to Anāthapiṇḍada, who intends to donate a place for a monastery. Interestingly, stanzas 18.62–66 are also quoted anonymously in Sanskrit manuscripts from Central Asia in the context of donation, as in SHT 141/2 (donation formula; see Lüders 1930, 9), SHT 191h (donation formula; Schlingloff 1955, 38, no. 38, lines 2–6) and in the Tocharian bilingual PK NS 14v1–4 (Couvreur 1970, 180). When we studied all this material in our manuscript reading group, Gudrun Melzer succeeded in identifying a manuscript fragment from Afghanistan, now in the Schøyen Collection (MS 2377/198), as preserving stanzas 18.77–87. Stanza 87 is the last one in chapter 18 of the *Buddhacarita*; since the fragment ends with *darśanasya cāpīti///* it is very likely that a chapter colophon followed, and this would mean that the fragment comes from a manuscript of the whole *kāvya* (it will

19.19–22 in chapter 30.3 (*Pañcasthāna-sūtra*)
20.34 in chapter 38.1 (*Āryikā-sūtra*)
24.13–45 in chapter 13.3 (*Śāriputraparinirvāṇa-sūtra*)
26.60 in chapter 15.3 (*Daśabala-sūtra*)
26.73ab in chapter 27.1 (*Kṣāranadī-sūtra*)

Saundarananda:
5.22 in chapter 30.3 (**Pañcasthāna-sūtra*)
7.49 in chapter 23.1 (**Śivapathikā-sūtra*)
8.31–33, 35, 38–40, 44 in chapter 7.1 (not yet identified)
9.7–15, 18, 22, 24–26, 28–33 in chapter 30.1 (**Pañcasthāna-sūtra*)
9.44, 46–48 in chapter 19.1 (SĀ 592)
10.19–63 in chapter 18.1 and 18.3 (SĀ 505)
11.24–58, 61–62 in chapter 35.3 (last sūtra in the *Itivṛttaka*, Taishō 765)
15.31–41 in chapter 22.1 (SĀ 1325)
16.4–41 in chapter 34.3 (*Dharmacakrapravartana-sūtra*)
16.95–96 in chapter 15.1 (SĀ 341)

In order to give a brief example of recovered verses,[25] I present five stanzas from chapter 24 of the *Buddhacarita*, where the Buddha, on the verge of entering parinirvāṇa, replies to Ānanda's doubts and grievances. The whole passage corresponds to section 14 in Waldschmidt's edition of the *Mahāparinirvāṇa-sūtra*,[26] and again, as in practically all the passages studied by Eltschinger, one observes verbal correspondences between the sūtra text and Aśvaghoṣa's verses.[27] They contain the famous phrase *ātmadvīpair vihartavyam*, where the underlying Middle Indic *attadīpa*, when Sanskritized, may be resolved into either *ātmadīpa*, "lamp for yourself," or *ātmadvīpa*, "island (= refuge) for yourself."[28] Whether they were aware of these two possibilities or not, the edi-

be edited by Gudrun Melzer in the next volume of the Buddhist Manuscripts in the Schøyen Collection series).

25. Meanwhile Kazunobu Matsuda published the verses *Buddhacarita* 16.88–91 (Matsuda 2019a, 5–6), 15.1–58 (Matsuda 2020), and 14.35–44, 19.19–22, 20.23, 24.13–45, 26.49, and 60 (Matsuda 2023); cf. also Matsuda 2024.

26. Waldschmidt 1950–1951, 192–202 = 14.1–26; *Tridaṇḍamālā* 26v5–27r1.

27. For this passage, see Eltschinger 2020, 141–144 (still without knowledge of the original Sanskrit text).

28. Cf. Karashima 2015, 176–177, who takes *dīpa* as a double entendre introduced by the Buddha himself.

tors responsible for the Central Asian version of the *Mahāparinirvāṇa-sūtra* followed a tradition that had *ātmadvīpa*, and so did the editor(s) of the manuscript of the *Tridaṇḍamālā*, despite the fact that in stanza 24.23 Aśvaghoṣa uses the image of a lamp when explaining the word *dharmadvīpa*. The translators of the Tibetan text of the *Buddhacarita*, however, consistently chose *sgron ma*, "lamp" (= Skt. *dīpa*).

deśito vo mayā mārggaḥ kṛtsno vivṛta eva ca |
ācāryamuṣṭir na hy asti buddhānām iti gṛhyatām || 24.19[29]

sthite mayy upaśānte vā kāryam etāvad eva tu |
ko 'rtho vo maccharīreṇa dharmmakāyās tathāgatāḥ || 24.20

saṃvignais tatparais tasmād adhunā mama cātyayāt |
ātmadvīpair vviharttavyan dharmmadvīpaiś ca nityaśaḥ || 24.21[30]

ātmadvīpā iti jñeyās tatparā dṛḍhavikramāḥ |
nirdvandvāḥ kuśalair ddharmmair na parāyattabuddhayaḥ || 24.22

dharmmadvīpāḥ punar jñeyā vidyāvanto vipaścitaḥ |
dīptayā prajñayā ghnanti pradīpeneva ye tamaḥ || 24.23

19.[31] I have explained the entire path to you and did nothing but reveal it; you should understand that Buddhas do not have the closed fist of a teacher (i.e., they withhold nothing).
20. Whether I remain or whether I pass to peace, there is only one thing to be done. Of what use is my mortal body to you? Tathāgatas have the body of the Dharma.
21. Now and after my demise you should live deeply moved,[32] fully

29. Cf. Waldschmidt 1950–1951, 14.14: (*na tatrānanda tathāgatasya dharmeṣv* ācāryamu)ṣṭi(r) *yaṃ tathāgataḥ praticchādayitavyaṃ manyeta* (here and in the following, unitalicized words denote those that are culled by Aśvaghoṣa from the canonical text).

30. Cf. Waldschmidt 1950–1951, 14.22: (tasmād) *ānand*aitarhi mam(a vā)tyayād ātmadvīpair vihartavyaṃ *ātmaśaraṇair* dharmadvīpair *dha*(*rmaśaraṇair* . . .).

31. As far as possible I follow the excellent translation from the Tibetan in Johnston 1937, 240, but it is instructive to see to what extent I have to deviate from it in view of the Sanskrit original.

32. "Deeply moved" is an attempt at giving a positive sense to the difficult *saṃvigna*; cf. "[religious] emotion" for the Tibetan translation *skyo ba* in Eltschinger 2020, 143, and "perturbation of mind (*saṃvega*)" in Johnston 1937, 240.

devoted, continuously having yourself for refuge and having the Dharma for refuge.

22. You should be known as those who have themselves for refuge, to be fully devoted, of steadfast courage, free of dispute due to the wholesome dharmas,[33] with the mind not depending on others.
23. Furthermore, you should be known as those who have the Dharma for refuge, to be possessed of learning, wise, to be those who ward off with blazing knowledge (the darkness of ignorance) like those who ward off darkness with a lamp.

Apart from Aśvaghoṣa's two Mahākāvyas—or, rather, their doctrinally relevant passages—that appear to form a major source of the *Tridaṇḍamālā*, there are, for example, verses from the *Ajātaśatrvavadāna* ascribed to Gopadatta (76–79) in chapter 34,[34] and chapter 24 contains the whole *Apramādavarga*, chapter 4 of the *Udānavarga*. Citations from other important works are to be expected. Interesting is another stanza connected with Aśvaghoṣa's name, the original source of which remains unknown. In his *Ratnaśrī*, a commentary on the *Kāvyādarśa*, the tenth-century Buddhist author Ratnaśrījñāna quotes a stanza from Aśvaghoṣa:[35]

ālasyaṃ yadi na bhavej jagaty anarthaḥ
ko vidvān hi na bhaved dhaneśvaro vā |

33. The exact meaning of *nirdvandvāḥ kuśalair ddharmmair* is difficult to determine, and the Tibetan rendering *rtsod med bdag gi don la mkhas* differs. It corresponds to a metrically possible *nirdvandvāḥ kuśalāḥ svārthe*, "indifferent, conversant with your own benefit," and is either based on a different Sanskrit original or the result of the translators' struggle with the passage (for the inferior quality of the Tibetan translation, see Jackson 1997, 39–40 and 49–50). Johnston translates it as "freed from the pairs, recognize your goal (*svārtha*)" (1937, 240). In Bc, *nirdvandva* is attested two more times: in 12.47c Johnston translates it as "free from the pairs of worldly life" (1936, 174) with a reference to 11.43a *dvandvāni* where it alludes to the four pairs of worldly dharmas (*lokadharma*). A third occurrence is found in 16.22; a part of this verse is preserved in a fragment from Central Asia edited by Friedrich Weller (1953, 7) as *maharṣir api nirdva(ndv)o*; Johnston translates the Tibetan as "the Great Seer, . . ., Who was freed from the pairs (*dvandva*)" (1937, 38). In all three cases Tibetan has *rtsod* for *dvandva* (12.47 *rtsod med*, 16.22 *rtsod bral*, 24.22 *rtsod med*; cf. Weller 1926, 198 and 270). Both translations, "free of dispute" and "free from (the four) pairs (of worldly dharmas)," make sense in all three places.

34. Cf. Hahn 1981, 274.

35. Thakur and Jha 1957, 61: *yathoktam ācāryāśvaghoṣeṇa*; for the dating of Ratnaśrījñāna, see Dimitrov 2011, 35–46.

> *ālasyād avanir iyaṃ sasāgarā hi*
> *saṃpūrṇā narapaśubhiś ca nirdhanaiś ca* ||
>
> If lassitude were not a misfortune in the world, who here would not be learned or rich? For through lassitude the Earth with (up to) its Ocean is filled with men who are like animals and poor (translation Warder 1974, 180, § 766).

This is a Praharṣiṇī with a metrical problem in *pāda* b. Surprisingly, the same stanza is found in the *Mokṣopāya*, a philosophical work of the seventh to ninth centuries from Kashmir.[36] Here, the metrical problem is solved (*ko na syād bahudhaniko bahuśruto vā*) and *pāda* c shows a rotation and a variant: *ālasyād iyam avanis sasāgarāntā*. Now Kazunobu Matsuda found the same stanza in the *Tridaṇḍamālā* (folio 30v2) in the first part of chapter 15, which contains the second *Daśabala-sūtra*[37] with *kausīdya* instead of *ālasya* in *pāda* a[38] (but *ālasya* retained in *pāda* c), another variant in *pāda* b and the same text in *pāda* c as in the *Mokṣopāya*:

> *kausīdyaṃ yadi na bhavej jagaty anarthaḥ*
> *ko na syād iha dhanavān bahuśruto vā* |
> *ālasyād iyam avaniḥ sasāgarāntā*
> *saṃpūrṇṇā narapaśubhiś ca nirdhanaiś ca* ||

How are these findings to be interpreted, and how are these three texts related to each other? There are at least two possible explanations. Either the stanza belongs to an unknown work of Aśvaghoṣa from which it was culled and inserted independently into both the *Tridaṇḍamālā* and the *Ratnaśrīṭīkā*. Or, alternatively, the stanza originally belonged to a text of unknown authorship, from which it was taken and inserted into the *Tridaṇḍamālā*, attributed to Aśvaghoṣa, and later used as a source by Ratnaśrījñāna. It is impossible to reconstruct how the stanza found its way into the *Mokṣopāya*, but it is known

36. Cf. Krause-Stinner 2011, 134, for the edition, and Steiner 2014, 182, for a German translation. I am grateful to Roland Steiner, who points me to the fact that the stanza is also preserved in the *Mahāsubhāṣitasaṃgraha* as no. 5293 (see Sternbach 1977, 1273); its wording is identical with that of the *Mokṣopāya*.

37. Waldschmidt 1958.

38. The two terms *ālasya* and *kausīdya* are closely related, and in the *Arthavistaradharmaparyāya* they appear as the first and second in a group of six factors detrimental to the recognition of suffering in impermanence (*anitye duḥkhasaṃjñā*); see SWTF, s.v. *kausīdya* (2:132) and *ālasya* in the addenda (4:558).

that the original version of this highly interesting work included Buddhist concepts.[39]

Even if not penned by Aśvaghoṣa, the *Tridaṇḍamālā* turns out to be a veritable mine of his stanzas. It contains priceless information, part of which concerns philologists and those interested in Buddhist literature: there are texts that were deemed lost in their Indian original, and some of them preserve readings of philological and dogmatic importance. However, it will also hopefully intrigue those who, like Gregory Schopen, are interested in the practice of Indian Buddhism. The actual practice, the rituals, and the everyday behavior of its proponents are extremely difficult to reconstruct from the surviving texts that are mostly normative, not descriptive. Here the *Tridaṇḍamālā* provides us with one of the rare windows into this realm. It is clearly a textbook designed for use in rituals, and the forty chapters would suggest that it was probably used in a wide variety of them. Regrettably, the text does not indicate the purpose or application of a specific chapter, or how to recite it; such matters must have been known to the officiating monk(s) who used it—not unlike a catechism, it seems. There is one chapter, however, which points to its possible application: chapter 25 contains the *Pravāraṇa-sūtra*,[40] itself a sūtra concerned with a ritual,[41] and in its third section the *Ekottarikastotra* ascribed to Mātṛceṭa is quoted, but with a telling adaptation. The ten Anuṣṭubh stanzas of this *stotra* contain epithets of the Buddha relating to the numbers one through ten, in ascending order, all in datives depending on the word *namas*, "homage to." In the *Tridaṇḍamālā* these epithets are consistently changed into genitives in agreement with the phrase *teṣām adya pravāraṇā*, "for them is now the Pravāraṇā (ceremony)," as, for example, in the second stanza:[42]

39. Cf. Slaje 2001, 772ff.; for the latest discussion of the stanza, see Dimitrov 2016, 193 (again, I owe this reference to Roland Steiner).

40. This spelling is attested in all the three colophons preserved in the Central Asian manuscripts.

41. In Central Asia the Sanskrit text is preserved in fragments from about ten manuscripts (a study and reconstruction of the text by the present author is finished, but unpublished). At least seven of them belong to composite manuscripts, since they contain the end of the *Pravāraṇa-sūtra* and the beginning of the following text. None of them represents a/the canonical order, and the other sūtras strongly suggest that the texts were assembled for apotropaic or ceremonial purposes. Despite many small differences, the Central Asian version and the one quoted in the *Tridaṇḍamālā* belong to the same recension, i.e., that of the (Mūla)Sarvāstivādins, if this term is helpful in a sūtra context.

42. The *Ekottarikastotra* is preserved in a Sanskrit manuscript from Tibet; cf. Matsuda 2019b, 23. For a comparative study of the *stotra*, its Tibetan translation, and the adaptation in the *Tridaṇḍamālā*, see Terzová 2019.

Ekottarikastotra:
dvipadānāṃ variṣṭhāya satyadvayavibhāvine |
advitīyasahāyāya namo 'stv advayabhāvine || 2 ||

Tridaṇḍamālā:
dvipadānāṃ variṣṭhānāṃ satyadvayavibhāvināṃ |
advitīyasahāyānāṃ teṣām adya pravāraṇā || 2 ||

Independent of the question whether Mātṛceṭa really is the author of the *stotra*, it is highly unlikely that the *stotra* was derived from the text in the *Tridaṇḍamālā*. Several terms—for example, *lokaikacakṣurbhūta* (verse 1) and *dvipadānāṃ variṣṭha* (verse 2)—are well-known epithets of the Buddha but not normally used for members of the saṅgha. This strongly speaks in favor of the *stotra* having been adapted, and therefore it is at least possible that chapter 25 was intended as a ceremonial text specifically designed to accompany the ritual of Pravāraṇā.

Amazing is the wide range of genres and literary styles that provided the building blocks, from the *Udānavarga* to the *Buddhacarita*, and no less amazing is the amount of sophisticated poetry that has been put to use in the collection; it is difficult to imagine that those who recited the text were not familiar, at least to a certain degree, with the works from which the citations came. Of course it is impossible to date the origin of the *Tridaṇḍamālā*, but Yijing's translation of the *Wuchang jing* 無常經 and his description of the *Tridaṇḍaka* demonstrate that, if not the *Tridaṇḍamālā* itself, at least its model was known already in the beginning of the eighth century and widely employed. I know of only a single reference to the work in a source that may be rather unexpected: Ratnākaraśānti in his *Muktikāvalī*, a commentary on the *Hevajra-tantra*, gives the *Avadānaśataka* and a/the *Tridaṇḍakamālā* as examples of works of the Śrāvakayāna: *tac ca śrāvakayānam avadānaśataka-tridaṇḍakamālādi*.[43] This is a peculiar combination, to say the least, and it is not clear whether Ratnākaraśānti references the two as examples of ritually employed texts, a possibility which may also hold for some of the texts he names in the following as examples of Mahāyāna sūtras. One should keep in mind that the whole passage starts with actions involving recitation and certain ritual elements—that is, the *poṣadha* and the ten *śikṣāpadas*. Regarding the title *Tridaṇḍakamālā*, it appears that the Tibetan translators of the *Muktikāvalī* either had a manuscript with the reading *Trimiśrakamālā* or understood the term *daṇḍaka* to

43. Isaacson 2013, 1039. I am grateful to Kazunobu Matsuda for bringing this reference to my attention.

mean something similar to this, since they translated the title as *spel ma gsum pa'i phreng ba*, "Garland of the triple mixture."[44]

Yet another interesting phenomenon might be mentioned. The *Anityatāsūtra* is included in the *Tridaṇḍamālā* as its eleventh chapter (starting on folio 201r4).[45] The accompanying verse passages, however, are not identical with those of the *Wuchang jing* 無常經. The verses before the sūtra are completely different, and those after the sūtra correspond only partly. This suggests a very open tradition, in which it was no problem at all to adapt the verse chapters of each *tridaṇḍa* to one's personal preferences or to specific ritual needs. The *Tridaṇḍaka* must have been a *Gebrauchstext*, a work for daily use of a highly fluid nature that allowed individual selection.[46] It also must have been a text used with enormous frequency and probably existed in countless different versions. This leads to the observation of an amazing discrepancy: If the *Tridaṇḍaka* was a kind of textbook used by monks in many rituals and for various purposes, one would expect to see this frequent use reflected in the number of surviving manuscripts. Why, then, do we know of only two textual witnesses, the *Tridaṇḍamālā* and the *Wuchang jing*? This is not easy to explain, but it may have been exactly due to its function as a textbook for daily use with a high degree of personal variation that its careful preservation was not necessary. Nonetheless, it is puzzling, since each manuscript, as one of its three *daṇḍa*s, would contain the word of the Buddha, something not easily treated with disrespect and negligence in its written form.

There are many references to the *Tridaṇḍaka* in the Vinaya section of the Tibetan canon (and, of course, in the corresponding texts in the Chinese Tripiṭaka), fewer in the Bka' 'gyur, but more than sixty in the Bstan 'gyur according to a search in an electronic version of the Sde dge edition. In both collections, the translation *rgyud chags gsum pa* alternates with *rgyun chags*

44. Sde dge 1189, Rgyud, vol. *ga*, 295b4–5; Peking 2319, Rgyud 'grel, vol. *tsa*, 361b1–4: *de nyid kyi nyan thos kyi theg pa ste gdams ngag brgya pa dang spel ma gsum pa'i phreng ba la sogs pa'i lung ngo*; interestingly, *Avadānaśataka* is translated as *gdams ngag brgya pa*, differing from the usual title *rtogs pa brjod pa brgya pa*.

45. This chapter is edited and translated into Japanese in Matsuda, Demoto, Ueno, Tanaka, and Fukita 2024.

46. This may also explain the curious text in a Tibetan manuscript from Dunhuang (IOL Tib J 466/3), which Lewis Doney describes as containing "praises to the Three Jewels, a paeon to a Tibetan emperor as both a ruler and a Buddhist, and a cosmology that includes both local deities and great Indian gods" (Doney 2018, 78). Although the text consists of three sections that are named *rgyud chags* and counted as *dang po*, *bar ma*, and *tha ma*, it does not follow the format of texts represented, e.g., by the *Tridaṇḍamālā*: The middle section does not consist of a canonical text, and it does not conclude with the dedication of merit. Interesting, however, is the reference to intonation (Doney 2018, 83, 85).

gsum pa. Not only is the meaning of each term opaque, but it is also difficult to decide which form could be the original one. This ambiguity is perfectly illustrated by the *Bod rgya tshig mdzod chen mo*, also quoted by Schopen in his footnote, where *rgyun chags gsum pa* serves as the lemma, but the definition then explains three *rgyud*. The most interesting reference with regard to its structure is perhaps one in the *Vinayavastuṭīkā*, where Kalyāṇamitra defines the *Tridaṇḍaka* along the lines of Yijing's description—without, however, mentioning Aśvaghoṣa:[47]

> *rgyun* (*rgyud* P) *chags gsum pa gdon* (*'don* P) *par bya'o zhes bya ba ni 'gyes kar dkon mchog gsum gyi rgyud dang | mdo sde'i rgyud dang | bsngo ba'i rgyud chags gsum gdon par bya'o || de yang dper na kun du rgyu dag gi ril ba'i* (*pa'i* D) *gzhi* (*rgyu* P) *shing bu gsum la brten pa dang 'dra bar dam pa'i chos gdon pa'i gzhi ni rgyun* (*rgyud* P) *chags gsum po 'di yin pas de'i phyir rgyun* (*rgyud* P) *chags gsum zhes bya ba'o* (*bya'o* P) *|| ran par gdon par bya'o | zhes bya ba ni ha cang mang ba yang ma yin te | ha cang nyung ba yang ma yin par ci ran cig gdon* (*gdong* D) *par bya ba'o || yon bshad par bya'o zhes bya ba ni rgyun* (*rgyud* P) *chags gsum pa bton pa'i 'og tu sbyin pa'i phan yon bshad par bya'o ||*

> "The *Tridaṇḍaka* is to be recited" means that separately three parts, a section on the Three Jewels, a section on the sūtra, and a section on the dedication (of the merit), are to be recited. In the same way as the Parivrājakas, for example, rely on the three wooden sticks as support for the pot, the support for reciting the holy Dharma is this "Triple Staff" (*tridaṇḍa*); therefore it is called *Tridaṇḍaka*. "It

47. Sde dge 4113, 'Dul ba, vol. *tsu*, 312a3–5; Peking 5615, 'Dul ba'i 'grel pa, vol. *dzu*, 361b1–4; for some remarks on the *Vinayavastuṭīkā* and its author Kalyāṇamitra, see Schopen 2010b, 228. Here Kalyāṇamitra comments on a passage in the *Poṣadhavastu*; see Hu-von Hinüber 1994, 292–294, § 21.1–3: *tṛdaṇḍako bhāṣitavyaḥ* <|> *atimahāntaṃ bhāṣante • bhagavān āha | nātimahān bhāṣitavyaḥ* <|> *te tv alpaṃ bhāṣante | bhagavān āha | nātyalpo bhāṣitavyaḥ* <|> *api tu parimaṇḍalo bhāṣitavyaḥ*; for a brief discussion of the meaning of *tṛdaṇḍaka*, see 209–210. For the manner of recitation, see also Schopen 2010a, 118n35: "Thus, the Proclamation of the Qualities of the Teacher and the recitation of the *Tridaṇḍaka* must be recited with measured intonation!" (*Kṣudrakavastu* [Sde dge 6, 'Dul ba, vol. *tha*, 46a7–b1; Peking 1035, 'Dul ba, vol. *de*, 43a8–b1]: *'di ltar ston pa'i yon tan yang dag par bsgrag* [*sgrag* P] *pa dang | rgyud* [*rgyun* P] *chags gsum pa gdon pa dag ni skad kyi gtang rag gis gdon par bya'o*), with a reference to *Vinayasūtra* 55.10: *kuryāt śāstṛguṇasaṃkīrttane tridaṇḍakadāne ca svaraguptim*. For the vocal technique in the recitation of the *Tridaṇḍaka*, see also Liu 2018, especially 728–730.

> is to be recited measuredly" means that it should not be recited too forcefully or too feebly. "The reward is to be assigned" means that after the *Tridaṇḍaka* has been recited the benefit of the gift is to be assigned.

This leads, finally, once more to the question of the exact meaning of the term *tridaṇḍa(ka)*. All the sources make it clear that *tri* refers to the threefold structure of the text or genre, but the exact meaning of *daṇḍa* remains somewhat mysterious. The *Vinayavastuṭīkā* indicates that the Brahmanical use of the term *tridaṇḍa* was not foreign to Buddhist texts.[48] Another example is found in the title of one of the discourses in the Śīlaskandha section of the Sanskrit *Dīrghāgama*. The text is known as the *Tridaṇḍi-sūtra*, and here it is evident that the name refers to a Brahmanical ascetic and his tripod. Śamathadeva in his *Abhidharmakośaṭīkā Upāyikā*, preserved only in Tibetan translation, quotes several times from the sūtra; three times *tridaṇḍin* is translated as *dbyug* (variants *dbu* and *dbyu*) *gu gsum pa*, but in a fourth citation, most likely also from the *Tridaṇḍi-sūtra*, it appears as *rgyud chags gsum pa*.[49] This must be a mistake of the translators, who unwittingly substituted the Buddhist for the Brahmanical meaning. Neither of the two Tibetan translations referred to above, *rgyud chags gsum pa* or *rgyun chags gsum pa*, helps us to understand the meaning of *daṇḍa(ka)*. Interestingly, the *Wörterbuch der tibetischen Schriftsprache* (WtS) gives under the entry for *rgyun chags* one of the meanings as "Bez[eichnung] für hypermetrische Verse, skt. *Daṇḍaka*"[50] and then refers to the *Mahāvyutpatti*, where *vṛtta* (1463), *chandas* (1464), *daṇḍaka* (1465), *grantha* (1466), and *parivāra* (1466) occur in a long list of classificatory terms used in literature.[51] For *rgyud chags*, the *Wörterbuch* refers to a passage from the *Pravrajyāvastu*, "*des ~ lṅa brgya bzlas so* 'er trug die 500 *rgyud chags* (skt. *tantraḥ*) vor,'" but the Sanskrit text edited in Vogel and Wille 1992, 75 (fol. 4r5) and 94, has *daṇḍa*.[52] As far as I can see, we have descriptions of the three parts of the *Tridaṇḍa(ka)*, but no definition of the term. In the absence

48. To the material adduced in notes 9 and 11 of Loukota Sanclemente's paper in this volume, one could add Zin 2018 for visual representations of such ascetics in Buddhist art.

49. Hartmann 1991, 269.

50. Cf. the title *Buddhabhaṭṭārakasya daṇḍakavṛttena stotram*, the "Hymnus auf den hochzuverehrenden Buddha im Daṇḍakaversmaß" (Hahn 1987, 52), translated into Tibetan as *Sangs rgyas rje btsun la rgyun chags kyi tshigs su bcad pas bstod pa*—unless, that is, it was retranslated into Sanskrit by the Tibetans, which would explain its grammatical peculiarities.

51. Sakaki 1916–1925, 112.

52. I owe this reference to one of the anonymous reviewers.

of better evidence, one can only speculate as to whether the Buddhists adopted the Brahmanical term that refers to the three staffs bound together and put it to use in a figurative sense, as the passage in the *Vinayavastuṭīkā* suggests.

Addenda

1. As mentioned above, our study of the *Tridaṇḍamālā* is a work in progress and constantly yields new insights. One such insight is worth mentioning here since it concerns Vinaya material. In May 2019, Kazunobu Matsuda noticed that Sāṅkṛtyāyana's excerpt of the first chapter contains verses known from the Mūlasarvāstivādin *Vinayavastu*.[53] Another Sanskrit version of these verses is found in the famous Gilgit manuscript of the *Vinayavastu*, more specifically in the *Cīvaravastu*,[54] and parts of them are preserved in an unpublished fragmentary manuscript of the *Vinayoddānagāthā* in the Schøyen Collection in Norway (MS 2381/51 verso, lines 2–4, and MS 2382/183 recto, line 1).[55]

2. Péter-Dániel Szántó was able to identify the forty stanzas of the *Śokavinodana*, a work so far only known from its Tibetan translation, *Mya ngan bsal ba* (Sde dge 4177 = 4505; Peking 5418 = 5677), in chapter 14 of the *Tridaṇḍamālā*. The colophon of the *Mya ngan bsal ba* ascribes the work to Aśvaghoṣa (*slob dpon rta dbyangs*). This finding led to two further identifications: first, a Sanskrit fragment from Central Asia in the German Turfan Collection (SHT 191 k and m, cf. note 24 above, and Schlingloff 1955, 38, nos. 41–44) by myself, and second, a Chinese translation, the *Jieyou jing* 解憂經 (Taishō 804), by Kazunobu Matsuda. Taishō 804 is a late translation by Fatian 法天 in the tenth century; it closely corresponds to the fourteenth *tridaṇḍa* of the *Tridaṇḍamālā*, thus adding a second Chinese example to Yijing's translation of the *Wuchang jing* (Taishō 801, see above).[56]

3. Meanwhile, we found four verses in the *Tridaṇḍamālā* that are also attested in the fragments of Aśvaghoṣa's *Śāriputraprakaraṇa*. One is contained in chapter 19.1 of the *Tridaṇḍamālā*, the second and third in chapter 19.3, and the fourth in chapter 27.3. For the first, see Lüders 1911b, 391 [= 1940, 193], fragment C 2, recto 3–4; for the second, Lüders 1911a, 79, fragment 51, b2, and 53, b1; for the third, Lüders 1911b, 391 [= 1940, 194], fragment C 2, verso 2–3; and for the fourth, Lüders 1911b, 393 [= 1940, 195], fragment K I, verso 3.

53. Sāṅkṛtyāyana 1938, 159–160.

54. Dutt 1942, 76.

55. "Schøyen Collection: Brāhmī." University of Oslo, Faculty of Humanities. Accessed June 29, 2019. https://www2.hf.uio.no/polyglotta/index.php?page=volume&vid=795.

56. See Hartmann, Matsuda, and Szántó 2022.

It is rather difficult to assess these findings, especially the fact that three of the four verses are found in close proximity to each other. Did the compilers of the *Tridaṇḍamālā* have a manuscript of the *Śāriputraprakaraṇa* at their disposal? This is unlikely, in my view. More probable is the possibility that they quoted from another source that also contained these verses. In light of all the evidence, it appears almost certain that the editors knew that the verses were connected with Aśvaghoṣa, wherever they sourced them. One possibility to be reckoned with—and strongly favored by Kazunobu Matsuda—could be Aśvaghoṣa's lost **Sūtrālaṃkāra*. We discuss the four stanzas and their possible source in another paper.[57]

4. In view of the fact that nearly all the verses identified so far are in one way or another connected to Aśvaghoṣa, the authorship of the *Ekottarikastotra* should be briefly reconsidered (see above in the context of the Pravāraṇā ceremony). Although the two sources (a separate Sanskrit manuscript and a Tibetan translation) unanimously ascribe it to Mātṛceṭa, we should perhaps not forget that from a certain time onward in the Indian Buddhist tradition Aśvaghoṣa and Mātṛceṭa were conflated.[58] This seems to be a late development: Atiśa mentions this conflation in the beginning of the eleventh century, and the *Prasādapratibhodbhava*, the second of Mātṛceṭa's two famous hymns, is credited to Aśvaghoṣa in its Tibetan canonical translation. If our version of the *Tridaṇḍamālā* is a late compilation—a possibility to be reckoned with—its compilers may have drawn on the *Ekottarikastotra* with the conviction that this text was also written by Aśvaghoṣa.

5. At present (April 2024), ten sūtras have been published:

TDM 5.2: an unidentified sūtra with partial parallels in SĀ 930, Taishō 99.2.237b–c, and the *Abhidharmakośavyākhyā* (Hartmann and Maue 2022, 71–74; Matsuda, Demoto, Ueno, Tanaka, and Fukita 2023, 65–67)

TDM 8.2: *Paramārthaśūnyatā-sūtra* (Matsuda 2024)

TDM 11.2: *Anityatā-sūtra* (Matsuda, Demoto, Ueno, Tanaka, and Fukita 2024, 10–13)

TDM 21.2: **Śivapathikā-sūtra* (Matsuda 2021)

TDM 26.2: *Āśīviṣa-sūtra* (Matsuda, Demoto, Ueno, Tanaka, and Fukita 2022)

TDM 27.2: *Kṣāranadī-sūtra* (partial edition, Hartmann 2022a; complete edition, Matsuda and Hartmann 2022)

57. See Hartmann and Matsuda 2024, 236–240.

58. See Hartmann 1987, 21, and Almogi 2020, 158ff.

TDM 29.2: *Aṣṭākṣaṇakṣaṇa-sūtra* (Ueno 2020)
TDM 30.2: **Pañcasthāna-sūtra* (Ueno 2021)
TDM 31.2: *Āryikā-sūtra* (Hartmann 2022b)
TDM 36.2: **Asāra-sūtra* (Ueno 2022)

Especially remarkable is the *Kṣāranadī-sūtra*, a Tibetan translation of which is preserved only in two of the so-called proto-Bka' 'gyurs, Gondhla and Tholing.

6. The appearance of stanzas from the second part of the *Buddhacarita* lost in Sanskrit had many repercussions and led to the identification of quotations especially in the manuscript fragments from Central Asia (see note 24 above for some examples). The most recent find concerns old Uigur literature. Three Sanskrit-Uigur bilingual manuscripts could be shown to contain text of the *Buddhacarita*.[59] All three share the same feature: not only the Sanskrit but also the Uigur text is written in a form of Indian Brāhmī and not in the usual Uigur script. Two of them (AtüHs I 25 and AtüHs II 115) belong to the German Turfan Collection, and the third (80 TBI 774b) to the collection of the Academia Turfanica.[60] The two German fragments overlap, and they must be derived from a common exemplar. Both excerpt the Sanskrit very unevenly: sometimes several words of a verse are excerpted and then several verses are skipped. The reason for this uneven selection process remains obscure. The first fragment, AtüHs I 25, contains words of verses from *Buddhacarita* 16.36 to at least 17.17, while the second, AtüHs II 115, covers words from verse 16.61 to at least 17.5. Since the TDM cites only the verses *Buddhacarita* 16.76 and 80–93, the quotations from those stanzas, which are not covered in the TDM, pose many problems, but the identification as such is beyond doubt. The fragment from Bezeklik, on the other hand, quotes more or less every word of the Sanskrit text but usually reduces it to its first *akṣara*. It preserves the text of Bc 15.27–38, which is fully quoted in the TDM.

7. Above (p. 238) the question was raised as to why we know only two textual witnesses, the *Tridaṇḍamālā* and the *Wuchang jing*, although the *Tridaṇḍaka* ritual provided a recitation pattern for all kinds of religious occasions throughout the year. A third witness, the *Jieyou jing*, was mentioned in addendum 2. Meanwhile, there are two more examples, both from the Silk Road, a Sanskrit manuscript and another Sanskrit-Uigur bilingual text. The first is SHT 4437 and 4438, two consecutive folios of a manuscript in the German Turfan Collection.[61] It corresponds to chapter 19 of the TDM and pre-

59. Hartmann, Wille, and Zieme 2022.

60. For the third, see Maue and Niu 2012.

61. Published in vol. 11 of the SHT series, pp. 33–35.

serves text of the last verse in section 1, the sūtra quotation in section 2, and the first eight Śārdūlavikrīḍita stanzas in section 3. This confirms the sequence and leaves no doubt as to the background of SHT 4438. Remarkably, the fragment contains glosses in Tocharian A and B, the local languages, which provide additional evidence for the practical use of the manuscript.

The second witness is TT VIII D found in Xočo.[62] This fragment belongs to a special group among the Uigur manuscripts: as in the case of the two Uigur manuscripts mentioned in addendum 6, the whole text is written in a Central Asian form of Indian Brāhmī script. It corresponds to chapter 5 of the TDM and covers parts of all three sections of this chapter. Of the first section, only the last verse is preserved, which carries the number 21 in the bilingual version. Although the late Indian manuscript of the TDM does not register verse numbers, its first section also contains exactly twenty-one stanzas. In the TDM, the full text of the sūtra is quoted, while the bilingual cites only two or possibly three excerpts. After that, the bilingual preserves remains of the first nine Vasantatilakā stanzas of the third section, again providing verse numbers, now starting with number 1. All this evidence leaves us with but one conclusion—namely, that the bilingual must be a version of at least chapter 5 of the TDM, if not of the whole text. Regrettably, so far only one of the verses in chapter 5 could be related to a third text, which, however, is hardly its source: the final verse 21 in the first section is also quoted in an introductory part contained in several manuscripts of the *Samādhirāja-sūtra*.[63] This introduction and the TDM share a number of verses, and therefore it is very likely that both draw on the same source, which could even be Aśvaghoṣa's lost *Sūtrālaṃkāra*.

8. The stanzas in the TDM reveal an amazing network of intertextuality, both in the sense of verses that appear verbatim in other sources and also in the sense of allusions or imitations. Some examples for the latter are collected in Hartmann and Matsuda 2024, section 6 (243–248). Some examples for the former are already given above, but many more could be added now. Here, we present only one, since its source was quite unexpected. Normally, a chapter of the TDM opens with three verses of homage to the *triratna* of Buddha, Dharma, and Saṅgha, and there are only a few exceptions. One of them is chapter 36, which begins with a single stanza of praise for all the three jewels in the form of a beautiful Śikhariṇī:

> *jayaty ādau tāvad daśabala*(101r2)*ravir dīptavacanaḥ*
> *prabhājālaḥ śrīmāṃs tribhuvanatamonāśanapaṭuḥ* |

62. Hartmann and Maue 2022.

63. Verse 33; see Matsunami 1975, 237 (identified by Péter-Dániel Szántó).

tato dharmāmbhodo hṛdayajarajaḥśāntijanano
jayaty āryaś cāgryo munivarasutānām iha gaṇaḥ ||

> Victorious is he first and foremost, the sun of ten powers, whose words are brilliant, who is surrounded by an abundance of light, the illustrious one, skilled in the removal of darkness in the three worlds; moreover, victorious is the cloud of the Dharma, which causes the stilling of passion born in one's heart, and [also] the noble and foremost group in this world [consisting] of the sons of the best ascetic.[64]

The same stanza is preserved at the beginning of an important copper scroll inscription found in Afghanistan that probably dates to the end of the fifth century.[65] Immediately after the verse, a sūtra is quoted, in this case a Mahāyāna work, the *Śrīmatībrāhmaṇīparipṛcchā*; in inscriptions, such a quotation seems unusual, but it connects at least vaguely with the format of the TDM. Regarding the origin of the verse, neither the TDM nor the inscription seem a probable candidate; most likely, both cite it from a third source, which again could be the lost *Sūtrālaṃkāra*.

9. There are now three sources that make a title form *Tridaṇḍa<ka>mālā* probable. One of these is the mention in Ratnākaraśānti's *Muktikāvalī* (see above with note 43); the other two are found in a text preserved in Uigur and Tocharian. For a detailed discussion, see Hartmann and Maue 2022, 52–54.

Works Cited

Abbreviations

AN *The Aṅguttara-Nikāya*. Edited by Richard Morris and E. Hardy. 5 vols. London: The Pali Text Society, 1885–1900.

AtüHs I See Maue 1996.

AtüHs II See Maue 2015.

Peking *Eiin Pekin-ban chibetto daizōkyō: Ōtani daigaku toshokan-zō* 影印北京版西藏大蔵経：大谷大学図書館蔵 (*The Tibetan Tripitaka:*

64. The translation is based on Melzer 2006, 267, but fills the gaps in her text.

65. Melzer 2006, 264 for the dating, and 267 for the edition of the verse.

Peking Edition. Kept in the Library of the Otani University, Kyoto). Edited by Chibetto Daizōkyō Kenkyūkai 西蔵大蔵経研究会. 168 vols. Tokyo: Chibetto daizōkyō kenkyūkai 西蔵大蔵経研究会, 1955–1961.

SĀ *Saṃyuktāgama* (Taishō Tripiṭaka no. 99)

Sde dge *The Sde-dge Mtshal-par Bka'-'gyur: A Facsimile Edition of the 18th Century Redaction of Si-tu Chos-kyi-'byuṅ-gnas Prepared under the Direction of H.H. the 16th Rgyal-dbaṅ Karma-pa*. 103 vols. Delhi: Delhi Karmapae Chodhey Gyalwae Sungrab Partun Khang, 1976–1979.

Sde-dge Bstan-'gyur Series, Published as Part of the Dgoṅs-rdzogs of H.H. the Sixteenth Rgyal-dbaṅ Karma-pa. 213 vols. New Delhi: Delhi Karmapae Chodhey, 1982–1986. Reprinted together as *The Tibetan Tripiṭaka, Taipei Edition*. 72 vols. Taipei: SMC Publishing, 1991.

SHT *Sanskrithandschriften aus den Turfanfunden*. Edited by Ernst Waldschmidt, Lore Sander, and Klaus Wille. 12 vols. Wiesbaden. Stuttgart: Franz Steiner Verlag, 1965–2017.

SWTF *Sanskrit-Wörterbuch der buddhistischen Texte aus den Turfan-Funden und der kanonischen Literatur der Sarvāstivāda-Schule*. Edited by Heinz Bechert, Klaus Röhrborn, and Jens-Uwe Hartmann. 4 vols. Göttingen: Vandenhoeck & Ruprecht, 1973–2017.

Taishō *Taishō shinshū daizōkyō* 大正新脩大藏經 (*The Buddhist Canon in Chinese, Newly Edited in the Taishō Era*). Edited by Takakusu Junjirō 高楠順次郎 and Watanabe Kaikyoku 渡邊海旭. 100 vols. Tokyo: Taishō issaikyō kankōkai 大正一切經刊行會, 1924–1935.

TDM *Tridaṇḍamālā*

WtS *Wörterbuch der tibetischen Schriftsprache*. Compiled by Petra Maurer and Johannes Schneider assisted by Samyo Rode and Nikolai Solmsdorf. Edited by Jens-Uwe Hartmann and Thomas O. Höllmann. Fascicles 1–. Munich: Verlag der Bayerischen Akademie der Wissenschaften in Kommission beim Verlag C. H. Beck, 2005–.

Almogi, Orna. 2020. *Authenticity and Authentication: Glimpses behind the Scenes of the Formation of the Tibetan Buddhist Canon*. Hamburg: Department of Indian and Tibetan Studies, Universität Hamburg.

Bandurski, Frank. 1994. "Übersicht über die Göttinger Sammlungen der von Rāhula Sāṅkṛtyāyana in Tibet aufgefundenen buddhistischen Sanskrit-Texte (Funde buddhistischer Sanskrit-Handschriften, III)." In *Untersuchungen zur buddhistischen Literatur*, 9–126. Sanskrit-Wörterbuch der buddhistischen Texte aus den Turfan-Funden, Beiheft 5. Göttingen: Vandenhoeck & Ruprecht.

Cousins, Lance S. 2003. "Sākiyabhikkhu/Sakyabhikkhu/Śākyabhikṣu: A Mistaken Link to the Mahāyāna?" *Saṃbhāṣā: Nagoya Studies in Indian Culture and Buddhism* 23: 1–27.

Couvreur, Walter. 1970. "Boeddhistische Sanskritfragmenten in Koetsjische Handschriftenverzamelingen." In *ANAMNHCIC: Gedenkboek Prof. Dr. E. A. Leemans*, 175–184. Brugge: Faculteit van de Letteren en Wijsbegeerte.

Cowell, Edward B., and Robert A. Neil. 1886. *The Divyâvadâna: A Collection of Early Buddhist Legends*. Cambridge: The University Press.

Dimitrov, Dragomir. 2011. *Śabdālaṃkāradoṣavibhāga: Die Unterscheidung der Lautfiguren und der Fehler*. 2 vols. Wiesbaden: Harrassowitz Verlag.

———. 2016. *The Legacy of the Jewel Mind: On the Sanskrit, Pali, and Sinhalese Works by Ratnamati. A Philological Chronicle (Phullalocanavaṃsa)*. Naples: Università degli studi di Napoli "L'Orientale," Dipartimento Asia Africa e Mediterraneo.

Doney, Lewis. 2018. "Imperial Gods: A Ninth-Century *Tridaṇḍaka* Prayer (*rGyud chags gsum*) from Dunhuang." *Central Asiatic Journal* 61.1: 71–101.

Dutt, Nalinaksha. 1942. *Gilgit Manuscripts*, vol. 3, part 2. Srinagar: Calcutta Oriental Press.

Eltschinger, Vincent. 2012. "Aśvaghoṣa and His Canonical Sources II: Yaśas, the Kāśyapa Brothers and the Buddha's Arrival in Rājagṛha (*Buddhacarita* 16.3–71)." *Journal of the International Association of Buddhist Studies* 35.1–2: 171–224.

———. 2013. "Aśvaghoṣa and His Canonical Sources I: Preaching Selflessness to King Bimbisāra and the Magadhans (*Buddhacarita* 16.73–93)." *Journal of Indian Philosophy* 41.2: 167–194.

———. 2018. "Aśvaghoṣa and His Canonical Sources (III): The Night of Awakening (*Buddhacarita* 14.1–97)." *Journal of Indian Philosophy* 47.2: 195–233.

———. 2020. "Aśvaghoṣa and His Canonical Sources: 4. On the Authority and the Authenticity of the Buddhist Scriptures." In *Archaeologies of the Written: Indian, Tibetan, and Buddhist Studies in Honour of Cristina Scherrer-Schaub*, edited by Vincent Tournier, Vincent Eltschinger, and Marta Sernesi, 127–169. Naples: UniorPress.

Hahn, Michael. 1981. "Ajātaśatrvavadāna—A Gopadatta Story from Tibet." In *K. P. Jayaswal Commemoration Volume*, edited by Jata S. Jha, 242–276. Patna: Kashi Prasad Jayaswal Research Institute.

———. 1987. "Sanskrittexte aus dem tibetischen Tanjur (I): Das Nāgārjuna zugeschriebene Daṇḍakavṛttastotra." *Berliner Indologische Studien* 3: 51–102.

Hartmann, Jens-Uwe. 1987. *Das Varṇārhavarṇastotra des Mātṛceṭa*. Göttingen: Vandenhoeck & Ruprecht.

———. 1991. "Untersuchungen zum Dīrghāgama der Sarvāstivādins." Habilitation thesis, Georg-August-Universität, Göttingen.

———. 2022a. "The (Re-)Appearance of the 'Discourse on the Salt River' (*Kṣāranadīsūtra*)." In *Guruparamparā: Studies on Buddhism, India, Tibet and More in Honour of Professor Marek Mejor*, edited by Katarzyna Marciniak, Stanisław Kania, Małgorzata Wielińska-Soltwedel, and Agata Bareja-Starzyńska, 145–155. Warsaw: University of Warsaw Press.

———. 2022b. "Trauer um die Großmutter und Trost vom Buddha: das *Āryikā-sūtra*." In *Connecting the Art, Literature, and Religion of South and Central Asia: Studies in Honour of Monika Zin*, edited by Ines Konczak-Nagel, Satomi Hiyama, and Astrid Klein, 153–160. New Delhi: Dev Publishers and Distributors.

———. 2023. "One or Many? The Commentaries on the *Bhadracaryāpraṇidhāna*." In *Burlesque of the Philosophers: Indian and Buddhist Studies in Memory of Helmut Krasser*, edited by Vincent Eltschinger, Jowita Kramer, Parimal Patil, and

Chizuko Yoshimizu, 1:129–152. Hamburg Buddhist Studies Series 19. Bochum and Freiburg: Projekt Verlag.

Hartmann, Jens-Uwe, and Kazunobu Matsuda. 2024. "The Case of the Appearing Poet: New Light on Aśvaghoṣa and the *Tridaṇḍamālā*." In *Buddhakṣetrapariśodhana: A Festschrift for Paul Harrison*, edited by Charles DiSimone and Nicholas Witkowski, 229–260. Marburg: Indica et Tibetica.

Hartmann, Jens-Uwe, Kazunobu Matsuda, and Péter-Dániel Szántó. 2022. "The Benefit of Cooperation: Recovering the *Śokavinodana* Ascribed to Aśvaghoṣa." In *Dharmayātrā: A Felicitation Volume in Honour of Venerable Tampalawela Dhammaratana*, edited by Mahinda Deegalle, 173–180. Paris: Nuvis Press.

Hartmann, Jens-Uwe, and Dieter Maue. 2022. "Ein sanskrit-uigurisches Fragment der *Tridaṇḍamālā* in Brāhmī-Schrift: Reedition des Texts TT VIII D." *Acta Asiatica Varsoviensia* 35: 39–130.

Hartmann, Jens-Uwe, Klaus Wille, and Peter Zieme. 2022. "Aśvaghoṣa's *Buddhacarita* in the Old Uigur Literature." *Annual Report of the International Research Institute for Advanced Buddhology at Soka University* 25: 173–189.

Hu-von Hinüber, Haiyan. 1994. *Das Poṣadhavastu: Vorschriften für die buddhistische Beichtfeier im Vinaya der Mūlasarvāstivādins*. Studien zur Indologie und Iranistik, Monographie 13. Reinbek: Wezler.

Isaacson, Harunaga. 2013. "Yogācāra and Vajrayāna according to Ratnākaraśānti." In *The Foundation for Yoga Practitioners: The Buddhist Yogācārabhūmi Treatise and Its Adaptation in India, East Asia, and Tibet*, edited by Ulrich Timme Kragh, 1036–1051. Cambridge, MA: Harvard University Press.

Iwamoto, Yutaka. 1937. *Mahāsāhasrapramardanī: Pañcarakṣā I*. Kyoto: Privately published by Iwamoto Yutaka.

Jackson, David P. 1997. "On the Date of the Tibetan Translation of Aśvaghoṣa's *Buddhacarita*." *Studia Indologiczne* 4: 41–62.

Johnston, E. H. 1928. *The Saundarananda of Aśvaghoṣa*. Lahore: Oxford University Press.

———. 1936. *The Buddhacarita: Or, Acts of the Buddha*, vol. 2. Panjab University Oriental Publications 32. Calcutta: Baptist Mission Press, published for The University of the Panjab, Lahore.

———. 1937. "The Buddha's Mission and Last Journey: *Buddhacarita*, xv to xxviii." *Acta Orientalia* 15: 26–62, 85–111, 231–252, 253–292.

———. 1939. "The Tridaṇḍamālā of Aśvaghoṣa." *Journal of the Bihar and Orissa Research Society* 25.1: 11–14.

Kanō Kazuo 加納和雄. 2020. "Chūsei chibetto no sōin ni okeru bonbun shahon no zōshorei: chun riwoche to pokan" 中世チベットの僧院における梵文写本の蔵書例：チュン・リウォチェとポカン (References to the Preservation of Sanskrit Manuscripts in Medieval Tibetan Monasteries: gCung Ri bo che and sPos khang). *Indogaku bukkyōgaku kenkyū* 印度學佛教學研究 (*Journal of Indian and Buddhist Studies*) 68.2: 194–200.

Karashima, Seishi. 2015. "Vehicle (*yāna*) and Wisdom (*jñāna*) in the Lotus Sutra—The Origin of the Notion of *yāna* in Mahāyāna Buddhism." *Annual Report of the*

International Research Institute for Advanced Buddhology at Soka University 18: 163–196.

Krause-Stinner, Susanne. 2011. *Mokṣopāya: Das Erste und Zweite Buch. Vairāgya-prakaraṇa. Mumukṣuvyavahāraprakaraṇa*. Wiesbaden: Harrassowitz Verlag.

Lin, Li-Kouang. 1949. *L'aide-mémoire de la vraie loi (Saddharma-smṛtyupasthāna-sūtra): Recherches sur un Sūtra Développé du Petit Véhicule*. Paris: Adrien-Maisonneuve.

Liu, Cuilan. 2018. "Reciting, Chanting, and Singing: The Codification of Vocal Music in Buddhist Canon Law." *Journal of Indian Philosophy* 46.4: 713–752.

Lüders, Heinrich. 1911a. *Bruchstücke buddhistischer Dramen*. Berlin: Georg Reimer.

———. 1911b. "Das Śāriputraprakaraṇa, ein Drama des Aśvaghoṣa." *Sitzungsberichte der Königlich Preussischen Akademie der Wissenschaften* 17: 388–411.

———. 1930. "Weitere Beiträge zur Geschichte und Geographie von Ostturkestan." *Sitzungsberichte der Preussischen Akademie der Wissenschaften, Philosophisch-Historische Klasse 1930*, 4–60. Berlin: Walter de Gruyter.

———. 1940. *Philologica Indica: Ausgewählte kleine Schriften, Festgabe zum 70. Geburtstage*. Göttingen: Vandenhoeck & Ruprecht.

Matsuda Kazunobu 松田和信. 2019a. "*Sankeishū* (*Tridaṇḍamālā*) ni okeru *Shōgikū-kyō* to *Buddacharita*" 三啓集 (*Tridaṇḍamālā*) における勝義空経とブッダチャリタ (The *Paramārthaśūnyatā-sūtra* and the *Buddhacarita* in the *Tridaṇḍamālā*). *Indogaku bukkyōgaku kenkyū* 印度學佛教學研究 (*Journal of Indian and Buddhist Studies*) 68.1: 1–11.

———. 2019b. "Ratonākarashānti no *Hannya haramitsu shujū shidai*" ラトナーカラシャーンティの般若波羅蜜修習次第 (Sanskrit Text of the *Prajñāpāramitā-bhāvanākrama* by Ratnākaraśānti). *Bukkyō daigaku bukkyō gakkai kiyō* 佛教大学仏教学会紀要 (*Bulletin of the Association of Buddhist Studies, Bukkyo University*) 24: 21–32.

———. 2020. "*Buddacharita* dai 15 shō '*Shotenbōrin*': bonbun tekisuto to wayaku" ブッダチャリタ第15章「初転法輪」：梵文テキストと和訳 (Sanskrit Text and Japanese Translation of the *Buddhacarita* Canto 15 'The First *Dharmacakra-pravartana*'). *Bukkyō daigaku bukkyō gakkai kiyō* 佛教大学仏教学会紀要 (*Bulletin of the Association of Buddhist Studies, Bukkyo University*) 25: 27–44.

———. 2021. "Fujōkan o toku *Chū-agon* 139 kyō: *Sankeishū* kara kaishū sareta bonbun tekisuto to wayaku" 不浄観を説く中阿含139経：三啓集から回収された梵文テキストと和訳 (Sanskrit Text and Japanese Translation of the *Madhyama-āgama* 139 [**Śivapathikā-sūtra*] Based on the *Tridaṇḍamālā* Manuscript). *Bukkyō daigaku bukkyō gakkai kiyō* 佛教大学仏教学会紀要 (*Bulletin of the Association of Buddhist Studies, Bukkyo University*) 26: 63–81.

———. 2023. "*Buddacharita* ansorojī: ushinawareta shi o bonbun *Sankeishū* shahon ni motomete" ブッダチャリタ・アンソロジー：失われた詩を梵文三啓集写本に求めて (*Buddhacarita* Anthology: Lost Verses of Aśvaghoṣa's *Buddhacarita* Discovered in Sanskrit Manuscript of the *Tridaṇḍamālā*). *Bukkyō daigaku bukkyō gakubu ronshū* 佛教大学仏教学部論集 (*Journal of School of Buddhism, Bukkyo University*) 107: 65–84.

———. 2024. "Ashuvagōsha no ātoman hihan: dai 8 sankeikyō '*Shōgikū-kyō*' no bonbun tekisuto to wayaku" アシュヴァゴーシャのアートマン批判：第8三啓経「勝義空経」の梵文テキストと和訳 (Aśvaghoṣa's Criticism on Ātman: Sanskrit Text and Japanese Translation of the 8th Tridaṇḍa *Paramārthaśūnyatā-sūtra*). *Bukkyō daigaku bukkyō gakubu ronshū* 佛教大学仏教学部論集 (*Journal of School of Buddhism, Bukkyo University*) 108: 1–22.

Matsuda Kazunobu 松田和信, Demoto Mitsuyo 出本充代, Ueno Makio 上野牧生, Tanaka Hironori 田中裕成, and Fukita Takanori 吹田隆徳. 2022. "Dokuja no tatoe: dai 26 sankeikyō no bonbun tekisuto to wayaku" 毒蛇の喩え：第26三啓経の梵文テキストと和訳 (Sanskrit Text and Japanese Translation of the 26th Tridaṇḍa: *Āśīviṣa*). *Bukkyō daigaku bukkyō gakkai kiyō* 佛教大学仏教学会紀要 (*Bulletin of the Association of Buddhist Studies, Bukkyo University*) 27: 47–78.

———. 2023. "Gomi no yama ni owaru keman no tatoe: dai 5 sankeikyō no bonbun tekisuto to wayaku" ごみの山に終わる華鬘の喩え：第5三啓経の梵文テキストと和訳 (The Simile of Garland Turning into Garbage: Sanskrit Text and Japanese Translation of the 5th Tridaṇḍa). *Bukkyō daigaku bukkyō gakkai kiyō* 佛教大学仏教学会紀要 (*Bulletin of the Association of Buddhist Studies, Bukkyo University*) 28: 55–80.

———. 2024. "Oi to byō to shi to: dai 11 sankeikyō *Mujō-kyō* no bonbun tekisuto to wayaku" 老いと病と死と：第11三啓経『無常経』の梵文テキストと和訳 (Aging, Illness and Death: Sanskrit Text and Japanese Translation of the 11th Tridaṇḍa *Anityatā-sūtra*). *Bukkyō daigaku bukkyō gakkai kiyō* 佛教大学仏教学会紀要 (*Bulletin of the Association of Buddhist Studies, Bukkyo University*) 29: 1–31.

Matsuda Kazunobu 松田和信 and Jens-Uwe Hartmann イェンス=ウヴェ・ハルトマン. 2022. "*Kega-kyō* (*Zō-agon* 1177 kyō) no bonbun genten to wayaku: <fu> genkei kangyuru no chibetto-go yaku tekisuto" 灰河経（雑阿含1177経）の梵文原典と和訳：〔附〕原型カンギュルのチベット語訳テキスト (Sanskrit Text and Japanese Translation of *Saṃyuktāgama* 1177 [*Kṣāranadī*] with Appendix: Tibetan Translation Preserved in Proto-Kanjur Manuscripts). *Bukkyōgaku seminā* 佛教學セミナー (*Buddhist Seminar, Otani University*) 116: 1–30.

Matsunami Seiren 松濤誠廉. 1975. "Bonbun *Gattō zanmai-kyō*" 梵文月燈三昧経 (Sanskrit Text of the *Yuedeng sanmei jing* [*Samādhirāja-sūtra*]). *Taishō daigaku kenkyū kiyō* 大正大学研究紀要 (*Memoirs of Taisho University*) 60: 244–188 (reverse pagination).

Maue, Dieter. 1996. *Alttürkische Handschriften*, vol. 1: *Dokumente in Brāhmī und tibetischer Schrift* [part 1]. Verzeichnis der orientalischen Handschriften in Deutschland XIII, 9. Stuttgart: Franz Steiner Verlag.

———. 2015. *Alttürkische Handschriften*, vol. 19: *Dokumente in Brāhmī und tibetischer Schrift*, part 2. Verzeichnis der orientalischen Handschriften in Deutschland XIII, 27. Stuttgart: Franz Steiner Verlag.

Maue, Dieter, and Ruji Niu. 2012. "80 TBI 774 b: A Sanskrit – Uigur Bilingual Text from Bezeklik." *Nairiku ajia gengo no kenkyū* 内陸アジア言語の研究 (*Studies on the Inner Asian Languages*) 27: 43–91.

Melzer, Gudrun. 2006. "A Copper Scroll Inscription from the Time of the Alchon Huns." In *Buddhist Manuscripts*, edited by Jens Braarvig et al., 3:251–278. Manuscripts in the Schøyen Collection. Oslo: Hermes Publishing.

Rotman, Andy. 2017. *Divine Stories. Divyāvadāna*, vol. 2. Somerville, MA: Wisdom Publications.

Sakaki Ryōzaburō 榊亮三郎. 1916–1925. *Bon-zō-kan-wa shiyaku taikō hon'yaku myōgi taishū (bon・zō sakuin)* 梵藏漢和四譯對校飜譯名義大集（梵・藏索引）(Mahāvyutpatti: *A Sanskrit-Tibetan-Chinese-Japanese Quadrilingual Collation [with Sanskrit and Tibetan Indices]*). 2 vols. Kyoto: Shingonshū kyōto daigaku 真言宗京都大学.

Sāṅkṛtyāyana, Rāhula. 1938. "Search for Sanskrit Mss. in Tibet." *Journal of the Bihar and Orissa Research Society* 24.4: 137–163.

Schlingloff, Dieter. 1955. *Buddhistische Stotras aus ostturkistanischen Sanskrittexten*. Berlin: Akademie-Verlag.

Schopen, Gregory. 1979. "Mahāyāna in Indian Inscriptions." *Indo-Iranian Journal* 21.1: 1–19. Reprinted in Schopen 2005, 223–246.

———. 1992. "On Avoiding Ghosts and Social Censure: Monastic Funerals in the *Mūlasarvāstivāda-vinaya*." *Journal of Indian Philosophy* 20.1: 1–39. Reprinted in Schopen 1997, 204–237.

———. 1997. *Bones, Stones, and Buddhist Monks: Collected Papers on the Archaeology, Epigraphy, and Texts of Monastic Buddhism in India*. Studies in the Buddhist Traditions. Honolulu: University of Hawai'i Press.

———. 2005. *Figments and Fragments of Mahāyāna Buddhism in India: More Collected Papers*. Studies in the Buddhist Traditions. Honolulu: University of Hawai'i Press.

———. 2010a. "On Incompetent Monks and Able Urbane Nuns in a Buddhist Monastic Code." *Journal of Indian Philosophy* 38.2: 107–131. Reprinted in Schopen 2014, 47–72.

———. 2010b. "On Some Who Are Not Allowed to Become Buddhist Monks or Nuns: An Old List of Types of Slaves or Unfree Laborers." *Journal of the American Oriental Society* 130.2: 225–234. Reprinted in Schopen 2014, 157–172.

———. 2014. *Buddhist Nuns, Monks, and Other Worldly Matters: Recent Papers on Monastic Buddhism in India*. Studies in the Buddhist Traditions. Honolulu: University of Hawai'i Press.

Seyfort Ruegg, David. 2004. "Aspects of the Study of the (Earlier) Indian Mahāyāna." *Journal of the International Association of Buddhist Studies* 27.1: 3–62.

Sferra, Francesco. 2008. *Sanskrit Texts from Giuseppe Tucci's Collection: Part I*. Manuscripta Buddhica 1. Serie Orientale Roma 104. Rome: Istituto Italiano per l'Africa e l'Oriente.

Skilling, Peter. 1994. *Mahāsūtras: Great Discourses of the Buddha*, vol. 1: *Texts*. Sacred Books of the Buddhists 44. Oxford: The Pali Text Society.

Slaje, Walter. 2001. "Observations on the Making of the *Yogavāsiṣṭha* (*caitta, nañartha* and *vaḥ*)." In *Le Parole e i Marmi: Studi in onore di Raniero Gnoli nel suo 70° compleanno*, edited by Raffaele Torella, 2:771–796. Serie Orientale Roma 92. Rome: Istituto Italiano per l'Africa e l'Oriente.

Steiner, Roland. 2014. *Der Weg zur Befreiung. Das Erste und Zweite Buch: Das Buch über die Leidenschaftslosigkeit. Das Buch über das Verhalten der Befreiungssucher*. Wiesbaden: Harrassowitz Verlag.

Sternbach, Ludwik. 1977. *Mahā-subhāṣita-saṁgraha: Being an Extensive Collection of Wise Sayings and Entertaining Verses in Sanskrit with Introduction, English Translation, Critical Notes and Indices*, vol. 3. Hoshiarpur: Vishveshvaranand Vedic Research Institute.

Szántó, Péter-Dániel. 2021. "Buddhist Homiletics on Grief (*Saddharmaparikathā, *ch. 11*)." *Indo-Iranian Journal* 64.4: 291–347.

Takakusu, J. 1896. *A Record of the Buddhist Religion as Practised in India and the Malay Archipelago (A.D. 671–695) by I-tsing*. Oxford: The Clarendon Press.

Terzová, Nicole. 2019. "Mātṛceṭas Ekottarikastava: Kritische Ausgabe und Übersetzung zweier Sanskrit-Handschriften unter Berücksichtigung der tibetischen Übersetzung." MA thesis, Ludwig-Maximilians-Universität, Munich.

Thakur, Anantalal, and Upendra Jha. 1957. *Kāvyalakṣaṇa of Daṇḍin (also Known as Kāvyādarśa) with Commentary Called Ratnaśrī of Ratnaśrījñāna*. Darbhanga: The Mithila Institute of Post-Graduate Studies and Research in Sanskrit Learning.

Tripathi, Ram Shankar, and Thakur Sain Negi. 2001. *Hevajratantram with Muktāvalī Pañjikā of Mahāpaṇḍitācārya Ratnākaraśānti*. Sarnath: Central Institute of Higher Tibetan Studies.

Tucci, Giuseppe (ツッチ, ジゥセッペ). 1956. "Chibetto oyobi nepōru ni oite arata ni hakken serareta bukkyō tenseki ni tsuite" チベット及びネポールにおいて新たに發見せられた佛教典籍について (Buddhist Literatures Newly Recovered in Tibet and Nepal). *Ōtani gakuhō* 大谷学報 (*Journal of Buddhology and Cultural Science, Otani University*) 36.1: 1–16.

Tzohar, Roy. 2019. "Reading Aśvaghoṣa Across Boundaries: An Introduction." *Journal of Indian Philosophy* 47.2: 187–194.

Ueno Makio 上野牧生. 2020. "Dai 29 sankeikyō (*Hachinan-kyō*) no bonbun tekisuto to wayaku" 第29三啓経（八難経）の梵文テキストと和訳 (Sanskrit Text and Japanese Translation of the 29th Tridaṇḍa Sūtra: The *Aṣṭākṣaṇakṣaṇasūtra*). *Bukkyōgaku seminā* 佛教學セミナー (*Buddhist Seminar, Otani University*) 111: 21–46.

———. 2021. "*Zōichi-agon* no ni kyōten (1): dai 30 sankeikyō (*Goji-kyō*) no bonbun tekisuto to wayaku" 増一阿含の二経典 (1)：第30三啓経（五事経）の梵文テキストと和訳 (Two *Ekottarikāgama* Sūtras [1]: Sanskrit Text and Japanese Translation of the 30th Tridaṇḍa Sūtra [**Pañcasthānasūtra*] from the *Tridaṇḍamālā* Manuscript). *Ōtani gakuhō* 大谷学報 (*Journal of Buddhist Studies and Humanities, Otani University*) 101.1: 1–28.

———. 2022. "*Zōichi-agon* no ni kyōten (2): dai 36 sankeikyō (*Fuken-kyō*) no bonbun tekisuto to wayaku" 増一阿含の二経典 (2)：第36三啓経（不堅経）の梵文テキストと和訳 (Two *Ekottarikāgama* Sūtras [2]: Sanskrit Text and Japanese Translation of the 36th Tridaṇḍa Sūtra [**Asārasūtra*] from the *Tridaṇḍamālā* Manuscript). *Ōtani gakuhō* 大谷学報 (*Journal of Buddhist Studies and Humanities, Otani University*) 102.1: 1–16.

Vogel, Claus, and Klaus Wille. 1992. "Some More Fragments of the Pravrajyāvastu Portion of the Vinayavastu Manuscript Found Near Gilgit." In *Sanskrit-Texte aus dem buddhistischen Kanon: Neuentdeckungen und Neueditionen II*, 65–109. Sanskrit-Wörterbuch der buddhistischen Texte aus den Turfan-Funden, Beiheft

4. Göttingen: Vandenhoeck & Ruprecht. Reprinted in Claus Vogel and Klaus Wille, eds. and trans. 2014. *The Pravrajyāvastu of the Mūlasarvāstivāda Vinaya*. Göttingen: Akademie der Wissenschaften zu Göttingen, Sanskrit-Wörterbuch der buddhistischen Texte aus den Turfan-Funden, 43–90. https://rep.adw-goe.de/handle/11858/00-001S-0000-0023-9A04-C (page references are to original edition).

———. 1996. "The Final Leaves of the Pravrajyāvastu Portion of the Vinayavastu Manuscript Found Near Gilgit, Part 1: Saṃgharakṣitāvadāna." In *Sanskrit-Texte aus dem buddhistischen Kanon: Neuentdeckungen und Neueditionen III*, 241–296. Sanskrit-Wörterbuch der buddhistischen Texte aus den Turfan-Funden, Beiheft 6. Göttingen: Vandenhoeck & Ruprecht. Reprinted in Claus Vogel and Klaus Wille, eds. and trans. 2014. *The Pravrajyāvastu of the Mūlasarvāstivāda Vinaya*. Göttingen: Akademie der Wissenschaften zu Göttingen, Sanskrit-Wörterbuch der buddhistischen Texte aus den Turfan-Funden, 91–146. https://rep.adw-goe.de/handle/11858/00-001S-0000-0023-9A04-C.

Waldschmidt, Ernst. 1950–1951. *Das Mahāparinirvāṇasūtra: Text in Sanskrit und Tibetisch, verglichen mit dem Pāli nebst einer Übersetzung der chinesischen Entsprechung im Vinaya der Mūlasarvāstivādins*. 3 vols. Berlin: Akademie-Verlag.

———. 1958. "Ein zweites Daśabalasūtra." *Mitteilungen des Instituts für Orientforschung* 6: 388–392, 395–396. Reprinted in Waldschmidt 1967, 353–357, 360–361.

———. 1967. *Von Ceylon bis Turfan: Schriften zur Geschichte, Literatur, Religion und Kunst des indischen Kulturraumes (Festgabe zum 70. Geburtstag)*. Göttingen: Vandenhoeck & Ruprecht.

Warder, A. K. 1974. *Indian Kāvya Literature*, vol. 2: *The Origins and Formation of Classical Kāvya*. Delhi: Motilal Banarsidass.

Weller, Friedrich. 1926. *Das Leben des Buddha: tibetisch und deutsch*. Leipzig: Eduard Pfeiffer.

———. 1953. "Zwei zentralasiatische Fragmente des Buddhacarita." *Abhandlungen der Sächsischen Akademie der Wissenschaften, Philologisch-historische Klasse*, Band 46, Heft 4. Berlin: Akademie-Verlag.

Willemen, Charles. 2019. "Yijing's *Scriptural Text about Impermanence* (*T.* 801)." In *Methods in Buddhist Studies: Essays in Honor of Richard K. Payne*, edited by Scott A. Mitchell and Natalie Fisk Quli, 67–76. New York: Bloomsbury.

Yamabe, Nobuyoshi. 2003. "On the School Affiliation of Aśvaghoṣa: 'Sautrāntika' or 'Yogācāra'?" *Journal of the International Association of Buddhist Studies* 26.2: 225–254.

Zin, Monika. 2018. "Some Details from the Representations of the Parinirvāṇa Cycle in the Art of Gandhara and Kucha: The Iconography of the Wandering Ascetics (Parivrājaka, Nirgrantha and Ājīvika)." *Art of the Orient* 7: 137–170.

The Double Life of *Gahapati**

Stephanie W. Jamison

MOST BODIES OF BUDDHIST literature know the figure of the *gahapati*, here cited in its Pāli form, usually translated as "householder," indeed often by the honorand of this volume himself. This rendering is perfectly appropriate on etymological grounds: the compound is transparently analyzable as "house-lord." But the role of the *gahapati* in the texts often goes beyond that of a mere head of household, as he provides considerable material support to the Buddha and his followers and engages seriously with them and with the social world in which he's embedded. There is thus a discrepancy between the assumed underlying meaning of the term and its function in the texts. In what follows I will argue that there are two senses of *gahapati* in the texts, that the bifurcation of the term into two senses significantly predates the Buddhist usages, and that the etymological "householder" sense is the recessive one. But before pursuing this line of argument I should first sketch a bit of the history of my engagement with this question, because the *gahapati* cannot be understood without contrasting this term with other apparent synonyms or near synonyms.

* In the course of the several years I've been fretting about these questions, I've had the benefit of discussions and correspondence with a number of people. I am especially indebted to two: Diego Loukota and Patrick Olivelle. I would like to thank Diego for many illuminating exchanges about the issues, and for drawing my attention to a number of primary passages in a wide variety of texts and languages, esp. the Kanaganahalli inscriptions, and of secondary treatments, esp. Chakravarti 1987, none of which I would have stumbled across on my own. Patrick clarified and expanded my thinking in the course of many exchanges over the years, and his comments on the first draft of this paper led to a sharpened and more strongly asserted presentation of my claims. Paul Dundas and Oskar von Hinüber have also given me the benefit of their expertise. The workshop on the Householder convened at the University of Texas by Patrick and Don Davis in February 2016 and the subsequent volume, edited by Patrick (Olivelle 2019), collecting the paper presented there as well as others on the topic, greatly stimulated my thinking and, especially, my rethinking. The papers in that volume by Oliver Freiberger and Claire Maes were especially influential. I regret that, given the destination of the volume in which this paper will appear, I could not consult the honorand. All remaining errors, false doctrines, and strayings from the path of true reason are, of course, my own.

In a recent article (Jamison 2019a) I discussed the curious history of the standard word for "householder" in Hindu dharma texts, Sanskrit *gṛhastha*. There I argued that this term, so deeply embedded in the orthodox dharma texts as the designation for the second, and especially crucial, stage in the *āśrama* system that parceled out the life-stages of the twice-born, was actually borrowed from Middle Indo-Aryan and from śramaṇic, especially Buddhist, discourse. The evidence for this claim is partly negative, partly positive. The negative evidence is that *gṛhastha* is not found anywhere in the voluminous Vedic corpus, not even in the *gṛhya* sūtras, the manuals of domestic ritual where we might expect it to be especially at home. The term appears in Sanskrit beginning only with the dharma sūtras and seemingly comes out of nowhere. The positive evidence is that MIA equivalents (*gihitha*, etc.) are found beginning in the Aśokan inscriptions and widely attested in Pāli, as well as in other MIA languages of Buddhism—Gāndhārī and Buddhist Hybrid Sanskrit—and also in Jaina materials in Ardhamāgadhī and could provide the source for the Sanskrit term. Investigating the history of **gṛhastha* (and its equivalents)[1] also required me to examine the early history of potentially equivalent terms, especially **gṛhapati*, which is well attested throughout the Vedic corpus, but *never* appears in the Hindu dharma literature. My implicit claim was that, at least in that literature, *gṛhastha* replaced *gṛhapati* as the standard word for householder.

Two factors have induced me to return to the question of the **gṛhapati*: (1) in the article mentioned above I did not pursue the post-Vedic use of this term or even cover the entire Vedic usage of it; (2) the volume containing the article (Olivelle 2019) includes a number of contributions, devoted to Buddhist and Jaina Middle Indic texts, as well as post-Vedic Sanskrit literature, that complicate the fairly simple claims I made about the relationship between **gṛhastha* and **gṛhapati* and that both support and challenge these claims. In this article, switching the focus from the former term to the latter, I will sketch a more complex picture than in the article cited, while standing by the substance of the original article. To anticipate the conclusions, I will argue that already in Vedic *gṛhapati* had developed two distinct usages and that devel-

1. Henceforth, I will use starred **gṛhastha* to refer to the lexical complex of related words, whether in Sanskrit or Middle Indo-Aryan languages (e.g., Aśokan *gahatha*, *grahatha*, etc.) and whatever form the "house" word takes as first member of this compound (e.g., *gaha*, *ghara*, *geha*, etc.). For discussion of these variations, see my article cited above. Unstarred *gṛhastha* will refer only to the Sanskrit word.

Similarly **gṛhapati* refers to the Sanskrit word and its MIA developments (Pāli *gahapati*, etc.), whereas *gṛhapati* will refer only to the Sanskrit word. I use **pravrajita* in the same way, for all possible forms of the word in the various languages.

opments of both usages are encountered in Buddhist and Jaina texts and in post-Vedic Sanskrit and MIA materials. Moreover, the dominant usage in all these texts is not that of the generic head of household, but of *gṛhapati* as a rich and prominent member of the community, a meaning that goes back to and derives from Vedic. Failing to distinguish the two senses leads to a too broad and generic assessment of the term, which muddies the interpretation of each individual occurrence.

Before turning to **gṛhapati*, I must first briefly summarize my previous treatment of the formation of **gṛhastha* and the reason it has the shape it has. As noted above, the first datable attestations of any form of **gṛhastha* are found in the Aśokan inscriptions (third century BCE). Assuming that the dharma sūtras are to be dated in the first centuries BCE, with the earliest at best around the same time as the Aśokan inscriptions or not much earlier,[2] it is unlikely that the Sanskrit form *gṛhastha* and its Hindu dharma context predate the Aśokan usage, with the Aśokan forms derived from the Sanskrit word and their usage adapted from the dharmic materials—despite our usual presumptions about the priority of Sanskrit to MIA forms. In fact, the earliest of the dharma sūtras (at least according to Olivelle), *Āpastamba*, barely uses the term,[3] which only becomes well established in the later dharma sūtras and in Manu, so that there may well be a larger chronological gap between Aśoka and the Hindu dharma use than at first appears. This suggests that the derivation and semantic adaptation went the other way, from Middle Indic to Sanskrit, with a MIA form like *gahattha* re-Sanskritized to *gṛhastha*; for speakers navigating a diglossic, multidialectal world like India in this period, the phonological conversion rules would have been automatic and second nature.

We should now consider the literal meaning of the compound **gṛhastha*, made up of a word for "house" plus a second member derived from √*sthā* "stand, stay." Unlike **gṛha-pati* "lord of the house," which assigns a certain social role or status to the person so designated, **gṛhastha* is a descriptor, and not a lofty one: "stay-at-home." However, this apparently humble epithet makes sense when we see the company it keeps, for **gṛhastha* often appears in an oppositional pairing with **pravrajita* "gone forth." This is clearest in the Aśokan Rock Edict XIIA, cited after Schneider 1978, 64–65:

RE XIIA Gi *devānaṃpiye piyad[a]si rājā savapāsaṃḍāni ca*
[pa]vajitāni ca gharastāni ca *pūjayati*
Ka . . . *pav[a]jitā[n]i gahathāni vā* . . .

2. For this dating see Olivelle 2000, 4–10, esp. 9–10.

3. See Brick 2019, Jamison 2019a.

Sh . . . *pravrajita[ni] grahathani ca . . .*
Ma . . . *[p]ravra[ji]tani gehathani ca . . .*

Bloch 1950, 121, ad loc.: Le roi ami des dieux au regard amical honore toutes les sectes, **les samanes et les laïques** [lit. the "gone forth" and the "stay-at home"].

But see also Pillar Edict Topra 7.25, which contains the same pairing with the addition of *pāṣaṃḍa*; the same pairing is found numerous times in Pāli and in other Buddhist MIA languages, Gāndhārī and Buddhist Hybrid Sanskrit among them, as noted above.[4] The term **gṛhastha* "stay-at-home" seems to have been coined in opposition to the "gone-forth," the wandering ascetic, the mendicant renouncer so characteristic of the śramaṇic sects of India in this era. The "stay-at-home" is his polar opposite and is also the *necessary* opposite to the wanderer, as the provider of alms and other material support. Thus, the source of the word should be sought in a religious system in which the non-stay-at-home, the wandering ascetic and renunciant, played a prominent role—namely, early Buddhism and similar movements. Vedic religion, at least in its vast textual record, shows little or no interest in or, perhaps more importantly, no institutional place for such figures. However, as Olivelle suggests to me, non-Vedic brahmaṇic groups, not strongly represented in the Vedic texts, may also have been part of the mix.

As sketched above, once the term **gṛhastha* was coined (in MIA dress, in my view), it made its way into Sanskrit and formed part of the newly crystallizing system of *āśrama*s as it took shape in the early dharma literature.[5] In that literature the break is neat and complete: the old term *gṛhapati* is absent, the new term *gṛhastha* holds sway, and we can reasonably speak of replacement of the first by the second. But this clean separation of spheres is not found elsewhere: **gṛhapati* and **gṛhastha* coexist in Buddhist, Jaina, and non-dharma Sanskrit texts, sometimes as apparent synonyms, and teasing apart the usage particularly of **gṛhapati* becomes a tricky business. In a way this coexistence is not surprising. Since **gṛhastha* was created as the oppositional member of a polarized pairing, it would originally have no reason to replace the more general term for "householder," which would cover a larger semantic field of roles and responsibilities than "stay-at-home" versus "gone-forth," and "stay-at-home" would only gradually and, perhaps, only partially come to occupy the full range of meanings of **gṛhapati*. Considered in this way, what is surprising is that the

4. For details and documentation see Jamison 2019a.

5. On the history of which see, of course, Olivelle 1993, esp. chapters 2–4.

change was not gradual and partial in the Hindu dharma literature, but sudden and complete. We will return to this below.

The largest and most important corpus in which to contrast the usages of **gṛhapati* and **gṛhastha* is furnished by the Pāli materials. In my article I cited some telling passages in which **gṛhastha* is contrastively paired with "gone-forth" or similar expressions—for example, *Khaggavisāṇa-sutta* (Rhinoceros Sutta) 9 *dussaṅgahā* ***pabbajitā*** *pi eke, atho* ***gahaṭṭhā*** *gharam āvasantā*; Vin III 89,35 *pūjita apacito* ***gahaṭṭhānaṃ c'eva pabbajitānaṃ ca***. The word *gahaṭṭha* is also contrasted with other words for the gone-forth ascetic; cf. *Suttanipāta* 134 [= *Vasala-sutta* 19] *yo buddhaṃ paribhāsati, atha vā tassa sāvakaṃ /* ***paribbājaṃ gahaṭṭhaṃ vā***, *taṃ jaññā vasalo iti*; *Dhammapada* 404 *asaṃsaṭṭhaṃ* ***gahaṭṭhehi anāgārehi*** ['homeless'] *cūbhayaṃ*.[6] But I did not further pursue **gṛhapati* in the Pāli corpus or contrast its usage with **gṛhastha*. Two important treatments of these issues should now be considered: an older one by Uma Chakravarti (1987), which discusses Pāli *gahapati* in its social context, and that of Oliver Freiberger in Olivelle's Householder volume (2019), produced in part in response to my original article. The two come to rather different conclusions, in part because they select different data to examine. I will treat Freiberger's contribution first.

Freiberger provides a thorough and necessary corrective to my quick and overly simplistic replacement scenario. He performed an exhaustive search for the relevant terms (*gahaṭṭha* and *gahapati*, as well as *gihin* and others) in the earliest layer of the Pāli canon. His most important immediate discovery is that *gahaṭṭha* is rather rare in this textual layer—considerably outnumbered by *gihin* and, especially, by *gahapati* (charted textually in the appendix "quantitative distribution of attested terms")—and that the three terms can be used to refer to the same (types of) persons, sometimes in the same passage.[7] His carefully marshaled evidence is responsible for my change from the implicit "quick and complete replacement" model in Pāli in the article cited to the "gradualist, partial replacement" model outlined above. In other words, I would now subscribe to the notion that **gṛhapati* remained in early Pāli as a general term for "householder," beside a fairly well-attested alternative,

6. With identical pairing, *mutatis mutandis*, in the parallel versions of the *Dhammapada*: Gāndhārī Dh 32, Patna 44, *Udānavarga* 33.20. The presence of the pair in all these versions in different languages of Buddhism suggests that the polarity belongs to a fairly early layer.

7. See his n13, citing a "terminologically complicated passage," in which *gahaṭṭha*, *gihin*, and *gahapati* can reference the same topic of discourse.

gihin,[8] and that **gṛhastha* was, initially at least, a semantically specialized variant whose move into the general slot was fairly late.

Indeed, on this point, Freiberger's work helps support my conjecture that **gṛhastha* was first coined to contrast with **pravrajita* (and similar terms for the mendicant ascetic), for from his discussion it appears that in his corpus **gṛhastha* is almost exclusively found in this pairing, judging from the fact that most of his discussion concerns "the contrastive pair of *gahaṭṭha* and ascetic (*pabbajita*, *anāgāra*, et al.)" (p. 62) and from his statement, after the main discussion, that (only) "in several passages *gahaṭṭha* appears independently, outside of the contrastive pair and unconnected to *pabbajita* or other terms for houseless ascetics" (p. 64).[9] As for Freiberger's treatment of *gahapati* as the quintessential householder, he treats all occurrences of the term as essentially referring to the same person playing the same role, and, though he cites numerous passages referring to the wealth and influence of certain *gahapati*s, their prominent role in the community, and their importance as lay-followers in supplying material support to the Buddha and his followers, he seems to consider these attributes as not characteristic of the *gahapati* but merely adventitious. I think this led him to disregard some important nuances that will lead us to identify two types of *gahapati* in the Pāli texts, with the dominant one being the "big man." The second type is well described in Chakravarti's work, which Freiberger does not refer to. It is also, as we will see, the standard usage of post-Vedic **gṛhapati* outside the early Pāli materials considered by Freiberger.

Before considering Chakravarti's treatment, let us take a detour through the other prominent śramaṇic religion, Jainism, and the treatment of the "householder" evidence there by Claire Maes in Olivelle 2019. Like Freiberger, she collected all the occurrences of **gṛhapati* (AM *gāhāvaï*[10]) and **gṛhastha*

8. Lit. "possessing a house," from **gṛhin*, an *-in*-stem possessive adj. to *gṛha* "house." Skt. *gṛhín* is found already in Vedic, in the *Taittirīyasaṃhitā* and later *brāhmaṇa* texts, and in post-Vedic texts, starting with Manu.

9. See also Cone's (2010, s.v.) definition of *gahaṭṭha*: "one who lives in a house; a householder; a lay-person (*very often contrasted with pabbajita*)" (my italics). As Freiberger points out, however, she also makes the same statement about *gihin*.

10. The phonological development from **gṛhapati* to AM *gāhāvaï* is not straightforward; we should probably expect *gahavaï* (which does appear; see below) or perhaps **gihavaï*. Pischel ([1900] 1981) explains the development with several ad hoc rules (for details, see Jamison 2019a, 19n35, and Maes 2019, 77–78). However, despite the phonological disturbance, there can be no doubt (at least as far as I can see) that *gāhāvaï* is the original AM equivalent of *gṛhapati* and that *gahavaï* is a later adaptation of **gṛhapati* borrowed either from Buddhist or Hindu dharma contexts.

It should be noted that one of the entries in the IAMD for *gāhāvaï* lists **gāthāpati* as one

(AM *gihattha*), as well as other words referring to householders, from the earliest texts of the Jaina canon in Ardhamāgadhī. Her results are quite similar to Freiberger's, and in fact the discrepancy between the relative frequency of attestation and the usage of the two terms is even stronger than in the early Pāli materials. As she clearly demonstrates, the earlier attested of the two terms and by far the most common is *gāhāvaï*, with eighty-five occurrences in her defined corpus, while *gihattha* is found only five times and only in the later parts of these early texts.[11] There are two distinct clumps (my word, not Maes's) of *gāhāvaï* attestations: by far the largest number is found in the *Ācārāṅga-sūtra*, especially Book 2; there is another, less numerous, group in the second book of the *Sūtrakṛtāṅga*. In the first and larger group the term *gāhāvaï* appears to have the generic "householder" sense found also in a number of occurrences of Pāli *gahapati*; as Maes describes, in this group of passages the *gāhāvaï* is seen only through the eyes of the mendicant, to whom he offers support:

> While these references confirm that a *gāhāvaï* was an important supporter of Jain mendicants, they unfortunately fail to provide much insight into the *gāhāvaï's* life, role, and status in the society. The multiple injunctions of the *Ācārāṅga Sūtra* never shift from the ascetic's perspective.[12]

But even in this cluster of passages the *gāhāvaï* is implicitly well-to-do, since a household just scraping by would be unlikely to be "an important supporter" of mendicants. The second smaller and later group of passages we will return to.

The use of *gihattha* is strikingly different from that of the equivalent term in Buddhist sources. As noted above, one of its striking features is its rarity, found once in the second book of the *Sūtrakṛtāṅga* and four times in the *Uttarādhyayana-sūtra*. Moreover, it does not generally participate in the polarized pairing so characteristic of the Buddhist occurrences (not only in Pāli but in other Buddhist MIA corpora). One passage (UD II.19; Maes 2019,

etymon or Sanskrit equivalent of the word. But, given the usage of the word, it is hard to see how "lord of verses/songs" could underlie it, and I assume that this reflects a commentarial puzzlement about the phonology that is similar to our own and an attempt to find a Sanskrit word that would more nearly reflect an AM *gāhā* phonologically.

11. For the exact statistics, as well as the characterization of the texts chosen to excerpt, see Maes 2019.

12. Maes 2019, 82.

84) does counsel one who "should wander" (*parivvae* [**parivrajet*]) to be "not attached to *gihatthas*" (*asaṃsatte gihatthehiṃ*; cf. UD 25.28), but, according to Maes (p. 86), "this binary construct, lying at the heart of the *śramaṇa* discourse, is in the early Jain texts more frequently expressed with the terms *agāra* and *anāgāra*." Most remarkable of all, Maes persuasively argues that at least two (UD 24, 25) of the five occurrences of *gihattha* seem to presuppose the usage found in the Hindu dharma literature and try to turn that usage to renunciant ends:

> . . . once the term *gṛhastha* did start to represent the central figure of the twice-born householder in the dharma literature, the term, or better, the Brahmanical worldview embedded in the term, circled back to the *śramaṇa* milieu, where its validity became contested.[13]
>
> [W]e have here [UD 25] an example of a lecture that should be read as a Jain response to the Brahmanical idea of "*gṛhastha*." This is an important conclusion, as it not only shows how Jains actively engaged with Brahmanical ideas, but also because it throws light on the relative chronology of (the different layers) of our texts.[14]

In other words, assuming my scenario of the original dharmic borrowing of a śramaṇic term, it has been *re*-borrowed from the dharma literature into śramaṇic discourse and consciously constructed against brahmaṇic discourse to serve as a cautionary example of what life not to lead. This is very different from the early Pāli materials, where *gahaṭṭha* seems perfectly at home in a Buddhist context, though overlaid on the older *gahapati* term. It therefore now appears to me that Buddhist and Jaina sources are not entirely parallel in their terminology about householders: they share the old term for householder, **gṛhapati*, also found in Vedic, but **gṛhastha* seems to have been a coinage that was only secondarily imported into Jainism, in some cases also trailing its newer dharmic connotations.[15]

Let us now return to **gṛhapati* and further explore the use of *gahapati* in Pāli, as presented by Uma Chakravarti (1987), in which she devotes a lengthy chapter (III: "The *Gahapati*," 65–93) to this figure. She considers *gahapati* pri-

13. Maes 2019, 86.

14. Maes 2019, 88.

15. As suggested in note 10, this secondary importation of Buddhist Middle Indic terms may also be seen in *gahavaï*, a transparent equivalent of Pāli *gahapati*, but, as far as I can see, is attested later and not frequently.

marily a designation of a particular social status and role with economic implications (p. 6); early in the chapter devoted to the term (pp. 66–67) she admits that *gahapati* can be used, like Skt. *gṛhapati*, in the literal sense of householder but argues that most of the occurrences evince further specialization:

> While early Buddhist texts *occasionally* use the word in this sense, *more often* this connotation is overshadowed by other implications of the term. . . . the definition of *gahapati* as householder is insufficient.[16]

There is no space here to produce even a brief summary of Chakravarti's rich discussion, richly documented, of the Pāli *gahapati* as an economic force, in which she charts the *gahapati*'s association with wealth and property, land and agriculture, compares and contrasts its usage with other terms like *seṭṭhi* and, especially, establishes the *gahapati*'s stable association with the terms *khattiya* and *brāhmaṇa* (see esp. pp. 66–69). She sees this trio as representing a threefold "conceptual categorization of society into the domain of power . . . the domain of religion . . . and the domain of the economy, represented by the *gahapati*" (p. 66). Although she considers this categorization "unique to the Buddhists" (p. 67), it is difficult not to be reminded of the *varṇa* system, and in fact Cone's definition of *gahapati* (2010, s.v.) contains two parts (separated by a semicolon): "the master of a house, the head of a family; one whose business is trade or agriculture (a member of the third class in society, after *khattiya* and *brāhmaṇa*)."[17] In other words, in one of its senses *gahapati* seems to be another word for what in Sanskrit would be *vaiśya*. Or rather, a particular set of *vaiśya*, those who are rich, successful, and socially prominent enough to deserve notice. The slotting in of the word *gahapati* in place of the older term may in part have resulted from linguistic accident, an unfortunate homonymy produced by Middle Indic sound laws. Skt. *vaiśya* should properly come out as *vessa* in MIA, which is a little too close to the expected outcome of *veśyā* "prostitute" (*vessā*) for semantic comfort. The term *vessa* for Vaiśya is indeed attested (see PED, s.v.) but seems not to be as widely used as *gahapati*. Phonologically close to it are *vesī* and *vesiyā*, both glossed by PED with a hybrid definition: "a woman of low caste, a harlot, prostitute," suggesting that the two words *veśyā* ("to be entered" → "prostitute") and *vaiśya* ("belonging to the *viś*" → "member of the third *varṇa*") had become at least partially conflated.[18] To

16. Chakravarti 1987, 66–67; my italics.

17. See also the extensive entry in the PED.

18. The same phonological rules seem to have caused the same problem in Ardhamāgadhī. See

avoid any chance of embarrassing confusion, *vessa* (< **vaiśya*) would tend to be avoided; this type of "taboo avoidance," which leads to the marginalization or loss of an innocent word that might be mistaken for a problematic homonym or near homonym, is widespread in the history of languages.[19] I therefore think the identification of the rich and influential *gahapati* with the Vaiśya *varṇa* is secondary and accidental: because of the taboo on *vessa*, another word was needed, and *gahapati* was available; its social usage was thus narrowed (at least in those circumstances). On the basis of the Vedic evidence to be discussed below, I assume that the original **gṛhapati* could have belonged to any of the twice-born *varṇas*.

As noted above, Freiberger (2019, 69–70) notes the co-occurrence of *gahapati* with *khattiya* and *brāhmaṇa* and in similar stock phrases indicating status and wealth, and he considers, only to dismiss, the *varṇa* significance of the triad as "probably . . . nothing more than a distant echo" (p. 69). Because he treats all occurrences of *gahapati* as representative of the same figure—a reasonable methodological approach, I certainly admit—the bifurcation of usages that we see expressed quite subtly by Cone's semicolon (see above) goes unremarked. But it seems clear to me from the passages adduced by him and by others that the attestations of *gahapati* cluster around two different poles of usage and that Chakravarti's *gahapati* as marker of socio-economic status is real.[20]

The bifurcation is also suggested in the Jaina usages discussed by Maes. Recall that her older and larger group of *gāhāvaï* passages (numbering sixty-six), in the *Ācārāṅga-sūtra*, portray a generic (if probably well-off) householder, supportive of and paired with the mendicant ascetics who approach him for material aid. But the reasonably substantial set of passages (numbering nineteen) in the *Sūtrakṛtāṅga* are, by her account, "different": "in *Sūtrakṛtāṅga* II, the *gāhāvaï* is clearly a well-respected member of society, very wealthy, a landowner, and a cattleman" (p. 83); "the *gāhāvaï* of the *Sūtrakṛtāṅga* coincides with the idea of a wealthy and influential citizen" (p. 84). In other words, the early Jaina attestations of the term show the same two distinct usages appar-

IAMD, s.v. *vessa*, which is attested marginally and defined as "Merchant; one of the 4 Varṇas," and *vessā*, "a prostitute," with its better-attested equivalent *vesā* "harlot."

19. A simple example is English *cock* for *rooster*.

20. This view is in fact a commonplace in the secondary literature on the social structure of this period. See, e.g., Yamazaki 2005, 131–134 and passim, relying primarily on Pāli sources, esp. the *jātakas*, and the Sanskrit *Divyāvadāna*; Jain [1947] 1984, 190–191, based on the Jain canon.

ent also in the early Pāli materials, but here distributed by text and, likely, chronology.[21]

Besides Pāli, another MIA Buddhist corpus attests both **gṛhapati* and **gṛhastha*—namely, Buddhist Hybrid Sanskrit. As noted above and in Jamison 2019a, in SP [*Saddharmapuṇḍarīka*] 291.11 (vs.), cited in BHSD, *gahastha*[22] contrasts with *pravrajita*, the same pairing we regularly find elsewhere. By contrast, *gṛhapati* in *gṛhapati-ratna* refers to "one of the 7 jewels of the cakravartin" (BHSD, s.v.) and thus represents only the "rich, prominent man" side of the word. See Edgerton's discussion there; he suggests that the equivalent figure in Pāli, *gahapati-ratana*, should be rendered "capitalist" (as opposed to PED "treasurer").[23] Whatever the exact rendering, it is clear that the generic householder has been left far behind.

The "rich, prominent" **gṛhapati* also shows up in the inscriptional record, in donative inscriptions in various forms of MIA. Given the context of donation, which requires a certain amount of wealth to participate, it is unlikely that the term refers to an ordinary householder but rather names a particular profession or social role, as do other such designations in donative inscriptions—and a profession whose members would control enough wealth to make notable, and noted, donations. For example, the online dictionary of Gāndhārī and its catalog of inscriptions lists several donative inscriptions with the donor a *grahavati* (CKI 172, 3) / *ga[ṃ]hapati* (CKI 249, 14e) or the daughter thereof (*grahavatisa dhita* CKI 172, 2; *grahavadi[dhita]* CKI 247, 1).[24] At a considerable geographical distance from Gandhāra are the Kanaganahalli inscriptions (Nakanishi and von Hinüber 2014), dated by them between the first or second and third century CE. Among the donors, a number of *gahapati*s are named; the editors consistently translate the term as "banker." Note, for example, IV.9 (Nakanishi and von Hinüber 2014, 107) N 2064 *]sa gahapatinā toḍ(e)sa ca na gahapatiput(e)sa sabhāriyesa sa[* "] by the banker]sa, the son of the banker

21. Diego Loukota also drew my attention to passages in the *Uvāsagadasāo* (= *Upāsakadaśā[ka]*) (§ 1.5, 17–21) relating the story of the *gāhāvaï* Āṇanda, who "unwittingly lists his various assets as he solemnly refrains from acquiring other property" (private communication, 3/26/18). The passages "trace a rich picture of what the ideal *gṛhapati* might have looked like: a good deal of personal wealth, split into a diversified portfolio that includes agricultural and commercial ventures, seems to be an essential characteristic, but also a position of social prominence and a role as the head of the extended family" (DL).

22. Note the truly hybrid form of the word, with MIA *gaha* but Sanskritized *-stha*.

23. Both Pāli and Ardhamāgadhī know the same figure. For the former, see Freiberger's discussion (pp. 69–70) and, e.g., PED and Cone, both s.v. *gahapati-ratana*; for the latter, see *gāhāvai-rayaṇa* "one of the 14 gems of a Chakravartī," s.v. the second entry for *gāhāvai* in IAMD.

24. Baums and Glass 2002–. Accessed July 22, 2018. https://www.gandhari.org/.

Toḍesacana (or: Sacana of the Toḍa family?), with his wife, with. . . ." The editors remark about this inscription, "The obviously fabulously rich Toḍa family made more than one donation at the Adhālaka-Caitya," and indeed a Toḍa *gahapati* is mentioned in another inscription (III.1.12, p. 89, N 3245). A *gahapati* is also mentioned directly next to a "merchant" (perhaps referring to the same person), V.2.18, p. 113, N. 3223 *gahapatino vāniga[sa]* "of the banker, the merchant."[25] In yet another part of the subcontinent, and at a somewhat earlier time, one Bhārhut inscription mentions a *gahapati* as donor (Lüders 1963, A 21, pp. 21–22): *bibikanadikaṭa budhino gahapatino.* Although Lüders translates the term as "householder," it obviously belongs with the other such inscriptions scattered about the subcontinent and refers to the same type of prominent individual. Thus, at least in the inscriptional record, as merely sampled here, the generic sense "householder" has been swamped by the "rich, prominent man" sense—not surprising given the usual contents of inscriptions.

Although this paper concentrates on the sources of the term **gṛhapati* and its early post-Vedic uses, it is worth noting that the "rich, prominent man" sense is widespread in later Sanskrit and MIA texts, both religious and secular. See, for example, Dezső 2019, 229, on the *Śreṣṭhijātaka*, no. 20 in Ārya Śūra's *Jātakamālā*, in which the Bodhisattva is referred to both as a *śreṣṭhin* and as a *gṛhapatiratna*, and other *jātaka*s in that collection in which the Bodhisattva is both *śreṣṭhin* and *gṛhapati*. Dezső concludes, "In these Jātakas the *gṛhapati* appears to be a wealthy citizen, a merchant or other kind of businessman, whose services are used by the king and who is a respected member of the society" (p. 231). Dezső also treats relevant passages in the Māhārāṣṭrī poetic anthology, the *Sattasaï*: "Another character we often meet in the *Sattasaī* is the *gahavaï* (Skt. *gṛhapati*). The word can simply mean 'husband' (e.g., in W 401), but in most of the cases it refers to a rich farmer or a landowner who also owns livestock" (p. 237). Similarly, "If we take a brief look at other Prakrit *kāvyas* possibly dating from a period before or around the fifth century CE, we see that both in the *Vasudevahiṇḍi* and in the *Paümacariya* the *gahavaï* is a rich man engaged in trade, agriculture or cattlebreeding" (p. 239).

The question that now arises is how did the one sense of **gṛhapati* give rise to the other—but this question does not usually seem to get asked. The tacit assumption is, I think, that enough householders, heads/lords of household, acquired enough material wealth and, with that, social prominence and influence to allow them to be named along with *khattiya*s and *brāhmaṇa*s,

25. And perhaps in II.4.1, p. 60, MASI CXXXI.6, though the "merchant" reading is "highly conjectural."

vāṇija and *seṭṭhi*, and to exert their economic force, and once this happened, such people would proudly use the word **gṛhapati* as a title and marker of status. This is not impossible, but it leaves the various steps necessary to change the meaning and reference of the term quite vague. And the change is not trivial, since it requires both narrowing and widening the semantic range: not all householders would be **gṛhapati* by the second set of criteria, which expanded to include qualities that had nothing directly to do with householding. The only scholar I know of who attempts to fill in these blanks is Chakravarti, in her section entitled "*Gahapati*: from householder to agriculturalist" (1987, 85–87), acutely framing the question as accounting for the term's "shift in meaning from a word that signified a householder, or head of the family unit, to one that signified an economic category and, more specifically [by her analysis], that of an agriculturalist" (p. 86). For her, to pose the question is to answer it (p. 87): if, as she argues, *gahapati*s were particularly associated with agriculture, they "were the owners and controllers of the primary means of production in the form of land." By their family's agricultural labor they gradually accumulated capital and "played a crucial role in the extension, and consolidation of the agricultural economy." But this explanation is circular: it assumes that the term *gahapati* is already an economic term rather than simply defining an intrafamilial role, and, in my opinion, also over-emphasizes the agricultural connection. In Pāli texts and other Middle Indic corpora the *gahapati* is as likely to be associated with the merchant (*seṭṭhi*, e.g., Vin I 16,11, Jāt IV 227,6, *vāṇija*, see above) as the farmer (*kassaka*, e.g., AN I 229,32), and certainly the early materials collected by Freiberger seem to show no particular connection to the land.

Because of the difficulties in motivating the semantic shift and because this shift seems to have already happened in all the corpora so far sampled, including (by inference) in Gāndhārī at some geographical distance, I think we need to project the semantic split further back and assume that already in Pāli and the other languages of Buddhism the term *gahapati* had two fairly distinct senses. And in fact we can see the lineaments—and, I will argue, the sources—of these separate usages already in Vedic.

I have already discussed the Vedic usage and evolution of *gṛhapati* in some detail (Jamison 2019a), or at least the portion that relates most directly to the generic "householder" sense. But in that article I merely mentioned (n23), only to postpone discussion, the usage of the term that may underlie the "rich, prominent man" sense. In what follows I will briefly summarize (from Jamison 2019a frequently cited already) the "householder" part, including the particular circumstances that made the term awkward in the middle and late Vedic religious climate, and then turn to the sense that, in my view, gives rise to the "rich, prominent man" sense. These two usages are essentially distinct by the middle Vedic period and found, generally, in separate texts, and the split was occasioned by the very awkwardness I just mentioned.

The most curious fact about Vedic *gṛhápati*[26] is that, though it is attested throughout the Vedic period, its career as a designation of an ordinary householder / head of household is limited, sporadic, and brief. To begin with, although the word is reasonably well attested in the *Ṛg Veda* (over twenty times), it is never used of a human.[27] Instead its referent is always the god Agni, the ritual fire in the household. Although it may be that Agni is called "lord of the house" in this text on the model of his putative human counterpart, there is no actual evidence for this, and it would not be surprising that the title "lord of the house" would be conferred on, and confined to, the prominent god who inhabited the dwelling and protected its occupants, rather than on the comparatively puny human.[28] Our second-oldest text, the *Atharva Veda*, contains only four occurrences of the term, but by this time it can be applied to the human houselord, and the household fire; in fact, three of the four occurrences are used of a human, with only one referring to Agni. But its application to Agni does not pass out of use: throughout the middle Vedic period this god is regularly identified as the *gṛhápati*, and often, when a human *gṛhápati* is mentioned, it is in the hopes that that human will acquire the traits that Agni displays in this role. The intertwining of god and man as *gṛhápati* is seen in an extremely widespread (prose) mantra, found, inter alia, in the White and Black Yajur Veda *saṃhitā*s, the *brāhmaṇa*s, and the *śrauta* sūtras:

> VS II.27[29] *ágne gṛhapate sugṛhapatís tváyāgne 'háṃ gṛhápatinā bhūyāsaṁ sugṛhapatís tváṃ máyāgne gṛhápatinā bhūyāḥ*

26. In the discussion of Vedic I will cite the word with accent, even though a number of the occurrences treated will come from Vedic texts transmitted without accents.

27. With a single possible exception, RV VI.53.2. This hymn exhibits a colloquial register and popular tone, and if the *gṛhápati* there is a human, this may reflect *Atharva Veda*-like usage. See ad loc. in my online commentary: http://rigvedacommentary.alc.ucla.edu.

28. In the article cited, I was more open to the possibility that the designation of Agni as *gṛhápati* was secondary to and based upon that of the human head of household. I now find that view unlikely.

29. VS (*Vājasaneyīsaṃhitā*) contains the mantras of the White Yajur Veda. A partial list of repetitions of this mantra includes passages in the White Yajur Veda *brāhmaṇa* (ŚB), Black Yajur Veda *saṃhitā*s (TS, MS, KS), and *śrauta* sūtras belonging to the *Ṛg Veda* (ŚŚS), White YV (KŚS), Black YV (BŚS), etc. For a complete list with passage numbers, see Franceschini 2007, 40. Note also the other mantras beginning *agne gṛhapate* collected there (pp. 40–41), and those beginning *agnir gṛhapatiḥ* (p. 25), *agniṃ gṛhapatiṃ* (p. 18), *agnaye gṛhapataye* (p. 10).

> O houselord Agni, might I become a good houselord with you as houselord, O Agni; might you become a good houselord with me as houselord, O Agni.

Throughout the middle Vedic period the most common referent of *gṛhápati* is Agni, generally in contexts that lack a human counterpart (unlike the mantra just cited) and often in connection with the wives of the gods,[30] as in

> KS I.10 (etc.) *agne gṛhapata upa mā hvayasva devānāṃ patnīr upa mā hvayadhvam*

> O houselord Agni, invite me; O wives of the gods, invite me.

After the brief flurry of human references in the AV, in the *brāhmaṇa* texts the word *gṛhápati* is almost never used of a human householder.[31] For example, that vast text, the *Śatapathabrāhmaṇa*, has two passages in which we can identify a human *gṛhápati*, each time in connection with the Householder's Fire (Gārhapatya): once in a curious, *gṛhya*-like passage (ŚBM II.4.1.13–14 = ŚBK I.4.2.8–9) in which a householder, returning from a journey and before entering his house, must "approach" the two ritual fires, the Āhavanīya and the Gārhapatya, lest the house get scared, tremble, and crush him and his family;[32] once when the question is asked what the danger is if the Gārhapatya fire goes out, with the response that the *gṛhápati* would die without proper knowledge of ritual procedure (ŚBM XI.5.1.9).

It is only in the *gṛhya* sūtras, the manuals of domestic ritual that come at the very end of the Vedic period, that the *gṛhapati* is found apart from his association with Agni and the Gārhapatya fire. As I showed in the article cited frequently above, insofar as the central figure of the *gṛhya* sūtras is named—and he often is not, since he is the default and therefore unnamed subject of all verbs of ritual action—the standard term is *gṛhapati* (cf. ŚGS I.1.2; PGS II.9.14–15; KhGS I.5.36, III.3.16, 24; GobhGS I.4.24). It is this usage especially

30. In Jamison 2019a, I discuss the striking pairing of the human housewife and the god Agni as *gṛhápati* already in the RV.

31. Save for *sattra* contexts; see below.

32. For the re-entry into the house after a journey in the *gṛhya* sūtras, see ŚGS III.7, HGS I.29, in both of which the returnee says to his house, "House, do not fear; do not tremble!" *gṛhā mā bibhīta mā vepadhvam* [HGS *vepiḍhvam*], a mantra found in variant forms from the AV onward (see Franceschini 2007, 686). In the *gṛhya* sūtra versions the returnee of course does not approach the *śrauta* fires, as the *gṛhápati* does in the ŚB.

that I think is continued in the generic "householder" use that we sometimes find in Pāli and other languages of Buddhism and in the early Jaina materials, as discussed extensively above.

But it is crucial to note that these texts, and therefore this usage, belong to the *gṛhya* side of the great ritual cleavage that defines Vedic religious practice after the *Ṛg Veda*: the division between the *śrauta* (high, solemn) and *gṛhya* (domestic) ritual systems. The former refers to the elaborate rites involving three ritual fires and multiple priests that can only be undertaken by twice-born men who "have established fires" (*āhitāgni*), the latter to the simpler life-cycle rituals requiring only a single fire that were available to all twice-born men.[33] And here enters the awkwardness alluded to above. As was recently noted, the word *gṛhápati*, starting with the *Ṛg Veda* and continuing all the way through the Vedic period, is inextricably bound up with the god Agni, frequently identified as *gṛhápati*, and with the ritual fire known as the Gārhapatya (*gā́rhapatya*), or "householder's fire," a transparent *vṛddhi* derivative of *gṛhápati*. But, embarrassingly, the householder's fire is a *śrauta* fire; it does not belong to the *gṛhya* system named with a different term derived from the "house" word and whose central figure is the *gṛhápati*. Instead, the Gārhapatya is one of the three *śrauta* fires, the foundational one, from which the others are "taken out," and the single ritual fire of the *gṛhya* system has to make do with other names (see Jamison 2019a, 14). So the terminology for the houselord is uncomfortably split: the human houselord is barely found in the *śrauta* texts, but the fire named after him is ubiquitous; by contrast, the leading ritual figure in the *gṛhya* texts is the *gṛhápati*, but he could not import his fire, or rather its name, into this distinct ritual system.

But there is another *gṛhápati* in the *śrauta* texts, besides the epithet of the fire god and the almost vanishingly rare generic householder—and this is the chief sacrificer of the set of rituals known as *sattra/satra*, "session." *Sattra*s are multi-day (twelve days or more) rites, and instead of having a single "sacrificer" (*yájamāna*) like most *śrauta* rituals, there are multiple sacrificers, and the usual practices regarding the sacrificer must be adjusted accordingly:

> All the performers must be consecrated and must be Brahmans: there is therefore no separate sacrificer: all share in the benefits of the offering: each bears the burden of his own errors. . . . One of them plays the part of sacrificer: the others hold on to him when he does those acts which only one man can perform.[34]

33. For some discussion of the differences and of the prehistory of the split, see Jamison 2019b.

34. Keith [1925] 1970, 349.

The one playing "the part of the sacrificer" is called the *gr̥hápati*, and it is from his Gārhapatya fire that the Offering fire (Āhavanīya), which serves for all the participants, is taken out (see, e.g., ŚB IV.6.8.5, 10, 13, 15; Hillebrandt [1879] 1981, 154). Almost all the human *gr̥hápati*s mentioned in the *brāhmaṇa* texts (i.e., the prose exegesis of the *śrauta* system) are actually participants in a *sattra*.[35] It is this role that in my opinion gave rise to the "rich, prominent man" usage of **gr̥hapati* in post-Vedic texts.

There are two major reasons for my view. On the one hand, considering this *gr̥hápati* from the human perspective, he is the leader of a group of otherwise equal sacrificers, all of whom are qualified by birth and attainments (having established their fires) to serve as *yájamāna* of their own sacrifices. Therefore the *gr̥hápati* in this ritual is truly *primus inter pares* ("first among equals"), and though I know of no passage that explains how and why he is chosen for this role, his wealth and/or prominence must fit him for it, preferentially over the others.

Moreover, the model for the *sattra* is a sacrifice performed by the gods. Different versions give different gods as the prototype for the human *gr̥hápati*. ŚB III.4.2.15, for example, names the *gr̥hápati* "as representative of Indra":

> ŚB III.4.1.15 ... *tásmād yádi bahávo dī́kṣeran gr̥hápataya evá ... práyaccheyuḥ sá hí téṣām indrabhājanáṃ bhávati*
>
> Therefore, if many should be consecrated, they should hand over (a particular offering) to the *gr̥hápati*, for of them he is the representation of Indra.

In a different section of the ŚB (VI.1.3.7) the "lord of beings" is the *gr̥hápati* in a different *sattra* (*bhūtā́nāṃ pátir gr̥hápatir ā́sīt*) and Dawn is the Sacrificer's Wife, whereas in AB V.25 the similar figure Prajāpati ("lord of creatures") is the gods' *gr̥hápati*. But of course the most stable divine association is with Agni, so often called *gr̥hápati* himself and, with his association with the Gārhapatya fire, the source for the title of the central sacrificer of the *sattra*, since the Offering fire is taken out of the *gr̥hápati*'s own Gārhapatya. Identification of the human *gr̥hápati* with any one of these divine figures would of course enhance his status.

Once the lead sacrificer at a *sattra* had come to be designated as *gr̥hápati*, the usage of the term could broaden to designate the same man outside his ritual role: someone prominent enough to be a ritual *gr̥hápati* could start being

35. E.g., ŚB III.4.2.15, IV.6.8.3ff., XI.4.2.17–18; AB V.25, VIII.21; JB III.4.

called *gṛhápati* in his non-ritual life and by non-coreligionists. As a courtesy title to begin with—just as an American football coach or boat captain can be addressed as "Coach" or "Capt." when he's buying groceries or playing golf, not just when he's directing players in a game or piloting a boat.[36] But because becoming a ritual *gṛhápati* required attributes like wealth and social prominence, the title *gṛhápati* could come to signify as its core meaning a person who has such attributes. As a parallel to the use of a religiously derived epithet as a general marker of status outside the religion proper, consider surnames like Dvivedi, Trivedi, which are in widespread use today and not restricted to a "Vedic" community.

To summarize my claims here, I argue that the two senses of **gṛhapati* that we find in post-Vedic, and particularly Buddhist MIA, literature have two distinct sources in Vedic. The generic "householder," which is recessive even in early Buddhist literature though perhaps more prominent in early Jaina texts, comes from the same generic use in Vedic, especially for the central figure of the *gṛhya* sūtras, the literal "lord of the house."[37] This literal meaning and generic usage are carried over into later literature, though this use is comparatively uncommon. But the "rich, prominent man" sense that is also found in early Buddhist and Jaina texts and that comes to dominate the Buddhist materials, the inscriptional evidence, and later secular literature comes out of the Vedic *śrauta* tradition. There the title is applied to the principal sacrificer in a *sattra*, a person of particular prominence, who owes his label not to a literal reading of the compound but rather to the long-entwined associations between the god Agni—often called *gṛhápati*—and the fundamental fire of the *śrauta* system, the Gārhapatya. On this analysis we don't have to account for a semantic change in post-Vedic literature but rather assume that the post-Vedic material was heir to these two senses of **gṛhapati* and kept them reasonably distinct.

36. Olivelle has suggested to me that the "rich man" sense of *gṛhápati* was the original one, and the "chief sacrificer of a *sattra*" is secondary to it, based on the already existing high social status of the *gṛhápati*—rather than the reverse, as I argue—on the grounds that it is somewhat improbable that the technical use of the term in Vedic ritual would give rise to the widespread use of the term for a rich man in non-Vedic materials. However, I find it difficult to account for the term without reference to the interrelationships of the god Agni Gṛhapati, the Gārhapatya fire of *śrauta* ritual, and the *gṛhápati* figure in the *sattra*. And see the *Mahābhārata* data about to be discussed and the explanation given in the text for the broadening of a courtesy title, esp. with regard to old religious titles like Trivedi.

37. It is, in fact, possible that the generic householder use in each tradition is independent and based on a sort of etymological back-formation, in which the compound is segmented and the two parts interpreted literally. Cf. the oft-quoted definition in the Pāli *Vinaya*: Vin III 212,36 *gahapati nāma koci agāraṃ ajjhāvasati* "a 'gahapati' is whoever inhabits a house."

Happily, the evidence for the householder in the *Mahābhārata*, assembled and discussed in Bowles 2019, provides support for this scenario. As he shows, the term *gṛhapati* in the MBh is vanishingly rare, occurring only six times in the constituted text of this enormous epic, as opposed to the considerably better attested *gṛhastha*. I will simply cite Bowles's characterization of the data and its semantic features (p. 177, several notes omitted):

> First, clearly for the *Mahābhārata* the term *gṛhastha* and its derivatives (mainly *gārhasthya*; occasionally *gārhastha*) have become the predominant terms marking the duties, lifestyles and "religious" obligations of the domestic life, most particularly in the case of Brahmins. The older term, *gṛhapati*, . . . has fallen almost totally into disuse. . . . Of its six appearances in the constituted text of the Critical Edition, two refer to its archaic meaning of Agni, the hypostasized ritual fire (3.212.4, 12.260.26), and three refer to the head of a *satra* sacrifice. . . . *Gṛhapati* in this sense is found at 1.4.11 in reference to Śaunaka at the head of the *sadasya* and *ṛtvij* priests attending his twelve-year *satra* at which the bard Ugraśravas recites to them the *Mahābhārata*; at 1.50.13 in reference to King Janamejaya in Āstīka's praise of the *sarpasatra* of which the king is patron; and at 13.85.25 where Varuṇa describes himself as the *gṛhapati* at his own *satra*. The one remaining occurrence, 12.235.27, introduces the human subjects—the "forest-dwelling (*vanaukas*) *gṛhapatis*"—of the third *āśrama*, which is subsequently described in 12.236, where such people are referred to as *vānaprasthas*. In the *Mahābhārata*, therefore, leaving aside one instance in the . . . *Viṣṇudharma* passage of the *Mahābhārata*,[38] the *gṛhapati* does not refer to the ideological construct of the householder, but rather, where its referent is a human, marks a ritual participant of high status, indeed, in most cases, a ritual leader.

Thus the data from the MBh strikingly conform to the distribution of *gṛhapati* in the middle Vedic *śrauta* texts just discussed—with half the occurrences referring to the chief sacrificer in a *sa(t)tra* ritual and two of the remaining three to the god Agni. The *gṛhya* use of the term for the householder celebrant of domestic ritual is found only once, in an appendix. Bowles devotes most of

38. Referring to a passage not found in the constituted MBh text, Bowles 2019, 177n7, writes: "Line 2585 in Appendix 1 No.4 of the *Āśvamedhikaparvan* defines the *gṛhapati* as *gṛhyakarmavaho yasmāt tasmād gṛhapatis tu saḥ*."

his paper to the use of *gṛhastha* (and its relatives) in what he felicitously terms "the basic binary" (beginning p. 182)—namely, the contrast between the "stay-at-home" and the "gone-forth" that I first identified in the Aśokan inscriptions—and he demonstrates that this binary "informs much of the data [of the *gṛhastha*] from the *MBh*."

One particularly nagging question remains: why did the Hindu dharma literature completely suppress the term *gṛhapati* in favor of *gṛhastha*, while the Buddhist, Jaina, and (semi-)secular literature in both MIA and Sanskrit keep **gṛhapati*, though predominately in the "rich, prominent man" sense? Even a body of text closely allied with the dharma material—namely, the *Arthaśāstra*—attests *gṛhapati*, though it is limited there to secret agents in the guise of *gṛhapati* (e.g., KAŚ I.1.4, 11.1, 9; II.35.8, etc.).[39] I do not have a clear or convincing answer, but I imagine that at least two factors contributed to this terminological rupture. On the one hand, the architects of the emerging dharma system, with its emphasis on the *āśrama* system (first as choices, then as life-stages) and its new incorporation of the renunciant ascetic into the set of acceptable orthodox roles, wanted to mark its break with the very different Vedic religious system by replacing the old word for the, or a, principal actor in it with one that expressed the polarity between the stay-at-home householder and the wandering ascetic. The other śramaṇic religions were already sufficiently distinguished from Vedic ritualism and did not feel the need to mark this distinction by abandoning the old term. And on the other, for those fashioning the new dharmic consensus, the awkward double sense of Vedic *gṛhápati*, with its feet in both the *śrauta* and the *gṛhya* systems, may have seemed more trouble than it was worth to untangle.

I will end by repeating my claims in the starkest possible terms. Most of the instances of **gṛhapati* we encounter in post-Vedic texts, including and perhaps especially Buddhist texts, have only a tangential and indirect relationship to the generic householder word; they do not continue the generic *gṛhápati* usage we find in the *gṛhya* sūtras and occasionally elsewhere in earlier Vedic. Instead they are direct continuators of an early specialization of Vedic *gṛhápati*—as the principal sacrificer, the big man, at a *sattra*—we could render it as "Mr. Big." They are not householders who got lucky and got rich; they are an entirely different social group and have been since middle Vedic times. Although both the generic householder word and the Mr. Big word are made up of the same lexical pieces, the pathways of their semantic derivation were quite distinct from the beginning. Failure to appreciate that distinction has populated post-Vedic

39. And, according to Olivelle (private communication), these *gṛhapati*s are most likely the rich, prominent men we meet elsewhere.

India with a remarkable number of householders who just happen to be rich—rather like assuming that the median income of households in Greenwich, Connecticut, or Malibu tells us something about American households in general. Our Mr. Big **gṛhapati* lives in Malibu; the standard average **gṛhapati* may be found struggling somewhere in, say, Nebraska.

I hope that I will be forgiven for having taken a major (though, given my interests, predictable) detour off the Buddhist path in order to explain some aberrancies in the usage of a term well attested in Buddhist literature. In following this roundabout route I take courage from the broad vision of our honorand, who has always taught that ancient Indian Buddhism must be approached as a piece with ancient Indian culture more generally, not as a country unto itself, and who, as we all know, has never shied away from unorthodox and iconoclastic positions. And I hope in this short piece to have provided one of his businessmen with a bit of history.

Works Cited

Abbreviations

AB	*Aitareyabrāhmaṇa*
AM	Ardhamāgadhī
AN	Aṅguttara Nikāya
AV	*Atharva Veda*
BHSD	*Buddhist Hybrid Sanskrit Dictionary*. See Edgerton [1953] 1985.
BŚS	*Baudhāyanaśrauta-sūtra*
CKI	Corpus of Kharoṣṭhī Inscriptions. Gāndhārī inscription, according to Catalog of Gāndhārī Texts. See Baums and Glass 2002–.
Gi	Girnar
GobhGS	*Gobhilagṛhya-sūtra*
HGS	*Hiraṇyakeśigṛhya-sūtra*
IAMD	*Illustrated Ardha-Magadhi Dictionary*. See Ratnachandraji Maharaj [1923] 2016.
Jāt	*Jātaka*
JB	*Jaiminīyabrāhmaṇa*
Ka	Kalsi
KAŚ	Kauṭilīya's *Arthaśāstra*
KhGS	*Khādiragṛhya-sūtra*
KS	*Kāṭhakasaṃhitā*
KŚS	*Kātyāyanaśrauta-sūtra*

MBh	*Mahābhārata*
MIA	Middle Indo-Aryan
MS	*Maitrāyaṇīsaṃhitā*
PED	*Pali-English Dictionary*. See Rhys Davids and Stede [1921–1925] 1979.
PGS	*Pāraskaragṛhya-sūtra*
RE	Rock Edict
RV	*Ṛg Veda*
ŚB	*Śatapathabrāhmaṇa*
ŚBK	*Śatapathabrāhmaṇa*, Kāṇva recension
ŚBM	*Śatapathabrāhmaṇa*, Mādhyaṃdina recension
ŚGS	*Śāṅkhāyanagṛhya-sūtra*
Sh	Shahbazgarhi
ŚŚS	*Śāṅkhāyanaśrauta-sūtra*
TS	*Taittirīyasaṃhitā*
UD	*Uttarādhyayana-sūtra*
Vin	Vinaya
VS	*Vājasaneyīsaṃhitā*

Baums, Stefan, and Andrew Glass. 2002–. "A Dictionary of Gāndhārī; Catalog of Gāndhārī Texts." https://www.gandhari.org/.

Bloch, Jules. 1950. *Les inscriptions d'Asoka traduites et commentées*. Paris: Les Belles Lettres.

Bowles, Adam. 2019. "The *Gṛhastha* in the *Mahābhārata*." In *Gṛhastha: The Householder in Ancient Indian Religious Culture*, edited by Patrick Olivelle, 173–203. New York: Oxford University Press.

Brick, David. 2019. "The Householder in Early Dharmaśāstra Literature." In *Gṛhastha: The Householder in Ancient Indian Religious Culture*, edited by Patrick Olivelle, 124–149. New York: Oxford University Press.

Chakravarti, Uma. 1987. *Social Dimensions of Early Buddhism*. New York: Oxford University Press.

Cone, Margaret. 2010. *A Dictionary of Pāli*, vol. 2. Bristol: The Pali Text Society.

Dezső, Csaba. 2019. "Householders and Housewives in Early *Kāvya* Literature." In *Gṛhastha: The Householder in Ancient Indian Religious Culture*, edited by Patrick Olivelle, 222–245. New York: Oxford University Press.

Edgerton, Franklin. [1953] 1985. *Buddhist Hybrid Sanskrit Grammar and Dictionary*, vol. 2: *Dictionary*. Reprint, Delhi: Motilal Banarsidass.

Franceschini, Marco. 2007. *An Updated Vedic Concordance: Maurice Bloomfield's A Vedic Concordance Enhanced with New Material Taken from Seven Vedic Texts*. 2 vols. Cambridge, MA: Dept. of Sanskrit and Indian Studies, Harvard University; Milan: Mimesis Edizioni.

Freiberger, Oliver. 2019. "*Gṛhastha* in the Śramaṇic Discourse: A Lexical Survey of House Residents in Early Pāli Texts." In *Gṛhastha: The Householder in Ancient Indian Religious Culture*, edited by Patrick Olivelle, 58–74. New York: Oxford University Press.

Hillebrandt, Alfred. [1879] 1981. *Ritual-Litteratur: Vedische Opfer und Zauber.* Reprint, Graz: Akademische Druck- u. Verlagsanstalt.

Jain, Jagdishchandra. [1947] 1984. *Life in Ancient India as Depicted in the Jain Canon and Commentaries: 6th Century BC to 17th Century AD.* 2nd revised and enlarged ed. New Delhi: Munshiram Manoharlal.

Jamison, Stephanie W. 2019a. "The Term *Gṛhastha* and the (Pre)history of the Householder." In *Gṛhastha: The Householder in Ancient Indian Religious Culture*, edited by Patrick Olivelle, 3–19. New York: Oxford University Press.

———. 2019b. "Vedic Ritual: The Sacralization of the Mundane and the Domestication of the Sacred." In *Self, Sacrifice, and Cosmos: Late Vedic Thought, Ritual, and Philosophy. Essays in Honor of Professor Ganesh Umakant Thite's Contributions to Vedic Studies*, edited by Lauren M. Bausch, 64–80. Delhi: Primus Books.

Keith, Arthur Berriedale. [1925] 1970. *The Religion and Philosophy of the Veda and Upanishads.* 2 vols. Harvard Oriental Series 31–32. Reprint, Delhi: Motilal Banarsidass.

Lüders, Heinrich, ed. 1963. *Bharhut Inscriptions.* Revised by E. Waldschmidt and M. A. Mehendale. Corpus Inscriptionum Indicarum 2.2. Ootacamund: Government Epigraphist for India.

Maes, Claire. 2019. "*Gāhāvaï* and *Gihattha*: The Householder in the Early Jain Sources." In *Gṛhastha: The Householder in Ancient Indian Religious Culture*, edited by Patrick Olivelle, 75–91. New York: Oxford University Press.

Nakanishi, Maiko, and Oskar von Hinüber, eds. 2014. *Kanaganahalli Inscriptions.* Supplement to *Annual Report of the International Research Institute for Advanced Buddhology at Soka University* 17. Tokyo: The International Research Institute for Advanced Buddhology, Soka University.

Olivelle, Patrick. 1993. *The* Āśrama *System: The History and Hermeneutics of a Religious Institution.* New York: Oxford University Press.

———, ed. and trans. 2000. *Dharmasūtras: The Law Codes of Āpastamba, Gautama, Baudhāyana, and Vasiṣṭha.* New Delhi: Motilal Banarsidass.

———, ed. 2019. *Gṛhastha: The Householder in Ancient Indian Religious Culture.* New York: Oxford University Press.

Pischel, R. [1900] 1981. *A Grammar of the Prākrit Languages.* Translated by Subhadra Jhā. Reprint, Delhi: Motilal Banarsidass.

Ratnachandraji Maharaj, Shatavadhani Jain Muni Shri, ed. [1923] 2016. *An Illustrated Ardha-Magadhi Dictionary: Literary, Philosophic and Scientific with Sanskrit, Gujrati, Hindi and English Equivalents, References to the Texts & Copious Quotations.* Reprint, Delhi: Motilal Banarsidass.

Rhys Davids, T. W., and William Stede, eds. [1921–1925] 1979. *The Pali Text Society's Pali-English Dictionary.* Reprint, London: Pali Text Society.

Schneider, Ulrich. 1978. *Die grossen Felsen-Edikte Aśokas: Kritische Ausgabe, Übersetzung und Analyse der Texte.* Wiesbaden: Otto Harrassowitz.

Yamazaki, Gen'ichi. 2005. *The Structure of Ancient Indian Society: Theory and Reality of the Varṇa System.* Toyo Bunko Research Library 6. Tokyo: The Toyo Bunko.

A Preliminary Report on the *Vinayasaṃgraha*: *Viśeṣamitra's Discussion Following *Pāyantikā* 72*

Ryōji Kishino

PROFESSOR GREGORY SCHOPEN'S major contributions to Vinaya research have been made possible by not only his skilled use of the *Mūlasarvāstivāda-vinaya* but also his frequent reference to its various commentaries and handbooks. There are approximately thirty Indian commentaries and handbooks on the *Mūlasarvāstivāda-vinaya* extant and available to us. Schopen has cited at least nineteen of them in his published papers and demonstrated that they can be useful for gaining more insight into the *Mūlasarvāstivāda-vinaya*.[1]

While most of the thirty or so Indian commentaries and handbooks on the *Mūlasarvāstivāda-vinaya* have come down to us only in Tibetan translations,[2] the principal text for this paper, *Viśeṣamitra's *Vinayasaṃgraha*, is an exception; it is fully preserved not only in Tibetan but also in Yijing's 義淨 (635–713) Chinese translation (Tib. *'Dul ba bsdus pa* [D 4105]; Chin. *Genben sapoduo bu lüshe* 根本薩婆多部律攝 [Taishō 1458]).[3] The *Vinayasaṃgraha* addresses

* I wish to thank Dr. Shayne Clarke and Mr. Dylan Luers Toda for their careful reading of a draft and insightful comments, and Mr. Warren Kadoya and Dr. Yao Fumi 八尾史 for many useful suggestions. They contributed significantly to the improvement of this paper. This acknowledgment, however, does not imply their entire approval or agreement. I alone remain responsible for all errors, inaccuracies, and inconsistencies. I would also like to express my gratitude to the Japan Society for the Promotion of Science for providing financial support (Grant-in-Aid for Scientific Research C 22K00065) and the Mitsubishi Foundation (Research Grants in Humanities, 2021).

1. Ende 2016, 84–85, 87–99.

2. Ōtani Cat., 263–288. Among the works on the *Mūlasarvāstivāda-vinaya* authored by Tibetan Buddhist scholars, those by Bu ston Rin chen grub (1290–1364) in particular are known for broadening our knowledge of the *Mūlasarvāstivāda-vinaya*. Cf. Kishino 2019, 108–109. Schopen is one of the first modern scholars to note the importance of Bu ston's works and to reference them in detail in studies of the Vinaya. See, for example, Schopen 1998, 178n67; cf. Ende 2016, 87.

3. The *Vinayasaṃgraha* was translated into Chinese by Yijing in 700 CE and into Tibetan by

each of the rules included in the *Bhikṣuprātimokṣa* of the *Mūlasarvāstivāda-vinaya* in the order that the rules are presented, and this is probably why it has been generally regarded as a commentary on the monks' *Prātimokṣa* of the *Mūlasarvāstivāda-vinaya*.[4]

As I will discuss below, the *Vinayasaṃgraha* has more significance than has been appreciated in modern scholarship. Few of the studies done to date,

---

Śīlendrabodhi and others early in the ninth century CE; Sasaki [1976] 1985, 150–151. A relatively large number of folios of the Tibetan translation of the *Vinayasaṃgraha* are preserved in the Pelliot Collection of Tibetan manuscripts from Dunhuang; see Yang 2012; cf. Clarke 2016, 190n11. It seems that the Tibetan translation of the *Vinayasaṃgraha* was revised or retranslated later by Jñānaśrībhadra and others; Ōtani Cat., 265 (no. 5606); Borgland 2014, 323n114. Tucci ([1932] 1988, 51) notes that this revision or retranslation was completed during the reign of King Rtse lde (r. ca. 1055–?); cf. Martin 2013, 257n36. Kun mkhyen Mtsho sna ba Shes rab bzang po (twelfth to thirteenth century CE) may have been referring to this dual translation process of the *Vinayasaṃgraha* in his commentary on the *Vinayasūtra*, *'Dul ba mdo rtsa'i rnam bshad nyi ma'i 'od zer legs bshad lung gi rgya mtsho*. He explains that the text consists of two translations, an earlier and a later one: *gzhan yang so sor thar pa'i 'grel pa* <u>*'Dul ba bsdus pa*</u> *slob dpon Khyad par bshes gnyen gyis mdzad pa ste* <u>*'gyur snga phyi gnyis*</u> *dang* / . . . (*'Dul ṭi ka nyi ma'i 'od zer legs bshad lung rigs kyi rgya mtsho*, 2:370, 16–17).

4. Sasaki ([1977] 1985, 168) explicitly refers to the *Vinayasaṃgraha* as a commentary on the monks' *Prātimokṣa*. However, his evidence for this claim is not clear. Sasaki says that he refers to six premodern Japanese works on the *Vinayasaṃgraha*, listing them: (1) *Konpon-satsubata-bu risshō kōgi* 根本薩婆多部律攝講義, 1 vol. (not found in KS; cf. BKDJ 3:532); (2) *Konpon-satsubata-bu risshō kōroku* 根本薩婆多部律攝講録, 3 vols. (cf. KS 3:624; KS 1:389, s.v. *ubu risshō kōroku* 有部律摂講録; not found in BKDJ); (3) *Ubu risshō bunka* 有部律攝分科 1 fasc. (cf. KS 1:389; BKDJ 1:213); (4) *Ubu risshō kikigaki* 有部律攝聞書 1 fasc. (cf. KS 3:718, s.v. *satsubata-bu risshō kikigaki* 薩婆多部律攝聞書; BKDJ 1:213: "U-bu-ris-shō-kiki-gaki"); (5) *Satsubata-bu risshō fugon inko* 薩婆多部律攝付言引拠 1 fasc. (cf. KS 3:718; BKDJ 4:49; Inaya 1987, 4); and (6) *Risshō kōroku* 律攝考録 1 fasc. (not found in KS or BKDJ). Accordingly, his reference to the *Vinayasaṃgraha* as a monks' *Prātimokṣa* commentary might be derived from these six. All of these six works are difficult to access, and I could only view a copy of the *Risshō kōroku* 律攝考録 preserved at Ryūkoku University in Kyoto (regarding this text, see Clarke 2006, 28). Although I cursorily surveyed the bibliographical description of the *Vinayasaṃgraha* in this text, I could not find any clear statement that it is a commentary on the monks' *Prātimokṣa*. Note, however, Tokuda (1974, 138) also suggests that the *Vinayasaṃgraha* is a commentary on the *Prātimokṣa* (戒本の随文解釈) in his excellent catalog of Vinaya texts extant in Japan. Likewise, MBD (2:1377, s.v. *konpon-setsuissaiu-bu binaya* 根本説一切有部毘奈耶) refers to the *Vinayasaṃgraha* as a commentary on the *Prātimokṣa* (戒本を解釋). In addition, in their forewords to Gakunyo's 學如 edition of the Chinese *Vinayasaṃgraha* (cf. note 23 below), Kōhan 弘範 (d. 1768) and Mitsumon 密門 (1719–1788) also refer to it as an exegesis of the *Prātimokṣa* (戒本ヲ釋シ); Kishino 2022, 24n9. Taking these views into consideration, it seems that the *Vinayasaṃgraha* has been traditionally regarded as a commentary on the monks' *Prātimokṣa* in Japan since at least the eighteenth century. In Tibetan Buddhist traditions, the *Vinayasaṃgraha* seems to have been regarded as a *Prātimokṣa* commentary by at least the time of Bu ston Rin chen grub; in his *'Dul ba spyi'i rnam par gzhag pa 'dul ba rin po che'i mdzes rgyan* (1357), he refers to it as *so so* [*sic*] *thar pa'i 'grel pa*; Kishino 2019.

for example, have paid sufficient attention to the Tibetan translation.[5] Even fundamental questions such as the relationship between the Chinese and Tibetan translations or the relationship of either to the *Mūlasarvāstivāda-vinaya* have yet to be adequately studied. My objective in this paper is to broaden our knowledge of the *Vinayasaṃgraha* based on both its Chinese and Tibetan translations. First, I will provide general information about the *Vinayasaṃgraha*, briefly discussing what is known about its author and date, and noting the conflicting attitudes toward it in Chinese and Tibetan Buddhist circles. Then, based on both its Chinese and Tibetan translations, I will analyze its content. However, I will not treat all of its content in detail; although the *Vinayasaṃgraha* is much more accessible than the *Mūlasarvāstivāda-vinaya* itself, it is by no means short, with Yijing's Chinese translation comprising fourteen *juan* 巻 or fascicles, and the extant Tibetan translation in the Bstan 'gyur thirteen *bam po*.[6] I therefore will cover only a

5. Sakaino 1932; Nishimoto 1933a; Sasaki [1976; 1977] 1985; Yang 2012. Apart from these three works, Shaku Keihō's two papers published in 1939 and 1940 might also be considered to be research on the *Vinayasaṃgraha*; cf. Clarke 2016, 190n12. Oddly enough, however, they provide little information about the text, despite their titles: "An Introduction to the *Mūlasarvāstivādin Vinayasaṃgraha*" (『根本説一切有部律攝』序説; 1939) and "A Survey of the *(Mūla)Sarvāstivādin Vinayasaṃgraha*" (有部律攝概説; 1940). Both papers are reprinted in Tamayama (1940, 1–25; 27–62) with a few changes in content and wording. According to Venerable Asai Shōzen 浅井證善 (personal communication, February 2022), Shaku and Tamayama are one and the same, although there is no such mention of this in Tamayama 1940.

6. The Chinese translation of the *Vinayasaṃgraha* is said to have circulated in two recensions: one in fourteen *juan* 巻, another in twenty *juan* 巻. Hirakawa (1960, 150) states that the latter is not available at present. It is reported, however, that the old manuscripts of Chinese Buddhist texts preserved in several temples in Japan, such as Ishiyamadera 石山寺 and Kōshōji 興聖寺, include full copies of the twenty *juan* 巻 recension of the Chinese *Vinayasaṃgraha*. Photographs of these manuscripts are fully preserved at the library of the International College for Postgraduate Buddhist Studies (Kokusai bukkyōgaku daigakuin daigaku 国際仏教学大学院大学) in Tokyo ("The Database of Old Buddhist Manuscripts in Japanese Collections." https://koshakyo-database.icabs.ac.jp/canons). I have not yet been able to see any of them. The Tibetan translation also seems to have circulated in two recensions: thirteen *bam po* and fifteen *bam po* recensions. This is mentioned by Bu ston in his *'Dul ba spyi'i rnam par gzhag pa* and *Chos 'byung*. For details, see Kishino 2019, esp. 122. It should also be noted that the Taishō edition of the fourteen *juan* 巻 recension refers to a large number of variant readings found in the Song 宋, Yuan 元, and Ming 明 editions. There are so many significant variant readings in the fourteenth *juan* 巻 of these editions that the Taishō edition adopts a unique method to show them. It provides two versions of the fourteenth *juan* 巻 in succession: the first is based primarily on the Second Koryŏ edition (再雕高麗版) (604b–610b), and the second is based on the Song, Yuan, and Ming editions (610b–617a). In his excellent study of the *Adhikaraṇavastu* of the *Mūlasarvāstivāda-vinaya*, Borgland (2014, esp. 33–34) refers to this Taishō *Vinayasaṃgraha* and wonders why it contains two explanations of the *Adhikaraṇaśamathadharmas* in succession. This is simply because it includes these two versions of the fourteenth *juan* 巻, and each

part of it, concentrating solely on its discussion following the seventy-second *pāyantikā* rule for bhikṣus of the *Mūlasarvāstivāda-vinaya*, comparing the Chinese and Tibetan translations.

There are several reasons why I focus on the *Vinayasaṃgraha*'s discussion following the seventy-second *pāyantikā*. First, the length of it is suitable for this paper; it is neither too long nor too short (Sde dge 4105, 'Dul ba, vol. *nu*, 239a6–245b7; Taishō 1458.24.597b18–600b26). Second, the discussion contains a variety of information about ordination, which is undoubtedly the most important ritual to the survival and prosperity of the Buddhist tradition, and therefore may be of particular interest to many Buddhists and scholars.[7] Third, the discussion deserves close attention since it includes a few controversial passages that led the Tibetan polymath Bu ston Rin chen grub (1290–1364) to doubt the authenticity of the work as a whole.[8]

General Information about the Text

The name of the author of the *Vinayasaṃgraha* is translated as Shengyou 勝友 in Yijing's 義淨 translation and Khyad par bshes gnyen in the Tibetan translation. These two translations may suggest several possible Sanskrit names. However, modern scholars usually take his name to be *Viśeṣamitra,[9] probably based on a Chinese source, which we will turn to immediately below. Following this convention, I will refer to the author of the *Vinayasaṃgraha* as *Viśeṣamitra throughout this paper.

As is often the case with Buddhist authors in early India, the exact dates of *Viśeṣamitra's life are unknown. It is only certain that he was born before 700 CE, when Yijing translated the *Vinayasaṃgraha* into Chinese. There are, however, at least two textual sources, one Tibetan and the other Chinese, that may provide further information.

In his *History of Buddhism in India*, Tāranātha (1575–1635) refers to Khyad

of them contains the explanation of the *Adhikaraṇaśamathadharmas*. A comparative study of the two versions of the fourteenth *juan* 卷 preserved in the Taishō edition is a desideratum.

7. The ordination procedures of the *Mūlasarvāstivāda-vinaya* tradition are relatively well studied. See, for example, Sakurabe 1964; Yamagiwa 1987; Schopen 2004b; a series of works by the Study Group of the *Pravrajyāvastu* in the *Vinayasūtra* (most recently, 2023); and Kishino 2015.

8. Kishino 2019.

9. Some modern scholars refer to the author of the *Vinayasaṃgraha* differently. Nanjio ([1883] 1975, 249, no. 1127) refers to him as Ginamitra (*sic*) in Sanskrit. Watters (1905, 169) assumes him to be *Jinamitra; cf. Pachow 1955, 5. Takai (1930, 23) and Nakamura (1980, 54–55n24) also suggest that the monk named Shengyou 勝友 in Chinese should be *Jinamitra. Martin (2013, 257n36) gives Viśeṣamitra or Viśiṣṭamitra.

par bshes gnyen as an Indian scholar-monk who lived during the reign of King "Go pā la,"[10] whom modern scholars regard as King Gopāla I, the founder of the Pāla dynasty.[11] Gopāla is commonly thought to have reigned in the middle of the eighth century CE.[12] If this is correct, and, in addition, if the monk named Khyad par bshes gnyen mentioned by Tāranātha was the author of the *Vinayasaṃgraha*, since Yijing translated the *Vinayasaṃgraha* in 700 CE, we could place *Viśeṣamitra from the middle of the seventh to the middle of the eighth century CE. This dating, however, seems to be somewhat unreasonable since it suggests that *Viśeṣamitra might have been born after Yijing 義淨 (635–713) and, moreover, that he had a very long life. If he completed the *Vinayasaṃgraha* at, for example, the age of fifty, this means that he lived for more than approximately one hundred years. Although not impossible, this seems unlikely.

On the other hand, the Chinese source seems to make a different, more reasonable suggestion. In the *Cheng weishi lun shuji* 成唯識論述記 (Taishō 1830), the major Chinese commentary on the *Cheng weishi lun* 成唯識論, author Ji 基 (632–682) lists all the so-called "Ten Great Masters" of the Vijñānavādin tradition and refers to a monk named Shengyou 勝友 as the eighth one.[13] More importantly, Ji 基 explains that the Indic name of Shengyou 勝友 is phonetically transcribed as Pishisha miduoluo 毘世沙蜜多羅.[14] This transcription almost certainly suggests that the Sanskrit behind Shengyou 勝友 is *Viśeṣamitra. Unfortunately, Ji 基 does not tell us anything about this monk except that he was a disciple of Hufa 護法 (Skt. *Dharmapāla),[15] who lived around the middle of the sixth century CE.[16] If we assume that this Shengyou 勝友/

10. Schiefner ([1869] 1963, 156–157): . . . *mtshan go pā lar gsol* / . . . *rgya po 'di'i sku che'i ring la* / . . . *khyad par bshes gnyen dang shes rab go cha dang* / *'dul 'dzin slob dpon dpa' po zhes bya ba rnams byung zhing* / . . . .

11. Teramoto 1928, 276–277; Chimpa and Chattopadhyaya 1970, 259; cf. Cabezón 2017, 448n1138.

12. Ikeda 2010, 158; Rajani 2016, 18.

13. Cf. Yang 2012, 16. Note that Xuanzang 玄奘 (602–664) also briefly refers to three of the "Ten Great Masters," including Shengyou 勝友, as eminent scholar-monks at Nālandā Monastery in his *Datang xiyuji* 大唐西域記; cf. Watters 1905, 165; Mizutani 1971, 299–300; Li 1996, 284.

14. Taishō 1830.43.232a4: 八, 梵云：毘世沙蜜多羅。唐言：勝友。

15. Taishō 1830.43.232a6: . . . 此後三論師, 並護法菩薩之門人也。

16. Takai 1930, 21–22: "528–560 A.D."; Mizutani 1971, 299n1: "d. ca 560"; Brown 1991, 299: "530–560 A.D."

Pishisha miduoluo 毘世沙蜜多羅 was the author of the *Vinayasaṃgraha*,[17] we may conclude that he lived during the sixth century CE. This suggests that *Viśeṣamitra was born before Yijing 義淨, and this seems more likely the case. According to these two textual sources, it seems possible for us to roughly estimate that the author of the *Vinayasaṃgraha* lived either from the middle of the seventh to the middle of the eighth centuries CE, or—more likely—as early as the sixth century CE.

We are unsure how much the *Vinayasaṃgraha* circulated or was used in India.[18] It seems certain, however, that there were conflicting attitudes toward the text in Chinese and Tibetan Buddhist circles. Yijing 義淨, who spent time at Nālandā, seems to have valued the *Vinayasaṃgraha* as much as the *Mūlasarvāstivāda-vinaya* itself. When he returned to China, he translated it before any of the canonical Vinaya texts.[19] In his travel record, furthermore, he quotes many passages from the *Vinayasaṃgraha* and the *Mūlasarvāstivāda-vinaya*.[20]

17. Given the close relationship between the *Mūlasarvāstivāda-vinaya* and the *Yogācārabhūmi*, it is possible that the monk named Shengyou 勝友 (Pishisha miduoluo 毘世沙蜜多羅), to whom Ji 基 refers as one of the Vijñānavādins in his *Cheng weishi lun shuji* 成唯識論述記, was the author of our *Vinayasaṃgraha* since the *Yogācārabhūmi* is known as one of the foundational texts of the Vijñānavādins. For several studies that suggest a close relationship between the *Mūlasarvāstivāda-vinaya* and the *Yogācārabhūmi*, see Kishino 2013, 364–365n142. It should also be noted that Yijing 義淨 translated not only *Viśeṣamitra's *Vinayasaṃgraha* but also two texts of the Vijñānavādins titled *Cheng weishi baosheng lun* 成唯識寶生論 (Taishō 1591) and *Guan suoyuan lun shi* 觀所縁論釋 (Taishō 1625), both of which are attributed to Hufa 護法 (*Dharmapāla). This may also suggest that *Viśeṣamitra and *Dharmapāla had a close relationship. That is, the author of the *Vinayasaṃgraha*, *Viśeṣamitra, might have been a disciple of a Vijñānavādin named *Dharmapāla.

18. Regarding the possibility that the *Vinayasaṃgraha* was closely studied in India, see note 20 below.

19. Sakaino 1932, 2.

20. Sasaki [1977] 1985, 175–176. Clarke 2012, 19, suggests that Yijing's positive attitude toward the *Vinayasaṃgraha* might be best understood by postulating that the text was widely propagated and read in Nālandā at least by the late seventh or early eighth century CE. In relation to this, it should be noted that the *Vinayasaṃgraha* is quoted in a *vṛtti* "commentary" on the *Bhikṣuṇīprātimokṣa* of the *Mūlasarvāstivāda-vinaya*, extant in the Tibetan translation, titled *Āryasarvāstivādimūlabhikṣuṇīprātimokṣasūtravṛtti* (BPSV), at least twice. BPSV (Sde dge 4112, 'Dul ba, vol. *tsu*, 35a1): *sde snod gcig nas gcig tu brgyud pa'i tshul gyis bstan pa yun ring du gnas pa'o zhes 'Dul ba bsdus pa las 'byung ngo //* ≈ *Vinayasaṃgraha* (Sde dge 4105, 'Dul ba, vol. *nu*, 100a1–2): *sde snod gcig nas gcig tu brgyud pa'i tshul gyis bstan pa yun ring du gnas pa'o //*; BPSV (Sde dge 4112, 'Dul ba, vol. *tsu*, 27b5–6): *'Dul ba bsdus pa las kyang / de la dgun dang / dpyid dang / dbyar rnams kyi zla ba phyed dang gsum dang / bdun pa ni gso sbyong bcu bzhi pa'o //* ≈ *Vinayasaṃgraha* (Sde dge 4105, 'Dul ba, vol. *nu*, 126b7–127a1): *thab krol byed par 'ong bar rig na gnas mal bsko bar bya ba ni gsum ste / dgun gyi dang / dpyid kyi dang / dbyar gyi'o //*.

Although it is uncertain whether the *Vinayasaṃgraha* was as widely read and referenced in China as Yijing would have wanted,[21] it certainly was valued in Japan at least approximately one thousand years after his death. The *Vinayasaṃgraha* was read as intensively as the *Mūlasarvāstivāda-vinaya* in the Edo 江戸 period (1603–1868), especially by monks of the Shingon 真言 school. These monks were aware that in his so-called *Sangaku roku* 三学録, the founder of their school, Kūkai 空海 (774–835), instructed his pupils to observe the *Mūlasarvāstivāda-vinaya* and referred to Yijing's Vinaya corpus, including the *Vinayasaṃgraha*, as a set of all-important texts.[22] One of these Shingon monks, Gakunyo 學如 (1716–1773), who strongly insisted that the school follow

---

These quotations may suggest that the *Vinayasaṃgraha* was widely read as an authoritative text by medieval Indian scholar-monks. It should also be noted that these quotations suggest that the *Vinayasaṃgraha* preceded the BPSV. Unfortunately, however, there is no information about the date of the BPSV. Neither the translator(s) nor the revisor(s) of the text are known; cf. Ōtani Cat., 270 (no. 5614). It too, like the Tibetan translation of the *Vinayasaṃgraha*, is well attested at Dunhuang; cf. Clarke 2015, 73. Note also that the Chinese translation of the *Vinayasaṃgraha* (Taishō 1458) refers to a certain verse, implying that it is from another text. The verse lists the eight colors that should not be used for dyeing robes by monks, and the same verse is found in the Chinese translation of the *Vinayakārikā* (Taishō 1459; cf. Clarke's contribution in the present volume). Taishō 1458.24.556b10–12: 然非法色, 有其二別。一謂：八種大色。何者是耶? 頌曰：紫礦紅藍鬱金香　朱沙大青及紅茜　黄丹蘇方八大色　苾芻不應將染衣。Compare Taishō 1459.24.627b22–23: 紫鑛紅藍鬱金香　朱砂大青及紅茜　黄丹蘇方八大色　苾芻不應將染衣。If this verse parallel means that the *Vinayasaṃgraha* quotes a verse from the *Vinayakārikā*, it follows that the *Vinayakārikā* preceded the *Vinayasaṃgraha*. However, this verse parallel is not found in the Tibetan *Vinayasaṃgraha* (D 4105) and the Tibetan *Vinayakārikā* (D 4123). Both of these Tibetan texts also list the eight colors (Sde dge 4105, 'Dul ba, vol. *nu*, 151b1–2; Sde dge 4123, 'Dul ba, vol. *shu*, 18a1–2), but the Tibetan *Vinayasaṃgraha* does not refer to the verse that is found in the Tibetan *Vinayakārikā*.

21. Currently, however, the *Vinayasaṃgraha* is used by nuns for their monastic lives at Nanlin Nisengyuan 南林尼僧苑 in Taiwan and Pushousi Temple 普壽寺 in Shanxi Province 山西省, China. See Chiu 2014, esp. 38–39; cf. Borgland 2017, 273n12.

22. Clarke 2006, esp. 25–28. Note also that there seem to have been several monks outside of the Shingon school who also recognized the importance of the *Mūlasarvāstivāda-vinaya* and studied the text. A Tendai 天台 monk, Ryōyū 亮雄 (Etaku 惠宅; b. 1740), for example, is known for having propagated the *Mūlasarvāstivāda-vinaya*: . . . また洛外華山元慶寺に亮雄阿闍梨(號惠宅和尚)あり . . . 兼て有部律を弘む (*Taigaku kaitei: kaimitsu kōyō* 台學階梯：戒密綱要, chapter 3, 43). Ryōyū seems to have made use of the *Vinayasaṃgraha* for the study of the *Mūlasarvāstivāda-vinaya*. In his *Sange ichijō kaigi zokuhen* 山家一乗戒儀続編 (Kansei 寛政 10 [= 1798 CE]; cf. BKDJ, q.v.; KS, s.v. *sange ichijō kaigi* 山家一乗戒儀), he mentions the utility of the *Vinayasaṃgraha*, saying that it provides ample information about rituals, and facilitates the reading and understanding of the *Mūlasarvāstivāda-vinaya* (*Sange ichijō kaigi zokuhen* 山家一乗戒儀続編, 21.6–8): 顧フニ夫レ吾儕根薄ク才拙シ。如何ソ難解ノ疏鈔ヲ學ヒ其精蘊ヲ究ルコトヲ得ンヤ。且ク有部〔ノ〕如キハ幸ニ律攝ナル者有。一十四巻ニシテ行事備足ス。更に廣律ヲ読ムモ読易ク解易シ。力及ハ不ル所ハ聖慈之レ頼ル。

Kūkai's 空海 instructions, highly valued the *Vinayasaṃgraha* and even published a revised edition.[23] The high esteem of the *Vinayasaṃgraha* within the Shingon tradition continued well into the Meiji 明治 period. It was included in a curriculum of texts to be studied as part of Shingon monks' education as late as 1888.[24] In Tibetan Buddhist traditions, however, the *Vinayasaṃgraha* seems to have been largely ignored, even despised. There seems to be little, if any, evidence that the *Vinayasaṃgraha* was ever studied in Tibet to the same degree as other Indian texts related to the *Mūlasarvāstivāda-vinaya* such as Guṇaprabha's *Vinayasūtra* and Viśākha(deva)'s *Vinayakārikā*.[25] More significantly, one of Tibet's most influential monks, Bu ston Rin chen grub, doubted the authenticity of the *Vinayasaṃgraha* and explicitly asserted that it was not trustworthy.[26]

The *Vinayasaṃgraha* is, thus, an interesting medieval Indian Buddhist text that was widely circulated within two large and distinct Buddhist circles where it received unequal receptions. To even begin to consider the reasons for these opposing evaluations will require paying much closer attention to the

23. Regarding Gakunyo's edition of the *Vinayasaṃgraha*, see Clarke 2006, 26–27; Baba 2016, 269–271; Kishino 2022.

24. For the Shingon school's curricula in the Meiji period, see Abe 2013.

25. For further information on this text, see Clarke's contribution in the present volume.

26. Kishino 2019. Note that Kun mkhyen Mtsho sna ba Shes rab bzang po (twelfth to thirteenth century CE; Tsedroen 1992, 76–77) refers to the *Vinayasaṃgraha* several times and to other Indian Buddhist texts related to the *Mūlasarvāstivāda-vinaya* in his *'Dul ba mdo rtsa'i rnam bshad nyi ma'i 'od zer legs bshad lung gi rgya mtsho*. When he mentions, for example, the list of the ten valid ordinations preserved in Vasubandhu's *Abhidharmakośabhāṣya*, he notes that the list is found in both the *Vinayakārikā* and the *Vinayasaṃgraha* (cf. § 3.3.2 in appendix): *dang po ni lung ma mo'i rjes su 'brangs te <u>mdzod 'grel</u> las* / (1) *sangs rgyas dang rang sangs rgyas rang byung gis bsnyen par rdzogs pa dang* / (2) *lnga sde bzang po ye shes khong du chud bas dang* / (3) *grags pa 'am mchog zung gcig lta bu tshur shog gis dang* / (4) *sde bzang drug cu'i tshogs skyabs 'gro lan gsum bzlas pas dang* / (5) *'ong srungs chen po ston par khas blangs pas dang* / (6) *bram ze sod ya legs sbyin dri bas mnyes pas dang* / (7) *skye dgu'i bdag mo chen mo la sogs pa shākya'i bud med lnga brgya lci ba'i chos brgyad spong bar khas blangs pas dang* / (8) *bu mo chos sbyin ma 'phrin gyis dang* / (9) *yul dbus kyi mi rnams bcu'i tshogs kyis dang* / (10) *mtha' 'khob kyi mi rnams lnga'i tshogs kyis bsnyen par rdzogs ba dang bcu'o* / *bcur 'byed lugs de kho na ltar per* (ms. 27b3: *be*) *śha ka'i* / <u>*Me tog phreng rgyud*</u> *dang* <u>*'Dul ba bsdus pa*</u> *las kyang bshad do* // (*'Dul ṭi ka nyi ma'i 'od zer legs bshad lung rigs kyi rgya mtsho*, 1:45.12–20) (for details about the list of the ten types of ordinations, see, inter alia, Hakamaya 2011). It should also be noted that according to a biography of Tsong kha pa Blo bzang grags pa (1357–1419), Tsong kha pa studied not only the *Vinayasūtra* but also various other Indian texts related to the *Mūlasarvāstivāda-vinaya*, including the *Vinayasaṃgraha*, when he was young; Odani and Tshul-khrims 1985, 22. These works might suggest that Tibetan Buddhist scholars other than Bu ston considered the *Vinayasaṃgraha* to be authoritative to some degree.

actual content of its Chinese and Tibetan translations. We will compare one part of these translations in the following section.

The Discussion Following Pāyantikā *72 in the* Vinayasaṃgraha

The seventy-second *pāyantikā* rule of the *Mūlasarvāstivāda-vinaya* makes it an offense for monks to ordain anyone who is under twenty years old:[27]

> *yang dge slong gang zag lo nyi shu ma lon pa dge slong gi dngos por rdzogs par bsnyen par byed na ltung byed do // gang zag de yang rdzogs par bsnyen par mi 'gyur la dge slong de dag kyang smad par 'gyur te de la de ni cho ga yin no //* [28]
>
> Further, if a monk ordains a person who has not reached twenty years old to monkhood, [the monk incurs] a *pāyantikā*. That person does not become ordained, whereas the monks will be blamed. In that case, that is the proper way.
>
> 若復苾芻, 知年未滿二十, 與受近圓, 成苾芻性者, 波逸底迦。此非近圓, 諸苾芻得罪。[29]
>
> Further, if a monk, knowing that [a candidate] has not reached twenty years old, ordains [him] to have him attain monkhood, [the monk incurs] a *pāyantikā*. This is not a [valid] ordination. The monks incur an offense.

The *Vinayasaṃgraha* begins its discussion of this rule with a brief outline of the rule's frame-story, the story that tells us how and why the rule was established by the Buddha, preserved in the *Vinayavibhaṅga*.[30] This is followed by comments on individual words or phrases in the wording of the rule.

27. For the Skt., see Clarke 2014, 232, fol. 201r2–3; cf. Banerjee 1977, 42: *yaḥ punar bhikṣur ūnaviṃśativarsaṃ* (Banerjee: *ūnaviṃśavarṣaṃ*) *pudgalaṃ bhikṣubhāvāyopasaṃpādaye* (Banerjee: *-saṃpādayeta*) *pāyantikā / sa ca pudgalo'nupasaṃpannas te ca bhikṣavo garhyā ayaṃ tatra samayaḥ //*; cf. Prebish (1975, 89): "Whatever monk should ordain a person less than twenty years old to the state of monkhood, that is *pāyantikā*. That person is not ordained and those monks are blameworthy. This is the proper course in this situation."

28. Sde dge 3, 'Dul ba, vol. *ja*, 284b3–4.

29. Taishō 1442.23.853a21–22.

30. There is a slight difference between the brief outline of the rule's frame-story preserved in Yijing's translation and that preserved in the Tibetan translation. Yijing's translation quotes the

The comments are centered around three underlined words or phrases in the rule: (1) *lo nyi shu ma lon pa* / 知年未滿二十, (2) *rdzogs par bsnyen par byed* / 與受近圓, and (3) *smad pa* / 諸苾芻得罪. Those concerning the first and the third phrases are very simple. The commentary on the first phrase briefly explains that a person who has not reached twenty years old should not be ordained because he cannot endure various hardships such as hunger and thirst.[31] This explanation is found in the frame-story of the rule (Sde dge 3, 'Dul ba, vol. *ja*, 283b4–284b3; Taishō 1442.23.853a9–20), and it is likely that *Viśeṣamitra is simply repeating it in his commentary. The commentary on the third phrase is just a rewording, stating that the phrase means that the monks have transgressed the Vinaya rule.[32] The commentary on the second phrase, *rdzogs par bsnyen par byed* / *yushou jinyuan* 與受近圓 (to ordain), however, is relatively long. It explains four aspects of ordination: (1) those who may confer ordination, (2) those who may be ordained, (3) how to ordain, and (4) the obligatory behavior of those who have been ordained.[33] Each of these four aspects is explained in detail.

---

seventy-second *pāyantikā* rule, whereas the Tibetan translation only refers to the number of the rule but does not quote it. As far as I can tell, this difference between the two translations is also found in the *Vinayasaṃgraha*'s discussions of other rules.

31. Sde dge 4105, 'Dul ba, vol. *nu*, 239a7: *lo nyi shu ma lon pa zhes bya ba ni bru ba tsha ba dang / skom pa la sogs pa'i sdug bsngal rnams mi bzod pa'i phyir ro //*. Regarding the phrase "having not reached twenty years old," it is because [the one who has not reached twenty years old] cannot endure hardships such as hunger and thirst. Taishō 1458.24.597b24–25: 言「知年未滿二十」者, 由其年小, 飢渴逼時, 不堪忍故。 Regarding the phrase "knowing that [a candidate] has not reached twenty years old," it is because he is young and therefore when faced with hunger and thirst, he cannot endure.

32. Sde dge 4105, 'Dul ba, vol. *nu*, 244b6: *smad pa zhes bya ba ni ltung byed kyi ltung ba byung ba zhes bya ba'i tha tshig go //*. Regarding the phrase "blamed," it means the same as [the phrase] "a *pāyantikā* offense has occurred." Taishō 1458.24.600a28–29: 言「諸苾芻得罪」者, 謂得越法罪。 The phrase "the monks incur an offense" means that [they] have committed a transgression (Skt. **sātisāro bhavati*; cf. Numata 1999, 67).

33. Sde dge 4105, 'Dul ba, vol. *nu*, 239a7–b1: *bsnyen par rdzogs par byed ces bya ba ni* (1) *gang bsnyen par rdzogs par byed pa dang* / (2) *gang la bsnyen par rdzogs par bya ba dang* / (3) *de ci ltar bsnyen par rdzogs par 'gyur ba* (4) *de bzhin du bsnyen par rdzogs pa'i gang kun du spyad ba de bsnyen par rdzogs ba'i mtshan nyid las rig par bya'o //*. Regarding the term "ordains," these [four] should be understood as the aspects of ordination: (1) those who may confer ordination, (2) those who may be ordained, (3) how to ordain him, and (4) the obligatory behavior of those who have been ordained in that way. Taishō 1458.24.597b25–26: 言「與授近圓」者, 謂:(1)能授、(2)所授、(3)進止威儀、(4)「所有行法」, 隨次當說。 Regarding the term "ordains," these [four] should be explained one by one: (1) those who may confer ordination, (2) those who may be ordained, (3) acts and movements [in the process of ordination], and (4) "the obligatory behavior [of those who have been ordained]."

In this way, we can understand the *Vinayasaṃgraha*'s explanations of the seventy-second *pāyantikā* rule as comprising three main sections, the second of which includes four subsections, in addition to a discussion of the frame-story. From this perspective, I have numbered the passages of these explanations of the seventy-second *pāyantikā* rule from § 1 to § 4.3 and created a table (appendix) providing an overview of their major topics, their exact locations in the Tibetan translation (Sde dge edition), and Yijing's Chinese translation (Taishō), and parallel texts I have found in the canonical Vinaya. With reference to this numbering, below I will provide more details on the content of these explanations.

As mentioned above, the commentary on the phrase "to ordain" (Tib. *rdzogs par bsnyen par byed* / Chin. 與受近圓) explains the four aspects of ordination. The first concerns the qualifications of those who are involved in conducting the ordination ceremony. They are classified into three categories: (1) the preceptor (*upādhyāya*), (2) the teacher (*ācārya*), and (3) the community (*saṅgha*) (§ 3.1).[34] These three are further explained one by one (§§ 3.1.1–3). In the explanation of the second aspect of ordination, the qualifications of those eligible to be ordained are clarified by a long description of those ineligible for ordination in six categories: (1) those who are mentally impaired (*āśayavipanna*[35]), (2) those whose foundation is impaired (**āśrayavikopana* [?]), (3) those who have genital impairment, (4) those who have impaired the Pure Dharma (*śukladharma*[36]), (5) those who are dependent on others (*paratantra*), and (6) those who are physically disfigured to the extent that they are unpleasant (**aprāsādika* [?][37])

34. Sde dge 4105, 'Dul ba, vol. *nu*, 239b1–2: *de la "gang bsnyen bar rdzogs par byed pa" ni* (1) *mkhan po dang* / (2) *slob dpon dang* / (3) *dge 'dun no* //. Regarding the phrase "those who confer ordination" there, [they are] (1) the preceptor (*upādhyāya*), (2) the teacher (*ācārya*), and (3) the community (*saṅgha*). Taishō 1458.24.597b26–27: 言「能授」者, 謂:(1)鄔波馱耶、(2)阿遮利耶、并(3)餘僧伽。Regarding the phrase "those who may confer ordination," [they are] (1) the preceptor (*upādhyāya*), (2) the teacher (*ācārya*), and (3) the rest of the community (*saṅgha*).

35. Cf. Hirakawa 1978, 310b.

36. Cf. MVP (Sakaki 1916–1925, 1117): Tib. dkar po'i chos *yongs su rdzogs pa* ≈ Skt. *paripūrṇaśukladharma*.

37. Chin. 醜惡不端嚴相; Tib. *mi dad par 'gyur ba* (see note 38 below). It is fairly certain that the Sanskrit behind the phrase "醜惡不端嚴相" in Yijing's translation is **aprāsādika*. However, the Tibetan *mi dad par 'gyur ba* suggests Sanskrit *aśraddha* "one who does not have religious faith." This Sanskrit, although possible, appears to be irrelevant to the context (§ 3.2.6). First, the examples of *mi dad par 'gyur ba* that *Viśeṣamitra provides in detail are those who are physically deformed. It seems unlikely that they coincide with those who do not have religious faith. Second, *Viśeṣamitra cites a well-known verse after these examples that refers to those who are physically pleasant (Skt. *prāsādika*; Tib. *mdzes pa*; Chin. 端正者) as worthy of entering the

(§ 3.2).[38] These six are further explained in detail individually (§§ 3.2.1–6). The explanation of the third aspect of ordination focuses on the ritual procedures for becoming a Buddhist monk (§ 3.3). The procedures for becoming a lay disciple,[39] a novice, and a monk are briefly provided in succession (§ 3.3.1), followed by a discussion about the validity of various irregular ordinations (§ 3.3.2). The explanation of the fourth aspect concerns two monastic conventions that are especially relevant to newly ordained monks. First, regulations regarding juniors showing reverence to seniors are provided (§ 3.4),[40] followed

---

religious life. For these reasons, I interpret Tib. *mi dad par 'gyur ba* here as an atypical translation of **aprāsādika*, albeit with some hesitation.

38. Sde dge 4105, 'Dul ba, vol. *nu*, 239b7–240a1: *"gang la bsnyen par rdzogs par bya" zhe na / (1) bsam pa nyams pa dang / (2) rten nyams pa dang / (3) skyes pa nyams pa dang / (4) dkar po'i chos nyams pa dang / (5) gzhan gyi dbang du gyur pa dang / (6) mi dad par 'gyur bas nyams pa ma yin no //*. Regarding the phrase "those who may be ordained," they are not (1) those who are mentally impaired (*āśayavipanna*), (2) those whose foundation is impaired (**āśrayavikopana* [?]), (3) those who have genital impairment, (4) those who have impaired the Pure Dharma (*śukladharma*), (5) those who are dependent on others (*paratantra*), and (6) those who are unpleasant (**aprāsādika* [?]). Taishō 1458.24.597c21–23: 言「所授」者, 有多種相。謂:(1)意樂損壞、(2)所依損壞、(3)丈夫損壞、(4)白法損壞、(5)繫屬他人、及(6)有醜惡不端嚴相。Regarding the phrase "those who are ordained," there are various forms [that they do not take]: (1) those who are mentally impaired, (2) those whose foundation is impaired, (3) those males who have [genital] impairment (4) those who have impaired the Pure Dharma, (5) those who depend on others, and (6) those who are ugly and unpleasant-looking.

39. Sde dge 4105, 'Dul ba, vol. *nu*, 241b1: *"ji ltar bsnyen par rdzogs par bya" zhe na / rab tu 'byung bar 'dod pa la bar chad kyi chos rnams dris te gzung bar bya'o // skyabs su 'gro ba dang / bslab pa'i gzhi lnga yang sbyin par bya'o //*. . . . Regarding the phrase "how to ordain," the one who desires to enter the religious life must be asked about any qualities that may be impediments to ordination (*antarāyikadharma*) and taken a hold of [so that he may not escape from the ordination ceremony]. The [Three] Refuges (*śaraṇa*) and five foundations of training (*śikṣāpada*) must also be given [to him]. . . . Taishō 1458.24.598b13–16: 言「進止威儀」者, 若有俗人, 求出家者, 應隨彼心, 詣一師處。其師即可問於障法。若清淨者, 當攝受之, 觀其意趣。有堪能者, 應授三歸、并五學處。. . . Regarding the phrase "acts and movements [in the process of ordination]," if there is a layman who seeks to enter the religious life, he should visit one teacher's place according to his intention. The teacher immediately can ask [him] about the qualities that may be impediments [to ordination]. If he is pure [regarding the qualities that are impediments to ordination], [the teacher] must take him in and observe his disposition. [When the teacher] deems him eligible [for ordination], [the teacher] should give the Three Refuges and five foundations of training [to him]. . . .

40. Sde dge 4105, 'Dul ba, vol. *nu*, 243a1: *"bsnyen par rdzogs pa'i kun tu spyad pa" ni gsar bus ches rgan pa la phyag bya'o // dang po lo grangs dri bar bya'o // dus tshod kyang ngo //*. . . . Regarding "the obligatory behavior of those who have been ordained," juniors must show reverence to seniors. [If two monks meet] for the first time, [they] must ask [each other] the length of time [that has passed since they were ordained], as well as the season [in which they were ordained]. Taishō 1458.24.599a12–13: 既近圓已,「所有行法」, 次下當說:小苾芻等, 應禮大者, 若初相見, 應問夏數, 及以受時。Once one's ordination is concluded (i.e., he is fully ordained),

by regulations regarding the dependence relationship with preceptors or teachers that novices and newly ordained monks must maintain (§ 3.5).

Characteristics of the Vinayasaṃgraha *Observable from the Discussion Following* Pāyantikā *72*

There are several points that can be immediately observed. First and foremost, there is little discrepancy between the Chinese and Tibetan translations with respect to both the topics and their order. There are certainly a few passages that appear in one translation but not in the other (§§ 3.1.1; 3.3.2; 3.4.4; 3.4.6; 3.5.3; 4.1). However, these do not affect the order of topics. The Chinese and Tibetan translations of the *Vinayasaṃgraha* correspond relatively well as far as the seventy-second *pāyantikā* rule is concerned.

It is equally apparent that the *Vinayasaṃgraha* includes plenty of information about ordination in its discussion following the seventy-second *pāyantikā* rule. Its comments on ordination are from four perspectives and in total account for more than 70 percent of the discussion that follows this rule. Also, these comments include many details on the ordination procedures that have little, if anything, to do with the seventy-second *pāyantikā* rule. This suggests that *Viśeṣamitra intended not only to clarify difficult or obscure wording of the rule to facilitate understanding but also to provide a variety of information related to ordination that he considered important. It should also be noted that, as the last column of the table in the appendix shows, *Viśeṣamitra seems to have collected information widely from various parts of the canonical Vinaya. He sometimes mentions the source of his information (§§ 3.2.4; 3.3.2).[41] Even when he does not specify the source, the textual parallels to the information he provides are not limited to the *Vinayavibhaṅga*, but are found also in the three other major parts of the *Mūlasarvāstivāda-vinaya*—that is, the seventeen *Vastus*, the *Kṣudrakavastu*, and the *Uttaragrantha*.

If these points observed about the discussion following the seventy-second *pāyantikā* rule are true of the *Vinayasaṃgraha* as a whole, we could say that the *Vinayasaṃgraha* does not include only explanatory comments on the

next, "the obligatory behavior [of those who have been ordained]" must be explained: Junior monks and so on should show reverence to seniors. When they see them for the first time, they should ask the number of summers [that have passed since they were ordained], as well as the time [of day in which they] received [ordination].

41. The texts of the canonical Vinaya that *Viśeṣamitra cited in §§ 3.2.4 and 3.3.2 appear not to be found in the *Mūlasarvāstivāda-vinaya* as it has come down to us. This may suggest that the textual tradition of the *Mūlasarvāstivāda-vinaya* that *Viśeṣamitra knew is different from the one that we know today.

Prātimokṣa rules themselves but instead provides various regulations that are preserved in the four major sections of the *Mūlasarvāstivāda-vinaya* even if they are not always closely related to the *Prātimokṣa* rules. Consequently, the *Vinayasaṃgraha* might cover a large number of important Mūlasarvāstivādin regulations. If this is true, it would not be entirely accurate to regard the *Vinayasaṃgraha* simply as a commentary on the *Prātimokṣa* rules but, rather, more an essential compendium of the *Mūlasarvāstivāda-vinaya*, even if it is structured in accordance with the format of the *Prātimokṣa*.[42]

It is likely, moreover, that the *Vinayasaṃgraha* was widely utilized by Japanese monks in the Edo 江戸 (1603–1867) and Meiji 明治 (1868–1912) periods precisely because it was regarded as an essential compendium. They surely knew that some texts of Yijing's Vinaya corpus were missing, since his translation projects had not been completed before his death.[43] Shingon monks may have highly valued the *Vinayasaṃgraha* because it includes important regulations from all sections of the *Mūlasarvāstivāda-vinaya*, including those missing from Yijing's Vinaya corpus, thereby revealing the important regulations that otherwise would have been inaccessible.

As an indication of directions for future research, I will briefly mention three other significant characteristics of the *Vinayasaṃgraha* that have come to light when analyzing its discussion that follows the seventy-second *pāyantikā* rule. First, *Viśeṣamitra gives word-commentaries on four Buddhist technical terms: *bhikṣuṇī-dūṣaka* (defiler of nuns), *steyasaṃvāsika* (interloper), *tīrthika-avakrāntaka* (a former monk who has gone over to another religious group), and *asaṃvāsika* (one who is no longer in communion) in § 3.2.4. The word-commentaries on these four words appear together with those on six words to which *Viśeṣamitra refers in his own discussion following the seventy-second *pāyantikā* rule. One is thereby led to think that these four words are used, along with the other six words, by *Viśeṣamitra in his discussion. These four words are, however, not found there. Moreover, they do not appear in the seventy-second *pāyantikā* rule either. That is to say, *Viśeṣamitra

42. In the entry on the Chinese translation of the *Vinayasaṃgraha* in BKDJ, Nishimoto (1933a) briefly notes that it cites many passages widely from the canonical Vinaya and serves as a compendium of the *Mūlasarvāstivāda-vinaya*.

43. For example, in the list of the Vinaya texts (*Ritsuzō mokuroku* 律蔵目録) included in the *Shōburuishū* 小部類集, widely attributed, although perhaps problematically, to Gakunyo 學如, Yijing's works are listed with a brief comment stating that Yijing died before some of his translations of the *Vastus* were revised and, as a result, are missing (*Shōburuishū* 小部類集, 4.4–6; original unpunctuated): 右二十三部、根本有部所用、義浄三蔵訳也。其餘、根本説一切有部婆窣都七八十巻有。未ダ再治ニ及ズ、三蔵入滅、今墜没ス。 Regarding the *Shōburuishū* 小部類集, see Kishino 2018, 102–103.

abruptly comments on four words in detail that appear neither in his own discussion nor in the seventy-second *pāyantikā* rule. It is not clear what exactly this abrupt instance of word-commentaries means. It might be simply one of *Viśeṣamitra's own peculiar ways of discussing the *Prātimokṣa* rules. It is also possible that the four words were originally preserved in his discussion about the seventy-second *pāyantikā* but disappeared for some reason in the process of transmission, and consequently that the current text of the *Vinayasaṃgraha* extant today differs from the original text. In any case, it should be investigated whether such apparently unrelated word-commentaries are found anywhere else in the *Vinayasaṃgraha*.

Second, *Viśeṣamitra mentions the views of others with regard to monastic regulations three times in his discussion following the seventy-second *pāyantikā* rule (§§ 3.4.4; 3.4.7; 4.1).[44] In § 3.4.7, for example, several ways of showing reverence are referred to as one of the views of others:

> *gzhan dag na re ston pa las* (Peking 5606, 317a7: *la*) *dkyil 'khor chen po lnga pas phyag bya'o // bla ma dang bla ma'i gnas lta bu la pus mo gzugs pa dang / 'dud par bcas pa'am / thal mo sbyar ba bcas pa'am / sgyid pa nas 'khyud pa'am / de bzhin du tsog pus 'dug pa'o // tshangs pa mtshungs par spyod pa gzhan rnams la ni mgo 'dud dam / thal mo sbyar ba'am / ngag yang dag par brjod pa'o zhes kyang zer ba'o //*[45]

> It is also said by others that one must show reverence to the Teacher (i.e., the Buddha) by [throwing down] the five parts of one's body (i.e., both knees, both hands, and forehead; cf. MVP [Sakaki 1916–1925] 9278) [on the ground]. To respectable ones (Skt. *guru*) and those who are worthy of respect (Skt. *gurusthānīya*) by either kneeling and maintaining a bowing posture, maintaining the gesture of supplication with one's hands, holding their knees in one's arms, or maintaining the posture of squatting, and to other coreligionists (Skt. *sabrahmacārin*) by either bowing one's head, maintaining the gesture of supplication with one's hands, or greeting with words.[46]

44. It might be common for medieval Indian scholar-monks to mention others' views in their exegetical works. See, for example, Vasubandhu's (fourth to fifth century CE; cf. Funayama 2021, 215–227) *Abhidharmakośabhāṣya* (Pradhan 1967, 3, 4, 9, 13, 15, 17, 21, etc. [text]; Sakurabe 1969, 151, 152, 154, 162, 163, 174, 175, 180, 186, etc. [translation]), and *Vyākhyāyukti* (Horiuchi 2009, 206 [text], 292 [translation]).

45. Sde dge 4105, 'Dul ba, vol. *nu*, 243b2–3.

46. Bu ston suggests that the way of showing reverence by kneeling mentioned here appears

> 有說：禮大師時，五輪至地。若尊及尊類，應手膝至地、或時曲躬低頭合掌、或捉腨、或蹲踞合掌。若對所餘同梵行者，若但合掌、或復低頭、或口云畔睇。[47]
>
> There are [these] views: when one shows reverence to the Teacher, one [should] throw down the five parts [of one's body] on the ground. [If one shows reverence] to respectable ones and those who are worthy of respect, one should either throw down one's body with one's hands and knees on the ground, or bend one's body and bow one's head with the gesture of supplication with one's hands, or hold their knees [in one's arms], or make the posture of squatting with the gesture of supplication with one's hands. If [one shows reverence] to others or to coreligionists, one [should] either simply make the gesture of supplication with one's hands, bow one's head, or say, "greetings."[48]

*Viśeṣamitra's references to the views of others in referring to monastic regulations are not exclusive to his discussion following the seventy-second *pāyantikā* rule. They are occasionally found in other places in the *Vinayasaṃgraha*.[49] There seems to be no doubt, therefore, that *Viśeṣamitra knew of other interpretations of monastic regulations or other Vinaya traditions. There is, however, still little that one can say about these views of others that *Viśeṣamitra mentions. His opinion of them is unclear; he does not clarify where they are from, nor does he express either criticism or approval. The source(s) of these views also need to be investigated further. I have yet to identify them in other Vinaya texts.

Third, *Viśeṣamitra explains that there are ten people to whom reverence must not be shown by ordained ones (§ 3.4.2):

> *bcu po dag gang la phyag mi bya zhe na / spo ba spyod pa la sogs pa bzhi dang / bslab pa byin pa dang / gnas nas phyung ba gsum ste / ltung*

---

neither in the *Mūlasarvāstivāda-vinaya* nor the *Vinayasūtra* and concludes that *Viśeṣamitra might have been confused or unfamiliar with the *Mūlasarvāstivāda-vinaya*. Note, however, *Viśeṣamitra refers to showing reverence by kneeling not as his own view but as one of the views of others. In this respect, Bu ston's criticism of *Viśeṣamitra seems to be not entirely reasonable. For details, see Kishino 2019.

47. Taishō 1458.24.599a25–28.

48. Chin. *pandi* 畔睇 ≈ Skt. *vandana*; cf. Nishimoto 1933b, 86n18.

49. See, for instance, Tib. (Sde dge 4105, 'Dul ba, vol. *nu*, 90a5, 154a3, 168b1–2, 175a5, 175b6) ≈ Chin. (Taishō 1458.24.526b8–10, 557c1–2, 563c23–24, 566c1–2, 566c20–22).

ba ma mthong ba dang / phyir mi 'chos pa dang / lta ba mi gtong ba 'di gsum gnas nas phyung ba dang / khyim pa dang / bsnyen par ma rdzogs pa'o //[50]

To which ten is reverence not to be shown? (1–4) Four [types of individuals who are on probation] such as one on the *parivāsa* probation, (5) the *pārājika* penitent (*śikṣādattaka*), (6–8) three [types of individuals] subject to suspension—that is, one who refuses to see his fault (*adarśana*), one who refuses to atone (*apratikarma*), and one who refuses to give up wrong views (*apratiniḥsṛṣṭapāpakadṛṣtigata*),[51] (9) a layman, and (10) one who is not fully ordained.

近圓有十種不應禮：行遍住等四人、授學人、三種被捨置人、諸在家人、及未近圓。是名為十。[52]

There are ten types [of people] to whom ordained ones should not show reverence: (1–4) four [types of individuals] who are on probation, such as one on the *parivāsa* probation, (5) the *pārājika* penitent (*śikṣādattaka*), (6–8) three [types of individuals] subject to suspension, (9) laymen, and (10) those who are yet to be fully ordained. These are the ten.

The *Śayanāsanavastu* of the *Mūlasarvāstivāda-vinaya* includes a similar passage that refers to ten people who must not be shown reverence by monks. They are, however, not completely the same as those mentioned in the *Vinayasaṃgraha*. In the *Śayanāsanavastu*, the types of individuals who are on probation are explained to be not four but five, and the *pārājika* penitent (*śikṣādattaka*) is not mentioned at all.[53] In this respect, we may see a

50. Sde dge 4105, 'Dul ba, vol. *nu*, 243a3–4.

51. Cf. Kishino 2013, 339nn64–66.

52. Taishō 1458.24.599a20–22.

53. Tib. (Sde dge 1, 'Dul ba, vol. *ga*, 188b4–6): *phyag mi bya ba bcu ste / bcu gang zhe na / spo ba dang / gzhi nas spo ba dang / spo ba spyad pa dang / mgu bar bya ba spyod pa dang / mgu bar bya ba spyad pa dang / ma mthong bas gnas nas phyung ba dang / phyir mi byed pas gnas nas phyung ba dang / sdig pa'i lta bar song ba mi 'dor ba gnas nas phyung ba dang / khyim pa thams cad dang / bsnyen par rdzogs pa ma yin pa thams cad do //*. Cf. Skt. (Gnoli 1978, 5.7–10): *daśāvandyāḥ; katame* <*daśa?*> *pārivāsiko mūlapārivāsikaḥ paryuṣitaparivāsaḥ mānāpyacārikaś caritamānāpyo 'darśanāyotkṣiptakaḥ apratikarmāyotkṣiptakaḥ apratinisṛṣṭe pāpake dṛṣṭigate utkṣiptakaḥ sarvo gṛhī* <*sarvāś*> *cānupasaṃpannaḥ*. Cf. Schopen 2000, 103: "Ten must not be shown deference. Which ten? One who is on probation; one whose probation has had to start over; one who has

discrepancy between the *Vinayasaṃgraha* and the canonical Vinaya.[54] The reason for this discrepancy is not clear. It might be because, as Bu ston concluded, *Viśeṣamitra was confused or unfamiliar with the *Mūlasarvāstivāda-vinaya*.[55] Alternatively, it might be due to there being multiple traditions of the *Mūlasarvāstivāda-vinaya*. That is to say, the extant recension of the *Śayanāsanavastu* of the *Mūlasarvāstivāda-vinaya* that we have today may differ from the one *Viśeṣamitra knew. It would require further examination of the discrepancies between the *Vinayasaṃgraha* and the canonical Vinaya to determine whether Bu ston's rejection of the *Vinayasaṃgraha* holds water.

In the future, I intend to discuss these three significant characteristics in some detail by analyzing *Viśeṣamitra's discussions that follow other *Prātimokṣa* rules.

undergone probation; one who is undergoing the procedure for becoming agreeable again; one who is suspended for not seeing a fault; one who is suspended for not correcting a fault; one who is suspended when reprehensible views are not abandoned; he who is a lay man; and one who is not ordained."

54. Note, however, that the list of ten people mentioned in the *Śayanāsanavastu* is also not exhaustive. The *Upāliparipṛcchā* in the *Uttaragrantha* of the *Mūlasarvāstivāda-vinaya* lists thirty-two types of people, including the *pārājika* penitent (*śikṣādattaka*), to whom reverence must not be shown: Sde dge 7, 'Dul ba, vol. *na*, 282a4–b4.

55. Regarding the disagreements in content between the *Vinayasaṃgraha* and the canonical Vinaya that led Bu ston to be skeptical about the authenticity of the former, see Kishino 2019.

Appendix: Contents of the Discussion Following Pāyantikā *72 in the* Vinayasaṃgraha

Appendix: Contents of the Discussion Following Pāyantikā *72 in the* Vinayasaṃgraha *(Sde dge 4105, 'Dul ba, vol.* nu, *239a6–245b7; Taishō 1458.24.597b18–600b26)*

	Major topics
§ 1	Brief outline of the frame-story of *pāyantikā* 72. Chinese includes wording of the rule.
§ 2	Word-commentary on "having not reached twenty years old" from the rule; explanation of why someone who has not reached twenty years old should not be ordained.
§ 3	Word-commentary on "ordination" from the rule; ordination should be understood from four perspectives: (1) those who confer ordination, (2) those who may be ordained, (3) how to ordain, and (4) the obligatory behavior of those who have been ordained.
§ 3.1	Word-commentary on "those who may confer ordination," to which *Viśeṣamitra refers in his own discussion; there are three categories: (1) the *upādhyāya*, (2) the *ācārya*, and (3) the *saṅgha*.
§ 3.1.1	The preceptor is classified into two categories: (1) one who has a candidate enter the religious life, and (2) one who has him fully ordained.
	The qualifications of the preceptor include having a ten-year career as a monk and mastery of the Vinaya in five respects: (1) knowing guilt, (2) knowing innocence, (3) knowing major offenses, (4) knowing minor offenses, and (5) the ability to recite the *Prātimokṣa* in detail.
	Verse summarizing five meritorious qualities that Vinaya masters gain.
	Enumeration of the qualities that the preceptor should possess.
	The monk who does not possess the aforementioned qualifications cannot be a preceptor, even if he has had a sixty-year career as a monk. Rather, he must maintain his relationship of dependence on his own preceptor; such a monk is named a "young-senior."
§ 3.1.2	The teacher is classified into five categories: (1) the teacher of a novice, who has the candidate declare that he will take the Three Refuges and follow the five foundations of training, (2) the monk-who-instructs-the-candidate-in-private (*raho'nuśāsaka*), (3) the monk-who-conducts-the-ritual (*karmakāraka*), (4) the one who initiates the relationship of dependence, and (5) the one who teaches recitation.
§ 3.1.3	The community is classified into two categories: (1) a community of ten members in a central region, and (2) a community of five members in a remote region.
	The validity of an ordination performed by five monks in a central region.

Tib.	Chin.	Parallels in the MSV
239a6–	597b18–	*Vinayavibhaṅga* (D 3 *ja* 283b4–284b3; T. 1442.23.853a9–20)
239a7	597b24–	*Vinayavibhaṅga* (D 3 *ja* 284a2–7; T. 1442.23.853a18–19)
239a7–	597b25–	
239b1–	597b26–	
239b2	597b28	*Pravrajyāvastu* (D 1 *ka* 49a1)
239b2–	597b29–	*Pravrajyāvastu* (D 1 *ka* 70a1–2; T. 1444.23.1031c7–10); *Śayanāsanavastu* (Gnoli 1978, 46; D 1 *ga* 216b3–b4)
239b3	n/a	cf. *Śayanāsanavastu* (Gnoli 1978, 45–46; D 1 *ga* 216a1–b5)
n/a	597c2–	
239b3–	597c5–	*Pravrajyāvastu* (D 1 *ka* 70a3–6; T. 1444.23.1031c11–17)
239b4–	597c9–	*Pravrajyāvastu* (D 1 *ka* 48b5–49a1); **Pañcaka* (D 7 *pa* 51a6–b2)
239b4–	597c1–	*Pravrajyāvastu* (D 1 *ka* 52a2)
239b6	597c16–	*Upālipariprcchā* (D 7 *na* 239a5–6); **Māṇavikā* (D 7 *pa* 221b6–222a1)

	Major topics
	The invalidity of an ordination performed when some of the members joining the ordination ceremony are replaced by the Buddha (i.e., an image of the Buddha?), a deaf person, and so on.
§ 3.2	Word-commentary on "those who may be ordained," to which *Viśeṣamitra refers in his own discussion; they may not be (1) mentally impaired (*āśayavipanna*), (2) those whose foundation is impaired (**āśrayavikopana*), (3) those who have genital impairment, (4) those who have impaired the Pure Dharma (*śukladharma*), (5) those who are dependent on others (*paratantra*), or (6) those who are physically disfigured to the extent that they are unpleasant (**aprāsādika*).
§ 3.2.1	Word-commentary on "those who are mentally impaired," to which *Viśeṣamitra refers in his own discussion; they include those who are fearful and worry about their lives.
§ 3.2.2	Word-commentary on "those whose foundation is impaired," to which *Viśeṣamitra refers in his own discussion; they are those who have a serious disease.
§ 3.2.3	Word-commentary on "those who have genital impairment," to which *Viśeṣamitra refers in his own discussion; they are categorized into five *paṇḍaka*s: (1) those who have no sexuality by nature, (2) those who alternate between male and female identities, (3) those who become aroused when they are hugged, (4) those who become aroused when they see others having sex, and (5) those whose sex organs are impaired by disease or injuries.
§ 3.2.4	Word-commentary on "those who have impaired the Pure Dharma," to which *Viśeṣamitra refers in his own discussion; they are all the non-Buddhists (*tīrthika*) except for the Śākya family and the Fire Worshippers (*āgneyajaṭila*).
	Word-commentary on "defiler of nuns" (*bhikṣuṇī-dūṣaka*), appearing in neither the rule nor *Viśeṣamitra's own discussion.
	Word-commentary on "interloper" (*steyasaṃvāsika*), appearing in neither the rule nor *Viśeṣamitra's own discussion.
	Citations from the **Māṇavikā* and the *Upāliparipṛcchā*.
	Word-commentary on "a former monk who has gone over to another religious group" (*tīrthika-avakrāntaka*), appearing in neither the rule nor *Viśeṣamitra's own discussion.
	List of monastics who should be expelled, such as patricides, matricides, arhaticides, schismatics, one who has shed the Buddha's blood, and one who has previously committed a grave offense.
	Word-commentary on "one who is no longer in communion" (*asaṃvāsika*), appearing in neither the rule nor *Viśeṣamitra's own discussion.

Tib.	Chin.	Parallels in the MSV
239b7	597c17–	cf. *Shisong lü* 十誦律 (T. 1435.23.397b14–16)
239b7–	597c21–	
240a1–	597c23–	cf. *Bhaiṣajyavastu* (Wille 1990, 94; D 1 *kha* 293a5; T. 1448.24.82b17–19)
240a2	597c25–	
240a2–	597c25–	*Pravrajyāvastu* (D 1 *ka* 95a5–b3)
240a4–	598a4–	*Pravrajyāvastu* (D 1 *ka* 72a4–b1; T. 1444.23.1031c25–28); *Kṣudrakavastu* (D 6 *da* 287b2–7; T. 1451.24.398c12–21)
240a6–	598a8–	cf. *Upāliparipṛcchā* (D 7 *na* 236a4–6)
240a7–	598a12–	*Pravrajyāvastu* (D 1 *ka* 94b1–2); *Vinayavibhaṅga* (D 3 *ja* 286a4–5; T. 1442.23.853c7–9)
240b1–	598a16–	Not identified
240b1–	598a16–	*Pravrajyāvastu* (Vogel and Wille 2002, 30; D 1 *ka* 120a6–7; T. 1443.23.1038c24–26)
240b2–	598a17–	*Pravrajyāvastu* (D 1 *ka* 121b6–129b6; T. 1444.23.1039b19–1040c17)
240b3–	598a22–	*Mātṛkā* (D 7 *pa* 278a7–b3)

	Major topics
§ 3.2.5	Word-commentary on "those who are dependent on others" (*paratantra*), to which *Viśeṣamitra refers in his own discussion: slaves, servants, those whose parents forbid them from entering the religious life, and so on.
§ 3.2.6	Word-commentary on "those who are physically disfigured to the extent that they are unpleasant" (**aprāsādika*), appearing in *Viśeṣamitra's own discussion; a detailed list of those who are physically deformed.
	Verse stating that attractive individuals (*prāsādika*) enter the religious life, and pure individuals (*pariśuddha*) are fully ordained.
§ 3.3	Word-commentary on "how to ordain," to which *Viśeṣamitra refers in his own discussion:
§ 3.3.1	Procedures for a man to become an upāsaka.
	Procedures for a lay disciple to become a śrāmaṇera.
	Procedures for a novice to become a bhikṣu.
§ 3.3.2	Five erroneous behaviors during the ordination ceremony that make it invalid: (1) the preceptor's name is not mentioned, (2) the candidate's name is not mentioned, (3) the community's name is not mentioned, (4) the motion is not proposed, and (5) the resolution with three proclamations is not completed.
	Several irregular situations that do not affect the validity of an ordination, such as an ordination for a male candidate conducted by a group of nuns, an ordination conducted without first asking the candidate whether he possesses any qualities that would impede his ordination, an ordination conducted without the preceptor, an ordination conducted by a preceptor who has not been fully ordained, and an ordination conducted with a preceptor who has transgressed the Vinaya rules.
	Citation from the *Upālipariprcchā*.
	The validity of an ordination of a candidate who possesses any qualities that would impede his ordination. The Tibetan translation says that it is valid, but the Chinese translation says it is invalid.
	The validity of an ordination rejected by the candidate in the middle of the ceremony.
	The validity of an ordination in which the candidate is deaf or a foreigner (**mleccha*).
	The validity of an ordination in which the preceptor or the group of monks conducting it has undergone a sex change.
	The validity of an ordination that is conducted for a candidate on the ground by a group of monks in the air.

Tib.	Chin.	Parallels in the MSV
240b6–	598a24–	*Pravrajyāvastu* (D 1 *ka* 77b1–2, 79a2–3, 84a7–b1; T. 1444.23.1033b19–21, c25–27, 1035b1–5); *Kṣudrakavastu* (D 6 *tha* 218b1–3; T. 1451.24.280c15–20)
240b7–	598a28–	*Kṣudrakavastu* (D 6 *da* 38a5–b7; T. 1451.24.328b11–18); cf. MVP (Sakaki 1916–1925, § CCLXX [8755])
241a7–	598b8–	*Pravrajyāvastu* (D 1 *ka* 63b6); *Kṣudrakavastu* (D 6 *da* 38b7; T. 1451.24.328b20–23)
241b1–	598b13–	
241b1	598b13–	*Pravrajyāvastu* (D 1 *ka* 49a2–b5)
241b1–	598b16–	*Pravrajyāvastu* (D 1 *ka* 49b5–51b6)
241b4–	598b29–	*Pravrajyāvastu* (D 1 *ka* 51b6–63b7)
242a1–	598c14–	**Pañcaka* (D 7 *pa* 54a2–3); cf. *Upāliparipṛcchā* (D 7 *na* 239b1–3)
242a2–	598c17–	*Upāliparipṛcchā* (D 7 *na* 235a4–5, 235a5–6, 240a1–2, 240a2–3, 235b4, 238a6–7, 241b3–4); *Muktaka* (Kishino 2016, § 1.1.3)
	n/a	
242a7–	598c23	*Upāliparipṛcchā* (D 7 *na* 235a6–b4); *Nidāna* (Kishino 2013, § 1.1.5)
242b1–	598c25–	*Muktaka* (Kishino 2016, § 1.1.3)
242b2–	598c26–	*Upāliparipṛcchā* (D 7 *na* 240b1–2, 240a5–7)
242b3	598c28–	*Upāliparipṛcchā* (D 7 *na* 241a6, b3)
242b3–	598c29	*Upāliparipṛcchā* (D 7 *na* 239a2–3)

	Major topics
	The definition of a valid ordination: it consists of one motion and the resolution with three proclamations.
	The number of candidates who may be ordained within a single boundary at the same time.
	A list of ten valid "historical" ordinations. There is some discrepancy between the Tibetan and Chinese lists. (1) the ordination of the buddhas and pratyekabuddhas with no teacher, (2) the ordination of the first five disciples of the Buddha through their enlightenment and the ordination of Sodāyin through his answer to the Buddha's query (Chinese translation: these two ordinations are separate), (3) the ordination of sixty disciples through the declaration of the Three Refuges (Chinese translation: this ordination is omitted), (4) the ordination of Mahākāśyapa through the acceptance of the teaching (Chinese translation: not through the acceptance of the teaching but through the [declaration of the Three] Refuges), (5) the ordination by a community of five members including a Vinaya master in a remote region, (6) the ordination by a community of ten members in a central region, (7) the ordination of Mahāprajāpatī through acceptance of the eight important rules, (8) the ordination of Dharmadinnā through a messenger, (9) the ordination by both communities, and (10) the ordination through the Buddha's saying, "Come, monk!"
§ 3.4.1	Word-commentary on "the obligatory behavior of those who have been ordained," to which *Viśeṣamitra refers in his own discussion. Juniors must show reverence to seniors. If they meet each other for the first time, they must ask one another their monastic age and the season in which they were ordained.
	A list of the five seasons: winter (*haimantika*), spring (*grīṣma*), the rains (*vārṣika*), the short rains (*mṛtavārṣika*), and the long rains (*dīrghavārṣika*).
§ 3.4.2	Reverence must be shown in four cases: (1) the world, including deities, must show reverence to the Tathāgata, (2) all lay people must show reverence to those who have entered the religious life, (3) fully ordained individuals must show reverence to those who were fully ordained before them (except for nuns), and (4) individuals who are not ordained must show reverence to those who are fully ordained.
	Monks must not show reverence to these ten: (1–4) the four types of individuals who are on probation, (5) the *pārājika* penitent (*śikṣādattaka*), (6–8) the three types of individuals subject to suspension, (9) a layman, and (10) one who is not fully ordained.
§ 3.4.3	There is no seniority between two or three individuals who have been ordained at the same time.

Tib.	Chin.	Parallels in the MSV
242b4	n/a	
242b4–	599a1–	cf. *Upālipariprcchā* (D 7 *na* 238b3–7)
242b5–	599a4–	*Mātṛkā* (D 7 *na* 234b7–235b3); cf. *Vinayakārikā* (D 4123, 3b7–4a2; T. 1459.24.618b9–21)
243a1	599a12–	*Śayanāsanavastu* (Gnoli 1978, 4; D 1 *ga* 188a6–b2); *Pravrajyāvastu* (D 1 *ka* 58a2–3)
243a1–	599a14–	
243a2–	599a16–	*Śayanāsanavastu* (Gnoli 1978, 4–5; D 1 *ga* 188b2–6)
243a4–	599a22–	
243a4–	599a22–	

	MAJOR TOPICS
§ 3.4.4	Others' views: six types of seniority: (1) seniority based on season, (2) seniority by nature (*dharmatā*), (3) seniority based on popularity, (4) seniority based on official positions, (5) seniority based on time, and (6) seniority based on bloodline.
§ 3.4.5	Two kinds of posture for showing reverence: (1) throwing one's whole body down on the ground and (2) holding in one's arms the knees of one to whom respect is shown.
§ 3.4.6	Definition of *vandana*: *vandana* is a salutation.
	Definition of **pūjana* (Tib. *mchod pa*): *pūjana* is a bow.
§ 3.4.7	Others' views: Reverence must be shown to the Buddha by throwing one's whole body down on the ground; to monks worthy of respect by either kneeling and maintaining a bowing posture, maintaining the gesture of supplication with one's hands, holding their knees in one's arms, or maintaining the posture of squatting; and to coreligionists (*sabrahmacārin*) by either bowing, maintaining the gesture of supplication with one's hands, or greeting with words.
§ 3.4.8	If reverence is shown by or to those who have bodily impurities, both those who show reverence and those to whom reverence is shown incur a fault.
	Two types of bodily impurity: (1) impurity of food and (2) impurity of excrement.
	Reverence should be shown according to the Vinaya rules even between those who are on bad terms.
	Reverence should not be shown by or to those who are wearing only a single cloth.
	When seniors sneeze, "I respect you" (*√*vand*) must be said to them. When juniors sneeze, "be healthy" (**arogya*), not "live [long]" (**saṃ*-√*jīv*), must be said to them. If those who entered the religious life in old age (*mahallaka*) or laymen sneeze, "live [long]" can be said to them.
	In a dark place, reverence should be shown not by bowing down but through salutation.
§ 3.5.1	How to request a relationship of dependence from a preceptor or a teacher.
§ 3.5.2	The disciple who maintains a relationship of dependence on his preceptor or a teacher may not travel. He is, however, able to travel if five years have passed since he was ordained and he has mastered the Vinaya rules in five respects (cf. § 3.1.1).
	When he travels and reaches his destination, he must acquire an alternative relationship of dependence on someone else within a few days.

Tib.	Chin.	Parallels in the MSV
243a5–	n/a	
243b1–	599a24–	*Kṣudrakavastu* (D 6 *tha* 194a5–6; T. 1451.24.273a26–27)
243b2	599a25	
	n/a	
243b2–	599a25–	
243b3–	599a29–	*Kṣudrakavastu* (D 6 *tha* 193b3–194a1; T. 1451.24.272c29–273a13)
243b4	599b1–	*Muktaka* (Kishino 2016, § 1.1.1)
243b4–	599b3–	*Muktaka* (Kishino 2016, § 1.1.1)
243b5	599b7–	*Kṣudrakavastu* (D 6 *da* 224a7–b2; T. 1451.24.381b22–23)
243b5–	599b8–	*Kṣudrakavastu* (D 6 *tha* 114b5–115b3; T. 1451.24.249b20–c23)
243b6	599b11–	*Kṣudrakavastu* (D 6 *tha* 184a6–7; T. 1451.24.270b8–9)
243b6–	599b12–	*Mātṛkā* (D 7 *pa* 268a1–4)
244a2	599b22–	*Pravrajyāvastu* (D 1 *ka* 71b1–2)
244a2–	599b25–	

	Major topics
	Even if he is an arhat, he must have an alternative relationship of dependence at his destination.
	Donations must be shared with the traveling monk for five days.
	Five deficient disciples who cannot be allowed to maintain a relationship of dependence: (1) those who do not have religious faith, (2) those who use vulgar language, (3) those who keep bad company, (4) those who are lazy, and (5) those who are not obedient.
	Five situations in which a relationship of dependence expires: (1) [either the preceptor or the disciple] moves out of the boundary, (2) [either the preceptor or the disciple] returns to secular life, (3) the preceptor returns from another place, (4) [either the preceptor or the disciple] defects to an opponent's side, and (5) [both the preceptor and the disciple] abandon the relationship of dependence.
	As soon as the disciple sees his preceptor, his relationship of dependence on another individual is terminated.
	If his own preceptor is approaching, the disciple must serve both him and the teacher with whom the disciple has an alternative relationship of dependence until the preceptor decides to stay.
	When either a disciple or his teacher has gone traveling and turns back halfway, their relationship of dependence remains intact.
	Acquiring a new relationship of dependence does not imply abandoning another relationship of dependence.
	When the preceptor or the teacher who has granted a relationship of dependence to a disciple passes away, the disciple must acquire an alternative relationship of dependence before two subsequent fortnightly *poṣadha* ceremonies take place.
	If the preceptor or the teacher who has granted a relationship of dependence to a disciple passes away before the rain retreat takes place, the disciple must not participate in the rain retreat. If the preceptor or the teacher passes away after the late rain retreat begins, the disciple must be observant of Vinaya rules and not remain there for more than two months.
§ 3.5.3	The preceptor or the teacher who grants a relationship of dependence must be visited by his disciple twice a month if they live 2.5 *yojana*s apart, once every five or six days if they live five *krośa*s apart, every day if they live one *krośa* apart, and three times a day if they live within the same boundary.
	If the preceptor and the teacher who grants a relationship of dependence have not finished the bowl and robe work, the disciple must complete the work first before he does his own bowl and robe work.*

*Tib. adds an obscure passage that I do not understand at all: *de nyid kyis kyang de'i'o //* (244b3).

Tib.	Chin.	Parallels in the MSV
244a3	599b27–	cf. *Pravrajyāvastu* (D 1 *ka* 71b2–5); *Nidāna* (Kishino 2013, § 2.8.2)
244a3	599b28–	*Nidāna* (Kishino 2013, § 2.8.2)
244a3–	599c1–	
244a4–	599c3–	*Mātṛkā* (D 7 *pa* 268a6–7); cf. *Sapoduo bu pini modeleqie* 薩婆多部毘尼摩得勒伽 (T. 1441.23.599c10–11); *Shisong lü* 十誦律 (T. 1435.23.416b27–c1)
244a5–	599c6–	*Kṣudrakavastu* (D 6 *tha* 214a7–215a6; T. 1451.24.279b14–c3)
244a6–	599c7–	cf. *Kṣudrakavastu* (D 6 *tha* 215a2–6; Chin. omits.)
244a6–	599c8–	*Kṣudrakavastu* (D 6 *tha* 215b3–216a4; T. 1451.24.279c14–280a2)
244a7–	599c10	
244a7	599c11–	*Kṣudrakavastu* (D 6 *tha* 229a1–230a1; T. 1451.24.284b3–21)
244a7–	599c12–	
244b1–	599c15–	*Nidāna* (Kishino 2013, § 3.1.3); cf. *Kṣudrakavastu* (D 6 *da* 215b1–3; T. 1451.24.279c10–13)
244b2	599c18–	*Kṣudrakavastu* (D 6 *tha* 227a5; T. 1451.24.382b19–20)

	Major topics
	A recitation instructor (*pāṭhācārya*) must also be taken care of by his disciples.
	If both the recitation instructor and the teacher who grants a relationship of dependence become sick, the latter must be taken care of.
	If a recitation instructor has many disciples, they must take care of him in turn.
	If a recitation instructor or the one who grants a relationship of dependence to a disciple is on bad terms with someone, the disciple must not have a close relationship with that person.
	The recitation instructor and the one who grants a relationship of dependence must be respectfully taken care of by their disciples.
	What a disciple who maintains a relationship of dependence is forbidden to do without permission from his preceptor or teacher: sprinkling water, bowl work, attending to visitors, and so on. In short, he requires permission to do anything except these five actions: (1) drinking water, (2) brushing his teeth, (3) defecating, (4) urinating, and (5) showing reverence to the *caitya* in the boundary.
	Restriction against asking the preceptor or a teacher for instructions and inquiring about their health at the same time.
	Detailed instructions about how to inquire about the health of the preceptor or a teacher.
	The good behavior expected of a disciple who maintains a relationship of dependence.
	A preceptor or a teacher must be vigilant of the behavior of a disciple with whom he keeps a relationship of dependence.
§ 4.1	Comment on "blamed"; it means that they have transgressed *pāyantikā* 72.
	Overview of the ten cases to which *pāyantikā* 72 may be applied that are mentioned in the *Vinayavibhaṅga*.
	Another case in which monks have ordained a candidate who is under twenty years old, having judged him to be over twenty years old.
	Another's view: monks who have ordained a candidate whom they deemed impure (Tib. *yongs su dag pa ma yin*) come to have a fault, even if he turns out to be pure.

Tib.	Chin.	Parallels in the MSV
244b3–	599c19–	*Kṣudrakavastu* (D 6 *tha* 214a3–7, 216a4–b1; T. 1451.24.279b5–13; 280a3–10)
244b4	599c23–	
244b4	599c24–	
244b5–	599c25–	*Pravrajyāvastu* (D 1 *ka* 64a2–5; T. 1444.23.1030c8–13)
n/a	600a4–	
	600a5–	cf. *Kṣudrakavastu* (D 6 *da* 225b7–226a4; 1451.24.382a5–16)
	600a12–	cf. *Kṣudrakavastu* (D 6 *da* 215b2–3; T. 1451.24.279c10–13)
	600a22–	
244b6	600a28–	
244b6–	600a29–	*Vinayavibhaṅga* (D 3 *ja* 284b7–287a2; T. 1442.23.853a27–c27)
245a7–	n/a	*Vinayavibhaṅga* (D 3 *ja* 287a2–5; T. 1442.23.853c28–854a1)
245b2	n/a	

	Major topics
§ 4.2	Four points for examination to see if a candidate is mature enough to be ordained: (1) his age, (2) his appearance and voice, (3) his underarm and pubic hair, and (4) his mind.
	A candidate's body must be inconspicuously checked for its physical maturity if he is unsure whether he is old enough to be ordained.
§ 4.3	Those who are over fifteen years old can be novices.
	Someone who is over seven years old and capable of chasing away crows can be appointed as a novice-who-can-chase-away-crows.
	The restriction against monks having two novices as pupils simultaneously. One of the novices should be left in the care of another monk.

Tib.	Chin.	Parallels in the MSV
245b2–	600b15–	
245b5	600b19–	*Muktaka* (Kishino 2016, § 1.1.3)
245b5	600b21	*Pravrajyāvastu* (D 1 *ka* 74b3–75b1; T. 1444.23.1032c7–29)
245b5–	600b22–	*Pravrajyāvastu* (D 1 *ka* 245b5–6); *Nidāna* (Kishino 2013, § 1.1.7)
245b6	600b24–	cf. *Wufen lü* 五分律 (T. 1421.22.115c19–21)

Works Cited

Abbreviations

BKDJ *Bussho kaisetsu daijiten* 佛書解説大辭典 (*Great Dictionary Explaining Buddhist Writings*). Edited by Ono Genmyō 小野玄妙. 11 vols. (1930–1932), with supplements (vols. 12–13) edited by Maruyama Takao 丸山孝雄 (1974–1977), an additional volume 別巻 (vol. 14) entitled *Bukkyō kyōten sōron* 佛教經典總論 (*General Theory on Buddhist Scriptures*) by Ono Genmyō (1936), and an author-title index *Choshabetsu shomei mokuroku* 著者別書名目録 (1988). Tokyo: Daitō shuppan 大東出版, 1930–1988.

BPSV *Āryasarvāstivādimūlabhikṣuṇīprātimokṣasūtravṛtti*

D = Sde dge *The Nyingma Edition of the sDe-dge bKa'-'gyur and bsTan-'gyur*. 120 vols. Sponsored by the Head Lama of the Tibetan Nyingma Meditation Center. Published by Dharma Mudranālaya under the direction of Tarthang Tulku. Oakland: Dharma Publishing, 1977–1983.

KS *Kokusho sōmokuroku* 国書総目録 (*General Catalog of the Nation's [Japan's] Books*). Edited by Iwanami shoten 岩波書店. Revised and supplemented ed. 9 vols. Tokyo: Iwanami shoten, 1989–1991.

MBD *Mochizuki bukkyō daijiten* 望月佛教大辭典 (*Mochizuki's Great Dictionary of Buddhism*). Edited by Mochizuki Shinkō 望月信亨. Enlarged and corrected ed. 10 vols. Reprint, Tokyo: Sekai seiten kankō kyōkai 世界聖典刊行協会, [1933–1936] 1954.

MSV *Mūlasarvāstivāda-vinaya*

MVP *Mahāvyutpatti*. See Sakaki 1916–1925.

Ōtani Cat. *Ōtani daigaku toshokan-zō chibetto daizōkyō tanjuru kandō mokuroku* 大谷大学図書館蔵西蔵大蔵経丹殊爾勘同目録 (*A Comparative Analytical Catalogue of the Tanjur Division of the Tibetan Tripitaka Kept in the Otani University Library*), vol. II.3. Compiled by Otani University 大谷大学. Kyoto: Otani Daigaku Shin Buddhist Comprehensive Research Institute, 1997.

Peking *Eiin Pekin-ban chibetto daizōkyō: Ōtani daigaku toshokan-zō* 影印北京版西蔵大蔵経：大谷大学図書館蔵 (*The Tibetan Tripitaka: Peking Edition. Kept in the Library of the Otani University, Kyoto*). Edited by Chibetto Daizōkyō Kenkyūkai 西蔵大蔵経研究会. 168 vols. Tokyo: Chibetto daizōkyō kenkyūkai 西蔵大蔵経研究会, 1955–1961.

Taishō = T. *Taishō shinshū daizōkyō* 大正新脩大藏經 (*The Buddhist Canon in Chinese, Newly Edited in the Taishō Era*). Edited by Takakusu Junjirō 高楠順次郎 and Watanabe Kaikyoku 渡邊海旭. 100 vols. Tokyo: Taishō issaikyō kankōkai 大正一切經刊行會, 1924–1935.

Japanese Texts

Risshō kōroku 律攝考録 (*A Record of an Investigation of the* Vinayasaṃgraha). n.d. Anon. 3 vols. Manuscript held at Ryūkoku University.

Sange ichijō kaigi zokuhen 山家一乗戒儀続編 (*Tendai's One Vehicle Ordination: Continuation*). 1798. Ryōyū 亮雄 (b. 1740). Manuscript held at Otani University.

Shōburuishū 小部類集 (*A Collection of Miscellaneous Papers*). n.d. Gakunyo 學如 [?] (1716–1773). 2 vols. Manuscript held at Fukuōji Temple 福王寺.

Taigaku kaitei: kaimitsu kōyō zen 台學階梯：戒密綱要 全 (*The Steps of Tendai Learning: The Essentials of Precepts and Esoteric Buddhism. Complete*). Edited by Tendai shūmu-chō kyōgaku-bu 天台宗務廳教學部. Tokyo: Sensō-ji shuppan-bu 浅草寺出版部, 1914.

Tibetan Texts

Kun mkhyen Mtsho sna ba Shes rab bzang po (ca. 13th century). *'Dul ṭi ka nyi ma'i 'od zer legs bshad lung rigs kyi rga mtsho*. 423 folios. Manuscript held at Otani University (Kikuchi Hōjun shi kizō zō-pa-bon bunken 菊池法純氏寄贈蔵巴梵文献 Collection).

———. *'Dul ṭi ka nyi ma'i 'od zer legs bshad lung rigs kyi rga mtsho*. 2 vols. Paṇ-chen Bsod-nams-grags-pa Literature Series 80–81. Delhi: Drepung Loseling Library Society, 1994.

Secondary Sources

Abe Takako 阿部貴子. 2013. "Meiji-ki ni okeru shingonshū no kyōiku karikyuramu: futsūgaku no dōnyū o megutte" 明治期における真言宗の教育カリキュラム：普通学の導入をめぐって (The Shingon School's Educational Curriculum during the Meiji Period: Surrounding the Introduction of Regular Subjects). *Gendai mikkyō* 現代密教 (*Journal of Contemporary Shingon Buddhism*) 24: 201–223.

Baba Hisayuki 馬場久幸. 2016. *Nikkan kōryū to kōraiban daizōkyō* 日韓交流と高麗版大蔵経 (*Japanese-Korean Exchanges and the Koryŏ Edition of the Chinese Buddhist Canon*). Kyoto: Hōzōkan 法藏館.

Banerjee, Anukul Chandra. 1977. *Two Buddhist Vinaya Texts in Sanskrit: Prātimokṣa Sūtra and Bhikṣukarmavākya*. Calcutta: The World Press Private Limited.

Borgland, Jens W. 2014. "A Study of the Adhikaraṇavastu: Legal Settlement Procedures of the Mūlasarvāstivāda Vinaya." PhD thesis, University of Oslo.

———. 2017. "Some Reflections on Thích Nhất Hạnh's Monastic Code for the Twenty-First Century." In *Buddhist Modernities: Re-inventing Tradition in the Globalizing Modern World*, edited by Hanna Havnevik, Ute Hüsken, Mark Teeuwen, Vladimir Tikhonov, and Koen Wellens, 259–281. New York: Routledge.

Brown, Brian Edward. 1991. *The Buddha Nature: A Study of the Tathāgatagarbha and Ālayavijñāna*. Delhi: Motilal Banarsidass.

Cabezón, José Ignacio. 2017. *Sexuality in Classical South Asian Buddhism*. Studies in Indian and Tibetan Buddhism. Somerville, MA: Wisdom Publications.

Chimpa, Lama, and Alaka Chattopadhyaya, trans. 1970. *Tāranātha's History of Buddhism in India*. Edited by Debiprasad Chattopadhyaya. Simla: Indian Institute of Advanced Study.

Chiu, Tzu-Lung. 2014. "Rethinking the Precept of Not Taking Money in Contemporary Taiwanese and Mainland Chinese Buddhist Nunneries." *Journal of Buddhist Ethics* 21: 9–56.

Clarke, Shayne. 2006. "Miscellaneous Musings on Mūlasarvāstivāda Monks: The *Mūlasarvāstivāda Vinaya* Revival in Tokugawa Japan." *Japanese Journal of Religious Studies* 33.1: 1–49.

———. 2012. "Multiple Mūlasarvāstivādin Monasticisms: On the Affiliation of the Tibetan Nuns' Lineages and Beyond." Paper delivered at Oslo Buddhist Studies Forum, June 12, 2012.

———, ed. 2014. *Vinaya Texts*. Gilgit Manuscripts in the National Archives of India: Facsimile Edition 1. New Delhi and Tokyo: The National Archives of India and The International Research Institute for Advanced Buddhology, Soka University.

———. 2015. "Vinayas." In *Brill's Encyclopedia of Buddhism*, vol. 1: *Literature and Languages*, edited by Jonathan A. Silk, Oskar von Hinüber, and Vincent Eltschinger, 60–87. Leiden and Boston: Brill.

Ende, Rein. 2016. "The *Mūlasarvāstivāda Vinaya*: An Attempt at an *Index Locorum* with a Focus on the Works of Gregory Schopen." MA project, McMaster University.

Funayama Tōru 船山徹. 2021. *Basubanzu-den: Indo bukkyō shisōka Vasubandu no denki* 婆藪槃豆伝：インド仏教思想家ヴァスバンドゥの伝記 (*The Biography of the Indian Buddhist Master Vasubandhu*). Kyoto: Hōzōkan 法藏館.

Gnoli, Raniero. 1978. *The Gilgit Manuscript of the Śayanāsanavastu and the Adhikaraṇavastu: Being the 15th and 16th Sections of the Vinaya of the Mūlasarvāstivādin*. Serie Orientale Roma 50. Rome: Istituto Italiano per il Medio ed Estremo Oriente.

Hakamaya Noriaki 袴谷憲昭. 2011. "10 shu no upasaṃpad(ā) to kaitai no mondai" 10種の upasaṃpad(ā) と戒体の問題 (The Problem of the Essence of the Precepts and the 10 Types of upasaṃpad[ā]). *Komazawa daigaku bukkyō gakubu kenkyū kiyō* 駒澤大學佛教學部研究紀要 (*Journal of the Faculty of Buddhism, Komazawa University*) 69: 1–45.

Hirakawa Akira 平川彰. 1960. *Ritsuzō no kenkyū* 律蔵の研究 (*A Study of the Vinayapiṭaka*). Tokyo: Sankibō busshorin 山喜房佛書林.

———. 1978. *Kusharon sakuin daisanbu* 俱舎論索引 第三部 (*Index to the Abhidharmakośabhāṣya [Peking Edition] Part Three, Tibetan-Sanskrit*). Tokyo: Daizō shuppan 大蔵出版.

Horiuchi Toshio 堀内俊郎. 2009. *Seshin no daijō bussetsu ron:* Shakukiron *daiyonshō o chūshin ni* 世親の大乗仏説論：『釈軌論』第四章を中心に (*Vasubandhu's Proof of the Authenticity of the Mahāyāna as Found in the Fourth Chapter of His* Vyākhyāyukti). Bibliotheca Indologica et Buddhologica 13. Tokyo: Sankibō busshorin 山喜房佛書林.

Ikeda Rentarō 池田練太郎. 2010. "Bukkyō kyōdan no tenkai" 仏教教団の展開 (The Development of the Buddhist Order). In *Bukkyō no keisei to tenkai* 仏教の形成と展開 (*Formation and Development of Indian Buddhism*), edited by Nara Kōmei 奈良康明 and Shimoda Masahiro 下田正弘, 119–164. Shin ajia bukkyōshi 02: Indo

II 新アジア仏教史 02: インド II (A New History of Buddhism in Asia 02: India II). Tokyo: Kōsei shuppansha 佼成出版社.

Inaya Yūsen 稲谷祐宣. 1987. "Aki Fukuōji to Gakunyo wajō (2): Gakunyo no chosaku ni tsuite" 安芸福王寺と学如和尚（二）：学如の著作について (Fukuōji Temple in Aki and Master Gakunyo [2]: On Gakunyo's Works). *Kōyasan jihō* 高野山時報 (*Kōyasan Times*) 2483 (December 1): 4–5.

Kishino, Ryōji. 2013. "A Study of the *Nidāna*: An Underrated *Canonical* Text of the *Mūlasarvāstivāda-vinaya*." PhD thesis, University of California, Los Angeles.

———. 2015. "The Concept of *sdom pa* in the *Mūlasarvāstivāda-vinaya*: On Possible Misunderstandings of the *Brahmocaryopasthāna-saṃvṛti*." *Bukkyō daigaku bukkyō gakkai kiyō* 佛教大学仏教学会紀要 (*Bulletin of the Association of Buddhist Studies, Bukkyo University*) 20: 147–192.

———. 2016. "A Further Study of the *Muktaka* of the *Mūlasarvāstivāda-vinaya*: A Table of Contents and Parallels." *Bukkyō daigaku bukkyō gakkai kiyō* 佛教大学仏教学会紀要 (*Bulletin of the Association of Buddhist Studies, Bukkyo University*) 21: 227–283.

———. 2018. "From Gyōnen 凝然 to Hirakawa Akira 平川彰: A Cursory Survey of the History of Japanese *Vinaya* Studies with a Focus on the Term *Kōritsu* 広律." *Bukkyō daigaku bukkyō gakkai kiyō* 佛教大学仏教学会紀要 (*Bulletin of the Association of Buddhist Studies, Bukkyo University*) 23: 85–118.

———. 2019. "The Implications of Bu ston's (1290–1364) Doubts about the Authenticity of the *Vinaya-saṃgraha*." *Memoirs of the Toyo Bunko* 77: 107–135.

———. 2022. "Gakunyo (1716–73) no hensan shita Gijō-yaku *Konpon-satsubatabu risshō* ni fuserareta Mitsumon (1719–88) no jobun to, soko ni kuwaerareta kakikomi ni tsuite" 學如 (1716–73) の編纂した義浄訳『根本薩婆多部律攝』に付せられた密門 (1719–88) の序文と、そこに加えられた書き込みについて (On Mitsumon's [1719–88] Prefatory Introduction Attached to Yijing's Translation of the *Vinayasaṃgraha* Compiled by Gakunyo [1716–73] and the Marginal Notes Added Thereto). *Seizan zenrin gakuhō* 西山禅林学報 (*Journal of Seizan Zenrin Studies*) 33: 55–186.

Li, Rongxi, trans. 1996. *The Great Tang Dynasty Record of the Western Regions*. BDK English Tripiṭaka 79. Berkeley: Numata Center for Buddhist Translation and Research.

Martin, Dan. 2013. "The Highland Vinaya Lineage: A Study of a Twelfth-Century Monastic Historical Source, the 'Transmission Document' by Zhing-mo-che-ba." In *Tibet after Empire: Culture, Society and Religion between 850–1000*, edited by Christoph Cüppers, Robert Mayer, and Michael Walter, 239–265. Lumbini: Lumbini International Research Institute. Reprinted in *Zentralasiatische Studien* 45 (2016): 279–308.

Mizutani Shinjō 水谷真成, trans. 1971. *Daitō saiikiki* 大唐西域記 (*Xuanzang's* Great Tang Dynasty Record of the Western Regions). Tokyo: Heibonsha 平凡社.

Nakamura Hajime. 1980. *Indian Buddhism: A Survey with Bibliographical Notes*. Osaka: KUFS (Kansai Univ. of Foreign Studies) Publication.

Nanjio, Bunyiu. [1883] 1975. *A Catalogue of the Chinese Translation of the Buddhist Tripiṭaka: The Sacred Canon of the Buddhists in China and Japan*. Reprint, San Francisco: Chinese Materials Center, Inc.

Nishimoto Ryūzan 西本龍山. 1933a. "*Konpon-satsubata-bu risshō*" 根本薩婆多部律攝 (*Mūlasarvāstivādin Vinayasaṃgraha*). In *Bussho kaisetsu daijiten* 佛書解說大辭典 (*Great Dictionary Explaining Buddhist Writings*), edited by Ono Genmyō 小野玄妙, 3:532. Tokyo: Daitō shuppansha 大東出版社.

———, trans. 1933b. "*Konpon-setsuissaiu-bu binaya*" 根本説一切有部毘奈耶 (*Mūlasarvāstivāda-vinaya*). Ritsu-bu 律部 (Vinaya Section) vol. 19 of *Kokuyaku issaikyō* 國譯一切經 (*Translation into the National Language, or Japanese, of the Entire Canon*). Tokyo: Daitō shuppansha 大東出版社.

Numata Ichiro 沼田一郎. 1999. "Harai sekkai no ichi kaishaku: *Konpon-setsuissaiu-bu binaya* no 'Upasena monogatari' ni tsuite" 波羅夷殺戒の一解釈：『根本説一切有部毘奈耶』の＜Upasena 物語＞について (One Interpretation of the Pārājika Precept of Killing: The Story of Upasena in the *Mūlasarvāstivāda-vinaya*). *Nippon bukkyō gakkai nenpō* 日本仏教学会年報 (*Journal of the Nippon Buddhist Research Association*) 64: 61–70.

Odani Nobuchiyo 小谷信千代 and Tshul-khrims Skal-bzang ツルティム・ケサン. 1985. "Geruku-ha shōshi (jō)" ゲルク派小史（上） (A Short History of dGe lugs pa: Part 1). *Bukkyōgaku seminā* 佛教學セミナー (*Buddhist Seminar, Otani University*) 41: 18–38.

Pachow, W. A. 1955. *A Comparative Study of the Prātimokṣa: On the Basis of Its Chinese, Tibetan, Sanskrit and Pali Versions*. Buddhist Tradition Series 31. Delhi: Motilal Banarsidass.

Pradhan, Prahlad. 1967. *Abhidharmakośabhāṣyam of Vasubandhu*. Tibetan Sanskrit Works Series 8. Patna: Kashi Prasad Jayaswal Research Institute.

Prebish, Charles S. 1975. *Buddhist Monastic Discipline: The Sanskrit Prātimokṣa Sūtras of the Mahāsāṃghikas and Mūlasarvāstivādins*. First Indian ed. Delhi: Motilal Banarsidass.

Rajani, M. B. 2016. "The Expanse of Archaeological Remains at Nalanda: A Study Using Remote Sensing and GIS." *Archives of Asian Art* 66.1: 1–23.

Sakaino Kōyō 境野黄洋, trans. 1932. "*Konpon-satsubata-bu risshō*" 根本薩婆多部律攝 (*Mūlasarvāstivādin Vinayasaṃgraha*). Ritsu-bu 律部 (Vinaya Section) vol. 17 of *Kokuyaku issaikyō* 國譯一切經 (*Translation into the National Language, or Japanese, of the Entire Canon*). Tokyo: Daitō shuppansha 大東出版社.

Sakaki Ryōzaburō 榊亮三郎. 1916–1925. *Bon-zō-kan-wa shiyaku taikō hon'yaku myōgi taishū (bon・zō sakuin)* 梵藏漢和四譯對校飜譯名義大集（梵・藏索引） (Mahāvyutpatti: *A Sanskrit-Tibetan-Chinese-Japanese Quadrilingual Collation [with Sanskrit and Tibetan Indices]*). 2 vols. Kyoto: Shingonshū kyōto daigaku 真言宗京都大学.

Sakurabe Hajime 櫻部建. 1964. "*Konpon-setsuissaiu-bu ritsu* kei no shohon ga tsutaeru shukke, ju gusokukai sahō" 根本説一切有部律系の諸本が傳える出家・受具足戒作法 (On the Initiation and Ordination Procedures Transmitted by the Various Texts Affiliated with the *Mūlasarvāstivāda-vinaya*). *Indogaku bukkyōgaku kenkyū* 印度學佛教學研究 (*Journal of Indian and Buddhist Studies*) 12.2: 496–504.

———. 1969. *Kusharon no kenkyū: kai, konpon* 俱舍論の研究：界・根品 (*A Study of the* Abhidharmakośa*: The Dhātu and Indriya Chapters*). Kyoto: Hōzōkan 法藏館.

Sasaki Kyōgo 佐々木教悟. 1976. "*Risshō* no kyōjo ni tsuite" 律摂の経序について (On the Introduction to the *[Prātimokṣa-]Sūtra* of the *Vinayasaṃgraha*). In *Okuda Jiō sensei kiju kinen: Bukkyō shisō ronshū* 奥田慈應先生喜寿記念：仏教思想論集 (*Studies in Buddhist Thought: Dedicated to Professor Jiō Okuda in Commemoration of His Seventy-Seventh Birthday*), edited by Okuda Jiō Sensei Kiju Kinen Ronbunshū Kankōkai 奥田慈應先生喜寿記念論文集刊行会, 987–1000. Kyoto: Heirakuji shoten 平楽寺書店. Reprinted in Sasaki 1985, 150–167.

———. 1977. "*Konpon-satsubata-bu risshō* ni tsuite" 根本薩婆多部律摂について (On the *Mūlasarvāstivādin Vinayasaṃgraha*). *Indogaku bukkyōgaku kenkyū* 印度學佛教學研究 (*Journal of Indian and Buddhist Studies*) 25.2: 587–594. Reprinted in Sasaki 1985, 168–184.

———. 1985. *Kairitsu to sōgya* 戒律と僧伽 (*Precepts/Vinaya and Saṅgha*). Indo, tōnan ajia bukkyō kenkyū インド・東南アジア仏教研究 (Indian and Southeast Asian Buddhist Studies) 1. Kyoto: Heirakuji shoten 平樂寺書店.

Schiefner, Antonius, ed. [1869] 1963. *Târanâthae de doctrinae Buddhicae in India propagatione*. Reprint, Tokyo: Suzuki Research Foundation.

Schopen, Gregory. 1998. "Marking Time in Buddhist Monasteries: On Calendars, Clocks, and Some Liturgical Practices." In *Sūryacandrāya: Essays in Honour of Akira Yuyama On the Occasion of His 65th Birthday*, edited by Paul Harrison and Gregory Schopen, 157–179. Indica et Tibetica 35. Swisttal-Odendorf: Indica et Tibetica Verlag. Reprinted in Schopen 2004a, 260–284.

———. 2000. "Hierarchy and Housing in a Buddhist Monastic Code: A Translation of the Sanskrit Text of the *Śayanāsanavastu* of the *Mūlasarvāstivāda-vinaya*. Part One." *Buddhist Literature* 2: 92–196.

———. 2004a. *Buddhist Monks and Business Matters: Still More Papers on Monastic Buddhism in India*. Studies in the Buddhist Traditions. Honolulu: University of Hawai'i Press.

———. 2004b. "Making Men into Monks." In *Buddhist Scriptures*, edited by Donald S. Lopez Jr., 230–251. London: Penguin Books. Reprinted in Schopen 2014, 175–193.

———. 2014. *Buddhist Nuns, Monks, and Other Worldly Matters: Recent Papers on Monastic Buddhism in India*. Studies in the Buddhist Traditions. Honolulu: University of Hawai'i Press.

Shaku Keihō 釋啓峰. 1939. "*Konpon-setsuissaiu-bu risshō* josetsu" 『根本説一切有部律攝』序説 (An Introduction to the *Mūlasarvāstivādin Vinayasaṃgraha*). *Mikkyō kenkyū* 密教研究 (*Esoteric Buddhist Studies*) 69: 18–36.

———. 1940. "*Ubu risshō* gaisetsu" 有部律攝概説 (A Survey of the [*Mūla*]-*Sarvāstivādin Vinayasaṃgraha*). *Mikkyō kenkyū* 密教研究 (*Esoteric Buddhist Studies*) 72: 48–69.

Study Group of the *Pravrajyāvastu* in the *Vinayasūtra* [*Ritsukyō 'Shukkeji'* Kenkyūkai 『律経』「出家事」研究会]. 2023. "*Ritsukyō 'Shukkeji'* no kenkyū (11)" 『律経』「出家事」の研究 (11) (The *Pravrajyāvastu* in the *Vinayasūtra* [11]). *Taishō daigaku sōgō bukkyō kenkyūsho nenpō* 大正大学綜合佛教研究所年報 (*Annual of the Institute for Comprehensive Studies of Buddhism, Taisho University*) 45: 145–162.

Takai Kankai 高井観海. 1930. "Yuishiki shisō no shiteki kōsatsu" 唯識思想の史的考察 (A Historical Investigation into Consciousness Only Thought). *Chisan gakuhō* 智山学報 (*Journal of Chisan Studies*) 2: 1–31.

Tamayama Ryūen 玉山隆莚. 1940. Ubu risshō *kōjutsu narabi ni* Shami-kai-kyō 有部律攝講述并沙彌戒經 (*A Lecture on the* [Mūla]Sarvāstivādin Vinayasaṃgraha *in Addition to the* Sūtra on Śrāmaṇera Precepts). Kōyasan: Shin-bessho Entsūji 眞別處圓通寺.

Teramoto Enga 寺本婉雅, trans. 1928. *Tāranātha* Indo bukkyōshi ターラナータ° 印度佛教史 (*Tāranātha's* History of Buddhism in India). Tokyo: Heigo shuppansha 丙午出版社.

Tokuda Myōhon 徳田明本. 1974. *Risshū bunken mokuroku*. 律宗文献目録 (*Bibliography of Publications on the Vinaya School*). Kyoto: Hyakka-en 百華苑.

Tsedroen, Jampa. 1992. *A Brief Survey of the Vinaya: Its Origin, Transmission and Arrangement from the Tibetan Point of View with Comparisons to the Theravāda and Dharmagupta Traditions*. Hamburg: Foundation for Tibetan Buddhist Studies.

Tucci, Giuseppe. [1932] 1988. *Rin-chen-bzaṅ-po and the Renaissance of Buddhism in Tibet Around the Millenium*. Translated from the Italian by Nancy Kipp Smith under the direction of Thomas J. Pritzker. Edited by Lokesh Chandra. New Delhi: Aditya Prakashan.

Vogel, Claus, and Klaus Wille, eds. and trans. 2002. "The Final Leaves of the Pravrajyāvastu Portion of the Vinayavastu Manuscript Found Near Gilgit, Part 2: Nāgakumārāvadāna and Lévi Text. With Two Appendices Containing a Turfan Fragment of the Nāgakumārāvadāna and a Kučā Fragment of the Upasaṃpadā Section of the Sarvāstivādins." In *Sanskrit-Texte aus dem buddhistischen Kanon: Neuentdeckungen und Neueditionen IV*, 11–76. Sanskrit-Wörterbuch der buddhistischen Texte aus den Turfan-Funden, Beiheft 9. Göttingen: Vandenhoeck & Ruprecht. Reprinted in Claus Vogel and Klaus Wille, eds. and trans. 2014. *The Pravrajyāvastu of the Mūlasarvāstivāda Vinaya*. Göttingen: Akademie der Wissenschaften zu Göttingen, Sanskrit-Wörterbuch der buddhistischen Texte aus den Turfan-Funden, 147–212. https://rep.adw-goe.de/handle/11858/00-001S-0000-0023-9A04-C.

Watters, Thomas, trans. 1905. *On Yuan Chwang's Travels in India 629–645 A.D.*, vol. 2. Edited, after his death, by T. W. Rhys Davids and S. W. Bushell. London: Royal Asiatic Society.

Wille, Klaus. 1990. *Die handschriftliche Überlieferung des Vinayavastu der Mūlasarvāstivādin*. Stuttgart: Franz Steiner Verlag.

Yamagiwa Nobuyuki 山極伸之. 1987. "Konpon-setsuissaiu-bu no shukke sahō ni okeru mondaiten" 根本説一切有部の出家作法における問題点 (Some Problems on Ordination in the Mūlasarvāstivāda School). *Indogaku bukkyōgaku kenkyū* 印度學佛教學研究 (*Journal of Indian and Buddhist Studies*) 36.1: 84–86.

Yang Benjia 杨本加. 2012. Genben sapoduo bu lüshe *yanjiu* 《根本萨婆多部律摄》研究 (*Research on the* Mūlasarvāstivādin Vinayasaṃgraha). Beijing: Minzu chubanshe 民族出版社.

Marginalia to an Endnote: More on the *Tridaṇḍaka*

Diego Loukota Sanclemente†

MOST OF WHAT USED to be known about the *Tridaṇḍaka* was collected by Gregory Schopen in a substantial endnote devoted to it. According to Schopen, the *Tridaṇḍaka* was "not a specific text, but a set form of recitation consisting of three parts" that would have been used "in a variety of different ritual contexts" according to the references to it contained in the *Mūlasarvāstivāda-vinaya*.[1] By all accounts, the recitation of the *Tridaṇḍaka* must have been fairly short, but the variety of its usage in the *Mūlasarvāstivāda-vinaya* suggests that it must have been rich in meaning. Schopen's endnote concludes with a desideratum for "further research" on the *Tridaṇḍaka*. In the pandemic years that intervened between the original writing of this piece and the present, much light has been thrown on the *Tridaṇḍaka* by means of the recent publications by scholars like Jens-Uwe Hartmann in this very volume, Matsuda Kazunobu 松田和信 (2019; 2020), and Tanaka Hironori 田中裕成 (2020) on a Sanskrit manuscript originally preserved in Tibet that contains a selection of forty *Tridaṇḍaka*s. The contents of the manuscript, which still awaits publication of a complete edition, have confirmed some of my own earlier speculations and dispelled others, making both redundant. Yet, other information that I had gathered on the *Tridaṇḍaka* is useful as a complement to the work published so far on the *Tridaṇḍaka* anthology, and it is in that interest that I will provide here a number of more or less independent marginalia.

Yijing and the Tridaṇḍaka

The testimony of the celebrated Chinese monk, traveler, and scholar Yijing 義淨 (635–713 CE) is central to any discussion on the *Tridaṇḍaka*, not only because Yijing translated a *Tridaṇḍaka* and also substantial portions of the *Mūlasarvāstivāda-vinaya* but also because he mentions the *Tridaṇḍaka* in at

1. Schopen 1992, 32–34n62; for the quotations, see 33 and 34, respectively.

least two places in his famous record of Buddhist monastic life in India and other areas of Asia, *A Record of the Inner Law Sent Home from the South Seas* (Taishō 2125; hereafter *Record*). Yijing, a lover of literature, strived to use in his translations and in his original writings a very literary form of Chinese with a terse diction. In order to evaluate his testimony, the passages in which he deals with the *Tridaṇḍaka*, although well known, can be fruitfully revisited.

The most crucial passage from Yijing's *Record* tells us that the *Tridaṇḍaka*—here referred to as a *jing* 經 (= sūtra)—is often chanted after the circumambulation of *caitya*s at dusk in Indian monasteries.[2] The wording of the passage is frustratingly ambiguous, and rather than attempting to translate it myself, I will provide and discuss the French translation of Sylvain Lévi and the English translation of Takakusu Junjirō 高楠順次郎. I will do so for two reasons: on the one hand, these translations have informed most modern information on the *Tridaṇḍaka*; on the other, an analysis of the interpretations of two supremely gifted scholars gives a clear idea of the difficulties that the text entails. Yijing says:

> 所誦之經多誦三啟，乃是尊者馬鳴之所集置。初可十頌許，取經意而讚歎三尊。次述正經，是佛親說。讀誦既了，更陳十餘頌，論迴向發願。節段三開，故云三啟。[3]

> Quant aux textes sacrés qu'on récite 誦, c'est surtout les Trois Ouvertures 三啟 qu'on récite. C'est un recueil dû au vénérable *Ma ming* (Aśvaghoṣa). La première partie compte dix vers; l'objet du texte est d'exalter les Trois Joyaux. Ensuite vient un texte sacré proprement dit, prononcé par le Bouddha en personne. Après l'hymne et la récitation, il y a encore plus de dix vers, qui ont trait à la déflexion des mérites (*pariṇāmanā*) et à la production du vœu (*praṇidhāna*). Comme il y a trois parties qui s'ouvrent successivement, on appelle ce texte sacré les Trois Ouvertures 三啟.[4]

> Among the scriptures which are to be read on such an occasion the "Service in three parts" is often used. This is a selection by the venerable Aśvaghoṣa. The first part containing ten ślokas consists of a hymn in praise of the three "Honourable Ones" (Triratna). The sec-

2. See the discussion below (pp. 325–329) on the Chinese terminology regarding the *Tridaṇḍaka* and the passages that allow for an equation of various Chinese terms with Sanskrit *tridaṇḍaka*.

3. Taishō 2125.54.227a13–17.

4. Lévi 1915, 434.

> ond part is a selection from some scriptures consisting of the Buddha's words. After the hymn, and after reading the words of the Buddha, there is an additional hymn, as the third part of the service, of more than ten ślokas, being prayers that express the wish to bring one's good merit to maturity. These three sections follow one another consecutively, from which its name—the Three-Part Service—is derived.[5]

As for *zunzhe Maming zhi suo jizhi* 尊者馬鳴之所集置, Lévi's "dû au vénérable *Ma ming* (Aśvaghoṣa)" is unnecessarily vague, as *jizhi* 集置 is transparently "to collect and arrange." Takakusu's rendering "[t]his is a selection by the venerable Aśvaghoṣa," although more direct, implies that Aśvaghoṣa's contribution in this case would have been limited to the selection of the material. This clause could be most straightforwardly understood to mean that Aśvaghoṣa on the one hand "collected" (*ji* 集) and on the other "arranged" the text (*zhi* 置), or that perhaps he "inserted" parts into it, which is yet another meaning of *zhi* 置. This would mean that Aśvaghoṣa took material from elsewhere and either arranged or padded it to create a composition.

A strictly literal rendering of *qu jingyi er zantan sanzun* 取經意而讚歎三尊 would be "[the ten or so stanzas] draw upon the meaning of [the] sūtra (or sūtras) and praise the Three Venerables."[6] Both Lévi's "l'objet du texte est d'exalter les Trois Joyaux" and especially Takakusu's "consists of a hymn in praise of the three 'Honourable Ones'" seem to miss the mark in the first part of the clause ("draw upon the meaning of the sūtra," *qu jingyi* 取經意), with one construing it in an oblique fashion (l'objet du texte est . . .) and the other ignoring it altogether. As for what "the sūtra" or "sūtras" referred to here might be, the following clause is enlightening: *ci shu zhengjing, shi fo qinshuo* 次述正經, 是佛親說, which Lévi renders very literally as "[e]nsuite vient un texte sacré proprement dit, prononcé par le Bouddha en personne." The choice of an indefinite article (*un*) here tells us that for Lévi the central portion was not fixed and could be filled with a variety of canonical texts or passages, an interpretation now supported by the *Tridaṇḍaka* anthology.

The other important testimonies of Yijing regarding the *Tridaṇḍaka* must be approached in tandem. On the one hand, in his *Record* Yijing mentions a "sūtra on impermanence" (*wuchang jing* 無常經) that is recited during monastic funerals in India and adds that he has attached that text to the

5. Takakusu 1896, 153, with minor stylistic updating of diacritics.

6. See in connection with this point, verse III.12b–c in the appendix below. There the author of the text states that he has "paraphrased" or "abridged according to the sūtra" (依經. . .略說).

Record itself (Taishō 2125.54.216c9–10; English translations in Takakusu 1896, 82, and Li 2000, 79). Yijing's *Record* in its extant versions has no such attachments, but a text under the name *Foshuo wuchang jing yi ming sanqi jing* 佛說無常經亦名三啟經 "Sūtra on Impermanence Spoken by the Buddha, also called *Tridaṇḍaka*," whose Chinese translation is attributed to Yijing in all extant versions, is contained in the oldest extant printed canon of Chinese-language Buddhist scriptures, the second Korean canon (Lancaster and Park 1979, § 870 = Taishō 801), and among the British Library holdings of Dunhuang manuscripts (Or.8210/S.274, Or.8210/S.3887, and Or.8210/S.153 = Taishō 2912). The contents of the text fit exactly the description in Yijing's *Record*, and the sūtra that serves as a central section is on the topic of impermanence. The text is listed under both titles in Zhisheng's 智昇 textual catalogue, redacted in 730 CE, where it is said that Yijing translated the text on the thirteenth day of the ninth month of the year 701 CE in Luoyang.[7]

The third British Library manuscript from Dunhuang (Or.8210/S.153 = Taishō 2912) is special in two ways: it records the title of the text as *Foshuo wuchang sanqi jing* 佛說無常三啟經, which lumps together the elements "impermanence" (無常 *wuchang*) and "*tridaṇḍaka*" (*sanqi* 三啟) into one single compound; the addition of *jing* 經, which conventionally translates the term *sūtra*, was likely mechanically added to the title simply to mark it as a Buddhist sacred text. The Dunhuang text ends with the following colophon:

> 初後讚歎乃是尊者馬鳴取經意而集造。中是正經, 金口所說。事有三開, 故云三啟也。[8]
>
> The initial and final hymns (*zantan* 讚歎) were collected and composed (*jizao* 集造) by the venerable Aśvaghoṣa by drawing on the meaning of the sūtra (or sūtras) (*qu jingyi* 取經意). The middle [section] is the sūtra in the proper sense, spoken by the Golden-Mouthed one. Because its matter has three openings, it is called *Tridaṇḍaka* (*sanqi* 三啟).

Notice here the remarkable affinities of this colophon with the wording of the passage from Yijing's *Record*. It is of course possible that someone could have fabricated this colophon on the basis of the *Record*, but the subtle deviations

7. Taishō 2154.55.567c21. On the context of Zhisheng's catalogue, see Chen 2007, 228–232, especially 231 and n56.

8. Taishō 2912.85.1459a8–9.

from the text of the *Record*, which might as well have been quoted verbatim, makes this, in my opinion, unlikely.

Charles Willemen (2019, 68–72) has recently translated Taishō 801, the text based on the recension of the second Korean canon; while preparing the initial draft of this article a few years back, I did my own English translation independently. Since I politely disagree with Willemen's translation on a number of points, and since the comparison between two published translations may allow the reader to glimpse the problems involved in disentangling the terse translational idiom of Yijing, I have appended to this article my own English translation. It provides, better than any description, an idea of what a *Tridaṇḍaka* may have looked like. References to this text ("Yijing's *Tridaṇḍaka*") will use the parsing of the text that I have adopted in the translation.

The Term Tridaṇḍaka

To the Sanskritist, the word *tridaṇḍa* or *tridaṇḍaka*, literally "triple staff," most immediately evokes the bound triple staff, to be occasionally unbound and mounted as a tripod, which served as a marker of initiation for many schools of Brahmanical asceticism. This kind of *tridaṇḍa[ka]* is still in use in India, and it was at least by the time of the texts of the so-called "Middle Period" of Indian Buddhism: Buddhist sources almost invariably use the term to characterize Brahmanical or, at the very least, non-Buddhist ascetics.[9] The *tridaṇḍa[ka]* in its sense of "tripod" was used by Buddhist and non-Buddhist authors alike also as a metaphor for stability and balance in cases where three conceptual parts or components were involved.[10] That the liturgical recitation that concerns us here may have been styled as a metaphorical tripod—as we have seen it was said to consist of three parts—is somewhat unlikely on account of the fact that the *tridaṇḍaka* staff was, as we mentioned, a clear marker of the Brahmanical ascetic.

Since the name *Tridaṇḍaka* is likely to be a reference to the three parts of

9. A rich discussion about the triple staff in the Brahmanical and Buddhist traditions can be found in Olivelle 1986–1987, 1:35–54. For further examples of the *tridaṇḍa* staff as a marker of a Brahmanical ascetic, see *Mahāvastu* (Senart 1890–1907, 3:393) and Āryaśūra's *Jātakamālā* (Kern 1891, 144.10). The title of the *Tridaṇḍi-sūtra* presented by Matsuda (2007) and Choi (2012) refers precisely to a Brahmanical ascetic with the "speaking" name Tridaṇḍin (i.e., the name of a literary character whose meaning alludes to characteristics of the character itself). As such, I have considered it to be unrelated to the *Tridaṇḍaka* we are dealing with here.

10. See *Mānavadharmaśāstra* 9.296b, 12.11a, 12.10d, with the relevant discussion in Olivelle 2005, 334n9.296.

the recitation, one possibility is that the *daṇḍa[ka]* in the compound is the vertical punctuation mark of the Brāhmī script and many of its derivatives, yielding "the text with the three marks of punctuation." The graphic sign is as old as Brāhmī itself, attested as it is, although sparingly, in the Kālsī edicts of Aśoka, but used more or less frequently only from the Guptas onward, at least epigraphically (Salomon 1998, § 2.5.2.3). However, among all modern Sanskrit dictionaries available to me, only the *Dictionnaire sanskrit-français* of Renou and his disciples (Stchoupak, Nitti, and Renou 1932) lists as an entry for *daṇḍa* "signe de ponctuation," explained as a "trait vertical qui sépare les phrases"; the *Dictionnaire* does not list, though, textual references. The term *daṇḍa* for the vertical punctuation sign may have crystallized only relatively late, perhaps even only in modern times.

A more promising line of inquiry stems from the entry for *daṇḍaka* in Böhtlingk and Roth's *Sanskrit-Wörterbuch* (Böhtlingk and Roth 1853–1875), which gives "eine ununterbrochen fortlaufende Reihe, Zeile" and gives as a reference scholia the *Śāṅkhāyanaśrauta-sūtra*, in which the reading of a passage as one single "*daṇḍaka*" by some exegetes is opposed to that of others as "*dvau ślokau*."

The Chinese and Tibetan translations of the term (*sanqi jing* 三啟經, *rgyud chags gsum* or *rgyun chags gsum*) are as opaque as the Sanskrit term they translate.[11] The Sanskrit-Tibetan lexicon *Mahāvyutpatti* gives *rgyun chags* as the equivalent of the elusive term *daṇḍaka* (Sakaki 1916–1925, § 1465) but also gives *rgyun chags par 'jug pa* for *saṃtānānuvṛtti* "continuous succession" (§ 2124) and *rgyun chags pa* for *anubandha* "sequence, succession" (§ 2179): "the three continuous [sections]" is what this lexical evidence would suggest regarding the Tibetan understanding of the term *tridaṇḍaka*.

As for the Chinese, *qi* 啟 (to be distinguished here from its Mandarin homophones with a subscript "1", i.e., "qi_1") has the general senses of "starting" or "opening." Lévi (1915, 434) renders $sanqi_1$ *jing* 三啟經 as "les Trois Ouver-

11. The identity of these three terms must be established through triangulation among passages of the *Mūlasarvāstivāda-vinaya*, and as often happens, the Tibetan translation has to act as a bridge. That Sanskrit *tridaṇḍaka* corresponds to Tibetan *rgyud chags gsum* or *rgyun chags gsum* is made clear by the following two passages: *Poṣadhavastu*, Hu-von Hinüber 1994, § 22.1, Dutt 1939–1959, III.4:80.5 = Sde dge 1, 'Dul ba, vol. *ka*, 136a5; *Cīvaravastu*, Dutt 1939–1959, III.2:120.6–8 = Sde dge 1, 'Dul ba, vol. *ga*, 102b5–6. The equivalence of Tibetan *rgyud chags gsum* or *rgyun chags gsum* with Chinese terms that include the element *sanqi [jing]* 三啟[經] can then be verified in the following passages: *Vibhaṅga*, Sde dge 3, 'Dul ba, vol. *cha*, 192b7–193a3 = Taishō 1442.23.753c18–25; Sde dge 3, 'Dul ba, vol. *cha*, 280b4 = Taishō 1442.23.776a16; *Kṣudrakavastu*, Sde dge 6, 'Dul ba, vol. *tha*, 46b1 = Taishō 1451.24.223b21.

tures," something like "the three openings" of the three sections of the text, in accordance with Yijing's understanding of the term.

An apotropaic Sanskrit text called *Dvādaśadaṇḍakanāmāṣṭaśatavimalī-karaṇā*,[12] known from Gilgit, Bāmiyān, and Qumtura throws interesting light on the term *daṇḍaka*. Luckily, the text has Chinese (Taishō 1253) and Tibetan (Tōhoku 193; Peking Cat. 860) versions that allow for triangulation. In the passage that concerns us here, the Buddha utters a *stotra* in honor of the goddess Śrī. The *stotra* consists simply of an enumeration of a hundred and eight epithets of the goddess, and the *stotra* is said to be *dvādaśadaṇḍaka* "consisting of twelve *daṇḍakas*." In the Sanskrit text, the Buddha asks rhetorically:

> *Katama* (*sic*) *dvādaśadaṇḍakaṃ nāmāṣṭaśataṃ vimalaprakhyaṃ nāma stotraṃ*?[13]
>
> What is the "Pure Renown" *stotra* of a hundred and eight names in twelve *daṇḍakas*?

The Chinese, translated by Amoghavajra (705–774 CE), adheres very closely to the Sanskrit:

> 云何十二契一百八名無垢讚歎？[14]

Here *dvādaśadaṇḍaka* "in twelve *daṇḍakas*" is rendered as *shi'er qi* 十二契 "in twelve *qi* 契." Qi_2 契 (different from qi_1 啟) as a verb means "to agree" and as a noun "contract" or "agreement," but it can designate in general any kind of written document. In medieval Buddhist Chinese there are a couple of compounds that incorporate qi_2 契 and designate generally a written document, like qi_2shu 契書 "document," and qi_2jing 契經 "religious scripture, sūtra." Qi_1 啟 and qi_2 契 shared one homophonic reading in Middle Chinese: *$k^hɛj$ (Pulleyblank 1991, s.vv.). Lin (1949, 305) noted, in fact, that the *Tridaṇḍaka* was referred to as $sanqi_2jing$ 三契經 and not as $sanqi_1jing$ 三啟

12. This text has been generally known since Dutt's editions of the Gilgit corpus as *Śrīmahā-devīvyākaraṇa*, but the late Seishi Karashima (2017, 17) suggested that this is a mistaken title given by Dutt on the basis of the Tibetan version, and that the text should more properly be called, in accordance with the Sanskrit colophons, *Dvādaśadaṇḍakanāmāṣṭaśatavimalīkaraṇā*.

13. Dutt 1939–1959, 1:98, line 5. The Bāmiyān text has here *(kata)mo* (*sic*) *dvādaśadaṃṇḍakaṃ nāmāṣṭaśataṃ (vima)laprakhyaṃ stotraṃ*? (Karashima 2017, folio 28r1). The Qumtura text is not extant for this passage.

14. Taishō 1253.21.254b4.

經 in the Chinese translation of the monumental *Abhidharmamahāvibhāṣā* of the Sarvāstivādins, and the form *sanqi*$_2$ *jing* 三契經 occurs also elsewhere. This latter point will be dealt with later: for the moment suffice it to say that Yijing's orthographical choice (*qi*$_1$ 啟 rather than the more transparent *qi*$_2$ 契) was idiosyncratic and against the mainstream.

Something is amiss in the Tibetan:

> *ming brgya rtsa brgyad dri ma med par grags pa zhes bya ba'i bstod pa brgyad cu gnyis pa gang zhe na?*[15]

Instead of *dvādaśadaṇḍaka/shi'er qi*$_2$ 十二契 "in twelve *daṇḍaka*s" we have here *brgyad cu gnyis pa* "eighty-second." The texts I have consulted are uniform here (with the exception of a banal *bcu* instead of *cu* in the Li thang), but it is tempting to conjecture here that *brgyad cu gnyis pa* is only an ancient corruption for *rgyud* (also often spelled *brgyud*) *bcu gnyis pa*, which would give a text fully consistent with the Sanskrit and the Chinese.

The manuscript from Gilgit (GBM, vol. 7, folio 1322, line 5–folio 1325, line 2) is neatly arranged in six lines per page—the Bāmiyān text is fragmentary—but the *stotra* occupies roughly sixteen lines, so it is unlikely that here *daṇḍaka* indicates what Renou in his *Dictionnaire* gives as another meaning of *daṇḍaka*: "*ligne (d'écriture).*" Since the auspicious number one hundred and eight is divisible by twelve (= nine), I assume that *daṇḍaka* may have been in this context a unit of textual length (as śloka was also used), every nine names constituting one *daṇḍaka*.

In his translation of portions of the *Mūlasarvāstivāda-vinaya*, Yijing translates *tridaṇḍaka* throughout as *sanqi*$_1$ *jing* 三啟經 and does not seem to use the word *qi*$_1$ 啟 in this meaning elsewhere, but the Tibetan version does use *rgyud chags* in passages that have no relation to the *Tridaṇḍaka*, and in those cases Yijing does not translate what corresponds to *rgyud chags*—that is, *daṇḍa* or *daṇḍaka* in the extant Sanskrit text—as *qi*$_1$ 啟 but as *song* 頌 "verse," and this, once again, echoes the general practice of measuring texts, and not only metrical ones, in ślokas. The passages in question describe the length of oral interventions during formal debates at the royal court;[16] these interventions are said to be "in *daṇḍa*s" or "*daṇḍaka*s of five hundred" (*pañcaśatiko daṇḍaḥ*/

15. Sde dge 193, Mdo sde, vol. *tsa*, 249a1; Lha sa, Mdo sde, vol. *ba*, 394a5; Li thang, Mdo sde, vol. *tsa*, 278b3.

16. *Pravrajyāvastu*, Vogel and Wille 1992, 4r5–5r10 = Sde dge 1, 'Dul ba, vol. *ka*, 9a4–12a7 = Taishō 1444.23.1022.b17–c16; *Vibhaṅga*, Sde dge 3, 'Dul ba, vol. *ca*, 169b4 = Taishō 1442.23.671c4.

daṇḍakaḥ; *rgyud chags lnga brgya*; *wubai song* 五百頌), which I hypothesize to be in this context a measure of discursive length too.

The evidence presented above suggests that *daṇḍaka* was at least understood by ancient exegetes to mean "connected section of a text," although the term may have been also used as a unit of textual length. *Tridaṇḍaka* would mean something like "the three connected parts," which matches the exegesis provided by Yijing. However unexciting, this understanding might better characterize this type of recitation: other interpretations of the meaning of the word fail, in my opinion, in their attempts to make sense of the word on the basis of limited evidence.[17]

Equally colorless is the name of a different recitation that bears striking resemblances to the *Tridaṇḍaka*: the *triskandhaka*, "the [text] in three sections." The *triskandhaka* is mentioned only in Mahāyāna sūtras and is richly treated by Jan Nattier (2003, 117–121). Like the *Tridaṇḍaka*, the *triskandhaka* was meant for "performance," and it "was a liturgical text [. . .] to structure a formal ritual of confession" (Nattier 2003, 120). This mahāyānic *triskandhaka* is, as Nattier concedes, not well understood, but the possibility that it might have been modeled somehow after the *Tridaṇḍaka* would highlight the relevance of the latter.

The Tridaṇḍaka *and the* Sūtra on Impermanence

The Tibetan translation of the *Mūlasarvāstivāda-vinaya* is rather consistent in its rendering of Indic terms, using always *rgyud* (or *rgyun*) *chags gsum* for *tridaṇḍaka*: Yijing—perhaps deliberately, and for the love of verbal variety—was all but consistent: although he mostly translates *Tridaṇḍaka* as *sanqi jing* 三啟經, on at least one occasion he uses the compounded form *sanqi wuchang jing* 三啟無常經 (Taishō 1451.24.287a2) where the Tibetan has simply *rgyun chags gsum* (Sde dge 6, 'Dul ba, vol. *tha*, 237a5–6). If Yijing had intended this as an enumeration ("the *Tridaṇḍaka* and the sūtra on impermanence")[18] one would expect something like **sanqi jing*, *wuchang jing* 三啟經、無常經.

17. See, for example, the entry on the *Tridaṇḍaka* in Nakamura 1975, s.v. *sankaikyō* 三契經: "chanting sūtras by dividing the tone into three sections (三段に調子を分けて経を諷詠すること)." This definition is clearly based only on the information provided by one single passage, i.e., *Kṣudrakavastu*, Sde dge 6, 'Dul ba, vol. *tha*, 41b4–44b6 = Taishō 1451.24.223b17–29, treated also below.

18. See, for example, the French translation of this passage by La Vallée Poussin (1937, 286–287): "Les bhikṣus qui font ce service funèbre (*song sang*) feront qu'un homme capable récite les trois 'informations,' *k'i* 啓 [et] le Sūtra sur l'impermanence."

Moreover, the preceding verse summary (*uddāna*) in Yijing's Chinese translation mentions the *Tridaṇḍaka* but not the "sūtra on impermanence," while the corresponding *uddāna* in Tibetan (Sde dge 6, 'Dul ba, vol. *tha*, 236b2) does not mention either. This raises the possibility that the Sanskrit text of the passage may have lacked a mention of a "sūtra on impermanence" too.

In his translations from the *Mūlasarvāstivāda-vinaya*, Yijing uses at least twice *wuchang jing* 無常經 "sūtra on impermanence" without *sanqi*$_1$ 三啟 (= *Tridaṇḍaka*), and both of these instances deserve examination.

The first one belongs to a well-known passage concerning the funerals of the monk Kālodāyin: the Tibetan text (Sde dge 3, 'Dul ba, vol. *nya*, 66a2–4) makes no mention of any recitation during the cremation of the body, but the corresponding passage in Yijing's translation adds a "recitation of the sūtra on impermanence" (*song wuchang jing* 誦無常經, Taishō 1442.23.864c7). Whether Yijing has inserted here what he knew or thought to be appropriate or whether the original from which he translated did include this detail is difficult to determine. It is interesting to note, though, that the association of the *Tridaṇḍaka* with the monastic funeral is, as we will see below, a well-established one in the *Mūlasarvāstivāda-vinaya*. Yijing seems to have used "*Tridaṇḍaka*" and "sūtra on impermanence" interchangeably. Moreover, as Schopen mentions in his endnote (1992, 33), the Buddha is said in the same Vinaya to have pronounced "teachings connected with impermanence" (*mi rtag pa dang ldan pa'i chos dag*) on the occasion of the funeral of his aunt, the nun Mahāprajāpatī.

The other instance of *wuchang jing* 無常經 without reference to the *Tridaṇḍaka* (*sanqi* 三啟) is particularly interesting because the Tibetan here also mentions a "sūtra on impermanence" or "sūtra related to impermanence" (*mi rtag pa nyid dang ldan mdo sde—Vibhaṅga*, Sde dge 3, 'Dul ba, vol. *cha*, 188b4 = Taishō 1442.23.752b18). Here we see the nun Dharmadinnā, who leads a faction of nuns specializing in the recitation of sūtras, and the nun Mahāprajāpatī, whose faction specializes in meditation, residing in the same convent. In collegial fashion, Dharmadinnā suggests topics of meditation to the meditating nuns, and Mahāprajāpatī suggests to the reciting ones the recitation of the "sūtra on impermanence." As we will see, the recitation of the *Tridaṇḍaka* was recommended to occupy moments of monastic leisure or inactivity.

The manuscript of the *Tridaṇḍaka* anthology contains forty examples of the genre, only one of which contains as its nucleus a sūtra on impermanence (Matsuda 2019, 3). Although much more needs to be known about the anthology, its contents show that a wide variety of texts could fill the central portion of the *Tridaṇḍaka*. Nevertheless, for Yijing in particular there seems to have been a definite association between canonical texts on impermanence and the *Tridaṇḍaka*. Matsuda, in fact, remarking on the *āgamic* texts excerpted in the *Tridaṇḍaka*s of the anthology, says that "as to whether there is any point of commonality among these sūtras, it is a fact that, as used for recitation, many of these sūtras lament the impermanence of the world" (Matsuda 2019, 9; my translation).[19]

The Uses of the Tridaṇḍaka

In his endnote, Schopen outlines some of the uses of the *Tridaṇḍaka*, and their variety highlights the important role the recitation may have had. One prominent occasion for the recitation of the *Tridaṇḍaka* is in, or in connection with, the monastic funeral. This funerary usage of the *Tridaṇḍaka* is clearly prescribed in one passage of the *Kṣudrakavastu*;[20] the "teachings connected with impermanence" that the Buddha pronounced at the funerals of Mahāprajāpatī,[21] and the "sūtra on impermanence" that Yijing reports to be customary during monastic funerals in India may, as we have seen, also refer to the *Tridaṇḍaka*. Most interesting in this respect is the account of the recitation of the *Tridaṇḍaka* as a suitable moment for the distribution of the estate of a dead monk. In other instances, the *Tridaṇḍaka* is used to appease or respectfully acknowledge the protective deities that rule and inhabit features of nature when the latter are to be used for human benefit: the monk in charge of works (*navakarmika*) must recite the *Tridaṇḍaka* before the felling of a tree;[22] also, a monk must recite the *Tridaṇḍaka* in the place where he has decided to spend the night.[23] What immediately precedes this last passage also rules that a monk on his way must either be silent or pronounce an "uttering of the Law" (*chos kyi gtam*), a category that possibly encompasses the *Tridaṇḍaka*.

The *Tridaṇḍaka* must be also recited during certain periods of monastic inactivity: a passage from the *Poṣadhavastu* rules that during the alms rounds or reception of meals from the community during the *poṣadha*, the

19. The original Japanese reads それらの経典に何らかの共通点があるのかといえば、読誦用として世の無常を嘆く経典が多いのも事実である。

20. *Kṣudrakavastu*, Sde dge 6, 'Dul ba, vol. *tha*, 237a5 = Taishō 1451.24.287a1–2. The funereal significance of the *Tridaṇḍaka* is richly documented in Tokiya 1985 and Terasaki 1991.

21. Schopen 1992, 33.

22. *Vibhaṅga*, Sde dge 3, 'Dul ba, vol. *cha*, 280b4 = Taishō 1442.23.776a15; see also Schopen 2009, 367n17, and Tokiya 1985, 169.

23. *Kṣudrakavastu*, Sde dge 6, 'Dul ba, vol. *tha*, 198b2.

monks must recite a *Tridaṇḍaka*; this is opposed to their "doing as they wish" (*yathāsukhaṃ kurvanti*; *ci bder byed*) during those recesses of time.[24] Beyond the realm of the *Mūlasarvāstivāda-vinaya*, in one of the Chinese versions of the *Legend of Aśoka* we are presented with a monk that "recited a *Tridaṇḍaka* wherever he went;"[25] in the Chinese *Lives of Eminent Monks* (*Gaoseng zhuan* 高僧傳) we hear about one monk, Bo Faqiao, who entered a village while reciting a *Tridaṇḍaka* and miraculously maintained his recitation for ninety years.[26]

As already mentioned, the massive and labyrinthine *Abhidharmamahāvibhāṣā* of the Sarvāstivādins (Taishō 1545) contains an interesting passage that mentions the *Tridaṇḍaka*.[27] It makes a binary distinction within the category of "offering" (*gongyang* 供養): there is "offering of wealth" (*caiyang* 財養) and "offering of the Law" (*fayang* 法養). Examples of the former include offering food and drink, perfumes, and flowers; the main example of the latter is the recitation of the *Tridaṇḍaka* (三契聲, 三契經偈).

The *Mahāvibhāṣā* does not specify that such recitation must be restricted to monastics, and there is, in fact, one passage in the *Mūlasarvāstivāda-vinaya* where a monastic encourages also the laity to recite the *Tridaṇḍaka* (*Vibhaṅga*, Sde dge 3, 'Dul ba, vol. *cha*, 192b7–193a3 = Taishō 1442.23.753c18–25):[28] here the nun Dharmadinnā recommends to the troops of King Prasenajit to recite the *Tridaṇḍaka* "wherever they should camp for the night" (*gang dang gang du 'brang 'debs pa*, 每於宿) as a salient element of a liturgy that ensures victory in battle. This remarkable passage is too long to be translated here and, moreover, the Chinese and the Tibetan are not in full agreement. What they agree on is that during the night before the siege, the troops must wake, recite the *Tridaṇḍaka*, and invoke the gods; eventually the gods descend to the aid of the troops and endow them with superhuman might and appearance, at the sight of which the besieged enemy surrenders without battle.

This passage constitutes, however, an interesting exception to a common trait of the vignettes presented above—namely, the recitation of the *Tridaṇḍaka* is the department of monastics. Just like the monastic community, though, the army constitutes a corporate institution ruled by an inner

24. *Poṣadhavastu*, Hu-von Hinüber 1994, § 22.1, Dutt 1939–1959, III.4:80.5 = Sde dge 1, 'Dul ba, vol. *ka*, 136a5.

25. Taishō 2042.50.121b3–7. On this passage, see also Yinshun 1981, 330.

26. Taishō 2059.50.413b25–c4.

27. Taishō 1545.27.153b2–5 (Buddhavarman's translation); Taishō 1546.28.117b25–c4 (Xuanzang's 玄奘 translation).

28. For other accounts of this episode, see also Sasaki 1971, 574, and Liu 2018, 739.

disciplinary code. The recitation of the *Tridaṇḍaka* among the military may have been, as among monastics, a highly disciplined—or at least discipline-instilling—collective enterprise.

Aśvaghoṣa and the Tridaṇḍaka

The story of the circa eleventh-century *Tridaṇḍamālā* manuscript, containing forty *Tridaṇḍaka*s and now being prepared for publication by Matsuda and Hartmann, is quite riveting. In the early twentieth century, enterprising scholars from three countries, Giuseppe Tucci, Rāhula Sāṅkṛtyāyana, and Gendun Chopel (Dge 'dun chos 'phel), saw independently, in the monastery of Spos khang in Tibet, a Sanskrit manuscript titled *Tridaṇḍamālā*.[29] The manuscript is not listed in the catalogue made by Wang Sen 王森 of the Sanskrit manuscripts from Tibet once kept at the Palace of Nationalities in Beijing,[30] nor in the unpublished catalogue that Luo Zhao 罗照 made of the holdings of the Potala and Norbulingka *in situ* in the 1980s.[31] So it is possible that it has been destroyed or lost, a conjecture further supported by anecdotal information collected in Spos khang by Kanō Kazuo 加納和雄 (Matsuda 2019, 2). Tucci's photographs of the manuscript are preserved, respectively, in Göttingen—of only seven folios (Bandurski 1994, 79)—and Rome—of all but one folio (Sferra 2008, § 47).[32] It was only in 2018 that Matsuda became interested in the manuscript and identified the photos of the *Tridaṇḍamālā* manuscript after sorting out some labeling errors (Matsuda 2019, 2).

That the colophon of the manuscript attributes the work to Aśvaghoṣa, "a *śākyabhikṣu*" and a "Sarvāstivādin," has been known since Sāṅkṛtyāyana's 1938 report on Sanskrit manuscripts in Tibet (Sāṅkṛtyāyana 1938, 160). What has only emerged now with the study of the photographs of the manuscript is that the *Tridaṇḍaka*s therein often do contain excerpts extracted from known works of Aśvaghoṣa, sometimes providing the lost Sanskrit text of substantial parts of his *Buddhacarita* (Matsuda 2019; 2020). Nevertheless, as scholars begin to unravel the mysteries and complexities of this rich manuscript, the role of Aśvaghoṣa in the composition of the anthology remains elusive, also because some of the identified quotations in the anthology belong not to

29. See Sāṅkṛtyāyana 1938, 139, 157–160, and Gendun Chopel 2014, 38.

30. Wang 2006.

31. Luo [1982?].

32. For more information on the photographs, see note 6 in Hartmann's contribution in this volume.

the works of Aśvaghoṣa but to those of Āryaśūra and Gopadatta (Matsuda 2019, 8).

Long ago, Lin (1949, 304) had already identified four verses of Yijing's *Tridaṇḍaka* that closely match others from Aśvaghoṣa's *Buddhacarita* and *Saundarananda*.[33] Weller (1950, 304–305), reviewing Lin's *Aide-mémoire de la vraie loi*, observed that the fact that the work contains verses from Aśvaghoṣa does not make it a work of Aśvaghoṣa, but he did not provide any other support for his curt dismissal of the possibility of Aśvaghoṣa's authorship. When Yijing talks about Aśvaghoṣa having "collected and arranged" (*jizhi* 集置) or "collected and composed" (*jizao* 集造) the metrical portions that frame the sūtra proper, could he have meant that Aśvaghoṣa had drawn from his own works?

An additional riddle is the fact that the eleventh *tridaṇḍaka* of the Spos khang manuscript, of which Prof. Matsuda kindly shared a preliminary transcription, overlaps, but only partially, with the *Tridaṇḍaka* translated by Yijing, with the central "sūtra on impermanence" and third section accounting for most of the direct parallelism. The fluidity involved here should not be surprising if one considers that the *Tridaṇḍaka* may have been nothing but a template whose slots could be filled with texts according to need and circumstance. Yet now various pieces of evidence point in the direction of Aśvaghoṣa—Yijing's testimony, the colophon of the Spos khang manuscript, the quotations from the *Buddhacarita* and the *Saundarananda* both in the translated *Tridaṇḍaka* and in the Spos khang manuscript—and the role that the celebrated poet may have had is an exciting question to which a comprehensive study of the Spos khang manuscript may offer new answers. One wonders if what was initially a work of Aśvaghoṣa eventually became a genre whose future developments and ancillary works were later attributed to the famous creator of the seminal work or corpus.[34]

33. I.9 = *Buddhacarita* 20.36 (Johnston 1937, 53); III.7 = *Saundarananda* 5.27 (Matsunami 1981); III.10 = *Saundarananda* 15.34 (Matsunami 1981); III.11 = *Buddhacarita* 6.46 (Johnston 1935–1936). The verse numbers of Yijing's *Tridaṇḍaka* correspond to those that I have adopted in my English translation included in the appendix below.

34. We might remark here in passing that Dalton (2016) and Doney (2018) have dealt with an interesting Tibetan text from Dunhuang titled *Rgyud chags gsum pa*, which, as we have seen, is the term that regularly renders the Sanskrit *tridaṇḍaka* in the Tibetan translation of the *Mūlasarvāstivāda-vinaya*. According to Dalton's analysis, this *Tridaṇḍaka* of tantric affiliation has elements like its tripartite overarching structure and the general theme of praise of the Three Jewels; distinctly Tibetan innovations seem to be the inclusion of praises to the local gods and to the Tibetan emperor. We will see below how, according to Kuiji, Indic *Tridaṇḍaka*s were the inspiration for poetic compositions in China. This Tibetan offshoot underscores the fact that

The *Tridaṇḍaka* was awarded, together with the recitation of the *Proclamation of the Qualities of the Teacher [= the Buddha]*,[35] a special status in the context of monastic recitation of the (Mūla)Sarvāstivādins. The Buddha is said to have allowed these two recitations to be chanted according to a special style, "measured intonation" (*svaragupti*; *skad kyi gtang rag gis*, *yinyong sheng*; 吟詠聲),[36] which was allegedly inspired by the recitation styles of non-Buddhist religious groups and was sufficiently melodic and ornamental to mislead the householder Anāthapiṇḍada into thinking that the Jetavana vihāra, which he had approached while the monks rehearsed the *Tridaṇḍaka*, had become either "the school of a musician" (*rol mo mkhan gyi brang*) or "the city of the gandharvas" (乾闥婆城) (*Kṣudrakavastu*, Sde dge 6, 'Dul ba, vol. *tha*, 41b4–44b6 = Taishō 1451.24.223b17–29); the gandharvas are, of course, the celestial musicians and synonymous with music. In China, the *Tridaṇḍaka* may in fact have been known mostly as a musical genre rather than a poetic one: commenting on a verse of Kumārajīva's *Lotus Sūtra*, the learned exegete Kuiji 窺基 (632–682) describes the *Tridaṇḍaka* (*sanqi*$_2$ 三契) as a heptatonic (*qisheng* 七聲)[37] form of religious song from the "western countries" that inspired the composition of similar songs in China.[38] He adds that the legendary śrāvaka Śroṇa Koṭīkarṇa, known also elsewhere for his musical skills,[39] is said to have practiced it.

The *Tridaṇḍaka* and the *Proclamation of the Qualities of the Teacher* may have been especially suited for artistic expression. In regard to the latter, one is inevitably reminded of the obscure origins of the Buddhist *stotra*, which erupts onto the literary landscape of ancient India already mature in the

the literary fortune of the *Tridaṇḍaka* in Buddhist Asia deserves more research and a separate treatment.

35. On the *Proclamation of the Qualities of the Teacher*, see another substantial note in Schopen 1996, 95–96n34.

36. Liu (2018) has richly expounded on the difference between spoken recitation and chanting in many Buddhist monastic traditions and has laid a special emphasis on the treatment of the *Tridaṇḍaka* in the *Mūlasarvāstivāda-vinaya*. Especially useful for the problem that interests us here is Liu's persuasive identification of the term *svaragupti* (occurring as such, among extant Indic texts, only in the *Vinayasūtra*) as the original Sanskrit expression that underlies the Chinese and Tibetan renderings that Schopen has rendered as "measured intonation" (pp. 728–730).

37. Heptatonic systems of musical scales are well attested for classical India, as also among the Tocharians (Widdess 1995, 15). Classical Chinese music theory is based, by contrast, in a pentatonic scale system still practiced today.

38. Taishō 1723.34.727b19–24.

39. Demiéville 1929, 93b.

works of Mātṛceta but whose origins may have been in ritual recitations that became increasingly elaborate and fit for literary experimentation. Perhaps rushing to conclusions, but following a similar trend of thought, Demiéville squarely identified Mātṛceta's *Śatapañcāśatkastotra* with an example of the *Proclamation of the Qualities of the Teacher* (Demiéville 1929, 94a). Yijing complains at one point in his *Record* about the fact that very little by way of good Indian poetry had reached China.[40] It is in fact remarkable that the very two Indian poetic texts of artistic intent that Yijing translated into Chinese,[41] the *Tridaṇḍaka* attributed to Aśvaghoṣa and Mātṛceta's *Śatapañcāśatka*, fit so nicely as possible instances of the *Tridaṇḍaka* and the *Proclamation of the Qualities of the Teacher*, the ubiquitous liturgical pair of recitations in the *Mūlasarvāstivāda-vinaya*.

Conclusions and Añjali

By way of concluding remarks to these disjointed addenda, I would draw the reader's attention to a number of points. Schopen's conjecture that the *Tridaṇḍaka* was a formulary—a template—rather than a specific text has been corroborated by the Spos khang *Tridaṇḍamālā*. In the case of Yijing, though, he seems to have had in mind, at least as the most venerable exemplar of the genre, a text on the topic of impermanence whose authorship, arrangement, or compilation he attributed to Aśvaghoṣa. The poet's involvement in the creation or practice of the *Tridaṇḍaka* seems now more likely than it did almost eight decades ago when the most devoted scholar of his work, E. H. Johnston, declared emphatically that the Spos khang manuscript, of which he knew only the colophon and a few brief excerpts, was unrelated to the author of the *Buddhacarita* and the *Saundarananda* (Johnston 1939, 13). I would also like to remark in passing that all the material that I have considered here is in some way or other related to the (Mūla)Sarvāstivāda: the *Tridaṇḍaka* may have been a distinctly sectarian tradition.

The material I have presented here represents only a humble set of marginalia to an endnote authored long ago by the honoree of this volume. Aspiring, as I do, to acquiring in my writing at least a fraction of his deep sense of struc-

40. Taishō 2125.54.227c6; English translation in Takakusu 1896, 158.

41. I have excluded from the category of "poetic texts with artistic intent" Yijing's translation of the *Vinayakārikā* (Taishō 1459), which aligns more closely with the tradition of didactic mnemonic verse (*kārikā*) than with the more ornate and artistically minded texts treated in this discussion.

ture, I offer this unstructured *tridaṇḍaka*-potpourri as a token of my gratitude and deep affection.

Appendix: The Tridaṇḍaka *Attributed by Yijing to Aśvaghoṣa*

This *Tridaṇḍaka* is preserved in several manuscript and printed witnesses.[42] A critical edition is also a desideratum for the future. For the purposes of this article, I have translated from the second Korean canon as presented in Taishō 801. Readers are encouraged also to see Charles Willemen's translation (2019, 68–72); the discrepancies between the two translations illustrate clearly the difficulties involved in deciphering Yijing's terse poetic idiom.[43]

> I bow to and take refuge in that unsurpassed man,
> always taking the magnificent vow of the great compassion,
> who, ferrying living creatures through the stream of birth and death,
> makes them reach the quiet place of nirvāṇa, ||I.1||[44]
> who performed the great departure, who resisted the lack of self-restraint tirelessly,
> who, through his wholehearted effort, his devices, and the power of his right wisdom,
> benefited himself as he benefited others, being perfect at both,
> who, for these reasons is called tamer of gods and men. ||I.2||
> I bow to and take refuge in the wonderful treasure of the Law,
> which with three, with four, with two, and with five discloses perfect understanding,
> which with seven and eight opens the door of the four truths,[45]
> all of whose practitioners attain the other shore of the unconditioned. ||I.3||
> The rain of the Law from the cloud of the Law soaks all creatures;

42. See pp. 321–325 above.

43. For an edition and Japanese translation of the *Anityatā-sūtra* from the eleventh *tridaṇḍa* of the *Tridaṇḍamālā*, see Matsuda, Demoto, Ueno, Tanaka, and Fukita 2024. For a recent translation of two versions of the *Anityatā-sūtra* from the Tibetan canon, see Skilling 2024, 131–132 and 137–140. For the Sanskrit text, see Yamada 1972.

44. I have divided the text into three sections, each identified with a Roman numeral. Verses within each of those sections are numbered instead with Arabic numerals.

45. Willemen (2019, 68) reads this verse, somewhat deictically, as a clear reference to several doctrinal categories. I feel inclined, instead, to leave it as a numerical riddle in the vein of the one in Aśvaghoṣa's *Buddhacarita* 2.41 (Johnston 1935–1936).

it can remove every suffering and purify illnesses;
it tames the disciple unwilling to transform;
it guides according to the occasion, without coercion. ||I.4||
I bow to and take refuge in the true and holy Assembly,
superior men in the eight stages[46] who released themselves from pollution;
the diamond mace of their knowledge smashes the mount of impiety;
it severs forever the links that have no beginning. ||I.5||
From the Deer Park to the Twin Trees,
they followed the Buddha's lifetime of spreading the true teachings.
When the conversions in the stories[47] named after each of them were achieved,
they turned their body to ashes and annihilated their consciousness, resting in no-rebirth. ||I.6||
I bow to and honor together these Three Venerable Jewels:
these are said to be the direct cause of universal salvation;
they prevent from drowning the fools lost in birth and death,
allowing each to escape and to attain enlightenment. ||I.7||
Those who are born will return to death,
comeliness changes and declines,
strength will be overcome by disease:
there is no one who can avert that. ||I.8||
Picture the great, wonderful mountain, Sumeru:
the eons will erode and scatter it.
The deep, bottomless ocean
will also be once dried up. ||I.9||
The great earth, the sun and moon
in time will recede into extinction.
There has not existed a thing
not devoured by impermanence. ||I.10||
Above, there is the place without thought;
below, the wheel-turning monarch,

46. The stages of "stream enterer" (*śrotaāpanna*), "once returner" (*sakṛdāgāmin*), "nonreturner" (*anāgāmin*), and arhat, each divided into one phase of ascent and one of consummation.

47. Other understandings of this verse are possible. I have interpreted *benyuan* 本緣 here in the common sense of "story, *avadāna*," although also "origin, cause" is possible. Willemen here takes this very differently: "Each in accordance with his former causality has practiced conversion."

the seven jewels constantly following his body,[48]
a thousand sons always surrounding him. ||I.11||
When his life be finished,
he will not be able to retain it even for a moment,
he will return to drift in the ocean of death,
about to receive sufferings according to causality. ||I.12||
The cycle of rebirth in the three worlds
is like the well-wheel
and also like the silkworm weaving her cocoon:
she spits silk to entangle herself. ||I.13||
All the unsurpassed World-Honored Ones,
those Enlightened Alone, and the Listeners
all had to relinquish their impermanent bodies:
how much more the common man? ||I.14||
Parents, wife, children,
siblings, and relatives:
seeing birth and death standing in between
how can one not be troubled? ||I.15||
Therefore all people are advised
to listen attentively to the true Law,
to abandon together this impermanent place,
and to march toward the immortal gate. ||I.16||
The Buddha's Law is like nectar,[49]
it relieves the heat and gives coolness.
With wholehearted effort one must listen well to it;
it can extinguish every affliction. ||I.17||

Thus have I heard. Once the *bhagavat*[50] stayed in Śrāvastī in the garden of the Jetavana of Anāthapiṇḍada. Then the Buddha told the monks: "There are three things that are not dear, lacking luster, unthinkable, disagreeable to the world. What are the three? Old age, disease, and death. Monks, these [things], old age, disease, and death, are verily not dear, verily lacking luster, verily unthinkable,

48. In all likelihood a reference to a list of seven "treasures" (*ratna*) of the universal monarch (*cakravartin*), whose most standard—although not fixed—members are wheel, elephant, horse, gem, queen, financier (*gṛhapati*), and general.

49. *Ganlu* 甘露 = *amṛta* "nectar, ambrosia."

50. *Bojiafan* (Middle Chinese **bagaban*) 薄伽梵, a rendering of the nominative singular form *bhagavān* from *bhagavat* "blessed, holy."

verily disagreeable to the world. If the world was without old age, disease, and death, the Tathāgata, Arhat, perfectly enlightened Buddha would not have gone into the world to preach to the creatures the Law and the matter of Discipline that he realized. For this reason, one must know that old age, disease, and death are not dear, lacking luster, unthinkable, disagreeable to the world. Because of these three things, the Tathāgata, Arhat, perfectly enlightened Buddha went into the world to preach to the creatures the Law and the matter of Discipline that he realized." Then the World-Honored One spoke again in verse:

"All external things, in all their ornament and color, will return to decay;
the body will age and change in the same way.
Only the victorious Law does not fade:
all the wise that there are should ponder [this] well. ||II.1||
These [things], old age, disease, and death, are all generally hateful,
their sight is loathsome, extremely despicable.
The face of youth lasts a moment:
before long it turns to decrepitude. ||II.2||
Imagine a lifespan that would last a hundred years:
at the end it would come, inevitably, under the sway of impermanence.
Old age, sickness, and death always follow
and always bring harm to creatures." ||II.3||

Then the World-Honored One finished preaching this sūtra. All the monks, nāgas, yakṣas, gandharvas, and asuras were enthused and determined to carry out the teaching.

Always pursuing the objects of the senses
does not lead to anything good.
Why, sheltering body and life,
do you not see death coming for conquest? ||III.1||
Breath, the very faculty of life, is spent,
the limbs disjointed.
Sufferings and death, together,
at this time can only in vain be cursed. ||III.2||
Both eyes turned upward:

the blade of death falls according to the deeds.[51]
Perception and confusion
are unable to redeem each other. ||III.3||
The chest is urged by a continuous, long cough,
short breath and dryness in the throat.
The king of death urges the Controller of Fate;[52]
the relatives try in vain to guard [the dying]. ||III.4||
All perception dimmed,
one enters a city of dangers.
Relatives and friends have all left.
[The moribund] comes to terms with departing, pulled by a rope.
||III.5||
When one is about to come to King Yama
it is according to the deeds that one receives a retribution.
Victorious causes engender the good path;
evil deeds precipitate one to hell. ||III.6||
No clear eyesight surpasses wisdom;
no darkness surpasses foolishness;
sickness is an invincible enemy;
no fear surpasses death. ||III.7||
All those with life must die:
those who crudely commit offenses stab their own bodies.
One must diligently ponder on the three kinds of deeds
and always cultivate merit and knowledge. ||III.8||
Relatives will go away;
wealth will be in someone else's power;
but when one upholds the roots of good,
the dangerous road will be filled with sustenance. ||III.9||
Just as on the road one stops by a tree,
resting briefly, not staying long,
chariot, horses, and so on, up to wife and child
do not last; they are all like this. ||III.10||
Like birds that roost together,

51. *Ye* 業 = *karman* "deed."

52. The "Controller of Fate" (*siming* 伺命) is, according to Zhang (2014, 115) an otherworldly "official who is in charge of people's lives," and who stems from indigenous Chinese tradition and can be traced back at least to the third-century BCE poetic collection *Chuci* 楚辭 (see p. 132, especially n173). Willemen here takes the words in their individual meaning (2019, 70) and has, very differently: "The king of death is on the lookout for your life."

gather at night, and part at dawn,
death separates those who love each other:
such is the nature of separation. ||III.11||
There is only the Buddha's enlightenment:
it is the true place to rely upon.
I have abridged according to the sūtra:
the wise should ponder it well. ||III.12||
Gods, asuras, yakṣas, and the like:
come to hear the Law with uplifted minds!
Protect the Law of the Buddha, make it last long!
May each [of you] diligently practice the teachings of the World-Honored One. ||III.13||
All the listening disciples that came to this place,
some on earth and some dwelling in heaven.
May they uphold the mind of compassion in the world of men;
day and night, may their whole selves take refuge in the Law. ||III.14||
May there be peace in every world.
May unlimited merit and wisdom fill the living.
May all the evil deeds be cleansed.
May one drive away sufferings and take refuge in perfect extinction. ||III.15||
Always using the perfume of the discipline to anoint the body brightly,
constantly keeping the garment of concentration to provide for oneself,
with the wonderful flower of enlightenment as universal ornament,
wherever one dwells [let there be] abiding ease. ||III.16||

Works Cited

Abbreviations

GBM *Gilgit Buddhist Manuscripts*. Edited by Lokesh Chandra and Raghu Vira. 10 vols. Śata-piṭaka Series 10. New Delhi: International Academy of Indian Culture, 1939–1974.

Peking Cat. *The Tibetan Tripitaka: Peking Edition: Catalogue & Index*. Edited by Daisetz T. Suzuki. Tokyo and Kyoto: Tibetan Tripitaka Research Institute, 1961.

Sde dge *The Sde-dge Mtshal-par Bka'-'gyur: A Facsimile Edition of the 18th Century Redaction of Si-tu Chos-kyi-'byuṅ-gnas Prepared under the Direction of H.H. the 16th Rgyal-dbaṅ Karma-pa.* 103 vols. Delhi: Delhi Karmapae Chodhey Gyalwae Sungrab Partun Khang, 1976–1979.

Taishō *Taishō shinshū daizōkyō* 大正新脩大藏經 (*The Buddhist Canon in Chinese, Newly Edited in the Taishō Era*). Edited by Takakusu Junjirō 高楠順次郎 and Watanabe Kaikyoku 渡邊海旭. 100 vols. Tokyo: Taishō issaikyō kankōkai 大正一切經刊行會, 1924–1935.

Tōhoku *A Complete Catalogue of the Tibetan Buddhist Canons (Bkaḥ-ḥgyur and Bstan-ḥgyur).* Edited by Hakuju Ui, Munetada Suzuki, Yenshō Kanakura, and Tōkan Tada. Tokyo: Tōhoku Imperial University, 1934.

Bandurski, Frank. 1994. "Übersicht über die Göttinger Sammlungen der von Rāhula Sāṅkṛtyāyana in Tibet aufgefundenen buddhistischen Sanskrit-Texte (Funde buddhistischer Sanskrit-Handschriften, III)." In *Untersuchungen zur buddhistischen Literatur*, 9–126. Sanskrit-Wörterbuch der buddhistischen Texte aus den Turfan-Funden, Beiheft 5. Göttingen: Vandenhoeck & Ruprecht.

Böhtlingk, Otto, and Rudolph Roth. 1853–1875. *Sanskrit-Wörterbuch.* 7 vols. Saint Petersburg: Imperatorskai͡a akademii͡a nauk.

Chen, Jinhua. 2007. *Philosopher, Practitioner, Politician: The Many Lives of Fazang (643–712).* Leiden: Brill.

Choi, Jin-kyoung. 2012. "The Two *Lohitya-sūtra*s in the Dīrghāgama Manuscript." *Indogaku bukkyōgaku kenkyū* 印度學佛教學研究 (*Journal of Indian and Buddhist Studies*) 60.3: 76–79.

Dalton, Jacob P. 2016. "How *Dhāraṇī*s WERE Proto-Tantric: Liturgies, Ritual Manuals, and the Origins of the Tantras." In *Tantric Traditions in Transmission and Translation*, edited by David B. Gray and Ryan Richard Overbey, 199–229. New York: Oxford University Press.

Demiéville, Paul. 1929. "Bombai." In *Hôbôgirin: Dictionnaire encyclopédique du bouddhisme d'après les sources chinoises et japonaises. Premier fascicule: A–Bombai*, edited by Sylvain Lévi, J. Takakusu, and Paul Demiéville, 93–96. Tokyo: Maison Franco-Japonaise.

Doney, Lewis. 2018. "Imperial Gods: A Ninth-Century *Tridaṇḍaka* Prayer (*rGyud chags gsum*) from Dunhuang." *Central Asiatic Journal* 61.1: 71–101.

Dutt, Nalinaksha, ed. 1939–1959. *Gilgit Manuscripts.* 4 vols. in multiple parts. Srinagar and Calcutta: Calcutta Oriental Press.

Edgerton, Franklin. 1953. *Buddhist Hybrid Sanskrit Grammar and Dictionary*, vol. 2: *Dictionary.* New Haven: Yale University Press.

Gendun Chopel (Dge 'dun chos 'phel). 2014. *Grains of Gold: Tales of a Cosmopolitan Traveler.* Translated by Thupten Jinpa and Donald S. Lopez Jr. Chicago: The University of Chicago Press.

Harrison, Paul. 2014. "Earlier Inventories of Sanskrit Manuscripts in Tibet: A Synoptic List of Titles." *From Birch Bark to Digital Data: Recent Advances in Buddhist Manuscript Research. Papers Presented at the Conference Indic Buddhist Manuscripts: The State of the Field, Stanford, June 15–19 2009*, edited by Paul Harrison and Jens-Uwe Hartmann, 279–290. Vienna: Verlag der Österreichischen Akademie der Wissenschaften.

Hu-von Hinüber, Haiyan. 1994. *Das Poṣadhavastu: Vorschriften für die buddhistische Beichtfeier im Vinaya der Mūlasarvāstivādins*. Studien zur Indologie und Iranistik, Monographie 13. Reinbek: Wezler.

Johnston, E. H. 1935–1936. *The Buddhacarita: Or, Acts of the Buddha*. 2 vols. Panjab University Oriental Publications 31–32. Calcutta: Baptist Mission Press, published for The University of the Panjab, Lahore.

———. 1937. "The Buddha's Mission and Last Journey: *Buddhacarita*, xv to xxviii." *Acta Orientalia* 15: 26–62, 85–111, 231–252, 253–292.

———. 1939. "The Tridaṇḍamālā of Aśvaghoṣa." *Journal of the Bihar and Orissa Research Society* 25.1: 11–14.

Karashima, Seishi. 2017. "Some Folios of the *Tathāgataguṇajñānācintyaviṣayāvatāra* and *Dvādaśadaṇḍakanāmāṣṭaśatavimalīkaraṇā* in the Kurita Collection." *International Journal of Buddhist Thought & Culture* 27.1: 11–44.

Kern, Hendrik. 1891. *The Jātaka-Mālā or Bodhisattvāvadāna-Mālā*. Cambridge, MA: Harvard University Press.

La Vallée Poussin, Louis de. 1937. "Staupikam." *Harvard Journal of Asiatic Studies* 2.2: 276–289.

Lancaster, Lewis R., and Sung-bae Park. 1979. *The Korean Buddhist Canon: A Descriptive Catalogue*. Berkeley: University of California Press.

Lévi, Sylvain. 1915. "Sur la récitation primitive des textes bouddhiques." *Journal asiatique*, 11th ser., 5.3: 401–447.

Li, Rongxi, trans. 2000. *Buddhist Monastic Traditions of Southern Asia: A Record of the Inner Law Sent Home from the South Seas*. BDK English Tripiṭaka 93-I. Berkeley: Numata Center for Buddhist Translation and Research.

Lin, Li-Kouang. 1949. *L'aide-mémoire de la vraie loi (Saddharma-smṛtyupasthāna-sūtra): Recherches sur un Sūtra Développé du Petit Véhicule*. Paris: Adrien-Maisonneuve.

Liu, Cuilan. 2018. "Reciting, Chanting, and Singing: The Codification of Vocal Music in Buddhist Canon Law." *Journal of Indian Philosophy* 46.4: 713–752.

Luo Zhao 罗照. [1982?]. "Budala gong, Luobulinka suocang beiyejing mulu" 布达拉宫罗布林卡所藏贝叶经目录 (Catalogue of the Sanskrit Holdings of the Potala and Norbulingka Palaces). Unpublished manuscript.

Matsuda Kazunobu 松田和信. 2007. "Bonbun jō-agon no *Tridaṇḍi-sūtra* ni tsuite" 梵文長阿含の *Tridaṇḍi-sūtra* について (On the *Tridaṇḍi-sūtra* of the Sanskrit *Dīrghāgama*). *Indogaku bukkyōgaku kenkyū* 印度學佛教學研究 (*Journal of Indian and Buddhist Studies*) 54.2: 129–136.

———. 2019. "*Sankeishū* (*Tridaṇḍamālā*) ni okeru *Shōgikū-kyō* to *Buddacharita*" 三啓集（*Tridaṇḍamālā*）における勝義空経とブッダチャリタ (The *Paramārthaśūnyatā-sūtra* and the *Buddhacarita* in the *Tridaṇḍamālā*). *Indogaku bukkyōgaku kenkyū* 印度學佛教學研究 (*Journal of Indian and Buddhist Studies*) 68.1: 1–11.

———. 2020. "*Buddacharita* dai 15 shō '*Shotenbōrin*': bonbun tekisuto to wayaku" ブッダチャリタ第15章「初転法輪」：梵文テキストと和訳 (Sanskrit Text and Japanese Translation of the *Buddhacarita* Canto 15 'The First *Dharmacakrapravartana*'). *Bukkyō daigaku bukkyō gakkai kiyō* 佛教大学仏教学会紀要 (*Bulletin of the Association of Buddhist Studies, Bukkyo University*) 25: 27–44.

Matsuda Kazunobu 松田和信, Demoto Mitsuyo 出本充代, Ueno Makio 上野牧生, Tanaka Hironori 田中裕成, and Fukita Takanori 吹田隆徳. 2024. "Oi to byō to shi to: dai 11 sankeikyō *Mujō-kyō* no bonbun tekisuto to wayaku" 老いと病と死と：第11三啓経『無常経』の梵文テキストと和訳 (Aging, Illness and Death: Sanskrit Text and Japanese Translation of the 11th Tridaṇḍa *Anityatā-sūtra*). *Bukkyō daigaku bukkyō gakkai kiyō* 佛教大学仏教学会紀要 (*Bulletin of the Association of Buddhist Studies, Bukkyo University*) 29: 1–31.

Matsunami Seiren 松濤誠廉. 1981. *Memyō* Tansei naru Nanda 馬鳴端正なる難陀 (*Aśvaghoṣa's* Saundarananda). Tokyo: Sankibō busshorin 山喜房佛書林.

Nakamura Hajime 中村元. 1975. *Bukkyōgo daijiten* 佛教語大辞典 (*Great Dictionary of Buddhist Vocabulary*). Tokyo: Tōkyō shoseki 東京書籍.

Nattier, Jan. 2003. *A Few Good Men: The Bodhisattva Path according to* The Inquiry of Ugra (Ugraparipṛcchā). Studies in the Buddhist Traditions. Honolulu: University of Hawai'i Press.

Olivelle, Patrick. 1986–1987. *Renunciation in Hinduism: A Medieval Debate*. 2 vols. Vienna: Institut für Indologie der Universität Wien.

———. 2005. *Manu's Code of Law: A Critical Edition and Translation of the Mānava-Dharmaśāstra*. South Asia Research. New York: Oxford University Press.

Pulleyblank, Edwin George. 1991. *Lexicon of Reconstructed Pronunciation in Early Middle Chinese, Late Middle Chinese, and Early Mandarin*. Vancouver: University of British Columbia Press.

Sakaki Ryōzaburō 榊亮三郎. 1916–1925. *Bon-zō-kan-wa shiyaku taikō hon'yaku myōgi taishū (bon・zō sakuin)* 梵藏漢和四譯對校飜譯名義大集（梵・藏索引）(Mahāvyutpatti: *A Sanskrit-Tibetan-Chinese-Japanese Quadrilingual Collation [with Sanskrit and Tibetan Indices]*). 2 vols. Kyoto: Shingonshū kyōto daigaku 真言宗京都大学.

Salomon, Richard. 1998. *Indian Epigraphy: A Guide to the Study of Inscriptions in Sanskrit, Prakrit, and the Other Indo-Aryan Languages*. South Asia Research Series. New York: Oxford University Press.

Sāṅkṛtyāyana, Rāhula. 1938. "Search for Sanskrit Mss. in Tibet." *Journal of the Bihar and Orissa Research Society* 24.4: 137–163.

Sasaki Kyōgo 佐々木教悟. 1971. "Konpon-setsuissaiu-bu to sankei *Mujō-kyō* ni tsuite" 根本説一切有部と三啓無常経について (On the *Mūlasarvāstivāda-vinaya* and the *Tridaṇḍaka/Anityatā-sūtra*). *Indogaku bukkyōgaku kenkyū* 印度學佛教學研究 (*Journal of Indian and Buddhist Studies*) 19.2: 570–577.

Schopen, Gregory. 1992. "On Avoiding Ghosts and Social Censure: Monastic Funerals in the *Mūlasarvāstivāda-vinaya*." *Journal of Indian Philosophy* 20.1: 1–39. Reprinted in Schopen 1997, 204–237.

———. 1996. "The Lay Ownership of Monasteries and the Role of the Monk in

Mūlasarvāstivādin Monasticism." *Journal of the International Association of Buddhist Studies* 19.1: 81–126. Reprinted in Schopen 2004, 219–259.

———. 1997. *Bones, Stones, and Buddhist Monks: Collected Papers on the Archaeology, Epigraphy, and Texts of Monastic Buddhism in India*. Studies in the Buddhist Traditions. Honolulu: University of Hawai'i Press.

———. 2004. *Buddhist Monks and Business Matters: Still More Papers on Monastic Buddhism in India*. Studies in the Buddhist Traditions. Honolulu: University of Hawai'i Press.

———. 2009. "The Urban Buddhist Nun and a Protective Rite for Children in Early North India." In *Pāsādikadānaṁ: Festschrift für Bhikkhu Pāsādika*, edited by Martin Straube, Roland Steiner, Jayandra Soni, Michael Hahn, and Mitsuyo Demoto, 359–380. Indica et Tibetica 52. Marburg: Indica et Tibetica Verlag. Reprinted in Schopen 2014, 3–22.

———. 2014. *Buddhist Nuns, Monks, and Other Worldly Matters: Recent Papers on Monastic Buddhism in India*. Studies in the Buddhist Traditions. Honolulu: University of Hawai'i Press.

Senart, Émile. 1890–1907. *Le Mahâvastu*. 3 vols. Paris: Imprimerie Nationale.

Sferra, Francesco. 2008. *Sanskrit Texts from Giuseppe Tucci's Collection: Part I*. Manuscripta Buddhica 1. Serie Orientale Roma 104. Rome: Istituto Italiano per l'Africa e l'Oriente.

Skilling, Peter. 2024. *Buddha's Words for Tough Times: An Anthology*. New York: Wisdom Publications.

Stchoupak, Nadine, Luigia Nitti, and Louis Renou. 1932. *Dictionnaire sanskrit-français*. Paris: J. Maisonneuve.

Takakusu, J. 1896. *A Record of the Buddhist Religion as Practised in India and the Malay Archipelago (A.D. 671–695) by I-tsing*. Oxford: The Clarendon Press.

Tanaka Hironori 田中裕成. 2020. "Sankeishū ni osamerareta *Saundarananda* no idoku ni tsuite" 三啓集に収められたサウンダラナンダの異読について (Variant Readings of the *Saundarananda* as Presented in the *Tridaṇḍamālā*). *Bukkyō daigaku bukkyō gakkai kiyō* 佛教大学仏教学会紀要 (*Bulletin of the Association of Buddhist Studies, Bukkyo University*) 25: 91–110.

Terasaki Keidō 寺崎敬道. 1991. "Konpon-setsuissaiu-bu ni tsuite no ichi kōsatsu: sankei *Mujō-kyō* no shūkyōteki imi" 根本説一切有部についての一考察：三啓無常経の宗教的意味 (A Study of the Mūlasarvāstivāda School: The Religious Meaning of the *Tridaṇḍaka/Anityatā-sūtra*). *Indogaku bukkyōgaku kenkyū* 印度學佛教學研究 (*Journal of Indian and Buddhist Studies*) 39.2: 566–568.

Tokiya Yukinori 釈舎幸紀. 1985. "Konpon-setsuissaiu-bu ni in'yō sareru *Mujō-kyō*" 根本説一切有部に引用される無常経 (The *Anityatā-sūtra* Quoted by the Mūlasarvāstivādins). *Indogaku bukkyōgaku kenkyū* 印度學佛教學研究 (*Journal of Indian and Buddhist Studies*) 34.1: 168–173.

Vogel, Claus, and Klaus Wille. 1992. "Some More Fragments of the Pravrajyāvastu Portion of the Vinayavastu Manuscript Found Near Gilgit." In *Sanskrit-Texte aus dem buddhistischen Kanon: Neuentdeckungen und Neueditionen II*, 65–109. Sanskrit-Wörterbuch der buddhistischen Texte aus den Turfan-Funden, Beiheft 4. Göttingen: Vandenhoeck & Ruprecht. Reprinted in Claus Vogel and Klaus Wille, eds. and trans. 2014. *The Pravrajyāvastu of the Mūlasarvāstivāda Vinaya*. Göttingen: Akademie der Wissenschaften zu Göttingen, Sanskrit-Wörterbuch der buddhistischen Texte aus den Turfan-Funden, 43–90. https://rep.adw-goe.de/handle/11858/00-001S-0000-0023-9A04-C.

Wang Sen 王森, comp. 2006. "Catalogue of the 259 Sanskrit Manuscripts Once Kept in the Palace of Culture of the Nationalities in Peking," appendix to "Some Remarks on the Sanskrit Manuscript of the Mūlasarvāstivāda-Prātimokṣasūtra Found in Tibet" by Haiyan Hu-von Hinüber. In *Jaina-itihāsa-ratna: Festschrift für Gustav Roth zum 90. Geburtstag*, edited by Ute Hüsken, Petra Kieffer-Pülz, and Anne Peters, 297–334. Marburg: Indica et Tibetica Verlag.

Weller, Friedrich. 1950. Review of *L'aide-mémoire de la vraie loi: Recherches sur un sūtra développé du petit véhicule*, by Lin Li-Kouang. *Sinologica* 2: 301–305. Reprinted in Friedrich Weller, *Kleine Schriften*, 1:606–610. Stuttgart: Franz Steiner Verlag, 1987.

Widdess, Richard. 1995. *The Rāgas of Early Indian Music: Modes, Melodies and Musical Notations from the Gupta Period to c. 1250*. Oxford: Clarendon Press.

Willemen, Charles. 2019. "Yijing's *Scriptural Text about Impermanence* (*T.* 801)." In *Methods in Buddhist Studies: Essays in Honor of Richard K. Payne*, edited by Scott A. Mitchell and Natalie Fisk Quli, 67–76. London: Bloomsbury.

Yamada, Isshi. 1972. "*Anityatāsūtra*." *Indogaku bukkyōgaku kenkyū* 印度學佛教學研究 (*Journal of Indian and Buddhist Studies*) 20.2: 996–1001.

Yinshun 印順. 1981. *Shuoyiqieyou bu weizhu de lunshu he lunshi zhi yanjiu* 說一切有部為主的論書和論師之研究 (*Research on the Treatises and Treatise Writers That Focused on the Sarvāstivāda*). Taipei: Huiri jiangtang 慧日講堂.

Zhang, Zhenjun. 2014. *Buddhism and Tales of the Supernatural in Early Medieval China: A Study of Liu Yiqing's (403–444)* Youming lu. Leiden: Brill.

Saṅghabheda: Monastic and Political

Patrick Olivelle

GREGORY SCHOPEN, a friend and colleague for close to four decades, is known for illuminating Buddhist texts and practices by looking at them through lenses provided by non-Buddhist sources less familiar to Buddhologists. His use of Brahmanical legal texts, the Dharmaśāstras, to understand and explain Buddhist Vinaya rules, especially those in the Vinaya of the Mūlasarvāstivāda, intersects with my own work on ancient Indian law. So, this paper is a small offering to the master who has taught us all to think outside the box.

In the vocabulary of Buddhist Vinaya, *saṅghabheda* is a technical term referring to the behavior of a monk that causes a conflict and dissension within a particular saṅgha or monastic community. Such a monk is called a *saṅghabhedaka* and is guilty of a *saṅghādisesa* offense and subject to punishment by the community. It is this *saṅghabheda* that has drawn the attention of scholars within the context of interpreting Aśoka's so-called Schism Edict.

In Buddhist studies, *saṅghabheda* is discussed primarily within the context of the Vinaya and its vocabulary. This paper attempts to bring other Buddhist and non-Buddhist sources that, I think, throw new light on the issue, or at least make us take a fresh look at the evidence. The central term *bheda* has been generally rendered "split" or "splitting," and less felicitously as "schism." Bechert (1982, 65) has shown the inaccuracy of the latter:

> It is now clear that *saṃghabheda* does not mean a "schism" in the sense known from Christian church history, where it nearly always implies dissensions in the interpretation of dogma. In Buddhist tradition, "splitting of the Sangha" always refers to matters of monastic discipline, because the validity of any *vinayakarma* depends on the validity of the *upasampadā* and the completeness of the bhikkhus within the *sīmā* during the performance of the particular ecclesiastic act.

I will attempt to show that "split"—in the sense of actually causing a separation—is also subject to misunderstanding. The only extra-Vinaya reference discussed in the literature I am aware of is the so-called Schism Edict of Aśoka, which deals with the Buddhist saṅgha and which also has several verbal forms of the roots √*bhid* and its cognate √*bhañj* but not the compound *saṅghabheda* itself. Much ink has been spilt over the interpretation of Aśoka's edict within the context of the Vinaya rules pertaining to *saṅghabheda* and the putative third council of Pāṭaliputra.[1] Indeed, the very misnomer "schism edict" is derived from a misunderstanding of the meaning of the term *bheda* that occurs in a spectrum of texts.

Even though, as Bechert's (1982) close study shows, Vinaya rules provide one significant lens through which to examine Aśoka's inscription, I think we need to cast our eyes more broadly to arrive at an adequate understanding of schism both in Aśoka and, perhaps, in the Vinaya itself. Norman ([1987] 1992, 210) also questions whether we can presume a strict adherence by Aśoka to Vinaya technical terminology: "What Bechert has not, however, shown beyond any shadow of doubt is that Aśoka was in fact using the words in their true Vinaya sense. It is not impossible that he was using them in a more general, less legalistic, sense."

There are two important documents dealing with *bheda* within a saṅgha, however, that are useful in this regard, and they have been totally and inexplicably ignored in scholarly discussions of *saṅghabheda*. The first is, in fact, a Buddhist text, the Pāli *Mahāparinibbāna-sutta*, which contains a long conversation between the Buddha and Vassakāra, a minister of King Ajātasattu, a conversation that focuses precisely on *saṅghabheda*. Although this text as currently preserved in the Pāli canon belongs to the Suttapiṭaka, in its original setting it was probably part of the Vinayapiṭaka, and it sets the scene for the rules of Vinaya.[2] The second, which sheds light on the import of the Vassakāra conversation, is Kauṭilya's *Arthaśāstra*. Its eleventh book is dedicated to discussing how a king can subvert and conquer a political saṅgha—that is, a confederacy.

1. For the use of Vinaya rules and vocabulary, see Bechert 1982 and 2001. Regarding the council of Pāṭaliputra, see Alsdorf 1959, Jayawickrama 1959, and Bechert's (1982, 62) discussion of their conclusions. Norman ([1987] 1992, 210) casts a skeptical eye on this claim: "There is no reference to the Third Council in the extant portions of the Schism Edict," and gives five possible reasons for this.

2. See Frauwallner 1956, and Lamotte's discussion of it ([1958] 1988, 176–178). For a discussion of the Pāli version of the Vassakāra episode, see Warder 1970, 67–69. Arguments for an early, perhaps pre-Mauryan, date for this text are given by von Hinüber 2008.

Kauṭilya's Arthaśāstra

I want to take up the *Arthaśāstra* first, because it gives the political science background to the Vassakāra conversation and the meanings of *saṅgha* and *bheda* within ancient Indian theories of political strategy. One issue that confronts us, however, is chronology. A large number of scholars have taken this text to have been authored by Cāṇakya, the prime minister to Candragupta, the founder of the Maurya dynasty at the end of the fourth century BCE and the grandfather of Aśoka. If we accept that date, then the *Arthaśāstra* broadly falls within the same chronological slot as the two other texts we are examining. But strong evidence places Kauṭilya sometime in the first century CE or thereabouts, several centuries after the two other documents, even though some of Kauṭilya's sources may predate him by several centuries.[3] I think, nevertheless, that, with respect to *saṅgha*, Kauṭilya is presenting established views of political science, views that probably long predated him. In fact, polities called saṅghas were already on the way out or even totally extinct during his time; we do not hear much about them in later literature. The views expressed in the *Arthaśāstra*, therefore, were probably the accepted political wisdom on the ways monarchs interacted with saṅgha polities. Kings knew how to deal with other kings, how to wage war against them. But they had difficulty figuring out the saṅgha polities.

First, the term *saṅgha* is not simply, and probably not originally, a term referring to the Buddhist monastic order. Indian legal literature uses several technical terms to refer to various kinds of associations, including those of artisans and merchants, terms such as *gaṇa*, *pūga*, *śreṇi*, and *saṅgha*. In ancient Indian political science, however, *saṅgha* referred more specifically to a particular kind of polity different from monarchy, a polity that was governed through consensus by leaders of extended family groups and can be called a confederacy. The eleventh book of the *Arthaśāstra* is named *saṅghavṛtta*, "Conduct Toward Confederacies." At the outset, Kauṭilya tells the king he is addressing, appropriately called *vijigīṣu*, "one bent on conquest," that a saṅgha is the most difficult polity to conquer: "Confederacies, because they are closely knit, are impervious to enemy assaults"—*saṃghā hi saṃhatatvād adhṛṣyāḥ pareṣām* (11.1.2). Note the close etymological connection between *saṅgha* and *saṃhata* ("closely knit"), both originating from *sam-√han*.

Kauṭilya uses the term *saṃhata* and its opposite *asaṃhata* frequently in various contexts. The former is used in at least two contexts, the first being

3. For detailed arguments in favor of this date, see Trautmann 1971, Olivelle 2013, and McClish 2019.

the close bond and unity among allies or chiefs within a kingdom. When traitorous chiefs band together (*saṃhata*) they pose a special danger to the king, and he is instructed not to confront them directly but to use "secret punishment"[4] to get rid of them (KAŚ 5.1.4). The fact they are *saṃhata* makes them especially dangerous and powerful, hence the need to deal with them surreptitiously and not in open conflict. At KAŚ 6.2.22 the term is applied to allies who are united and at 7.4.6 to the subjects or the constituents of a kingdom who are united. Another typical context for its use is an army. At 9.2.10, Kauṭilya says that when an army is *asaṃhata* because it is drawn from different places, enemies can divide it and sow dissension within it: it is thus *bhedya*, subject to internal conflict and disunity. But this is not possible in an army whose soldiers are taken from the same region, caste, and profession; such an army is *saṃhata*. A more literal meaning of *saṃhata* is found in the description of a military battle formation: *saṃhatānīka* is a compact and dense military formation (KAŚ 10.3.5), while an *asaṃhatavyūha* is a battle formation that is spread out (10.3.53; 10.6.38).

In the context of a political saṅgha, the term *saṃhata* is used in the sense of cohesion and unity of purpose forged by family bonds. Unlike an army, however, a saṅgha is always and by nature *saṃhata* and cannot be easily defeated by traditional military means. The best and perhaps the only way to defeat a hostile saṅgha is to create dissension and disunity—that is, *bheda*—within it. Kauṭilya (11.1.3) is explicit:

> *tān anuguṇān bhuñjīta sāmadānābhyām, viguṇān bhedadaṇḍābhyām* |
>
> He [the king] should exploit the ones [saṅghas] that are favorably disposed through conciliation and gifts, and those not favorably disposed by sowing dissension and using military force.

Now, the concept of *bheda* is not confined to a king's dealings with saṅghas. It is part of a set of four strategies called *upāya* (KAŚ 2.10.47): conciliation (*sāma*), gifts (or bribes, *dāna*), creating dissension (*bheda*), and using military force (*daṇḍa*).[5] The above passage asks the king to deploy the first two when a particular saṅgha is friendly and susceptible to such overtures and the last two when it is hostile. But as the rest of book eleven shows, Kauṭilya's view is

4. Called *tūṣṇīṃdaṇḍa* or *upāṃśudaṇḍa*, this involves secret assassinations made to look like accidents or the result of quarrels (see Olivelle 2013, 478).

5. See also MDh 7.198.

that the best option for subduing a saṅgha is *bheda*—that is, to sow dissension and create enmity and internal strife. That is when a saṅgha becomes no longer *saṃhata* and thus vulnerable. Sowing dissension is done through various strategies and the deployment of secret agents. Here is one example:

> *sarveṣām āsannāḥ sattriṇaḥ saṃghānāṃ parasparanyaṅga-dveṣavairakalahasthānāny upalabhya kramābhinītaṃ bhedam upacārayeyuḥ "asau tvā vijalpati" iti | evam ubhayatobaddharoṣāṇāṃ vidyāśilpadyūtavaiharikeṣv ācāryavyañjanā bālakalahān utpādayeyuḥ* |[6]
>
> Secret agents operating nearby should find out the grounds for mutual abuse, hatred, enmity, and quarrels among all members of saṅghas and sow dissension (*bheda*) in anyone whose confidence they have gradually won, saying: "That person defames you." When ill will has thus been built up among adherents of both sides, agents posing as teachers should provoke quarrels among their young boys with respect to their knowledge, skill, gambling, and sports.

Kauṭilya gives further telling examples of how *bheda* within a saṅgha can be instigated. Quite naturally sex figures prominently in the efforts to sow dissension.

> *kārtāntikavyañjano vā kanyām anyena vṛtām anyasya prarūpayet "amuṣya kanyā rājapatnī rājaprasavinī ca bhaviṣyati, sarvasvena prasahya vainām labhasva" iti | alabhyamānāyāṃ parapakṣam uddharṣayet | labdhāyām siddhaḥ kalahaḥ* ||
>
> *bhikṣukī vā priyabhāryaṃ mukhyaṃ brūyāt "asau te mukhyo yauvanotsikto bhāryāyāṃ māṃ prāhiṇot, tasyāhaṃ bhayāl lekhyam ābharaṇaṃ gṛhītvāgatāsmi, nirdoṣā te bhāryā, gūḍham asmin pratikartavyam"* ||[7]
>
> An agent working undercover as an astrologer should describe to one man a girl who has been chosen by another: "That man's daughter is bound to become the wife of a king and the mother of a king. Get her by giving all you have got or by using force." If he fails to

6. KAŚ 11.1.6–7.

7. KAŚ 11.1.49–52.

get her, he should stir up the opponent's side. If he gets her, a quarrel is assured.

Or else, a female mendicant should tell a chief who loves his wife: "That chief, arrogant due to his youth, sent me to your wife. Because I fear him, I have come carrying this letter and ornaments. Your wife is innocent. You should deal with him secretly."

Kauṭilya gives several other examples of this kind and concludes his discussion with this advice to a king wishing to conquer a saṅgha: "A sovereign king should behave in this manner toward saṅghas;" and to a saṅgha: "Saṅghas too should guard themselves in this manner against these kinds of deceptive practices perpetrated by a sovereign king"—*saṅgheṣv evam ekarājo varteta | saṅghāś cāpy evam ekarājād etebhyo 'tisaṃdhānebhyo rakṣayeyuḥ* | (KAŚ 11.1.54–55).

The centrality of *bheda* in political strategy, especially with regard to confederacies, is important to understanding the conversation between the Buddha and Vassakāra. When there is internecine conflict within a saṅgha polity, it is destabilized and weakened from within. Although this technical term is not used by Kauṭilya, what he proposes is essentially *saṅghabheda*.

Vassakāra and the Buddha

Just like Kauṭilya's *vijigīṣu* king, King Ajātasattu of Magadha was planning an attack on the Vajjīs, which in the Sanskrit form *vṛjika* is listed as a confederacy or saṅgha by Kauṭilya (11.1.5). Ajātasattu's belligerent talk reminds one of Kauṭilya's *vijigīṣu*, a king bent on conquest. The king is cautious, and with reason, as Kauṭilya points to the difficulty of defeating a saṅgha in open combat. So he sends his minister, Vassakāra, to talk to the Buddha, because he always tells the truth and from his statements Ajātasattu would be able to judge whether his expedition will be a success. Vassakāra informs the Buddha of Ajātasattu's plan to attack the Vajjīs:

> *rājā bho gotama māgadho ajātasattu vedehiputto vajjī abhiyātukāmo. so evam āha: āhañhi 'me vajjī evaṃmahiddhike evaṃmahānubhāve ucchejjāmi vajjī vināsessami vajjī anayavyasanam āpādessāmi vajjī ti.*[8]

> The Māgadha king, Ajātasattu, son of the Videha queen, Venerable Gotama, wants to attack the Vajjīs. He said this: "These Vajjīs—

8. DN II 73,18–21.

so prosperous and so powerful—I will annihilate the Vajjīs! I will destroy the Vajjīs! I will bring them to utter perdition!"

Clearly, Ajātasattu's boast sounds hollow. He is concerned, for, as Kauṭilya notes, saṅgha confederacies are notoriously difficult to subdue by force of arms. He wants to find out the Buddha's prediction. The Buddha's reply to the minister, by way of an aside with Ānanda, is instructive with regard to *saṅghabheda*:

> *yāvakīvañ ca ānanda vajjī abhiṇhaṃ sannipātā sannipātabahulā bhavissanti, vuddhi yeva ānanda vajjīnaṃ pāṭikaṅkhā no parihāni. . . . yāvakīvañ ca ānanda vajjī samaggā sannipatissanti samaggā vuṭṭhahissanti samaggā vajjikaraṇīyāni karissanti, vuddhi yeva ānanda vajjīnaṃ pāṭikaṅkhā no parihāni.*[9]

> So long, Ānanda, as the Vajjīs will continue to sit together at meetings constantly and to hold such meetings frequently, the Vajjīs should be expected to prosper, Ānanda, and not to decline. . . .
>
> So long, Ānanda, as the Vajjīs will continue to sit together at meetings in unity (*samaggā*), and to rise in unity, and carry out the affairs of the Vajjīs in unity, the Vajjīs should be expected to prosper, Ānanda, and not to decline.

Vassakāra's parting words to the Buddha are reminiscent of Kauṭilya's advice with regard to the means of conquering a confederacy. Note the identification of instigating sedition and causing dissension (*bheda*) as the best methods of conquering a confederacy.

> *akaraṇīyā va bho gotama vajjī raññā māgadhena ajātasattunā vedehiputtena yadidaṃ yuddhassa aññatra upalāpanāya aññatra mithubhedā.*[10]

> Venerable Gotama, the Vajjīs cannot be subdued by the Māgadha king, Ajātasattu, son of the Videha queen—that is, through war

9. DN II 73,29–74,5–8.

10. DN II 76,2–4.

> except through instigations[11] and through mutual dissension (*bheda*).[12]

As soon as Vassakāra leaves, the Buddha turns to the monks to instruct them about the conditions for the welfare of the Buddhist saṅgha, conditions that parallel those for the political saṅgha:

> *yāvakīvañ ca bhikkhave bhikkhū abhiṇhaṃ sannipātā sannipātabahulā bhavissanti, vuddhi yeva bhikkhūnaṃ pāṭikaṅkhā no parihāni. yāvakīvañ ca bhikkhave bhikkhū samaggā sannipatissanti*

11. The Pāli *upalāpana* is translated by Rhys Davids (1910, 81) as "diplomacy." The verbal form is used with the meaning of coaxing or cajoling, and that is closer, I think, to the meaning. In a note to this term Rhys Davids explains: "Upalāpana, which I have only met with here, must mean 'humbug, cajolery, diplomacy;' . . . Sum. Vil. explains it, at some length, as making an alliance, by gifts, with hostile intent, which comes to much the same thing." I do not think it "comes to much the same thing." The commentator, I think, has intuited the meaning correctly when he says "with hostile intent." Cone (2001, s.v. *upalāpana*) gives the meaning of "persuading (to friendship), winning over (with gifts)." She gives similar meanings to the verbal form *upalāpeti* and provides further citations not noticed by Rhys Davids. The Pāli *upalāpana* corresponds in meaning to the Sanskrit *upajāpa* used frequently by Kauṭilya in the sense of instigating someone to sedition. The term *upalāpana*, or any cognate verbal form, is not found in Sanskrit, although Cone notes the occurrence of the term in Buddhist Hybrid Sanskrit.

12. This passage, including the phrase *aññatra mithubhedā*, is found only in the Pāli version. It is absent in other versions preserved in Sanskrit, Chinese, and Tibetan. See Waldschmidt 1951, 118–119. The question is whether the Pāli added this statement or the Sanskrit traditions omitted it. Von Hinüber (2008) argues for the antiquity of the Pāli version but does not address this particular phrase. I think the Pāli is probably closer to the original, especially because of the inclusion of a hapax term (*upalāpana*) and the way this statement corresponds to the political science views about saṅghas. In a recent private communication, Professor von Hinüber agreed that the Pāli is probably closer to the original and gave some reasons, although he emphasized that his conclusions are very tentative: "The Sanskrit wording is abbreviated here also in the part of the text kept in Sanskrit. Moreover, *akaraṇīya* is replaced by *agamanīya*. This might point to an attempt to tone down the still rather aggressive mood expressed by Vassakāra's final statement even after the Buddha's advice. It is no longer a threatening 'we still will deal with the Vajjīs, if not by war, then by tricks' as in Pāli, but 'we must not approach them (at all).' Thus, the political conclusion of Vassakāra's answer (the reference to the *upāyas*) is suppressed. If this is done, the advice of the Buddha really preserves peace (in Sanskrit), which he ultimately fails to do in Pāli. If this guess is correct, the Pāli version is the original and the Sanskrit is a developed milder and here more peaceful text as happens so often. A very good example for this kind of development is the Ājīvika's answer to the Buddha after the latter's first speech after enlightenment: A doubtful *huveyya* 'may be' in Pāli turns into enthusiastic approval *sādhu sādhu* in Sanskrit in course of the text tradition. Another reason for suppressing the wording may be the slightly unusual syntax perhaps not really understood by the Sanskrit redactors."

> *samaggā vuṭṭhahissanti samaggā saṅghakaraṇīyāni karissanti, vuddhi yeva bhikkhave bhikkhūnaṃ pāṭikaṅkhā no parihāni.*[13]
>
> So long, O bhikkhus, as the bhikkhus will continue to sit together at meetings constantly and to hold such meetings frequently, the bhikkhus should be expected to prosper and not to decline.
>
> So long, O bhikkhus, as the bhikkhus will continue to sit together at meetings in unity (*samaggā*), and to rise in unity, and carry out the affairs of the saṅgha in unity, O bhikkhus, the bhikkhus should be expected to prosper and not to decline.

Kauṭilya's and the Buddha's views on how a saṅgha can prosper and resist external assaults are identical. What keeps a saṅgha—whether it is political or monastic—strong and prosperous is unity, concord, and taking decisions by consensus: the *saṃhata* of Kauṭilya and *samaggā* of the Buddha. This is confirmed by the use of the parallel Magadhan Prakrit form *samage* by Aśoka.

Aśoka's Letter on Saṅghabheda

Kauṭilya's discussion of political saṅghas and the Buddha's conversation with Vassakāra provide us an extra pair of lenses to examine Aśoka's inscriptions about monks who instigate *bheda* within the Buddhist monastic saṅgha. Versions of the edict are found in three locations: Allāhābād, Sārnāth, and Sāñcī. All three are seriously damaged, and the text can be reconstructed only through comparison of the three and through some educated conjectures.[14] I give below the one reconstructed by Alsdorf (1959, 163):

> *devānaṃpiye ānapayati kosaṃbiyaṃ mahāmātā vataviyā. saṃghe samage kaṭe. saṃghasi no lahiye bhede. ye saṃghaṃ bhākhati bhikhu vā bhikhuni vā, se pi cā odātāni dusāni saṃnaṃdhāpayitu anāvāsasi āvāsayiye.*
>
> The Beloved of the Gods orders. The high officers of Kosambi should be commanded. The unity of the saṅgha has been instituted. In the saṅgha no dissension is to be tolerated. Whoever divides the saṅgha,

13. DN II 76,31–77,2.

14. For the discovery and the early attempts to accurately read and interpret this inscription, see Norman [1987] 1992.

be it a monk or a nun, that person should be made to put on white clothes and to reside in a nonmonastic residence.

Three elements in this order by Aśoka have been noted by scholars: (1) the term *bhede* as also its verbal equivalent *bhākhati*; (2) the term *samage*; and (3) the expelling of offending monks and nuns, who are made to wear white clothes (i.e., give up the monk's ocher robe and wear civilian clothes) and live in what is called an *anāvāsa*.

It is the term *bheda* that has been interpreted as "schism" or "split" within the saṅgha. In the Vinaya, someone causing a *saṅghabheda* is guilty of a *saṅghādisesa* (Skt. *saṅghāvaśeṣa*) offense and is suspended from the community for a specific period of time. The term *bheda* as used by Kauṭilya and in the Buddha's conversation with Vassakāra refers not to any split or schism but to causing discord or disrupting the unity of a saṅgha, whether it is political or monastic. Such discord was viewed by both Kauṭilya and the Buddha as detrimental to the saṅgha, leading to its weakening and causing internal rot and collapse. For Kauṭilya's king this was a desirable outcome; he would find it easy to conquer such a saṅgha.

Bechert (1982) interprets the Prakrit *samage* of Aśoka and the Pāli *samaggā* in the Buddha's conversation with Vassakāra within the context of the Vinaya rules regarding the boundary, or *sīmā*, of a monastery. According to him, *samaggā* means the totality of the monks living within a particular *sīmā*; before any official act (*saṅghakamma*) can be undertaken the saṅgha of that particular monastery must be "complete"; that is, all the resident monks must be present. This is clearly the etymological meaning of the term. However, I think the term as it appears in the Buddha's conversation with Vassakāra with reference to the Vajjī confederation means more than simply the presence of all the members—that is, a full quorum. It means, over and above that, the agreement, unity, and concord of the members as they sit down for meetings and get up from them at their conclusion. It is this concord and unity of the membership that is disrupted by the *bheda*, whether internally generated as in the Vinaya and Aśoka, or externally instigated as in Kauṭilya.

With regard to the third point, the expelling or the punishment of the offending members, Kauṭilya and the Buddha's conversations with Vassakāra are silent. The punishment of a member guilty of an offense listed in the *Pātimokkha* by the community of monks poses little problem. The issue that has puzzled scholars is Aśoka's instruction to defrock and expel a monk guilty of *saṅghabheda*. First, expelling such a member goes against the Vinaya rule that sets a much lesser punishment. Second, it indicates a brazen interference in monastic discipline by the government. To understand why Aśoka orders expulsion of monks guilty of *saṅghabheda* we must look at two issues. First, the general rules of ancient Indian law regulating corporate entities, often called precisely "saṅghas." Second—and this is bound to be speculative—what was the subtext of Aśoka's order? What occasioned his letter and directives to the high officials?

Norman (1993) refers to Sasaki's (1989) article, which presents evidence from the Chinese translation of the *Mahāsāṅghika-vinaya* that co-opts powerful upāsakas to "talk to" and even bribe a monk causing discord in a monastery. As Norman rightly observes, this Vinaya does not tell us much about what was happening during the third century BCE, but it does open up the possibility of lay intervention in monastic disputes. The so-called "cover letter" of Aśoka accompanying his edict, which is inscribed only at Sārnāth, indicates that, besides high government officials, local upāsakas may also have been involved in Aśoka's effort to rid the monasteries of dissident monks. The cover letter (Hultzsch 1925, 162) reads:

> The Beloved of Gods declares as follows: Let one copy of this edict remain with you, deposited in the bureau, and have one copy of it deposited with the Upāsakas. And let these Upāsakas come on every Uposatha-day so that trust may be developed in this decree; and consistently on every Uposatha-day let respective Mahāmātras come to the Uposatha-ceremony so that trust may be developed in this decree and attention paid to it. And as far as your jurisdiction extends, you should dispatch officers everywhere in accordance with the provisions of this directive. Likewise, in accordance with the provisions of this directive, you should have officers dispatched to all the areas around forts.[15]

Laws governing the internal administration of professional groups, whether they are traders, artisans, or religious professionals, are subsumed in the Dharmaśāstras under the category of *samaya*.[16] The state recognized the legitimacy of such corporate laws, and the corporations were authorized to discipline their members when they broke those laws. Manu clearly states that the king should be involved in punishing a person who breaks corporate laws (*samayabhedin*): "Next, I will explain the Law relating to persons

15. My translation.

16. For *samaya* in Dharmaśāstras, see Davis 2005. Sometimes kings ratified charters of corporate groups, such as the Charter of Viṣṇuṣeṇa recorded in an inscription and edited in Wiese and Das 2019.

who breach a contract. When a man belonging to a village, region, or corporate entity (saṅgha) enters into a contract truthfully and then breaks it out of greed, the king should banish that man from his realm"—*ata ūrdhvaṃ pravakṣyāmi dharmaṃ samayabhedinām* || *yo grāmadeśasaṅghānāṃ kṛtvā satyena saṃvidam* | *visaṃvaden naro lobhāt taṃ rāṣṭrād vipravāsyet* || (MDh 8.218–219). Yājñavalkya (2.196) also says: "That is the rule also for guilds, traders' unions, religious orders, and associations. The king should safeguard their unique characteristics and uphold their traditional modes of life"—*śreṇinaigamapāṣaṇḍigaṇānām apy ayaṃ vidhiḥ* | *bhedaṃ*[17] *caiṣāṃ nṛpo rakṣet pūrvavṛttiṃ ca pālayet* || (YDh 2.196; see also NSm 10.2–3). But the king is expected to intervene when serious breaches of law, and especially the sowing of dissension (*bheda*), occur. Nārada says: "Those who cause dissension in corporate entities should be punished in a special way"—*pṛthag gaṇāṃś ca ye bhindyus te vineyā viśeṣataḥ* || (NSm 10.6). Even though the person inflicting the punishment is not stated, the subject of all verbs in the sections on legal procedure is the king or judge. Similar statements regarding individuals who sow dissension in corporate entities are given also in other Dharmaśāstras.[18]

So, from a purely legal standpoint—assuming that the provisions of the Dharmaśāstras were operative in the third century BCE—Aśoka's intervention when monks were causing disunity within the saṅgha is nothing remarkable. However, Indian law also assumed that corporations would generally police themselves without royal intervention. It is only when they are unable to do so, or when a serious crime required corporal punishment or execution, that a corporation may request judicial intervention. This is where the background to and the subtext of Aśoka's order to his high officials become significant. Did he simply one day think of sending this order? That is highly improbable. More than likely there was a particular reason for his doing so. Could it have been requests made by one or more saṅghas for royal intervention and legal remedy with regard to some recalcitrant monks? This is the background for the council of Pāṭaliputra recorded in later Buddhist texts and assumed to have been undertaken under the auspices of Aśoka by some scholars. Irrespective of the historicity of such a council, this or a similar situation within at least some elements of the contemporary Buddhist saṅgha may have been the reason for Aśoka's order recorded in these inscriptions.

Now, as we have seen, expelling monks from a monastery is not what is

17. The term *bheda* here may be confusing, but within this context the term refers to the differences between various civil groups.

18. *Bṛhaspatismṛti* 17.16 (ed. in Aiyangar 1941; tr. in Jolly 1889); *Kātyāyanasmṛti* 672 (ed. and tr. in Kane 1933).

required for a *saṅghabheda* offense within the extant Vinaya rules. But could there have been times when, as a matter of practical necessity, more extraordinary measures were required? Or was this Vinaya rule in existence in precisely this form in the third century BCE? Clearly, later Indian law codes, as we saw earlier in Manu (8.219), have provisions for actually exiling members of corporate entities from the kingdom itself. So simply taking them out of the monastery can be seen as a milder form of punishment.

Concluding Postscript

This brief survey shows that it is at the very least useful to view *saṅghabheda* in both Aśoka's edict and the Vinaya rules within a broader discussion of *bheda* in political confederations (saṅghas) and in corporate units, whether they are identified as *saṅgha*, *gaṇa*, *pūga*, or with some other term. That discussion includes material from the *Arthaśāstra*'s discussion of political saṅghas, the Buddha's own conversation with Vassakāra on the eve of King Ajātasattu's attack on the saṅgha of the Vajjīs, and corporate law in ancient Indian legal codes.

It is clear from Kauṭilya's discussion of political saṅghas and the Buddha's conversation with Vassakāra that dissension (*bheda*) and lack of cohesion and unity are detrimental to a saṅgha. Both Aśoka's statement and the Vinaya rule show that unity (*samage*, *samaggā*) was also viewed as very important for the proper functioning and perhaps even for the very existence of a Buddhist monastic saṅgha. In the broadest sense, these provisions against *bheda* reflect the old saying: "One bad apple spoils the whole barrel." When one monk becomes the source of conflict and acrimony, the whole community may soon experience disunity and internal strife. In the case of a political saṅgha, as Kauṭilya's advice to a king shows, such disunity can offer opportunities to foreign enemies to undermine and conquer that saṅgha.

That is certainly the reason for insisting on *samage* or *samaggā*. As I have already noted, this notion cannot simply refer to the legal requirement that all monks living within the monastic boundary (*sīmā*) should be present at any monastic gathering to conduct business (*saṅghakamma*). If that were the case, Aśoka's statement that the saṅgha has been made *samage* makes little sense. It also makes little sense within the conversation between the Buddha and Vassakāra. There the emphasis is on their sitting down at meetings and rising up in concord. So *samage* refers, beyond the presence of all the monks, to this inner quality of unity and cohesion among all members of the saṅgha.

I think we can relate Aśoka's *samage* and the Buddha's *samaggā* to Kauṭilya's *saṃhata*. The first, *samage* (Sanskrit *samagra*), refers etymologically to "totality." So, the totality of the community or the confederacy indicates—beyond Bechert's presence of all the monks—that there are no dissenting voices; there is unanimity and concord. The second, *saṃhata*, seems to come at it from a different angle; we have seen its military use with regard to battle formations that are tight and close. It is this compactness that is indicated by *saṃhata* when it relates to a saṅgha and its unity. It is close-knit without gaps.

Aśoka is thus saying that his activities with respect to the Buddhist saṅgha have already made the saṅgha a community that is unified and in concord. Unfortunately, he does not tell us what those activities were. He wants to maintain this unity in the future by taking action against monks or nuns who may cause disruptions and disunity within the saṅgha. And this action includes the banishment of such individuals from the monastic community, effectively reducing them to the lay status.

Why Aśoka did not let the specifically Vinaya remedy of a probationary period (*mānatta*), if such a rule did exist during Aśoka's time, to take place is difficult to answer. The Vinaya remedy is effective against individual transgressors who acknowledge their offense and accept the punishment. However, we can visualize situations where a group may have been guilty of a *saṅghabheda* but may not have been willing either to acknowledge their offense or to accept the punishment, which is the situation considered by the *Mahāsāṅghika-vinaya* noted earlier. They may, indeed, have accused the other monks of being guilty of precisely the offense charged against them. Things can get messy quickly. This is when the civil authority can intervene on the side of one party, probably the establishment party, and expel the troublemakers.

What Kauṭilya and the Buddha in his comments to Vassakāra point out is the central importance of unity and concord (*samage* or *saṃhata*) for the success of a saṅgha, political or monastic. It is the assault on this unity and concord that the term *bheda* refers to. The *bheda* in a political saṅgha, as Kauṭilya points out, can be engineered by outside forces intent on disrupting and ultimately conquering that polity. In the case of the monastic saṅgha, the rot sets in from within when dissension is generated by the behavior, words, and actions of individual monks.

Works Cited

Abbreviations

DN	*The Dīgha Nikāya*. Edited by T. W. Rhys Davids and J. Estlin Carpenter. 3 vols. London: The Pali Text Society, 1890–1911.
KAŚ	Kauṭilya's *Arthaśāstra*. Ed. in Kangle [1960] 1969. Tr. in Olivelle 2013.
MDh	*Mānavadharmaśāstra*. Ed. and tr. in Olivelle 2005.
NSm	*Nāradasmṛti*. Ed. and tr. in Lariviere [1989] 2003.
YDh	*Yājñavalkyadharmaśāstra*. Ed. and tr. in Olivelle 2019.

Aiyangar, K. V. Rangaswami. 1941. *Bṛhaspatismṛti (Reconstructed)*. Gaekwad's Oriental Series 85. Baroda: Oriental Institute.

Alsdorf, L. 1959. "Aśokas Schismen-Edikt und das Dritte Konzil." *Indo-Iranian Journal* 3.3: 161–174.

Bechert, Heinz. 1982. "The Importance of Aśoka's So-Called Schism Edict." In *Indological and Buddhist Studies: Volume in Honour of Professor J. W. de Jong on His Sixtieth Birthday*, edited by L. A. Hercus, F. B. J. Kuiper, T. Rajapatirana, and E. R. Skrzypczak, 61–68. Canberra: Faculty of Asian Studies, Australian National University.

———. 2001. "Sanghabheda and Nikāyabheda in Buddhist Law." *Indian International Journal of Buddhist Studies* 2: 9–14.

Cone, Margaret. 2001. *A Dictionary of Pāli*, vol. 1. Oxford: The Pali Text Society.

Davis, Donald R., Jr. 2005. "Intermediate Realms of Law: Corporate Groups and Rulers in Medieval India." *Journal of the Economic and Social History of the Orient* 48: 104–106.

———. 2007. "The Non-Observance of Conventions: A Title of Hindu Law in the *Smṛticandrikā*." *Zeitschrift der Deutschen Morgenländischen Gesellschaft* 157.1: 103–124.

Frauwallner, Erich. 1956. *The Earliest Vinaya and the Beginnings of Buddhist Literature*. Serie Orientale Roma 8. Rome: Istituto Italiano per il Medio ed Estremo Oriente.

von Hinüber, Oskar. 2008. "Hoary Past and Hazy Memory: On the History of Early Buddhist Texts." *Journal of the International Association of Buddhist Studies* 29.2: 193–210.

Hultzsch, Eugen. 1925. *Inscriptions of Asoka: New Edition*. Corpus Inscriptionum Indicarum 1. Oxford: Clarendon Press, for the Government of India.

Jayawickrama, N. A. 1959. "A Reference to the Third Council in Aśoka's Edicts?" *University of Ceylon Review* 17: 61–72.

Jolly, Julius. 1889. *The Minor Law-Books*. Part I: *Nārada, Bṛhaspati*. Sacred Books of the East 33. Oxford: Clarendon Press.

Kane, P. V. 1933. *Kātyāyanasmṛti on Vyavahāra (Law and Procedure)*. Poona: Oriental Book Agency.

Kangle, R. P. [1960] 1969. *The Kauṭilīya Arthaśāstra*. Part I: *A Critical Edition and Glossary*. 2nd ed. Bombay: University of Bombay.

Lamotte, Étienne. [1958] 1988. *History of Indian Buddhism from the Origins to the*

Śaka Era. Translated from the French by Sara Webb-Boin. Louvain: Institut Orientaliste.

Lariviere, Richard W. [1989] 2003. *The Nāradasmṛti*. 2 vols. Reprint, in one volume, Delhi: Motilal Banarsidass.

McClish, Mark. 2019. *The Ages of the Arthaśāstra: Sovereignty and Sacred Law in Ancient India*. Cambridge: Cambridge University Press.

Norman, K. R. 1987. "Aśoka's 'Schism' Edict." *Bukkyōgaku seminā* 佛教學セミナー (*Buddhist Seminar, Otani University*) 46: 1–33. Reprinted in K. R. Norman, *Collected Papers* 3:191–218. Oxford: The Pali Text Society, 1992.

———. 1993. "Aśoka and Saṅghabheda." In *Studies in Original Buddhism and Mahāyāna Buddhism in Commemoration of Late Professor Dr. Fumimaro Watanabe*, edited by Egaku Mayeda, 1:9–29. Kyoto: Nagata Bunshodo. Reprinted in K. R. Norman, *Collected Papers* 5:205–229. Oxford: The Pali Text Society, 1994.

Olivelle, Patrick. 2005. *Manu's Code of Law: A Critical Edition and Translation of the Mānava-Dharmaśāstra*. South Asia Research. New York: Oxford University Press.

———. 2013. *King, Governance, and Law in Ancient India: Kauṭilya's* Arthaśāstra. New York: Oxford University Press.

———. 2019. *Yājñavalkya: A Treatise on Dharma*. Murty Classical Library of India. Cambridge, MA: Harvard University Press.

Rhys Davids, T. W. 1910. *Dialogues of the Buddha*, vol. 2. London: Oxford University Press.

Sasaki, Shizuka. 1989. "Buddhist Sects in the Aśoka Period (I): The Meaning of the Schism Edict." *Bukkyō kenkyū* 仏教研究 (*Buddhist Studies*) 18: 181–202.

———. 1992. "Buddhist Sects in the Aśoka Period (2): *Saṃghabheda* (I)." *Bukkyō kenkyū* 仏教研究 (*Buddhist Studies*) 21: 157–176.

———. 1993. "Buddhist Sects in the Aśoka Period (3): *Saṃghabheda* (2)." *Bukkyō kenkyū* 仏教研究 (*Buddhist Studies*) 22: 167–199.

Trautmann, Thomas. 1971. *Kauṭilya and the Arthaśāstra: A Statistical Investigation of the Authorship and Evolution of the Text*. Leiden: Brill.

Waldschmidt, Ernst. 1951. *Das Mahāparinirvāṇasūtra: Text in Sanskrit und Tibetisch, verglichen mit dem Pāli nebst einer Übersetzung der chinesischen Entsprechung im Vinaya der Mūlasarvāstivādins*, vol. 2. Berlin: Akademie-Verlag.

Warder, A. K. 1970. *Indian Buddhism*. Delhi: Motilal Banarsidass.

Wiese, Harald, and Sadananda Das. 2019. *The Charter of Viṣṇuṣeṇa*. Halle an der Saale: Universitätsverlag Halle-Wittenberg.

The Evolution of the First *Nissaggiya-pācittiya* and the *Bodhisattvabhūmi*

Shizuka Sasaki

An "offense requiring confession and forfeiture" (*nissaggiya-pācittiya*) is the fourth of seven categories of offenses in the *Pātimokkha*. This kind of offense requires punishment for the illegal possession of objects.[1] Bhikkhus and bhikkhunīs who have committed these offenses must forfeit the illegal objects and confess in front of the other monks or nuns. However, the forfeited items are often returned to them.

In this study, I examine an expedient called *vikappanā* ("assignment"), which allows bhikkhus to keep items without committing a *nissaggiya-pācittiya* offense. Assignment appears in the first *nissaggiya-pācittiya* rule of the *Suttavibhaṅga* for monks. Using the results of my investigation into *vikappanā*, I clarify one aspect of the evolution of Vinaya literature.

Among the extant Vinayas, the way of carrying out assignment of prohibited objects in the *Mūlasarvāstivāda-vinaya* is unique, suggesting that its procedure was first introduced by the group of monastics that used that Vinaya. Additionally, there is clear evidence that the particular procedure of assignment stipulated in the *Mūlasarvāstivāda-vinaya* was actually carried out in the saṅgha in which the *Bodhisattvabhūmi* was compiled. This suggests that the saṅgha in which the *Bodhisattvabhūmi* was transmitted used the *Mūlasarvāstivāda-vinaya* as its formal Vinaya or, at least, used the procedure that is found only in the *Mūlasarvāstivāda-vinaya*. The *Bodhisattvabhūmi* thus contains the oldest record of actual use of the *Mūlasarvāstivāda-vinaya*'s method of assignment in a Buddhist saṅgha.

1. In principle, Pāli technical terms are used throughout this paper. Equivalents in other languages, such as Sanskrit, are supplied as appropriate.

Summary of the First Group of Rules Concerning Offenses Requiring Confession and Forfeiture (Nissaggiya-pācittiya *1*)[2]

According to the *Suttavibhaṅga* of the *Mahāvihāra-vinaya*, the Buddha was at Gotamaka Cetiya in Vesālī when he declared that a bhikkhu should possess only three robes. At that time, the group of six bad monks (the *chabbaggiyas*), who had many sets of three robes, changed them depending on the situation. The good bhikkhus saw this and condemned the group of six bad monks. When the Buddha became aware of this, he established the following rule (*sikkhāpada*):[3]

> *yo pana bhikkhu atirekacīvaraṃ dhāreyya, nissaggiyaṃ pācittiyaṃ.*[4]
>
> If a bhikkhu keeps an extra robe, it is an offense requiring confession and forfeiture [of the extra robe].

At that time, Ānanda obtained an extra robe and decided to give it to Sāriputta. However, Sāriputta was at Sāketa, far from Vesālī, and Ānanda could not give him the robe immediately. Thus, Ānanda would violate the first rule if he kept the robe. When Ānanda consulted with the Buddha, the Buddha asked him, "How many more days will it be before Sāriputta returns?" Ānanda replied, "He will return within ten days." So the Buddha revised the previous rule, establishing a new one:[5]

> *niṭṭhitacīvarasmiṃ bhikkhunā ubbhatasmiṃ kaṭhine dasāhaparamaṃ atirekacīvaraṃ dhāretabbaṃ. taṃ atikkāmayato nissaggiyaṃ pācittiyaṃ.*[6]
>
> After the work of making the robes is finished and *kaṭhina* has been removed by a bhikkhu, an extra robe may be kept for at most

2. In this paper, *nissaggiya-pācittiya* refers in general to *nissaggiya-pācittiya* for bhikkhus.

3. Some *sikkhāpadas* are established through a plurality of steps. *Nissaggiya-pācittiya* 1 is one such rule.

4. Vin III 195,18–19.

5. A similar story and rule appear in *nissaggiya-pācittiya* 21 concerning "possession of an extra alms bowl."

6. Vin III 196,9–10.

ten days.[7] For him who exceeds that period, there is confession and forfeiture.[8]

After the amendment of the initial ruling as above, various terms and phrases in the rule are analyzed and explained. Then the conditions for establishing guilt are given, such as: "If a bhikkhu keeps the robe for more than ten days and knows that [more than ten days] have passed, it is an offense requiring confession and forfeiture."[9] Finally, eleven cases in which there is no guilt are explained (non-offense clauses). One of these cases is when the monk "assigns" (*vikappeti*) the robe to another monastic.[10]

This paper focuses on the word "assignment" (*vikappanā*; verb: *vikappeti*) and follows the evolution of the understanding of "confession and forfeiture" (*nissaggiya-pācittiya*). *Vikappanā* is a noun indicating the formal giving away of extra robes to others. In fact, however, the monk does not really give up the robe. *Vikappanā* can be interpreted to mean that, once a bhikkhu assigns his extra robes to another monastic, the one to whom it is assigned is the owner. The new owner can then give the bhikkhu the rights to the robe, and he can keep it for more than ten days without there being a transgression.

In what follows, the term "assignment" is used to refer to the fairly complex procedure described above.

Rule Classification Related to Assignment

In the *Mahāvihāra-vinaya*, the word *vikappanā* "assignment" does not appear in the *sikkhāpada* of the first *nissaggiya-pācittiya*. The canonical text only stipulates that an extra robe may be kept for at most ten days by a bhikkhu, and if that period is exceeded, there is confession and forfeiture for him. Assignment appears for the first time in one of the non-offense clauses in the *Suttavibhaṅga*: "There is no offense if an extra robe is assigned."[11] Similarly,

7. There is some disagreement concerning the meaning of the phrase "the work of making the robes is finished"; see Hirakawa 1993, 63; Horner 1940, 6; von Simson 2000, 184; Banerjee 1977, 25; Ochiai 2011, 37; Satō 1963, 70.

8. Pruitt and Norman 2001, 29.6–9, translate this sentence as follows: "The robe material having been used up, the *kaṭhina* frame having been removed by a bhikkhu, an extra robe is to be worn for ten days at the most. For one exceeding that, there is an offence entailing expiation with forfeiture." See also Kieffer-Pülz 2013, 908–933.

9. Vin III 197,15: *dasāhātikkante atikkantasaññī, nissaggiyaṃ pācittiyaṃ.*

10. Vin III 197,18–28.

11. Vin III 197,28–30: *anāpatti anto dasāhaṃ adhiṭṭheti vikappeti vissajjeti nassati vinassati*

in the *Mahīśāsaka-*, *Mahāsāṅghika-*, and *Sarvāstivāda-vinaya*s, the canonical ruling (*śikṣāpada*) itself does not contain the word "assignment" (*vikappanā* or equivalents). Rather, the word appears first in the *Sūtravibhaṅga* explanation of one of the exemptions. The relevant passages are as follows:[12]

Mahīśāsaka-vinaya (*nissaggiya* 1):

> 若比丘三衣竟捨迦絺那衣已。長衣乃至十日。若過尼薩耆波逸提。
>
> After [the work of making] the three robes is finished and *kaṭhina* has been removed by a bhikṣu, an extra robe [may be kept] for at most ten days. [For him who] exceeds that period, there is confession and forfeiture.[13]

Mahāsāṅghika-vinaya (*nissaggiya* 1):

> 若比丘衣已竟。迦絺那衣已捨。若得長衣得至十日畜。過十日者。尼薩耆波夜提。
>
> *kṛtacīvarehi bhikṣūhi uddhatasmin kaṭhine daśāhaparamaṃ bhikṣuṇā atirekacīvaraṃ dhārayitavyaṃ. taduttariṃ dhāreya nissargikapācattikaṃ.*
>
> After *kaṭhina* has been removed by bhikṣus who have finished the work of making the robes, should an extra robe come into possession it may be kept for at most ten days by a bhikṣu. For him who exceeds ten days, there is confession and forfeiture.[14]

ḍayhati acchinditvā gaṇhanti vissāsaṃ gaṇhanti, ummattakassa, ādikammikassā 'ti. Horner 1940, 10: "There is no offence if, within ten days, it is allotted, assigned, bestowed, lost, destroyed, burnt, if they tear it from him, if they take it on trust; if he is mad, if he is the first wrong-doer."

12. Another example of a text that does not include the word "assignment" in the rule is *Jietuo jie jing* 解脫戒經 (Taishō 1460.24.661b2).

13. Taishō 1421.22.23b25–26.

14. Taishō 1425.22.292a26–27; Tatia 1975, 13.16–17.

Sarvāstivāda-vinaya (*niḥsargikā* 1):

若比丘衣竟。已捨迦絺那衣。畜長衣得至十日。若過是畜者。尼薩耆波夜提。

niṣṭhitacīvareṇa bhikṣuṇā uddhṛte kaṭhine daśāhaparamam atiriktaṃ cīvaraṃ dhārayitavyaṃ tata uttaraṃ dhārayen niḥsargikā pātayantikā.

After *kaṭhina* has been removed by a bhikṣu who has finished the work of making the robes, should an extra robe come into possession it may be kept for at most ten days by a bhikṣu. For him who keeps it exceeding that period, there is confession and forfeiture.[15]

However, unlike the other four Vinayas, the *Dharmaguptaka-* and *Mūlasarvāstivāda-vinaya*s include the word "assignment" in the *śikṣāpada* itself.

Dharmaguptaka-vinaya (*nissaggiya* 1):

若比丘衣已竟迦絺那衣已出畜長衣經十日不淨施得畜。若過十日尼薩耆波逸提。

After the robes have been completed and *kaṭhina* has been removed by a bhikṣu, an extra robe may be kept for ten days without assignment. If it exceeds ten days, there is [an offense requiring] confession and forfeiture.[16]

Mūlasarvāstivāda-vinaya (*naisargikā* 1):

若復苾芻作衣已竟羯恥那衣。復出得長衣齊十日。不分別應畜。若過畜者。泥薩祇波逸底迦。

niṣṭhitacīvareṇa bhikṣuṇā uddhṛte kaṭhine daśāhaparamaṃ atirekacīvaram avikalpitaṃ dhārayitavyaṃ tataḥ uttari dhārayen naisargikā pāyantikā.[17]

15. Taishō 1435.23.30a28–b1; von Simson 2000, 184.4–5.

16. Taishō 1428.22.602a11–12.

17. Hu-von Hinüber 2003, 22–23: *niṣṭhitacīvareṇa bhikṣuṇā uddhṛte kaṭhine daśāhaparamam*

> *dge slong chos gos zin pas sra brkyang phyung na zhag bcu'i bar du gos lhag pa rung bar ma byas pa bcang bar bya'o / de las 'das pa 'chang na spang ba'i ltung byed do //*
>
> After *kaṭhina* has been removed by a bhikṣu who has finished the work of making the robes, an extra robe may be kept for at most ten days without assignment. For him who keeps it exceeding that period, there is confession and forfeiture (*naisargikā pāyantikā* = *nissaggiya-pācittiya*).[18]

Some Vinayas include the word "assignment" in the *śikṣāpada* of the first *nissaggiya-pācittiya*, while others do not. Evidence from elsewhere in the Vinayas suggests that the word "assignment" was not originally included in the wording of the first rule requiring confession and forfeiture.

The fifty-ninth *pācittiya* in the *Mahāvihāra-vinaya* states that when a bhikkhu gives a robe to another member of the saṅgha by way of assignment, if he makes use of it without the recipient's permission, then the bhikkhu must confess it. Since the recipient formally owns the robe, the donor cannot use it without permission of the recipient or his agent. Therefore, the fifty-ninth *pācittiya* states that if the donor wears the assigned robe that has not been formally given up by the one to whom it was assigned, he must perform the confession. Here it is important to note that either the phrase "having been assigned" (*vikappetvā*) or corresponding wording appears in the *śikṣāpada*s of all Vinayas. An example can be found in the *Mahāvihāra-vinaya*:

> *yo pana bhikkhu bhikkhussa vā bhikkhuniyā vā sikkhamānāya vā sāmaṇerassa vā sāmaṇeriyā vā sāmaṃ cīvaraṃ vikappetvā apaccuddhārakaṃ paribhuñjeyya, pācittiyan ti.*
>
> If any bhikkhu, having assigned a robe to a bhikkhu, bhikkhunī, sikkhamānā, sāmaṇera, or sāmaṇerī, should make use of it without it having been formally given up by the one to whom it was assigned, there is an offense requiring confession (*pācittiya*).[19]

atirekacīvaram avikalpitaṃ dhārayitavyaṃ / tata uttari dhārayen naiḥsarggikapāyattikā //.

18. Taishō 1442.23.711c14–16; Clarke 2014, 238, fol. 13r6–v2; Banerjee 1977, 25; Sde dge 3, 'Dul ba, vol. *cha*, 41b4–5; Peking 1032, 'Dul ba, vol. *je*, 38a7.

19. Vin IV 121,30–33.

The *Dharmaguptaka-*, *Mahīśāsaka-*, and *Mahāsāṅghika-vinaya*s all say the same thing.[20] The Chinese translation of the *Sarvāstivāda-vinaya* also agrees with those three Vinayas and the *Mahāvihāra-vinaya*. However, among the Sanskrit manuscripts of the Sarvāstivāda *Prātimokṣa-sūtra*, there is another manuscript group, designated as "Version B" by Georg von Simson.[21]

Sarvāstivāda-vinaya (*pātayantikā* 68):

> 若比丘與他比丘比丘尼式叉摩尼沙彌沙彌尼衣。他不還。便強奪取著。波逸提。[22]
>
> (von Simson: Version A) *yaḥ punar bhikṣur bhikṣoḥ vā bhikṣuṇyā vā śikṣamāṇāyā vā śrāmaṇerasya vā śrāmaṇerikāyā vā cīvaram uddiśya tataḥ paścād apratyuddhārya paribhuṃjīta pātayantikā.*
>
> (von Simson: Version B) *yaḥ punar bhikṣur bhikṣoḥ pātraṃ vā cīvaram vā dat(t)vā tataḥ paścād apratyuddhārya paribhuṃjīta pātayantikā.*[23]

Version B lacks the list of other monastics to whom the robe may be assigned (*viz.*, bhikṣuṇī, śikṣamāṇā, śrāmaṇera, śrāmaṇerī). Moreover, not only robes but also bowls are covered by the rule. The gerunds meaning "having assigned" are *uddiśya* in Version A and *dat(t)vā* in Version B.

In the *Mūlasarvāstivāda-vinaya*, the *śikṣāpada* is as follows:

> 若復苾芻受他寄衣。後時不問主輒自著用者。波逸底迦。[24]

20. *Dharmaguptaka-vinaya* (Taishō 1428.22.676a28–b1): 若比丘與比丘比丘尼式叉摩那沙彌沙彌尼衣。後不語主還取著者波逸提。; *Mahīśāsaka-vinaya* (Taishō 1421.22.69b16–17): 若比丘與比丘比丘尼式叉摩那沙彌沙彌尼淨施衣還奪波逸提。; *Mahāsāṅghika-vinaya* (Taishō 1425.22.379a8–10): 若比丘與比丘比丘尼。式叉摩尼沙彌沙彌尼衣。後不捨而受用者。波夜提。; *yo puna bhikṣu bhikṣusya vā bhikṣuṇīye vā śrāmaṇerasya vā śrāmaṇerīye vā śikṣamāṇāye vā cīvaraṃ datvā apratyuddhareya paribhuṃjeya apratyuddhāraparibhoge pācattikaṃ* (Tatia 1975, 26.3–5).

21. Von Simson 2000, 2–15.

22. Taishō 1435.23.114c24–26.

23. Von Simson 2000, 226, 5–6.

24. *Pācittiya* 68, Taishō 1442.23.851c13–14.

> *yaḥ punar bhikṣur bhikṣoś cīvaraṃ datvā tataḥ paścād apratyuddhārya paribhuṃjīta pāyantikā.*[25]
>
> *yang dge slong gang dge slong la gos byin nas de'i 'og tu rdeng med par snyod na ltung byed do* //[26]
>
> If a bhikṣu, having given (*datvā*) a robe to a bhikṣu, should later make use of it without it having been formally given up by the one to whom it was assigned, it is an offense requiring confession (*pāyantikā*).

The Mūlasarvāstivādin version differs from all the other Vinayas mentioned (*Mahāvihāra-*, *Dharmaguptaka-*, *Mahīśāsaka-*, and *Mahāsāṅghika-vinaya*s) and von Simson's Sarvāstivāda Version A in that it contains no mention of assignment to a bhikṣuṇī, śikṣamāṇā, śrāmaṇera, or śrāmaṇerī. Thus, two possible versions of this rule can be distinguished.

One version, found in the *Mahāvihāra-*, *Dharmaguptaka-*, *Mahīśāsaka-*, and *Mahāsāṅghika-vinaya*s and von Simson's Sarvāstivāda Version A, mentions all five types of monastics (bhikṣu, bhikṣuṇī, śikṣamāṇā, śrāmaṇera, and śrāmaṇerī) as possible recipients to whom robes can be assigned. The other version, found in the *Mūlasarvāstivāda-vinaya* and von Simson's Sarvāstivāda Version B *Prātimokṣa-sūtra*, limits the possible recipients to bhikṣus. Below I will try to explain this divergence.

So far, I have shown that this *pācittiya* (the fifty-ninth *pācittiya* in the *Mahāvihāra-vinaya*) presupposes the expedient of assignment. This rule is found in different places in the *Prātimokṣa*s of different Vinayas, and the number of the *pācittiya* rule varies from one school to another. For convenience, below I will refer to this rule simply as the *vikappanā*-rule.

In the *vikappanā*-rule, gerunds ("having given") are used to express assignment: *vikappetvā* in the *Mahāvihāra-vinaya*, *uddiśya* or *dat(t)vā* in the Sarvāstivāda *Prātimokṣa-sūtra*, and *datvā* in the *Mūlasarvāstivāda-vinaya*. At this stage, it is unclear whether these verbs differ significantly in meaning, but at the very least, it is obvious from the context that they are used to express the same action. A Pāli commentary to the *Mahāvihāra-vinaya*, the *Samantapāsādikā*, uses the verb *dammi* to mean "assign."[27]

25. Clarke 2014, 232, folio (18)r3. In Banerjee 1977, 42, we find the word *vikalpya* instead of *datvā*.

26. Sde dge 3, 'Dul ba, vol. *ja*, 276a4; Peking 1032, 'Dul ba, vol. *nye*, 258a6.

27. Sp III 648,26–649,3.

The word analysis in the *Suttavibhaṅga* of the *vikappanā*-rule describes specific types of assignment and procedures used during the assignment. In the case of the *Mahāvihāra-vinaya*, it says, "There are two types of assignment: assignment in person (*sammukhāvikappanā*) and assignment in the presence of another (*parammukhāvikappanā*)."[28] Although a brief explanation of the procedures for conducting these two types of assignment are given in the word analysis in the *Suttavibhaṅga*, a more detailed account can be found in the *Samantapāsādikā*, to which we now turn.

The *Samantapāsādikā* comments upon the word "assignment" in the *Mahāvihāra-vinaya* not in the commentary on the fifty-ninth *pācittiya* but in the commentary on the first *nissaggiya-pācittiya*, where the word "assignment" first appears. There the two types are explained in greater detail as follows:

1a. Assignment in person: A bhikkhu having an extra robe (hereafter, "the donor") says to another bhikkhu, "I assign this robe to you." At this point, the donor has the right to deposit the robe, but not to use it, to give it away, or formally take possession of it. If the other bhikkhu says, "You may do with my robe as you like," at that point, the donor has the right to use it as he wishes.

1b. Assignment in person: The donor stands before another bhikkhu and names one of the five types of monastics (bhikkhu, bhikkhunī, sikkhamānā, sāmaṇera, sāmaṇerī) who is not present. The donor says, "I assign this robe to So-and-so." At this point, the donor has the right to deposit (*nidheti*) the robe. If the other bhikkhu before him says, "You may do with So-and-so's robe as you wish," at that point, the donor has the right to use it as he wishes.

2. Assignment in the presence of another: The donor stands before another bhikkhu and says, "I give this robe to you so that you may assign it." The other bhikkhu asks, "Who is your friend?" If the donor names one of the five types of monastics "So-and-so," then the other bhikkhu says, "I give this robe to So-and-so." At this point, the donor has the right to deposit the robe. If the other bhikkhu says, "You may do with So-and-so's robe as you like," at that point, the donor has the right to use it as he wishes.[29]

In this way, the word analysis in the *Suttavibhaṅga* of the *vikappanā*-rule describes the types and procedures related to assignment.

28. Vin IV 122,9–16.

29. Sp III 648,3–649,28.

In addition to the *Mahāvihāra-vinaya*, the *Sūtravibhaṅga* explanation of the *vikappanā*-rule in the *Dharmaguptaka*- (Taishō 1428.22.676b2), *Mahīśāsaka*- (Taishō 1421.22.69a10), *Mahāsāṅghika*- (Taishō 1425.379a10), and *Sarvāstivāda-vinayas* (Taishō 1435.23.114c29) also explain the procedures of assignment.[30]

Strangely, however, in the case of the *Mūlasarvāstivāda-vinaya*, the *Sūtravibhaṅga* explanation of the *vikappanā*-rule includes no description of how to make an assignment.[31] We do not find descriptions of the actual procedure of assignment anywhere in the *Mūlasarvāstivāda-vinaya*.[32] Why is it that the *Mūlasarvāstivāda-vinaya* is the only text that does not explain how to make an assignment of an extra robe? An answer to this problem shall be proposed in the second half of this paper.

As noted above, some Vinayas include a term for assignment in the wording of the ruling of the first *nissaggiya-pācittiya*, while others do not. If the term "assignment" had been included in the wording of the first *nissaggiya-pācittiya* from the beginning, we would expect the *Vibhaṅga* word-commentary to explain it. However, none of the Vinayas contains such an explanation. Although the act of making an assignment is not explained, common knowledge of the process is assumed in statements such as "There is no offense if an extra robe is assigned."

Accordingly, we must conclude that the *śikṣāpada* of the first *nissaggiya-pācittiya* did not originally include the term for assignment. Rather, it simply stated, "Using an extra robe for more than ten days is an offense requiring confession and forfeiture." Later, a process was devised for making an assignment as an expedient to enable a monk to keep an extra robe semi-permanently. The *vikappanā*-rule that includes the assignment as an essential factor was made after this stage.

As explained above, specific procedures for assignment were first discussed in the *Sūtravibhaṅga* explanation of the *vikappanā*-rule. Under the influence of the *vikappanā*-rule, a new exclusion was added to the *Sūtravibhaṅga* of the first rule requiring confession and forfeiture, stating that a monk, if he had assigned a robe to another person, could use the robe for longer than ten days without committing an offense. Vinayas such as the *Mahāvihāra-vinaya* include such an exclusion. Later, the *śikṣāpada* of the first rule requiring confession and forfeiture itself was influenced by the words of the *Sūtravibhaṅga*, and the term

30. However, unlike the other Vinayas, the *Sarvāstivāda-vinaya* allows only *parammukhā-vikappanā* and forbids *sammukhāvikappanā*.

31. Taishō 1442.23.851b25; Sde dge 3, 'Dul ba, vol. *ja*, 276a4–b2; Peking 1032, 'Dul ba, vol. *nye*, 258a6–b3.

32. Yamagiwa 2009, 247–248.

"assignment" was incorporated into the *śikṣāpada* of some, but not all, Vinayas: the *Mahāvihāra-*, *Mahīśāsaka-*, *Mahāsāṅghika-*, and *Sarvāstivāda-vinaya*s all preserve the original form; the *śikṣāpada*s preserved in the *Dharmaguptaka-* and *Mūlasarvāstivāda-vinaya*s include a term for assignment.[33]

Thus, we have determined which Vinayas are older and which are more recent in this respect, depending on whether or not they include a term for assignment in the first rule requiring confession and forfeiture. Next, we will examine the peculiarities of the *Mūlasarvāstivāda-vinaya* with regard to the first rule requiring confession and forfeiture and the *vikappanā*-rule.

Features of Assignment in the Mūlasarvāstivāda-vinaya

Three particular points regarding the *Mūlasarvāstivāda-vinaya* have been discussed so far:

1. In the *Mūlasarvāstivāda-vinaya*, as in the *Dharmaguptaka-vinaya*, the *śikṣāpada* of the first *naisargikā* includes the word *datvā*, "having given," with the meaning of assigning an extra robe to another monastic. As discussed above, this mention of assignment is a later addition.
2. The *vikappanā*-rule in other Vinayas states, "If a bhikṣu, having assigned a robe to a bhikṣu, bhikṣuṇī, śikṣamāṇā, śrāmaṇera, or śrāmaṇerī, should make use of it without it having been formally given up by the one to whom it was assigned, there is an offense requiring confession and forfeiture." However, in the *Mūlasarvāstivāda-vinaya*, assignment is limited only to bhikṣus. The words *bhikṣuṇī*, *śikṣamāṇā*, *śrāmaṇera*, or *śrāmaṇerī* do not appear. The only other Vinaya that mentions exclusively bhikṣus in the *śikṣāpada* is Version B of the Sarvāstivādin *Prātimokṣa-sūtra*.
3. In the *vikappanā*-rule of all Vinayas except the *Mūlasarvāstivāda-vinaya*, the *Sūtravibhaṅga*s present specific procedures for assigning a robe. However, these explanations are not found in the *vikappanā*-rule of the *Mūlasarvāstivāda-vinaya*.

How can these distinctive points in the *Mūlasarvāstivāda-vinaya* be explained? Let us begin by examining the origin story of the first *naisargikā*

33. This shows that *Prātimokṣa* rules were not devised all at once, but rather were created over time. At the very least, we can determine that the wording of the first *nissaggiya-pācittiya* was enacted first without the *vikappanā*-rule, and only after that was the *vikappanā*-rule introduced.

in the *Mūlasarvāstivāda-vinaya*, which is similar to the story in the *Mahāvihāra-vinaya*.

According to the story preserved in the Tibetan translation, monks had many robes that they wore for different occasions such as going on alms rounds or meeting their *upādhyāya* and *ācārya*, and so on.[34] A slightly covetous bhikṣu, on seeing this, criticized them, and the Buddha established the initial rule, which reads as follows:

> When a robe has been made, a bhikṣu shall keep three robes if his *kaṭhina* has been removed. Keeping more of these robes is an offense entailing confession and forfeiture.

Later on, a householder wished to donate a beautiful robe to Mahākāśyapa but did not have the chance to meet him, and so the householder went to Ānanda with the robe and asked him to give it as an offering when Mahākāśyapa visited on the *uposatha* day. Ānanda knew it would be an offense of the first rule to take the robe, but not taking it would interfere with the householder's giving of an offering and be harmful to Mahākāśyapa. Therefore, Ānanda, seeking the counsel of the Buddha, took the robe to him and explained the situation. The Buddha then declared, "A bhikṣu is allowed to have an extra robe for up to ten days without assigning it."[35]

Soon after this, the Buddha modified the rule. This amended rule is the final version of the first *naisargikā*:

> When a robe has been made and a bhikṣu's *kaṭhina* has been removed, he may keep an extra robe for ten days without having undergone the procedure of assignment. For one who exceeds that period, there is an offense entailing confession and forfeiture.[36]

The story line is quite natural. However, in the Chinese translation of the Mūlasarvāstivādin *Bhikṣuvibhaṅga*,[37] the story on which the amended rule

34. Sde dge 3, 'Dul ba, vol. *cha*, 39a7–41b4; Peking 1032, 'Dul ba, vol. *je*, 36a5–38a7.

35. Sde dge 3, 'Dul ba, vol. *cha*, 41b2: *de lta bas na dge slong gis zhag bcu'i bar du gos lhag pa rung bar ma byas pa bcang bar rjes su gnang ngo //*.

36. Sde dge 3, 'Dul ba, vol. *cha*, 41b4: *dge slong chos gos zin pas sra brkyang phyung na zhag bcu'i bar du gos lhag pa rung bar ma byas pa bcang bar bya'o / de las 'das par 'chang na spang ba'i ltung byed do //*. The Tibetan text includes a long annotation on this rule, but I do not discuss it here.

37. Taishō 1442.23.711c5–16: 阿難陀便持彼衣詣世尊所。禮雙足已具以白佛。佛告阿難陀。善哉善哉阿難陀。我未聽者今汝預知。若有婆羅門居士施苾芻衣者。彼諸苾芻須應爲受。

is based differs greatly from the Tibetan translation. The Chinese does not include the statement, "A bhikṣu is allowed to have a robe for up to ten days without assigning it." Instead, it says something completely different.

In the Chinese version of the story, Ānanda was perplexed by what to do with the robe and thus sought the counsel of the Buddha, who declared, "If a *brāhmaṇa* or a householder donates robes, the bhikṣus may receive them, dispose of robes they had previously, and keep the new robes."[38] Then the bhikṣus did not know what to do with the old robes that had been disposed of. The Buddha directed, "Keep and use the old robes and extra robes, considering them to be entrusted to [your] *upādhyāya* or *ācārya*." However, since a bhikṣu kept the robes for a long time without assigning them, the Buddha amended the initial rule, the Chinese text of which is similar to the Tibetan translation.

There are two problems. First, the flow of the story in the Chinese version does not make sense. Ānanda went to the Buddha for counsel regarding the disposal of the extra robe he was supposed to give to Mahākāśyapa. According to the Tibetan, the Buddha said, "An extra robe may be kept for ten days" (i.e., until the arrival of Mahākāśyapa). However, according to the Chinese, the Buddha declared, "If a *brāhmaṇa* or a householder donates robes, the bhikṣus may receive them, dispose of robes they had previously, and keep the new robes." In the Chinese, the Buddha's declaration is completely unrelated to Ānanda's dilemma.

Second, the Buddha declared, "Keep and use the old robes and extra robes, considering them to be entrusted to [your] *upādhyāya* or *ācārya*." In other words, extra robes were to be assigned to the *upādhyāya* or *ācārya*. This instruction is peculiar to this text and is not found in other Vinayas or in the Tibetan translation of the *Mūlasarvāstivāda-vinaya*.

These contradictions point to a problem with the text. Given that this portion exists only in the Chinese version and not in the Tibetan, we can conclude that it was inserted in the original text of the Chinese version after the *Mūlasarvāstivāda-vinaya* split into two recensions, as represented by the Tibetan and Chinese versions, respectively.[39]

應捨舊衣當持新者。時諸苾芻雖聞此語仍未解了。所捨舊衣欲何所作。佛言所有舊衣及餘長衣。應於親教師及軌範師處。作委寄想而持用之。時諸苾芻不爲分別經久持畜。世尊知已告諸苾芻曰。我觀十利重爲汝等。制其學處應如是說。若復苾芻作衣已竟羯恥那衣。復出得長衣齊十日。不分別應畜。若過畜者。泥薩祇波逸底迦。

38. Taishō 1442.23.711c7–8: 若有婆羅門居士施苾芻衣者。彼諸苾芻須應爲受。應捨舊衣當持新者。

39. Scholars have noted other cases where the Chinese version of the *Mūlasarvāstivāda-vinaya* has more revisions to rules than the Tibetan version (e.g., Sasaki 2018).

Notable here is the instruction to entrust an extra robe to an *upādhyāya* or *ācārya*. No other Vinaya specifies to which of the five types of monastics a robe should be assigned, and nowhere else is assignment limited to an *upādhyāya* or *ācārya*. This regulation is unique to the Chinese translation of the *Mūlasarvāstivāda-vinaya*.[40] It seems that the reference to *upādhyāya* and *ācārya* was added to the origin story of the original text of the Chinese version in order to give the regulation greater authority. We find similar passages in a number of other Mūlasarvāstivādin materials.

In Viśeṣamitra's *Vinayasaṃgraha*, for instance, we read:

> "If a bhikṣu has an extra robe, it must be assigned" means that whether it is a finished robe or an unfinished robe, it should be assigned by entrusting it to an *ācārya* or *upādhyāya*. Otherwise, it can be assigned to some other noble person or fellow practitioner. [If] those to whom the robes are entrusted maintain good conduct, are well informed, and are more virtuous in every way than [the donor] himself, then entrusting it is good. [During assignment,] say the following words: "Venerable, please remember these words. I, Bhikṣu So-and-so, have this extra robe that I have not yet assigned. It must be assigned. I assign it now to an *upādhyāya* and keep it by myself with the *upādhyāya* as the trustee." Repeat this again, and then a third time.[41]

Here, the *ācārya* or *upādhyāya* is the preferred person to whom an assignment of the robe is made. The words of the bhikṣu who is performing the assignment make it clear that the assignment should be made to his *upādhyāya*. Here too, then, the regulation to make an assignment to an *ācārya* or *upādhyāya* is found. The Tibetan translation of this text agrees with the Chinese.[42]

In the *Muktaka* of the *Mūlasarvāstivāda-vinaya*, we find the following:

> And [Upāli] said to the Buddha, "I do not know what to say if there are other robes apart from these thirteen robes." The Buddha said, "Keep them after assigning them to an *ācārya* or *upādhyāya* as the

40. Nishimoto was the first to notice this fact (1933, 300).

41. Taishō 1458.24.553b28–c6: 若苾芻有餘長衣。合分別者。或已成衣。或未成衣。應於阿遮利耶鄔波馱耶處。作委寄意而分別之。或餘尊人。或同梵行者。其委寄人持戒多聞所有德行。過於己者委寄爲善。應如是說。具壽存念。我苾芻某甲有此長衣。未爲分別。是合分別。我今於鄔波馱耶處。而作分別。以鄔波馱耶作委寄者。我今持之。第二第三亦如是說。

42. *Vinayasaṃgraha*, Sde dge 4105, 'Dul ba, vol. *nu*, 143a2–5.

> trustee. Assign them like this. Turn to a bhikṣu and say these words: 'Venerable, please remember these words. I, Bhikṣu So-and-so, have this extra robe that I have not yet assigned. It must be assigned. Now, in the Venerable's presence, I assign this to my *upādhyāya* as the trustee. I will now keep it.' Say it three times."[43]

The Tibetan translation is the same as the Chinese: the bhikṣu should keep (*bsngos la bcang bar bya ste*) an extra robe by specifying an *ācārya* or *upādhyāya* or some other trustworthy person (*yid gcugs pa rnams*) as the trustee.[44]

The *Ekottarakarmaśataka* gives the following:

> "Reverend, what should I do if there is an extra robe apart from these thirteen requisite robes?" The Buddha said, "[One] should entrust the extra robe apart from the thirteen robes to the two types of teachers (*ācārya* and *upādhyāya*) or another type of exemplary person. [One] should hold the object [in one's hand] and say these words to another bhikṣu: 'Venerable, please remember these words. I, So-and-so, have this extra robe that I have not yet assigned. It must be assigned. I assign it now in the presence of the Venerable to [my] *upādhyāya* as the trustee. I will now keep it.' Repeat this a second and then a third time."[45]

This is nearly the same as the passage from the *Muktaka*: it consists of an instruction to assign an extra robe to specific types of people. The *ācārya* and *upādhyāya* are the preferred recipients of the assignment. Also notable here is Yijing's annotation: "When assigning a robe, there is no 'indirect assignment (*parammukhāvikappanā*)' or 'true assignment (*sammukhāvikappanā*).' Even though other texts may state that there are [these types of assignment], that

43. Taishō 1452.24.448a5–10: 復白佛言。此十三衣外更有餘衣。不知云何。佛言。應於軌範師及親教師而作委寄分別持之。應如是分別。對一苾芻作如是說。具壽存念。我苾芻某甲。有此長衣未爲分別。是合分別。我今於具壽前而爲分別。以鄔波馱耶作委寄者。我今持之三說。

44. *Vinayottaragrantha*, Sde dge 7, 'Dul ba, vol. *pa*, 180b1–4; Peking 1037, 'Dul ba, vol. *phe*, 174b8–175a3.

45. Taishō 1453.24.498a24–b2: 大德。此十三資具衣外自餘長衣。此欲如何。佛言。十三衣外自餘長衣。應於二師及餘尊類。而作委寄。應持其物對餘苾芻作如是說。具壽存念。我某甲有此長衣。未爲分別。是合分別(舊云說淨者取意也)我今於具壽前而作分別。以鄔波馱耶作委寄者。我今持之。第二第三亦如是說。

is not the teaching of this *nikāya*."[46] A similar description can be found in the *Karmavācanā* from Gilgit.[47]

From this passage, we can see that in various texts belonging to the Mūlasarvāstivādin Vinaya tradition, the notion that an *ācārya* or *upādhyāya* should be the recipient of an assignment was common. Statements on which this idea is based are inserted into the origin stories of the Chinese translation of the *Mūlasarvāstivāda-vinaya*. Thus, it follows that this method of assignment was newly introduced in the *Mūlasarvāstivāda-vinaya*.

In the earlier regulations, the five types of monastics were eligible to receive an assignment; there was no mention of *ācārya* or *upādhyāya* as trustee. Therefore, there is a discrepancy with the older regulation, especially with the *vikappanā*-rule quoted above, according to which there is an offense entailing confession if a bhikṣu, having assigned a robe to a bhikṣu, bhikṣuṇī, śikṣamāṇā, śrāmaṇera, or śrāmaṇerī, uses it without permission.

This rule clearly states that assignment is to be made to the five types of monastics; thus, the new regulation either contradicts or narrows the scope of the *vikappanā*-rule. Accordingly, for it to be implemented, the *vikappanā*-rule would have to be changed to conform to the new regulation.

In fact, only the *Mūlasarvāstivāda-vinaya*'s *vikappanā*-rule, as we have seen above, does not mention bhikṣuṇīs, śikṣamāṇās, śrāmaṇeras, or śrāmaṇerīs. This does not conflict with the regulation that assignment be made to an *ācārya* or *upādhyāya* (or other exemplary person). Thus, we must infer that the reason why bhikṣuṇīs, śikṣamāṇās, śrāmaṇeras, and śrāmaṇerīs are not mentioned in the *vikappanā*-rule in the *Mūlasarvāstivāda-vinaya* is that the procedure of assignment had changed within a *nikāya* or group that used the *Mūlasarvāstivāda-vinaya*.

In addition, the *Mūlasarvāstivāda-vinaya*, unlike the *Sūtravibhaṅga* explanation of the *vikappanā*-rule in all other Vinayas, does not include a specific procedure for assignment, let alone specific types of assignment such as *sammukhāvikappanā* and *parammukhāvikappanā*, which can be found in the *Mahāvihāra-vinaya*. As we have seen, Yijing noted that the *Mūlasarvāstivāda-vinaya* did not accept this kind of *vikappanā*.

On the other hand, handbooks such as the **Ekottarakarmaśataka* clearly include a regulation that the recipient of an assignment should be an *ācārya*, *upādhyāya*, or other exemplary person. If this were the original form of assign-

46. Taishō 1453.24.498b4: 分別衣法更無展轉眞實之事。設有餘文故非斯部之教。

47. Von Hinüber 1969, 112: *samanvāharāyuṣmaṃn aham evaṃnāmā bhikṣur idaṃ cīvaram atirekam avikalpitaṃ vikalpanārham upādhyāyasya vikalpayāmy upādhyāyasya viśvāsena dhārayāmi.*

ment and it had been modified later to "assignment to one of the five types of monastics" as in the *Mahāvihāra-vinaya*, there would have to have been some descriptions that explain the "assignment to *ācārya* or *upādhyāya*" with consistency in the *Mūlasarvāstivāda-vinaya* itself. However, we do not have any such descriptions.

On the other hand, if the assignment shown in the *Mahāvihāra-vinaya* and elsewhere were the original and had been replaced later with the new type of assignment—assignment to *ācārya* or *upādhyāya*—in the *nikāya* where the *Mūlasarvāstivāda-vinaya* was used, the present situation would seem quite natural.

Assignment in the Bodhisattvabhūmi

It is clear from the above that new forms of assignment were implemented in the *Mūlasarvāstivāda-vinaya*. When and by whom might the original form have been modified? Chapter 10 (*Śīlapaṭala*) of the *Bodhisattvabhūmi* can help answer these questions.

> Regarding this [point], the following represents skillful means: A bodhisattva has from the outset dedicated and entrusted with a pure attitude all his or her possessions and objects suitable for practicing charity to the buddhas and bodhisattvas throughout the ten directions in the same way that a fully ordained monastic dedicates his or her robes to a teacher or preceptor. Because of [having made] this dedication, even though [such an individual] may have obtained an extensive and varied quantity of possessions and objects that are suitable for practicing charity, he or she is referred to as "a bodhisattva who abides in the *ārya* lineage."[48]

In the explanation of *dānapāramitā* (perfection of giving), it is taught that bodhisattvas are to assign their possessions to buddhas and bodhisattvas

48. Engle 2016, 223. *Yujia shidi lun* 瑜伽師地論 (*Bendifen zhong pusadi* 本地分中菩薩地) (Taishō 1579.30.508c1–7): 云何施設方便善巧。謂諸菩薩先於所畜一切資具一切施物。爲作淨故以淨意樂捨與十方諸佛菩薩。譬如苾芻於己衣物爲作淨故。捨與親教軌範師等。如是菩薩淨施因縁。雖復貯畜種種上妙一切資具一切施物。猶得名爲安住聖種。Wogihara [1930–1936] 1971, 128.12–18; Dutt 1978, 89.9–13: *tatredam upāya-kauśalaṃ. prāg eva bodhisattvena sarvapariṣkārāḥ sarva-deya-dharmā daśasu dikṣu viśuddhen' āśayena buddha-bodhisattvānāṃ nisṛṣṭā bhavaṃti vikalpitāḥ tad-yathā nāma bhikṣur ācāryāya vā upādhyāyāya vā sva-cīvaraṃ vikalpayet. sa evaṃ vikalpa-hetoḥ sarva-citrodāra-pariṣkāra-deya-dharma-saṃnidhi-prāpto 'py ārya-vaṃśa-vihārī bodhisattva ity ucyate.*

of the ten directions just as a bhikṣu should assign his robe to an *ācārya* or *upādhyāya*. This description can be found in all three Chinese translations of the *Bodhisattvabhūmi*: *Bodhisattvabhūmi* of *Yogācārabhūmi* (Taishō 1579), *Pusa dichi jing* 菩薩地持經 (Taishō 1581), and *Pusa shanjie jing* 菩薩善戒經 (Taishō 1582), and the Tibetan version and Sanskrit text.[49] Though the exact date of the Chinese translation of the *Pusa dichi jing* is unclear, we know that it was translated between the years 414 and 426 CE, and it is one of the oldest *vijñaptimātratā* texts translated into Chinese. The *Pusa shanjie jing* was translated into Chinese in 431. The distinctive regulations regarding the assigning of robes to one's *ācārya* or *upādhyāya* found in the Chinese translation of the *Bhikṣuvibhaṅga* of the *Mūlasarvāstivāda-vinaya* and the Mūlasarvāstivādin *Uttaragrantha* and various digests appear in the earliest Yogācāra literature.[50]

This passage presupposes that bhikṣus in the saṅgha of the authors of the *Bodhisattvabhūmi* were actually assigning their robes to *ācārya*s or *upādhyāya*s. Thus, in the area where the *Bodhisattvabhūmi* was composed, the procedure for assignment was that of the *Mūlasarvāstivāda-vinaya*, according to which *ācārya*s or *upādhyāya*s are the recipients.

Among the extant Vinayas, the only references to this type of assignment are in the *Mūlasarvāstivāda-vinaya*; thus, we can confirm that the earlier Yogācāra text, the *Bodhisattvabhūmi*, was not composed in a saṅgha that used the *Mahāvihāra-*, *Dharmaguptaka-*, *Mahīśāsaka-*, *Mahāsāṅghika-*, or *Sarvāstivāda-vinaya*s. Yijing noted that the *nikāya* that used the

49. *Pusa dichi jing* 菩薩地持經 (Taishō 1581.30.908b15–22): 云何菩薩方便不施。不忍直言必定不與。要以軟語開解發遣。作是方便有而不施。菩薩本來所畜衆具一切施物。以清淨心於一切十方諸佛菩薩捨作淨施已。譬如比丘以己衣物於和上阿闍梨所捨作淨施。如是作淨施因縁故。得畜種種無量財物。故名住聖種菩薩。; *Pusa shanjie jing* 菩薩善戒經 (Taishō 1582.30.981a12–19): 復次菩薩聞求者來。即出承迎爲施床座。既得相見先意共語軟言問訊。隨所須物事事供施。菩薩摩訶薩初發心時自言。我今所有之物當施十方諸佛菩薩及諸衆生。譬如弟子以衣鉢物奉施於師。師雖不取而此弟子得福無量。菩薩亦爾。所有之物奉施諸佛及諸菩薩。諸佛菩薩雖不受取。亦令施者得無量福。

50. Much research has been published on the relationship among *Bodhisattvabhūmi*, *Pusa dichi jing* (Taishō 1581), *Pusa shanjie jing* (Taishō 1582), and *Youposai jie jing* 優婆塞戒經 (Taishō 1488): Ōno 1954; Hirakawa 1960b; Naitō 1962; Tsuchihashi 1968; Okimoto 1973; Kitazuka 1997. A comprehensive investigation into Vinaya sources quoted in the *Poshalun* 婆沙論 (= *Apidamo dapiposha lun* 阿毘達磨大毘婆沙論, Taishō 1545) reveals that while some are quotations from the *Sarvāstivāda-vinaya* and some are from the *Mūlasarvāstivāda-vinaya*, in many cases no corresponding passages can be found in the extant Vinayas. Thus, the Vinaya used by the editor of the *Poshalun* might be an unknown Sarvāstivādin Vinaya (Sasaki 2000). Other research has pointed out that the *Sarvāstivāda-vinaya* was used by the Vaibhāṣikas of Kaśmīr, and the *Mūlasarvāstivāda-vinaya* was used by the Sautrāntikas (Sasaki 2018). It is hoped that further examination—considering these facts and the result of this article—will lead to a more detailed understanding of the history of the Sarvāstivādins.

Mūlasarvāstivāda-vinaya rejected other types of assignment, such as *parammukhāvikappanā* or *sammukhāvikappanā*, which appear in the Vinayas of other *nikāyas*. In light of his comment, we can be virtually certain that the *Bodhisattvabhūmi* was created in a saṅgha where the *Mūlasarvāstivāda-vinaya* or its prototype was used.

Version B of the Sarvāstivāda *Prātimokṣa-sūtra* does not mention the five types of monastics in the *śikṣāpada* of its *vikappanā*-rule and thus agrees with the *vikappanā*-rules of the *Mūlasarvāstivāda-vinaya*. Therefore, we can surmise that Version B of the Sarvāstivāda *Prātimokṣa-sūtra* was somehow contaminated through contact with the *Mūlasarvāstivāda-vinaya*.

Conclusion

The *Mahāvihāra-*, *Mahīśāsaka-*, *Mahāsāṅghika-*, and *Sarvāstivāda-vinayas* do not have a phrase for assignment (*vikappanā*) in the wording of the first offense requiring confession and forfeiture. On the other hand, the *Dharmaguptaka-* and *Mūlasarvāstivāda-vinayas* include it in their version of the rule. Thus, originally, *vikappanā* was not included in the wording of the first *nissaggiya-pācittiya*. The wording of the first *nissaggiya-pācittiya* was established before assignment had been devised as an expedient way to allow monks to keep more property than previously allowed.

Later, the idea of assignment was created. Then the *vikappanā*-rule, the regulation on assignment, was set forth. This newly created idea of assignment was incorporated into the *Suttavibhaṅga* of the first *nissaggiya-pācittiya* to maintain logical consistency. Later, the *Dharmaguptaka-* and *Mūlasarvāstivāda-vinayas*, under the influence of the adoption of the expedient of assignment into the *Sūtravibhaṅga* of earlier Vinayas, included assignment in the wording of their own first *nissaggiya-pācittiya*.

The procedure of assignment in the *Mūlasarvāstivāda-vinaya* differs from that in the other Vinayas in that the recipient is limited to an *ācārya* or *upādhyāya*. This limitation was implemented in the *Mūlasarvāstivāda-vinaya* at a later time. When this new procedure was introduced, several changes occurred: the *śikṣāpada* of the *vikappanā*-rule was modified in the Vinaya of the Mūlasarvāstivādins; the descriptions of the procedures for performing original assignment were removed from the *Sūtravibhaṅga* explanation of the *vikappanā*-rule of the proto-*Mūlasarvāstivāda-vinaya*; the descriptions of the new type of assignment were incorporated into other sections of the *Mūlasarvāstivāda-vinaya* such as the *Vinayottaragrantha*. Finally, the reference to the new type of assignment was added to the origin story of the first *nissaggiya-pācittiya* in order to give the procedure greater authority.

The new procedure for assignment introduced in the *Mūlasarvāstivāda-vinaya* can be found in the *Bodhisattvabhūmi*, a very early *vijñaptimātratā* text. Due to this, we can confirm that the procedure described in the *Mūlasarvāstivāda-vinaya* was in fact in use in the saṅgha in which the *Bodhisattvabhūmi* was composed. The *Bodhisattvabhūmi* contains the oldest record of the actual use of a Vinaya procedure that is found only in the *Mūlasarvāstivāda-vinaya*.

Works Cited

Abbreviations

Peking	*Eiin Pekin-ban chibetto daizōkyō: Ōtani daigaku toshokan-zō* 影印北京版西蔵大蔵経：大谷大学図書館蔵 (*The Tibetan Tripitaka: Peking Edition. Kept in the Library of the Otani University, Kyoto*). Edited by Chibetto Daizōkyō Kenkyūkai 西蔵大蔵経研究会. 168 vols. Tokyo: Chibetto daizōkyō kenkyūkai 西蔵大蔵経研究会, 1955–1961.
Sde dge	*The Tibetan Tripiṭaka: Taipei Edition*. Edited by A. W. Barber. 72 vols. Taipei: SMC Publishing, 1991.
Sp	*Samantapāsādikā* (*Vinaya-aṭṭhakathā*). Edited by Junjirō Takakusu and Makoto Nagai. 7 vols. London: The Pali Text Society, 1924–1947.
Taishō	*Taishō shinshū daizōkyō* 大正新脩大藏經 (*The Buddhist Canon in Chinese, Newly Edited in the Taishō Era*). Edited by Takakusu Junjirō 高楠順次郎 and Watanabe Kaikyoku 渡邊海旭. 100 vols. Tokyo: Taishō issaikyō kankōkai 大正一切經刊行會, 1924–1935.
Vin	*The Vinaya Piṭakaṃ*. Edited by Hermann Oldenberg. 5 vols. Reprint, London: The Pali Text Society, [1879–1883] 1969–1982.

Banerjee, Anukul Chandra. 1977. *Two Buddhist Vinaya Texts in Sanskrit: Prātimokṣa Sūtra and Bhikṣukarmavākya*. Calcutta: The World Press Private Limited.

Clarke, Shayne, ed. 2014. *Vinaya Texts*. Gilgit Manuscripts in the National Archives of India: Facsimile Edition 1. New Delhi and Tokyo: The National Archives of India and The International Research Institute for Advanced Buddhology, Soka University.

———. 2015. "Vinayas." In *Brill's Encyclopedia of Buddhism*, vol. 1: *Literature and Languages*, edited by Jonathan A. Silk, Oskar von Hinüber, and Vincent Eltschinger, 60–87. Leiden and Boston: Brill.

Dutt, Nalinaksha, ed. 1978. *Bodhisattvabhūmiḥ: Being the XVth Section of Asaṅgapāda's Yogācārabhūmiḥ*. 2nd ed. Patna: Kashi Prasad Jayaswal Research Institute.

Engle, Artemus B. 2016. *The Bodhisattva Path to Unsurpassed Enlightenment: A Complete Translation of the Bodhisattvabhūmi*. Boulder, CO: Snow Lion.

von Hinüber, Oskar. 1969. "Eine Karmavācanā-Sammlung aus Gilgit." *Zeitschrift der Deutschen Morgenländischen Gesellschaft* 119.1: 102–132.

Hirakawa Akira 平川彰. 1960a. *Ritsuzō no kenkyū* 律蔵の研究 (*A Study of the Vinaya-piṭaka*). Tokyo: Sankibō busshorin 山喜房佛書林.

———. 1960b. "Daijōkai to *bosatsukai-kyō*" 大乗戒と菩薩戒経 (Mahāyāna Precepts and the *Bodhisattvaprātimokṣa-sūtra*). In *Fukui hakase shōju kinen: tōyō shisō ronshū* 福井博士頌寿記念：東洋思想論集 (*Festschrift for Dr. Fukui: Collected Papers on Eastern Thought*), edited by Fukui Hakase Shōju Kinen Kankōkai 福井博士頌寿記念刊行会, 522–544. Tokyo: Fukui hakase shōju kinen kankōkai 福井博士頌寿記念刊行会.

———. 1993. *Nihyaku gojikkai no kenkyū* 二百五十戒の研究 (*A Study of the 250 Precepts*), vol. 2. Tokyo: Shunjūsha 春秋社.

———. 1998. *Bikuni ritsu no kenkyū* 比丘尼律の研究 (*A Study of the Bhikṣuṇīvinaya*). Tokyo: Shunjūsha 春秋社.

Horner, I. B. 1940. *The Book of the Discipline*, vol. 2. Oxford: The Pali Text Society.

Hu-von Hinüber, Haiyan. 2003. "Das Bhikṣu-Prātimokṣasūtra der Mūlasarvāstivādins, anhand der Sanskrit-Handschriften aus Tibet und Gilgit sowie unter Berücksichtigung der tibetischen und chinesischen Übersetzungen kritisch herausgegeben." Unpublished manuscript available at https://freidok.uni-freiburg.de/data/9535.

Kieffer-Pülz, Petra. 2013. *Verlorene Gaṇṭhipadas zum buddhistischen Ordensrecht: Untersuchungen zu den in der Vajirabuddhiṭīkā zitierten Kommentaren Dhammasiris und Vajirabuddhis*, vol. 2. Wiesbaden: Harrassowitz Verlag.

Kitazuka Mitsunori 北塔光昇. 1997. Ubasokukai-kyō *no kenkyū* 優婆塞戒経の研究 (*A Study of the Sūtra on Upāsaka Precepts*). Kyoto: Nagata bunshōdō 永田文昌堂.

Naitō Ryūō 内藤龍雄. 1962. "*Bosatsu-zenkai-kyō* ni okeru ni san no mondai" 菩薩善戒經における二三の問題 (Some Problems on the *Pusa shanjie jing* [*Bodhisattvacaryānirdeśa*]). *Indogaku bukkyōgaku kenkyū* 印度學佛教學研究 (*Journal of Indian and Buddhist Studies*) 10.1: 130–131.

Nishimoto Ryūzan 西本龍山, trans. 1933. "*Konpon-setsuissaiu-bu binaya*" 根本說一切有部毘奈耶 (*Mūlasarvāstivāda-vinaya*). Ritsu-bu 律部 (Vinaya Section) vol. 19 of *Kokuyaku issaikyō* 國譯一切經 (*Translation into the National Language, or Japanese, of the Entire Canon*). Tokyo: Daitō shuppansha 大東出版社.

Ochiai Takashi 落合隆 (Phra Takashi Pahapungnyo), ed. 2011. *Pāṭimokkha: Pātimokka 227 kaikyō, Tai tērawāda bukkyō biku haradaimokusha Pāṭimokkha:* パーティモッカ二二七戒経, タイ・テーラワーダ仏教・比丘波羅提木叉 (*Pāṭimokkha: The Sutta of 227 Precepts. Thai Theravāda Buddhism: Bhikkhu Pātimokkha*). Doitao, Chiangmai: Wat Phraputthabat-tamo.

Okimoto Katsumi 沖本克巳. 1973. "*Bosatsu-zenkai-kyō* ni tsuite" 菩薩善戒経について (A Study on the *Pusa shanjie jing*). *Indogaku bukkyōgaku kenkyū* 印度學佛教學研究 (*Journal of Indian and Buddhist Studies*) 22.1: 373–378.

Ōno Hōdō 大野法道. 1954. *Daijō kaikyō no kenkyū* 大乗戒経の研究 (*Research on Mahāyāna Precept Sūtras*). Tokyo: Risōsha 理想社.

Pruitt, William, and K. R. Norman, eds. and trans. 2001. *The Pātimokkha*. Oxford: The Pali Text Society.

Sasaki Shizuka 佐々木閑. 2000. "Basharon to ritsu" 婆沙論と律 (Vinayas Quoted in the *Vibhāṣā*). *Indogaku bukkyōgaku kenkyū* 印度學佛教學研究 (*Journal of Indian and Buddhist Studies*) 49.1: 86–94.

———. 2018. "Who Used the Sarvāstivāda Vinaya and the Mūlasarvāstivāda Vinaya?" In *Reading Slowly: A Festschrift for Jens E. Braarvig*, edited by Lutz Edzard, Jens W. Borgland, and Ute Hüsken, 357–373. Wiesbaden: Harrassowitz Verlag.

Satō Mitsuo 佐藤密雄. 1963. *Genshi bukkyō kyōdan no kenkyū* 原始仏教教団の研究 (*A Study of the Early Buddhist Order in the Vinaya Piṭaka*). Tokyo: Sankibō busshorin 山喜房佛書林.

von Simson, Georg, ed. and trans. 2000. *Prātimokṣasūtra der Sarvāstivādins*, Teil II: *Kritische Textausgabe, Übersetzung, Wortindex sowie Nachträge zu Teil I*. Sanskrittexte aus den Turfanfunden 11. Abhandlungen der Akademie der Wissenschaften in Göttingen. Philologisch-historische Klasse, Dritte Folge 238. Göttingen: Vandenhoeck & Ruprecht.

Tatia, Nathmal. 1975. *Prātimokṣasūtram of the Lokottaravādimahāsāṅghika School*. Tibetan Sanskrit Works Series 16. Patna: Kashi Prasad Jayaswal Research Institute.

Tsuchihashi Shūkō 土橋秀高. 1968. "Jukai girei no hensen" 授戒儀礼の変遷 (Transitions of the Precept Conferral Ceremony). In *Bukkyō kyōdan no kenkyū* 仏教教団の研究 (*Research on the Buddhist Order*), edited by Yoshimura Shūki 芳村修基, 95–166. Kyoto: Hyakka-en 百華苑.

Wogihara, Unrai, ed. [1930–1936] 1971. *Bodhisattvabhūmi: A Statement of Whole Course of the Bodhisattva (Being Fifteenth Section of Yogācārabhūmi)*. Reprint, Tokyo: Sankibo Buddhist Book Store.

Yamagiwa Nobuyuki 山極伸之. 2009. "Ritsuzō ga shimesu jōse no shujusō" 律蔵が示す浄施の種々相 (Pāli *vikappanā* and Chinese *jing-shi* in the Various Vinayapiṭakas). *Nippon bukkyō gakkai nenpō* 日本仏教学会年報 (*Journal of the Nippon Buddhist Research Association*) 74: 231–252.

Part 3
Epigraphical and Art-Historical Studies

King Pūrṇavarman's Fiery Feet*

Robert L. Brown

King Pūrṇavarman ruled a kingdom or city called Tārumānagara, located in western Java, in the fifth or sixth century CE.[1] Pūrṇavarman left us seven Sanskrit rock inscriptions, four of which have sculptures carved on the stone as well. The sculptures on two of the inscribed rocks (Jambu and Ciaruteun) are footprints identified as those of Pūrṇavarman (plates 1 and 2); on a third inscribed rock (Kebon Kopi) is a set of footprints of the king's elephant (plate 3), and on the fourth inscribed rock (Tegu) is carved a staff.

On the Ciaruteun relief a curious design associated with the footprints has never been identified. My paper suggests that the designs indicate light emanating from the king's feet, based on evidence from Indian texts and inscriptions. It also looks at evidence from the court of the Indian king Harṣavardhana who ruled in the seventh century CE, and at whose court the Chinese monk Xuanzang stayed, leaving us a description of the king's demeanor and the role of the king's personal elephant.

The footprints on the Ciaruteun rock have very unusual designs that appear to be attached to the king's footprints (plate 2). The two designs consist of central circles with straight lines radiating from the circle, and with a single line carved as if connecting the rayed circle to the foot. The two designs are not entirely similar, as the number of rays appears to vary, perhaps ten to twelve.

There have been two interpretations by scholars: either they are spiders or lotuses. Neither explanation is convincing. Some ninety years ago Jean Philippe Vogel gave us one of the most complete analyses of the two possibilities and concluded that neither fits particularly well.[2] Most obviously the designs look nothing like spiders or lotuses. In order to associate these with

* The text of inscriptions and their translations included herein has been updated to conform to modern conventions (e.g., use of diacritics) and reproduced with minor stylistic variation.

1. Griffiths 2014.

2. Vogel 1925, 22–24.

the footprints, scholars have consistently looked to evidence of Brahmanical or Hindu religion. Indeed, religious interpretations are also the way in which Pūrṇavarman's sculptures and inscriptions have usually been interpreted by scholars. My suggestion is to consider them in terms of royal imagery, emphasizing that the footprints are not those of Viṣṇu but are those of a king. In this perspective, my interpretation is that the rayed forms represent the light and splendor of King Pūrṇavarman's feet.

Scholars draw their interpretation of the footprints as those of Viṣṇu directly from the Sanskrit inscription on the stone. It reads in Vogel's edition and translation:

> *vikkrāntasyāvanipateḥ*
> *śrīmataḥ Pūrṇṇavarmaṇaḥ*
> *Tārūmanagarendrasya*
> *Viṣṇor iva padadvayam*
>
> Of the valiant lord of the earth, the illustrious Pūrṇavarman, [who is] the ruler of the town of Tārūma, [is this] the pair of foot-prints like unto Viṣṇu's.[3]

Based on the reference to Viṣṇu, scholars have tended to identify Viṣṇu as the deity whom Pūrṇavarman worshipped and concluded that the footprints themselves are conterminous with those of Viṣṇu. Furthermore, the word *vikrānta*, translated above as "valiant," can have "a special meaning which is connected with the three steps of Viṣṇu."[4] Indeed, the word is found again in another inscription of Pūrṇavarman, the Cidanghiang inscription that was found in 1947:

> *vikrānto 'yaṃ vanipateḥ prabhuḥ satyapara[k]rā[maḥ]*
> *narendrasya bhūtena śrīmataḥ pūrṇṇavarmmaṇaḥ*
>
> This is the conqueror of the 3 worlds (with his three steps), his majesty king Pūrṇavarman, the great king, the hero, (and) to be the banner of all kings in the world.[5]

Hariani Santiko's essay "The Religion of King Pūrṇawarman of Tārumā-

3. Vogel 1925, 22.

4. Santiko 2001, 424.

5. Santiko 2001, 425.

nagara" (2001) expands on the idea of the three strides (*trivikrama*) that Viṣṇu takes to conquer the three worlds of the earth, the ether, and the sky, suggesting that King Pūrṇavarman may have ceremonially performed the three strides and that "He wanted to become Viṣṇu and gain the world."[6]

While I feel Santiko has overstated the connection between Pūrṇavarman and Viṣṇu, there is no question that the king was aware of Viṣṇu's three strides. Rather my point is that the footprints that are carved on the stone along with his inscriptions are not those of Viṣṇu but are clearly stated to be those of the king. Viṣṇu's footprints are mentioned in the inscriptions as a simile for those of the king: the king's footprints are like those of Viṣṇu. The question in my paper is how to identify the circular rayed designs that are connected to his feet on the Ciaruteun inscription. Scholars, assuming the footprints are those of Viṣṇu, have until now failed to find a convincing interpretation.

Before discussing how considering the footprints to be those of the king and not those of Viṣṇu may open up another interpretation of the designs, we should look at one more of Pūrṇavarman's inscriptions, that of Jambu:

> *Śrīmān dātā kṛtajño narapatir asamo yaḥ purā [Tā]r[u]māya[ṃ] nāmnā śrī-Pūrṇṇavarmmā pracuraripuśarābhedyavikhyātavarmmo*
> *tasyedam pādavimbadvayam arinagarotsādane nityadakṣam bhaktānāṃ yandripāṇām bhavati sukhakaraṃ śalyabhūtaṃ ripūṇām.*

> Illustrious, munificent, and true to his duty was the unequalled lord of men—the illustrious Pūrṇavarman by name—who once [ruled] at Tārumā and whose famous armour (*varman*) was impenetrable by the darts of a multitude of foes. His is this pair of foot-prints which, ever dexterous in destroying hostile towns, is salutary to devoted princes, but a thorn in the side of his enemies.[7]

The Jambu inscription clearly states that the footprints that accompany the inscription are those of the king. The actual sculptures of the feet are damaged. Already in 1925 when Vogel was writing, he mentioned that this pair of footprints are on top of the rock and are partly broken away. There are apparently no designs in association with them. I am not sure why Santiko states that "in the Jambu inscription it symbolizes the act of performing 'three steps' by king

6. Santiko 2001, 431.

7. Vogel 1925, 25.

Pūrṇawarman similar to the act of the god Viṣṇu," as I do not see any such reference.[8] The comparison of the king's footprints to those of Viṣṇu occurs only in the Ciaruteun inscription.

The feet of a king are a constant trope in Indic inscriptions and texts indicating his power, strength, and beauty. The king is often described as sitting with his feet raised on his throne or on a footstool so they are clearly in view. The placement of the head beside or under a person's feet is indicative of honor and submission, metaphorically representing that the purest and most honored part of the person giving honor, the head, is equivalent to the lowest and most impure, the feet, of the person being honored. This imagery is seen in many contexts in Indic-related symbolism, from honoring one's teacher to honoring a conquering hero or a deity. In bowing in defeat at the feet of a triumphant king, the flower garlands and jewels on the crown of the vassal kings fall onto the dominant king's feet. For example, the Rīsthal inscription of 515 CE says:

> [The King Prakāśadharman] falsified in battle the Hūṇa (Hun) overlord's title of "Emperor", which (had) become established on earth up to (the time of) Toramāṇa, whose footstool was colored by the rays of light from the jewels in the crowns of kings.[9]

Another inscription, the Aphsad inscription by Sūkṣmaśiva, describes King Ādityasena's feet as if igniting in flames with the touch of the defeated kings' heads:

> [King Ādityasena] Whose arms are swollen and twitch due to the splitting of the temples of rutting elephants in war, whose halo of fame [. . .] by the power of the various enemies whom he had destroyed, whose feet are like a wild and sparkling fire (as they are touched) by the crowned heads of all the kings that he had cast down, whose renowned and spotless glory is his pride in battle, (that) king is possessed of Fortune.[10]

While these quotations from inscriptions might be interpreted as literary grandiosity, we have the poet Bāṇa's description of his audience with King Harṣavardhana in around 613 CE. While there is no doubt Bāṇa's description

8. Santiko 2001, 426.

9. Salomon 1989, 8.

10. Bakker 2014, 131.

inflates the visual scene and flatters the king, Bāṇa is overcome with joy and awe when first sighting Harṣa. Bāṇa writes:

> His [King Harṣa's] left foot was playfully placed on a large costly footstool made of sapphires, girt round with a band of rubies,—as if it were the (dark) head of Kali the demon of the iron age,—while the surface of the ground was dyed by the rays which fell on it; like the youthful Kṛiṣṇa when he planted his foot on the circle of hoods of the serpent Kāliya, he dignified the earth by the spreading rays of his toe-nails, white like fine linen, as with the tiara of his chief queen. His feet were very red as with wrath at unsubmissive kings, and they shed a very bright ruby-light on the crowded crests of the prostrate monarchs, and caused a sunset of all the fierce luminaries of war and poured streams of honey from the flowers of the crest garlands of the local kings. . . .[11]

I take my interpretation of the footprints of King Pūrṇavarman from these and similar inscriptions and textual sources. We can imagine King Pūrṇavarman's feet visualized "like a wild and sparkling fire," and his toenails spreading rays "white like fine linen." The two designs attached to Pūrṇavarman's sculptured feet spread in a circle of rays from a circular center indicating rays of sparkling fire and light. The bursts of rays are connected to the king's feet by the threads that go to the big toes. This indicates the source of and relationship between the burst of light and the foot and indeed appear to link directly to the big toes and their nails. The nails of kings are referred to frequently in the inscriptions and the texts as being reflective and producing light.

For example, using again Bāṇa's *Harṣacarita*, when the "goddess of the Royal Prosperity" was given a promise of protection by King Harṣa, he was "waited on reverentially by the reflected images of a fair handmaid standing near, which fell on his toe-nails, as if they were the ten directions of space impersonate."[12] That is, the king's protection, personified by the reflected images, is seen everywhere, in all spatial directions. The reflective toenails of kings were seen not only on King Harṣa's feet but on other kings mentioned in the *Harṣacarita* as well. For example, when the conquered vassal chiefs were presented to King Harṣa, some hung their heads so that their faces were

11. Cowell and Thomas [1897] 1968, 58–59.

12. Cowell and Thomas [1897] 1968, 57.

reflected in their toenails, while others "seemed to present chowries in obsequious service under the form of the rays issuing from their nails."[13]

The artists of Pūrṇavarman's carved feet produced a clever solution to creating visual imagery of a penumbra of exploding light. The importance of Pūrṇavarman's feet as indicating the king's valor and power is demonstrated in his Jambu inscription: "His [Pūrṇavarman's] is this pair of foot-prints which, ever dexterous in destroying hostile towns, is salutary to devoted princes, but a thorn in the side of his enemies."[14] Further, the Kebon Kopi inscription that identifies the sculpture of two feet of the king's elephant stresses the king's role as a warrior: "Here appeareth the pair of foot-prints of the . . . . Airāvata(?)-like elephant of the lord of Tārumā [who is] great in . . . . . . and(?)victory."[15] The sculpture of two of the feet of Pūrṇavarman's elephant (plate 3) is a clear visual link to these two inscriptions and the king's identification as a warrior and conquering hero.

It is noteworthy that only two feet of Airāvata are carved on the rock. Was the rock simply too small for four? While I do not have an explanation, I can point out that the two footprints appear to be of the front feet of the elephant. The prints clearly show that the elephant has five toes; Asian elephants have five toes on their front feet and four on their back feet. This may be of little help in showing why only two feet were depicted, but at least it orients us to visualize Airāvata's massive head and we do not have to ponder which end of the elephant those massive feet upheld.

Interestingly, it is information about King Harṣavardhana, the seventh-century Indian king mentioned above as the topic of Bāṇa's poem the *Harṣacarita*, that helps us understand the significance of King Pūrṇavarman's elephant. Bāṇa describes in great detail Harṣa's royal court that he visited around 613 CE. Bāṇa gives a long description of the swirl of people and animals that surrounded the inner court where Harṣa sat. Before Bāṇa was allowed to enter into the presence of Harṣa, he spent a long period admiring Harṣa's royal elephant, Darpaśāta, who had his own enclosure. Bāṇa's guide told him: "This is his majesty's favourite elephant, his external heart, his very self in another birth, his vital airs gone outside from him, his friend in battle and in sport. . . ."[16] The importance of a king's personal elephant cannot be exaggerated.

13. Cowell and Thomas [1897] 1968, 48.

14. Vogel 1925, 25.

15. Vogel 1925, 28.

16. Cowell and Thomas [1897] 1968, 51.

A second historical witness to King Harṣa was the Chinese Buddhist monk Xuanzang, who met Harṣa several times. Xuanzang was highly regarded by Harṣa and accompanied the king in 643 on his tour to Prayāga to celebrate a universal act of charity in which the king gave away all of his wealth in order to increase his merit. The 643 celebration was the sixth and last of these elaborate events that Harṣa had held every five years during his long reign.[17] Xuanzang reports that Harṣa, dressed as the god Indra, gathered his audience of those invited to the distribution at Kanauj and appeared riding on an elephant while throwing treasure to the people.[18] The acts of charity continued for seventy-five days. The sculptured footprints of Pūrṇavarman's elephant beside the Kebon Kopi inscription likens them to those of Airāvata, Indra's elephant. This implies that Pūrṇavarman can be likened to Indra, a similar visualization that King Harṣa created in his playacting at Kanauj.

What both Bāṇa's and Xuanzang's eyewitness accounts add to our understanding of King Pūrṇavarman's inscriptions and sculptures is how embedded they are in Indic royal symbolism. Thus, through his footprints Pūrṇavarman presents himself in words and art in terms that would have been readily understandable in royal courts in both India and Java. Cédric Ferrier and Judit Törzsök, in their article "Meditating on the King's Feet? Some Remarks on the Expression *Pādānudhyāta*," make the argument that scholars have wrongly regarded Indian kingship as dominated by its sacred or divine aspects. They write that "in our opinion the king was not considered a god, and he was certainly not seen as a divine being in the Gupta period, even if there can be shared features of a god and the king."[19] The authors focus on the Sanskrit phrase *pādānudhyāta*, which is used frequently in epigraphical and textual sources and has been translated by scholars as "who meditates on the feet of" and used to indicate the worship of the feet, usually of a king. Their corrected translation is "favoured by the revered" and indicates a secular relationship, as between a son and his father. After a lengthy review of the use of the term, the authors conclude that "the expression *pādānudhyāta* did not imply religious devotion to the king in the beginning, but came to be associated with it after the tenth century, and even then, perhaps only occasionally."[20] For our purposes, the implication of this research is that Pūrṇavarman's sculptured feet and design, dating to the Gupta period, would be unlikely to be associated

17. Li 1996, 143–144.

18. Li 1996, 147–148.

19. Ferrier and Törzsök 2008, 110.

20. Ferrier and Törzsök 2008, 110.

with the worship of Viṣṇu. The final sentence of the article by Ferrier and Törzsök may, in this regard, be applicable to my study. The authors hope their reconsideration of traditional interpretations "shall contribute not only to a more correct analysis of inscriptional sources, but also to a better understanding of the nature of kingship and the delegation of royal power."[21]

In conclusion, I will introduce Pūrṇavarman's Tugu inscription that is accompanied by a sculpture. The inscription is the most discussed by scholars of Pūrṇavarman inscriptions, as it is the longest and most detailed that lays out gifts that he supplied, including the digging of a river ("the charming river Gomatī pure of water"[22]) and presentation of a thousand cows to the brahmins. Of interest for us is that there is a sculpture on the stone of a staff, perhaps a *triśūla*, that would suggest a Śaivite association.[23] For us the point is that there is no reference to Viṣṇu in the inscription; it is again Pūrṇavarman as the king who is the subject and actor in the inscription. Indeed, none of the inscriptions of Pūrṇavarman speaks of him as worshipping any deity.

My interpretation of the rayed symbols beside the feet of King Pūrṇavarman is associated with the footprints being those of a king. While other scholars have focused on the reference in the inscription that the footprints are like those of Viṣṇu, and then proceeded to connect the symbols to Viṣṇu, I have used the reference to Viṣṇu as a simile that does not turn the footprints into those of Viṣṇu. The footprints can best be contextualized by using the rich Indian tradition of inscriptional and textual references regarding how the feet of kings were used and visualized. As such, the repeated references to a king's feet being able to produce light, even sometimes described as emitting rays (as Bāṇa speaks of Harṣa's toenails in the quotation above), appear a likely explanation for the visual symbols emitting from King Pūrṇavarman's feet.

Works Cited

Auboyer, Jeannine. 1987. "A Note on 'The Feet' and Their Symbolism in Ancient India." In *Kusumāñjali: New Interpretation of Indian Art &*

21. Ferrier and Törzsök 2008, 111.

22. Vogel 1925, 32.

23. See Bosch 1961.

Culture. Sh. C. Sivaramamurti Commemoration Volume, edited by M. S. Nagaraja Rao, 1:125–127. Delhi: Agam Kala Prakashan.

Bakker, Hans T. 2014. *The World of the Skandapurāṇa: Northern India in the Sixth and Seventh Centuries*. Leiden: Brill.

Boisselier, Jean. 1959. "Le Viṣṇu de Tjibuaja (Java occidental) et la statuaire de Sud-Est asiatique." *Artibus Asiae* 22.3: 210–216.

Bosch, F. D. K. 1961. "Guru, Trident and Spring." In *Selected Studies in Indonesian Archaeology*, 155–170. The Hague: Martinus Nijhoff.

de Casparis, J. G. 1986. "Some Notes on the Oldest Inscriptions of Indonesia." In *A Man of Indonesian Letters: Essays in Honour of Professor A. Teeuw*, edited by C. M. S. Hellwig and S. O. Robson, 242–256. Dordrecht: Foris.

Chhabra, B. Ch. 1965. *Expansion of Indo-Aryan Culture During Pallava Rule (as Evidenced by Inscriptions)*. Delhi: Munshi Ram Manohar Lal.

Cowell, E. B., and F. W. Thomas, trans. [1897] 1968. *The Harṣa-carita of Bāṇa*. Reprint, Delhi: Motilal Banarsidass, 1968.

Ferrier, Cédric, and Judit Törzsök. 2008. "Meditating on the King's Feet? Some Remarks on the Expression *Pādānudhyāta*." *Indo-Iranian Journal* 51.2: 93–113.

Fleet, John Faithfull, ed. 1888. *Inscriptions of the Early Gupta Kings and Their Successors*. Corpus Inscriptionum Indicarum 3. Calcutta: Superintendent of Government Printing, India.

Griffiths, Arlo. 2014. "Early Indic Inscriptions of Southeast Asia." In *Lost Kingdoms: Hindu-Buddhist Sculpture of Early Southeast Asia*, edited by John Guy, 53–57. New York: Metropolitan Museum of Art.

Li, Rongxi, trans. 1996. *The Great Tang Dynasty Record of the Western Regions*. BDK English Tripiṭaka 79. Berkeley: Numata Center for Buddhist Translation and Research.

Salomon, Richard. 1989. "New Inscriptional Evidence for the History of the Aulikaras of Mandasor." *Indo-Iranian Journal* 32.1: 1–36.

Santiko, Hariani. 2001. "The Religion of King Pūrṇawarman of Tārumānagara." In *Fruits of Inspiration: Studies in Honour of Prof. J. G. de Casparis, Retired Professor of the Early History and Archeology of South and Southeast Asia at the University of Leiden, the Netherlands, on the Occasion of His 85th Birthday*, edited by Marijke J. Klokke and Karel R. van Kooij, 423–433. Groningen: Egbert Forsten.

Vogel, J. Ph. 1925. "The Earliest Sanskrit Inscriptions of Java." In *Publicaties van den Oudheidkundigen Dienst in Nederlandsch-Indië* 1: 15–35.

Making Room for the Buddha: The Rise of the Buddhist Image Cult at the Kānherī Caves

Robert DeCaroli

THE EMERGENCE OF BUDDHIST image use in South Asia is still not entirely understood.[1] Over the years, Gregory Schopen's research has clarified many aspects of its development and demonstrated that, for at least some adherents, the Buddha was made present through his images.[2] Professor Schopen primarily discusses these developments as they are presented in the *Mūlasarvāstivāda-vinaya*, a Buddhist monastic code that was developed in the northwest of the Indian subcontinent in the early centuries of the Common Era. This territory at the time was held by the Kuṣāṇa dynasty, whose empire encompassed both the regions of Gandhāra and Mathurā. It was in these regions, in the first century CE, that we find the earliest evidence of image production, and it was from here that the Buddhist image tradition appears to have spread.[3]

Although not without controversy, the emergence of the Buddhist image cult is fairly well studied in the Kuṣāṇa empire. Its development in other parts of South Asia has received far less attention, however, and is in many ways less understood. Looking at rock-cut Buddhist sites in the western Deccan, for example, it can be challenging to identify the earliest images and the circumstances under which they were accepted as a part of regional Buddhist practice. Nevertheless, it is clear that images of the Buddha eventually came to dominate the sculptural programs of the western monasteries.

Not only were they included within the caves, but by the fifth century CE images of the Buddha proliferated even on the caves' exteriors. Prominent Buddha images and, in some cases, entire shrines were added by supportive donors. These so-called "intrusive" images were sculpted onto preexisting

1. For a discussion, see DeCaroli 2015, 147–153.

2. Schopen 1990.

3. Schopen 1988–1989. For more on the emergence of the image cult, see van Lohuizen-de Leeuw 1981 and Rhi 1994.

sites, whose original plans did not include any images of the Buddha.[4] It is tempting to see these caves as frozen in time at the moment of their creation, yet these additions and alterations remind us of their continued significance and use. These changes also document the importance of visual forms and the desire to update long-established sites of devotion. This pattern of renovation is traceable across the western Ghats and even further inland at sites like Ajaṇṭā.

It is also true that the earliest monastic sites in the region, such as the second- and first-century BCE caves at Bhājā, Kondivite, and Bedsā, for instance, had very limited sculptural decoration (if any) and were totally devoid of Buddha images. The trajectory toward increased complexity in ornament is, therefore, clear, and the inclusion of Buddha images appears to have been a significant part of that process. With these two points as our chronological brackets, the period between the first and fifth centuries is where we must look for evidence of the first tentative steps toward regional image use.

The Sātavāhana kings held most of the Deccan from the late first century BCE to the third century CE (with occasional losses to the Kṣatrapas in the north). Much like the Kuṣāṇas, it appears that the Sātavāhanas were only rarely direct patrons of Buddhist sites but provided the political, cultural, and religious context in which these innovative developments occurred. There is good evidence to suggest that the earliest Buddha images from Andhra were created when the Sātavāhanas ruled the region.[5] It is therefore worth considering if a similar development occurred in the western Deccan. With this historical context in mind, what does one look for when trying to identify an incipient figural tradition? One location that may provide us some insight into this process is the well-known *caitya* hall at Kānherī, Cave 3.

The Right-hand Column at Kānherī Cave 3: Early Buddhas

I am not the first to suggest that this cave, one of over a hundred located in the hills above Mumbai, may hold a special place in the emergent figural tradition. Marilyn Leese and Susan Huntington have both argued that it displays one of the earliest sculptural Buddha images in the region.[6] These authors rightly single out two small images for discussion. Both are located on an exterior attached pillar (*stambha*) located at the right of the courtyard, and they bear a striking resemblance to early Mathurān-style images of Śākyamuni (figures

4. Morrissey 2009.

5. Shimada 2013, 109–110.

6. Leese 1979, 83–85, and Huntington 1985, 172–173.

Figure 1. Standing Buddha and attendants from the lower portion of the right-hand exterior pillar at Cave 3. Kānherī, India, mid-second century CE. Photo by Robert DeCaroli.

1 and 2). The first of these images stands with a rigid, frontal stance, and the second image is seated, but both exhibit the *abhaya-mudrā*. Their plump faces, wide-eyed gaze, clinging robes, and broad shoulders make a compelling stylistic comparison with second-century images from Mathurā, thereby strengthening the argument for assigning them an early date.

It is also important to note that both images appear as part of a triad and are flanked by attendant figures carrying flowers. Because they are raised in relief from the surface of the stone, they must have been sculpted when the pillar was first created. Had they been added later, it would have been necessary to carve them below the level of the surrounding stone. It is curious that both of these early images appear on an exterior pillar. Typically, we would expect an image of the Buddha to be given a place of prominence within the cave. This exterior placement might therefore indicate the experimental nature of this foray into new subject matter. Adding to the unique characteristics of Cave

Figure 2. Seated Buddha and attendants from the upper portion of the right-hand exterior pillar at Cave 3. Kānherī, India, mid-second century CE. Photo by Robert DeCaroli.

3 is the presence of a third triad (this one damaged), located inside the *caitya* (figure 3).

For reasons that remain unclear, this interior triad was sculpted on the fifth column on the left side of the cave's apsidal hall. Perhaps because of its unusual placement and badly damaged state this triad is often overlooked in discussions of images at the site.[7] Although the attendant figures are fairly well preserved, the central image was thoroughly defaced at some point in the cave's history. Nevertheless, the placement of the figures on separate facets of the octagonal pillar and the attendants' full-bodied appearances and up-raised arms closely resemble the sculptures on the exterior column.[8]

The fact that only the central image of the interior triad was singled out for destruction merits some consideration. It was presumably a figure of the Buddha, and it is curious that only it, and not the attendant figures, were effaced. If this defacement occurred at an early time, it may speak to the contentious nature of new practices. Images of local deities, such as yakṣas, were already

7. I know of no comparable image placement in the western caves.

8. For a detailed image, see Leese 1979, fig. 11.

Figure 3. Interior with view of the columns. Note the damaged sculptural triad on the left (fourth column in the photo). Cave 3. Kānherī, India, ca. mid- to late second century CE. Photo by Mohit S. Wikimedia Commons.

a familiar sight in the region, but images of the Buddha were certainly new. The innovative nature of this central figure may explain why it alone drew the attention of vandals. Although we may never know when or why that image was actually destroyed, we can say that changes in decoration at the caves overwhelmingly point to the eventual triumph of image-based practices, and none of the later images appears to have suffered intentional defacement.

To summarize, Cave 3 at Kānherī displays three triads: two on an exterior pillar that represent the Buddha flanked by attendants and one on an interior pillar in which the central figure has been effaced. Given the level of the surrounding stone, each of these must have been added when the pillars were originally created. Yet, determining the age of these pillars requires some analysis because, as described in the inscriptions left by the donors, this cave had a particularly complicated history.

Construction on this cave began rather ambitiously. The *caitya* extends over thirty meters into the mountainside, and (disregarding the fifth-century additive or "intrusive" images) many of the cave's most ornate features can be dated to this initial phase.[9] The courtyard, its pillars, nāga guardians, and railing motifs were carved in this first period of construction. The same is

9. My analysis of construction at Cave 3 is largely consistent with what Vidya Dehejia proposes. See Dehejia and Rockwell 2016, 64–66. It is notable that S. Nagaraju developed a very different sequence for the construction of the *caitya*. The author posits three phases of construction, of which the latest corresponds to both the sculpting of the forecourt pillars and the reign of Śrī Yajña Sātakarṇi. Nagaraju proposes that the exterior portions of the cave were left unfinished as builders moved to complete the deepest parts first. Therefore, he argues that the more elaborate ornamentation is later. While it is tempting to see the simple forms as earlier, it seems more reasonable to me that the carvers would have worked from front to back and that the inscription (Gokhale's number 5) addresses only one donation and not three. See Nagaraju 1985, 48–49.

most likely true for the massive *mithuna* figures (loving couples) that grace the entryway. Turning to the interior, it becomes apparent that funding began to falter, because only the first six pillars on the left and right were ever fully completed (figure 3). These finished pillars exhibit octagonal shafts set in large pots resting on step-shaped bases. The upper portions of these pillars invert this arrangement and are typically crowned by capitals depicting beautifully sculpted animals and riders (the second pillar on each side breaks from the standard portrayal of riders and instead shows elephants and nāgas lustrating a stūpa). The artists subsequently turned their attention to the next set of five pillars on the left (pillars 7–11) but had only completed the decorative upper portions of the columns when the work stopped. Subsequent construction at the site was far more austere, as exemplified by the unadorned, slender octagonal pillars that were carved throughout the remaining portions of the cave's interior. Even the bases of the partially finished pillars were narrowed and smoothed. This decision by the sculptors was a decisive one, because by removing this stone it precluded any possibility that the bases of these pillars would ever match the earlier ones.

The historical circumstances behind this situation are only partially explained in a damaged inscription on the right-hand gate post (which Shobhana Gokhale numbers as inscription 5). It describes the efforts of two merchant brothers, Gajasena and Gajamitra, who we are told completed this cave during the reign of a Sātavāhana king whose name begins "Gotam" and that Gokhale reconstructs as "Gotam(iputa Sāmi-Siri Yaṇa) Sotakaṁṇi."[10] This is likely a reference to the Sātavāhana king Śrī Yajña Sātakarṇi. This identification is supported by a number of coins cataloged by Alexander Cunningham in which this ruler's full name is presented as Gotamiputa siri Yajña Satakani.[11] Further support can be found in an inscription (Gokhale's number 25) from outside Cave 21 at Kānherī. The inscription is from the sixteenth regnal year of a king whose full name is Gotamiputa sāmi-siri-Yaña Sātakaṇi.[12] This can be no one other than Śrī Yajña Sātakarṇi, and this inscription provides further precedent for the matronymic designation "Gautamīputra" appearing at the start of his name.[13] If this attribution is correct, and it seems fairly secure,

10. Gokhale 1991, 47–52; text, translation, and discussion on 51. I have removed the genitive case endings in Gokhale's reconstruction.

11. Gokhale 1991, 51. For the coins of Śrī Yajña Sātakarṇi, see Cunningham 1891, 102–110.

12. Gokhale 1991, 75, and Lüders 1912, 108 (# 1024).

13. Although the name in the Kānherī Cave 21 inscription is clear, there is a possibility that the Cave 3 inscription refers to Gautamīputra Śrī Sātakarṇi, after whom Śrī Yajña Sātakarṇi was third or fourth to take the throne. This earlier king is believed to have been a contemporary of

the mention of this Sātavāhana king allows us to place Gajasena's and Gajamitra's act of patronage in the mid- to late second century (roughly 170–200 CE), which fits well with the cave's stylistic qualities.

The cave's inscriptions also mention the efforts of other individuals, including an elder monk (*thera*), five reverends (*bhadaṃta*), and a merchant (*negamo*), who were also instrumental in completing the cave. The exact relationship between the merchant brothers and the other named individuals is far from clear. The fact that they are listed together in a single inscription (number 5) suggests that their efforts were in some way connected, which has led Dehejia to suggest that the monks and other unnamed individuals all provided additional funds for the construction project.[14] It is rare for one inscription to list so many donors, but Dehejia's interpretation is certainly plausible. Even if one were inclined to quibble about the exact identities of the donors, the inscription clarifies the sequence of construction at the cave. Specifically, the nineteenth line of the inscription states that these named individuals (or some of them) "completed" (*samāpitā*) the cave, which means that they are likely responsible for the later, austere portions of the cave rather than for the more elaborate earlier work located toward the entrance.[15]

It might seem counterintuitive that the simpler artwork is later, but we know that sculptors at rock-cut sites typically began with the upper and forward portions of the cave and gradually worked their way down and back.[16] That this was the case here is corroborated by the lack of bases on five pillars with ornate capitals. The bases were intentionally trimmed after the capitals had already been completed, thereby precluding any further sculptural adornment. Additionally, the pillars located toward the cave's entrance are thicker than those at the back, which means their decoration must have been planned from the outset. This too points to them being earlier, because one universal truth of rock-cut architecture is that one can always remove stone but never add more, which is to say that the thicker, ornate columns are likely what was originally intended for the cave.

Nahapāna and is known from inscriptions at Nāsik. He is therefore associated with caves and political events that predate Kānherī Cave 3, making him unlikely to be the king named in the inscription. Nevertheless, Cribb argues that the two kings' reigns were separated by only thirty-seven years. See Cribb 1998, 173–175.

14. Dehejia and Rockwell 2016, 63–67.

15. Gokhale 1991, 51, line 19. For the analysis of its implications, see Dehejia and Rockwell 2016, 65.

16. For other examples of how simplified decoration can characterize the later parts of an excavation, see Spink 1991, 83–85.

The decision to simplify the shape and style of the remaining interior pillars is not quite as odd or drastic as it may first appear. In fact, there is good reason to believe that in the original plan for the cave, at least some of the pillars were intended to be unadorned and octagonal, an architectural choice that also may help us pin down the date of the cave. If we consider the ground plans for the *caitya*s at Nāsik (Cave 18), Kārlā, and Junnar (Leṇyādri Cave 3) it becomes apparent that each has six pillars (or seven in the case of Kārlā), located around the apse, which lack the ornamentation present on the other pillars.[17] The somewhat hidden location of these plain, octagonal pillars located behind the stūpa presumably made it unnecessary to ornament them in a lavish fashion. If we can assume that the left-hand pillars at Kānherī were all completed, then the finished cave at Kānherī would have had eight unadorned pillars behind the stūpa and eleven ornamented pillars on each side of the hall. This architectural practice of including two types of pillars in a single cave seems to have been in style for a limited time. The elaborate pillar decoration at fifth-century sites like Ajaṇṭā Caves 19 and 26, for example, are not limited in this fashion. Likewise, earlier (second to first centuries BCE) caves like Bedsā, Bhājā, and Ajaṇṭā Cave 10 utilize simple, octagonal pillars throughout. This still leaves us with a span of several centuries (first to fourth centuries CE). If we want to establish the early date of Kānherī Cave 3 and its Buddha images, we should consider ways to narrow this further.

Scholars such as James Burgess, James Fergusson, and Vidya Dehejia have attempted to develop a chronological sequence for these *caitya* caves.[18] They have considered morphological changes in the paleography, stylistic changes in the sculpture (with special attention to the *mithuna* couples), and developments in architectural form. On this last point, the presence of wooden beams or of construction that closely mimics wooden architecture is viewed as indicating an early date, because it is presumed that the architects had not yet fully learned to trust the stone. Based on these criteria, both chronologies identify Nāsik as the earliest in the sequence and Kānherī as the latest.[19] Dehejia differs from the other scholars over the dating of Kārlā, and I agree with her that it must be earlier than Junnar. This view has been strengthened due to the re-dating of King Nahapāna, whose nephew donated to the mon-

17. For the ground plans, see Dehejia 1972, 74.

18. Dehejia 1972, 148–185. Although Dehejia here dates Śrī Yajña Sātakarṇi's reign to 152–181 CE, she has subsequently revised her dating of the Sātavāhana ruler to 174–203 CE (Dehejia and Rockwell 2016, 65). See also Fergusson and Burgess [1880] 1988, 181–186. Fergusson and Burgess place all of the excavation at Kānherī between 100 BCE and 150 CE.

19. Fergusson and Burgess [1880] 1988, 348–353, and Dehejia 1972, 132–133, 183–184.

astery at Kārlā.[20] It now appears that Nahapāna lived in the middle of the first century CE, which places Kārlā among the earliest. Of particular note is that these scholars all identify the *caitya* at Kānherī as the latest in this sequence.

Unfortunately, only two of the caves, Kārlā and Kānherī, have dated inscriptions. The Kānherī inscription that most probably refers to Śrī Yajña Sātakarṇi places the first phase of construction, and the early Buddha images, before or during his reign, 170–200 CE.[21] Kārlā, by contrast, has an inscription by Uṣavadāta (Usabhadāta), the son-in-law of the great Kṣatrapa king Nahapāna, who is recorded as donating a village to support the monastery.[22] Inscriptions mentioning Uṣavadāta have also been found at Nāsik, and there is one recorded by his minister at Junnar. These provide the dates 41, 42, and 46 of an unspecified era. Early scholarship has assumed this was a date in the Śaka Era, and if we accept 78 CE as the start of that era, he would have been active between 118 and 123 CE.[23] The recent reassessment of Nahapāna's date has called into question his use of the Śaka Era, as it seems likely that he predated the use of that system for recording dates.[24] Therefore, even though the date of this king is not fixed, it is reasonable to place him, and Uṣavadāta's donation, in the middle of the first century, roughly 50 CE. Because Kārlā originally contained no images of the Buddha and exhibits earlier stylistic features, the first phase of construction at Kānherī almost certainly postdates it. We can conclude that construction at Kānherī began after the work at Kārlā was complete. The Kānherī Buddha images were, therefore, likely created at some point between 50 and 200 CE. This is still a substantial span of time, but stylistic comparisons with sculpture from other regions can help us refine this further.

20. Cribb 1992 proposes a mid-first-century reign for Nahapāna. Bhandare (1998, 168–178) proposes that Nahapāna reigned 32–78 CE. See also Shimada 2013, 50–51.

21. There are disagreements over the dates of Śrī Yajña Sātakarṇi's reign. Andrew Ollett gives 171–199 CE, Ajay Mitra Shastri prefers 170–198 CE, Vidya Dehejia settled on 174–203 CE, Joe Cribb makes a case for 106–132 CE, and Umakant Shailendra Bhandare and Akira Shimada both argue for 170–200 CE. Based on stylistic comparisons to inscribed Sātavāhana-era sculpture from Andhra, I also prefer 170–200 CE. For further references, see Ollett 2017, 189–198; Shastri 2008; Dehejia and Rockwell 2016, 65; Cribb 1998; Bhandare 1998, 305–324; and Shimada 2013, 48–58. Additional analysis can be found in Nakanishi and von Hinüber 2014, 20–22.

22. Lüders 1912, 118 (# 1099).

23. See Dehejia 1972, 22–23. For Usabhadāta, Usabhadata, and Ushavadāta, see Lüders 1912, 117–118 (# 1097 and # 1099), 123–124 (# 1125), 125–127 (## 1131–1135); for minister Ayama at Junnar, 134 (# 1174).

24. Cribb 1992 and 1998. See also Bhandare 1998, 168–178, and Shimada 2013, 50–51.

The Kānherī images' small size and badly weathered condition make any sort of stylistic analysis challenging, but a few salient features of the Buddhas and their attendants can be identified. The Buddha images' broad shoulders and frontal stance with weight evenly distributed on both legs suggest an early date because of similarities to second-century examples from Mathurā. The smooth heads of the figures also support this conclusion, because curly hair on Buddha images first appears on dated images in Mathurā around the start of the third century.[25] The flattened clothing of the figures, particularly the way that it stands rigidly away from the body and bunches up around the left arm of the seated figure, also invites comparisons with the Mathurān style. For example, consider the statue of the bodhisattva from Sārnāth that was donated by Bhikṣu Bala and his disciples in 130 CE.[26] The way the garment on the bodhisattva image is pressed against its broad, rigid body makes an apt comparison to the Kānherī examples. Similarly, the upright posture, *abhayamudrā*, and heavy cloth over the left arm of the Kānherī seated image have points of commonality with the Katrā and Ahicchatra images of Śākyamuni. The Katrā image is often assigned a second-century date based on its style. We can be more precise regarding the Ahicchatra image because it has an inscription dating it to year 32. This year is presumably of the Kaniṣka era, which provides a date of circa 158 CE.[27] Taken collectively, these comparisons point to a date in the mid-second century.

Comparative examples from Amarāvatī produce similar results. Stylistically, the Buddhas at Kānherī resemble the very earliest Buddha images from Andhra. These are found on the second type of dome slabs, as designated in Akira Shimada's chronology of Amarāvatī, and coincide with the rise of Sātavāhana control in the region.[28] Shimada notes that the Buddha figures at Amarāvatī invariably have hair in snail-shell curls, which, based on comparisons to Mathurān examples, suggests a possible date in the late second or early third century.[29] Despite the rough state of the Kānherī examples, there do not seem to be any traces of the curled hair. This stylistic feature links them to the examples from Mathurā mentioned earlier and indicates a slightly earlier date for the Kānherī images.

25. Shimada 2013, 102–104.

26. Schopen 1988–1989, 159–162.

27. The image is in the National Museum, New Delhi. The date is based on Harry Falk's (2004) dating of the Kaniṣka era.

28. Shimada 2013, 102–104, 109–110.

29. Shimada 2013, 101–104. Shimada proposes 200 CE as a working date for the transition to snail-shell curls in Mathurā.

An inscription on a dome slab from Amarāvatī helps to solidify a late second-century date for the very first Buddha sculptures at the site. It records a date in the reign of Śrī Yajña Sātakarṇi, the same king that is likely named at Kānherī Cave 3. Shimada characterizes the art from this second phase as having the same sturdy and solid forms found in earlier art and as being mostly aniconic. Yet it is during this transitional moment at the inception of the phase-three railing style that we find the first three instances in which the Buddha is represented in figural form.[30] Therefore, the first images at Amarāvatī, like the first images at Kānherī, were created before or during the early portion of Śrī Yajña Sātakarṇi's reign. Based on the hair style and the content of the inscriptional evidence, I would place the Kānherī Buddhas slightly before those at Amarāvatī. This chronology supports the likelihood that the first period of construction at Kānherī occurred before 170 CE, and the first images at Amarāvatī can subsequently be dated to a little after 200 CE. These estimations are contingent on the dates assigned to Śrī Yajña Sātakarṇi's reign, but most of these differ by no more than seventy years.[31]

The attendant figures from Kānherī compare well with similarly dated figures. The Kānherī attendants have few clear features, but the fact that they hold bouquets of flowers and wear no cloth over their shoulders distinguishes them from other examples. Likewise, the large loops of fabric that project out from their waists are distinctive. To my eye, the best comparisons can be found at Amarāvatī and are associated with the second type of casing stones from the stūpa dome.[32] These examples share the bare shoulders and belt loops found at Kānherī. And while most do not hold bouquets, they do have a propensity for holding a variety of offerings in their upraised right hands. One of these slabs bears the inscription naming Śrī Yajña, which allows us to place this style between 170 and 200 CE. When compared to examples from Nāgārjunakoṇḍa, which Elizabeth Rosen Stone dates to 225–240 CE, we can see that the projecting belt loops and flowers still remain, but their naturalism and relaxed poses suggest a later date for the Nāgārjunakoṇḍa attendant figures.[33] The general sequence suggested by this comparison places the Kānherī sculpture slightly before those from Amarāvatī, which, in turn, precede the naturalistic developments at Nāgārjunakoṇḍa.

To summarize, the two extant Śākyamuni images at Kānherī both date to

30. Shimada 2013, 109–110.

31. Shastri 2008 and Cribb 1998 both date his reign to before 170.

32. Shimada 2013, 109–110, figs. 43, 44, and 47.

33. Stone 1994, 24–31 and figs. 41, 44.

the first phase of construction at the site and must predate or coincide with the early years of "King Gotam[iputa Sāmi-Siri Yaṇa]" presumably Śrī Yajña Sātakarṇi, which points to a date before 200 CE and later than 60 CE, after the Kārlā *caitya* was made. We can narrow this further by pointing out similarities with sculptures from Mathurā and Andhra. The stylistic and iconographic features of the reliefs at Kānherī Cave 3 suggest that these images slightly precede Amarāvatī's examples dated to the year 170 and that they are close in date to those produced further north. Therefore, a mid-second-century date circa 150 CE for the creation of the Kānherī images seems likely.

The early style, small scale, and unusual placement of these images all support the idea that these are among the first displayed publicly in the region. Furthermore, evidence suggests that image use spread within the caves after this initial experimentation. If I am correct, image use was far more extensive at Kānherī than previously recognized.

The Left-hand Column at Kānherī Cave 3: Sockets and Niches

Although I previously stated that one cannot add more stone to rock-cut architecture, that was not entirely accurate. It is more precise to say that one cannot add more stone without leaving a trace. In this case, I am referring to the sockets used to fit new stonework or woodwork and to affix repairs when portions of the original excavation break. Although the pillar on the right-hand portion of the Kānherī Cave 3 courtyard has received a great deal of scholarly attention due to the presence of its Buddha images, the left-hand column has been largely ignored. I have seen no mention of two slender sockets and the traces of a third that were added to the upper portions of the column's base (figure 4). These sockets are located just above a nāga image and occupy three separate facets of the octagonal shaft. In this arrangement, they exactly mirror the placement of the standing Buddha and his attendants on the facing right-hand pillar. These sockets are quite shallow. The well-preserved left-hand example is 13 cm long, has a width of only 5.5 cm, and extends 7 cm deep. The central socket is 18 cm long and has both a width and a depth of 7 cm. The stone on the socket closest to the cave entrance is broken, but the length of the cut appears to have been approximately 14 cm. Given the shallow and slender nature of these sockets it is hard to imagine them serving a structural function. Indeed, it is hard to imagine them being used for any purpose other than attaching sculptural adornments. The placement of these slots parallels the placement of sculptural decoration on the pillar facing it across the courtyard, which suggests an attempt to bring the left-hand pillar in line with the decoration on the right.

Figure 4. Detail of narrow sockets on left-hand exterior pillar. Lines were added to highlight the location of the sockets. Cave 3. Kānherī, India, ca. late second to third century CE. Photo by Robert DeCaroli.

Similar socketing was used elsewhere at Kānherī. One need only look further up the pillar to find an example: if one climbs the hill and looks down at the uppermost portions of the columns, the large sockets cut into the capitals of both columns are immediately apparent. Such mortices may have been used to support a wooden superstructure that parallels what we find in stone at the

Figure 5. Bench with mortice in Cave 34. Kānherī, India, ca. third to fourth century CE. Photo by Robert DeCaroli.

first-century BCE cave site of Bedsā. It is also possible that these attached columns were originally capped by sculptural ornaments of the sort seen at Kārlā or on the famous Aśokan pillars that were their precedent and inspiration. A loose sculpture depicting a lion found near Cave 3 may possibly have been placed atop the pillars, but its badly damaged state makes any sort of meaningful assessment impossible.

Figure 6. Arched niche at the back of Cave 53. Kānherī, India, ca. fourth century CE. Photo by Robert DeCaroli

There are over a hundred caves of varying size at Kānherī, and at least eight of them contain sockets that could have allowed the residents retroactively to add sculpture to the site. These alterations could have been added at any point in the caves' history and serve as reminders that these were inhabited spaces, updated and reshaped to meet the changing institutional and ritual needs of the community. Given the long occupation of the site, which has a documented history that stretches from the first century BCE into the eleventh century CE, it is not unexpected to find evidence of renovation.[34] Notably these niches are often found in caves that otherwise lack ornamentation. I believe that these examples may indicate a transitional stage after the introduction of image use but before it became common to overcut earlier caves.

Notable among these are mortices placed on a platform located next to a stūpa in Cave 36 and carved into a bench in Cave 34 (figure 5). These sockets are prominently located within the caves and have no apparent architectural function; their placement suggests decorative or ritual use. Other examples can be found in Caves 50 and 53 (figure 6). While these arched niches could arguably have been used for a number of purposes, the presence of a remarkably similar

34. Dehejia 1972, 184.

Figure 7. Arched niche with Buddha image in Cave 54. Kānherī, India, ca. fifth century CE. Photo by Robert DeCaroli.

niche in Cave 54, which contains a sculpted Buddha image, indicates how similar niches were used (figure 7). Likewise, the unique profile of the indentation carved into the back of Cave 101 leaves little doubt that it was intended for a seated image (figure 8).

Cave 26 contains a bench running along the back wall that bears two sockets. The placement of an "intrusive" seated Buddha, sculpted into the wall directly above the central socket, is suggestive of the cave's function as a place of devotion. Dhavalikar identifies the cave as early (ca. first century BCE), based in part on the octagonal pillars on the verandah. However, a later third- or fourth-century inscription at the site reveals continued engagement from the community long after the period when images became commonplace.[35]

Although plentiful, this evidence of continued embellishment is unfortunately circumstantial. As far as I am aware the only loose sculptures found at Kānherī were the previously mentioned lion and a tenth-century wooden image of Tārā reported by M. G. Dikshit.[36] In the absence of sculptural exam-

35. Dhavalikar 1984, 52–54.

36. Dikshit 1942 is unpublished, but the findings are cited in Dhavalikar 1984, 66.

Figure 8. Distinctively shaped mortice in Cave 101. Kānherī, India, ca. third to fourth century CE. Photo by Robert DeCaroli.

ples, my case hinges primarily on the size and placement of the mortices and tantalizing comparisons with later caves in which relief sculptures still remain.

Supporting evidence can, however, be found in the fifth-century Buddhist caves at Bāgh. Caves 1, 3, 7, and 8 each contain sockets similar to those found at Kānherī. The examples in Bāgh Cave 3 are particularly relevant because traces of wall painting provide contexts for the sockets, indicating what they may

Figure 9. Sockets on the floor in front of the stūpa in Cave 3. Kānherī, India, late second to third century CE. Photo by Robert DeCaroli.

have once held. In the left rear chamber, a painted throne with elephants and *makaras* is visible and a large mandorla with an empty center was positioned on the right-hand wall. These decorations were both painted around sockets that were presumably used to affix images. It seems very likely that they held a seated Buddha and a standing Buddha, respectively.[37] This evidence offers further indication that some sockets were used to accommodate images and points to a process by which figural images were added to locations after the caves had already been completed.

If we return to the interior of Cave 3 and look to the back, we see that an arrangement of three sockets was, at some point, carved into the floor of the *caitya*, placed evenly along the front of the stūpa (figure 9). If these were made to accommodate images—and they would have to have been substantial images—this would hint at the growing centrality and importance of the image cult in regional practice.

It is interesting to note that at Junnar, specifically at Cave 6 of the Leṇyādri group, we see a similar situation. This *caitya* hall, which, based on its style, can

37. Spink 1976–1977, 63–64. See also Owen 2001, 48–49. The sockets are now filled with cement.

be identified as being only slightly younger than Cave 3 at Kānherī, also shows evidence of later sculptural elaborations. The primary difference is that at Junnar, only one rectangular socket was added to the cave floor, just in front of the stūpa. A related arrangement can be seen in Bāgh Cave 7. Three holes, a deep central one flanked by two shallow ones, were added to a lip of stone in front of the stūpa.[38] Obviously, these sockets need not have been used to accommodate a Buddha image, but in light of the other evidence it is certainly a strong possibility.

This assertion finds some support based on what we know about later developments in the region. Specifically, the fifth-century *caitya*s at Ajaṇṭā (such as Caves 19 and 26) feature large Buddha images that were sculpted onto the primary stūpas at the time of the caves' excavations. In fact, the fifth century seems to have seen a proliferation in the use of Buddha images. At Ajaṇṭā Cave 11, the fifth-century sculptors abandoned work on an unfinished stūpa and converted it into a Buddha image, which suggests that images had become a priority. Many sites show evidence of this change in practice. Even at Kānherī, donors added intrusive Buddha images to the stūpa in Cave 4. Inscriptional evidence places the stūpa's construction in the second century, but the image can be dated to the early fifth century on stylistic grounds.[39] Such examples reveal the trajectory of ornamentation at the site and provide weight to the idea that these mortices are associated with sculptural additions.[40]

Despite these clear changes over time, dating the sockets at Kānherī still remains complicated. The Bāgh Caves date to mid- to late fifth century, so even if their sockets were added shortly after the caves were created, it suggests that sockets were in use at approximately the same time that images and shrines were being recut into monastery walls across western India.[41] Ultimately, this presents two possibilities for Kānherī. Either there was a great burst of interest in the fifth century and both the sockets and intrusive images are contemporaneous, or there was a gradual and long-lasting process during which images were added first with sockets and later by using a variety of techniques. Although this question remains unresolved, the modest scale and exterior placement of the Kānherī Cave 3 pillar sockets are significantly different from the large size and prominence of sockets placed in other locations. This

38. Owen 2001, 48, and Spink 1976–1977, 64, 84.

39. Gokhale 1991, 62.

40. This process parallels the way fifth-century artists painted Buddha images in the first-century BCE caves at Ajaṇṭā. These paintings are particularly apparent in Caves 9 and 10. See Zin 2003, 20, 22.

41. Owen 2001, 45–47.

may be indicative of a cautious early attempt at adding figural imagery to the site. If this is so, then Kānherī Cave 3 may have been at the forefront of innovation twice—once for sculpting Buddha images and again for adding them.

Conclusions

Admittedly, it is not easy to pin down the inception of an artistic tradition. Locating evidence for the emergence of the Buddhist image cult in the western Deccan is complicated by the monasteries' histories of renovation and defacement. Kānherī complicates this task further because of its exceptionally long period of habitation and relative paucity of inscriptions. Nevertheless, there is strong stylistic evidence that the two extant early Buddha images (and possibly a third) from Cave 3 are among the earliest in the western caves. Furthermore, it appears that this process began in the mid-second century, slightly before the reign of Śrī Yajña Sātakarṇi. This precedes a strikingly similar process in Andhra, where the earliest Buddha images were created during the reign of the same Sātavāhana king.

Multiple sockets and niches in places of high visibility appear to have been used to affix sculptural imagery. Such evidence points to a change in image-based practice that took hold in the mid-second century and, over time, was accommodated by adapting the early caves to suit new needs. Professor Schopen taught us that the Buddha's images were at times viewed as residents of the monastery. But before the Buddha could reside, he had to be invited in. We know that the image cult had great success in the western Deccan, and Kānherī appears to have played a central role in getting it started.

Works Cited

Bhandare, Umakant Shailendra. 1998. "Historical Analysis of the Satavahana Era: A Study of Coins." PhD thesis, University of Mumbai.

Cribb, Joe. 1992. "Numismatic Evidence for the Date of the 'Periplus.'" In *Indian Numismatics, History, Art and Culture: Essays in the Honour of Dr. P. L. Gupta*, edited by D. W. MacDowall, Savita Sharma, and Sanjay Garg, 1:131–145. New Delhi: Agam Kala Prakashan.

———. 1998. "Western Satraps and Satavahanas: Old and New Ideas of Chronology." In *Ex Moneta: Essays on Numismatics, History and Archaeology in Honour of Dr. David W. MacDowall*, edited by Amal Kumar Jha and Sanjay Garg, 1:167–182. Nashik: Harman Publishing House.

Cunningham, Alexander. 1891. *Coins of Ancient India from the Earliest Times Down to the Seventh Century A.D.* London: B. Quaritch.

DeCaroli, Robert. 2015. *Image Problems: The Origin and Development of the Buddha's Image in Early South Asia.* Seattle: University of Washington Press.

Dehejia, Vidya. 1972. *Early Buddhist Rock Temples: A Chronological Study.* London: Thames and Hudson.

Dehejia, Vidya, and Peter Rockwell. 2016. *The Unfinished: Stone Carvers at Work on the Indian Subcontinent.* New Delhi: Roli Books.

Dhavalikar, M. K. 1984. *Late Hinayana Caves of Western India.* Poona: Deccan College Postgraduate and Research Institute.

Dikshit, M. G. 1942. "Buddhist Establishments in Western India." PhD thesis, University of Bombay.

Falk, Harry. 2004. "The Kaniṣka Era in Gupta Records." *Silk Road Art and Archaeology* 10: 167–176.

Fergusson, James, and James Burgess. [1880] 1988. *The Cave Temples of India.* 2nd Indian ed. New Delhi: Munshiram Manoharlal.

Gokhale, Shobhana. 1991. *Kanheri Inscriptions.* Pune: Deccan College Post Graduate and Research Institute.

Huntington, Susan L. 1985. *The Art of Ancient India.* With contributions by John C. Huntington. New York and Tokyo: Weatherhill.

Leese, Marilyn. 1979. "The Early Buddhist Icons in Kaṇheri's Cave 3." *Artibus Asiae* 41.1: 83–93.

van Lohuizen-de Leeuw, Johanna E. 1981. "New Evidence with Regard to the Origin of the Buddha Image." In *South Asian Archaeology, 1979: Papers from the Fifth International Conference of the Association of South Asian Archaeologists in Western Europe Held in the Museum für Indische Kunst der Staatlichen Museen Preussischer Kulturbesitz Berlin*, edited by Herbert Härtel, 377–400. Berlin: Dietrich Reimer Verlag.

Lüders, Heinrich. 1912. *A List of Brāhmī Inscriptions from the Earliest Times to about A.D. 400 with the Exception of Those of Aśoka*. Appendix to *Epigraphia India and Record of the Archeological Survey of India* 10, edited by Sten Konow and V. Venkayya. Calcutta: Superintendent of Government Printing.

Morrissey, Nicolas Michael. 2009. "*Śākyabhikṣus*, Palimpsests and the Art of Apostasy: The Emergence and Decline of Mahāyāna Buddhism in Early Medieval India." PhD thesis, University of California, Los Angeles.

Nagaraju, S. 1985. "The Kanheri Caitya Hall and Its Foundation Inscription: A Reëxamination (*sic*)." In *Indian Epigraphy: Its Bearing on the History of Art*, edited by F. M. Asher and G. S. Gai, 47–53. New Delhi: Oxford and IBH Publishers.

Nakanishi, Maiko, and Oskar von Hinüber, eds. 2014. *Kanaganahalli Inscriptions*. Supplement to *Annual Report of the International Research Institute for Advanced Buddhology at Soka University* 17. Tokyo: The International Research Institute for Advanced Buddhology, Soka University.

Ollett, Andrew. 2017. *Language of the Snakes: Prakrit, Sanskrit, and the Language Order of Premodern India*. Oakland: University of California Press.

Owen, Lisa Nadine. 2001. "Constructing Another Perspective for Ajaṇṭā's Fifth-Century Excavations." *Journal of the International Association of Buddhist Studies* 24.1: 27–59.

Rhi, Ju-hyung. 1994. "From Bodhisattva to Buddha: The Beginning of Iconic Representation in Buddhist Art." *Artibus Asiae* 54.3–4: 207–225.

Schopen, Gregory. 1988–1989. "On Monks, Nuns and 'Vulgar' Practices: The Introduction of the Image Cult into Indian Buddhism." *Artibus Asiae* 49.1–2: 153–168. Reprinted in Schopen 1997, 238–257.

———. 1990. "The Buddha as an Owner of Property and Permanent Resident in Medieval Indian Monasteries." *Journal of Indian Philosophy* 18.3: 181–217. Reprinted in Schopen 1997, 258–289.

———. 1997. *Bones, Stones, and Buddhist Monks: Collected Papers on the Archaeology, Epigraphy, and Texts of Monastic Buddhism in India*. Studies in the Buddhist Traditions. Honolulu: University of Hawai'i Press.

Shastri, Ajay Mitra. 2008. "Sātavāhana-Kṣaharāta Chronology and Art History." In *South Asian Archaeology, 1999: Proceedings of the 15th International Conference of the European Association of South Asian Archaeologists, Held at the Universiteit Leiden, 5–9 July, 1999*, edited by E. Raven, 341–351. Groningen: Egbert Forsten.

Shimada, Akira. 2013. *Early Buddhist Architecture in Context: The Great Stūpa at Amarāvatī (ca. 300 BCE–300 CE)*. Leiden: Brill.
Spink, Walter M. 1976–1977. "Bāgh: A Study." *Archives of Asian Art* 30: 53–84.
———. 1991. "The Archaeology of Ajaṇṭā." *Ars Orientalis* 21: 67–94.
Stone, Elizabeth Rosen. 1994. *The Buddhist Art of Nāgārjunakoṇḍa*. Buddhist Tradition Series 25. Delhi: Motilal Banarsidass.
Zin, Monika. 2003. *Guide to the Ajanta Paintings*, vol. 2: *Devotional and Ornamental Paintings*. New Delhi: Munshiram Manoharlal.

Sambhoga-grāma in the Jetavanārāma Sanskrit Inscription*

Petra Kieffer-Pülz

THE JETAVANĀRĀMA SANSKRIT INSCRIPTION was found in 1894 in Anurādhapura (Sri Lanka), north of the Twin Ponds (Kūṭṭam-pokunā). At that time its find-spot was considered to be part of the Jetavanārāma—hence the name of this inscription. Later it was understood to belong to the Abhayagiri monastery. This granite slab inscription is incomplete; its beginning must have been on a separate stone. Since the introductory part is missing, it is unknown whether it was set up by the monastery or by some secular authority.[1] The inscription is composed in Sanskrit and written in the Siddhamātṛkā script.[2] Based on paleographical reasons it is dated to the first half of the ninth century CE[3] and considered to most probably fall within the reign of Sena I (833–853).[4] The script resembles the paleographic forms of inscriptions of this time in the Bihar-Bengal area, which made Gunawardana assume that the scribe either came from that area or was familiar with it.[5] The remains of the building in the vicinity of the inscription's find-spot, according to Gunawardana,[6] have "a ground-plan unique in the architectural tra-

* I feel honored to be able to make a small contribution to this volume in honor of Gregory Schopen as a sign of my respect for a scholar who exemplarily combined textual, epigraphical, and archeological approaches. I thank Shayne Clarke for his corrections and suggestions, and for improving my English. Thanks also go to the anonymous peer-reviewer for comments and corrections.

1. See also Schmiedchen 2016, 571.

2. Wickremasinghe 1904–1912, 2: "variety of the Magadha Nāgarī"; "Kuṭila Nāgarī alphabet"; Gunawardana 1979, 250: "Nagarī script of the 'nail-headed' variety"; Salomon 1998, 151: "northern Indian scripts"; Gethin 2012, 51: "Siddhamātṛka(!) script"; 53: "north Indian script."

3. Wickremasinghe 1904–1912, 2, 4; Gunawardana 1966, 58.

4. Gunawardana 1966, 61.

5. Gunawardana 1966, 61.

6. Gunawardana 1966, 57, based on *Archaeological Survey of Ceylon. Annual Report 1894*, 3.

dition of Sri Lanka" that is "strongly reminiscent of the style represented by the ruins at Paharpūr in the Rājshāhi District of Bengal,"[7] which refers to the Somapuravihāra.[8]

The inscription was edited and translated by the Sinhalese epigraphist Don Martino de Zilva Wickremasinghe in the first volume of *Epigraphia Zeylanica* (1904–1912).[9] Since then several scholars have dealt with it. All of them nearly exclusively focused on the final passage, which says that one hundred monks, twenty-five of each of the four *nikāya*s, are residents (*naivāsika*[10]) in that monastery. The identification of the four schools (*nikāyas*) was at the center of interest.[11] In 1966, Gunawardana assumed that the four *nikāya*s are the "Mahāsāṅghikas, Sarvāstivādins, Sthaviravādins"—represented by the Sinhalese school of the Abhayagirivāsin—"and the Sammitīyas."[12] This position he still held in 1979.[13] In 1970, Kalupahana, in response to Gunawardana's article, identified the four *nikāya*s and equated them with the three Lankan schools as the Sthaviravāda (Mahāvihāra), Sautrāntika (Abhayagiri), Sarvāstivāda (Jetavana), and Mahīśāsaka (Jetavana).[14] His interpretation was refuted by Bechert in 1982 as being based on a complete misunderstanding of the nature of the term *nikāya*.[15] Although Bechert considered Gunawardana's interpretation more compatible with the facts than Kalupahana's, he thought that the "four *nikāya*s" cannot be identified with certainty "as

7. Gunawardana 1979, 250.

8. For instance, Mitra 1971, 40, fig. 11.

9. Wickremasinghe 1904–1912, 1–9.

10. For a discussion of the term *naivāsika* in relation to *āvāsika*, see Silk 2008, 150–151, with older literature.

11. Walters 2000, 132–133, states: "Sena I apparently built a hall at the Abhayagiri monastic complex devoted to reconciliation among equal numbers of representatives from the four major divisions of the interregnal Buddhist world as construed by Sarvāstivādins of the period: the Sarvāstivādins, Mahāsāṃghikas, Saṃmatīyas, and Sthaviravādins (those of Abhayagiri, I assume)." He refers to Gunawardana 1979, 247–255, as a source. Neither the inscription nor Gunawardana speaks of a "reconciliation" of the various schools. Whether or not there is a continuity of the mention of the four *mahānikāya*s and earlier epigraphic formulas stating the donation for the benefit of the community of the four directions (*caturdiśasaṅgha*) (Tournier 2017, 263n29) is a topic for future research.

12. Gunawardana 1966, 63.

13. I conclude this from the fact that he included this article nearly verbatim in Gunawardana 1979, 247–256.

14. Kalupahana 1970, 188–190.

15. Bechert 1982, 60–76.

long as no additional evidence is available."[16] Nevertheless, he considered the Mahīśāsaka a more likely candidate than the Mahāsāṅghika.[17] Gethin added another element to the discussion—namely, the mention of the four *nikāyas* in Dhammapāla's subcommentary to the Dīgha Nikāya. In light of the given evidence he considered Gunawardana's identification the most plausible.[18] Tournier refers to the fact that other texts identify the four *mahānikāyas* with the "Mahāsāṅghika, Sthāvira, Sarvāstivādin (ou Mūlasarvāstivādin, selon les sources) et Sāṁmitīya."[19]

As an inscription belonging to the category of "monastic organizational guidelines" (*vihārakatikāvata*)[20] the Jetavanārāma Sanskrit Inscription covers several topics in addition to the passage just mentioned. Concerning these other topics not much seems to have been written, apart from the discussion of some of the terms used.[21] One portion or another of this inscription is quoted here and there, mostly in Wickremasinghe's translation,[22] rarely in original attempts to render the text,[23] but there seem to be no further studies of it. In the present contribution, I will roughly outline the contents of this inscription and then focus on the term *sambhoga-grāma* used in one of the regulations.

Outline of the Contents of the Inscription

In the first three lines this inscription deals with wages to be given to monastics stationed in villages (novices, and monks in charge of new building activities). It is likely that this topic began on the lost slab, because the function

16. Bechert 1982, 74.

17. Bechert 1982, 74–76.

18. Gethin 2012, 50–54.

19. Tournier 2017, 263n29.

20. Ratnapāla 1971, 7; Bechert 1982, 62.

21. On the term *vārika* in the Jetavanārāma Sanskrit Inscription: Gunawardana 1979, 121–122; Ranawella 1998, 113–115. To this can be added the investigation by von Hinüber 2012, 373–389, which is based on the usage of this term in the textual traditions. For the tasks of *vārikas*, see also Silk 2008, 101–125, and Kieffer-Pülz 2010, 78–79. On the term *parivahana*, see Gunawardana 1979, 102–103, 105–106; Ranawella 1999n165; Ranawella 2005, 14.

22. Coomaraswamy 1909, 45–46; Perera 2001, 275. Guṇavardhana 2004 deals with the historical value of the inscription. Gunawardana 2017 summarizes some of the contents of the inscription based on Wickremasinghe's translation.

23. Gunawardana 1966, 61; 1979, 251, summarizes the portion concerning the four *nikāyas*; Carrithers 1984, 139, translates one sentence from the beginning of this inscription, Gethin 212, 53, the passage with the four *nikāyas*, and Schmiedchen 2016, 571–572, longer portions from the beginning of the inscription.

of the novices in the villages remains unclear. The next section deals with the administration of ten villages (eight mentioned by name), arranged in four groups,[24] connected in some way or another to the vihāra in which the inscription was set up (lines 3–10).[25]

The subsequent section lists people prohibited from living in this vihāra and types of behavior to be avoided (lines 10–25). In addition to quite general statements such as "one living improperly (*mithyājīvinā*) or supporting a woman ([*strīpoṣa*]*kena*) must not live here" (line 12), there are also more specific regulations. They allow such monks, who had received their ordination in a different vihāra but had given up their entitlement to food and residence there and did not carry out any matters connected with that other vihāra, to live in the vihāra with the Jetavanārāma Sanskrit Inscription (lines 10–11). Thus, implicitly this regulation prohibits monks ordained in other vihāras from living in the present monastery when they had not previously given up their relation to their former monastery. Monks are further prohibited from living there when they assist another vihāra (*anyavihārasāhāyyaṃ kurvatā*, lines 13–14) if they had been ordained elsewhere and then left the order in Lanka (*atra deśe kāṣāyaṃ parityajya*) and were again ordained as novices (*punaḥ pravrajitena*, lines 15–16), when they were singled out[26] (*nirdhārita*) by another vihāra (lines 17–18), and so on.

The next section describes the attitude of guards (*vārika*) and workers (*karmakara*) vis-à-vis householders (lines 23–24); then follows a description of the equipment of a village in charge of new constructions and renovations (*navakarma-grāma*) with stone cutters, carpenters, overseers, workers (? *karma*[*kāraka*]),[27] and so on, their rewards, and how their work should be checked and entered in the register (lines 25–33).

24. Monks in the monastery of Lahasikā had to care for Lahasikā, Urulgoṇi, and the villages appointed for robes and building repairs (lines 3–8); monks in the monastery of Huṇālā were responsible for the villages Ambila, Huṇālā, and Ulavaṇṇarīkhaṇṭi (lines 8–9); the third group comprised Kīrā and Pallāya (line 9); and the last group consisted of Sunagrāma only (lines 9–10).

25. Whether these villages were owned by the monastery as Schmiedchen states (2016, 71: "Acht Dörfer im Besitz der monastischen Einrichtung") or they were linked to the monastery by some tenure system, by rewards or tributes, is unclear from the inscription.

26. Wickremasinghe 1904–1912, 7, understands this to mean that one is expelled from another monastery.

27. In literary sources, *karmakāraka* is the designation for a monk who is responsible for legal acts (*karman*; Silk 2008, 68n110, with older literature). In the Jetavanārāma Sanskrit Inscription there are two instances where Wickremasinghe supplements *ka* (line 22) and *karma* (line 29) to read *karmakāraka*. In line 29 *karma*(*kāraka*) definitely is used in the meaning "worker";

Finally, there follows the paragraph stating that twenty-five monks from each of the four *nikāya*s are residents (*naivāsika*), that forty monks who are experts in the śāstras have taken tutelage (*niśraya*) void of any *nikāya* differences (?),[28] and so on. This is elaborated in some detail in the subsequent lines. The final two lines (39–40) of the preserved part of the inscription[29] according to Wickremasinghe (1904–1912, 5n19) are unintelligible with the exception of some characters here and there, which he, however, did not transliterate. The ink-impression reproduced in the article is not helpful, but perhaps a glance at the original stone might reveal one or another *akṣara*.

The Term Sambhoga-grāma

The compound *sambhoga-grāma* appears in a regulation that is included in the section prohibiting certain kinds of people from living in the monastery. In the immediately following regulation only *sambhoga* is used, which, however, most probably stands for *sambhoga-grāma* too. The rules run as follows:[30]

thus it either has been wrongly supplemented or has a different meaning here than in the literary sources. The inscription otherwise mentions workers and so on by the words *karmakara* (line 24) "workers," *karma(kāra)ya* (lines 27–28) "supervisors (?) of work," and *karmakṛt* (line 31) "workers" or "supervisors of work."

28. Wickremasinghe 1904–1912, 9, understands these forty to be part of the previously mentioned one hundred residents: "[There shall reside] twenty-five monks from each of the four great fraternities (*nikāya*), thus [making] one hundred residents [in all]. [Of these, there shall be] forty monks who are versed in the *śāstra*. [They shall be] those who have received tutelage void of any sectarian difference." Lines 33–34: *cāturmahānikāyeṣu pañcaviṃśatiḥ pañcaviṃśatis tapasvinaḥ tena śatan naivāsikānāṃ | catvāriṃśat śāstrābhiyuktās tapasvinaḥ | nikāyabhedam vināpi gṛhītaniśrayāḥ*.... Gethin 2012, 53, follows Wickremasinghe in his assumption that the śāstra experts are part of the hundred aforementioned ascetics. But the hundred monks are said to belong to the four *nikāya*s. If the sentence with the forty śāstra experts is to be connected to the subsequent sentence (as Wickremasinghe, but not Gethin, argues), then the śāstra specialists are characterized as having taken *niśraya* without any *nikāya* difference. Thus they could not be part of the previous hundred who are sorted according to *nikāya*s, but must be additional monks. Unlike Wickremasinghe, Gethin does not understand the śāstra experts to be the subject of the subsequent sentence concerning the tutelage void of sectarian differences. Gethin (2012, 53) translates, "forty [of these should be] ascetics versed in the *śāstras*. Those who have received tutelage irrespective of division into schools...."

29. It is not certain that the inscription ended after line 40, since the lower edge of the stone seems to be nowhere preserved.

30. Wickremasinghe 1904–1912, 5. As explained in the preface to *Epigraphia Zeylanica* 1 (1904–1912), v, Wickremasinghe used parentheses to mark doubtful letters and those supplied doubtfully. In the present passage the characters in parentheses are mere reconstructions; the respective portions of the inscription are white empty spots in the ink-impression.

asyārāmasya sambho[21]*gagrāmādau yeṣāṃ bhikṣūṇāṃ śrāmaṇerā-ṇām vā jñātayaḥ* (*santi tair yatibhi*)*r api na vastavyaṃ* | *ihārāme* | [22] *yeṣām vā ārāme sambhogādau kuṭṭumbibhir gaṇakena ka*(*rmakārakāṇām?*) *putrādau nāma kriyate tair api* [23] *na vastavyaṃ* |

This is translated by Wickremasinghe as:

> Moreover [this Vihāra] shall not be inhabited (by those brothers), whether monks (*bhikṣu*) or novices (*śrāmaṇēra*), whose relatives (live) in the villages and so forth belonging to this monastery. It shall not be inhabited also by those [superintendents of work?], whose sons and so forth are named by the astrologer after the householders of the villages and so forth belonging to their monastery or to the monastery here.[31]

Wickremasinghe was not certain what *sambhoga* stood for, and so he simply translated *sambhoga-grāma* as "villages." In a footnote he tried to link *sambhoga-grāma* to Sinhalese *ninda-gama*, a village or field in exclusive possession or use by the grantee,[32] without giving any evidence for this relation. The term *sambhoga-grāma* possibly appears a second time in inscriptions, but the reading is uncertain. In the Sinhalese Raṁbāva slab-inscription of Mahinda IV (956–972 CE), we find the word (*sambho*)*ga gamu*. This inscription deals with "the grant of certain lands" to one person and his family "for the purpose of supplying oil to illuminate the stone image of the Buddha at the Sacred Bodhi-tree." Among the lands granted, the (*sambho*)*ga* village Vaňgurupiṭi[33] "together with the fields situated therein and gardens attached thereto, but exclusive of what is dedicated to the Saṅgha"[34] is listed. Tambiah mentions this same inscription, but with the reading *saṃgha-bhoga-gama*[35] and with-

31. Wickremasinghe 1904–1912, 8; concerning "villages," Wickremasinghe (1904–1912, 8n1) states: "*Sambhoga-grāma*, probably Sinhalese *ninda-gama*. For an account of the different kinds of villages according to the system of land tenure in mediaeval Ceylon, see Bell's *Report on the Kégalla District* (Ceylon Sessional Papers, xix, 1892), pp. 115–9. Cf. also Hoernle's translation of the *Uvāsagadasāo*, p. 14, note (25), on *upabhōga* and *paribhōga*."

32. Wickremasinghe 1904–1912, 8n1 (see note 31 above), and 244; Paranavitana 1934–1941, 54n7.

33. Wickremasinghe 1912–1927, 68: (*Va*)*nguru*-(*pi*)*ṭi* (*sambho*)*ga gamu*.

34. Wickremasinghe 1912–1927, 69.

35. According to Tambiah 1968, 188, the inscription reads "*saṁghabhoga-gama*," which he

out hinting at Wickremasinghe's deviating reading.[36] From the context in the inscription it is clear that this village was not given to the saṅgha as property. Only some rights to some payments or a percentage of its income were intended for the saṅgha for some unspecified purpose. Otherwise it would not have been possible to give this village—with the exclusion of whatever fiscal or proprietary rights were transferred to the saṅgha previously—to another person.

Gunawardana assumed that *sambhoga gamu* would correspond to Pāli **sambhoga-gāma*, a term which he states is not found in the *Chronicles*. In fact, **sambhoga-gāma* is traced nowhere in Pāli literature to my knowledge. Gunawardana further states that "it is very tempting to connect" *sambhoga-gāma* "with *bhogagāma* . . . ," used frequently in the *Chronicles*. But he finally rejects this idea.[37]

The term *bhoga-gāma* appears in a number of Pāli commentaries and in the Sri Lankan *Chronicles*, generally describing a village given for the use of someone, either secular or monastic.[38] Geiger translates it as "maintenance village,"[39] Bhikkhu Bodhi as "tributary village."[40] **Saṅgha-bhoga-gāma*[41] would thus describe a village given for the use of a saṅgha, without specification of the use and purpose of this donation.[42]

---

equates with Tamil *sarvamaniyam* "complete exemption from tax." For his claim that "in the *Mahāvaṃsa* the word commonly used for a village granted by the king to the priesthood is *samghabhoga-gama* and to others is *bhogagama*," Tambiah gives Mhv 54.28 as a reference. But there we find only *saṃghabhoga*. Wickremasinghe 1912–1927, 68, gives the reading as (*sambho*)*ga gamu*, which shows that most of the first part is restored. Only the length could be quite well estimated.

36. Most probably he has taken the *saṃ* as an abbreviation for *saṅgha*, as in *saṅgamu* (Sinhalese for **saṅgha-grāma* or Pāli **saṅgha-gāma*). See Ilangasinha 1992, 85. The quality of the reproduction of the ink-impression of this inscription in Wickremasinghe 1912–1927, 68, does not allow a decision.

37. Gunawardana 1979, 62–63.

38. Gunawardana 1966, 55, 61–62.

39. Geiger [1960] 1986, § 136, and Geiger [1927] 1992, 355 (index) with references; Geiger [1925] 1992, 16n4, explains that *bhogā* means "the produce taxes of certain lands."

40. Bodhi 2000, 1441n5.

41. Not used in Pāli, *pace* Tambiah 1968, 188.

42. *Saṅghabhoga* appears several times in the *Mahāvaṃsa* and twice in Pāli commentaries, with explanations in the corresponding subcommentaries. Mp-nṭ II 53: *tattha* ***saṅghabhogassā*** *ti* (Mp II 156,4) *saṅghassa catupaccayaparibhogatthāya dinnakhettavatthutaḷākādikassa, tato uppannadhaññahiraññādikassa ca saṅghassa bhogassa*. "There, '**of the *saṅghabhoga***' means: of the fields, sites, reservoirs, and so on, given for the sake of the usage of the four requisites of the saṅgha, and of the grain, gold, and so on, that accrued therefrom [that is] **of the wealth**

There is, however, no doubt concerning the reading *sambhoga-grāma* in the Jetavanārāma Sanskrit Inscription. Thus, it is the term *sambhoga* that qualifies the village, not *saṅgha-bhoga*.

Sambhoga is a term well known in early Jain and Buddhist texts.[43] Its basic meaning is "enjoyment" or "joint enjoyment." It is used as a simplex and in compounds in secular[44] and monastic contexts. In a monastic context it especially refers to the "joint meals" of monks.[45] In the Theravāda *Vinaya* the term *sambhoga* appears in the younger layer of the *Suttavibhaṅga*, in the word analysis to *pācittiya* rules 69 and 70[46] (in the explanation of *sambhuñjeyya*). There it is differentiated into *āmisa-sambhoga* ("joint enjoyment of material goods") and *dhamma-sambhoga* ("joint enjoyment of the Dhamma").[47] This differentiation is also common in other Vinayas.[48] Otherwise *sambhoga* is found several times in the *Cullavagga* and *Mahāvagga* of the Theravāda *Vinaya*. Although it appears in various compounds as well, it is not prominent in the Pāli tradition.[49]

Sambhoga often appears together with the term *saṃvāsa*.[50] As such we find it in the introduction to the *Mahāsāṅghika-Lokottaravāda-prātimokṣa*[51]

(*bhoga*) of the ***saṅgha***." Spk-ṭ II 332: ***saṅghabhogan*** *ti* (≠ Spk III 34,5) *saṅghasatakaṃ bhogagāmaṃ gantvā*. "***Saṅghabhogaṃ*** means: having gone to the maintenance village which is saṅgha property." Interestingly, here the quoted text is only found in the Burmese edition of the *Sāratthappakāsinī* (*saṅghabhogaṃ katvā*). The Sinhalese edition has *saṅghabhogatthāya gantvā*; the Roman edition *sambhogaṃ katvā* (Spk III 34,5).

43. Hu-von Hinüber 2016; Hu-von Hinüber 2018, 15–30 (shorter English version).

44. For instance, *accharā-sambhoga*; Masefield 1994, 456 with note 137.

45. Hu-von Hinüber 2016; an example from the Theravāda commentarial tradition is Sp VI 1264,4: *sace khuddako vihāro hoti, sabbe bhikkhū ekasambhogā*. "If the monastery is small, all monks eat together."

46. Vin IV 137,30–35, and 140,17–18; see Hu-von Hinüber 1996, 45–46.

47. Hu-von Hinüber 2016, 46, considers this to refer to the *Pātimokkha* only, but that probably is too narrow an interpretation.

48. For instance, in the *Pravrajyāvastu* of the Mūlasarvāstivāda (Vogel and Wille [2002] 2014, 165, 180): "enjoyment of (worldly) goods"; "enjoyment of the Law"; in the *Bhikṣuṇīvinaya* of the Mahāsāṅghikas (Hirakawa 1982, 116): "food of the Dharma (teaching)," "material food."

49. Most passages are discussed by Hu-von Hinüber 2016, 42–67.

50. Hu-von Hinüber 2016, 54–55.

51. Tatia 1975, 4, lines 17–20, vv. 20–21:
yeṣāṃ ca vasati hṛdaye śāstā dharmo gaṇottamo |
śikṣā uddeśo saṃvāso saṃbhogo śāstuno vacanaṃ ||
teṣām upoṣadho [']dya aparityaktāni yehi etāni |
paricarya dharmarājaṃ te yānti asaṃskṛtaṃ sthānaṃ || 20–21 ||

and in the conclusion of the *pārājika* section of the *Sarvāstivāda-*[52] and *Mūlasarvāstivāda-prātimokṣa*s[53] but not in the conclusion of the *pārājika* sections of the *Mahāsāṅghika-Lokottaravāda-prātimokṣa* or the *Theravāda-pātimokkha*.[54] *Saṃvāsa* in this context refers not simply to the residential community[55] but to that community's capability to carry out legal acts (*karman*) together, to recite the *Prātimokṣa* together, and so on.[56] A person who may not participate in this "[legal] communal life" (*asaṃvāsa*) is also excluded from the joint meals of the monks, because they are distributed according to seniority and thus presuppose a valid ordination age. The addition of the term *sambhoga* in the concluding *pārājika* sections of the *Prātimokṣa*s of the Sarvāstivāda and Mūlasarvāstivāda thus simply makes this explicit, but strictly speaking, it would not have been necessary.

According to Hu-von Hinüber, *sambhoga* also appears in the *Kṣudrakavastu*

"And [there is] now the Observance for those in whose hearts the Teacher, the Dharma, and the best of groups (i.e., the saṅgha) dwell; training, recitation, communal life, joint meals [and] the word of the Teacher, those who have not abandoned them, having honored the King of Dharma, reach the unconditioned stage."

As the verse is printed in Tatia 1975, two hemistichs of the Āryā stanzas quoted are not metrical. The first hemistich of st. 20 becomes so if *ca* is supplied after *dharmo*, and in the first hemistich of st. 21 *adya* should probably be read. Thanks to the anonymous peer reviewer for these suggestions.

52. Von Simson 2000, 165: *uddiṣṭā mayāyuṣmantaś catvāraḥ pārājikā dharmā yeṣāṃ bhikṣur anyatamānyatamaṃ dharmaṃ āpanno na labhate bhikṣubhiḥ sārdhaṃ saṃvāsaṃ vā saṃbhogaṃ vā yathā pūrvaṃ tathā paścāt pārājiko bhavaty asaṃvāsyaḥ*. "Recited by me, venerable sirs, are the four rules entailing defeat. A monk who commits [a transgression of] one or other of these rules, does not obtain the [legal] communal life or joint eating together with the monks. As [he was] before so [he is] thereafter; he becomes expelled [from the community, incurs] the loss of the [legal] communal life."

53. Hu-von Hinüber 2003, 10: ... *na labhate bhikṣubhiḥ sārddhaṃ samvāsam vā sambhaugam* [v.l. *saṃbhogaṃ*] *vā*. ... The Tibetan equivalent to *sambhoga* is *longs spyod*; see Vidyabhusana 1915, 80, line 12. See also Das [1902] 1985, s.v. *longs spyod*, which gives *bhoga* and *sambhoga* as Sanskrit equivalents.

54. Both the *Mahāsāṅghika-prātimokṣa* (Tatia 1975, 8, lines 13–14) and the *Theravāda-pātimokkha* (Pruitt and Norman [2001] 2008, 10, line 11) only have *saṃvāsa* there. But *sambhoga* appears in an *anāpatti* formula transmitted in the *Mahāvagga* (Vin I 97,33–34; 98,9–10.23–24: *alabbhamānāya sāmaggiyā anāpatti sambhoge saṃvāse*. "If completeness [of the saṅgha] has not been obtained (for carrying out a legal act of suspension against a monk), [there is] no offense [for this monk] in joint eating and in [legal] communal life (with the other monks)."

55. So argues von Simson 2000, 272, who translates *saṃvāsaṃ vā saṃbhogaṃ vā* as "Wohn- und Essensgemeinschaft."

56. See, for instance, Kieffer-Pülz 1992, 52–53, 62–63.

of the *Mūlasarvāstivāda-vinaya*. She bases her investigation on the Chinese translation by Yijing. The story is about a vihāra's endangered supply of material goods when its owner is put into jail.[57]

> Wenn der (Kloster)herr nach fünf Jahren zurückkehrt, ist es gut. Wenn er nicht zurückkommt, soll man bis zu zehn Jahren(!) genau so eine gemeinsame Versorgung, aber eine getrennte Prātimokṣa-Rezitation durchführen.[58]

The same story was previously dealt with by Schopen based on the Tibetan translation in 1996.[59] Schopen renders the corresponding passage slightly differently.

> If after five years the Owner of the *Vihāra* is released, that is good. But if he is not released then, after performing a formal act of two-fold motion, those who are the guardians of *vihāras* in the neighborhood of that *vihāra*, and their common acquisitions, and their fortnightly meetings, should remain distinct for five more years.[60]

Hu-von Hinüber's *sambhoga* (Chin. *tongliyang* 同利養)[61] corresponds to Schopen's "and their common acquisitions" (Tib. *rnyed pa thun mong dang*).[62] But whether or not *rnyed pa thun mong* reflects *sambhoga* is unclear, since *rnyed pa* normally stands for *lābha*[63] and *sambhoga* in the *Mūlasarvāstivāda-prātimokṣa* corresponds to Tibetan *longs spyod*.[64] This needs further investigation.

In the school of the Dharmaguptakas, *sambhoga* receives a more prominent place. In this school the concept of *sīmā* ("monastic boundary") is extended compared to most other schools. A *sīmā* regularly defines the space within

57. See Hu-von Hinüber 2016, 101–106.

58. Hu-von Hinüber 2016, 105. In her English version, Hu-von Hinüber (2018, 23) only summarizes the contents.

59. Schopen 1996.

60. Schopen 1996, 109–110. The final sentence is misunderstood. The being distinct (*tha dad pa*) only refers to the *poṣadha* ceremony "with their distinct fortnightly assembly." If the monks of the vihāra whose owner is in prison should keep distinct from those of the neighboring vihāra throughout, then the whole paragraph would be meaningless.

61. Hu-von Hinüber 2016, 101.

62. Schopen 1996, 111.

63. Das [1902] 1985, s.v. *rnyed pa* gives *lābha, pūraṇa, parigata, udaya.*

64. See note 53 above.

which the legal acts (*karman*) of the community are carried out. In addition, it can be determined as the space within which some of the robe rules are rescinded. The Dharmaguptakas seem to extend the functions of the *sīmā*, in that in special cases they combine the question of the supply of goods with the determination of a boundary for the observance (*poṣadha*),[65] so that the *sīmā* also defines the area of goods' supply. This again appears to be reflected in the *Shanjianlü piposha* (fifth century CE), a Chinese translation of the Pāli *Samantapāsādikā*,[66] enriched with Dharmaguptaka elements. According to Hu-von Hinüber (2016, 98), here the relation of the boundary within which monks are not considered separated from their three robes (even if they are) (Pāli *avippavāsa-sīmā*) to the *poṣadha-sīmā* (*busa jie*) and the **sambhoga-sīmā* (*tongliyang jie*) is explained.[67] In a footnote she states that the text reads **bhoga-sīmā* (*liyang jie* 利養界), which should be understood as an abbreviation for "boundary for the joint supply of food" (**sambhoga-sīmā*, Chin. *tongliyang jie* 同利養界).[68] The relevant passage of the *Shanjianlü piposha* has little concurrence with Sp V 1136,1ff. In the commentary to the words "he gives to a *sīmā*" (*sīmāya deti*) the commentator lists fifteen types of boundaries, which are also given in the *Shanjianlü piposha*. There we have a *lābha-sīmā* (Sp V 1136,9.24–31; 1137,17) but neither a *bhoga-* nor a *sambhoga-sīmā*. The passage quoted and

65. Dealt with in detail in Hu-von Hinüber 2016, 68–97. There are various formulas (*karmavācanā*) in this Vinaya that allow two residences (*āvāsa*) to determine a joint observance (*poṣadha*) and supply (*sambhoga*), or a joint *poṣadha* with separate supply, or a separate *poṣadha* with joint supply, or a separate *poṣadha* and a separate supply. In order to change the *poṣadha*, earlier boundaries (*sīmā*) have to be abolished and new ones determined. In the case that both *āvāsa*s want a joint *poṣadha* and supply, the *āvāsa*s determine a joint *sīmā*, which functions as a *sīmā* for the *poṣadha* and for the supply area. In cases where a different supply area is wished for, the formulas mention that the *sīmā* is determined for one *poṣadha* but with different supplies. If the regulation concerning the *poṣadha* remains unchanged and only the regulation concerning the supply is altered, the old *sīmā*s are not abolished and no new ones are determined. This shows that the *sīmā* is valid for the *poṣadha* and other legal acts (Hu-von Hinüber 2016, 84). But the linking of the *sīmā* and the supply (be it in the positive or negative) in the formulas for determining the *sīmā* for a *poṣadha* connected the *sīmā* to the supply area. This function of a *sīmā* in East Asian Buddhism is discussed more closely by Jung (2019, 269–276), who hints at the fact that the *sīmā* for supply, or food boundary, as he calls it, is not identical with the *sīmā* within which the monks have to assemble but that it refers to a smaller area within the latter (271). For a further development, see the mention of a **bhoga-sīmā* in the *Shanjianlü piposha* (see above).

66. Hu-von Hinüber 2016, 98–100, and 2018, 23.

67. Hu-von Hinüber 2016, 98: "In diesem Zusammenhang wird das Verhältnis der Grenze für das Nichtgetrenntsein von den drei Gewändern (不失衣界) zu der **poṣadha-sīmā* (布薩界 *busa-jie*) und der **saṃbhoga-sīmā* (同利養界 *tongliyang-jie*) erläutert."

68. Hu-von Hinüber 2016, 98.

translated by Hu-von Hinüber[69] is only faintly reminiscent of the Pāli original.[70] Thus it seems to belong to those sections adapted to the Dharmaguptaka tradition. From the point of view of content, the statements there make sense only when we assume that the boundary for the *poṣadha* also indicates the area of the supply of goods or—if the area of the supply of goods and *poṣadha* are not identical—that the boundary of the area for the supply of goods now is called *sīmā*. This needs further investigation.[71]

The Mahīśāsaka tradition seems to have taken a similar route, because in the formula (*karmavācanā*) for determining the boundary within which monks are not considered separated from their three robes (even if they are), the *sīmā* is mentioned as a "*sīmā* for the same communion, for one common *poṣatha*, and for the distribution of (the goods accrued to the community)."[72]

Sambhoga in the Vinaya context thus seems to refer mostly to the supply of material goods, though in a narrower sense it may be used for food only. The term has a more prominent position in the texts of the Sarvāstivāda, Mūlasarvāstivāda, Dharmaguptaka, and possibly Mahīśāsaka traditions than in that of the Theravāda. Though we cannot say that it is non-Theravāda Vinaya terminology, since it is not foreign to that tradition, its usage in the Jetavanārāma inscription would go well together with the fact that the monastery to which this inscription belongs accommodated one hundred monks from four *nikāya*s, which most probably represented four *nikāya*s prevalent in India at that time (see above). The *sambhoga-grāma* of the Jetavanārāma Sanskrit Inscription thus in all probability refers to villages whose task it was to provide the saṅgha in the *ārāma* with material goods, or perhaps exclusively with food.[73] The *sambhoga-grāma* then would be a "[goods or food] supply

69. Similarly translated into English by Bapat and Hirakawa 1970, 521.

70. Sp V 1137,15–19: *"samānasaṃvāsasīmāya dammī" ti dinnaṃ pana khaṇḍasīmā-sīmantarikāsu ṭhitānaṃ na pāpuṇāti. avippavāsasīmā-lābhasīmāsu dinnaṃ, tāsu sīmāsu antogatānaṃ pāpuṇāti. gāmasīmādisu dinnam pana, tāsaṃ sīmānaṃ abbhantare baddhasīmāya ṭhitānaṃ pi pāpuṇāti.* "But [something] given [with the words]: 'I give to the boundary for the same communion (*samāna-saṃvāsa-sīmā*)' does not reach those who stay within the boundary for a part [of the community] (*khaṇḍa-sīmā*) and in the interval between [two] boundaries (*sīmantarikā*). [Something] given to the boundary for the not-being-separated [from the three robes] (*avippavāsa-sīmā*) and to a benefit boundary (*lābha-sīmā*) reaches those staying within these boundaries. But [something] given to a village boundary (*gāma-sīmā*) and so on reaches even those staying within a determined boundary (*baddha-sīmā*) inside these boundaries."

71. For some insights, see Jung 2019, 278–279.

72. Chung and Kieffer-Pülz 1997, 44. Here too a closer examination of this tradition is necessary.

73. The tasks of villages are explicitly mentioned in calling them *cīvaranavakarmaṇe niyuktāṃś ca grāmān* (Wickremasinghe 1904–1912, 4, lines 4–5), Sinhalese *sivur-gam* corresponding to

village." The two regulations containing the word *sambhoga* therefore can be translated as follows:

> Those monks and novices whose relatives [live] in the [goods'] supply villages and so on of this *ārāma* also must not live here in the *ārāma*.
>
> Or those [monks] who are *ka*[*rmakāraka*]s (?) whose sons and so on are named by the astrologer (?) after the householders (?) in the *ārāmā*, in the [goods'] supply [villages], and so on, also must not live [here].[74]

The second sentence is not completely clear, since the word qualifying the monastics is destroyed except for the *ka* in the beginning. If it is restored to *karmakārakāṇāṃ* as tentatively done by Wickremasinghe, and if this term was used in its usual meaning (see note 27 above), then unlike in the preceding sentence only bhikṣus could have been spoken of here. The first sentence clearly shows that relations between monks and novices in the *ārāma* on the one side and people in the supply villages on the other were considered an impediment for living in this *ārāma*. This likely is the case, because it held a considerable risk of preferential treatment of those monks by their relatives. If the second sentence is understood correctly, this points in the same direction. Monks with direct offspring named after some of the householders either staying in the *ārāma* or in the supply villages may be suspected of having a special relationship with these householders, which again implied the danger of favoritism. However, it seems quite unlikely that such a rule would be applied only to monks who are *karmakārakas*. Therefore, the supplementation of this word by Wickremasinghe is quite unlikely, and the question of which types of monastics are meant here must be left open.

In the sentence with the term *sambhoga-grāma*, the monastery in which the Jetavanārāma Sanskrit Inscription is placed is designated as *ārāma*, as also in the subsequent regulation. In the preceding sections of this inscription it

Skt. *cīvara-grāma* (Wickremasinghe 1904–1912, 187, line 28; 189n11; 244). So it may be that the provision with robes was not included in the term *sambhoga-grāma*.

74. For Wickremasinghe's translation of this sentence, see p. 428 above.

was constantly designated as *vihāra*.[75] Otherwise, only the word *parṇaśālā*[76] is used—namely, for the monasteries of the monks in the villages connected to the present monastery in one way or another.[77] Only in the two sentences that contain the word *sambhoga* is the monastery designated as *ārāma*. Whether *ārāma* and *vihāra* are synonyms here—both have been used to denote entire monasteries since the fifth century CE at the latest—or whether *ārāma* describes the entire monastic complex whereas the vihāra with the inscription was only a smaller entity within it remains unclear. But the first alternative is the more likely, since this inscription regulates the conditions for living in the monastery with the Jetavanārāma Sanskrit Inscription. Thus it is improbable that regulations concerning different areas within a larger unit would be contained in it.

Works Cited

Abbreviations

Mhv	*Mahāvaṃsa* (and *Cūḷavaṃsa*). Edited by Wilhelm Geiger. 3 vols. London: The Pali Text Society, 1908, 1925–1927.
Mp	*Manorathapūraṇī* (*Aṅguttaranikāya-aṭṭhakathā*). Edited by Max Walleser and Hermann Kopp. 5 vols. London: The Pali Text Society, 1936–1957.
Mp-nṭ	*Sāratthamañjūsā* (*Manorathapūraṇī-navaṭīkā*). Rangoon: Chaṭṭhasaṅgīti, 1961.
Sp	*Samantapāsādikā* (*Vinaya-aṭṭhakathā*). Edited by Junjirō Takakusu and Makoto Nagai. 7 vols. London: The Pali Text Society, 1924–1947.
Spk	*Sāratthappakāsinī* (*Saṃyuttanikāya-aṭṭhakathā*). Edited by Frank Lee Woodward. 3 vols. London: The Pali Text Society, 1929–1937.
Spk-ṭ	*Sāratthappakāsinī-ṭīkā*. Rangoon: Chaṭṭhasaṅgīti, 1961.
Vin	*The Vinaya Piṭakaṃ*. Edited by Hermann Oldenberg. 5 vols. London: Williams and Norgate, 1879–1883.

75. But the term *vihāra* is also used in this inscription with respect to monasteries not identical with the one where the Jetavanārāma Sanskrit Inscription stood. See the mention of such other vihāras in lines 2, 5, 11, 13, and 17.

76. Whether *parṇaśālā* stands for a monastery or a kind of hermitage covered with leaves is unclear.

77. Wickremasinghe 1904–1912, 4, 6, lines 4, 8.

Bapat, P. V., and A. Hirakawa, trans. 1970. *Shan-Chien-P'i-P'o-Sha: A Chinese Version by Saṅghabhadra of Samantapāsādikā. Commentary on Pali Vinaya*. Bhandarkar Oriental Series 10. Poona: Bhandarkar Oriental Research Institute.

Bechert, Heinz. 1982. "On the Identification of Buddhist Schools in Early Sri Lanka." In *Indology and Law: Studies in Honour of Professor J. Duncan M. Derrett*, edited by Günther-Dietz Sontheimer, 60–76. Beiträge zur Südasienforschung 77. Wiesbaden: Steiner.

Bodhi, Bhikkhu, trans. 2000. *The Connected Discourses of the Buddha: A New Translation of the Saṃyutta Nikāya*. Pali Text Society Translation Series 47. Oxford: The Pali Text Society in association with Wisdom Publications.

Carrithers, Michael B. 1984. "'Sie werden die Herren der Insel sein': Buddhismus in Sri Lanka." In *Die Welt des Buddhismus*, edited by Heinz Bechert and Richard Gombrich, 133–146. Munich: Verlag C. H. Beck.

Chung, Jin-il, and Petra Kieffer-Pülz. 1997. "The *karmavācanās* for the Determination of *sīmā* and *ticīvareṇa avippavāsa*." In *Dharmadūta: Mélanges offerts au Vénérable Thích Huyền-Vi à l'occasion de son soixante-dixième anniversaire*, edited by Bhikkhu T. Dhammaratana and Bhikkhu Pāsādika, 13–56. Paris: Librairie You-Feng.

Coomaraswamy, Ananda K. 1909. *The Indian Crafts-Man*. London: Probsthain & Co.

Das, Sarat Chandra. [1902] 1985. *A Tibetan-English Dictionary*. Reprint, New Delhi: Gaurav Publishing House.

Geiger, Wilhelm, trans. [1925] 1992. *Cūḷavaṃsa: Being the More Recent Part of the Mahāvaṃsa*. Part 1. Reprinted together with part 2 in one volume. Oxford: The Pali Text Society.

———, trans. [1927] 1992. *Cūḷavaṃsa: Being the More Recent Part of the Mahāvaṃsa*. Part 2. Reprinted together with part 1 in one volume. Oxford: The Pali Text Society.

———. [1960] 1986. *Culture of Ceylon in Mediaeval Times*, edited by Heinz Bechert. 2nd unrevised ed. Veröffentlichungen des Seminars für Indologie und Buddhismuskunde der Universität Göttingen 4. Stuttgart: Franz Steiner Verlag.

Gethin, Rupert. 2012. "Was Buddhaghosa a Theravādin?" In *How Theravāda Is Theravāda? Exploring Buddhist Identities*, edited by Peter Skilling, Jason A. Carbine, Claudio Cicuzza, and Santi Pakdeekham, 1–63. Chiang Mai: Silkworm Books.

Guṇavardhana, Nadiṣā Ṣarmalī. 2004. "Jētavanārāma Saṃskṛta Śilālipiya (The Jetavanārāma Sanskrit Inscription)." In *Sarasavi: Samājīya Vidyā Śāstrīya Lipi Saṃgrahaya*, edited by Herat Mādana Baṇḍāra and Priśānta Guṇavardhana, 2:138–145. Kälaṇiya: Kelaṇiya University's Department of Archaeology.

Gunawardana, Nadeesha. 2017. "Historical Facts Revealed From the Two Slab Inscriptions of Mihintalē in Sri Lanka." *Humanities and Social Sciences Review* 7.2: 185–190.

Gunawardana, R. A. L. H. 1966. "Buddhist Nikāyas in Medieval Ceylon." *Ceylon Journal of Historical and Social Studies* 9: 55–66.

———. 1979. *Robe and Plough: Monasticism and Economic Interest in Early Medieval Sri Lanka*. The Association for Asian Studies: Monographs and Papers 35. Tucson: The Association for Asian Studies by the University of Arizona Press.

von Hinüber, Oskar. 2012. "Buddhistische Mönche als Verwalter ihrer Klöster. Die Entstehung des Begriffs 'vārika' in der Tradition der Theravādins." *Zeitschrift der Deutschen Morgenländischen Gesellschaft* 152.2: 373–389.

Hirakawa, Akira. 1982. *Monastic Discipline for the Buddhist Nuns: An English Translation of the Chinese Text of the Mahāsāṃghika-Bhikṣuṇī-Vinaya*. Tibetan Sanskrit Works Series 21. Patna: Kashi Prasad Jayaswal Research Institute.

Hu-von Hinüber, Haiyan. 2003. "Das Bhikṣu-Prātimokṣasūtra der Mūlasarvāstivādins, anhand der Sanskrit-Handschriften aus Tibet und Gilgit sowie unter Berücksichtigung der tibetischen und chinesischen Übersetzungen kritisch herausgegeben." Unpublished manuscript available at https://freidok.uni-freiburg.de/data/9535.

———. 2016. *Saṃbhoga: Die Zugehörigkeit zur Ordensgemeinschaft im frühen Jainismus und Buddhismus*. Studia Philologica Buddhica, Monograph Series 33. Tokyo: The International Institute for Buddhist Studies of the International College for Postgraduate Buddhist Studies.

———. 2018. "Saṃbhoga: The Affiliation with a Religious Order in Early Jainism and Buddhism." In *Jaina Studies: Select Papers Presented in the 'Jaina Studies' Section at the 16th World Sanskrit Conference Bangkok, Thailand & the 14th World Sanskrit Conference Kyoto, Japan*, edited by Nalini Balbir and Peter Flügel, 15–30. 16th World Sanskrit Conference 8. New Delhi: D. K. Publishers & Distributors.

Ilangasinha, H. B. M. 1992. *Buddhism in Medieval Sri Lanka*. Delhi: Sri Satguru Publications.

Jung, Ghichul. 2019. "'Natural Land Is Too Weak to Sustain the Great Dharma': Daoxuan's Commentary on the *Sīmā* and Medieval Chinese Monasticism." *Journal of the International Association of Buddhist Studies* 42: 265–314.

Kalupahana, D. J. 1970. "Schools of Buddhism in Early Ceylon." *Ceylon Journal of the Humanities* 1: 159–190.

Kieffer-Pülz, Petra. 1992. *Die Sīmā: Vorschriften zur Regelung der buddhistischen Gemeindegrenze in älteren buddhistischen Texten*. Monographien zur indischen Archäologie, Kunst und Philologie 8. Berlin: Dietrich Reimer Verlag.

———. 2010. Review of *Managing Monks*, by Jonathan A. Silk. *Indo-Iranian Journal* 53.1: 71–88.

Masefield, Peter. 1994. *The Udāna Commentary* (*Paramatthadīpanī nāma Udānaṭṭhakathā*), vol. 1. Sacred Books of the Buddhists 43. Oxford: The Pali Text Society.

Mitra, Debala. 1971. *Buddhist Monuments*. Calcutta: Sahitya Samsad.

Paranavitana, S. 1934–1941. "No. 6. Vihāregama Pillar-Inscription." *Epigraphia Zeylanica* 4: 50–54.

Perera, Lakshman S. 2001. *The Institutions of Ancient Ceylon from Inscriptions*, vol. 2: *From 831 to 1016 A.D.*, pt. 1: *Political Institutions*. Kandy: International Centre for Ethnic Studies.

Pruitt, William, and K. R. Norman, eds. and trans. [2001] 2008. *The Pātimokkha*. Reprint, with corrections, Oxford: The Pali Text Society.

Ranawella, Sirimal. 1998. "Supplementary Information on the Interpretation of the Word *Variyan vide Sesquicontennial* [*sic*] *Volume of the Royal Asiatic Society of Sri Lanka* 1845–1995, 1995, pp. 141–157." *Journal of the Royal Asiatic Society of Sri Lanka*, n.s., 43: 113–115.

———. 1999. *Inscriptions of Āpā Kitagbo and Kings Sena I, Sena II, and Udaya II*. Dehiwala: Sridevi.

———. 2005. *Sinhala Inscriptions in the Colombo National Museum*. Sri Lanka: Department of National Museums.

Ratnapāla, Nandasena, ed. and trans. 1971. *The Katikāvatas: Laws of the Buddhist Order of Ceylon from the 12th Century to the 18th Century*. Münchener Studien zur Sprachwissenschaft, Beiheft N. Munich: R. Kitzinger.

Salomon, Richard. 1998. *Indian Epigraphy: A Guide to the Study of Inscriptions in Sanskrit, Prakrit, and the Other Indo-Aryan Languages*. South Asia Research Series. New York: Oxford University Press.

Schmiedchen, Annette. 2016. "13.6 Indien." In *Enzyklopädie des Stiftungswesens in mittelalterlichen Gesellschaften*, vol. 2: *Das soziale System Stiftung*, edited by Michael Borgolte, 567–680. Berlin: Walter de Gruyter.

Schopen, Gregory. 1996. "The Lay Ownership of Monasteries and the Role of the Monk in Mūlasarvāstivādin Monasticism." *Journal of the International Association of Buddhist Studies* 19.1: 81–126. Reprinted in Schopen 2004, 219–259.

———. 2004. *Buddhist Monks and Business Matters: Still More Papers on Monastic Buddhism in India*. Studies in the Buddhist Traditions. Honolulu: University of Hawai'i Press.

Silk, Jonathan A. 2008. *Managing Monks: Administrators and Administrative Roles in Indian Buddhist Monasticism*. Oxford: Oxford University Press.

von Simson, Georg, ed. and trans. 2000. *Prātimokṣasūtra der Sarvāstivādins*, Teil II: *Kritische Textausgabe, Übersetzung, Wortindex sowie Nachträge zu Teil I*. Sanskrittexte aus den Turfanfunden 11. Abhandlungen der Akademie der Wissenschaften in Göttingen. Philologisch-historische Klasse, Dritte Folge 238. Göttingen: Vandenhoeck & Ruprecht.

Tambiah, Henry Wijayakone. 1968. *Sinhala Laws and Customs*. Colombo: Lake House Investments.

Tatia, Nathmal. 1975. *Prātimokṣasūtram of the Lokottaravādimahāsāṅghika School*. Tibetan Sanskrit Works Series 16. Patna: Kashi Prasad Jayaswal Research Institute.

Tournier, Vincent. 2017. *La formation du Mahāvastu et la mise en place des conceptions relatives à la carrière du bodhisattva*. École française d'Extrême-Orient Monographies 195. Paris: École française d'Extrême-Orient.

Vidyabhusana, Satis Chandra. 1915. "So-sor-thar-pa; or, a Code of Buddhist Monastic Laws: Being the Tibetan Version of Prātimokṣa of the Mūla-sarvāstivāda School." *Journal of the Asiatic Society of Bengal*, n.s., 11: 29–139.

Vogel, Claus, and Klaus Wille, eds. and trans. 2002. "The Final Leaves of the Pravrajyāvastu Portion of the Vinayavastu Manuscript Found Near Gilgit, Part 2: Nāgakumārāvadāna and Lévi Text. With Two Appendices Containing a Turfan Fragment of the Nāgakumārāvadāna and a Kučā Fragment of the Upasaṃpadā Section of the Sarvāstivādins." In *Sanskrit-Texte aus dem buddhistischen Kanon: Neuentdeckungen und Neueditionen IV*, 11–76. Sanskrit-Wörterbuch der buddhistischen Texte aus den Turfan-Funden, Beiheft 9. Göttingen: Vandenhoeck & Ruprecht. Reprinted in Claus Vogel and Klaus Wille, eds. and trans. 2014. *The Pravrajyāvastu of the Mūlasarvāstivāda Vinaya*. Göttingen: Akademie der Wissenschaften zu

Göttingen, Sanskrit-Wörterbuch der buddhistischen Texte aus den Turfan-Funden, 147–212. https://rep.adw-goe.de/handle/11858/00-001S-0000-0023-9A04-C.

Walters, Jonathan. 2000. "Buddhist History: The Sri Lankan Pāli Vaṃsas and Their Commentary." In *Querying the Medieval: Texts and the History of Practices in South Asia*, edited by Ronald Inden, Jonathan Walters, and Daud Ali, 99–164. Oxford: Oxford University Press.

Wickremasinghe, Don Martino de Zilva. 1904–1912. "No. 1. Jētavanārāma Sanskrit Inscription." *Epigraphia Zeylanica* 1: 1–9.

———. 1904–1912. "No. 15. Puliyan̲-kuḷam Slab-Inscription (C/8) of Udā Mahayā." *Epigraphia Zeylanica* 1: 182–190.

———. 1904–1912. "No. 21. Vēvälkäṭiya Slab-Inscription of Mahinda IV (*circa* 1026–1042 A.D.)." *Epigraphia Zeylanica* 1: 241–251.

———. 1912–1927. "No. 12. Ram̆bǟva Slab-Inscription." *Epigraphia Zeylanica* 2: 64–70.

Plate 1. Footprints of king at Ciaruteun. Photo OD 6889, courtesy of the Kern Institute, Leiden University Library; cf. Vogel 1925, plate 29. Here and below (plate 3), these scans of prints and Vogel's plates all derive ultimately from the same negative.

Plate 2. Detail of footprints of king at Ciaruteun. Photo courtesy of Pierre-Yves Manguin, EFEO.

Plate 3. Footprints of elephant at Kebon Kopi. Photo OD 6887, courtesy of the Kern Institute, Leiden University Library; cf. Vogel 1925, plate 33.

Plate 4. The bodhisattva Akṣayamati's offering of pearls, painted scene on interior pillar, Cave 10. Ajaṇṭā, India, late fifth century CE. Photo by Nicolas Morrissey.

Plate 5. *Caitya* hall interior, Cave 9. Ajaṇṭā, India, late fifth century CE. Photo by Nicolas Morrissey.

Plate 6. Painted composition, interior rear wall, Cave 9. Ajaṇṭā, India, late fifth century CE. Photo by Nicolas Morrissey.

Plate 7. Detail views of painted composition, interior rear wall, Cave 9. Ajaṇṭā, India, late fifth century CE. Photo by Nicolas Morrissey.

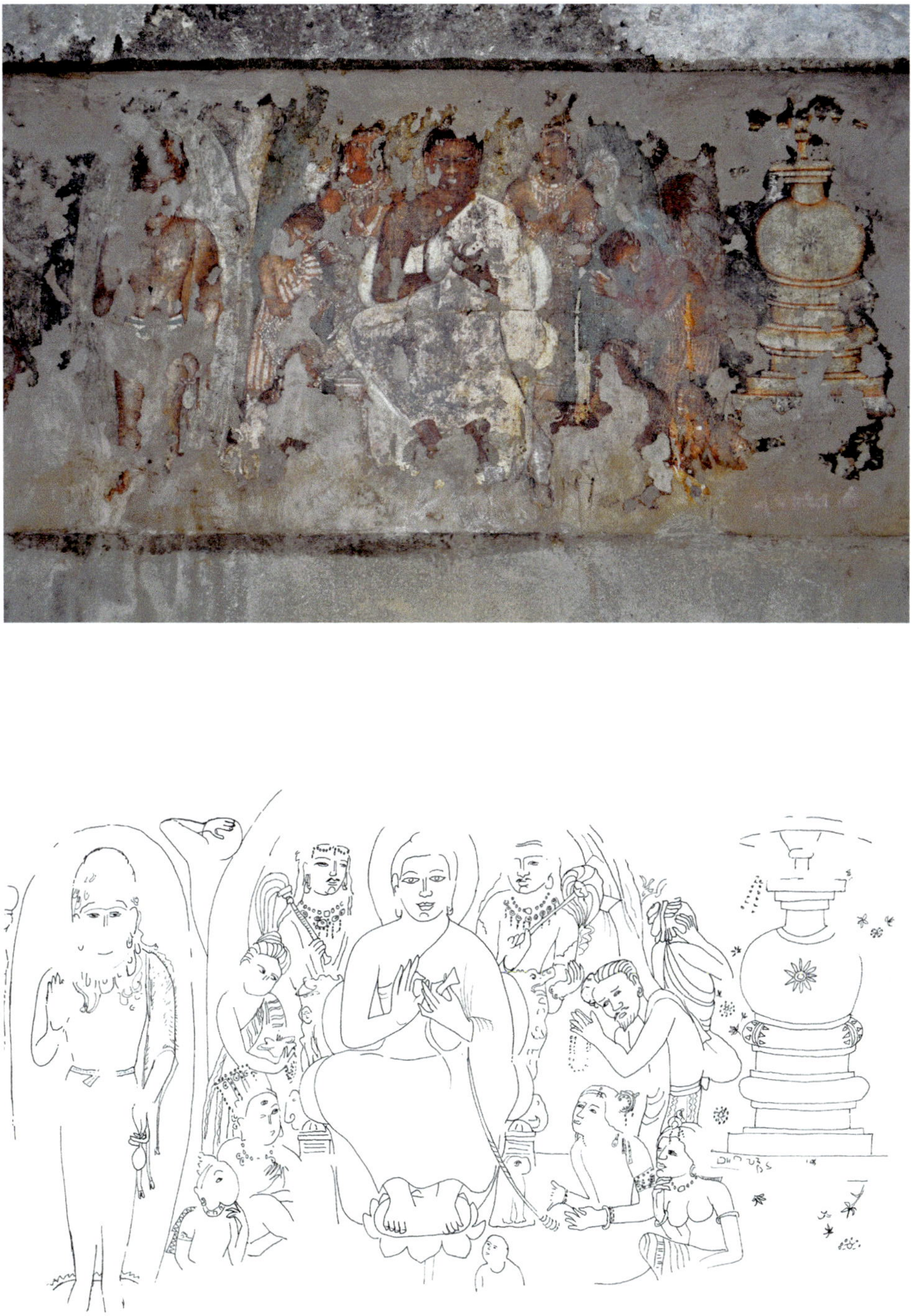

Plate 8. Central scene of painted composition, interior rear wall, Cave 9. Ajaṇṭā, India, late fifth century CE. Photo by Nicolas Morrissey with corresponding drawing provided courtesy of Dieter Schlingloff and Monika Zin.

Plate 9. The bodhisattva Akṣayamati, painting on interior rear wall, Cave 9. Ajaṇṭā, India, late fifth century CE. Photo by Nicolas Morrissey.

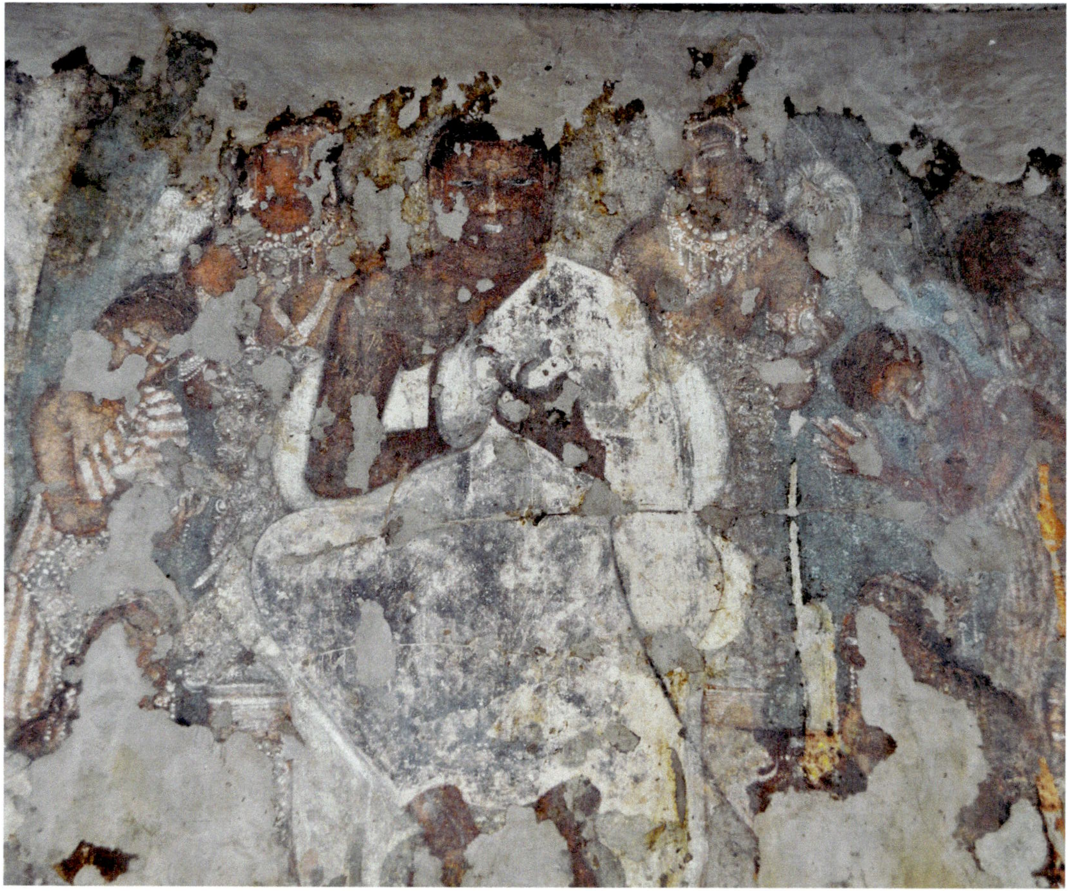

Plate 10. The bodhisattva Akṣayamati's offering of pearls, painted scene on interior rear wall, Cave 9. Ajaṇṭā, India, late fifth century CE. Photo by Nicolas Morrissey.

Plate 11. The bodhisattva Avalokiteśvara, painting on interior rear wall, Cave 9. Ajaṇṭā, India, late fifth century CE. Photo by Nicolas Morrissey with corresponding drawing provided courtesy of Dieter Schlingloff and Monika Zin.

Plate 12. The opening of the jeweled stūpa of Prabhūtaratna, painted scene on interior rear wall, Cave 9. Ajaṇṭā, India, late fifth century CE. Photo by Nicolas Morrissey with corresponding drawing provided courtesy of Dieter Schlingloff and Monika Zin (red lines and gray shaded areas to highlight details of stūpa interior added by Nicolas Morrissey).

Plate 13. Śākyamuni and Prabhūtaratna, painted scene on interior rear wall, Cave 9. Ajaṇṭā, India, late fifth century CE. Photo by Nicolas Morrissey with corresponding drawing provided courtesy of Dieter Schlingloff and Monika Zin.

Plate 14. Śākyamuni preaching on Vulture Peak and the "Parable of the Burning House," painted scene on interior rear wall, Cave 9. Ajaṇṭā, India, late fifth century CE. Photo by Nicolas Morrissey with corresponding drawing provided courtesy of Dieter Schlingloff and Monika Zin.

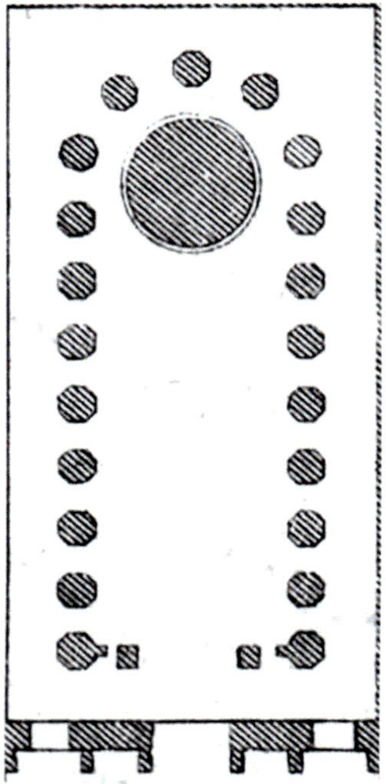

Plate 15. Painted composition, interior rear wall, Cave 9. Ajaṇṭā, India, late fifth century CE. Photo by Nicolas Morrissey with Cave 9 plan showing alignment of painted stūpa with central rock-cut stūpa in the *Caitya* hall (after Fergusson and Burgess [1880] 1988, plate XXVIII).

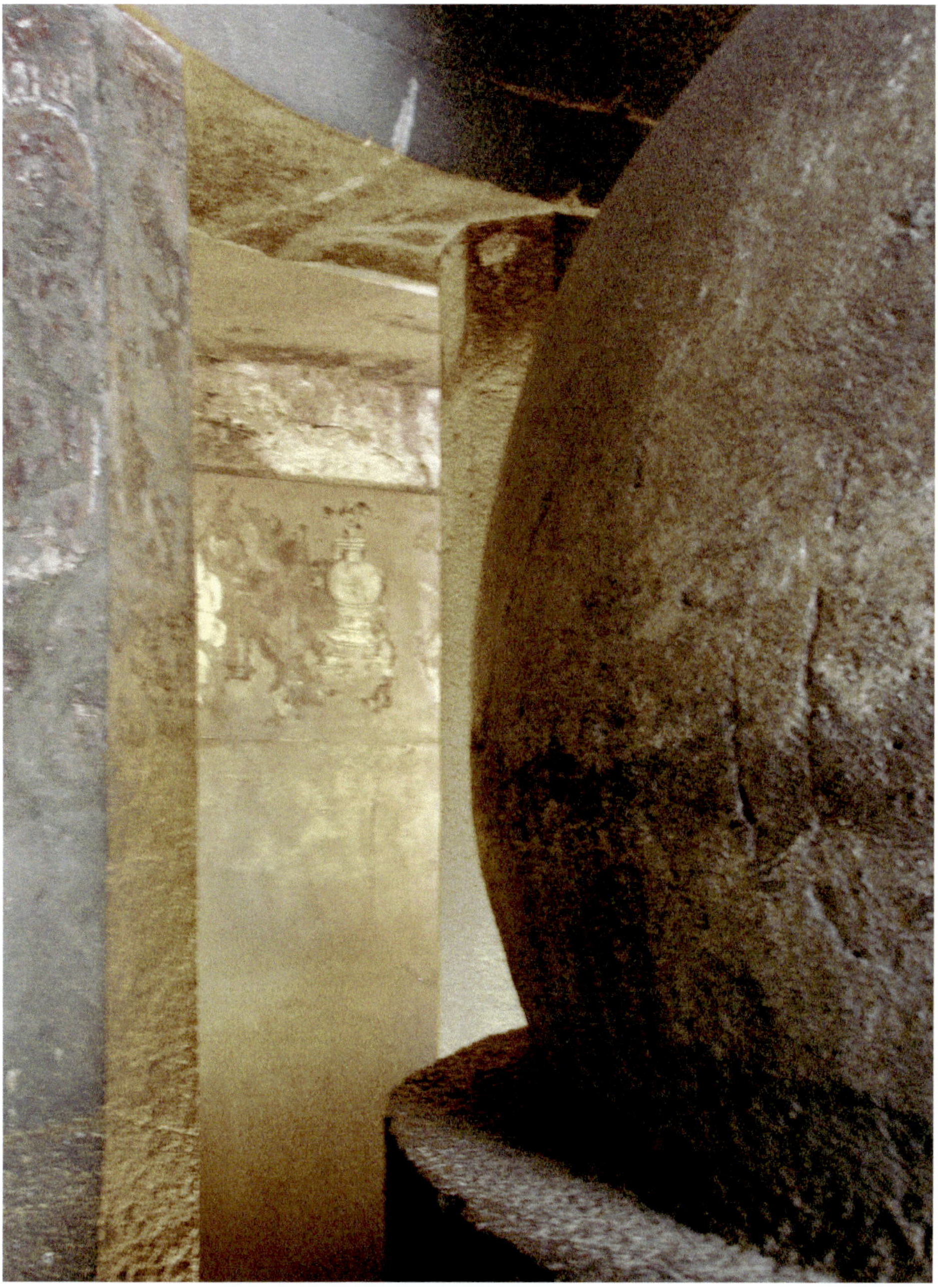

Plate 16. Main stūpa and painted stūpa alignment, Cave 9 interior. Ajaṇṭā, India, late fifth century CE. Photo by Nicolas Morrissey.

Plate 17. Main stūpa, Cave 9 interior. Ajaṇṭā, India, late fifth century CE. Photo by Nicolas Morrissey.

Plate 18. Painted stūpa, interior rear wall, Cave 9. Ajaṇṭā, India, late fifth century CE. Photo by Nicolas Morrissey.

Plate 19. Painted buddha images on interior triforium, Cave 9. Ajaṇṭā, India, late fifth century CE. Photo by Nicolas Morrissey.

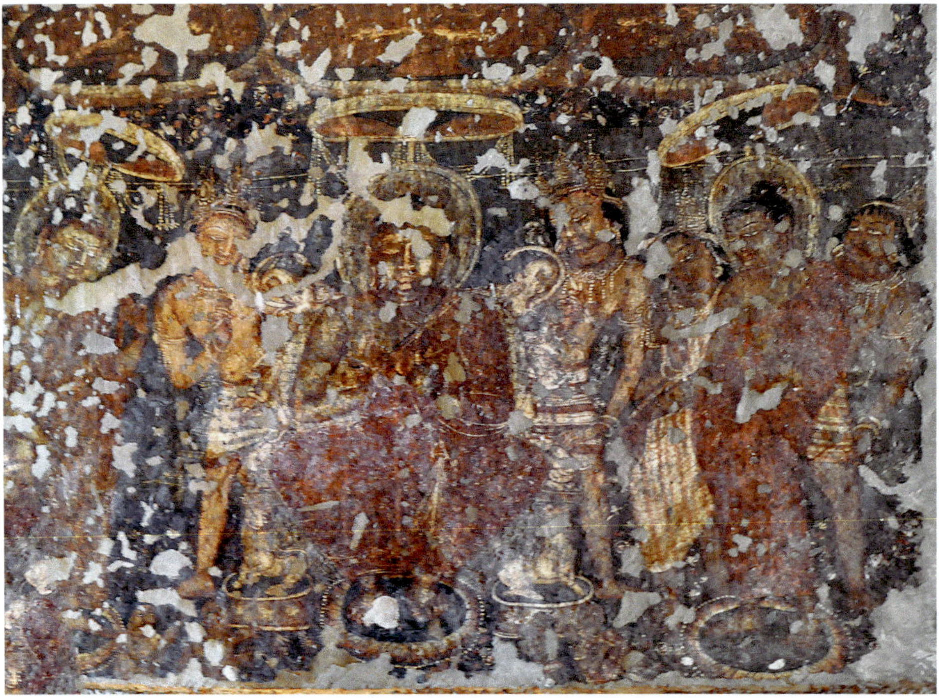

Plate 20. Painted buddha images on interior triforium, Cave 9. Ajaṇṭā, India, late fifth century CE. Photo by Nicolas Morrissey.

Plate 21. Painted buddha images on interior left aisle wall, Cave 9. Ajaṇṭā, India, late fifth century CE. Photo by Nicolas Morrissey.

Plate 22. Painted buddha images on left interior pillars, Cave 9. Ajaṇṭā, India, late fifth century CE. Photo by Nicolas Morrissey.

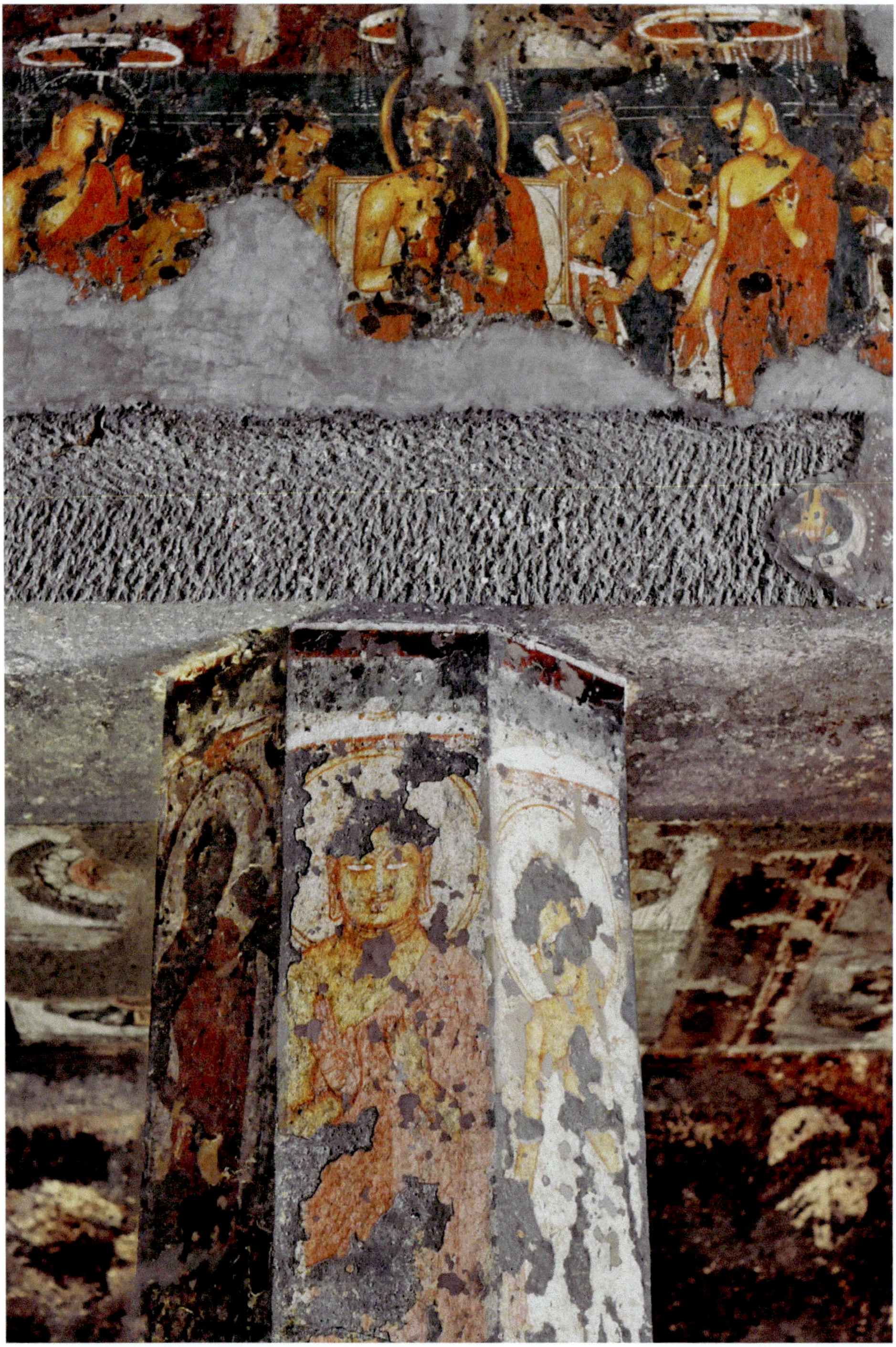

Plate 23. Painted buddha images on right interior pillar and triforium, Cave 9. Ajaṇṭā, India, late fifth century CE. Photo by Nicolas Morrissey.

Plate 24. Amitābha's Sukhāvatī. Dunhuang Mogao Cave 220, China, 642 CE.
Reproduced from ZSDM 1: plate 24.

Plate 25. Amitābha triad and fifty bodhisattvas. Dunhuang Mogao Cave 332, China, ca. 698 CE. Reproduced from ZSDM 1: plate 94.

Plate 26. Amitābha triad in the Tachibana miniature shrine. Hōryūji, Japan, late seventh century CE. Reproduced from Uehara 1968, figure 16.

Plate 27. Amitābha triad and fifty bodhisattvas. Hōryūji mural, Japan, end of the seventh century CE. Reproduced from KSH.

Plate 28. Preaching buddha stele. Muhammad Nari, Gandhāra, third century CE. Lahore Museum. Photo by Juhyung Rhi.

Plate 29. Wuliangshou (Amitāyus, Amitābha) triad. Binglingsi Cave 169, China, ca. 420 CE. Reproduced from ZYSB, plate 21.

Plate 30. Wuliangshou triad. Wanfosi, Chengdu, China, 483 CE. Sichuan Museum. Reproduced from CK, plate 8.

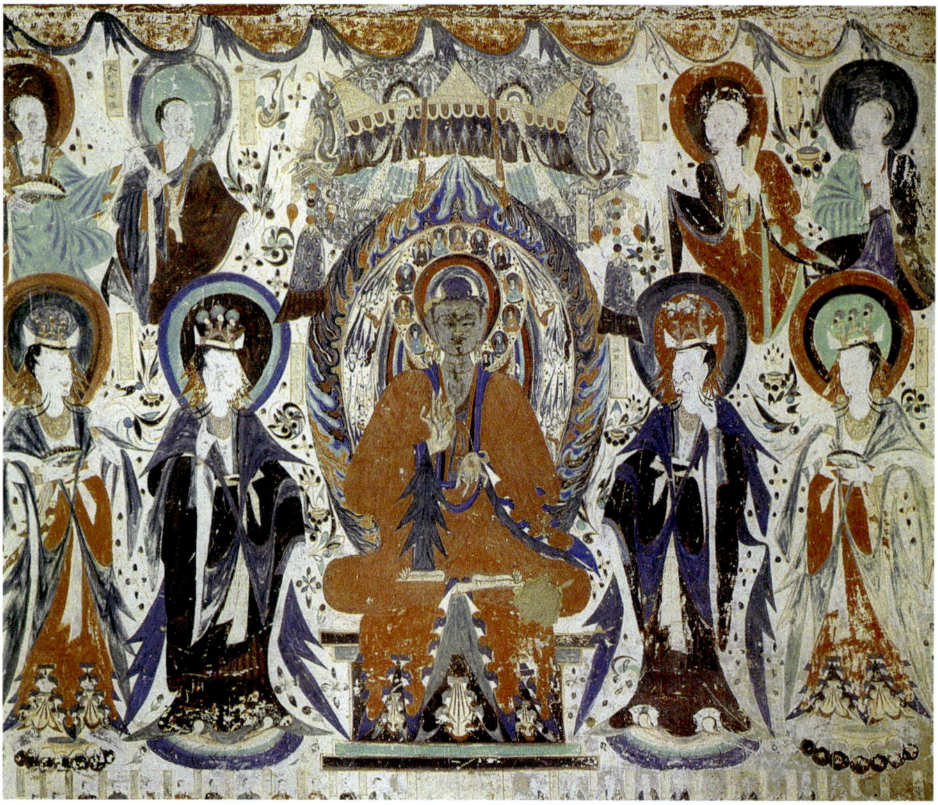

Plate 31. Wuliangshou Buddha. Dunhuang Mogao Cave 285, China, 539 CE. Reproduced from ZSDM 1: plate 125 detail.

Plate 32. Jiaye (Kāśyapa) Buddha. Dunhuang Mogao Cave 285, China, 539 CE. Reproduced from ZSDM 1: plate 125 detail.

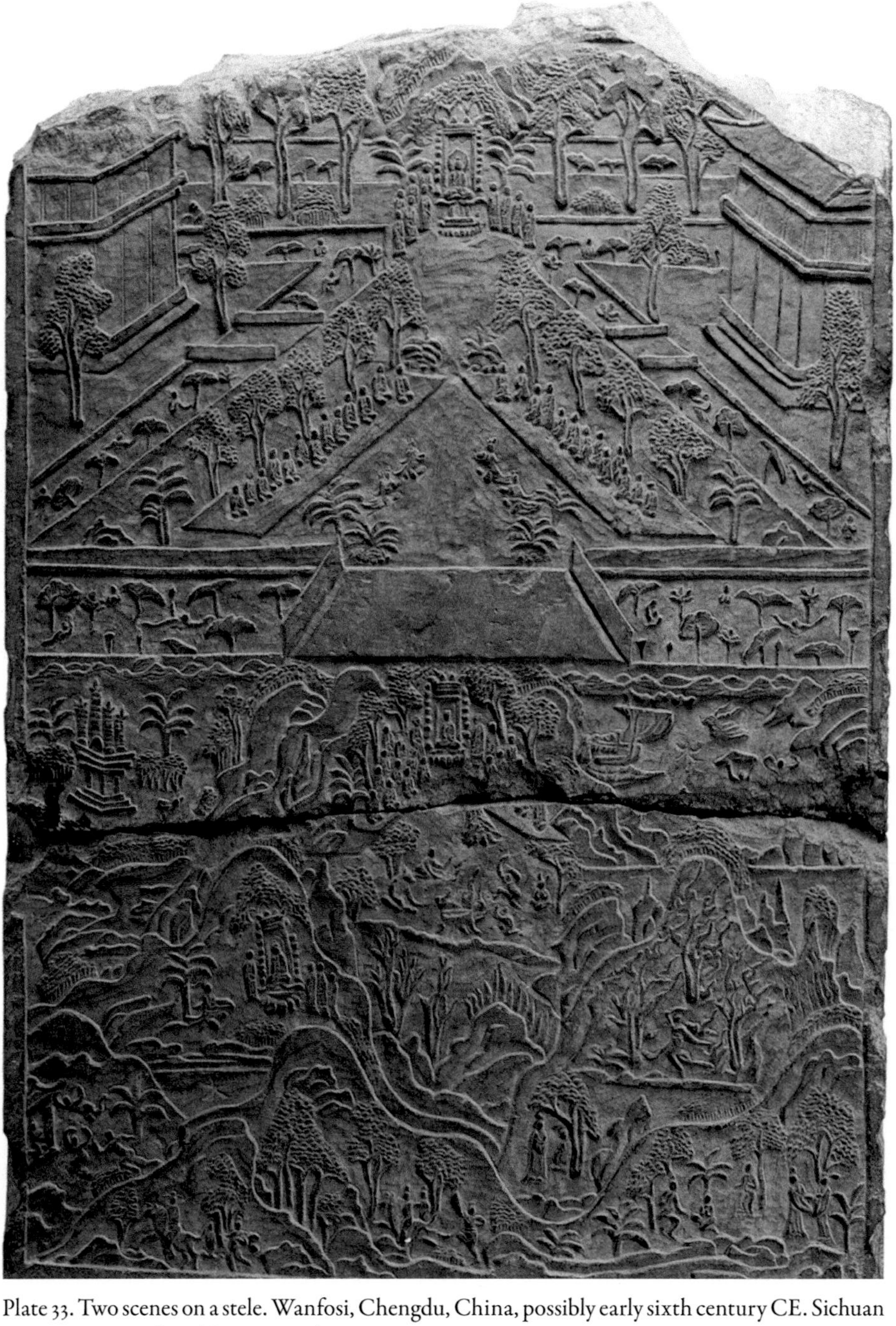

Plate 33. Two scenes on a stele. Wanfosi, Chengdu, China, possibly early sixth century CE. Sichuan Museum. Reproduced from CK, plate 31.

Plate 34. Amitābha's Sukhāvatī. Southern Xiangtangshan Cave 2, China, late sixth century CE.
National Museum of Asian Art, Smithsonian. Photo by Juhyung Rhi.

Plate 35. Preaching buddha relief. Kānherī Cave 89, India, sixth century CE. Photo by Juhyung Rhi.

Art and Practice in a Fifth-Century Indian Buddhist Cave Temple: A New Identification of an Old Mahāyāna Painting at Ajaṇṭā*

Nicolas Morrissey

THE STATUS OF THE *Saddharmapuṇḍarīka-sūtra* within Indian Buddhist communities—monastic or otherwise—of any time period and region remains unclear. There are, as is well known, multiple Chinese translations of this sūtra dating as early as the third century CE, along with substantial and fairly early manuscript witnesses of Sanskrit recensions from Gilgit and Central Asia and, though significantly later in date, numerous complete exemplars preserved from Nepal.[1] Yet it has been noted, for example—and on more than one occasion—that the *Saddharmapuṇḍarīka-sūtra* seems

* This paper has taken an unusually long, circuitous, and at times uncertain route to appear in print. As Professor Schopen was the earliest advocate of the ideas presented here though, even if he may neither admit nor recall such as fact (I suspect the former), it is certainly fitting that they now find place in this volume celebrating his many contributions as a scholar and teacher. Many thanks are due to Dieter Schlingloff and Monika Zin for very kindly sharing with me the drawings of the paintings included here. I would also like to express my gratitude to Peter Skilling and Vincent Tournier who—despite their hesitancy about the cogency of the overall argument—both long ago generously offered many constructive observations that resulted in markedly improving the work, even if its current form remains, perhaps, unlikely to persuade them to change their minds.

1. The range of scholarship on the extant textual corpus of the *Saddharmapuṇḍarīka* is far too extensive to cite fully here, but see at least for some sense of the Sanskrit materials Yuyama 1970, Tsukamoto 2007, and more recently Nishi 2022, esp. i–vii. The edition of Kern and Nanjio [1908–1912] 1992, based on a group of Nepalese manuscripts supplemented by alternative readings of an unprovenienced Central Asian manuscript (long referred to as the "Kashgar" or "Petrovskij" Manuscript but likely from Khotan; see von Hinüber 2014 and Wille 2000, 159–183), remains the standard Sanskrit text, though some of its lapses have been recognized at least since Baruch 1938, 7–12, and affirmed by Filliozat 1938, 346: "... cette édition sont souvent insuffisamment complètes et arbitrairement choisies"; for the Gilgit recension, see Watanabe 1975 and von Hinüber 2012; for the Central Asian recension, see Toda 1981; the dated Nepalese manuscripts are summarized in Vogel 1974.

not to have been a particularly important source within Indian Buddhist scholastic circles, that "while known" to śāstric authors, it "left precious few traces in Indian texts."[2] In addition, to date, only a single example of art-historical evidence from India persuasively connected to the *Saddharmapuṇḍarīka* has come to light—a small, seemingly isolated painting in Cave 10 at Ajaṇṭā dated to the late fifth century CE first identified by Gregory Schopen in a paper drafted between 1982 and 1983 but published only in 2005 (plate 4).[3] Such indications of the apparent lack of influence of the *Saddharmapuṇḍarīka-sūtra* would seem to make it difficult to disagree with the assertion that this text in "the Indian cultural sphere . . . stimulated relatively little debate, analysis, literary production, or artistic reflection."[4] Nevertheless, if Schopen's identification of the painting in Ajaṇṭā Cave 10 as a depiction of a narrative scene from the *Saddharmapuṇḍarīka-sūtra* stands, then this would at least establish that a version of the text, or a portion thereof, "was actually known at this remarkable site, and this provides the impetus to look elsewhere at Ajaṇṭā for other

2. Silk 2014, 158; cf. Silk 2001, 91, where it is also suggested that the *Saddharmapuṇḍarīka* was not "a main scriptural source" for Indian śāstric exegetes and was only "in fact relatively rarely referred to." However, see Mochizuki 2011 and Apple 2015, both indicating that the number of such references may not actually be so negligible.

3. Schopen 2005b, where he identifies this painting as a possible depiction of a narrative episode in chapter 24 of the *Saddharmapuṇḍarīka-sūtra* (*Samantamukha*) in which the bodhisattva Akṣayamati presents a gift of a necklace of pearls "worth a hundred thousand" to the bodhisattva Avalokiteśvara. There have been previous efforts to identify examples of Indian art that exhibit influence from the *Saddharmapuṇḍarīka-sūtra*, but these are far from definitive; for two interesting examples, see Taddei 1987 and, though problematic, Pandit 2016. The *Saddharmapuṇḍarīka* has also been persistently invoked in various interpretations of a much-discussed stele from Muhammad Nari; for convenience, see the various references assembled and reviewed in Harrison and Luczanits 2012. A potentially more viable association with the *Saddharmapuṇḍarīka* might be found in material from Gilgit, including an interesting bronze statue dating to the era of the Palola Ṣāhis and a petroglyph from Hodur; see von Hinüber 2004, fig. 5; Hauptmann 2008, 353, fig. 2 and 357; von Hinüber 2012, 59–60; and now Hu-von Hinüber 2019. Additionally, there has been a longstanding assumption that images depicting a bodhisattva along with the so-called "*aṣṭamahābhaya*," of which there are numerous examples in both sculpture and painting throughout the rock-cut monasteries of the Deccan, represent Avalokiteśvara as described in chapter 24 of the *Saddharmapuṇḍarīka*, but this identification, however intriguing or plausible, has yet to be fully established on the basis of a careful study of specific individual images and their respective correspondence to the text—such a study remains a desideratum; cf. Schlingloff 1988, esp. 177, where he notes: "It therefore does not appear that the [Ajaṇṭā] artists modeled their pictorial representations of the dangers from which Avalokiteśvara rescues beings on descriptions given in any particular textual tradition." See also de Mallmann 1948, 28–36 and 136–141; Leese 1988; Divakaran 1989; Silk 2001, 92; Bautze-Picron 2004; and Brancaccio 2011, 160–166, and 2014.

4. Teiser and Stone 2009, 3.

traces of that same text."[5] In this regard, there is another, and far more extensive, wall painting there that may turn out to be of considerable significance.

The painting in question is located in one of the early phase (ca. first century BCE to first century CE) caves at Ajaṇṭā, a relatively diminutive *caitya* hall designated as Cave 9 (plate 5).[6] Housing within its interior a monolithic rock-cut stūpa, this hall has generally been characterized as a congregational center for the early Buddhist community at Ajaṇṭā, utilized presumably for the performance of a range of activities, such as formal assemblies of the saṅgha, observance of the *poṣadha* and various other liturgical practices, doctrinal discourse, exposition and recitation, communal meditation, as well as myriad forms of cult-oriented or ritual behaviors, including the presentation of offerings (*dāna*) and circumambulation (*pradakṣiṇa*) along the path demarcated by the cave's interior pillars—practices that may be grouped into the rather amorphous category of "pūjā."[7] Situated at the midway point of the circumambulatory path within this cave is a substantial painting covering almost the entire span of the interior rear wall (approximately eighteen feet in length and three feet in height, see plates 6 and 7). This particular area of painting in Cave 9 belongs not to the early phase of occupation at Ajaṇṭā but to the later

5. Schopen 2005b, 294, who observes further that if his identification of the painting from Cave 10 at Ajaṇṭā were to be accepted, it would represent "the first, and so far only, known illustration of a Mahāyāna *sūtra* narrative in Indian art"; though see also Kim 2009 and Luczanits 2010, 567–578, for a discussion of what might be illustrations of the story of Sadāprarudita from the *Aṣṭasāhasrikā* preserved on several twelfth-century manuscript folios from eastern India; also see Losty 1989 for an interesting series of narrative illustrations found in a manuscript of the *Kāraṇḍavyūha* also dated to the twelfth century CE.

6. The precise date of the early *caitya* halls at Ajaṇṭā remains undetermined, at least in part due to the comparative paucity of inscriptions from this period of occupation at the site. Cave 9 at Ajaṇṭā, for example, has not a single inscription dating prior to the Vākāṭaka period. See Dehejia 1972, 157–158, who places the excavation of Cave 9 at Ajaṇṭā at 70–50 BCE; and Nagaraju 1981, 100, who has suggested a date for Cave 9 as early as the second century BCE; cf. Qureshi 2010, 38–39.

7. Even though the different types of activities undertaken within the communal public spaces of *caitya* halls at the western cave monasteries cannot be known with any specificity, there can be little question that the stūpas within them functioned as a central locus of worship for both monastics and laity; see Bareau 1962 and Schopen 1985, esp. 17. Depictions of various types of devotional activities at stūpa sites are frequently represented in early Buddhist sculpture; for some examples, see the discussion in Huntington 2012, esp. 12–28, and Becker 2015, 23–77. Note that although practices performed by the laity are emphasized by Huntington, she still observes that: "... *puja* fits conceptually within the framework of merit-increasing activities appropriate to Buddhist practitioners, whether members of the lay or monastic community"; see also van Kooij 1995; Trainor 1996, esp. 20; Walters 1997; and Pagel 2007. For a late description of Indian monks conducting daily stūpa worship, see Takakusu [1896] 1982, 152.

Vākāṭaka period (ca. late fifth century CE) and therefore appears to reflect an endeavor to renovate or perhaps update the interior of this early *caitya* hall, which, following several centuries of abeyance, if not outright abandonment, would almost certainly have been regarded as archaic.[8]

Even though considerable parts of the painting on the rear wall of Cave 9 are unfortunately quite abraded, it may still be possible to discern—in contrast to longstanding prior interpretations—a single, unified composition that once included a sequence of narrative episodes exclusive to the *Saddharmapuṇḍarīka-sūtra*. Perhaps significantly, however, the potential relationship between this narrative composition in Cave 9 and the *Saddharmapuṇḍarīka-sūtra* may extend beyond simply providing additional, and previously unnoticed, evidence that this text was known at Ajaṇṭā during the late fifth century CE. The highly specified and ordered arrangement of the individual narrative scenes included in this elaborate painting, which covers almost the entirety of the interior rear wall, arguably reveals a purposeful, intentionally conceived visual and conceptual alignment with not only this cave's central and most prominent architectural feature, its rock-cut stūpa, but also all of the other new paintings introduced into this *caitya* hall during the late fifth century CE. This remarkably cohesive articulation of interior space strongly suggests that the introduction of this painted composition into Cave 9 at Ajaṇṭā may have been the central component of a much broader initiative during the late fifth century CE to thoroughly transform the interior of this *caitya* hall. This initiative, moreover, appears to have been undertaken by a markedly specific and homogeneous group of patrons. Of the extant donative inscriptions from Cave 9 belonging to the Vākāṭaka period in which the status of the donor can be determined, all except one record gifts of paintings offered by monks, and of these, all except one identify the monastic donor with the title *śākyabhikṣu*, an epithet that, if not exclusive to adherents of Mahāyāna Buddhism, was one very frequently utilized by them.[9] There

8. Despite a general consensus that the major monasteries of the western Deccan were abandoned after the cessation of patronage attendant to the decline of the Sātavāhanas beginning in the late second century CE, the actual basis for this presumption has not been extensively investigated. See Dhavalikar 1984 for discussion of a series of excavations that might indicate that the post-Sātavāhana period in the western Deccan may not have been completely inactive; cf. Owen 2001. Disruptions to patronage seem also to have impacted the excavation and occupation of Buddhist monasteries in the Deccan even during the Sātavāhana period; see Rees 2009.

9. The painted composition on the rear wall of Cave 9 did at one time possess as many as five separate donative records, but lamentably none have survived sufficiently intact to convey any specific information about the identity of this painting's patrons. For a sense of the very fragmentary state of these painted inscriptions, including what has been lost, see Patel 2007, esp.

is a distinct possibility, therefore, that the refurbishment of Cave 9 at Ajaṇṭā during the late fifth century CE was deliberately overseen by a predominately monastic and Mahāyāna-oriented group aiming to co-opt and fully reappropriate this preexisting but long-unoccupied sacred space at the site.[10] Furthermore, as will be shown here, the demonstrably prominent, if not singular,

60, and Cohen 2006, 287–288, nos. 23–26. Note that Cohen's ins. no. 25 (cf. Burgess 1879, 49) may—though the record was never copied and is no longer extant—contain a reference to a possible donor as a *paramopāsaka*, which presents the distinct possibility that at least one of the patrons of the Cave 9 rear wall composition may have been an adherent of Mahāyāna Buddhism; for the potential Mahāyāna association of the titles *paramopāsaka* and *śākyabhikṣu* in Indian inscriptions, see Schopen 1979; 1987, 123; 2000, 16; Cohen 2000; Khettry 2010–2011; Prasad 2013, 186–189; and McCombs 2014. One attempt to deflect the potential Mahāyāna association of the latter title can be found in Cousins 2003, but see the response in Schopen 2005a, 244–246. Additionally, although Vincent Tournier has recently claimed—largely on the basis of Cousins's contribution along with others containing what he admittedly describes as "obvious weaknesses"—that the association of the title *śākyabhikṣu* with adherents of the Mahāyāna has been "disproved" and "shown to be untenable," such assertions are at present perhaps more than a bit precipitous. While Tournier is certainly accurate to note that this title on its own should not automatically and definitively be in all instances understood as a "code name" for individuals associated with bodhisattva soteriology, there is still undeniable evidence from the fifth century onward that a very substantial proportion, the majority even, of *śākyabhikṣus* known in Indian inscriptions were either explicitly identified as followers of the Mahāyāna (e.g., *mahāyānika-śākyabhikṣu/pravaramahāyānayāyina-śākyabhikṣu*), or aspiring, along with all beings, to supreme awakening (*anuttarajñāna*), or, at the very least, directly adjacent to other generalized Mahāyāna ideas and material culture; see Tournier 2018, 45n70, and 2023, 411–412, and cf. Schopen 1979, esp. 15, Morrissey 2013, and McCombs 2014, esp. 315–348. Elsewhere in Cave 9 there are eleven extant donative records, each of which is associated with the donation of an individual painted buddha or bodhisattva image placed on the cave's pillars and triforium—images which, as will be shown, are to be viewed as conceptually and thematically related to the rear wall composition. Of these eleven records, eight identify donors with the epithet *śākyabhikṣu*; see Cohen 2006, 287–294, nos. 22, 27, 29–37. The correspondence between the patronage activities of *śākyabhikṣus* at Ajaṇṭā and the presence of imagery seemingly associated with the *Saddharmapuṇḍarīka-sūtra* was not, however, confined to Cave 9 at the site. In Cave 10, which houses the painting first identified by Schopen as a narrative representation of the bodhisattva Akṣayamati's gift of pearls, there are fifteen extant donative records, each again associated with the donation of individual paintings of buddha images. Although the painting depicting Akṣayamati's gift was not inscribed, in nine of the fifteen records in this cave the donor is identified by the title *śākyabhikṣu*; see Cohen 2006, 297–305, nos. 44–45, 46, 48, 51–61. In this area of Ajaṇṭā then, where imagery associated with the *Saddharmapuṇḍarīka* is notably present, a proportionately significant number of active patrons—at least three quarters—can be identified as *śākyabhikṣus*.

10. The presence of multiple individual donors contributing to a cohesive, unified program of decoration in Cave 9 at Ajaṇṭā in the late fifth century would appear to mark the continuation (or re-emergence) of the modes of collective patronage well known at early stūpa complexes throughout India, with the notable exception that lay donors appear conspicuously underrepresented in the reoccupation and renovation of Cave 9; see Dehejia 1992. For another example

representation of themes drawn specifically from the *Saddharmapuṇḍarīka-sūtra* in the paintings of the updated decorative program in Cave 9 may, in turn, reflect an attempt by this same specific group to reconceive this *caitya* hall into an entirely new cultic *imaginaire*—a location that was efficacious for, and oriented toward, accommodating ritual and/or devotional activities at least informed by, but also perhaps more intensively derived from, structured around, and even directly focused on, this specific Mahāyāna text.[11] In light of these possibilities, it would certainly seem that the extant fifth century CE paintings in Cave 9 at Ajaṇṭā merit being considered anew. And if these possibilities might prove compelling, then the status of the *Saddharmapuṇḍarīka-sūtra* during the late fifth century CE within at least one Indian Buddhist monastery in the Deccan, and, more generally, that of Mahāyāna Buddhism there, if not beyond, may too merit reconsideration.[12] Indeed, some of the current perceptions in regard to both may be in need of revision.

The extant corpus of paintings belonging to the Vākāṭaka period at Ajaṇṭā has been dealt with most thoroughly—and authoritatively—by Dieter Schlingloff. He has identified the painting on the rear wall of Cave 9 not as a discrete composition, however, but as a series of eight marginally connected narrative scenes

of a group of patrons collectively appropriating a cave during the late Vākāṭaka period at Ajaṇṭā, see the discussion of Cave 22 at the site in Spink 2005, 172–188.

11. Cf. Abe 1990, 1, which serves as an important, yet still too frequently neglected, reminder: "Studies of Buddhist art have often focused on the task of aligning imagery with Buddhist texts. Buddhist art, however, functioned not only as an illustration of written text but as an integral element of ritual practice."

12. Though not always recognized, the fifth century CE certainly appears to have been a pivotal moment of transition for Mahāyāna movements in India. While there can be little question that the discoveries of Mahāyāna texts such as those among the manuscripts now preserved in the Split and Bajaur Collections confirm that Mahāyāna sūtras were being composed as well as others copied during the early centuries of the Common Era, definitive evidence in sources outside of these texts, such as Buddhist art, architecture, or inscriptions that might further attest to the measurable influence or circulation of Mahāyāna ideas, or the existence of actual, discrete Mahāyāna groups, is still virtually absent throughout India until the fifth century CE. On the discoveries of early Mahāyāna manuscripts, see Boucher 2009, and, now for convenience, Schlosser 2022, esp. 16–17, for the sources cited therein. On the evidence for the emergence of identifiable Mahāyāna communities in India beginning in the fifth century CE, but not before, see Schopen 1979 and 2000; cf. Boucher 2008, 83–84, and Morrissey 2013. See now, also, Tournier 2020, 178, who notes that "... evidence of various kinds concurs in identifying the late fourth to early sixth century as marking a shift, when the ideas propounded by the Bodhisattva movement became, so to speak, the 'main stream.'"

depicting events attendant to the conversion of the brahmin ascetic Kāśyapa through a public display of miraculous powers by the Buddha Śākyamuni.[13] Textual iterations of this narrative cycle are attested in a substantial number of disparate literary sources, but Schlingloff has privileged the version preserved in the *Catuṣpariṣat-sūtra*.[14] Very uncharacteristically, however, Schlingloff's overall identification of this painted composition, and particularly his treatment of each of the various individual elements included within it, is somewhat tenuous, as he admits that only a single scene "can be assigned with certainty to the Kāśyapa cycle. All the other scenes show the Buddha in the fashion of an image of worship, seated, standing, or walking, in a stereotyped environment. The composition even reflects, to some extent, images of Buddha-worship that refer to other events in the Buddha's life."[15] In spite of this marked ambiguity in regard to seven of the eight scenes in the composition, Schlingloff remains sufficiently confident to assert that "their identification as well as their assignment to the Kāśyapa legend according to the *CPS* [*Catuṣpariṣat-sūtra*] tradition seems obvious."[16] Beyond the rather gossamer foundation of this assertion, however, the viability of Schlingloff's attribution of the entire painted composition to the Kāśyapa narrative cycle of the *Catuṣpariṣat-sūtra* is undermined by his interpretation of the central section of the painting (plate 8), which he proposes is a single narrative scene depicting the Buddha preaching enclosed within what he describes as two "Szenentrenner" or "scene-dividers," a representation of the bodhisattva Avalokiteśvara on the left and a stūpa on the right.[17] By using this term Schlingloff contends that neither of these two images plays a narrative function and that, consequently, they are separate from the enclosed scene, which he identifies as the visit of various classes of deities to the Buddha during the second night of his stay at Kāśyapa's hermitage. If these two images were actually intended to serve as scene-dividers, though, they would be wholly unique within the extensive corpus of narrative

13. For a concise and accessible presentation of his identification of this painting, as well as some very useful composite drawings (no. 67), see Schlingloff 2013, 381–395, and 1999, 23.

14. For a discussion of the extant manuscript witnesses for the *Catuṣpariṣat-sūtra* (which appears to have been wholly extracted from—or inserted into—the *Mūlasarvāstivāda-vinaya*, albeit at an indeterminate point in time) and their textual parallels, see Kloppenborg 1973, xi–xiii, and the sources cited therein; for a translation of the conversion of Kāśyapa narrative in the text, see Kloppenborg 1973, 50–72, which is based on the edition prepared by Waldschmidt 1952–1960.

15. Schlingloff 2013, 384.

16. Schlingloff 2013, 384; cf. Spink 2006, 245–250, who has also expressed certain doubts about Schlingloff's identification of this painting as overly "hopeful," if not "controversial."

17. Schlingloff 2013, 390–392.

painting preserved at Ajaṇṭā.[18] Moreover, Schlingloff's exclusion of these two elements from the narrative content of this scene is particularly problematic as there is a well-known episode from a Buddhist text in which the bodhisattva Avalokiteśvara, the Buddha Śākyamuni, and a stūpa all play a part. This narrative episode, however, is found not in the *Catuṣpariṣat-sūtra* but rather in a Mahāyāna source—namely, the *Saddharmapuṇḍarīka-sūtra*.

At the beginning of the prose section of chapter 24 of the *Saddharmapuṇḍarīka-sūtra* (*Samantamukha*) there is a series of passages in which the bodhisattva Akṣayamati asks the Buddha Śākyamuni a series of questions in regard to the various qualities of the bodhisattva Avalokiteśvara, including the origin of his name and the nature of his ability to remain in the world and preach the Dharma. After hearing Śākyamuni extol the extent of the salvific abilities of the bodhisattva Avalokiteśvara, the merits of worshiping him, and the myriad forms he is able to manifest in the service of others, the narrative culminates with a passage describing the response of the bodhisattva Akṣayamati, in which he respectfully entreats Śākyamuni for permission to offer a "gift of piety" (*dharmācchādam*) to Avalokiteśvara. The Buddha agrees to this request, and Akṣayamati then removes from his own neck a pearl necklace and presents it to Avalokiteśvara. Although he initially refuses the gift, Avalokiteśvara eventually accepts the necklace but divides it into two parts, one of which he gifts to Śākyamuni and the other he presents to the jeweled stūpa of the Blessed One Prabhūtaratna (*pratigṛhya ca dvau pratyaṃśau kṛtavān kṛtvā caikaṃ pratyaṃśaṃ bhagavate śākyamunaye dadati sma dvitīyaṃ pratyaṃśaṃ bhagavataḥ prabhūtaratnasya . . . ratnastūpe samupanāmayāmāsa*).[19] Part of this sequence of events was, if Schopen's identification and analysis holds, already the subject of a small painting at Ajaṇṭā on a pillar in Cave 10, a *caitya* hall immediately adjacent to the west of Cave 9 (plate 4). A slightly variant and far more elaborate visual presentation of this narrative, however, appears to occupy the central section of the painted composition on the rear wall of Cave 9 (plate 8). In this section of painting there is a scene depicting an enthroned Buddha wearing a white robe, attended by two regally attired chowrie bearers and shown in the act of teaching or preach-

18. Cf. Spink 2006, 248, who notes in regard to the painting in Cave 9 that "such a precise organization of narrative episodes, separated with what Schlingloff calls 'scene dividers' is also not at all characteristic of the 'free-flowing' mural compositions made during Ajanta's heyday. . . ." For the various narrative conventions utilized at Ajaṇṭā, and especially the noteworthy absence at the site of the "sequential narrative" technique, which relies on various types of "scene dividers," see Dehejia 1997, 3–35 and 207–237.

19. Kern and Nanjio [1908–1912] 1992, 446.8–10; Watanabe 1975, B 286.12–14; Toda 1981, 428a6–b1; translated in Kern [1884] 1963, 412.

ing, with his hands displaying *dharmacakra-mudrā*. On the viewer's left of this triad is another figure with the *jaṭā* or matted locks of an ascetic, dressed in a long red and white striped robe, shown standing and leaning forward slightly while gazing upward toward the seated Buddha with a necklace of pearls clasped in the joined palms of his hand. Further to the viewer's left is a representation that, following Schlingloff, can be identified as the bodhisattva Avalokiteśvara, who is shown surrounded by a full-bodied halo, also with an elaborate *jaṭā* hairstyle, an animal skin draped over his left shoulder, and carrying in his left hand a *kamaṇḍalu* or water flask. On the viewer's right of the seated Buddha is another, virtually identical, depiction of a standing ascetic-type figure wearing the same red and white striped robe and with the *jaṭā* hairstyle, but who is now shown more deliberately bending forward with the palms of his hands held together and the necklace of pearls threaded over the bases of his joined thumbs and dangling from his two bottom fingers.[20] To the right of this element of the composition is a depiction of a white stūpa with a large *harmikā* and a multi-tiered base, which also has a distinctive decorative motif perceptible on the center of its drum (see plates 8, 9, and 18).[21]

Through the employment of a compositional technique characteristic of Ajaṇṭā's fifth-century paintings, which Dehejia has described as "synoptic narration including conflation," this central section of the painting on the rear wall in Cave 9 effectively condenses into a single scene the full sequence of narrative events recounted in the *Samantamukha* chapter of the *Saddharmapuṇḍarīka*.[22] With Śākyamuni positioned in the center of the scene, shown seated on a throne while preaching, the bodhisattva Akṣayamati is first depicted on his proper right in his role as interlocutor, who, having risen to his feet, asked the Buddha to explain the various qualities of the bodhi-

20. It is difficult to ascertain in either instance if the necklace in this painting comprises a double strand or one single longer strand folded twice over the ascetic figure's hand. Although the representation of the necklace in Cave 9 differs from the Cave 10 painting discussed by Schopen, it is still clear in both cases that each necklace is made up of the same white, elongated bead-like forms identifiable as pearls. Both can easily be distinguished from other examples of beaded objects found in the extant paintings of the Vākāṭaka period at Ajaṇṭā, such as, most commonly, rosaries or *akṣamālā*, which are invariably composed of very different black or dark brown, round seed-like beads tightly strung together with an overtly circular form. For a good photograph of a typical example from Cave 1 at the site, see Behl 1998, 86; also cf. Morrissey 2013, 81, fig. 4.

21. This painted stūpa once had an inscription written on its base, now unfortunately indecipherable aside from traces of several *akṣaras*; what little remains legible though may indicate the beginning syntax [*(d)eyadharm(m)a*] of a type of formulaic expression often found in the donative inscriptions at Ajaṇṭā; cf. Cohen 2006, 287–288, no. 24.

22. For a description of the synoptic and conflated narrative modes in Buddhist art, see Dehejia 1997, 21–27.

sattva Avalokiteśvara. As the primary subject of Śākyamuni's discourse in this chapter of the sūtra, Avalokiteśvara is prominently represented immediately on the proper right of Akṣayamati and the Buddha (see plates 8 and 11). The bodhisattva Akṣayamati is then again depicted on the proper left of the seated Buddha in a posture of deference or supplication with the necklace of pearls clasped between his joined palms, here portrayed at a later point in the narrative, asking Śākyamuni's permission to offer it as a gift (plates 9 and 10).[23] All three eventual recipients of the gift of pearls have also been creatively incorporated sequentially into this same scene: first the bodhisattva Avalokiteśvara (plate 11), who initially accepts the necklace but then divides it into two parts in order to offer one part first to Śākyamuni and then the other to the jeweled stūpa of the Buddha Prabhūtaratna, which has been placed at the far right of this scene in the composition (plates 7 [upper register] and 8) and which here does not function as a "scene-divider" but, along with Śākyamuni and Avalokiteśvara, is included as an integral part of the narrative composition. The distinctive motif on the center of the stūpa in the painting can be interpreted as either a representation of an actual jewel set into the architectural fabric of the stūpa or, more obliquely, an attempt by the artist to convey the luster of the stūpa described as "made from seven precious substances" (*saptaratnamaya*). Significantly, there are several additional elements in the painting that seem to parallel the description of Prabhūtaratna's stūpa found in the text, which further indicates that this image was indeed intended to depict it, not only, it would seem, in order for it to play a pivotal role within this particular narrative scene but also to serve as a unifying thematic component of the entire composition.

23. For additional examples of Buddhist narrative art that include the repetition of the same figure within a single narrative scene, including others at Ajaṇṭā, see Dehejia 1997, 25–26 and 218–219. It is perhaps curious that the representation of Akṣayamati in the painted composition on the rear wall of Cave 9 (plates 8–10) diverges from the figure identified as Akṣayamati by Schopen (2005b, 279) in the Cave 10 painting, which is clearly identifiable as a monk (see plate 4). In all the available Sanskrit versions of the *Saddharmapuṇḍarīka*, though, Akṣayamati is never explicitly identified as a monk but is, rather, consistently referred to in the same manner as Avalokiteśvara—as a bodhisattva, mahāsattva. In this regard, Miyaji has suggested that securely identifiable representations of this latter bodhisattva at Ajaṇṭā usually exhibit iconographic traits associated with ascetics, such as "... the hairstyle of *jaṭāmukuṭa*, the *dhotī* of ankle length and the absence of any ornaments" (2005, 87). Though not discussed by Miyaji, the figure identifiable as Avalokiteśvara in the Cave 9 painted composition possesses this ascetic-type iconography, and there is little reason to presume, therefore, that another bodhisattva also depicted by an artist at Ajaṇṭā could not also have exhibited these same iconographic markers. For the role of ascetic attributes in the iconographic development of representations of bodhisattvas at Ajaṇṭā and many of the other major cave monasteries of the Deccan, see the discussion of Maitreya in Kim 1997, 139–191.

In the *Saddharmapuṇḍarīka-sūtra*, the stūpa of the Buddha Prabhūtaratna first appears at the beginning of chapter 11, entitled *Stūpasaṃdarśana*:

> Then there arose a stūpa made from seven precious substances from the middle of the assembly, from the spot of earth in front of the Blessed One, five hundred *yojanas* in height and proportionate in circumference. After appearing, the stūpa remained in midair in the sky, sparkling, beautiful, fully ornamented with five thousand terraces of flowers, adorned with many thousands of arches, decorated with thousands of victory banners, ornamented with thousands of jeweled garlands and gilded bells, emitting an aroma of sandalwood and bay leaf which pervaded the entire world. Its row of umbrellas extended so high it seemed to touch the celestial abodes of the four great kings. It was made from seven precious substances—namely, gold, silver, beryl, white coral, emerald, red coral and quartz. The gods of the thirty-three heavens honored and covered this stūpa with divine *mandārava* and great *mandārava* flowers. And from that stūpa emanated this voice: "Excellent! Excellent! Blessed One, Śākyamuni, this discourse on Dharma (*dharmaparyāya*), the *Saddharmapuṇḍarīka*, is well spoken by you. Indeed it is so Blessed One, indeed Sugata."[24]

Described in such elaborated terms, this stūpa would certainly not, by any means, be easily rendered into artistic representation. Nevertheless, it does appear that in this section of the painted composition the artist has with some creativity attempted to provide an accurate, or at least functional, depiction of it, though the end result is perhaps not as vibrant as its effusive literary description. In addition to the jewel-like image on the drum of the painted stūpa, it has been placed in an elevated position within the composition, clearly floating above the ground level of the rest of the scene. The painted stūpa is also shown surrounded by numerous white flowers, what may be "the divine *mandārava* and great *mandārava* flowers" showered upon it by the gods.[25]

24. Kern and Nanjio [1908–1912] 1992, 239.1–240.4; Watanabe 1975, B 234.1–3; Toda 1981, 226a7–227b7; translated in Kern [1884] 1963, 227. All translations included below are by the author and, unless otherwise noted, based on Kern and Nanjio's edition.

25. Monier-Williams [1899] 2022, 788, s.v. *mandāra*, lists the Indian coral tree, *Erythrina indica*, a white variety of *Calotropis gigantea*, and the thorn apple as potential options for identifying this type of flower. The two latter species are well known for their white flowers, while the former is perhaps more associated with those that are red, hence the name; there is, however, at least one variety of the Indian coral tree, *Erythrina variegata alba*, not uncommon in modern

Though difficult to perceive, there is also in this area of the composition immediately to the left side of the painted stūpa a representation of a kneeling male figure, depicted looking upward and with his hands pressed up against the sides of his head (see plate 9). This physical posture and gesture can reasonably be interpreted as an effective visual idiom to express this figure's (as well as the collective audience's) sense of wonder and amazement in response to witnessing a jeweled stūpa appear out of the ground, float into midair, be showered with various flowers by the gods, and with a perceptible voice issuing from inside it. This type of response by the assembly to the appearance of the jeweled stūpa is, as a parallel, articulated in Kern and Nanjio's edition of the text with the phrases "filled with gladness, delight, satisfaction, and joy" (*saṃjñātaharṣāḥ prītiprāmodyaprasādaprāptāḥ*) and "filled with intense curiosity" (*kautūhalaprāptaṃ*), and it may have been this extraordinary sense of awe, delight, curiosity, and wonder that this particular figure in the painting was intended to convey visually.[26] If, in light of these elements, the painted stūpa on the rear wall of Cave 9 can be recognized as a representation of the jeweled stūpa of the Buddha Prabhūtaratna, then this both aligns with and helps to identify the remaining scenes included in the composition, which also appear to have been derived from the narrative of the *Stūpasaṃdarśana* chapter of the *Saddharmapuṇḍarīka*.

After the spectacular entrance of the jeweled stūpa in the opening passage of this chapter, the bodhisattva Mahāpratibhāna asks Śākyamuni on behalf of the understandably captivated assembly about the specific cause for its appearance and whose voice emanated from within it. Śākyamuni responds that "within this great jeweled stūpa the complete body of a tathāgata sits undivided. This stūpa is his; he causes this sound to emanate" (*mahāratnastūpe tathāgatasyātmabhāvas tiṣṭhaty ekaghana tasyaiṣa stūpaḥ / sa eṣa śabdaṃ*

Maharashtra, which is known particularly for having white flowers. Though it is unclear if the artist(s) intended to represent a specific type of flower in the painting, it is worth noting at least that all of them have been rendered white, and the form of several incorporated into this scene as well as elsewhere throughout the composition can even be recognized as quite naturalistic representations of coral tree flowers.

26. Kern and Nanjio [1908–1912] 1992, 240.5–8; Watanabe 1975 (not extant); Toda 1981, 228a2. The Kashgar manuscript adds here the interesting phrase "filled with aesthetic shock." Note as well that another figure with a similar gesture (having one hand [possibly both?] raised and pressed against the side of his head covering an ear) is discernible immediately above the representation of the bodhisattva Avalokiteśvara in the painting (see plate 11), which was perhaps intended to further emphasize both the aural and visual impact of the series of events attendant to the preaching of the *Saddharmapuṇḍarīka*, which in this scene pairs the miraculous and salvific nature of the bodhisattva Avalokiteśvara and his appearance in this world with the equally miraculous appearance of the jeweled stūpa of Prabhūtaratna.

niścārayati /).[27] Śākyamuni then recounts that this perfectly and completely awakened tathāgata was named Prabhūtaratna, who, in another distant world sphere (*lokadhātu*) called Ratnaviśuddhā, had formerly made the following vow at the time of his complete nirvāṇa:

> This was the former vow (*pūrvapraṇidhāna*) of the Blessed One (Prabhūtaratna): When I was pursuing the bodhisattva path I had not yet arrived at unsurpassed, perfect and complete awakening as at that time I had not heard the instruction for bodhisattvas, the discourse on Dharma, the *Saddharmapuṇḍarīka*. But when I heard this discourse on Dharma, the *Saddharmapuṇḍarīka*, then from that point forward I became fully established in unsurpassed, perfect and complete awakening. . . . Monks! At the time of my complete liberation, one great jeweled stūpa for the manifest form of the complete body (*ātmabhāvavigraha*) of the Tathāgata is to be made.[28] All other stūpas, however, are to be made for me in name [only].[29]

This initial vow was, in turn, followed with and empowered by a "continuing declarative resolution" (*adhiṣṭhāna*) made by Prabhūtaratna that his stūpa, containing the "manifest form of my [i.e., Prabhūtaratna's] complete body" (*mamātmabhāvavigraha*) was to "arise in whatever buddhafields in the ten directions of all world spheres the discourse on Dharma (*dharmaparyāya*), the

27. Kern and Nanjio [1908–1912] 1992, 240.11–12; Watanabe 1975 (not extant); Toda 1981, 228b1–2; translated in Kern [1884] 1963, 228.

28. The precise sense of the term *ātmabhāva* and the related compound *ātmabhāvavigraha* in this passage, as well as others throughout the text, is far from clear. Kern, in his translation ([1884] 1963), has consistently rendered these terms as "proper body" and "proper bodily frame" respectively, which closely parallels Burnouf, who similarly translated *mamātmabhāvavigraha*, for example, as "la propre forme de mon corps" (for one instance, see [1852] 1973, 146). Although Edgerton, in his entry on *ātmabhāva* ([1953] 1993, 92), remarked that "The fact has not been recognized sufficiently clearly that this is a quite plain and simple synonym of *śarīra*, 'body,'" Conze has noted in response that this translation results in "murdering its finer metaphysical meaning," and he is perhaps more accurate to emphasize that the term *ātmabhāva* was meant to refer to the "whole person" or "the sum total of all that seems to be built around a self"; Conze 1957, 100; cf. Silk 2006, 60–75, Skilling 2005, 301–302, and Tsukamoto 2007, 119–122. Throughout the narrative development of the *Saddharmapuṇḍarīka*, though, it is certainly clear that the *ātmabhāva* of Prabhūtaratna that is contained within the jeweled stūpa, and so dramatically revealed by Śākyamuni, is not an ordinary body or bodily relic preserved after his nirvāṇa in the long-distant past, but an enduring, complete, and fully preserved living presence.

29. Kern and Nanjio [1908–1912] 1992, 240.14–241.1–3, 6–7; Watanabe 1975, B 234.7–11; Toda 1981, 228b6–229a3, 5–7; translated in Kern [1884] 1963, 229.

Saddharmapuṇḍarīka, would be illuminated by any blessed ones, buddhas, and remain in the sky above the assembly while those blessed ones, buddhas recite the discourse on Dharma, the *Saddharmapuṇḍarīka* . . . and give a shout of approval to them. . . ."[30] The appearance in the midst of the assembly and suspension in the air of the stūpa, and the voiced expression of approval from within it concomitant to the former vow (*pūrvapraṇidhāna*) and continuing declarative resolution (*adhiṣṭhāna*) of Prabhūtaratna are, however, only a precursor to a more extensive secondary solemn vow (*praṇidhānaṃ gurukaṃ*) also made by this buddha in the distant past in regard to his stūpa. The full extent of that vow as recounted by Śākyamuni to the bodhisattva Mahāpratibhāna reads:

> This was his vow: Whenever in other buddhafields buddhas, blessed ones, would preach this discourse on Dharma (*dharmaparyāya*), the *Saddharmapuṇḍarīka*, then may this stūpa containing the manifest form of my complete body be near to the tathāgatas to hear the *dharmaparyāya*, the *Saddharmapuṇḍarīka*. When, moreover, those buddhas, blessed ones, having revealed this manifest form of my complete body, would desire to show it to the fourfold community, then, having assembled from the ten directions, from various buddhafields, all those manifest forms of tathāgatas with various names who have been created by [other] tathāgatas from [their own] complete bodies, who are preaching the Dharma to beings in each of those buddhafields, then, together with those manifest forms of tathāgatas, created from the complete bodies [of other tathāgatas], having opened this stūpa containing the manifest form of my own complete body, it should be shown to the fourfold community.[31]

Following this reiteration of the twofold vow (*pūrvapraṇidhāna* "former vow"/*praṇidhānaṃ gurukaṃ* "solemn vow") and "continuing declarative resolution" (*adhiṣṭhāna*) made in the past by the Buddha Prabhūtaratna, the next section of the *Stūpasaṃdarśana* chapter contains a lengthy description of the various machinations through which Śākyamuni effects the fulfillment of its

30. Kern and Nanjio [1908–1912] 1992, 41.8–12; Watanabe 1975, B 234.11–15; Toda 1981, 229b1–7. Both the general sense and potential implications of the term *adhiṣṭhāna* in this context and how it might be differentiated from the terms *praṇidhāna* and *pūrvapraṇidhāna* remain unresolved here; for useful discussions on the term *adhiṣṭhāna*, see Eckel 1992, 90–94, and Tournier 2014, 5–18.

31. Kern and Nanjio [1908–1912] 1992, 242.4–11; Watanabe 1975, B 234.18–22; Toda 1981, 230b1–231a4; translated in Kern [1884] 1963, 230–231.

various components. First, the gathering of innumerable forms of miraculously created (*nirmitāḥ*) tathāgatas who are preaching the *Saddharmapuṇḍarīka* in buddhafields of countless other world spheres, their arrival along with other innumerable buddhas and their attendants from every single direction at the assembly and their accommodation on elaborate lion-thrones at the foot of jeweled trees (*siṃhāsanaṃ ratnavṛkṣamūle*), for which "Śākyamuni, in order to make room for the tathāgatas who were arriving one after the other, purified two million *nayuta*s of *koṭi*s of other world spheres, in every single direction, (... *aparāṇi viṃśatilokadhātukoṭīnay*[*u*]*taśatasahasrāṇy ekaikasyāṃ diśi śākyamunis tathāgataḥ pariśodhayati sma / teṣāṃ tathāgatānām āgatāgatānām avakāśārthaṃ* ...).[32] Subsequently, the climactic scene of this chapter—and arguably of the text as a whole—ensues, which has Śākyamuni use a finger of his right hand to open the jeweled stūpa, which then splits into two parts. Crucially, for both the internal development of the narrative of the sūtra and its impact on its audience, what is dramatically revealed inside the opened jeweled stūpa is the completely and perfectly preserved *living* Buddha Prabhūtaratna, who, even though he had achieved nirvāṇa and been interred long before in the immeasurably distant past, is described in Yuyama's suggested emendation of Kern and Nanjio's text as "... *siṃhāsanopaviṣṭaḥ paryaṅkaṃ baddhvāpariśuṣka gātro 'saṃghaṭṭitakāyo yathā samādhisamāpannas* /" (seated cross-legged on a lion-throne, with a nourished [*apariśuṣka*, lit. "not dried"] body, a fully constituted [i.e., complete] physical form, as though fully absorbed in samādhi).[33] So revealed, the fully animated Buddha Prabhūtaratna immediately speaks in order to proclaim his enthusiasm for the preaching of the *Saddharmapuṇḍarīka* to the assembled audience by Śākyamuni and to affirm the singularity of his intention to be present in order to hear it.[34] Prabhūtaratna then invites Śākyamuni to share his seat on the lion-throne within the jeweled stūpa, following which the latter recommences his preaching of the *Saddharmapuṇḍarīka* to the expansive audience comprising manifested forms of tathāgatas, their acolytes, and the fourfold assembly, all of whom, through his magical power (*ṛddhibalena*), had become raised in the air to witness the ongoing exposition.

Intriguingly, the dramatic moments coincident with the opening of

32. Kern and Nanjio [1908–1912] 1992, 246.11–247.2; Watanabe 1975 (not extant); Toda 1981, 237a3–5; translated in Kern [1884] 1963, 234–235.

33. Yuyama 1989, esp. 183; Kern and Nanjio [1908–1912] 1992, 249.5–6; Watanabe 1975 (not extant); Toda 1981, 240b2–3; translated in Kern [1884] 1963, 236.

34. Kern and Nanjio [1908–1912] 1992, 249.6–9; Watanabe 1975, B 235.21–23; Toda 1981, 240b4–7; translated in Kern [1884] 1963, 236–237.

the jeweled stūpa by Śākyamuni to reveal the manifest, complete body (*ātmabhāvavigraha*) of the living Buddha Prabhūtaratna, fully preserved and constituted in form (*apariśuṣka gātro 'saṃghaṭṭitakāyo*), appear as the main subject of at least two contiguous scenes in the painted composition in Cave 9 (plates 12 and 13). The first scene is placed in the section of painting immediately adjacent to the episode of Akṣayamati's gift of the pearl necklace, directly to the right of the representation of Prabhūtaratna's magically arisen, jeweled stūpa. There is a partially abraded but still identifiable image of a haloed buddha figure wearing white robes and standing beneath a jeweled umbrella. This buddha figure is not depicted frontally—that is, toward the viewer—but is rather shown turned at a noticeably sideways angle. His left hand is raised to hold a fold of robe and his lower right arm is elevated almost ninety degrees from the elbow with the palm extended outward in a pronounced manner and facing away from his body, the fingers of this hand rather oddly distributed but in a way that appears to show either the index or middle finger visibly curled upward.[35] Positioned in the foreground of the scene in this way, this buddha figure can be seen quite distinctly motioning with his right hand directly toward—and thereby effectively directing the viewers' gaze to—a representation of another haloed buddha included in this section of the painting, also wearing white robes but depicted seated on an elaborately decorated golden throne with his legs pendent on a stylized lotus cushion and his hands joined together in a typical form of *dharmacakra-mudrā*. The relationship between these two buddhas—a rare, if not entirely unique, occurrence of two buddhas represented within a single narrative episode—is clarified by a distinctive visual element in this scene used by the artist(s) to illustrate a rendered cross section of the external structure and interior architectural space of a stūpa (see the drawing in plate 12 with this feature outlined in red and gray shading). The intention appears to have been to utilize this visual strategy in order to depict the interior of the jeweled stūpa that had been opened by Śākyamuni "with a finger of his right hand" that then "split into two parts" to reveal within it

35. This somewhat unusual treatment of the right arm seems a slight variant of what is commonly referred to within the Ajaṇṭā corpus of painting and sculpture as the gift-giving gesture (*varada-mudrā*), usually expressed in sculpted figures with the right arm lowered completely and parallel to the side, the palm of the hand flat and facing directly outward with the fingers pointing downward. While there can be, in general, considerable variation in the representation of *varada-mudrā* in painted figures at Ajaṇṭā, the treatment of the right arm in this particular buddha in the Cave 9 painting conforms fully to neither of these two consistent and characteristic elements, perhaps signaling that the intention was to depict this figure engaged in an activity more specific than the bestowal of a gift or benediction.

the living Buddha Prabhūtaratna seated on a throne.[36] This was effectively—and creatively—achieved perspectively by the employment of this cross sectional form, which in the painting demarcates in light gray color the contours of the bifurcated edges of the opened stūpa in between the two buddhas (outlined in red in the drawing in plate 12), while an area of darker gray shading extends around and behind the seated Buddha Prabhūtaratna, thereby visibly enclosing him within a clearly defined, built architectural form.[37] The rather anomalous placement of a flying kinnara-type figure in front of the external architectural frame of the stūpa and in between the two buddhas may, additionally, have been inserted into this scene to provide the sense that, as repeatedly emphasized in the text, after the jeweled stūpa of Prabhūtaratna had appeared, it remained above the assembly "standing in midair in the sky" (*vaihāyasamantarīkṣe sthitaṃ*). Also revealing are the recognizable forms of several multi-petaled white coral tree flowers embellishing the outer edges of the stūpa frame, and even in the hand of a figure behind the proper left of the seated Buddha Prabhūtaratna, quite possibly a visual allusion to the *mandārava* flowers showered upon the jeweled stūpa by the gods.

The adjacent and final scene in the composition, located on the section of the rear wall of Cave 9 farthest to the viewer's right, follows the narrative sequence of events articulated in the *Stūpasaṃdarśana* chapter with remarkable precision (see plate 13). In this badly damaged area of painting both buddhas are once again seen together in close proximity to each other, each positioned partly in front of, and enclosed by, a stone architectural structure indicated primarily by an extended plane of flat gray shading visible in the background of the scene, which is surmounted by what appears to be a horizontal coping stone. The haloed buddha figure standing under a bejeweled umbrella now positioned on the right, identifiable as Śākyamuni, is shown with his palm extended again in a rather exaggerated form of *varada-mudrā*, gesturing demonstratively toward a seated buddha, identifiable as Prabhūtaratna,

36. Although the manner in which Prabhūtaratna is described in the text, *siṃhāsanopaviṣṭaḥ paryaṅkaṃ baddhvā*, is typically translated as "cross legged," *paryaṅkāsana* has in some instances been described as having the legs pendent; see for example Banerjea [1956] 1974, 272: "... a sitting posture in which both the legs are made to dangle down from whatever type of seat the figure sits on"; cf. Haussig 1984, 91–92, fig. 7.

37. It is important to emphasize that the areas of gray shading discernible in this motif are without doubt indicative of an architectural structure built from stone, and therefore must be distinguished from natural rock formations such as mountains, which are uniformly represented in the Ajaṇṭā paintings by very conspicuous horizontal layers of stylized, rectilinear geometric forms; for an example of this type of representation, see plate 14 and the discussion on p. 459 below.

on the left. The use of this gesture is effective in visually underscoring the pivotal nature of the moment when Śākyamuni pointedly reveals the living Buddha Prabhūtaratna to the entire assembly, fully confirming his specific identity and the consequent fulfillment of the past vows that resulted in his miraculous appearance. The Buddha Prabhūtaratna, also haloed and under an elaborate umbrella, is shown seated on a throne displaying *dharmacakramudrā*, reiterating, as described in the text, his enthusiasm for listening to the preaching of the discourse of the *Saddharmapuṇḍarīka* and, perhaps, then inviting Śākyamuni to sit with him on a throne inside the jeweled stūpa. As both buddhas have not been depicted seated side-by-side within the stūpa, what may have been represented in this section of the composition is the moment following the opening of the stūpa just prior to the former Buddha Prabhūtaratna ceding a portion of his seat to Śākyamuni, after which the latter recommences with his preaching of the *Saddharmapuṇḍarīka* to the assembled congregation.[38] The division of these two scenes in this way therefore appropriately constitutes a direct parallel to the twofold prescription of the Buddha Prabhūtarata's solemn vow (*praṇidhānaṃ gurukaṃ*) that, first, his stūpa is opened by Śākyamuni to reveal the manifest form of his complete body and, second, it is to be shown to the fourfold assembly.

Although each of the three painted scenes described above exhibits a plausible connection with narrative episodes from the *Saddharmapuṇḍarīka-sūtra*, there is still a fairly large section of the left portion of the composition on the rear wall of Cave 9 that has not yet been addressed but also appears to include specific episodes drawn directly from this sūtra. Divided into two registers, this area of painting comprises the opening narrative scenes of the overall composition. The first register, at the farthest left of the rear wall, depicts a scene situated in a mountainous locale, the prominently visible horizontal layers of blue-and-gray-colored, block-like geometric forms being a well-established and easily recognizable convention in the paintings at Ajaṇṭā for represent-

38. Representations of paired buddhas within the jeweled stūpa of Prabhūtaratna are well attested in early medieval Chinese art; for some representative examples, see Davidson 1954, figs. 2, 4, 17, 20, and Wang 2005, 3–52, plates 2, 10, 17, 19. There is a comparative illustration of this particular scene in a miniature painting at the beginning of the *Stūpasaṃdarśana* chapter in one of the Khotanese manuscripts of the *Saddharmapuṇḍarīka* housed in St. Petersburg (SI P 10 folio 287B); see for convenience the image reproduced in the facsimile edition published in Mizufune 2013, SI P 10 folio 287B; it is also discussed in von Hinüber 2015, 227, and fig. 5, and Hu-von Hinüber 2019, 383, and fig. 7 (though note that the image is mislabeled there). Within South Asian contexts, representations of paired buddhas seated in the jeweled stūpa of Prabhūtaratna are exceptionally rare; only two late examples have been found in miniature illustrations in medieval Nepalese manuscripts of the *Saddharmapuṇḍarīka*; see Mizufune 2009, folio 1b, and Hu-von Hinüber 2019, figs. 5 (again, mislabeled) and 6.

ing this type of setting (plate 14). Atop this mountainous landscape is a depiction of a buddha in a white robe seated on a stone bench or dais with his legs pendent and resting on an elevated stone platform, next to which rests a water vessel (*kamaṇḍalu*). The buddha is shown preaching with his hands arranged in *dharmacakra-mudrā* to an audience of several seated figures, at least two of whom, and possibly a third, hold their hands in respectful salutation (*añjali-mudrā*). Schlingloff has contended that this scene can be identified as the Buddha addressing the aged brahmin Kāśyapa and two of his disciples, yet this seems unwarranted as the figures in the seated audience cannot be recognized as Brahmanical ascetics.[39] Rather, as two of the preserved figures both have distinctive shaven heads and are shown wearing robes typical of monastics, they can be firmly identified as Buddhist monks. This visual depiction of both the setting and the audience, therefore, mirrors with considerable accuracy the much-heralded mountain location of Vulture Peak (Gṛdhrakūṭa), where the preaching of the *Saddharmapuṇḍarīka-sūtra* (and, of course, numerous other Mahāyāna sūtras) takes place as described in the introductory passages of the text. Although multiple spectacles and miracles certainly transform the setting throughout the development of the narrative, it is important to note that the location remains consistent throughout the sūtra, which in its basic structure remains simply a record of the events surrounding an extended sermon delivered by the Buddha to an audience—one that exponentially increases as the narrative progresses—assembled on Vulture Peak mountain.

In this regard, one of the most enduring and characteristic elements of this extended sermon, the so-called "Parable of the Burning House" expounded by the Buddha in chapter 3 of the sūtra, has been conspicuously included as the subject of the second narrative scene of the painted composition.[40] In this familiar parable, the Buddha describes to the monk Śāriputra, the central interlocutor of this chapter, the skillful actions taken by an aged, wealthy householder in order to save his young children, who had become unwittingly trapped in their home that was engulfed in flames. Though initially unresponsive to their father's pleas for them to flee, the children were eventually convinced to escape the burning house by a ruse. Their father, less than truthfully, told the children that he had placed their favorite toys—bullock carts, goat carts, and deer carts—outside of the house for them to play with. The children naturally flee from the house to safety in expectation of the opportunity to play with the toys, which, they subsequently realize, are not there. Relieved

39. Schlingloff 2013, 384.

40. Kern and Nanjio [1908–1912] 1992, 72.9–77.3; Watanabe 1975, A 29.14–31.27; Toda 1981, 77a6–82b7; translated in Kern [1884] 1963, 72–76.

that he was able to save his children, even if through apparently untoward but well-intentioned means, the wealthy householder then gifts to each of them the same lavishly decorated and appointed bullock carts, "the greatest, most magnificent vehicles" (*mahāyānāny eva . . . udārayānāny eva dattāni*).[41] With remarkable economy, this parable elucidates a fundamental theme integral to the overall message contained in the *Saddharmapuṇḍarīka-sūtra*: it is an allegorical narration of the Buddha's use of expedient means (*upāyakauśalya*) to offer his followers seemingly different paths to escape *saṃsāra*, the eponymous "burning house," when ultimately there is only a single path, the Mahāyāna. The inferior carts represent the vehicles of the śrāvakas and pratyekabuddhas, while the magnificent carts that all the children receive in the end represent the path of the bodhisattva leading to the distinctly Mahāyāna soteriological goal, the attainment of buddhahood.[42] The area of the painted composition (plate 14) that once contained an illustration of a truncated version of the episode from the text in which Śākyamuni narrates this parable is, unfortunately, quite deteriorated. Even though many of the details of this particular section of painting are obscured due to its fragmentary condition, there is still discernible a pillared structure depicted ablaze—small remnants of flames appear within this scene emerging from the building to the right of the upper portion of a pillar and adjacent to a ladder (see this area highlighted with a circle in plate 14). The immolation of the building is also further confirmed explicitly by the presence of several figures climbing a ladder and each carrying a large pot, presumably filled with water, in what can only be read as an attempt to extinguish a fire by a group that might be accurately described as an ancient Indian fire brigade. In the foreground, there is a standing buddha shown addressing several seated figures, two of whom are recognizable as ascetics due to their *jaṭā* and another image of a figure in monastic dress that is perhaps identifiable as a representation of the monk Śāriputra. Schlingloff, again basing his interpretation on the narrative of the *Catuṣpariṣat-sūtra*, has identified these figures as the "aged" or "very old brahmin" Kāśyapa together with three of his disciples, to whom the Buddha is showing his alms bowl into which he had forced a poisonous snake that he had subdued in Kāśyapa's fire house.[43] Although two of the figures do appear to be representations of

41. Kern and Nanjio [1908–1912] 1992, 76.6–7; Watanabe 1975, A 31.16; Toda 1981, 82a1; translated in Kern [1884] 1963, 74.

42. For a thorough treatment of this parable, see the still useful discussions in Fujita 1975 and Pye 1978; also more recently Bielefeldt 2009 and Apple 2014. For an interesting analysis of the possible wordplay between *yāna* and *jñāna* in this parable, see Karashima 2015, esp. 174–181.

43. Schlingloff 2000, 385. It is not apparent what, if anything, the Buddha in this scene may

ascetics, both of them are clearly much more youthful than aged, and consequently neither can persuasively be identified as the elder Kāśyapa. Alternatively, in light of the limited amount of space devoted to this scene within the overall composition, these seated figures might be interpreted as representations of the disparate members of the assembly in front of which the Buddha Śākyamuni preaches this parable to Śāriputra, which is described at this early stage in the narrative development of the text (i.e., long before the audience dramatically increases) as including groups of ascetics and *brāhmaṇa*s amid a host of other beings.[44]

In light of the interpretation of the individual scenes described here, it would appear that, in terms of both content and physical space, the predominant part of the painted composition on the rear wall of Cave 9 was devoted to illustrating multiple narrative scenes drawn from the *Saddharmapuṇḍarīka-sūtra* involving the stūpa of the former Buddha Prabhūtaratna. There is, as we have seen, a series of dramatic events in which this stūpa serves as a focal point within the narrative of the text represented across several of the composition's painted scenes: its initial appearance in the midst of the assembly and subsequent levitation (plates 8 and 9); the bodhisattva Akṣayamati's gift of the pearl necklace to Avalokiteśvara, which he in turn gifts to Śākyamuni and the magically arisen stūpa (plates 8–10); the climactic moment when the stūpa is opened to reveal the living presence of the Buddha Prabhūtaratna (plate 12); and the two buddhas, Śākyamuni and Prabhūtaratna, engaging with one another just prior to sharing a seat within the stūpa, following which the former resumes his preaching (plate 13).

The relative importance of the stūpa of the former Buddha Prabhūtaratna is further emphasized by its precise placement in the center of the painted composition. This conspicuous location, moreover, situates the painted image of the stūpa in direct juxtaposition with the *caitya* hall's centrally placed, rock-cut stūpa. The former is placed in the middle of the rear wall immediately behind the latter and is clearly visually aligned with it along the main axis of the cave (plates 15 and 16). In addition to this telling spatial correspondence there is also an undeniable similarity between the architectural form of the painted image and the actual stūpa within the cave, particularly in terms of

be holding in his hands. If it is a bowl, as Schlingloff's drawing and discussion emphasize, this would not be an unusual or even unexpected attribute for a Buddha. There is, however, certainly no visible trace of a snake, yet another missing element seemingly essential to the viability of Schlingloff's interpretation of the narrative scene illustrated in this section of the painted composition.

44. Kern and Nanjio [1908–1912] 1992, 64.9; Watanabe 1975, B 205.19; Toda 1981, 69a4; translated in Kern [1884] 1963, 65.

the rounded shape of the drum (*aṇḍa*) and multi-tiered *harmikā* (plates 17 and 18). Such an explicit alignment and similarity in form is quite unlikely to have been mere coincidence. It would seem evident that the fifth-century artists and patrons of Cave 9 devised the painted composition in order for it to articulate visually a specific relationship to the central object of worship in the cave, the rock-cut stūpa, and perhaps also to facilitate a specific type of interaction between the two. Given the precise nature of the spatial and visual correspondence between the painted representation of the stūpa of the Buddha Prabhūtaratna and the rock-cut stūpa of Cave 9, the intention was almost certainly directed at establishing the shared identity of these two stūpas through the medium of the painted composition on the rear wall. If the placement of this element of the painted stūpa was indeed conceived to function in this way, then the individual narrative scenes within the composition might be recognized as collectively comprising a visual *māhātmya* or sacred biography of the rock-cut stūpa within Cave 9, oriented toward, in part at least, elaborating its religious meaning and establishing its cultic efficacy.[45]

In the narrative development of the *Saddharmapuṇḍarīka-sūtra*, there are two points of emphasis that serve to establish the cultic significance of the stūpa of the Buddha Prabhūtaratna, and both of these seem to have been intentionally included in the narrative scenes of the painted composition or visual *māhātmya* on the rear wall of Cave 9. First, in both the text and the painted composition there is an explicit emphasis on the significance of what the stūpa contained—the "living" presence of the manifest form of the complete body (*ātmabhāvavigraha*) of the Buddha Prabhūtaratna—the revelation of which takes up the better part of an entire chapter of the sūtra and also two complete scenes of the composition in Cave 9, almost half the space of the overall painting on the rear wall. Second, also evident in the text and the narratives of the painted composition is an emphasis on the relationship between the jeweled stūpa of the Buddha Prabhūtaratna and the power of the oral and aural presence of the *Saddharmapuṇḍarīka-sūtra*. As narrated by Śākyamuni's reit-

45. On *māhātmyas* as a genre of Sanskrit Purāṇa literature and their relationship with sacred sites in India, see Granoff 1993, esp. the sources cited in 92n8 and the series of papers that focus on various regional *māhātmyas* collected in Bakker 1990. Slusser has described a series of scroll or banner paintings from a later period in medieval Nepal that were displayed in monastic contexts as the "pictorial equivalents" of *māhātmya* texts, and these might provide a potentially informative parallel for the manner in which the painted composition in Cave 9 may have functioned; see Slusser 1979 and 1985. Alfred Foucher also long ago recognized the relationship between artistic representation and *māhātmyas* and the use of both by Buddhists ". . . pour établir et perpétuer ce qu'on pourrait appeler la topographie de leurs légendes"; see Foucher [1949] 1987, 18.

eration of the twofold vow and declarative resolution made by the Buddha Prabhūtaratna, it was specifically in order for him to be present at the occasion of the preaching of the *Saddharmapuṇḍarīka* that inspired Śākyamuni's instructions to his disciples to construct a stūpa for Prabhūtaratna following his nirvāṇa—so that it could appear on each such occasion and thereby enable Prabhūtaratna to repeatedly experience the very source of his initial attainment of unsurpassed, perfect and complete awakening. Additionally, it is of some import to recognize that all of the miraculous events associated with the stūpa of the Buddha Prabhūtaratna narrated in the text and depicted in the scenes of the painted composition in Cave 9 were both occasioned and impelled by the preaching of the *Saddharmapuṇḍarīka* by Śākyamuni: its sudden and dramatic appearance, its rising in the air above the assembly, being showered with celestial flowers by the gods, Akṣayamati's and Avalokiteśvara's gift of piety, and its opening to reveal his living presence. The importance of the association between the proclamation of the *Saddharmapuṇḍarīka* and the stūpa of the Buddha Prabhūtaratna is underscored visually in Cave 9 by the placement of the scene depicting Śākyamuni preaching to an audience on Vulture Peak as the first narrative element of the painted composition. Located prominently on the far left of the rear wall, the primary position of this scene is appropriate in terms of narrative progression as it corresponds to the opening setting of the text, but it also effectively establishes Śākyamuni's extended discourse as the fundamental source or catalyst for all of the ensuing miraculous events depicted in the remainder of the composition in which the stūpa of the Buddha Prabhūtaratna becomes completely transformed.[46]

There is, however, one consistent narrative element shared by all of the scenes involving the stūpa of the former Buddha Prabhūtaratna in the *Saddharmapuṇḍarīka-sūtra* that is noticeably absent in the painted composition. There is no perceptible indication of an attempt by the artist(s) to include the myriad forms of tathāgatas (*tathāgatavigrahāḥ*) and their attendants brought by Śākyamuni from other buddhafields and world spheres in every direction to the assembly to witness the opening of the jeweled stūpa

46. The ability to see the Buddha Śākyamuni preaching on Vulture Peak is also presented in chapter 16 of the *Saddharmapuṇḍarīka* as a confirmation of a devotee's faith in the sūtra: "when, Ajita, a son or daughter of good family, who, having heard the *dharmaparyāya* . . . is faithfully devoted to it, then for that one this sign of faith will be known: he will see me preaching the Dharma on Vulture's Peak . . ." (*yadā cājita sa kulaputro vā kuladuhitā . . . dharmaparyāyaṃ śrutvādhyāśayenādhimucyate tadā tasyedam adhyāśayalakṣaṇaṃ veditavyaṃ yad uta gṛdhrakūṭaparvatagataṃ māṃ dharmaṃ nirdeśayantaṃ drakṣyati . . .*); Kern and Nanjio [1908–1912] 1992, 337.9–10; Watanabe 1975, A 124.15–18; Toda 1981, 324a1–3; translated in Kern [1884] 1963, 320–321.

and the revelation of the living Buddha Prabhūtaratna from within it, and who remain as part of the audience for the ongoing preaching of the sūtra. Significantly, though, a large number of painted images of standing and seated buddhas—some individually depicted and others more elaborately portrayed with attendants—were, during the late fifth century CE, placed in what appear to have been discrete groups throughout almost all of the interior areas of Cave 9, once covering most of the aisle walls, triforium, and pillars (plates 19, 21, 22, and 23).[47] It is entirely plausible that, collectively, the carefully organized arrangement of these numerous images may have been intended to represent the diffusely gathered assembly so elaborately described in the text. The well-preserved groups of enthroned buddhas with multiple attendants (at least one on a clearly discernible lion-seat) painted along the upper interior triforium are particularly striking in this regard, as their elevation above the main floor of the cave effectively conveys the distinct impression that they were, along with their attendants, suspended in the air after having "all arrived together from the ten directions and taken up seats in the eight quarters . . . each on their own lion-throne" (see plates 19, 22, and 23).[48] These painted images distributed throughout the interior of Cave 9 seem quite distinctly and, therefore, purposefully linked both visually and conceptually to the narrative scenes of the painted composition on the rear wall and, in turn, to the cave's centrally placed rock-cut stūpa.

When viewed as a conceptually unified, cohesive program, it becomes possible perhaps to more fully appreciate the extent to which the late fifth-century paintings in Cave 9 at Ajaṇṭā resulted in the creation of a unique and innovatively devised sacred space that preserved the traditional architectural form of the *caitya* hall but managed to quite radically reorient the nature of the devotional focus within it. Any devotee who performed circumambulation within the cave, for example, would have been able (if they were familiar with the narrative content of the *Saddharmapuṇḍarīka* or were instructed about it) to apprehend the identity of its archaic rock-cut stūpa as the one constructed for the Buddha Prabhūtaratna in the long-distant

47. Cf. Spink 2006, 251–259, who argues that these images were initially part of a planned redecoration scheme for the hall's interior, which was at a certain point curtailed but continued toward completion by individual donors.

48. Kern and Nanjio [1908–1912] 1992, 248.1–3; Watanabe 1975 (not extant but cf. B 235.5–16); Toda 1981 (not extant, but cf. 236b–237a). See Zin 2003, 2, plates 20 and 21, for a useful plan of Cave 9 with drawings of the best preserved of these images and their location within the cave.

past.[49] In addition, through encountering the painted composition on the rear wall, devotees performing circumambulation would also have been able to see a representation of the Buddha Śākyamuni preaching on Vulture Peak, along with a visual marker identifying the specific content of that preaching as the *Saddharmapuṇḍarīka*, a perhaps easily recognizable scene depicting the "Parable of the Burning House." As devotees continued to proceed along the circumambulatory path, they would then have progressively encountered vivid visual representations of the miraculous events that transformed the stūpa of the Buddha Prabhūtaratna instigated by the preaching of the *Saddharmapuṇḍarīka*: its magical levitation above the assembly and adornment with celestial *mandārava* flowers by numerous gods, the gift of pearls by the bodhisattva Akṣayamati to Avalokiteśvara, who then presents it to Śākyamuni and the magically arisen jeweled stūpa, and finally Śākyamuni dramatically opening the stūpa to reveal the living Buddha Prabhūtaratna. Additionally, the numerous painted images on the interior walls, pillars, and triforium of Cave 9 would have provided for a devotee a potentially powerful vision of the expansive collective audience of buddhas and bodhisattvas from manifold other worlds described in the text that had gathered to hear the preaching of the *Saddharmapuṇḍarīka* by Śākyamuni and to witness the miraculous appearance and opening of Prabhūtaratna's stūpa precipitated by it.[50]

49. Kern and Nanjio [1908–1912] 1992, 240.13; Watanabe 1975, B 234.6–7; Toda 1981, 228b4; translated in Kern [1884] 1963, 229. One might imagine that the stūpa in Cave 9 would have been painted or decorated in some manner to further establish this identification, but no such painting is extant; cf. Spink 2006, 241: "Needless to say, in any redecoration scheme, the monolithic stupa would surely have been given very high priority. . . . because of its exposed position, the new painting on it . . . has totally disappeared."

50. The performative contexts of potential ritual behaviors that may have been enacted in Cave 9 at Ajaṇṭā are, of course, inaccessible. Though somewhat afield, it might be productive to consider as a potentially informative parallel—and only that—certain so-called visualization sūtras and meditation manuals preserved in Chinese and dating to the fifth century CE that outline ritual practices singularly focused on the recitation of the *Saddharmapuṇḍarīka*, which also incorporate, intriguingly, the invocation of distinct visual components aligned with the imagery included in the Ajaṇṭā Cave 9 composition, including, specifically: Śākyamuni preaching on Mount Gṛdhrakūṭa, the appearance of the stūpa of Prabhūtaratna, the myriad buddha emanations attending the spectacle of its levitation, and the dramatic opening of it by Śākyamuni to reveal the fully preserved living presence of the Buddha Prabhūtaratna. See, for example, both the *Siwei lüeyao fa* (Taishō 617.15.297c–300c) and the *Guan puxian pusa xingfa jing* (Taishō 277.9.389b–394b); Mukhopadhyaya 1950; Soper 1959, 222–223; Katō, Tamura, and Miyasaka 1975; Beyer 1977, 338–339; Stevenson 1986, esp. 67–72, and 2009; Fujita 1990; Silk 1997; Yamabe 1999a, 1999b, 1999c, 2002, 2005, 2009; Wang 2004 and 2005, 6–23; Mai 2009; Greene 2012; Willemen 2012; Chen 2014; and Howard and Vignato 2015.

Interpreted in this way, the process of reconfiguring the interior decorative program of Cave 9 established a sacred space that was, in terms of cultic significance, inseparable from the narrative world of the *Saddharmapuṇḍarīka-sūtra*. The carefully ordered arrangement of paintings within this cave made available the veneration of a stūpa first constructed for a buddha from the distant past and another world sphere, Prabhūtaratna, a figure who is both central to the narrative of the *Saddharmapuṇḍarīka* and exclusive to this single textual source. The updated painting program in Cave 9 also made it possible, through the ritual veneration of this stūpa, for a devotee to "see," or perhaps even directly experience, the numinous power attendant to the proclamation of the *Saddharmapuṇḍarīka-sūtra* by Śākyamuni amid a vast audience of buddhas and bodhisattvas, which both instigated the miraculous levitation of the stūpa and manifested from within it the fully preserved, living Buddha Prabhūtaratna.[51]

Conclusion

The interpretation of the art-historical, textual, and epigraphic material considered here allows for certain tentative conclusions in regard to the status of the *Saddharmapuṇḍarīka-sūtra* within at least one historically localized Indian Buddhist community. This text appears to have been the primary, and perhaps even instigating, influence for the establishment of what might be the first identifiable sanctuary at an Indian Buddhist monastic site designed specifically to accommodate Mahāyāna-oriented ritual practices, which was accomplished through the reoccupation and extensive redecoration of Cave 9 at Ajaṇṭā during the late fifth century CE. The central component of this redecoration initiative was a painted composition on the rear wall of Cave 9 that incorporated no less than five major narrative scenes particular to the *Saddharmapuṇḍarīka-sūtra*. These narrative scenes were organized within the composition to align, both visually and conceptually, with both the painted images of buddhas and bodhisattvas dispersed throughout the *caitya* hall's interior and the main stūpa of the cave, in a manner that promoted the identification, or reimagining, of the latter as the archaic stūpa constructed in the long-distant past to house the living, manifest form of the complete body (*ātmabhāvavigraha*) of the Buddha Prabhūtaratna. This carefully constructed pictorial program in Cave 9 at Ajaṇṭā may, in addition, have been

51. There is an interesting literary parallel in this regard to be found in the Nepalese *Śṛṇgabheryavadāna*, in which a jeweled *caitya* appears in the sky while a devotee is performing pūjā to a *caitya* constructed out of sand; see Lewis 1994 and 2000, 29–36.

designed to function in tandem with the performance of a range of ritual activities developed from, and directly involving, the *Saddharmapuṇḍarīka*, such as the public preaching of the sūtra by *dharmabhāṇaka*s, various forms of individual and/or communal recitation, and quite possibly, practices of meditative absorption (samādhi), each of which, for practitioners interacting with the paintings, would have been accompanied by ritually potent visions of the miraculous events narrated in the sūtra, including Śākyamuni preaching on Vulture Peak, the appearance and levitation of the jeweled stūpa, and the dramatic revelation from within it of the fully constituted, living Buddha Prabhūtaratna.

This reading of the art-historical evidence from Cave 9 at Ajaṇṭā certainly seems to underscore that in any attempt to locate Mahāyāna ritual practices at Indian Buddhist sites, it might be important, crucial even, to more fully acknowledge that evidence for these types of practices might have manifested in modes and contexts far more discursive than have been previously considered. It might be important, for example, to consider more critically the possibility that practices that may be reflective of the existence of an individual Mahāyāna sūtra cult—or what some might more readily identify as an example of a Mahāyāna cult of the book—would almost certainly have included an expansive range of activities enacted at an equally expansive number of locations, both divergent from, and of course in addition to, public or domestic spaces where an actual Mahāyāna sūtra in manuscript form, a portion of one, or even a representation of one, was set up or established in some way to be venerated.[52]

52. As is well known, more than forty years ago Schopen recognized the consistent appearance of passages employing the same or parallel formulaic vocabulary across a not insignificant range of early or early-middle Mahāyāna sūtras, including the *Saddharmapuṇḍarīka*, that sought to elevate specific locations where individual sūtras were made present orally (through recitation, teaching, illumination, preaching, and so on) or were set up or stored in material form as a book and where various forms of worship were performed to them, as sanctified by becoming a shrine or *caitya* (*caityabhūto bhavet*). It was on the basis of these passages, accordingly, that Schopen first suggested that the places where individual Mahāyāna sūtras circulated and were venerated—that is, the specific locations where what he identified as localized instances of a broader cult of the book were practiced—may have served as discrete "organizational centers" at which different individual Indian Mahāyāna communities coalesced. What has not been effectively addressed in the long interim to the present though, and which consequently remains quite unclear, is the extent to which, if at all, this particular cultic innovation so seemingly prominent in early and early-middle Mahāyāna literature may have instigated a discernible impact on the material culture of Buddhist sites in South Asia—that is to say, whether or not any communal Mahāyāna "organizational center" associated with a single specific sūtra cult was actually ever established in India in a form potentially accessible or visible to the historian, and if so, when or where and at what type of site and by what particular type of group. It might be

At any rate, it is sufficiently clear from the material discussed here that the historical currency of the *Saddharmapuṇḍarīka-sūtra* within Indian Buddhism needs to be seriously revisited. At Ajaṇṭā during the fifth century CE at least, there is now every indication that this text—and the seemingly Mahāyāna-oriented group of *śākyabhikṣu*s aligned with it—may have been much more influential than previously thought, if only momentarily.[53] Where

---

conceivable, however, in light of the discussion here, to recognize Cave 9 at Ajaṇṭā during the late fifth century CE as one such possible center, at which the *Saddharmapuṇḍarīka* served as the focal point of communal cultic worship and practice for a Mahāyāna-oriented group. See Schopen 1975 and cf. 2010, but also note that Schopen has in recent years emended his position somewhat, seeing now in the formulaic language of the "*sa pṛthivīpradeśaś caityabhūto bhavet*" passages the construction of "what was probably at first a metaphor" aimed at shifting "the religious focus from cult and giving to doctrine, to send monks, nuns, and even laymen quite literally back to their books" (2004, 497). But Schopen has continued to maintain though, and this is of some significance, that regardless of whether or not the original intent may have been metaphorical, these formulaic passages can also still be read explicitly as an "attempted redefinition of Buddhist sacred sites" (2000, 23) by the authors of Mahāyāna sūtras, which subsequently resulted, at least in part, in "an attempt by the 'new' movement to substitute one similar cult (the cult of the book) for another similar cult (the cult of relics)" (2004, 497); cf. Nattier 2003, 185–186. Cf. Kinnard 2002; Schopen 2010; and Kim 2013, 1–72, esp. 36–41.

53. The precise chronological position of the painting in Cave 9 within the overall progression of decoration at Ajaṇṭā during the Vākāṭaka period is difficult to determine. Spink has argued that the extent and quality of execution evident in the rear wall composition, as well as its narrative content, suggests that it was first begun during what he identifies as "the Programmatic Phase" of Vākāṭaka patronage. However, the association of a number of individual donative inscriptions with this painting may indicate, according to Spink, that it was at some point abandoned by its initial sponsors, then taken over and completed by "intrusive patrons" during his so-called "Period of Disruption." Either way, this composition on the rear wall would appear to belong to a very late period of activity at the site. The redecoration of Cave 9, then, seems to have occurred amid the final years of occupation at Ajaṇṭā during a period characterized by considerable confusion and disarray, when administrative control was largely absent and its elite, courtly Vākāṭaka patrons had moved on. Prior to this, Cave 9 was apparently neither occupied by any of the site's major patrons nor placed under active worship, indicating that this old, first-century BCE cave "left in bad repair" was certainly available for appropriation. The availability of this unoccupied *caitya* hall, and perhaps especially its interior stūpa, may have been particularly attractive to a fledgling Mahāyāna group that may have had only limited access to the resources necessary to sponsor their own entirely new foundation. It is certainly intriguing, at any rate, that the new program of paintings introduced into this archaic and long-neglected *caitya* at this time so clearly reflects a concerted effort to transform this cave in a way that rendered it specifically meaningful and ritually efficacious for those that could only have been intimately familiar with, and in some way, therefore, committed to, the *Saddharmapuṇḍarīka-sūtra*. However, the reoccupation and subsequent Mahāyāna-oriented transformation of Cave 9 seems to have taken place in the most nebulous of circumstances, when it was not part of any major patron's original plans, and undertaken only a short while in advance of the "sudden and decisive" end of activity at the entire Ajaṇṭā monastic complex. See the extended discussion in Spink 2006, 167–173 and 239–272 (esp. 245–250).

else in India the *Saddharmapuṇḍarīka-sūtra* may have circulated and been influential though, if anywhere, remains to be seen.[54]

54. Cf. von Hinüber 2012, 62–63, who has described the *Saddharmapuṇḍarīka* as "firmly embedded in the Buddhist culture of Gilgit" and noted its "universal veneration" there during the sixth to eighth centuries CE. Similarly Fussman 1996, 779, where he suggests that the Gilgit manuscript finds of this sūtra "prouve à lui seul la grande popularité" of the text there. Although there may be as many as four separate manuscript witnesses of the *Saddharmapuṇḍarīka* extant from Gilgit and two dispersed examples of art-historical evidence (one metal sculpture and one graffiti-like rock drawing) dating to the early medieval period that may exhibit potential influence from certain themes contained within it, what this material can firmly establish beyond indicating that the *Saddharmapuṇḍarīka* was known in the region at this time, especially in terms of its precise status or extent of popularity, remains, at present, unclear. See now also the discussion of this material in Hu-von Hinüber 2019.

Works Cited

Abe, Stanley. 1990. "Art and Practice in a Fifth-Century Chinese Buddhist Cave Temple." *Ars Orientalis* 20: 1–31.

Apple, James B. 2014. "The Single Vehicle (*ekayāna*) in the *Avaivartikacakrasūtra* and *Lotus Sūtra*." *Bulletin of the Institute of Oriental Philosophy* 30: 13–43.

———. 2015. "Candrakīrti and the *Lotus Sutra*." *Bulletin of the Institute of Oriental Philosophy* 31: 97–122.

Bakker, Hans, ed. 1990. *The History of Sacred Places in India as Reflected in Traditional Literature: Papers on Pilgrimage in South Asia (Panels of the VIIth World Sanskrit Conference, Kern Institute, Leiden August 23–29, 1987).* Leiden: E. J. Brill.

Banerjea, Jitendra Nath. [1956] 1974. *The Development of Hindu Iconography.* Reprint, New Delhi: Munshiram Manoharlal.

Bareau, André. 1962. "La construction et le culte des stūpa d'après les *vinayapiṭaka*." *Bulletin de l'École française d'Extrême-Orient* 50.2: 229–274.

Baruch, W. 1938. *Beiträge zum Saddharmapuṇḍarīkasūtra*. Leiden: E. J. Brill.

Bautze-Picron, Claudine. 2004. "The Universal Compassionate Bodhisattva: Miscellaneous Aspects of Avalokitasvara/Avalokiteśvara in India." *Silk Road Art and Archaeology* 10: 225–290.

Becker, Catherine. 2015. *Shifting Stones, Shaping the Past: Sculpture from the Buddhist Stūpas of Andhra Pradesh.* Oxford: Oxford University Press.

Behl, Benoy. 1998. *The Ajanta Caves: Artistic Wonder of Ancient Buddhist India*. London: Thames and Hudson.

Beyer, Stephen. 1977. "Notes on the Vision Quest in Early Mahāyāna." In *Prajñāpāramitā and Related Systems: Studies in Honor of Edward Conze*, edited by Lewis Lancaster, 329–340. Berkeley: Berkeley Buddhist Studies Series.

Bielefeldt, Carl. 2009. "Expedient Devices, the One Vehicle, and the Life Span of the Buddha." In *Readings of the Lotus Sūtra*, edited by Stephen Teiser and Jacqueline Stone, 62–82. New York: Columbia University Press.

Boucher, Daniel. 2008. *Bodhisattvas of the Forest and the Formation of the Mahāyāna: A Study and Translation of the* Rāṣṭrapālaparipṛcchā-sūtra. Studies in the Buddhist Traditions. Honolulu: University of Hawai'i Press.

———. 2009. "What Do We Mean by 'Early' in the Study of the Early Mahāyāna—And Should We Care?" *Bulletin of the Asia Institute*, n.s., 23: 33–41. Actually published 2013.

Brancaccio, Pia. 2011. *The Buddhist Caves at Aurangabad: Transformations in Art and Religion*. Leiden: Brill.

———. 2014. "Aṣṭamahābhaya Avalokiteśvara in the Western Deccan: Buddhist Patronage and Trade between the Fifth and Sixth Century CE." In *Changing Forms and Cultural Identity: Religious and Secular Iconographies*, edited by Deborah Klimburg-Salter and Linda Lojda, 91–98. South Asian Archaeology and Art 1. Turnhout: Brepols.

Burgess, James. 1879. *Notes on the Bauddha Rock-Temples of Ajanta*. Bombay: Government Central Press.

Burnouf, Eugène. [1852] 1973. *Le lotus de la bonne loi: traduit du sanscrit, accompagné d'un commentaire et de vingt et un mémoires relatifs au buddhisme*. Reprint, Paris: Imprimerie Nationale.

Chen, Jinhua. 2014. "Meditation Traditions in Fifth-Century Northern China: With a Special Note on a Forgotten 'Kaśmīri' Meditation Tradition Brought to China by Buddhabhadra (359–429)." In *Buddhism across Asia: Networks of Material, Intellectual and Cultural Exchange*, edited by Tansen Sen, 101–130. Nalanda-Sriwijaya Research Series 1. Singapore: Institute of Southeast Asian Studies.

Cohen, Richard. 2000. "Kinsmen of the Sun: Śākyabhikṣus and the Institutionalization of the Bodhisattva Ideal." *History of Religions* 40.1: 1–31.

———. 2006. "Ajanta's Inscriptions." In *Arguments about Ajanta*, by Walter Spink, 273–339, vol. 2 of *Ajanta: History and Development*. Leiden: Brill.

Conze, Edward, ed. and trans. 1957. *Vajracchedikā Prajñāpāramitā*. Serie Orientale Roma 13. Rome: Istituto Italiano per il Medio ed Estremo Oriente.

Cousins, Lance S. 2003. "Sākiyabhikkhu/Sakyabhikkhu/Śākyabhikṣu: A Mistaken Link to the Mahāyāna?" *Saṃbhāṣā: Nagoya Studies in Indian Culture and Buddhism* 23: 1–27.

Davidson, J. Leroy. 1954. *The Lotus Sūtra in Chinese Art: A Study in Buddhist Art to the Year 1000*. New Haven: Yale University Press.

Dehejia, Vidya. 1972. *Early Buddhist Rock Temples: A Chronology*. Ithaca: Cornell University Press.

———. 1992. "Collective and Popular Bases of Early Buddhist Patronage: Sacred Monuments, 100 BC–AD 250." In *The Powers of Art: Patronage in Indian Culture*, edited by Barbara Stoler Miller, 35–45. Delhi: Oxford University Press.

———. 1997. *Discourse in Early Buddhist Art: Visual Narratives of India*. New Delhi: Munshiram Manoharlal.

Dhavalikar, M. K. 1984. *Late Hinayana Caves of Western India*. Poona: Deccan College Postgraduate and Research Institute.

Divakaran, Odile. 1989. "Avalokiteśvara—From the North-West to the Western Caves." *East and West* 39.1–4: 145–178.

Eckel, Malcolm David. 1992. *To See the Buddha: A Philosopher's Quest for the Meaning of Emptiness*. Princeton: Princeton University Press.

Edgerton, Franklin. [1953] 1993. *Buddhist Hybrid Sanskrit Grammar and Dictionary*, vol. 2: *Dictionary*. Reprint, Delhi: Motilal Banarsidass.

Fergusson, James, and James Burgess. [1880] 1988. *The Cave Temples of India*. 2nd Indian ed. New Delhi: Munshiram Manoharlal.

Filliozat, Jean. 1938. Review of *Beiträge zum Saddharmapuṇḍarīkasūtra*, by W. Baruch. *Journal asiatique* 230: 346–347.

Foucher, Alfred. [1949] 1987. *La vie du Bouddha d'après les textes et les monuments de l'Inde*. Reprint, Paris: Librairie d'Amérique et d'Orient.

Fujita, Kōtatsu. 1975. "One Vehicle or Three?" *Journal of Indian Philosophy* 3.1–2: 79–166.

———. 1990. "The Textual Origins of the *Kuan Wu-liang-shou ching*: A Canonical Scripture of Pure Land Buddhism." In *Chinese Buddhist Apocrypha*, edited by Robert E. Buswell Jr., 149–173. Honolulu: University of Hawai'i Press.

Fussman, Gérard. 1996. "Histoire du monde indien." In *Annuaire du Collège de France 1995–1996: Résumé des cours et travaux*, 779–786. Paris: Collège de France.

Granoff, Phyllis. 1993. "Halāyudha's Prism: The Experience of Religion in Medieval Hymns and Stories." In *Gods, Guardians, and Lovers: Temple Sculptures from North India A.D. 700–1200*, edited by Vishakha N. Desai and Darielle Mason, 66–93. New York: The Asia Society Galleries.

Greene, Eric. 2012. "Meditation, Repentance, and Visionary Experience in Early Medieval Chinese Buddhism." PhD thesis, University of California, Berkeley.

Harrison, Paul, and Christian Luczanits. 2012. "New Light on (and from) the Muhammad Nari Stele." In *Special International Symposium on Pure Land Buddhism, 4th August 2011, Otani University*, 69–127. International Symposium Series 1. Kyoto: Ryukoku University Research Center for Buddhist Cultures in Asia.

Hauptmann, Harald. 2008. "Felsbildkunst am Oberen Indus." In *Gandhara—Das buddhistische Erbe Pakistans: Legenden, Klöster und Paradise*, edited by Christian Luczanits, 352–357. Mainz: Verlag Philipp von Zabern.

Haussig, Hans Wilhelm. 1984. *Wörterbuch der Mythologie*, vol. 5: *Götter und Mythen des Indischen Subkontinents*. Stuttgart: Klett-Cotta.

von Hinüber, Oskar. 2004. *Die Palola Ṣāhis: Ihre Steininschriften, Inschriften auf Bronzen, Handschriftenkolophone und Schutzzauber. Materialien zur Geschichte von Gilgit und Chilas*. Antiquities of Northern Pakistan. Reports and Studies 5. Mainz: Verlag Philipp von Zabern.

———. 2012. "The Saddharmapuṇḍarīkasūtra at Gilgit: Manuscripts, Worshippers, and Artists." *Journal of Oriental Studies* 22: 52–67.

———. 2014. "A Saddharmapuṇḍarīkasūtra Manuscript from Khotan: The Gift of a Pious Khotanese Family." *Journal of Oriental Studies* 24: 134–156.

———. 2015. "Three *Saddharmapuṇḍarīkasūtra* Manuscripts from Khotan and Their Donors." *Annual Report of the International Research Institute for Advanced Buddhology at Soka University* 18: 215–234.

Howard, Angela F., and Giuseppe Vignato. 2015. *Archaeological and Visual Sources of Meditation in the Ancient Monasteries of Kuča*. Leiden: Brill.

Huntington, Susan. 2012. *Lay Ritual in the Early Buddhist Art of India: More Evidence Against the Aniconic Theory*. Amsterdam: Royal Netherlands Academy of Arts and Sciences.

Hu-von Hinüber, Haiyan. 2019. "From the Upper Indus to the East Coast of China: On the Origin of the Pictorial Representation of the Lotus Sūtra." *Annual Report of the International Research Institute for Advanced Buddhology at Soka University* 22: 377–390.

Karashima, Seishi. 2015. "Vehicle (*yāna*) and Wisdom (*jñāna*) in the Lotus Sutra—The Origin of the Notion of *yāna* in Mahāyāna Buddhism." *Annual Report of the International Research Institute for Advanced Buddhology at Soka University* 18: 163–196.

Katō, Bunnō, Yoshirō Tamura, and Kōjirō Miyasaka, trans. 1975. *The Threefold Lotus Sutra: Innumerable Meanings, The Lotus Flower of the Wonderful Law, and Meditation on the Bodhisattva Universal Virtue*. Tokyo and New York: Kōsei Publishing Co. and Weatherhill Inc.

Kern, Hendrik, trans. [1884] 1963. *Saddharma-Puṇḍarīka; or The Lotus of the True Law*. Reprint, New York: Dover Publications.

Kern, Hendrik, and Bunyiu Nanjio, eds. [1908–1912] 1992. *Saddharmapuṇḍarīka*. Bibliotheca Buddhica 10. Reprint, New Delhi: Motilal Banarsidass.

Khettry, Sarita. 2010–2011. "Sakyabhikshu of Bronze Image Inscriptions of Bengal (West Bengal and Bangladesh)." *Proceedings of the Indian History Congress* 71: 148–153.

Kim, Inchang. 1997. *The Future Buddha Maitreya: An Iconological Study*. New Delhi: D. K. Printworld.

Kim, Jinah. 2009. "Iconography and Text: The Visual Narrative of the Buddhist Book-Cult in the Manuscript of the Ashṭasāhasrikā Prajñāpāramitā Sūtra." In *Kalādarpaṇa: The Mirror of Indian Art. Essays in Memory of Shri Krishna Deva*, edited by Devangana Desai and Arundhati Banerji, 255–272. New Delhi: Aryan Books International.

———. 2013. *Receptacle of the Sacred: Illustrated Manuscripts and the Buddhist Book Cult in South Asia*. Berkeley: University of California Press.

Kinnard, Jacob N. 2002. "On Buddhist 'Bibliolaters': Representing and Worshiping the Book in Medieval Indian Buddhism." *The Eastern Buddhist*, n.s., 34.2: 94–116.

Kloppenborg, Ria, trans. 1973. *The Sūtra on the Foundation of the Buddhist Order (Catuṣpariṣatsūtra)*. Leiden: Brill.

van Kooij, Karel R. 1995. "Remarks on Festivals and Altars in Early Buddhist Art." In *Function and Meaning in Buddhist Art: Proceedings of a Seminar Held at Leiden University 21–24 October 1991*, edited by K. R. van Kooij and H. van der Veere, 33–43. Groningen: Egbert Forsten.

Leese, Marilyn. 1988. "Ellora and the Development of the Litany Scene in Western India." In *Ellora Caves: Sculpture and Architecture (Collected Papers of the University Grants Commission's National Seminar)*, edited by Ratan Parimoo et al., 164–179. New Delhi: Books and Books.

Lewis, Todd. 1994. "Contributions to the History of Buddhist Ritualism: A Mahāyāna *Avadāna* on *Caitya* Veneration from the Kathmandu Valley." *Journal of Asian History* 28.1: 1–38.

———. 2000. *Popular Buddhist Texts from Nepal: Narratives and Rituals of Newar Buddhism*. Albany: State University of New York Press.

Losty, Jeremiah P. 1989. "An Early Indian Manuscript of the Kāraṇḍavyūhasūtra." In *Studies in Art and Archaeology of Bihar and Bengal: Nalinīkānta Śatavārṣikī, Dr. N. K. Bhattasali Centenary Volume (1888–1988)*, edited by Debala Mitra and Gouriswar Bhattacharya, 1–21. Delhi: Sri Satguru Publications.

Luczanits, Christian. 2010. "In Search of the Perfection of Wisdom: A Short Note on the Third Narrative Depicted in the Tabo Main Temple." In *From Turfan to Ajanta: Festschrift for Dieter Schlingloff on the Occasion of His Eightieth Birthday*, edited by Eli Franco and Monika Zin, 2:567–578. Bhairahawa, Nepal: Lumbini International Research Institute.

Mai, Cuong T. 2009. "Visualization Apocrypha and the Making of Buddhist Deity Cults in Early Medieval China." PhD thesis, Indiana University.

de Mallmann, Marie-Thérèse. 1948. *Introduction à l'étude d'Avalokiteçvara.* Paris: Presses Universitaires de France.

McCombs, Jason. 2014. "Mahāyāna and the Gift: Theories and Practices." PhD thesis, University of California, Los Angeles.

Miyaji, Akira. 2005. "The Historical Transition of the Iconography of Bodhisattva Maitreya: The Iconographic Relationship between Maitreya and Avalokiteśvara." *Journal of Studies for the Integrated Text Science* 3.1: 67–102.

Mizufune, Noriyoshi, ed. 2009. *Sanskrit Lotus Sūtra Manuscript from the British Library (Or. 2204): Facsimile Edition.* Lotus Sutra Manuscript Series 9. Tokyo: Soka Gakkai.

———, ed. 2013. *Sanskrit Lotus Sūtra Manuscripts from the Institute of Oriental Manuscripts of the Russian Academy of Sciences: Facsimile Edition.* Lotus Sutra Manuscript Series 13. Tokyo: Soka Gakkai.

Mochizuki, Kaie. 2011. "How Did the Indian Masters Read the *Lotus Sūtra*?" *Indogaku bukkyōgaku kenkyū* 印度學佛教學研究 (*Journal of Indian and Buddhist Studies*) 59.3: 1169–1177.

Monier-Williams, Monier. [1899] 2022. *A Sanskrit-English Dictionary: Etymologically and Philologically Arranged with Special Reference to Cognate Indo-European Languages.* Reprint, New Delhi: Munshiram Manoharlal.

Morrissey, Nicolas. 2013. "Shakyabhikshus at the Brazen Glen: Mahayana Reoccupation of an Old Monastery at Pitalkhora." In *Living Rock: Buddhist, Hindu and Jain Cave Temples in the Western Deccan*, edited by Pia Brancaccio, 77–91. Mumbai: Marg.

Mukhopadhyaya, Sujitkumar. 1950. "An Outline of Principal Methods of Meditation." *Visva-Bharati Annals* 3: 110–150.

Nagaraju, S. 1981. *Buddhist Architecture of Western India (C. 250 B.C.–C. A.D. 300).* Delhi: Agam Kala Prakashan.

Nattier, Jan. 2003. *A Few Good Men: The Bodhisattva Path according to* The Inquiry of Ugra (Ugraparipṛcchā). Studies in the Buddhist Traditions. Honolulu: University of Hawai'i Press.

Nishi, Yasutomo. 2022. *Saddharmapuṇḍarīka: Kern-Nanjio's Edition in Roman Script with Complemented Footnotes.* Philosophica Mahāyāna Buddhica, Monograph Series 6: Kern-Nanjio's Edition Romanized Text 1. Tokyo: Chuo Academic Research Institute.

Owen, Lisa Nadine. 2001. "Constructing Another Perspective for Ajaṇṭā's Fifth-Century Excavations." *Journal of the International Association of Buddhist Studies* 24.1: 27–59.

Pagel, Ulrich. 2007. "Stūpa Festivals in Buddhist Narrative Literature." In *Indica et Tibetica: Festschrift für Michael Hahn. Zum 65. Geburtstag von Freunden und Schülern überreicht*, edited by Konrad Klaus and Jens-Uwe Hartmann, 369–394. Vienna: Arbeitskreis für Tibetische und Buddhistische Studien Universität Wien.

Pandit, Suraj A. 2016. "A Unique Sculptural Panel from Kanheri Cave 90." In *Temple Architecture and Imagery of South and Southeast Asia. Prāsādanidhi: Papers Presented to Professor M. A. Dhaky*, edited by Parul Pandya Dhar and Gerd J. R. Mevissen, 273–279. New Delhi: Aryan Books International.

Patel, Divia. 2007. "Copying Ajanta: A Rediscovery of Some Nineteenth-Century Paintings." *South Asian Studies* 23: 39–62.

Prasad, Birendra Nath. 2013. "Cultic Relationships Between Buddhism and Brahmanism in the 'Last Stronghold' of Indian Buddhism: An Analysis with Particular Reference to Votive Inscriptions on the Brahmanical Sculptures Donated to Buddhist Religious Centres in Early Medieval Magadha." *Buddhist Studies Review* 30.2: 181–199.

Pye, Michael. 1978. *Skilful Means: A Concept in Mahayana Buddhism*. London: Duckworth.

Qureshi, Dulari. 2010. *The Rock-Cut Temples of Western India*. Delhi: Bharatiya Kala Prakashan.

Rees, Gethin. 2009. "A Hiatus in the Cutting of Buddhist Caves in the Western Deccan." *Ancient Asia* 2: 119–134.

Schlingloff, Dieter. 1988. *Studies in the Ajanta Paintings: Identifications and Interpretations*. Delhi: Ajanta Publications.

———. 1999. *Guide to the Ajanta Paintings*, vol. 1: *Narrative Wall Paintings*. New Delhi: Munshiram Manoharlal.

———. 2000. *Ajanta. Handbuch der Malereien/Handbook of the Paintings: Erzählende Wandmalereien/Narrative Wall-Paintings*, vol. 1: *Interpretation*. Wiesbaden: Harrassowitz Verlag.

———. 2013. *Ajanta: Handbook of the Paintings/Narrative Wall Paintings*, vol. 1: *Interpretation*. New Delhi: Aryan Books International.

Schlosser, Andrea. 2022. *Three Early Mahāyāna Treatises from Gandhāra: Bajaur Kharoṣṭhī Fragments 4, 6, and 11*. Gandhāran Buddhist Texts 7. Seattle: University of Washington Press.

Schopen, Gregory. 1975. "The Phrase '*sa pṛthivīpradeśaś caityabhūto bhavet*' in the *Vajracchedikā*: Notes on the Cult of the Book in Mahāyāna." *Indo-Iranian Journal* 17.3–4: 147–181. Reprinted in Schopen 2005a, 25–62.

———. 1979. "Mahāyāna in Indian Inscriptions." *Indo-Iranian Journal* 21.1: 1–19. Reprinted in Schopen 2005a, 223–246.

———. 1985. "Two Problems in the History of Indian Buddhism: The Layman/Monk Distinction and the Doctrines of the Transference of Merit." *Studien zur Indologie und Iranistik* 10: 9–47. Reprinted in Schopen 1997, 23–55.

———. 1987. "The Inscription on the Kuṣān Image of Amitābha and the Character of the Early Mahāyāna in India." *Journal of the International Association of Buddhist Studies* 10.2: 99–134. Reprinted in Schopen 2005a, 247–277.

———. 1997. *Bones, Stones, and Buddhist Monks: Collected Papers on the Archaeology, Epigraphy, and Texts of Monastic Buddhism in India*. Studies in the Buddhist Traditions. Honolulu: University of Hawai'i Press.

———. 2000. "The Mahāyāna and the Middle Period in Indian Buddhism: Through a Chinese Looking-Glass." *The Eastern Buddhist*, n.s., 32.2: 1–25. Reprinted in Schopen 2005a, 3–24.

———. 2004. "Mahāyāna." In *Encyclopedia of Buddhism*, edited by Robert E. Buswell Jr., 2:492–499. New York: Macmillan Reference USA.

———. 2005a. *Figments and Fragments of Mahāyāna Buddhism in India: More Col-*

lected Papers. Studies in the Buddhist Traditions. Honolulu: University of Hawai'i Press.

———. 2005b. "The Ambiguity of Avalokiteśvara and the Tentative Identification of a Painted Scene from a Mahāyāna *Sūtra* at Ajaṇṭā." In Schopen 2005a, 278–298.

———. 2010. "The Book as a Sacred Object in Private Homes in Early or Medieval India." In *Medieval and Early Modern Devotional Objects in Global Perspective: Translations of the Sacred*, edited by Elizabeth Robertson and Jennifer Jahner, 37–60. New York: Palgrave Macmillan.

Silk, Jonathan A. 1997. "The Composition of the *Guan Wuliangshoufo-jing*: Some Buddhist and Jaina Parallels to Its Narrative Frame." *Journal of Indian Philosophy* 25.2: 181–256.

———. 2001. "The Place of the *Lotus Sūtra* in Indian Buddhism." *Journal of Oriental Philosophy* 11: 87–105.

———. 2006. *Body Language: Indic śarīra and Chinese shèlì in the Mahāparinirvāṇa-sūtra and Saddharmapuṇḍarīka*. Tokyo: The International Institute for Buddhist Studies of the International College for Postgraduate Buddhist Studies.

———. 2014. "Taking the *Vimalakīrtinirdeśa* Seriously." *Annual Report of the International Research Institute for Advanced Buddhology at Soka University* 17: 157–188.

Skilling, Peter. 2005. "Cutting Across Categories: The Ideology of Relics in Buddhism." *Annual Report of the International Research Institute for Advanced Buddhology at Soka University* 8: 269–322.

Slusser, Mary Shepherd. 1979. "Serpents, Sages, and Sorcerers in Cleveland." *The Bulletin of the Cleveland Museum of Art* 66.2: 67–82.

———. 1985. "On a Sixteenth-Century Pictorial Pilgrim's Guide from Nepal." *Archives of Asian Art* 38: 6–36.

Soper, Alexander Coburn. 1959. *Literary Evidence for Early Buddhist Art in China*. Ascona: Artibus Asiae.

Spink, Walter M. 2005. *Ajanta: History and Development*, vol. 3: *The Arrival of the Uninvited*. Leiden: Brill.

———. 2006. *Ajanta: History and Development*, vol. 2: *Arguments about Ajanta*. Leiden: Brill.

Stevenson, Daniel B. 1986. "The Four Kinds of Samādhi in Early T'ien-t'ai Buddhism." In *Traditions of Meditation in Chinese Buddhism*, edited by Peter Gregory, 45–98. Honolulu: University of Hawai'i Press.

———. 2009. "Buddhist Practice and the Lotus Sūtra in China." In *Readings of the Lotus Sūtra*, edited by Stephen Teiser and Jacqueline Stone, 132–150. New York: Columbia University Press.

Taddei, Maurizio. 1987. "Non-Buddhist Deities in Gandharan Art—Some New Evidence." In *Investigating Indian Art: Proceedings of a Symposium on the Development of Early Buddhist and Hindu Iconography Held at the Museum of Indian Art Berlin in May 1986*, edited by Marianne Yaldiz and Wibke Lobo, 349–362. Berlin: Staatliche Museen Preussischer Kulturbesitz.

Takakusu, J. [1896] 1982. *A Record of the Buddhist Religion as Practised in India and the Malay Archipelago (A.D. 671–695) by I-tsing*. Reprint, New Delhi: Munshiram Manoharlal.

Teiser, Stephen, and Jacqueline Stone. 2009. "Interpreting the Lotus Sūtra." In *Readings of the Lotus Sūtra*, edited by Stephen Teiser and Jacqueline Stone, 1–61. New York: Columbia University Press.

Toda, Hirofumi, ed. 1981. *Saddharmapuṇḍarīkasūtra. Central Asian Manuscripts: Romanized Text*. Tokushima: Kyoiku Shuppan Center.

Tournier, Vincent. 2014. "Mahākāśyapa, His Lineage, and the Wish for Buddhahood: Reading Anew the Bodhgayā Inscriptions of Mahānāman." *Indo-Iranian Journal* 57.1–2: 1–60.

———. 2018. "A Tide of Merit: Royal Donors, Tāmraparṇīya Monks, and the Buddha's Awakening in 5th–6th-Century Āndhradeśa." *Indo-Iranian Journal* 61.1: 20–96.

———. 2020. "Stairway to Heaven and the Path to Buddhahood: Donors and Their Aspirations in Fifth- and Sixth-Century Ajanta." In *Mārga: Paths to Liberation in South Asian Buddhist Traditions*, edited by Cristina Pecchia and Vincent Eltschinger, 177–248. Vienna: Verlag der Österreichischen Akademie der Wissenschaften.

———. 2023. "A 4th/5th-Century *sūtra* of the Saṁmitīya Canon? On the So-Called 'Continental Pāli' Inscription from Devnimori." In *Proceedings of the Third International Pali Studies Week Paris 2018*, edited by Claudio Cicuzza, 403–470. Material for the Study of the Tripiṭaka 18. Bangkok and Lumbini: Fragile Palm Leaf Foundation and Lumbini International Research Institute.

Trainor, Kevin. 1996. "Constructing a Buddhist Ritual Site: Stupa and Monastery Architecture." In *Unseen Presence: The Buddha and Sanchi*, edited by Vidya Dehejia, 18–35. Mumbai: Marg.

Tsukamoto, Keishō. 2007. *Source Elements of the Lotus Sutra: Buddhist Integration of Religion, Thought and Culture*. Tokyo: Kōsei Publishing.

Vogel, Claus. 1974. *The Dated Nepalese Manuscripts of the Saddharmapuṇḍarīkasūtra*. Nachrichten der Akademie der Wissenschaften in Göttingen. Philologisch-historische Klasse, Jahrgang 1974, Nr. 5. Göttingen: Vandenhoeck & Ruprecht.

Waldschmidt, Ernst, ed. 1952–1960. *Das Catuṣpariṣatsūtra: Eine kanonische Lehrschrift über die Begründung der buddhistischen Gemeinde: Text in Sanskrit und Tibetisch, verglichen mit dem Pāli nebst einer Übersetzung der chinesischen Entsprechung im Vinaya der Mūlasarvāstivādins*. 3 vols. Berlin: Abhandlungen der Deutschen Akademie der Wissenschaften.

Walters, Jonathan. 1997. "*Stūpa*, Story, and Empire: Constructions of the Buddha Biography in Early Post-Aśokan India." In *Sacred Biography in the Buddhist Traditions of South and Southeast Asia*, edited by Julianne Schober, 160–194. Honolulu: University of Hawaiʻi Press.

Wang, Eugene. 2004. "Oneiric Horizons and Dissolving Bodies: Buddhist Cave Shrine as Mirror Hall." *Art History* 27.4: 494–521.

———. 2005. *Shaping the Lotus Sūtra: Buddhist Visual Culture in Medieval China*. Seattle: University of Washington Press.

Watanabe, Shōkō, ed. 1975. *Saddharmapuṇḍarīka Manuscripts Found in Gilgit*. Part Two: *Romanized Text*. Tokyo: The Reiyukai.

Wille, Klaus. 2000. *Fragments of a Manuscript of the Saddharmapuṇḍarīkasūtra from Khādaliq*. Lotus Sutra Manuscript Series 3. Tokyo: Soka Gakkai.

Willemen, Charles. 2012. *Outlining the Way to Reflect (T.XV 617) Siwei lüeyao fa* 思惟略要法. Buddhist Studies Series 1. Mumbai: Somaiya.

Yamabe, Nobuyoshi. 1999a. "The *Sūtra on the Ocean-Like Samādhi of the Visualization of the Buddha*: The Interfusion of the Chinese and Indian Cultures in Central Asia as Reflected in a Fifth Century Apocryphal Sūtra." PhD thesis, Yale University.

———. 1999b. "The Significance of the '*Yogalehrbuch*' for the Investigation into the Origin of Chinese Meditation Texts." *Bukkyō bunka* 仏教文化 (*Buddhist Culture*) 9: 1–74.

———. 1999c. "An Examination of the Mural Paintings of Toyok Cave 20 in Conjunction with the Origin of the Amitayus Visualization Sūtra." *Orientations* 30.4: 38–44.

———. 2002. "Practice of Visualization and the *Visualization Sūtra*: An Examination of Mural Paintings at Toyok, Turfan." *Pacific World: Journal of the Institute of Buddhist Studies*, 3rd ser., 4: 123–152.

———. 2005. "Visionary Repentance and Visionary Ordination in the Brahmā Net Sūtra." In *Going Forth: Visions of Buddhist Vinaya. Essays Presented in Honor of Professor Weinstein*, edited by William Bodiford, 17–39. Honolulu: University of Hawai'i Press.

———. 2009. "The Paths of Śrāvakas and Bodhisattvas in Meditative Practices." *Acta Asiatica* 96: 47–75.

Yuyama, Akira. 1970. *A Bibliography of the Sanskrit Texts of the Saddharmapuṇḍarīkasūtra*. Canberra: Centre of Oriental Studies in association with Australian National University Press.

———. 1989. "The Tathāgata Prabhūtaratna in the Stūpa." In *Amalā Prajñā: Aspects of Buddhist Studies (Professor P. V. Bapat Felicitation Volume)*, edited by N. H. Samtani and H. S. Prasad, 181–185. Delhi: Sri Satguru Publications.

Zin, Monika. 2003. *Ajanta. Handbuch der Malereien: Devotionale und ornamentale Malereien*. 2 vols. Wiesbaden: Harrassowitz Verlag.

The Visuality of Sukhāvatī, Chinese Depictions, and Early Indian Images*

Juhyung Rhi

Questions about the Amitābha Cult and the Images of Sukhāvatī in India

In an article published in 1987, Gregory Schopen points out the limited significance of an image inscription of Amitābha, from Govindnagar in Mathurā, as evidence for the cult of Amitābha in the period of its dedication in the twenty-sixth year of Kaniṣka, which can be equated with around 152 CE in the current consensus on the Kaniṣka era.[1] After carefully examining the contents of the inscription, Schopen states:

> ... the concern with Amitābha which produced our inscription in the 2nd century A.D. was not only, as we have seen, very limited and uninfluential—a minor preoccupation—it also was not a part of a wholly independent movement. It expressed itself half in old and established idioms, and half in not yet finished new formulae that would come to characterize not a cult of Amitābha, but the

* A Korean version of this paper was published in *Bulgyohak rivyu* 佛敎學리뷰 (*Critical Review for Buddhist Studies, Geumgang University*) 26 (2019). The English version was written and submitted earlier than the Korean version.

1. Schopen also refutes the suggestion of several scholars to link the Amitābha image, or its inscription, to the *dhyāni* buddha tradition (1987, 111–116). As he rightly argues, the *dhyāni* buddha system, as it is commonly called, or the system of *pañcabuddha* (five buddhas) of esoteric Buddhism, is obviously a later development in Indian Buddhism, though it might have been the sole context in which Indian Buddhist art specialists had been familiar with Amitābha before the discovery of this damaged Amitābha statue from Govindnagar.

> Mahāyāna as a whole; it dictated the production of a new image, but for—in part at least—an old and established purpose.[2]

Given the conventional nature and phrasing of dedicatory inscriptions, it is true that there is nothing in this inscription that may be distinctively linked to the idea, if not necessarily the cult, of Amitābha as we know it through early scriptures on Amitābha. The formula *anuttaraṃ buddhajñānaṃ* in the inscription, which was identified by Schopen as specific to the Mahāyāna, may tell us only that the image was related to the overall Mahāyāna movement that was slowly evolving during this period. Further, following this inscription, we find virtually no trace of Amitābha in India proper until this buddha appears in an inscription, possibly from the seventh century, which mentions "Lokanātha bearing Amitābha (on the head)" (Majumdar 1940, 394–395, no. 842). This evidence appears to reflect an understanding of Amitābha as related to Lokanātha (Avalokiteśvara) within a system of the four celestial buddhas, prompted by the rise of esotericism in Indian Buddhism, which obviously represents a different phase in the conception of Amitābha. Faced with this discouraging situation, yet nevertheless stimulated by the enormous popularity of the cult of Amitābha in East Asia, scholars have continued to search for its origins in the material and visual evidence of Indian Buddhism.[3] Especially on the basis of the visual features of Sukhāvatī delineated in detail in the textual tradition, which were apparently formulated into a distinctive theme in later East Asian visual traditions, some scholars (Minamoto 1926; Higuchi 1950; Huntington 1980; Iwamatsu 1994; Quagliotti 1996; Harrison and Luczanits 2012) have attempted to identify Amitābha or his buddhafield, Sukhāvatī, in visual representations from the northwest of the subcontinent—if not India proper—which a number of scholars suspect to be the place of origin for early texts on Amitābha (Fujita 1970, 222–258). Nonetheless, we have good reason to question whether the visuality[4] of Sukhāvatī in the early textual tradition was distinctive or cogent enough to prompt visual depictions of it as an idiosyncratic iconographic theme in early Indian Buddhism. Additionally, one may wonder whether the examples proposed by scholars as possible depictions

2. Schopen 1987, 123.

3. I admit that the popularity of Amitābha in the Western Pure Land in early China must also have been related to the prevalent cult of the Queen Mother of the West, which was on the rise during the Han dynasty (220 BCE–206 CE).

4. By *visuality* in this paper I mean "the quality or state of being visual" (following the definition at merriam-webster.com; consulted on October 22, 2018) or "the extent of such quality or state."

of Sukhāvatī should be considered as such. In this paper, I will explore these questions by carefully reading the descriptions of Sukhāvatī in the accounts of Sukhāvatī texts and by examining whether the visual depictions of Sukhāvatī from East Asia can be used as grounds supporting the identification of the alleged Indian examples.

The Visuality of Sukhāvatī in the Textual Accounts

Sukhāvatī is extensively described in both the *Larger Sukhāvatīvyūha* (LSV) and the *Smaller Sukhāvatīvyūha* (SSV). The accounts in the LSV are much longer and more detailed than those in the SSV. Furthermore, we have for the LSV the versions that appear to be earlier than those of the SSV, which are more useful for understanding the early development of ideas about Sukhāvatī. Approximately a third of the LSV is dedicated to the visual features of Sukhāvatī, which suggests the importance of visuality in this text.

Fujita Kōtatsu, who has extensively studied the textual tradition of Amitābha[5] and Sukhāvatī in India, has enumerated the visual features of Sukhāvatī primarily based on the accounts in the *Wuliangshou jing* 無量壽經 (likely translated by Buddhabhadra and Baoyun 寶雲 around 421;[6] Taishō 360) in comparison with six other extant versions (Fujita 2007, 356–360).[7]

5. For the name of Amitābha, an alternative, Amitāyus, also appears prominently in the textual tradition (for a comprehensive list of the texts in Chinese translations referring to Amitābha/Amitāyus and Sukhāvatī, see Fujita 1970, 141–161). Among the major recensions of the LSV and the SSV that will be consulted in this paper, the *Amituo sanyesanfo saloufotan guodu rendao jing* 阿彌陀三耶三佛薩樓佛檀過度人道經 (Taishō 362) uses "Amituo 阿彌陀" (Amitābha) only, and the *Wuliang qingjing pingdengjue jing* 無量清淨平等覺經 (Taishō 361) mainly uses "Wuliang qingjing 無量清淨" (most likely Amitābha). In the Sanskrit and Tibetan recensions, Amitābha is invariably used. However, in the *Wuliangshou jing* 無量壽經 (Taishō 360), the *Wuliangshou rulai hui* 無量壽如來會 of the *Da baoji jing* 大寶積經 (Taishō 310[5]), and the *Dasheng wuliangshou zhuangyan jing* 大乘無量壽莊嚴經 (Taishō 363), "Wuliangshou 無量壽" (Amitāyus) is almost exclusively found. In the Govindnagar inscription discussed by Schopen (1987, 101), it is written as Amitābha. Since it is clear that the two names refer to the same buddha, I will use Amitābha throughout this paper regardless of the original words. For the complex problems surrounding these two names, see Fujita 1970, 287–335, and Fujita 2007, 235–255.

6. For the translator and date, see Fujita 2007, 76–87; cf. Fujita 1970, 62–77.

7. Cf. Fujita 1970, 442–457. Kagawa Takao presented a similar list, also noting differences in seven extant recensions (1993, 192–193). Kagawa's list enumerates the following (I have added a letter after each numeral when Kagawa lists two items under a single numeral, by which he apparently distinguishes diverging accounts between two or three groups among the seven recensions): (1) Amitābha Buddha exists and gives a sermon at present; (2A) Sukhāvatī is made of the seven precious substances; (2B) Sukhāvatī is prosperous; (3) there are no four seasons

Twenty-one items are cited below with notes on their occurrences in the earlier and later groups (marked E and L respectively) of the extant versions of the LSV as well as the *Wuliangshou jing* (marked W), which can be placed between the two groups, though closer to the later group.[8] The earlier group includes the *Amituo sanyesanfo saloufotan guodu rendao jing* 阿彌陀三耶三佛薩樓佛檀過度人道經 (trans. Zhi Qian 支謙 or Lokakṣema during the early third or late second century;[9] Taishō 362) and the *Wuliang qingjing pingdengjue jing* 無量清淨平等覺經 (trans. Bo Yan 帛延 or Dharmarakṣa during the mid-third century or in 373;[10] Taishō 361), whereas the later group includes the *Wuliangshou*

and neither cold nor heat; (4A) there are bathing ponds made of the seven precious substances; (4B) there are rivers; (5) the temperature of the water of the rivers can be adjusted as desired; (6A) inside the lakes there are fragrant flowers; (6B) inside the rivers (or lakes) there are fragrant lotuses; (6C) along the rivers there are sandalwood trees, which emit fragrant scents; (7) the islands in the middle of the rivers are adorned with birds; (8) the flow of water makes exquisite sounds; (9) those who lecture on the sūtra and those who recite the sūtra attain the four fruits; (10) there are no sounds of evil (*akuśala*) or suffering; (11A) bowls made of the seven precious substances are naturally filled with food of all kinds of taste; (11B) living beings in Sukhāvatī do not need to consume food; (12) incense, flowers, and clothing appear as desired; (13A) there is no distinction between celestial beings and humans; (13B) all the living beings miraculously acquire bodies like empty space, bodies that are not surpassed; (14) there are prayers for women to attain rebirth; (15) the lecture hall and the vihāra of Amitābha are made of the seven precious substances; (16) there is no sun, no moon, and no stars; (17) the lifespan of Amitābha is extremely long; (18) fragrant water, flowers, and gems fall from the heavens, and musical instruments from the heavens are played; (19) there is a huge bodhi tree; (20) bodhisattvas in Sukhāvatī are all at the rank of *ekajātipratibaddha*; and (21) there are gardens and groves as well as lotus lakes.

8. The classification of the extant LSV versions into two groups is also based on Fujita 2007, 87–93; cf. Fujita 1970, 167–194. Paul Harrison considers that the twofold division by Fujita "does not convey the full complexity of the differences between the various versions" (1998, 563–564). However, it cannot be denied that there are remarkable correspondences within each of the two groups classified by Fujita.

9. For the translator and date of the *Amituo sanyesanfo saloufotan guodu rendao jing*, see Fujita 2007, 39–46 (cf. Fujita 1970, 51–62); Harrison 1998, 556–557; Harrison, Hartmann, and Matsuda 2002, 179–181; Nattier 2008, 86–87.

10. For the translator and date of the *Wuliang qingjing pingdengjue jing*, see Fujita 2007, 46–56; cf. Fujita 1970, 35–51; Harrison 1998, 556–557 and n18. Regarding the translators of the Chinese versions, Luis Gómez (1996, 130) cites Fujita as the "most respected authority" on this issue and notes that he questions the relative chronology of the Chinese versions in the sequence of "Zhi Qian, Loujiachen [Lokakṣema], Bodhiruchi and Sanghavarman (exact relationship between these two is debatable), and Faxian." Unlike Fujita, he still seemingly considers the *Wuliang qingjing pingdengjue jing* as Lokakṣema's translation and, if combining Bodhiruci and Saṅghavarman is a mistake and the two should be separated, accepts the traditional attribution of the *Wuliangshou jing* to Saṅghavarman, not Bo Yan or Dharmarakṣa as argued by Fujita. Placing Bodhiruci (seventh century) before Saṅghavarman (third century)

rulai hui 無量壽如來會 of the *Da baoji jing* 大寶積經 (*Mahāratnakūṭa-sūtra*) (trans. Bodhiruci in the early eighth century; Taishō 310[5]), the *Dasheng wuliangshou zhuangyan jing* 大乘無量壽莊嚴經 (trans. Faxian 法賢 in the late tenth century; Taishō 363), the extant Sanskrit recension,[11] and the Tibetan translation (trans. Jinamitra, Dānaśīla, and Ye shes sde in the first half of the ninth century; Tōhoku 49, Peking 760[5]).

1. Sukhāvatī is located in the west, one hundred trillion buddhafields away from the Sahā world. (E, W, L)
2. There are neither hells nor existences as animals and asuras. (E, W, L)
3. The land is made from the seven precious substances, like those of the sixth heaven (Paranirmitavaśavartina), and is broad and extensive without limit. (E, W)
4. There are neither mountains, such as Sumeru, nor large or small seas. (E, W, L)
5. There are no four seasons and neither heat nor cold. (E, W)
6. Sukhāvatī is adorned with trees made from the seven precious substances. (E, W, L)
7. When the wind blows, the trees make pleasing sounds. (E, W, L)
8. There is a great bodhi tree. (W, L)
9. When the wind blows, the bodhi tree emits the sound of teaching. (W, L)
10. The most beautiful music in the world systems of the ten directions is heard. (E, W)
11. There are lecture halls, vihāras, palatial halls, and pavilions made from the seven precious substances. (E, W)
12. There are bathing ponds filled with water with eight good qualities. (E, W)
13. The water depth of the ponds is adjusted as desired. (E, W, L)
14. The temperature of the water is adjusted as desired. (W, L)
15. The waves of the water make the sound of diverse teachings. (W, L)
16. All of the desired objects are prepared, as in the sixth heaven. (E, W, L)

must also be a mistake. For the question about the historicity of Saṅghavarman as the third-century translator, see Nattier 2008, 158–159.

11. Fujita (2007, 19–34) enumerates thirty-nine extant Sanskrit manuscript versions. The earliest one, from Afghanistan, seems to date from the sixth to seventh century on paleographical grounds, and two others were copied in the twelfth century, while all of the rest are from the mid-eighteenth century to the first half of the twentieth century. In content, these Sanskrit versions are clearly later than most of the extant Chinese translations.

17. Bowls of the seven precious substances are naturally filled with food with diverse tastes. (E, W)
18. Even though food is ready, there is no need to consume the food. (W, L)
19. Clothing, food, perfumes, and ornaments appear as desired. (W, L)
20. As the wind blows, the ground is carpeted with flowers. (E, W, L)
21. Light emanates from lotus flowers, and from the tip of each of the rays of light myriads of buddhas emerge and preach the Dharma. (W, L)

Items 3, 5, 10, 11, 12, and 17 do not appear in the later group, whereas items 8, 9, 14, 15, 18, 19, and 21 do not appear in the earlier group, though all of the other items are present in both groups and in the *Wuliangshou jing*.

Fujita has done the same for the SSV based on the *Amituo jing* 阿彌陀經 translated by Kumārajīva (dated 402; Taishō 366) in comparison with another Chinese translation by Xuanzang 玄奘 and extant versions in Sanskrit and Tibetan. Fujita's study yields only eight items, mostly identical to those from the LSV, with minor differences, such as references to the sevenfold railings, silk nets, and the birds making the sound of Dharma (Fujita 2007, 360–362; cf. Fujita 1970, 457–462).[12] All four of the extant versions of the SSV are apparently later than the LSV versions of the earlier group (Fujita 2007, 107–128; cf. Fujita 1970, 97–115).

Scholars have explored from early on the origins of Amitābha and Sukhāvatī both inside and outside the Buddhist tradition. Various theories have been put forward, including some occasionally farfetched suggestions (summarized in Fujita 1970, 261–286; Kagawa 1993, 155–171; Fujita 2007, 368–381; see also Karetzky 1997). We may easily expect that not only the idea of a paradisiacal land but also its visual descriptions were naturally affected by, if not directly derived from, other earlier traditions—unless the idea of Sukhāvatī was an age-old legend. Especially noteworthy are its parallels in the Buddhist tradition, which

12. Fujita lists the following eight features from the SSV, which appear in all of the four extant versions: (1) Sukhāvatī is located in the west, one hundred trillion buddhafields away (Fujita's LSV list, no. 1); (2) there are neither hells nor existences as animals and asuras (no. 2); (3) the ground of the land is made of the seven precious substances (no. 3); (4) there are sevenfold railings, silk nets, and rows of trees; (5) there are lotus ponds made of the seven precious substances, which are filled with water endowed with eight good qualities and grand lotuses and aligned with flights of steps and trees of the seven precious substances (no. 12); (6) heavenly music is heard, and flowers fall like rain from the heavens (no. 10); (7) birds make sounds of Dharma, and those who hear the sounds reflect on the Three Jewels; and (8) the wind blows from the trees made of precious substances and makes pleasurable sounds, while those who hear the sounds reflect on the Three Jewels (no. 9).

were probably familiar to many Buddhists of this same period and possibly had a significant impact on the visuality of Sukhāvatī. Kuśāvatī, Uttarakuru, and celestial realms such as Trāyastriṃśa and Paranirmitavaśavartina are prominent in those that show considerable affinities to Sukhāvatī.[13]

Kuśāvatī (Kusāvatī) is mentioned in the *Mahāsudassana-suttanta* of the Dīgha Nikāya (Rhys Davids 1899–1921, 2:199–232) as well as the extant Sanskrit version and their equivalents in Chinese translations. Śākyamuni Buddha suggests that Kuśinagara was formerly Kuśāvatī, the royal city of King Mahāsudarśana (Mahāsudassana), and describes how it looked and how the king made it even more beautiful and pleasant:

> The royal city Kusāvatī, Ānanda, was surrounded by Seven Rows of Palm Trees. . . . And when those rows of palm trees, Ānanda, were shaken by the wind, there arose a sound sweet, and pleasant, and charming, and intoxicating. . . .[14]

A remarkable similarity between this section and the account of Sukhāvatī was early on observed by its translator, T. W. Rhys Davids, who cites for comparison the following passage from the LSV (Sanskrit version) translated by Max Müller:[15]

> And again, O Śāriputra, when those rows of palm trees and strings of bells in that Buddha country are moved by the wind, a sweet and enrapturing sound proceeds from them. . . .[16]

The description of Kuśāvatī in the *Mahāsudassana-suttanta* continues, with remarks on the king's beautification of the city. He created lotus ponds in spaces between the palm trees, which were then furnished with four flights of steps and double railings. Flowers of every season were planted in the lotus ponds, and people bathed in them. A palatial mansion, with elaborate decora-

13. Early on, for a variety of suggestions regarding parallels to Sukhāvatī in Brahmanical and Buddhist traditions, I was indebted to Fujita 2007, although several other works, including those cited by Fujita, such as Rhys Davids 1899–1921, Matsumoto [1904] 2006, and Mochizuki [1932] 1977, later informed my pursuit of this problem.

14. Rhys Davids 1899–1921, 2:201, with minor stylistic modification.

15. Following Rhys Davids's comment, Matsumoto Bunzaburō presented a detailed discussion of the similarities between Kuśāvatī and Sukhāvatī in comparison with textual descriptions in the LSV, the SSV, and various versions of the *Mahāsudassana-suttanta* ([1904] 2006, 254–297).

16. Rhys Davids 1899–1921, 2:201n1, with minor stylistic modification, quoting Müller 1880, 170.

tions, called Dharma was built. A grove of palm trees was made at the entrance to counteract the heat. Two networks of bells, which make sweet and pleasant sounds, were hung in the palace. Seven kinds of instruments produced sweet and pleasant sounds. Though Kuśāvatī is a secular city of a *cakravartin*, its various elements show a remarkable resemblance to Sukhāvatī.

As is well known, Uttarakuru is a continent located in the north of the Sahā world in Buddhist cosmology (Anālayo 2008). However, it was conceived of as a paradisiacal land from an earlier period in the Brahmanical tradition (Kirfel 1920, 108–109), as attested in references to it in the *Aitareyabrāhmaṇa*, the *Rāmāyaṇa*, and the *Mahābhārata* (Bhattacharya 2000). The *Rāmāyaṇa* provides the following descriptions:

> Go, most excellent monkeys, to those illustrious Uttara Kurus, who are liberal, prosperous, perpetually happy, and undecaying. In their country there is neither cold nor heat, nor decrepitude, nor disease, nor grief, nor fear, nor rain, nor sun.[17]

> There are rivers by the thousands there, their waters brimming with beds of golden lotuses, rich with leaves sapphire and emerald. The ponds there sparkle for they are adorned with clusters of red lotuses made of gold, bright as the newly risen sun. The whole region is covered with bright clusters of blue lotuses, with leaves like precious jewels, and filaments shining like gold. There splendid, glittering mountains, golden and bright as fire, full of all kinds of jewels, plunge down to rivers in which shoals of round pearls, precious gems, and gold have arisen. And there trees crowded with birds, always laden with fruit and flowers, whose fragrance, taste, and touch are heavenly, yield every desire. Other magnificent trees bring forth garments of every appearance as well as ornaments glittering with pearls and emeralds, for both women and men. Still others bear fruits to enjoy in every season. Others yield wonderful precious golden beds with bright-colored coverings; while other trees produce garlands that delight the heart, and all sorts of costly drinks and foods. . . . Sounds of singing and musical instruments and loud laughter are constantly heard there, delighting the hearts

17. Bhattacharya 2000, 194. Bhattacharya cites this passage from Muir 1871, 325, adding that it is found in the Gauḍīya (Bengali) and northwestern recensions only (Bhattacharya 2000, 194n11).

of all beings. No one is unhappy there, no one lacks a beloved. These virtues that delight the heart increase day by day.[18]

Such a perception of Uttarakuru probably existed from the earlier period and affected the Buddhist tradition.[19] The *Āṭānāṭiya-suttanta* of the Dīgha Nikāya (Rhys Davids 1899–1921, 3:192–194) describes it as a highly pleasant place for one's life and livelihood. Among its virtues, for instance, its inhabitants possess neither goods nor women, and there is no need to toil to produce food. The *Āṭānāṭiya-suttanta* also provides a brief description of its cities, which mainly concerns trees, birds, and a lake.

The *Lokasthāna-sūtra* of the *Dīrghāgama*, preserved in Chinese translations, contains more detailed descriptions of Uttarakuru. Among the four extant Chinese translations of the *Lokasthāna*, the *Daloutan jing* 大樓炭經 (trans. Fali 法立 and Faju 法炬 in 290–306; Taishō 23) and the *Shiji jing* 世記經 of the *Chang ahan jing* 長阿含經 (trans. Buddhayaśas and Zhu Fonian 竺佛念 in 412–413; Taishō 1[30]) are earlier and thus more relevant to our purpose.[20] The accounts in these two translations (Taishō 23.1.279c25–281a3; Taishō 1[30].1.117c13–119b23)[21] are largely the same but exhibit minor differences, which seem to reflect slightly distinct traditions in transmission. The descriptions of Uttarakuru include bathing ponds and gardens, typical elements in such paradisiacal places. A bathing pond known as Nanda is decorated with four precious substances—gold, silver, beryl (*vaiḍūrya*), and crystal (*sphaṭika*)—and diversely colored lotus flowers whose roots and stems emit sweet nectars, resplendent light, and fragrant scents. The four gardens placed in the four directions of the Nanda pond are embellished with sevenfold railings and various trees made from the four precious substances. The trees exude diverse fragrances and bear flowers and fruits alongside all kinds of clothing,

18. Lefeber 2016, 153–154. Bhattacharya's work (2000, 194–195), which I initially consulted, cites a passage from Shastri 1957, 284–285, remarking: "This passage is more or less common to all recensions" (Bhattacharya 2000, 195n12). I cite here a more recent translation by Lefeber. The divisions of ślokas and their numbers are removed.

19. Affinities between the accounts of Sukhāvatī and Uttarakuru in various texts were first noted by Matsumoto ([1904] 2006, 297–306) and later treated in greater detail, with more sources from the Buddhist side, by Mochizuki ([1932] 1977, 630–637).

20. Two other Chinese translations are the *Qishi jing* 起世經 (by Jñānagupta, 585–600; Taishō 24) and the *Qishi yinben jing* 起世因本經 (by Dharmagupta, 605–616; Taishō 25). Interestingly, there is no equivalent of the *Lokasthāna* in the Dīgha Nikāya.

21. An English translation of the *Shiji jing* (except for chapters 9–12) is found in Howard 1986, 115–156.

jewelry, floral wreaths, and music. On the four sides of Uttarakuru are four pleasantly decorated Anavatapta lakes. As the *Shiji jing* describes them:

> Their waters are pure and without defilements. The lakes are surrounded by walls made of seven precious substances, and there are countless birds singing harmoniously and compassionately to each other.[22]

Unlike Sukhāvatī, Uttarakuru in the *Lokasthāna* possesses both mountains and rivers. Its benefits, such as longevity, a constant supply of food, casual sexual encounters, and the spontaneous disposal of bodily waste, are clearly related to the mundane and material needs of humans. Yet most of the visual features closely resemble those we are already familiar with in the account of Sukhāvatī.

In elucidating the rise and fall of the world system, the *Lokasthāna* also provides detailed descriptions of diverse celestial realms, such as the abode of the four heavenly kings (Cāturmahārājakāyika) and the Trāyastriṃśa heaven. In Cāturmahārājakāyika, the city of each of the four heavenly kings is beautifully decorated with sevenfold ramparts, railings, jewel-strewn curtains, and trees (Taishō 23.1.293b12–294a20; Taishō 1[30].130b1–131a2; cf. Howard 1986, 146–148). Every part of the buildings and trees is made from the seven precious substances. The gardens have pavilions and bathing ponds. All kinds of trees emanate fragrances and bear fruit. Various birds sing harmoniously and compassionately to each other. For Trāyastriṃśa, such accounts are repeated, expanded, and elaborated for various buildings and gardens (Taishō 23.294a28–300a19; Taishō 1[30].131a3–137a23; cf. Howard 1986, 148–155). Buildings and trees are adorned with the seven precious substances. There are also garden pavilions and numerous birds that sing harmoniously, which are described in an identical manner in both Cāturmahārājakāyika and Uttarakuru. The same words are repeated using stock phrases throughout this text.

Similar descriptions for buildings and trees are also found for Māra's celestial palace, located between the Paranirmitavaśavartina and Brahmakāyika heavens,[23] in the *Lokasthāna*: "At the bathing pond all kinds of trees with

22. Howard 1986, 121, with slight modifications; cf. Taishō 1[30].1.117c24–25.

23. The *Daloutan jing* initially recounts that Māra's heaven is located above the Brahmakāyika heaven and, following a long description, says incongruously that the Brahmakāyika heaven is above Māra's heaven (Taishō 23.1.277b11–12, 277c7). The first remark is evidently a mistake by the Chinese translator. The *Shiji jing* does not have a sentence that corresponds to the first remark in the *Daloutan jing*.

variegated leaves, foliage, and fruits exude various fragrant scents, and manifold birds each sing compassionately" (Taishō 23.1.277b12–c7, esp. 277c5–7 for this citation; cf. Taishō 1[30].1.115a29–b2; Howard 1986, 117).[24] In fact, such phrases are not reserved for these heavens or for Uttarakuru but are also found for places imagined to be palatial or highly pleasant for living—such as the cities of *cakravartins* and nāgas, and even the palaces of asuras or King Yama in the hells (Taishō 23.1.281c17–19, 281c24–25, 286a6–11, 287b21–26, 288b9–10, 288b14–28; Taishō 1[30].1.120a2–4, 126b10–12, 127b3–5, 129b8–13).[25]

Such textual descriptions of various paradisiacal or semi-paradisiacal places are essentially no different from the major visual features found in the textual accounts of Sukhāvatī (for example, nos. 3, 6, 7, 11, 12, 16, 17, 19, 20 in Fujita's LSV list cited above). They are obviously common elements, universally employed in describing paradisiacal places in the early Indian textual tradition, including Akṣobhya's buddhafield, Abhirati, from the *Akṣobhyavyūha* (Taishō 313.11.755c9–756c21), and suggest that there is little distinctive or special in the accounts of Sukhāvatī. In the LSV, however, we do find attempts to distinguish Sukhāvatī from other paradisiacal places. For example, the LSV states that Sukhāvatī has "neither hells, nor existences as animals and asuras" (no. 2 in Fujita's list; see Kagawa 1984, 190–191).[26] This may only be a modest—and conceivable—enhancement of the earlier traditions of describing paradisiacal lands, because Sukhāvatī needed to offer more advanced traits as a religious goal in a spiritual ascension. Not incidentally, a similar account on "no three evil modes of existence—that is, no hells, no animals, and no hungry ghosts" is found for Abhirati in the *Akṣobhyavyūha* (Taishō 313.11.755c7–8). The absence of women is also a feature of Sukhāvatī (not present in Fujita's list; see Kagawa 1984, 225),[27] likely to promote the image of Sukhāvatī as free from

24. Howard translates *motian* 摩天 in the *Shiji jing* as "Brahmā *deva*." However, this *motian* must be a scribal error for *motian* 魔天 (Māra) in the Chinese original, because the latter is enumerated after Paranirmitavaśavartin at the last place in the list of twelve kinds of living beings in Kāmadhātu, i.e., at its topmost place before the transition to the Rūpadhātu (Taishō 1[30].1.135c27–136a2). The same reference to twelve kinds of living beings in the Kāmadhātu is also found in the *Daloutan jing* (Taishō 23.1.299a19–24).

25. Anomalously, in corresponding parts in the *Shiji jing*, remarks on lotus ponds are invariably missing.

26. For the comparison of the accounts of Sukhāvatī in various versions of the LSV, I use Kagawa 1984, which presents the complete collation of all of the seven extant versions passage by passage. References to the LSV will be made through Kagawa's work. The remark on "neither hells nor existences as animals and asuras" is also found in the eighth vow of Dharmākara, the previous incarnation of Amitābha (Kagawa 1994, 108–109).

27. The account of "no women" in the two earliest Chinese translations is missing in the

sexual desire.[28] The idea of "neither mountains, nor seas large or small" (no. 4; Kagawa 1984, 200–201), for which a parallel is found in the remark of "the land is level . . . there are no high or low places, and there are no mountains, no hills, and no gorges" in the *Akṣobhyavyūha* (Taishō 313.11.755c9–10), must be another attempt to present Sukhāvatī as an ideal terrestrial place.[29] The two earliest Chinese translations of the LSV even state that there are no rivers, including the Ganges (Kagawa 1984, 201). But, likely given its oddity, this remark vanishes from later versions, which instead report that there are riv-

---

corresponding places for all of the other versions. The remark on the same condition, that in Sukhāvatī there are no women and that those who wish to be reborn there must be first made men, is also found in the second vow of Dharmākara in the two earliest Chinese translations (Kagawa 1984, 138–139). However, again, this remark is absent from all other versions. The *Wuliangshou jing*, however, contains the following passage in the thirty-fifth vow: "May I not gain possession of perfect awakening if, once I have attained buddhahood, any woman in the measureless, inconceivable world systems of all the buddhas in the ten regions of the universe, hears my name in this life and single-mindedly, with joy, with confidence and gladness resolves to attain awakening, and despises her female body, and still, when her present life comes to an end, she is reborn as a woman" (Gómez 1996, 170; cf. Taishō 360.12.268c21–24). The same passage is found in all later versions (Kagawa 1984, 138–139). Perhaps the specification of "no women" for Sukhāvatī may have been deemed too negative and was thus somewhat downplayed in later versions. In a detailed assessment of this problem, Paul Harrison asks, "Could it be that as Pure Land Buddhism became more popular, the *Sukhāvatī-vyūha* was rewritten in such a way as to soften the hardline stance of the early tradition? Can it be that whereas the early text reflects the uncompromising anti-female sentiments of the male ascetics who composed it, the later text breathes a softer, more ambiguous and inclusive spirit to a wider and more diverse audience?" and explores the ramifications of this discrepancy in the earlier tradition for our understanding of early Mahāyāna texts (1998, especially 564–565). Xiao Yue (2013) suggests that the declaration that there are "no women" in the *Amituo sanyesanfo saloufotan guodu rendao jing* may have been inserted by the Chinese translators.

28. This shows a conspicuous contrast to an account about sexual pleasure that appears in the middle of the passage from the *Rāmāyaṇa* I cited above (though I omitted the particular part there): "There are splendid women there distinguished by their beauty and youth. There *gandharvas*, *kinnaras*, perfected beings [*siddhas*], great serpents, and *vidyādharas*, all shining like the sun, make love with these women. All have performed virtuous deeds, all are intent on sexual delight, all live with young women, enjoying pleasures and wealth" (Lefeber 2016, 154).

29. Jan Nattier points out that "[t]he absence of mountains is a regular feature of ideal lands in Indian Buddhist literature, including Amitābha's world, the future worlds of the various *śrāvakas* predicted to Buddhahood in the *Lotus Sūtra*, and even our own Jambudvīpa during the time of the future Buddha Maitreya," and suspects, citing Bruce Lincoln's suggestion, that the motif was not indigenous to India but borrowed from the Iranian religious tradition, where it was possibly associated with "a leveling of social status and the promise of an egalitarian society" (Nattier 2000, 81n23; Lincoln 1983). Perhaps reflecting the external derivation of the motif, in other paradisiacal places mentioned in Indian Buddhist sources, such as those in the celestial realm, mountains and rivers are usually treated as indispensable parts of their terrains, probably given their naturalness.

ers though no seas (Kagawa 1984, 200–201). The remark on "no four seasons" found in the two earliest Chinese translations of the LSV and the *Wuliangshou jing* (Kagawa 1984, 201) is probably an interpolation or an unwarranted change by the translators. Also, the idea of "neither heat nor cold" (Kagawa 1984, 201), which is also mentioned for Abhirati (Taishō 313.11.756a27–28), is nothing new, as we find a parallel attribute for Uttarakuru in the *Shiji jing* version of the *Lokasthāna* (Taishō 1[30].1.118a5, 118c13, 120c26; Howard 1986, 122–124). The miraculous birth (*upapāduka*) in the lotus pond is a theme emphatically stated in the LSV and the SSV (Kagawa 1984, 138–139, 223, 248–253). However, *upapāduka* is not exclusive to Sukhāvatī but universal to birth in all of the celestial realms.[30] The birth on the lotus also has precedents in the Brahmanical tradition (Tsukamoto 1979). But perhaps the embellishment of *upapāduka*, by suggesting that it takes place on a lotus, may have been first adopted in the LSV within the Buddhist tradition and soon followed in other Mahāyāna sūtras (Rhi 1991, 133–134).

Overall the descriptions of Sukhāvatī in the LSV and the SSV follow the earlier accounts of paradisiacal places in both their structure and their many details. Those who composed the LSV acknowledge as much, repeatedly noting that diverse elements in Sukhāvatī are identical to those of the sixth heaven (Paranirmitavaśavartina) or Trāyastriṃśa, or superior to them, but without any specification (for example, Taishō 362.12.301b6, 301c12, 303b26, 303c7, 304c28, 305b21).[31] Descriptions of paradisiacal lands like those of Sukhāvatī must have been familiar to Buddhists of this period, and the visuality of Sukhāvatī was likely perceived as nothing new or special to Sukhāvatī. It is doubtful whether the lengthy, though trite, description of Sukhāvatī in the LSV or the SSV would have been impressive enough to prompt its visual recreation in images. Even if the textual description of Sukhāvatī had been transferred to visual images (though this is purely conjectural), it would have been hard to distinguish such images of Sukhāvatī from visual images of other paradisiacal places, such as Abhirati.

Admittedly, the LSV does touch on the visualization of Sukhāvatī. In the

30. For example, the *Ekottarikāgama* (Taishō 125.2.632a7–19), in defining the four modes of birth, explains that *upapāduka* pertains to all celestial beings, those in the great hells, hungry ghosts, some humans, and some animals.

31. Śākyamuni Buddha's following words in the two earliest Chinese translations succinctly sum up the method taken in the LSV: "All the lecture halls and the residential halls in Amitābha's buddhafield are superior to the residence of the lord of the sixth heaven by a hundred quadrillion times" (Taishō 362.12.308b3–4; cf. Taishō 361.12.290a5–6). Despite this emphatic claim, however, this superiority is only substantiated by an ambiguous reference to a numerical exaggeration.

two earliest Chinese translations, Śākyamuni Buddha instructs Ānanda to face the direction of the sunset in the west and venerate Amitābha Buddha by prostrating and reciting homage to the buddha (*namo amituo sanyesanfotan* 南無阿彌陀三耶三佛檀 or *namo wuliang qingjing pingdengjue* 南無無量清淨平等覺). Then Amitābha, from far away in Sukhāvatī, emits light, and the entire audience in Śākyamuni's assembly is able to view the buddhafield of Amitābha made from the seven precious substances. Afterward Śākyamuni asks Ānanda and Ajita:

> I had told you about Amitābha, all the bodhisattvas and arhats, and the buddhafield made of the seven precious substances [in Sukhāvatī]. Are there any differences [between my words and the vision you just had]?[32]

The question is, of course, answered in the negative. But this is all that is said about the actual visualization of Sukhāvatī, and it is interesting that the visualization is treated so briefly. Moreover, the function of the visualization serves only to confirm Śākyamuni's description of Sukhāvatī rather than to encourage a deliberate visionary experience of the buddhafield.

In the Sanskrit version of the LSV, the description of Sukhāvatī is expanded by the insertion of a seemingly compressed passage drawn originally from a longer description mentioned earlier in the text:

> Do you see, Ajita, the perfect array of ornaments and good qualities in that buddha-field? Above in the open sky there are enchanting parks, luscious forests, charming gardens, and graceful rivers, and lotus ponds scattered with blue water lilies, lotuses, white water lilies, and white lotuses, all made of many kinds of jewels. Below, from the earth to the abode of the Akaniṣṭha deities, the sky is covered with flowers, ornamented with wreaths of flowers, filled with rows of many bejeweled columns, frequented by flocks of all kinds of birds created by the Tathāgata. Do you see this?[33]

This passage, which is found in neither the two earliest Chinese translations nor the *Wuliangshou jing* or the *Wuliangshou rulai hui* of the *Mahāratnakūṭa-sūtra* but in the *Dasheng wuliangshou zhuangyan jing* of the late tenth cen-

32. Taishō 362.12.316c28–317a1; cf. Taishō 361.11.299a1–2. This passage is not found in other versions of the LSV, including the *Wuliangshou jing*.

33. Gómez's translation of the Sanskrit version (1996, 103).

tury (Taishō 363.12.325b5–12), obviously reflects a later development. The visualization of Sukhāvatī is evidently not presented here as a religious practice to be followed. It exhibits little of the importance we might think necessary for a visual representation. Furthermore, the account of the visualization of Sukhāvatī at the end of the two earliest Chinese translations of the LSV is accompanied by a passage about diverse living beings saved from agonies and hardships by the radiating light emanating from Amitābha (Taishō 362.12.316c11–28; Taishō 361.11.298c14–29), which seems to reflect part of the intention of including this passage, though it disappears in later versions, perhaps with a shift in emphasis.

The visualization of Amitābha or Sukhāvatī is also recounted in the explanation of rebirth for the three types of believers in the LSV (Kagawa 1984, 248–253). In the two earliest Chinese translations, Śākyamuni says that those of the superior and intermediate types might experience the vision of Amitābha surrounded by bodhisattvas and arhats in a dream, though no further description is provided. What is more interesting is his explanation concerning those who are less competent, the intermediate and inferior types. If they repent for their laziness, they might be reborn in Sukhāvatī. But they cannot directly head there. They must first find a city made of the seven precious substances on the way and be reborn there (through *upapāduka* on the lotus). The city is beautifully adorned with bathing ponds, trees, and sounds and is stocked with a variety of foods. The highest enjoyments are provided in the city, in a way comparable to Trāyastriṃśa. However, due to their foundering sincerity and faith, they may only reach Sukhāvatī after they have resided there for five hundred lives. No description of Sukhāvatī follows, not to mention words extolling the superiority of Sukhāvatī. Intriguingly, this pleasurable city is mentioned only as an intermediate expediency, not as a final destination. The visualization of Sukhāvatī does not play a significant role in this passage. Interestingly enough, even this account disappears in later versions of the LSV, beginning with the *Wuliangshou jing*, possibly because this description of the interim place so closely resembles Sukhāvatī that it undermines the visual superiority of Sukhāvatī, which may have been taken more seriously during a later period.

East Asian Depictions of Sukhāvatī and Their Relevance to Indian Images

It has been commonly assumed that visual elements such as the exuberant palatial mansions, pleasurable lotus ponds, and splendid lotus seats are distinctive features of depictions of Sukhāvatī. But our perception has clearly been shaped in large part by both the prevalence of such visual elements in depictions of Sukhāvatī in East Asia and the flourishing of the theme itself. For instance, a mural in Mogao Cave 220 of Dunhuang dated 642 shows a spectacular depiction of Sukhāvatī with diverse visual elements mentioned above as well as Avalokiteśvara and Mahāsthāmaprāpta, two principal attendant bodhisattvas of Amitābha, living beings reborn on lotuses, and musicians and dancers (plate 24). In another example, a mural in Mogao Cave 332 dated 698, we find a somewhat different scene: there are no architectural structures, such as pavilions and railings, but the entire composition is occupied by water, in which Amitābha sits on a lotus flanked by two standing bodhisattvas and surrounded by a number of seated figures on lotuses (plate 25). We may also recall prominent examples from Japan, though lacking large-scale settings, such as an Amitābha triad in the Tachibana miniature shrine (plate 26) and the mural of an Amitābha triad inside the golden hall of Hōryūji (plate 27). The acquaintance with such examples has encouraged scholars to attempt to identify their origin on the Indian subcontinent, especially in its northwestern corner in Gandhāra (Minamoto 1926; Higuchi 1950). A stele from Muhammad Nari in Lahore Museum (plate 28), which was once identified as a representation of the Great Miracle at Śrāvastī, has drawn considerable attention ever since some scholars connected it to Sukhāvatī in recent years (Huntington 1980; Quagliotti 1996).[34] The scene on the stele shows some resemblance to the mural from Mogao Cave 332. The following discussion will examine the relevance of East Asian depictions of Amitābha and Sukhāvatī to early Indian Buddhist art, focusing on the lotus pond and the lotus seat and in relation to textual descriptions.

The lotus pond and the lotus seat for Amitābha are often thought of as hallmarks of the visual depiction of Sukhāvatī. As we have seen, however, the lotus pond was not distinctive or exclusive to Sukhāvatī but a common motif generically employed in imagining a paradisiacal land in early Indian religious traditions. In early Indian Buddhist art, representations of the lotus pond are extremely rare outside the ordinary narrative context, except for steles from Gandhāra of a preaching buddha with two bodhisattvas or in the middle of a multitude of figures who are possibly bodhisattvas. The best-known example is the Muhammad Nari stele (plate 28), in which a buddha is seated on a gigan-

34. John Huntington does not explicitly point out the resemblance of the Muhammad Nari stele to East Asian depictions of Sukhāvatī but focuses more on a comparison with textual descriptions of Sukhāvatī from the LSV, which I have assessed critically elsewhere (Rhi 1991, 130–136; Rhi 2003, 171–174). However, he is fully aware of Amitābha images from East Asia, such as those from Dunhuang and Hōryūji (Huntington 1980, 656–657, 663–664). Without knowledge of East Asian images, I suspect, no scholar would have linked the stele to Amitābha.

tic lotus standing in the water. In the middle of rolling waves, lotuses support smaller figures, fish swim, and nāgas—clearly not humans reborn—apparently venerate the buddha above. The water might be a lotus pond, but even if so, one wonders whether it is the same sort of lotus pond that is supposed to be found in Sukhāvatī, which are invariably for bathing, like those mentioned in other paradisiacal places. In most of the depictions of Sukhāvatī that scholars have been able to securely identify, which were found later in China (from the late sixth century onward), the lotus ponds are represented as domestic structures furnished with railings and bridges. Further, strictly speaking, the lotus ponds of Sukhāvatī cannot have animals such as nāgas or fish, as stated in the LSV. The water in the Muhammad Nari stele is reminiscent, instead, of a larger lotus pond or lake like those mentioned in other contexts in the Buddhist textual tradition. For example, the Anavatapta lake is often referred to as a setting for the sermon of Śākyamuni Buddha in Buddhist scriptures. In the *Ekottarikāgama*, Śākyamuni stays at the Anavatapta lake and, taking a seat on a golden lotus whose stem is made of the seven precious substances, preaches to the monks, who also sit on lotuses (Taishō 125.2.708c11–709a4). In the *Bhaiṣajyavastu* of the *Mūlasarvāstivāda-vinaya*, Śākyamuni moves to the Anavatapta lake with 499 monks, and all sit on a thousand splendid lotuses created by the nāgas Nanda and Upananda for Śākyamuni's sermon on their previous lives (Taishō 1448.24.76c–77a).[35] The presence of nāgas or fish in the Anavatapta lake of course presents no problem. These two examples describe Śākyamuni addressing monks, unlike the Muhammad Nari stele, and I have no intention to link them directly to visual examples. But the water in the Muhammad Nari stele looks more like an aquatic place outside a domestic setting. One may even wonder whether this represents a pond or a lake. I previously suggested that it might connote something greater, such as an ocean as a primordial basis for the emergence of a buddha (Rhi 2013, 8–10).

Chinese depictions of Sukhāvatī often feature a large, eye-catching lotus seat for Amitābha. However, in the LSV and the SSV, the reference to the lotus as a seat for Amitābha is almost negligible. Surprisingly, only one reference to it exists in each of the two earliest Chinese translations among various versions of the LSV, while there are none in the SSV:

35. The number of monks accompanying the Buddha is given as 499 and 999 in two different references in this account (Taishō 1448.24.76c13, 77a1). The latter appears to be a typographical error in the Koryŏ edition on which the Taishō was based. I would like to thank Shayne Clarke for pointing this out.

> Amitābha Buddha and all the bodhisattvas and arhats, having finished bathing [in the ponds], take seats on a large lotus. Then, tumultuous winds blow naturally from the four directions.[36]

This short remark appears following the account of the depth of water being adjusted according to one's desire when bathing and continues to an account of the winds. It is mentioned in passing, apparently without any particular religious import. Given our often tacit presumptions about its prominence in the text, the lotus seat is surprisingly treated in the two earliest Chinese translations of the LSV in an almost negligible manner. Moreover, even this remark disappears in all later versions of the LSV. This means that the lotus seat for Amitābha was not a serious consideration in the textual tradition of the LSV.

In the *Wuliangshou jing* and other later versions, we find instead the following passage:

> Moreover, many jewel lotuses fill this world system. Each jewel blossom has a hundred thousand million petals. The radiant light emanating from their petals is of countless different colors. . . . From every flower issue thirty-six hundred thousand million rays of light. From each one of these rays issue thirty-six hundred thousand million buddhas. Their bodies have the color of purple gold [refined gold] and in them the major marks and minor signs that adorn buddhas and bodhisattvas are rare and extraordinary. Moreover, each one of those buddhas emits hundreds of thousands of rays of light that spread out everywhere in the ten quarters and proclaim the subtle and sublime Dharma. In this way, each of these buddhas firmly establishes innumerable living beings in the Buddha's True Way.[37]

Obviously, this depiction has nothing to do with the idea of the lotus seat for Amitābha, but it incorporates the notion of myriad buddhas miraculously appearing on lotuses or rays of light for teaching living beings, accounts that are found in diverse forms in numerous textual accounts of both Mahāyāna and non-Mahāyāna.[38]

36. Taishō 362.12.305c3–4; cf. Taishō 361.12.285b16–18.

37. Gómez 1996, 186; cf. Taishō 360.12.272a22–b2; Kagawa 1984, 199–200. This passage is found in all of the later versions, except for the tenth-century Chinese translation, *Dasheng wuliangshou zhuangyan jing* (Taishō 363).

38. This type of miraculous feat is often performed by a buddha (usually Śākyamuni) or, to a lesser extent, by a divine bodhisattva (such as Mañjuśrī and Samantabhadra) and commonly

It is evident that, in the early textual tradition concerning Sukhāvatī, neither the lotus pond nor the lotus seat for Amitābha were given great importance. Moreover, they were certainly not given enough importance to be considered salient motifs in visual depiction, even if there had been an urge for the visual image of Sukhāvatī—though I remain skeptical about this presupposition as well. This is also attested in early representations of Amitābha in Chinese Buddhism. The earliest extant example of Amitābha in Chinese Buddhist art is a triad of painted clay images of Amitābha with Avalokiteśvara and Mahāsthāmaprāpta, all inscribed with their names, in Cave 169 of Binglingsi 炳靈寺 (plate 29; ZSYB, 204, no. 21).[39] This triad is dated to the Western Qin (385–431), possibly around 420, if it is contemporaneous with an inscription on the adjoining rock face (ZSYB, 205, no. 28, 255). Amitābha is seated at the center meditating on a lotus throne. The lotus seat is not in blossom but is presented in a stylized form with inverted petals, a common convention in early Chinese Buddhist images. During this period and afterward, this type of seat for buddhas or bodhisattvas was regularly used irrespective of their

takes the form of myriads of buddhas appearing in the rays of light emanating from the buddha/bodhisattva or on lotuses miraculously created by the buddha/bodhisattva. It appears prominently in Mahāyāna sūtras but not in those from the earliest phase. It seems to have become conspicuous in texts that may date from the fourth century or afterward, such as the *Avataṃsaka-sūtra* or the *Prajñāpāramitā-sūtra* (Xuanzang's translation, Taishō 220). See, for example, Taishō 278.9.407b14–c5; Taishō 220.5.2a29–b9. A miracle of essentially the same nature is found in the account of Śākyamuni Buddha performing the great miracle at Śrāvastī told in such apparently non-Mahāyāna texts as the *Mūlasarvāstivāda-vinaya* and the *Divyāvadāna* as well as the *Xianyu jing* 賢愚經 (Taishō 202) and the *Fobenxing jing* 佛本行經 (Taishō 193), although the Indian origin of the latter two texts is questionable (Rhi 1991, 249, 268, 282–283, 303–305). Another text of interest in this regard is the *Guan fosanmeihai jing* 觀佛三昧海經, which includes a number of passages describing numerous buddhas placed in virtually every ray of light emanating from various parts of the buddha (for example, Taishō 643.15.663–693). Intriguingly, many of these texts, including the sixty-fascicle edition of the Chinese *Avataṃsaka* and the *Guan fosanmeihai jing*, are translations by Buddhabhadra, who also translated the *Wuliangshou jing*. Unless the account of the miraculous occurrence in the *Wuliangshou jing* is an interpolation, such accounts garnered popular attention in the period of Buddhabhadra. In any case, it reflects a later development in the description of the LSV.

39. The inscriptions are written as *Wuliangshou fo* 无量壽佛 (Amitāyus Buddha), *Guanshiyin pusa* 觀世音菩薩 (Avalokiteśvara [or Avalokitasvara] bodhisattva), and *Dedashizhi pusa* 得大勢志菩薩 (Mahāsthāmaprāpta bodhisattva) (ZSYB, 255, Cave 169, no. 6). Another inscription of *Wuliangshou fo* is found for a seated buddha painted on the eastern side of the Amitābha triad just mentioned. Because the buddha is placed between two groups of figures on each side, one of which is identified in inscriptions as Vimalakīrti, the buddha with the two groups may have originally been derived from a scene based on the *Vimalakīrtinirdeśa-sūtra*, and the inscription of *Wuliangshou fo* is most likely a mistake (ZSYB, plates 36, 37; 205, no. 37; 257, Cave 169, no. 11).

names, and without the inscription it would have been impossible to identify this image as Amitābha. Two other early examples, a small gilt-bronze statuette with the inscribed date of 464 (Matsubara 1995, plate 32) and a stone statue with the inscribed date of 476, show Amitābha seated in the meditation pose (Matsubara 1995, plates 51, 52). For the stone statue, the pedestal has been damaged, but the gilt-bronze statuette sits on a so-called Meru-type throne, which features a series of horizontally piled slabs that diminish in size before increasing in size downward. In any case, the two are iconographically indistinguishable from other buddhas bearing different names, most of whom are Śākyamuni. Another seated Amitābha in stone, dated 483 from Sichuan, features a throne covered with robes, though it is apparently not a lotus (plate 30; Matsubara 1995, text vol., 250–251, no. 6). The right hand is raised in *abhaya-mudrā*, while the left hand is lowered with the palm revealed. In the murals of Mogao Cave 285 of Dunhuang dated 539, three buddhas are identified as Amitābha in the accompanying inscriptions (plate 31; ZSDM 1:215–217 and plates 122–124, 139). All are identical in form, seated on square pedestals and displaying in the right hand a gesture resembling the so-called *vitarka-mudrā* while the left hand is lowered. In the row of eight buddhas painted on the western wall that includes two Amitābha Buddhas, two buddhas other than Amitābha are seated on lotuses. One of them is Kāśyapa, one of the seven buddhas of the past and the predecessor of Śākyamuni (plate 32). The other, though not inscribed, is part of a pair consisting of Śākyamuni and Prabhūtaratna based on the *Saddharmapuṇḍarīka-sūtra*. Early Chinese examples clearly indicate that the lotus was not perceived as a distinctive seat for Amitābha in this early period in China. It is only in the late sixth century that we find Amitābha seated on a lotus blossom—in the depiction of Sukhāvatī on a larger scale, as seen in a relief from the Southern Xiangtangshan 南響堂山 caves in the National Museum of Asian Art, Smithsonian (plate 34). It should also be noted that in this period there was no practice of iconographically distinguishing buddhas; instead, buddhas with different names, including Amitābha, shared buddha image types (Rhi 2011).

The earliest known example of the depiction of Sukhāvatī in China may be a fragment from a stele found at Wanfosi 萬佛寺 in Chengdu, Sichuan, which is preserved only in a rubbing (Liu and Liu 1958, plate 31). A late nineteenth-century record (*Tianrangge biji* 天壤閣笔記 cited in Liu and Liu 1958, 3) shows that the stele had an inscribed date from the reign of Yuanjia 元嘉 of Song (424–452). But the credibility of this early date has been questioned, and the stele may be from as much as a century later (Wong 1998–1999, 57–60). Only a small portion of the scene of Sukhāvatī remains from the upper part of the fragment, showing a lotus pond with a bridge crossing over it. There seems to be no tie between this scene and the scene in the lower part of the fragment, which has been variously identified as an illustration of *jātaka*s, *avadāna*s, or the chapter on Avalokiteśvara of the *Saddharmapuṇḍarīka* (Kim 2003, 8–10). Although it would be difficult to assert that this fragmentary scene portrays Sukhāvatī, a similar scene appears on the back of another stele also from Wanfosi, which represents two bodhisattvas on the obverse (plate 33; Wong 1998–1999, fig. 2A). It has no inscribed date but is thought to have originated in the second quarter or the middle of the sixth century (Wong 1998–1999, 57; Kim 2003, 6n9). In a symmetrical composition, two diagonal lines run downward to the lower corners in each side from the upper center, where what appears to be a buddha is seated. He is on neither a lotus seat nor a pond. Along the diagonal lines are rows of trees and seated figures. The compound is surrounded by lotus ponds with tiny figures who may have been reborn or who might be swimming.[40] The murals of Cave 127 of Maijishan 麥積山 in Tianshui dated to the Western Wei (535–556) depict a similar scene, though this seems to lack lotus ponds (ZSTM, 239 and plate 161). In these examples, all dated to the first half of the sixth century, we might witness the beginning of the depiction of Sukhāvatī in China. Moreover, the lotus pond emerges as a prominent motif in these scenes, probably for the first time in Buddhist art. Nonetheless, these examples in no way resemble what has been suggested as depictions of Sukhāvatī from Gandhāra, such as the Muhammad Nari stele.

The depiction of Sukhāvatī in China advances to a more elaborate and clearly distinguishable form during the late sixth century, as we can see in a relief from the Southern Xiangtangshan caves (plate 34).[41] It reaches a fully developed stage in the Dunhuang murals of the seventh century. Possibly the earliest extant example, a mural in Mogao Cave 220 dated 642 (plate 24), depicts a lotus seat in full blossom for Amitābha with exuberantly adorned lotus ponds along with various other elements, such as monumental pavilions and beautifully embellished trees. The inclusion of various elaborate features of Sukhāvatī seems to be a product of a meticulous reading of the textual accounts of the LSV and the SSV as well as the *Guan wuliangshou jing* 觀無量壽經 (Tō 1980, 14–21; Katsuki 1992; Okada 2000, 184–185). The buddha in the center shows *dharmacakra-mudrā* in a manner similar to that of the famous

40. Dorothy Wong considers the scenes in the upper portions of the two steles from Wanfosi as depictions of Sukhāvatī (1998–1999). However, Yoshimura Rei suggests that they represent a purified buddhafield mentioned in the *Saddharmapuṇḍarīka* along with the lower-portion scenes based on the same sūtra (1985, 23–24).

41. A mural in Mogao Cave 393 dated to the Sui period (581–618) is also identified as a depiction of Sukhāvatī by some scholars (Li 1984, 165–166, fig. 8; Katsuki 1992, 69).

buddha of the First Sermon from Sārnāth (Huntington 1985, fig. 10.20). It is worth noting that *dharmacakra-mudrās* of this type were never employed in buddha images identified as Amitābha before this time. Beginning with the mural in Mogao Cave 220, we find a number of depictions of Sukhāvatī at Dunhuang in this typical composition (for a list of examples in Dunhuang murals, see Katsuki 1992, 73). From the late seventh century, the depiction of Sukhāvatī was further embellished with the addition of smaller subsidiary scenes, such as the sixteen visualizations, based on the *Guan wuliangshou jing*, on each side and at the bottom of the central scene, thus establishing the so-called *Guan jing bianxiang* 觀經變相 (*Visualization Sūtra bianxiang*) (Kawahara 1968; see for example ZSDM 3: plates 103, 136).[42]

The mural in Mogao Cave 332 dated 698 (plate 25), however, differs significantly from the usual depictions of Sukhāvatī at Dunhuang. There are neither palatial halls, pavilions, nor architecturally embellished lotus ponds. A buddha showing *dharmacakra-mudrā* is seated under a canopy and on a large lotus in full bloom on the water with two standing bodhisattvas and numerous seated figures, all on lotuses. Interestingly, the water is bordered, in its upper edges, by mountain ridges.[43] This is not an ordinary depiction of Sukhāvatī but a theme known as "Amitābha and fifty bodhisattvas" of Sukhāvatī (ZSDM 3:231, no. 94; Katsuki 1994; Okada 2000, 162).[44] The "Amitābha and fifty bodhisattvas" is one of the themes categorized as *ruixiang* 瑞像 (literally an "auspicious image") in Chinese Buddhism, which denotes images of miraculous origin, often claimed to be from India, in sculptural or pictorial form, or their representations. According to two Chinese sources, the *Ji shenzhou sanbao gantong lu* 集神州三寶感通錄 (dated 664; Taishō 2106.52.421a17–b3) and the *Fayuan zhulin* 法苑珠林 (dated 668; Taishō 2122.53.401a17–b4), a bodhisattva at Kukkuṭārāma in Magadha who was proficient in five supernatural powers prayed for the advent of Amitābha in the Sahā world—in the time of the absence of the buddha image—and obtained images of Amitābha and

42. The Xiaonanhai 小南海 middle cave (dated 550), near Anyang, Henan, has inscribed depictions in relief carvings of the rebirths of believers in nine grades, apparently based on the *Guan wuliangshou jing* (Katsuki 1996). The central icon is a buddha triad, in which all three of the images, including the buddha, are standing rather than seated. It is thus evident that the rebirths in nine grades are not presented as part of a usual depiction of Sukhāvatī. However, this shows that the *Guan wuliangshou jing* was being incorporated into visual images already in this period.

43. As to this anomaly, Hida Romi suggests that this theme may represent the descent of Amitābha and his retinue to the Sahā world (Hida 1997; cf. Okada 2000, 200n24).

44. Naitō Tōichirō (1931, 121–132) is said to have first identified the Mogao Cave 332 mural as the theme of "Amitābha and fifty bodhisattvas" on the basis of the account in the *Ji shenzhou sanbao gantong lu* (Hida 1997, 98).

fifty bodhisattvas sent by Amitābha himself, the pictorial representations of which he disseminated. When Buddhism reached China during the reign of Emperor Ming (57–75) of the Han dynasty, a copy was transmitted but soon forgotten. During the reign of Emperor Wen (581–604) of the Sui dynasty, however, a painting on the same theme was discovered by the monk Mingxian 明憲, who distributed copies of it all over the country. This story is also recorded in an inscription dated to 634 for a sculpted scene in a cave on Mount Wolong 臥龍 in Zitong 梓潼, Sichuan, which appears to be identical in composition to the Mogao Cave 332 mural and thus confirms the identity of the latter (Katsuki 1994; Okada 2000, 166–173). This theme was particularly popular in the Sichuan area, where a number of examples still exist, and spread to other areas in China and other parts of East Asia (Okada 2000; Ch'oe 2004). In Japan, the famous mural of Amitābha (no. 6) in Hōryūji has been known as a depiction of this theme (plate 27). The Tachibana-shrine Amitābha triad (plate 26) might also have been inspired by this theme from China.[45]

We cannot, of course, assume that the story recorded in the two Chinese sources has a historical basis, and it was likely contrived to justify the creation of a new iconographic type—possibly near the end of the sixth or the early seventh century, as Mingxian is identified as a monk from the Sui dynasty (581–618) (cf. Okada 2000, 12). However, the iconographic type apparently incorporates a number of motifs from India, such as the buddha in *dharmacakra-mudrā*, the lotus throne, the water, and multiple figures on lotuses. Considering that the phase of Buddhist art in Gandhāra in which such objects as the Muhammad Nari stele were made—which cannot be later than the fourth century in my assessment—is separated from the period of Chinese invention of this type by more than two centuries, it seems most likely that the inspiration came from western Deccan or the middle Gangetic valley, where Buddhist art was still flourishing during the sixth century. For instance, lotus thrones appear prominently in Buddhist images from Sārnāth and in relief carvings in western Deccan caves, such as Aurangabad and Kānherī (plate 35).[46] In the latter, the buddha is often surrounded by a multitude of figures in celestial attire, apparently placed on water.

This brief survey of early depictions of Amitābha and Sukhāvatī in China

45. Wong suggests that the two Japanese examples show the parallel development with the depiction of Amitābha in Mogao Cave 332, rather than the former being derivations of the latter (2008, esp. 162).

46. Hida draws attention to the similarity of the Mogao Cave 332 mural to the depiction of the Great Miracle at Śrāvastī on a stele from Sārnāth (Hida 1997, 99 and fig. 10; or, for the stele, see Williams 1975, fig. 8).

tells us two important things, which may also cast light on our endeavor to explore the situation in Indian Buddhism. First, although images of Amitābha were made in small numbers in pictorial or sculptural form from as early as the fifth century in China, they usually took the form of a single image or belonged within a triad but were not combined with the depiction of Sukhāvatī as a setting. According to the material evidence, an interest in the visuality of Sukhāvatī only appears as early as the sixth century and gradually becomes prominent in the latter half of that century. Huiyuan 慧遠 of Lushan 廬山 (334–416), who is thought to have initiated devotional interest in Amitābha in Chinese Buddhism, apparently paid little attention to the visuality of Sukhāvatī but instead focused on the samādhi practice of reciting the name of Amitābha based on the *Pratyutpannasamādhi-sūtra*. It was shortly after the death of Huiyuan that the two translations of the Sukhāvatī sūtras that had an enormous influence on the Amitābha cult later in East Asia first appeared: the *Wuliangshou jing* (probably translated by Buddhabhadra and Baoyun around 421, certainly not by Saṅghavarman in 252 according to traditional attribution) and the *Guan wuliangshou jing* (traditionally known as a translation by Kālayaśas in 424–442 and often called *Guan jing* in East Asian scholarship).[47] The *Guan jing* 觀經, which was most likely created outside India, especially reflects a growing enthusiasm for the visuality of Amitābha and Sukhāvatī in presenting detailed codification of the visual features of the Amitābha triad and Sukhāvatī together with a prescription for practicing their visualization. Probably with the supposed translation (or composition) of the *Guan jing*, interest in the visuality of Sukhāvatī was slowly on the rise and began to find its expression in images during the sixth century. Second, during the early phase of imagery for Amitābha, in the fifth and sixth centuries, no fixed iconographic form existed, and Amitābha was represented in a manner indistinguishable from other buddhas. As we have seen, Amitābha is unrecognizable without a clear inscription. Only in the latter half of the sixth century was a specific iconography for the depiction of Sukhāvatī explored and devised, before it reached an established form in the early seventh century.

47. Fujita observes: "Because Huiyuan, seeking friendly relationship with Kumārajīva, repeated questions and answers in letters to him, he must have known the *Amituo jing* [translation of the SSV by Kumārajīva], but there is no trace that he relied on the sūtra in [the formation of] his thought. Some twenty years after the *Amituo jing* came out, the current *Wuliangshou jing* was translated, and the *Guan wuliangshou jing* appeared. All these took place after the passing of Huiyuan. He elucidated on the samādhi of reciting [Amitābha] Buddha without any relationship to the three major sūtras of Pure Land Buddhism." He continues with a remark that Huiyuan left little direct impact on the development of Pure Land Buddhism in China until he was revived as the founder of one of its lineages during the tenth century (2007, 565–566).

This development is clearly related to Chinese Buddhists' avid reading and careful examination of textual accounts of Sukhāvatī in the period, including those of the *Guan jing*. After all, for the Chinese, Buddhist texts supposedly from India were the only authoritative sources for information regarding sacred entities, unlike in Indian Buddhism, where diverse textual accounts were being created, almost in competition, during the early centuries of the Common Era.[48] Along with this process, a new iconographic type transmitted from India was sometimes interpreted anew or labeled with the creation of a new legend according to the contemporary needs of Buddhists, as we can see in the invention of the theme of "Amitābha and fifty bodhisattvas."

It seems obvious that there is no direct tie between these Chinese examples and the images that have been considered by some scholars as their precedents in India, especially in Gandhāra. The examples we have seen from China were most likely invented in China as the depiction of Sukhāvatī, but they were not simple adoptions of iconographic types transmitted with fixed identities. They do not support the popular anticipation that there must already have been images of Amitābha or Sukhāvatī. According to our current evidence, the depiction of Sukhāvatī, if not the image of Amitābha, in all likelihood does not appear to have existed in Indian Buddhism before this distinctive iconographic type was developed in China.

Amitābha Buddha and Indian Buddhism

Moving one step further, we might raise a question about the nature of the cult of Amitābha in early Indian Buddhism. For instance, an image inscription from Govindnagar in Mathurā is our lone unequivocal material evidence from Indian Buddhism for Amitābha from the early centuries of the Common Era; no other epigraphical, sculptural nor pictorial evidence exists until the seventh century in India proper. In this regard, an inscription on a small triad stele from Gandhāra, which supposedly contains the names Amitābha and Avalokiteśvara (Brough 1982), also deserves special attention. Scholars have debated the reading of this inscription and whether or not it truly contains either of those names or only one of them (Avalokiteśvara) (Salomon and

48. I admit that besides the translated texts, the oral tradition must also have played an important role, especially in the early period. However, by the latter half of the sixth century, when the iconography of Amitābha and Sukhāvatī was being formulated, the textual accounts established through translated scriptures must have been the most important source for such a task. I am grateful to Daniel Boucher for reminding me of this problem.

Schopen 2002).[49] Even if one were to accept the reading of Amitābha in this inscription, I suspect that this name was given, more or less arbitrarily, to an image of a type that was commonly used for any buddha, as this was a prevalent practice in early Buddhist art in both India and in China, of which we saw examples above (Rhi 2011).

Besides these two inscriptions, five examples referring to Amitābha can be found among numerous inscriptions carved on rocks in the Chilas-Thalpan area in northern Pakistan. They are all written in Brāhmī and datable to the fifth century or later (Tsukamoto 1996–2003, 3: Chilas 129, 135, Thalpan 43, 44, 53). Because of the relative proximity of the location, they might have a distant relationship to early Gandhāran Buddhism.[50] All contain short phrases offering homage in the form of "*namo Amitābhāya* (*Amitāyuto*)." Two are dedicated to Amitābha alone. However, the three others mention Amitābha along with other buddhas. In the inscription Chilas 135, homage is simultaneously paid to Ratnaśikhin, Śākyamuni, and Akṣobhya. The set of these four buddhas and its format "*namo* . . . " is analogous to what we find in the *Suvarṇaprabhāsa-sūtra*, which refers to Akṣobhya (east), Ratnaketu (south), Amitāyus/Amitābha (west), and Dundubhisvara (north) (Bagchi 1967, 4, 63; Taishō 665.16.404c15–17, 423c7–9, 439b26–28; cf. Tsukamoto 1996–2003, 3:142). In the *Suvarṇaprabhāsa*, the buddha in the south is Ratnaketu, not Ratnaśikhin, but the two are similar; the buddha in the north is Dundubhisvara, not Śākyamuni. Despite these differences, the two sets are similar in composition and context. In each of the two other inscriptions, Amitābha is mentioned alongside two other buddhas: Śikhin and (Śa)tapatmanayanacūḍāpratihatavelāṃburaśmirāja in Thalpan 43 and Saṃpuṣpitasālarāja and Samantaraśmivyudgataśrīkṛpana in Thalpan 53. In these inscriptions, Amitābha is clearly not presented as an object of individual worship but is

49. The inscription of the stele, which is currently in the John and Mable Ringling Museum of Art in Sarasota, Florida, was read by John Brough (1982, 66) as "*budhamitrasa olo'iśpare danamukhe budhamitrasa amridaha*. . ." meaning "The Avalokeśvara of Buddhamitra, a sacred gift, the Amṛtābha of Buddhamitra. . ." and by Salomon and Schopen (2002, 27) as "*dhamitrasa oloiśpare danamukhe budhamitrasa amridae* ///" with a differing translation, "Gift of Dhamitra [*sic*] at Oloiśpara [?], for the immortality [i.e. *nirvāṇa*] of Buddhamitra. . . ," though Salomon does not entirely rule out the possibility that it still contains at least "Avalokiteśvara" (personal communication with Salomon). More recently, Karashima Seishi presented a view that agrees with the revised reading by Salomon and Schopen but supports a translation close to Brough's (Karashima 2017).

50. I call the relationship "distant" because I believe that by this period—or from the fifth century on—Gandhāra and its adjacent areas, especially the northern region in Swāt and Gilgit, were in a phase clearly distinguishable from the earlier one in various cultural and religious aspects that include visual styles.

one of many buddhas to be venerated together. In the Chilas-Thalpan area, there are altogether twenty-two inscriptions of this format referring to fifteen buddhas (Tsukamoto 1996–2003, 3: Chilas 121, 130–132, 134, Thalpan 35, 45–51, 54, 56–58), of which Amitābha (or Amitāyus) is merely one. It is evident that in this context, Amitābha has no special place as the object of a cult.

Returning to the earlier period, it is worth reiterating that we simply cannot be positive that even Amitābha in the Govindnagar inscription was the object of a cult. The image could have been named merely as one of the many buddhas to be venerated in the present rather than the buddha who greets devotees to be reborn in Sukhāvatī. We might equally have doubts as to whether *that* Amitābha is based on such central texts on Amitābha as the LSV or the SSV. It is equally likely that this particular Amitābha was either derived from other texts that mention Amitābha, though not as a central object of interest—for example, other major Mahāyāna sūtras, such as the *Saddharmapuṇḍarīka* (Dharmarakṣa's translation, Taishō 263.9.92a29, 126c8)—or that it had no such distinct textual basis. The reference to Amitābha is found in many texts from the early centuries of the Common Era. By the time of Buddhabhadra, who translated the *Wuliangshou jing* around the early fifth century, more than sixty texts in Chinese translations mention Amitābha in diverse ways (Fujita 1970, 141–144). There is no question, then, that Amitābha was widely known as a representative of numerous buddhafields conceived of by Buddhists during the early centuries of the Common Era. However, was it really the object of an ardent devotional cult? Intriguingly, there is little trace of it in tangible evidence, even if that were the case. Or was it largely treated as a "generalized religious goal"[51] that many Buddhists eagerly selected as an exemplar, even in

51. Schopen presents the idea of Sukhāvatī as a generalized religious goal in one of his early articles (1977). After examining a number of accounts that refer to rebirth in Sukhāvatī apparently in contexts not directly related to Amitābha in diverse Mahāyāna sūtras, he concludes that "rebirth in Sukhāvatī became a generalized religious goal open to the Mahāyāna community as a whole" perhaps as early as the second century CE with "not a large time gap between the appearance of the latter [LSV] and the beginning of the process of generalization" (1977, 204). Still, he admits that the Amitābha cult based on the LSV may have preceded the process of generalization. However, it is possible that, even in the supposed phase prior to generalization, ideas about Amitābha may not have existed as a cult to the extent we commonly presume. Interestingly enough, the exact same phenomenon of generalization is also observed in early Chinese Buddhism through dedicative inscriptions from the fifth to late sixth centuries (Kuno 1989). Only at the end of the sixth century can we detect an independent cult of Amitābha arising before it was institutionalized through textual interpretations and visual forms. Does this mean that Chinese Buddhists received the idea concerning Amitābha and Sukhāvatī in the form of generalization as it was in practice in contemporaneous Indian Buddhism during the fifth century and revived it as a separate cult more than a century after? I would imagine, instead, that ideas about Amitābha and Sukhāvatī never developed or were not established into a cult in

discourses of various other paths within the overall Mahāyāna? Was it perhaps like a magic city created by a guide (*nāyaka*) who leads a group of tired traveling merchants—in order for them to rest and gain strength to proceed to the ultimate destination—as in a parable told in the *Pūrvayoga* chapter of the *Saddharmapuṇḍarīka* (Taishō 263.9.92b16–c26, 94a2–b19)?[52] It is worth noting that this parable exhibits a remarkable resemblance to the account in the two earliest Chinese translations of the LSV of Śākyamuni leading the intermediate and inferior believers first to a pleasurable but interim place before they reach Sukhāvatī, which disappears in later versions (see p. 493 above). Having carefully read the LSV and the SSV, I increasingly wonder whether they are really about a cult, especially in the versions of the early phase. Our perceptions of Amitābha and Sukhāvatī have inevitably and immensely been affected by the flourishing of the Amitābha cult in East Asian Buddhism and, no less, in modern-day Japan, where devotion to Amitābha is both institutionally and personally prominent even among academics. We need, perhaps, to examine the ideas underlying Amitābha and Sukhāvatī in early Indian Buddhism from a fresh perspective rather than projecting back our knowledge of their consequent development in later East Asian Buddhism.

Works Cited

Abbreviations

CK	*Chūgoku kokuhōten* 中国国宝展 (*Exhibition of National Treasures from China*). Tokyo: Asahi shinbunsha 朝日新聞社, 2000.
E	Earlier groups of the extant versions of the LSV

Indian Buddhism before their transmission to China. After citing Schopen's suggestion in his discussion of the transmission and reception of the three major Pure Land sūtras, Fujita (2007, 506) criticizes it: "Although, surely, we cannot deny the presence of such aspect [as argued by Schopen], it is problematic philologically to conclude monolithically on diverse developments of the Pure Land thought in India solely on the basis of Sanskrit and Tibetan materials without consulting various accounts presented in a large number of texts in Chinese translations." Unfortunately, he fails to present his own interpretation of the phenomenon.

52. The verse part of the parable of a magical city describes the city in the familiar words of the guide: "Now I would rather exhibit supernatural power and magically create an extensive city with walls. I will decorate ten million people and build rooms beautifully adorned. I will create a great river, gardens, and bathing ponds where flowers and fruits will grow plentiful. I will decorate the towers, buildings, and walls with silk" (Taishō 263.9.94a2–b19).

KSH	*Kondō hekiga saigen kinen hōrūjiten* 金堂壁画再現記念法隆寺展 (*The Hōryūji Exhibition Commemorating the Reconstruction of the Murals of the Golden Hall*). Tokyo: Asahi shinbunsha 朝日新聞社, 1968.
L	Later groups of the extant versions of the LSV
LSV	*Larger Sukhāvatīvyūha*
Peking Cat.	*The Tibetan Tripitaka: Peking Edition: Catalogue & Index*. Edited by Daisetz T. Suzuki. Tokyo and Kyoto: Tibetan Tripitaka Research Institute, 1961.
SSV	*Smaller Sukhāvatīvyūha*
Taishō	*Taishō shinshū daizōkyō* 大正新脩大藏經 (*The Buddhist Canon in Chinese, Newly Edited in the Taishō Era*). Edited by Takakusu Junjirō 高楠順次郎 and Watanabe Kaikyoku 渡邊海旭. 100 vols. Tokyo: Taishō issaikyō kankōkai 大正一切經刊行會, 1924–1935.
Tōhoku	*A Complete Catalogue of the Tibetan Buddhist Canons (Bkaḥ-ḥgyur and Bstan-ḥgyur)*. Edited by Hakuju Ui, Munetada Suzuki, Yenshō Kanakura, and Tōkan Tada. Tokyo: Tōhoku Imperial University, 1934.
W	*Wuliangshou jing*
ZSDM	*Zhongguo shiku: Dunhuang mogaoku* 中国石窟：敦煌莫高窟 (*Chinese Caves: Mogao Caves of Dunhuang*). Edited by Dunhuang wenwu yanjiusuo 敦煌文物研究所. 5 vols. Beijing and Tokyo: Wenwu chubanshe 文物出版社 and Heibonsha 平凡社, 1982–1987.
ZSTM	*Zhongguo shiku: Tianshui maijishan* 中国石窟：天水麦积山 (*Chinese Caves: Maijishan of Tianshui*). Edited by Tianshui maijishan shiku yishu yanjiusuo 天水麦积山石窟艺术研究所. Beijing and Tokyo: Wenwu chubanshe 文物出版社 and Heibonsha 平凡社, 1998.
ZSYB	*Zhongguo shiku: Yongjing binglingsi* 中国石窟：永靖炳灵寺 (*Chinese Caves: Binglingsi of Yongjing*). Edited by Gansusheng wenwu gongzuodui, binglingsi wenwu baoguansuo 甘肃省文物工作队、炳灵寺文物保管所. Beijing and Tokyo: Wenwu chubanshe 文物出版社 and Heibonsha 平凡社, 1989.

Anālayo. 2008. "Uttarakuru." In *Encyclopaedia of Buddhism*, edited by W. G. Weeraratne, 8:460–461. Colombo: Government of Sri Lanka.

Bagchi, S., ed. 1967. *Suvarṇaprabhāsasūtra*. Buddhist Sanskrit Texts 8. Darbhanga: The Mithila Institute of Post-Graduate Studies and Research in Sanskrit Learning.

Bhattacharya, Ramkrishna. 2000. "Uttarakuru: The (E)utopia of Ancient India." *Annals of the Bhandarkar Oriental Research Institute* 81.1–4: 191–201.

Brough, John. 1982. "Amitābha and Avalokiteśvara in an Inscribed Gandhāran Sculpture." *Indologica Taurinensia* 10: 65–70.

Ch'oe Sŏna (Choi Sun-ah) 崔善娥. 2004. "Tong Asia 7–8 segi chŏnbŏmnyunin amit'abul chwasang yŏn'gu: Anapchi ch'ult'o kŭmdong samjon p'anbul ŭi tosanghakchŏk wŏllyu wa kwallyŏn hayŏ" 東아시아 7–8世紀 轉法輪印 阿彌陀佛坐像 硏究：雁鴨池 出土 金銅三尊板佛의 圖像學的 源流와 관련하여

(Study of Seated Amitābha Buddha Images Showing the *Dharmacakra-mudrā* from the 7th–8th Centuries in East Asia: In Relation to the Iconographical Origin of a Buddha Triad on a Gilt Bronze Plate from Anapchi). *Misulsahak yŏn'gu* 美術史學研究 (*Korean Journal of Art History*) 244: 33–64.

Fujita Kōtatsu 藤田宏達. 1970. *Genshi jōdo shisō no kenkyū* 原始浄土思想の研究 (*A Study of Early Pure Land Buddhism*). Tokyo: Iwanami shoten 岩波書店.

———. 2007. *Jōdo sanbukyō no kenkyū* 浄土三部経の研究 (*A Study of the Three Pure Land Sūtras*). Tokyo: Iwanami shoten 岩波書店.

Gómez, Luis O. 1996. *The Land of Bliss: The Paradise of the Buddha of Measureless Light*. Honolulu and Kyoto: University of Hawai'i Press and Higashi Honganji Shinshū Ōtaniha.

Harrison, Paul. 1998. "Women in the Pure Land: Some Reflections on the Textual Sources." *Journal of Indian Philosophy* 26.6: 553–572.

Harrison, Paul, Jens-Uwe Hartmann, and Kazunobu Matsuda. 2002. "Larger Sukhāvatīvyūhasūtra." In *Buddhist Manuscripts*, edited by Jens Braarvig et al., 2:179–214. Manuscripts in the Schøyen Collection 3. Oslo: Hermes Publishing.

Harrison, Paul, and Christian Luczanits. 2012. "New Light on (and from) the Muhammad Nari Stele." In *Special International Symposium on Pure Land Buddhism, 4th August 2011, Otani University*, 69–127. International Symposium Series 1. Kyoto: Ryukoku University Research Center for Buddhist Cultures in Asia.

Hida Romi 肥田路美. 1997. "Hōryūji kondō hekiga ni egakareta sangakukei no igi" 法隆寺金堂壁画に画かれた山岳景の意義 (The Significance of Mountain Landscape Painted in the Murals of the Golden Hall of Hōryūji). *Bukkyō geijutsu* 佛教藝術 (*Ars Buddhica*) 230: 91–114.

Higuchi Takayasu 樋口隆康. 1950. "Amida sanzonbutsu no genryū" 阿弥陀三尊仏の源流 (The Origin of the Amitābha Triad). *Bukkyō geijutsu* 佛教藝術 (*Ars Buddhica*) 7: 108–113.

Howard, Angela Falco. 1986. *The Imagery of the Cosmological Buddha*. Leiden: E. J. Brill.

Huntington, John C. 1980. "A Gandhāran Image of Amitāyus' Sukhāvatī." *Annali dell'Istituto Orientale di Napoli* 40 (n.s. 30): 651–672 and plates 1–16.

Huntington, Susan L. 1985. *The Art of Ancient India*. With contributions by John C. Huntington. New York and Tokyo: Weatherhill.

Iwamatsu Asao 岩松浅夫. 1994. "Gandāra chōkoku to amidabutsu" ガンダーラ彫刻と阿弥陀仏 (Gandhāran Sculpture and Amitābha Buddha). *Tōyō bunka kenkyūsho kiyō* 東洋文化研究所紀要 (*Memoirs of the Institute for Advanced Studies on Asia*) 123: 209–246.

Kagawa Takao 香川孝雄. 1984. Muryōju-kyō *no shohon taishō kenkyū* 無量寿経の諸本対照研究 (*A Comparative Study of Various Versions of the* Sukhāvatīvyūha). Kyoto: Nagata bunshōdō 永田文昌堂.

———. 1993. *Jōdokyō no seiritsushiteki kenkyū* 浄土教の成立史的研究 (*A Study on the Formation of Pure Land Buddhism*). Tokyo: Sankibō busshorin 山喜房佛書林.

Karashima, Seishi. 2017. "On *Avalokitasvara* and *Avalokiteśvara*." *Annual Report of the International Research Institute for Advanced Buddhology at Soka University* 20: 139–165.

Karetzky, Patricia Eichenbaum. 1997. "The Evolution of the Symbolism of the Paradise of the Buddha of Infinite Life and Its Western Origins." *Sino-Platonic Papers* 76.

Katsuki Gen'ichirō 勝木言一郎. 1992. "Tonkō bakkōkutsu dai 220 kutsu amida jōdo hensōzu kō" 敦煌莫高窟第220窟阿弥陀浄土変相図考 (On the Representation of Amitābha's Pure Land in Mogao Cave 220 of Dunhuang). *Bukkyō geijutsu* 佛教藝術 (*Ars Buddhica*) 202: 67–92.

———. 1994. "Chūgoku ni okeru amida sanzon gojū bosatsuzu no zuzō ni tsuite: Garyūzan senbutsugan no sakurei shōkai to sono igi" 中国における阿弥陀三尊五十菩薩図の図像について：臥龍山千佛巖の作例紹介とその意義 (On the Iconography of the Amitābha Triad and Fifty Bodhisattvas in China: Introducing an Example at Qianfoyan on Mount Wolong and Exploring Its Significance). *Bukkyō geijutsu* 佛教藝術 (*Ars Buddhica*) 214: 61–73.

———. 1996. "Shōnankai sekkutsu chūkutsu no sanbutsu zōzō to kuhon ōjōzu ukibori ni kansuru ichi kōsatsu" 小南海石窟中窟の三仏造像と九品往生図浮彫に関する一考察 (Study on Three Sets of a Buddha Triad and Relief of the Depictions of the Rebirths in Nine Grades in the Xiaonanhai Middle Cave). *Bijutsushi* 美術史 (*Journal of the Japan Art History Society*) 139: 68–86.

Kawahara Yoshio 河原由雄. 1968. "Tonkō jōdo hensō no seiritsu to tenkai" 敦煌浄土変相の成立と展開 (The Formation and Development of the Representation of the Pure Land at Dunhuang). *Bukkyō geijutsu* 佛教藝術 (*Ars Buddhica*) 68: 85–107.

Kim Hyewŏn (Kim Haewon) 金惠瑗. 2003. "Chungguk ch'ogi chŏngt'o p'yohyŏn e taehan koch'al: Sach'ŏnsŏng Sŏngdo palgyŏn chosang ŭl chungsim ŭro" 中國 初期 淨土 表現에 대한 考察：四川省 成都 發見 造像을 중심으로 (Study of Representations of the Pure Land in Early Chinese Buddhist Art: With a Focus on the Finds from Chengdu in Sichuan Province). *Misulsa yŏn'gu* 美術史研究 (*Journal of Art History*) 17: 3–29.

Kirfel, W. 1920. *Die Kosmographie der Inder nach den Quellen dargestellt*. Bonn and Leipzig: Kurt Schroeder.

Kuno Miki 久野美樹. 1989. "Zōzō haikei to shite no shōten, takushō saihō ganbō: Chūgoku nanbokuchōki o chūshin to shite" 造像背景としての生天、託生西方願望：中国南北朝期を中心として (Aspiration for Rebirth in a Heaven or the Western Pure Land as a Background for Making Images in the Northern and Southern Dynasties Period of China). *Bukkyō geijutsu* 佛教藝術 (*Ars Buddhica*) 187: 25–59.

Lefeber, Rosalind. 2016. *The Rāmāyaṇa of Vālmīki: An Epic of Ancient India*, vol. 4: *Kiṣkindhākāṇḍa*. Princeton: Princeton University Press.

Li Qiqiong 李其琼. 1984. "Suidai de mogaoku yishu" 隋代的莫高窟艺术 (Art in Mogao Caves of the Sui Dynasty). In ZSDM 2:161–170.

Lincoln, Bruce. 1983. "'The Earth Becomes Flat'—A Study of Apocalyptic Imagery." *Comparative Studies in Society and History* 25: 136–153.

Liu Zhiyuan 刘志远 and Liu Tingbi 刘廷壁. 1958. *Chengdu wanfosi shike yishu* 成都万佛寺石刻艺术 (*Art of Stone Carving from Wanfosi in Chengdu*). Beijing: Zhongguo gudian yishu chubanshe 中国古典艺术出版社.

Majumdar, N. G. 1940. "The Inscriptions." In *The Monuments of Sāñchī*, by John Marshall and Alfred Foucher, 1:261–396. London: Probsthain.

Matsubara Saburō 松原三郎. 1995. *Chūgoku bukkyō chōkoku shiron* 中国仏教彫刻史論 (*Study of the History of Chinese Buddhist Sculpture*). 4 vols. Tokyo: Yoshikawa kōbunkan 吉川弘文館.

Matsumoto Bunzaburō 松本文三郎. [1904] 2006. *Gokuraku jōdoron* 極楽浄土論 (*A Study of the Pure Land of Sukhāvatī*). Reprinted in *Miroku jōdoron, Gokuraku jōdoron* 弥勒浄土論・極楽浄土論 (*A Study of the Pure Land of Maitreya and a Study of the Pure Land of Sukhāvatī*), edited by Maeda Kōsaku 前田耕作, 211–364. Tokyo: Heibonsha 平凡社.

Minamoto Toyomune 源豐宗. 1926. "Jōdohen no keishiki" 浄土變の形式 (The Form of the Representation of the Pure Land). *Bukkyō bijutsu* 佛教美術 (*Buddhist Art*) 7: 60–73.

Mochizuki Shinkō 望月信亨. [1932] 1977. *Jōdokyō no kigen oyobi hattatsu* 浄土教の起源及び発達 (*The Origin and Development of Pure Land Buddhism*). Reprint, Tokyo: Sankibō busshorin 山喜房佛書林.

Muir, J. 1871. *Original Sanskrit Texts on the Origin and History of the Peoples of India*. London: Trübner & Co.

Müller, F. Max. 1880. "On Sanskrit Texts Discovered in Japan." *Journal of the Royal Asiatic Society* 12.2: 153–188.

Naitō Tōichirō 内藤藤一郎. 1931. *Hōryūji hekiga no kenkyū* 法隆寺壁画の研究 (*Study of Hōryūji Murals*). Osaka: Tōyō bijutsu kenkyūkai Ōsaka shibu 東洋美術研究会大阪支部.

Nattier, Jan. 2000. "The Realm of Akṣobhya: A Missing Piece in the History of Pure Land Buddhism." *Journal of the International Association of Buddhist Studies* 23.1: 71–102.

———. 2003. "The Indian Roots of Pure Land Buddhism: Insights from the Oldest Chinese Versions of the *Larger Sukhāvatīvyūha*." *Pacific World: Journal of the Institute of Buddhist Studies*, 3rd ser., 5: 179–201.

———. 2008. *A Guide to the Earliest Chinese Buddhist Translations: Texts from the Eastern Han* 東漢 *and Three Kingdoms* 三國 *Periods*. Bibliotheca Philologica et Philosophica Buddhica 10. Tokyo: The International Research Institute for Advanced Buddhology, Soka University.

Okada Ken 岡田健. 2000. "Shotōki no tenbōrin-in amida zuzō ni tsuite no kenkyū" 初唐期の転法輪印阿弥陀図像についての研究 (Study on the Iconography of Amitābha Showing the *Dharmacakra-mudrā* of the Early Tang Period). *Bijutsu kenkyū* 美術研究 (*Journal of Art Studies*) 373: 159–205.

Quagliotti, Anna Maria. 1996. "Another Look at the Mohammed Nari Stele with the So-Called 'Miracle of Śrāvastī.'" *Annali dell'Istituto Orientale di Napoli* 56.2: 274–289.

Rhi, Juhyung. 1991. "Gandhāran Images of the 'Śrāvastī Miracle': An Iconographic Reassessment." PhD thesis, University of California, Berkeley.

———. 2003. "Early Mahāyāna and Gandhāran Buddhism: An Assessment of the Visual Evidence." *The Eastern Buddhist*, n.s., 35.1–2: 152–202.

———. 2011. "Tosanghak ŭn chŏngmal chungyohan'ga? Milgyo ch'urhyŏn ijŏn pul-sang ŭi chonmyŏng kyujŏng/p'anbyŏl e kwanhayŏ" 圖像學은 정말 중요한가? 密敎 出現 以前 佛像의 尊名 規定/判別에 관하여 (Does Iconography Really Matter? Iconographical Identification of Buddha Images Before the Rise of Esotericism). *Misulsa wa sigak munhwa* 美術史와 視覺文化 (*Art History and Visual Culture*) 10: 220–263; a Korean translation of a paper for "New Research on Buddhist Sculpture," Victoria and Albert Museum, London, 8 November 2010. An expanded version of the English paper was published as Rhi 2023.

———. 2013. "Presenting the Buddha: Images, Conventions, and Significance in Early Indian Buddhism." In *Art of Merit: Studies in Buddhist Art and Its Conservation*, edited by David Park et al., 1–26. London: Archetype Publications.

———. 2018. "Looking for Mahāyāna Bodhisattvas: A Reflection on Visual Evidence in Early Indian Buddhism." In *Setting Out on the Great Way: Essays on Early Mahāyāna Buddhism*, edited by Paul Harrison, 243–273. Sheffield, UK: Equinox Publishing.

———. 2023. "Does Iconography Really Matter? Iconographical Specification of Buddha Images in Pre-Esoteric Buddhist Art." In *Gandhāran Art in Its Buddhist Context: Papers from the Fifth International Workshop of the Gandhāra Connections Project, University of Oxford, 21st–23rd March, 2022*, edited by Wannaporn Rienjang and Peter Stewart, 12–41. Oxford: Archaeopress Archaeology.

Rhys Davids, T. W., trans. 1899–1921. *Dialogues of the Buddha*. 3 vols. London: Oxford University Press.

Salomon, Richard, and Gregory Schopen. 2002. "On an Alleged Reference to Amitābha in a Kharoṣṭhī Inscription on a Gandhāran Relief." *Journal of the International Association of Buddhist Studies* 25.1–2: 3–32.

Schopen, Gregory. 1977. "Sukhāvatī as a Generalized Religious Goal in Sanskrit Mahāyāna Sūtra Literature." *Indo-Iranian Journal* 19.3–4: 177–210. Reprinted in Schopen 2005, 154–189.

———. 1987. "The Inscription on the Kuṣān Image of Amitābha and the Character of the Early Mahāyāna in India." *Journal of the International Association of Buddhist Studies* 10.2: 99–134. Reprinted in Schopen 2005, 247–277.

———. 2005. *Figments and Fragments of Mahāyāna Buddhism in India: More Collected Papers*. Studies in the Buddhist Traditions. Honolulu: University of Hawai'i Press.

Shastri, Hari Prasad, trans. 1957. *The Ramayana of Valmiki*, vol. 2. London: Shanti Sadan.

Tō Kengo 鄧健吾 (later known as Higashiyama Kengo 東山健吾). 1980. "Tonkō bakkōkutsu dai 220 kutsu shiron" 敦煌莫高窟第220窟試論 (Study on Mogao Cave 220 of Dunhuang). *Bukkyō geijutsu* 佛教藝術 (*Ars Buddhica*) 133: 11–33.

Tsukamoto Keishō 塚本啓祥. 1979. "Rengejō to rengeza" 蓮華生と蓮華座 (Rebirth on Lotus and Lotus Seat). *Indogaku bukkyōgaku kenkyū* 印度學佛教學研究 (*Journal of Indian and Buddhist Studies*) 28.1: 1–9.

———. 1996–2003. *Indo bukkyō himei no kenkyū* インド仏教碑銘の研究 (*A Comprehensive Study of the Indian Buddhist Inscriptions*). 3 vols. Kyoto: Heirakuji shoten 平楽寺書店.

Williams, Joanna G. 1975. "Sārnāth Gupta Steles of the Buddha's Life." *Ars Orientalis* 10: 171–192.

Wong, Dorothy C. 1998–1999. "Four Sichuan Buddhist Steles and the Beginning of Pure Land Imagery in China." *Archives of Asian Art* 51: 56–79.

———. 2008. "Reassessing the Wall Paintings of Hōryūji." In *Hōryūji Reconsidered*, edited by D. C. Wong, 131–190. Newcastle, UK: Cambridge Scholars Publishing.

Xiao Yue 肖越. 2013. "*Daiamida-kyō* no honganmon ni okeru 'nyonin' to 'in'itsu no kokoro': honganmon no seiritsu o chūshin ni" 『大阿弥陀経』の本願文における「女人」と「淫泆之心」：本願文の成立を中心に (The Reference to Women and Lascivious Mind in the Text of the Original Vows in the *Amituo sanyesanfo saloufotan guodu rendao jing*: With a Focus on the Formation of the Text of the Original Vows). *Indogaku bukkyōgaku kenkyū* 印度學佛教學研究 (*Journal of Indian and Buddhist Studies*) 61.1: 987–990.

Yoshimura Rei 吉村怜. 1985. "Nanchō no hoke-kyō fumonbon hensō: Ryūsō genka ninen-mei sekkoku gazō no naiyō" 南朝の法華経普門品変相：劉宋元嘉二年銘石刻画像の内容 (The Illustration of the *Samantamukha* Chapter of the *Lotus Sūtra* in the Southern Dynasties of China: The Content of the Stone Carved Relief Images Dated in the Second Year of Yuanjia of the Liu Song). *Bukkyō geijutsu* 佛教藝術 (*Ars Buddhica*) 162: 11–27.

Schism and Sectarian Conflicts as Revealed—and Concealed—in Indian Buddhist Inscriptions

Richard Salomon

Aśoka's Schism Edict

It is well known that schism (*saṅghabheda*) was viewed as a problem, perhaps even the single greatest problem, that faced the Buddhist communities in antiquity, apparently from the earliest times. But Indian inscriptions rarely—with one notable exception—allude directly to such problems. In several instances, though, conflicts between Buddhist monastic communities are alluded to indirectly or even revealed unintentionally in inscriptions. This article points out a few such examples and is dedicated to the honoree of this volume as a tribute to his groundbreaking achievements in revealing the historical realities of Indian Buddhism, often by digging out what is visible only between the lines of its records.

The "notable exception" referred to above is of course the well-known schism edict of Aśoka, whose text is recorded in varying forms on the pillars at Allāhābād (Kosam), Sāñcī, and Sārnāth, with a lengthy postscript in the latter version.[1] But it is not clear, and it has been debated at length for many years, exactly what instance or type of *saṅghabheda* this text refers to. The inscription opens with a phrase that, following Alsdorf (1959, 162), can be securely reconstructed as *(*saṃghe) samage kaṭe*, "The saṅgha has been made united." This clause, phrased in the preterite indicative, would seem to be a reference to a specific contemporary historical event—unless, as suggested by Norman in a footnote ([1987] 1992, 211n1), it means "The Order was made united (when

1. The literature on the schism inscription is too vast to be cited in detail here. Standard though outdated editions are provided in Hultzsch 1925, xix–xxii and 159–164, and Bloch 1950, 152–153. Important improvements and reconstructions of the several lacunae were offered in Alsdorf 1959. Further references are listed in Falk 2006, 160–161, 205, and 213–214 (to which should be added Tieken 2000).

it was founded)." But the rest of the text is prescriptive rather than descriptive, expressed with verbal forms in the future, optative, gerundive, and (in the Sārnāth version) subjunctive, as in the oft-quoted proclamation (according to the Sāñcī version), "One who would split the saṃgha, whether monk or nun, is to be clad in white robes and made to dwell in a place where monks and nuns may not dwell" (*ye saṃghaṃ bhākhati bhikhu vā bhikhuni vā odātāni dusāni sanaṃdhāpayitu anāvāsasi vāsāpetaviye*).

But whether the *saṅghabheda* referred to was a matter of procedural differences or doctrinal disputes, whether it affected only the saṅgha under Aśoka's immediate purview or the entirety of Buddhist communities in his vast realm, whether or not it was related in any way to the third council as described in the literature of the Theravādin school—these and other issues have been debated at length, but for the most part inconclusively. However this may be, this record, like Aśoka's inscriptions in general, stands out as unique, and nothing like it occurs in later inscriptions; for in terms of format, contents, and style, there is a near-complete break in the Indian "epigraphical habit" after Aśoka.[2] With regard to the topic in question here, schism is rarely if ever directly referred to in later inscriptions. Yet there are several later Buddhist inscriptions that hint at rivalries and conflicts between adherents of different schools and communities, and the rest of this article will be dedicated to the presentation and analysis of several such examples.

The Mathurā Lion Capital: Sarvāstivādins vs. Mahāsāṅghikas

An early and well-known but controversial instance occurs in the inscriptions on the Mathurā lion capital, datable to around, probably slightly after, the beginning of the Common Era. Even after many years of study and multiple editions and discussions,[3] the interpretation of this long Kharoṣṭhī inscription remains problematic and controversial in many respects, including with regard to the passages relevant to the topic at hand. I will refer only to the two most recent editions, by Falk (2011, 122) and Baums (2012, 219–222). It is now agreed (Falk 2011, 122; Baums 2012, 219n41) that the lion capital actually bears two separate inscriptions written at different times. The first inscription mentions only the Sarvāstivādins, as the recipients of a donation of relics of the Buddha Śākyamuni plus a stūpa and monastic residence (lines A14–16, *thuva ca sagharama ca caṯ<*u>dis̲asa saghasa sarvastivaṯana parigrahe*). The second inscription, which was probably added a decade or more later (Falk 2011, 134;

2. See Salomon 2009a.

3. For a comprehensive bibliography on the Mathurā lion capital, see CKI no. 048.

Baums 2012, 219n41), refers again to the Sarvāstivādins—three times—but also once, near the end, to the Mahāsāṅghikas. This reference to two schools in the same inscription is in itself highly unusual, and although the nature of the relationships between them that it implies is still controversial and uncertain, it certainly refers to some kind of rivalry or conflict.

The second inscription records another donation of land (*kadhavaro*, literally "camp") to "the Sarvāstivādins" but also refers twice to a particular Sarvāstivādin monk, one Budhila (*ayariasa budhilasa naḵaraḵasa bhikhusa sarvastivaṯasa*), apparently acting as the individual recipient on behalf of the Sarvāstivādins. The tract of land had been, according to Falk's interpretation (127), "separated . . . having taken it out of the *sīmā* (of the community to which it formerly belonged)" (*palichina nis̱imo karita*). The most important phrase for our subject (lines N3–4) is read by Falk (128) as *na mahasaghiana prañaviṯave*, "(It) must not be offered to the Mahāsaṅghikas [*sic*]," but by Baums (220–221) as *mahasaghiana prañaviṯave*, "[The act of possession] . . . should be announced to the Mahāsāṃghikas." The contrast between the negative in Falk's translation versus Baums's positive wording reflects different interpretations of the (unmarked) word boundaries. Baums, following Konow (1929, 48), takes the *na* at the beginning of line N3 as the last syllable of the word continued from the end of the previous line and reads *pa<*ri>gra/na*, whereas Falk reads the word at the end of line N2 merely as *pagra* and interprets it as "just a shortened version for *pratigrahe*"—that is, the usual term (*parigraha* or *pratigraha*) denoting the receiving of possession of a particular place or object by a monastic entity. Both readings are difficult in that they do not agree with the standard formulation, but I am inclined to favor Falk's interpretation on the grounds that taking the word in question as an abbreviated form of the usual term in the locative (i.e., as *pa<*ri>gra<*he>*) seems more likely than the nominative form of an otherwise unattested and etymologically unlikely *pa<*ri>grana*, "the act of possession."

A second issue with regard to the crucial phrase *(na) mahasaghiana prañaviṯave*[4] is the correct rendition of *prañaviṯave*. Falk, reading it with the preceding *na* as a negative command, translates "(It) must not be offered to the Mahāsaṅghikas," taking *prañaviṯave* (= Sanskrit **prajñapayitavya-*) in

4. Falk (2011, 128) introduced another important revision of this passage: "All readings later than Bühler" have a *ma* at the beginning of line N4, so that, for example, Konow (1929, 48–49) read *pragrana mahasaghiana prama ñavit(r)avave* "to teach the foremost Mahāsāṁghikas the truth." But Falk, on the basis of his direct examination of the lion capital in the British Museum (2011, 121), takes "this hook-like *ma* to be a break in the stone." Baums, apparently deferring to Falk's hands-on experience, accepts this revision without comment.

something like its characteristically Buddhist sense of "arranges, provides."[5] But Baums, taking the phrase as a positive statement, translates "should be announced," explaining in a footnote (221n46) that "the more literal translation of the verb as 'announce' yields a satisfactory meaning; the Mahāsāṃghikas were the predominant Buddhist group in Mathura at the time (Falk 2011: 132), and it was therefore particularly important that the new Sarvāstivāda monastery declare its existence to its powerful neighbors." Here, as in so many parts of this bewildering inscription, a completely satisfactory interpretation continues to elude us, despite the several improvements introduced in these two new editions. Neither Falk's nor Baums's translation of *prañavit̲ave* corresponds exactly with the particularly Buddhist senses of the verb *pra-√jñā*,[6] but Baums's "more literal translation" seems, in balance, somewhat more likely.

In any case, what is clear and what concerns us here is that the lion capital inscriptions explicitly refer to some sort of institutional conflict in Mathurā between the Sarvāstivādins and the Mahāsāṅghikas in or around the early first century CE. According to Falk's interpretation (p. 127), the phrase *nis̲imo karita niyat̲it̲o* (lines J1–2), translated as ". . . was presented, after having taken it out of the *sīmā* (of the community to which it formerly belonged)," indicates that "The donation process is twofold: first the land is removed from the *sīmā* of a monastery, then it is given."[7] Thus Falk (p. 132) depicts a scenario in which the Saka rulers, newly arrived into midland India from the far northwest, were patronizing the Sarvāstivādins, who had been prominent in their previous realm, at the cost of the Mahāsāṅghikas, who had hitherto dominated in the Mathurā area. Apparently, the Saka overlords, after first endowing a Sarvāstivādin monastery, some years later provided another such donation, and this one was (following Falk's interpretation) actually confiscated from another community—no doubt the Mahāsāṅghikas—and transferred into the possession of the Sarvāstivādins.

If the scenario presented above is correct, it confirms what we would have suspected *a priori*—namely, that shifts in the fortunes of the various Buddhist *nikāya*s depended to a great extent on winning the favor of local ruling elite, and that the competition for their favor was accordingly intense. From the prominent position of the monk Budhila, mentioned twice as the direct recipient of the second endowment, it would appear that individual monks

5. Edgerton, *Buddhist Hybrid Sanskrit Dictionary*, s.v. *prajñapayati*.

6. See for example the discussion in Oguibenine 1983. I am indebted for this and several other helpful references and comments to the anonymous reviewer of this article.

7. Here again, Baums's rendering is different: ". . . outside the monastic boundary; and (it) is offered by him."

who gained the ear of the ruler played a major role in the success of their institutions; and this is hardly surprising, as we can easily get the same impression from Buddhist literature.

The Wardak Inscriptions: Heretics and True Believers (?)

From a slightly later period—that is, during the glory days of the Kuṣāṇa empire in the second and early third centuries CE—we have several examples of inscriptions that can be interpreted as referring to disputes or disagreements between different Buddhist communities. The first case involves the Wardak (or Khawat) Kharoṣṭhī inscription (CKI no. 159), recording on a bronze bowl the dedication of relics of the Buddha Śākyamuni by one Kamagulyaputra Vagamarega, apparently a member of the ruling Kuṣāṇa elite, in his own monastery. Recently a semi-duplicate inscription recording a similar donation by Vagamarega's daughter has been discovered (Falk 2008a; CKI no. 509). Both inscriptions are dated in the year 51 of an unstated era, no doubt the era of Kaniṣka. Following Falk's now widely accepted epoch year of 127–128 CE, this would correspond to around 178–179 CE, during the reign of Kaniṣka's successor, Huviṣka.

These inscriptions refer, in one case fairly clearly, in another more controversially, to sectarian rivalry. The more certain example appears at the end of both inscriptions, in the last member of an expanded version of the standard declaration of the intended beneficiaries of the merit of the dedication.[8] In the first version, it reads *mithyagaṣa ca agrabhaga bhavatu*, translated by Konow (1929, 170) as "and may there also be a principal lot for the man of false belief," and by Baums (2012, 244) as "and may there be a best lot for the one who is wrong." The new semi-duplicate inscription adds the word *bahula* at the beginning of the phrase, thus reading *bahulamithyagaṣa ca agrabhagadae bhavatu*, translated by Falk (2008a, 74) as "Also to him who holds many wrong views shall be the state of pre-eminence," and more accurately by Baums (2012, 246) as "and may it be for the best lot of the one who holds many wrong views."

We are left to guess the identity of this "one who is wrong" or "one who holds many wrong views," but two points make it very likely that he is a member of a rival Buddhist school rather than some non-Buddhist (*anyatīrthika*). First, there is the example of the Mathurā lion capital, which records, at a slightly earlier period, a dispute that is directly presented as between two Buddhist schools. Second, the phrase in question in the first Wardak/Khawat inscription is followed immediately by an additional sentence (absent in the

8. On the formulae and contents of such declarations, see Salomon 2012, 188–194.

Figure 1. The Wardak (Khawat) bronze bowl. Note the fourth line ("This monastery is the possession of the Mahāsāṅghika masters") written in larger characters.

second), seemingly a sort of postscript, which is inscribed in much larger letters just below the three grooves around the circumference of the bowl that otherwise would have marked off the end of the inscription. This supplementary phrase proclaims, loud and clear, "This monastery is the possession of the Mahāsāṅghika masters" (*eṣa vihara acaryaṇa mahasaṃghigaṇa parigraha*). Here we can hardly fail to hear an echo of the debates and arguments that must have taken place between monastics belonging to competing institutions affiliated with different *nikāyas*, all seeking the favor of the ruling Kuṣāṇa elite. In this case, the Mahāsāṅghikas were presumably in competition with the Sarvāstivādins (as at Mathurā) and probably also the Dharmaguptakas, both of which schools are known from inscriptions to have been widespread in the Greater Gandhāra region (Salomon 1999, 167–178).

The second apparent reference to sectarian rivalry in the Wardak inscriptions is less certain. The phrase in question appears near the end of the text of the first version (again absent from the second version), as the member of the list of intended beneficiaries that immediately precedes the one discussed above. Konow (1929, 170) read it as *sada sarviṇa avaṣaḍ(r)igaṇa sa parivara ca agrabhagapaḍ(r)iyaṃśae* and translated "always for all who are not heretics; and may also the surrounding structure be for the sharing of the principal lot," taking *avaṣaḍ(r)igaṇa* as the equivalent of Sanskrit *apāṣaṇḍikānām*. But Falk proposed a revision of Konow's reading of the word he translated as "who are not heretics," *avaṣaḏigaṇa* (in modernized transcription), to *avaṣatriga*, on the grounds that "The shape of the letter *tri* is clearly different from *ḏri* found twice before" (2008a, 73).[9] This observation is justified on purely visual grounds, as the letter in question has a curved angle at the upper right corner like *tri*, rather than coming to a point as it clearly does in the other instances of the syllable *ḏri*. But the resulting reading *avaṣatriga* is difficult to explain; Falk suggests "either **āvarṣatrika*, 'umbrella-bearer', cf. *āvarṣa/varṣa* and *varṣatra*, or *ā varṣatrikānāṃ*, i.e. *ā* with genitive," but neither etymology is very convincing. Baums nevertheless translates accordingly: "and may it always be for the best lot and share . . . with all umbrella-bearers" (2012, 244).

But in view of the philological problems with the revised reading, it is tempting to retain Konow's reading *avaṣaḍ(r)igaṇa* and dismiss the slight paleographic inconsistency as a variant form or a copyist's or engraver's slip. If so, retaining the interpretation of the word in question[10] as "for those who are not heretics," we have a sense that perfectly anticipates the following reference to "the one who holds (many) wrong views." In this formulation, the sequence of beneficiaries listed by the donor follows a logical and more or less familiar pattern, beginning with the king, the donor's parents, his brother, his other relatives, himself, and all living beings. This is followed by a sort of postscript in which he also designates a large share of merit (*agrabhagapaḏiyaṃśa*), first to those "who are not heretics," and finally—grudgingly, it would seem—to "the one who holds (many) wrong views." It is striking that this last beneficiary, unlike the preceding ones, is phrased in the singular. Does this mean that it refers to a particular individual, perhaps a personal rival of the donor, or more likely of the monk who sponsored or solicited the donation?

In the end though, it remains uncertain whether the first Wardak inscription really does refer to "those who are not heretics." But it is clear that both of them do refer to "the one who holds (many) wrong views," implying an

9. I.e., in *gaḏigeṇa*, line 1 and *agrabhagapaḏiyaṃśae*, line 3.

10. In other regards, Falk's and Baums's interpretations of the passage are clearly an improvement on Konow's, but those details do not concern us here.

atmosphere in which the composer's compatriots were conceived and categorized in terms of correct versus incorrect doctrines. As we have seen above, these categories probably refer to groups and individuals within, rather than beyond, the Buddhist community as a whole.

Tampering with Inscriptions at Sārnāth: Sarvāstivādins vs. Sāṃmitīya-Vātsīputrīyas

While the interpretation of the instances discussed above as indicative of sectarian rivalries is admittedly open to question, we also have other cases in which strife between rival *nikāya*s is presented right before our eyes. I refer particularly to a few clear instances of inscriptions in which the name of one school that had been recorded as the original recipient of the benefaction has been erased or altered to that of another.[11]

A particularly interesting series of such altered inscriptions provides a unique window into the rivalry between the Sarvāstivādin and Sāṃmitīya-Vātsīputrīya *nikāya*s at Sārnāth. The materials concerned are seven related inscriptions in Brāhmī script and hybrid Sanskrit, dating between about the second and fourth centuries. In at least four of them, the name of one of these two sects has been changed or excised. Two of these inscriptions (A-1 and A-2 in the list below) were added onto the Aśokan pillar containing the schism edict discussed in the first part of this article. Two others (B-1 and B-2) are on a unique monolithic stone railing[12] located in a niche at the south side of the "main shrine." This railing "was hewn from one single block of stone and chiselled with that extraordinary precision and accuracy which characterises all Mauryan work. . . . The railing is in fact a remarkable 'tour de force', and was undoubtedly erected, in the first instance, on some especially hallowed space" (Marshall and Konow 1909, 89). Moreover, Falk (2012, 211–216) has plausibly argued that the railing is not only indeed of Mauryan antiquity but was originally an enclosure for the sacred tree at Lumbini marking the place where the Buddha was born, and which had been moved to Sārnāth at some later date.[13]

11. These examples were discussed briefly in Salomon 2009b, 11–18.

12. The railing is illustrated in Falk 2006, 214, figs. 22–23, and Falk 2012, 212, fig. 9.7.

13. Falk prudently begins his argument with the admonition that "This proposal is not as far-fetched as it may appear at first," and in what follows he does make a strong if not conclusive case for the origin of the railing at Lumbini. Possibly relevant to Falk's hypothesis are the three inscriptions prominently displayed (with some variation in the text) on three of the four gateway *toraṇa*s of the great stūpa at Sāñcī (Marshall and Foucher 1940, 1:340–342, inscriptions 389, 396, 404), warning that anyone who removes or causes to be removed any of the stonework (*selakame*, no. 404; *toraṇa vedikā va* "gate or railing" in no. 396) and transfers it to "another

Finally, the three remaining inscriptions in this group (C-1, C-2, C-3) are on the top steps of the south and east stairways on the Dhamekh or "Jagat Singh stūpa"—that is, the huge stūpa at the southern side of the archeological site. Thus it is evident from the outset that these three sets of inscriptions were recorded on monuments of particular importance and prominence, and this fact no doubt explains their unusual history.

In order to clarify the somewhat complicated situation, I list here the seven inscriptions concerned, together with a brief summary of their contents:

Group A: Inscriptions on the Aśokan pillar
- A-1: Ostensibly recording the possession [of the pillar] by the Sāṃmitīya-Vātsīputrīyas[14]
- A-2: Dated in the year 40 of King Aśvaghoṣa, recording the possession [of the pillar] by [name removed][15]

Group B: Inscriptions on the monolithic railing
- B-1: Ostensibly recording the possession [of the railing] by the Sarvāstivādins[16]
- B-2: Recording the possession [of the railing] by the Sarvāstivādins[17]

Group C: Inscriptions on the stairs of the Dhamekh stūpa
- C-1: Recording the possession [of the stūpa] by the Sarvāstivādins[18]

ācariya-kula" will be guilty of the five great sins, including causing *saṅghabheda*. The sense of *ācariya-kula* here is uncertain: N. G. Majumdar (in Marshall and Foucher 1940, 1:341–342) translates "Church," but Schopen (1994, 550–551) prefers the more literal "house of the teacher." In any case, these inscriptions do imply the existence—perhaps the prevalence—of another form of rivalry and competition between adherents of different institutions, including possibly different *nikāyas*—namely, the appropriation and reuse of architectural components or other physical objects.

14. Vogel 1906, 172 + fig. i-f; Sahni 1914, 30; Tsukamoto 1996, 896 (Sārnāth 3); Falk 2006, 214; Salomon 2009b, 118.

15. Vogel 1906, 171–172 + fig. i-e; Venis 1912; Fleet 1912; Sahni 1914, 30; Suenaga 1937; Tsukamoto 1996, 896 (Sārnāth 2).

16. Oertel 1908, 68; Marshall and Konow 1909, 96–97; Tsukamoto 1996, 928 (Sārnāth 168); Salomon 2009b, 118; Falk 2012, 213.

17. Marshall and Konow 1909, 96 + pl. XXX.iv; Salomon 2009b, 118; Falk 2012, 213–214.

18. Marshall and Konow 1911, 73 + pl. XXI.1; Tsukamoto 1996, 935 (Sārnāth 230).

C-2: Recording the possession [of the stūpa] by the Sarvāstivādins[19]

C-3: "Deliberately defaced" and presumably illegible[20]

Figure 2. Inscription (A-1) on the Aśokan pillar at Sārnāth (from *Epigraphia Indica* 8, plate between pp. 176–177, fig. i-f).

Inscription A-1 (fig. 2), on the Aśokan pillar with the schism edict, was originally read by Vogel (1906, 172) as *ā[cā]ryyaṇaṃ sa[mmi]tiyānaṃ parigraha vātsīputrikānāṃ* and translated "Homage of the masters of the **Sammitiya** (?) sect (and) of the **Vâtsîputrika** school." The obvious defects in his translation can be attributed to the less advanced state of knowledge of Buddhist epigraphy and history at the time. First, *parigraha*, mistranslated by Vogel as "homage," is now widely attested in Buddhist donative inscriptions as designating the recipients of the gift and translated as "in the possession of" or "in the keeping of."[21] The term is typically, as here, preceded by *ācāryāṇāṃ* plus the name of the *nikāya* with which the recipient "masters" are affiliated.

Secondly, Vogel's insertion of "(and)" in the translation is obviously wrong, since it is nowadays clear that *sammitiya-* and *vātsīputrika-* refer to the same *nikāya*—that is, the Sāṃmitīya-Vātsīputrīyas.[22] But Vogel did have some suspicion of this, remarking (172) that "Unfortunately the second syllable of the second word is uncertain. If the proposed reading be correct, it would afford an interesting proof of the correctness of a Tibetan tradition, according to which the **Vâtsîputrîyas** were a subdivision of the **Sammitîya** sect."

19. Hargreaves 1920, 129; Tsukamoto 1996, 935 (Sārnāth 230). Here Tsukamoto seems to have combined the nearly identical inscriptions C-1 and C-2 under Sārnāth 230. They are correctly listed as separate items in Shizutani 1965, 126 (nos. 1693–1694).

20. Hargreaves 1920, 129 (no published illustration).

21. Compare Salomon 2012, 194–195.

22. On the name of the Sāṃmitīya *nikāya*, its variant forms, its relation to the associated term Vātsīputrīya/Vātsīputrika, and the problem of which term is primary and which secondary, see Skilling 2016, 3–4, 21–22, and 46n1. I follow Skilling's adoption of the forms Sāṃmitīya and Vātsīputrīya as the standard spellings.

It is the peculiar appearance of the second word that particularly concerns us here. The second syllable was read by Vogel as *mmi* but placed in square brackets indicating his uncertainty. The next syllable, *ti*, is also blurred and somewhat misshapen.[23] *Yā* is more or less normally shaped, but the otherwise smooth and polished surface around it has been cut into and abraded.[24] The reason for the peculiar appearance of this word was shown by Falk: "A close look at the text shows that it has been reworked: an original *sarvvāstivādinaṃ* has been changed to *sammatīyānaṃ*" (2006, 214; compare p. 212, fig. 15). The peculiar shape of the syllables *mmi* (as read by Vogel) or *mma* (Falk) and *tī* is due to their having been altered from *rvvā* and *sti* respectively. The following *yā* appears more or less normal but occupies a wider space than usual because it has been substituted for the two syllables *-vādi-* of *sarvvāstivādinaṃ*. The first and last syllables of this word are, on the other hand, normally formed, since they are the same in the substituted word *sammatīyānaṃ* as in the original *sarvvāstivādinaṃ* and hence did not need to be altered.

If there were any doubt about the matter, the tampering alleged by Falk is proven by the wording *parigraha vātsīputrikānāṃ* at the end of the inscription. Normally in such formulae, *parigraha* would be the last word; that is, the usual order would have been **sammaḷitīyānaṃ vātsīputrikānāṃ parigraha*. Here, *vātsīputrikānāṃ* was obviously added after *parigraha* because there was not sufficient space in the original text before it, which had had only the single word *sarvvāstivādinaṃ*.

Inscription A-2[25] on the Aśokan pillar (figs. 3–5 below) is dated in the fortieth year of the reign of the otherwise-unknown[26] King Aśvaghoṣa. It is written in hybrid Sanskrit and Brāhmī characters of about the second century CE. The inscription was read and translated by Vogel (1906, 171) as ..... *rpârigeyhe rajña aśvaghoṣasya catariśe savachare hematapakhe prathame divase dasame*,

23. This is clearer in the photographic detail image shown in Falk 2006, 212, fig. 15, than in the estampage of the full inscription reproduced here.

24. This again is more clearly discernible in Falk 2006, 212, fig. 15.

25. This short inscription is presented here in three separate images because there is no published illustration of the text as a whole, as far as I have been able to determine. The beginning of the inscription is extracted from Vogel's image of the Aśokan edict; see the editor's (E. H. = Eugen Hultzsch) note in Vogel 1906, 171n3. The separate image of the end of the inscription will be offered below.

26. The only other record of King Aśvaghoṣa is a very fragmentary Sārnāth inscription on a stone slab (Vogel 1906, 172) that is too short to yield any useful information. Some speculation as to his historical position will be presented below.

Figure 3. Inscription (A-2) of King Aśvaghoṣa, year 40, on the Aśokan pillar at Sārnāth: beginning of the inscription (from *Epigraphia Indica* 8, detail of plate facing p. 168).

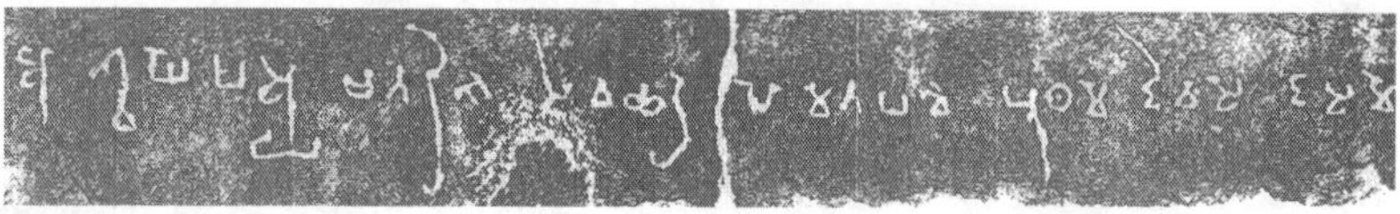

Figure 4. Inscription (A-2) of King Aśvaghoṣa, year 40, on the Aśokan pillar at Sārnāth: middle of the inscription (from *Epigraphia Indica* 8, plate between pp. 176–177, fig. i-e).

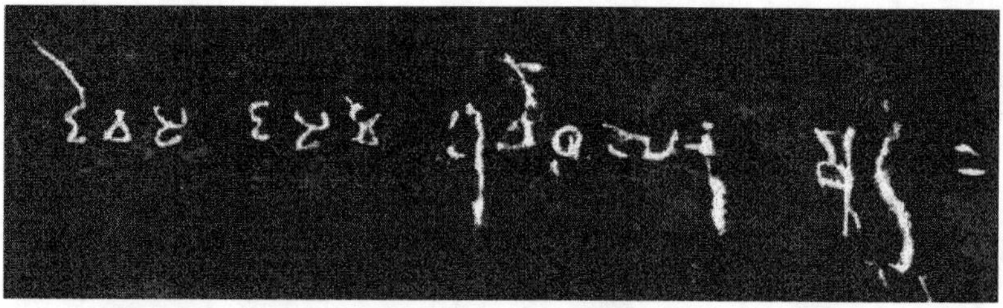

Figure 5. Inscription (A-2) of King Aśvaghoṣa, year 40, on the Aśokan pillar at Sārnāth: end of the inscription (from *Journal of the Royal Asiatic Society of Great Britain and Ireland* 1912, plate facing p. 700).

"[In the fortunate reign] of Râjan Aśvaghôsha, in the fortieth year, in the first fortnight of winter, on the tenth day."[27]

As for the beginning of the inscription, represented by him with ellipsis dots, Vogel refers to "the first word which is partly destroyed," suggesting that "it is probable that at the beginning there was some expression equivalent to the *vardhamâna-kalyâṇa-vijaya-rājyê* of later inscriptions." But, besides the (admitted) anachronism of this formula, there is not nearly enough room for anything like it; by comparison to the text that follows, there would have been room for about five or six *akṣaras*.

27. Here, Vogel seems to leave *rpārigeyhe* untranslated, instead of mistranslating it as in the preceding inscription.

It must be noted that, except for the illegible portion at the beginning of the inscription and the disturbed portion at the end (to be discussed below), the rest of the pillar face and the inscriptions on it, though incomplete, are perfectly preserved. It is therefore clear that the illegible section at the beginning, which Vogel described as "partly destroyed," was in fact intentionally defaced. This point has gone unnoticed except by Arthur Venis, who correctly observed that "Intentional injury would seem to have been the cause of . . . the complete obliteration of the opening letters of the Aśvaghosha epigraph" (1912, 702).

At this point, by comparing this inscription with A-1 (and with the other Sārnāth inscriptions discussed below, which will point to the same conclusion), we can make a good guess as to what word had been suppressed at the beginning of A-2: it was no doubt again *sarvvāstivādinaṃ* (or the like). Evidently, the "possession" of the Aśokan pillar had originally been granted, perhaps by King Aśvaghoṣa himself, to the local Sarvāstivādin masters, until at some later time it somehow came into the hands of the Sāṃmitīya-Vātsīputrīyas, who saw fit to adjust the record by obliterating one reference to their rivals (A-2) and altering the other one (A-1).

The following word in A-1, read by Vogel as *rpārigeyhe*,[28] is presumably to be understood as the gerundive of the verb *pari-√grah* (= Sanskrit *parigṛhya-*)[29] that is the source of the noun *parigraha* discussed above. I would therefore propose that the inscription originally stated "[This pillar] is to be put in the possession of the Sarvāstivādins, in the fortieth year of King Aśvaghoṣa," and so on.

However, in 1912 Venis pointed out for the first time that Vogel's presentation of the inscription was incomplete.[30] After *divase dasame* at the end of Vogel's copy, there are four or five more *akṣaras* (see fig. 5) and then, supposedly, two numerical figures. Venis read this as *sutithaye 4 200, 9* and translated "on the auspicious tithi, the fourth; in the year 209" (1912, 702). He explained the number 209 as referring to a year of the Mālava era of 58/7 BCE, equivalent to 151 CE. However, Fleet (1912) correctly criticized and rejected Venis's reading and interpretation (which Venis himself duly admitted was "frankly

28. Vogel's reading of the first syllable as *rpā* is phonetically unlikely, even given the aberrant sandhi sometimes found in Buddhist/epigraphic Hybrid Sanskrit (see, e.g., Salomon 1998, 84). The extra stroke above the right upper stem of the *p* is perhaps just an incidental mark or slip of the engraver's chisel rather than a pre-consonantal *r*.

29. In a footnote (p. 171n4), Vogel correctly associated this word with the root *grah* by reference to Pischel's *Grammatik der Prâkrit-Sprachen*, § 572.

30. According to Sahni (1914, 30n4), this was because the estampages that had been made available to Vogel were incomplete and did not show the entire text.

conjectural and invites correction") and presented a tentative alternate reading for the first word, "suggested to me by Professor Lüders" (1912, 706), as *sukhathaya* "for the sake of happiness." Fleet also doubted that the apparent numerical figures following this word indicated a date, concluding, "How the remaining letters should be read, I do not venture to say" (707).

Important for our purposes is Venis's observation that "the blurring of the letters which are the subject of this note"—that is, the concluding portion, which was missing in Vogel's edition—were also caused by "intentional injury." This suggests that we should look to the other erased or altered inscriptions, such as inscription A-1 discussed above, for an explanation of the partially obliterated words at the end of A-2. With this in view, it would seem that the defaced remnants of the first word in this group (following the undamaged *dasame*, visible in fig. 5) look rather similar to *ācāryānaṃ* or the like. The initial syllable, which Venis and Fleet/Lüders read as *u*, also matches quite well with *a* as it appears in *aśvaghoṣa* at the beginning of the inscription (figs. 3, 4). The next letter is comparable to the *c* of *catariśe*, and after it are what could be the remnants of a fractured *y*. This word, set off by a space, is followed in Venis's estampage with only two characters, and then two short parallel horizontal lines. Not much can be made of this, but on the basis of inscription A-1 we would expect *samma/itiyānaṃ* or the like. The first syllable could well be *sa*, although the second looks more like *ra* or *ri* than *ma*, and what follows is apparently incomplete. It would seem that this word was never finished (or perhaps incompletely copied in Venis's estampage?). Thus we can only guess, on the basis of the parallels, that the Sāṃmitīyas had obliterated the name of the Sarvāstivādins at the beginning of the inscription and replaced it, or intended to replace it, with their own name at the end.

But even if this is what happened, it remains to be explained why the altered reading at the end of the inscription was also, like the beginning, subjected to "intentional injury," in Venis's terms. Perhaps we are dealing with a back-and-forth battle here. For example, maybe the original reference to the Sarvāstivādins was totally obliterated by the Sāṃmitīyas, who tried to substitute their own name, but this in turn was partially vandalized but not completely excised by some other parties—most likely the Sarvāstivādins again, to judge from the other relevant inscriptions. It may be significant in this connection that although Venis was correct that both the beginning and the end of this inscription has been subjected to "intentional injury," the degree of the damage is quite different at the beginning and the end. This makes it seem that we are dealing with two separate acts of vandalism at two different times, as part of an ongoing struggle for control of the Aśokan pillar.

Whatever the details, it is clear that the peculiarities of the two inscrip-

Figure 6. Inscription (B-1) on the monolithic stone enclosure at Sārnāth (from *Archæological Survey of India. Annual Report 1904–5*, pl. XXXII.ix).

tions on the Sārnāth Aśokan pillar reflect a rivalry between the Sāṃmitīyas and the Sarvāstivādins, with the former group altering the text at the cost of the latter. In inscription B-1 (fig. 6) on the monolithic stone railing, we have another example of exactly the same sort of tampering—but in the opposite direction! This inscription was read in Oertel (1908, 68) as *ācā(*ryā)-naṁ sarvvāstivādinaṁ. . . . parigahetāvaṁ*, "Homage to the masters of the *Sarvāstivādin* sect." The reading is presumably due to Sten Konow, cited as "S. K." in footnote 1 on the same page, where it is pointed out that "the inscription consists of two distinct parts in different characters. The beginning belongs to the third or fourth century A.D. The final portion, *parigahe tāvaṁ* [*sic*], is older by about four centuries.[31] It appears that the first part of the earlier inscription has been erased, and a different beginning substituted."[32] In light of the inscriptions on the Aśokan pillar, it is easy to guess that the word that had been excised at the beginning of the inscription would have been *saṃmitīyānaṃ* or the like, and Marshall and Konow hinted at but did not directly state this: "[T]he facts show that the Sarvāstivādins must at that period have been trying to assert themselves as a prominent sect at Sārnāth. That they should have scratched out the name of some other sect and written their own instead indicates that their predominance cannot have been of long standing. . . . It seems therefore that the Sarvāstivādins and the Sammatiyas were both settled in Sārnāth about the year 300, but that the latter sect later on succeeded in asserting itself as the leading one" (1909, 96–97).

31. Falk (2012, 213) remarks on this point that "In fact, the difference in time seems to be much shorter," but he does not offer a specific alternative figure.

32. These observations about inscription B-1 were repeated and elaborated in Marshall and Konow in connection with their discussion of a similar Sarvāstivādin possession inscription, our B-2: "The end of the inscription discovered by Mr. Oertel is, however, quite different. It is written in a form of Prakrit, and in an older alphabet, which may be roughly assigned to the first or second century B.C. Now, the stone shows distinct signs of an erasure before the Prakrit portion, and the inference seems unavoidable that the Sarvāstivādins have substituted their own name for that of another sect, which they had previously struck out" (1909, 96).

In fact, although Marshall and Konow did not note it, the Sāṃmitīya hypothesis is supported by the empty space between *ācā(*ryā)naṃ sarvvāstivādinaṃ* and *parigahetāvaṃ*, which was indicated by ellipsis dots in the edition in Oertel 1908. This space (fig. 6) consists of a section where some *akṣaras* have been struck out but nothing added in their place.[33] The original inscription might have had here *vātsīputrikānaṃ* or the like, following the *saṃmalitīyānaṃ* that has been rewritten as *sarvvāstivādinaṃ*. The difference in length between the names of the two schools (*sarvvāstivādinaṃ* vs. *saṃmal-itīyānaṃ vātsīputrikānaṃ*) might explain the blank space, although there does not seem to be enough room for the full term *vātsīputrikānaṃ*; perhaps some shorter version of the name had been inscribed there. Moreover, there actually are some faintly discernible traces of the original *saṃmitīyānaṃ*, or some such reading, near the beginning of the inscription. For instance, the second syllable looks like it has been altered from an original *mmi* to *rvvā*, and the third *akṣara* was probably changed from *ti* to *sti*.

Figure 7. Inscription (B-2) on the monolithic stone enclosure at Sārnāth (from *Archæological Survey of India. Annual Report 1906–7*, pl. XXX.iv).

Finally, the last word of inscription B-1 was read by Konow (in the footnote to Oertel 1908, 68) as *parigahe tāvaṃ* (but correctly as a single word, *parigahetāvaṃ*, in the main text of the same page) and (mis-)translated as "Homage of. . . ." This can now be clarified by reference to *pārigeyhe* in inscription A-2. Like *pārigeyhe*, *parigahetāvaṃ* must be intended as a gerundive, with the suffix element *-tāvaṃ* representing a Prakrit equivalent of Sanskrit *-tavya* developed through degemination and compensatory lengthening (*-tavyam* > *-tavvaṃ* > *tāvaṃ*). Thus the inscription originally said, "[This monument] is

33. The visual impression is similar to that given by the Barabar and Nagarjuni Hill cave inscriptions of Aśoka and his successor, Daśaratha, where four times the name of the recipients, the Ājīvikas, has been chiseled off. But in these cases no other name was substituted, and the archeological evidence suggests that the caves were taken over by Hindus (Salomon 2009b, 121–122) rather than Buddhists, so that the case falls outside the scope of this article.

to be put into the possession of the Sāṃmitīya-Vātsīputrikas" but was subsequently altered to say ". . . of the Sarvāstivādins."

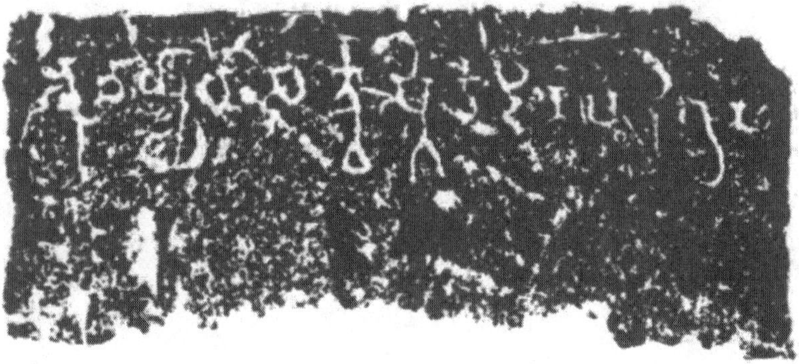

Figure 8. Inscription (C-1) on the south stairway of the Dhamekh stūpa, Sārnāth (from *Archæological Survey of India. Annual Report 1907–8*, pl. XXI.1).

Finally, inscription B-2 (fig. 7) on the same monolithic railing similarly records its possession by the Sarvāstivādins (*ācāryy[ā]ṇaṃ sarvvāstivādinaṃ parigrahe*). This one does not appear to have been altered.[34] It was presumably added to the ensemble at the time of, or after, the alteration of inscription B-1, as if to confirm the ownership of the Sarvāstivādins.

Turning now to the three inscriptions on the stairway of the Dhamekh stūpa: the first one, inscription C-1 (fig. 8), is inscribed "on the topmost step of the stone stairs on the south side of the Jagat Singh [= Dhamekh] Stūpa" (Marshall and Konow 1911, 73). The text, proclaiming the "possession" of the Sarvāstivādins, is virtually identical to that of inscription B-2 on the monolithic railing: *ācāryyāṇaṃ sarvvāstivādinaṃ parigraha*. The script, according to the editors, "may safely be assigned to the third, or more probably, to the second century A.D." (Marshall and Konow 1911, 73).

34. The inscription is divided into two parts, "one on each side of the central bar of the south side of the railing" (Marshall and Konow 1909, 96), which appear, at least in the rubbing on the accompanying pl. XXX.iv, to have a rather different quality, with the first part appearing thin and spidery, the second much thicker and firmer. But this may have to do with a different quality of the stone on the two crossbars, or may just reflect the quality of the estampage. I previously (Salomon 2009b, 118) suspected that this inscription, too, had "apparently been tampered with," but I now doubt that. However, Falk, who has examined the original inscription, notes my earlier remark and says that it "shows traces of reworking" (2012, 214), so the question remains open.

Inscription C-2 was found in an analogous position on the east side of the Dhamekh stūpa, "On the extreme right edge of the top step of the monolithic stairs on the east side" (Hargreaves 1920, 129). No illustration is provided, but the text is described and presented as identical to the previous one.

Finally, inscription C-3 is mentioned by Hargreaves (1920, 129), who reported that "On the right hand side of the sloping edge of the same stairs are traces of an earlier inscription deliberately effaced and probably by the Sarvāstivādins," with a footnote referring to Marshall and Konow 1911, 73. Hargreaves's suspicion is surely correct, and by comparison with the previous set of inscriptions we can confidently surmise that the effaced inscription (unfortunately not illustrated) had proclaimed the possession of the stūpa by the Sāṃmitīya-Vātsīputrīyas. Thus the situation corresponds to that at the monolithic railing: the earlier occupiers, no doubt the *ācārya*s of the Sāṃmitīya-Vātsīputrīya school, were displaced by the Sarvāstivādins at some time before the third century CE. The Sarvāstivādins marked their control by altering the Sāṃmitīyas' record and recording their own corresponding text in two duplicate inscriptions, deliberately placing them in marked positions on the "topmost step[s]" of the eastern and southern stairways of the Dhamekh stūpa.

In conclusion, these seven inscriptions provide testimony of a sectarian struggle between the Sarvāstivādin and the Sāṃmitīya-Vātsīputrīya *nikāya*s over three particularly important monuments at the Sārnāth complex. (Quite possibly other *nikāya*s as well were involved in the competition at Sārnāth at various times, although I have not found any direct epigraphic evidence of this.) Apparently the Sāṃmitīya-Vātsīputrīyas at some point and by some means wrested possession (*parigraha*) of the Aśokan pillar from the Sarvāstivādins, while the latter, perhaps by way of retribution, took over control of the monolithic railing pillar and the great Dhamekh stūpa from the former. Obviously, we are not dealing here with a trivial turf war but with a dispute over major symbols of authority—especially if Falk's interpretation of the stone fence as a relic of the Buddha's birthplace is correct.[35]

35. Such sectarian conflicts are of course by no means unique to Buddhism, nor limited to epigraphic evidence, and in some places similar archeological evidence of them has been noticed. For example, the south Indian Hindu site of Mahābalipuram (Māmallapuram) presents numerous instances of the erasure or alteration of images. In the Mahīṣamardinī cave at Mahābalipuram the features of the door guardian figures (*dvārapāla*s) have been altered from their originally Vaiṣṇava forms into Śaivite figures (Dehejia and Davis 2010, 7; Francis 2014, 188). The sectarian struggle that this implies is confirmed by the appearance, in four different locations at Mahābalipuram, of a curse on those "in whose hearts Rudra (Śiva) does not dwell" (*dhik teṣāṃ dhik teṣāṃ punar api dhig dhig dhig astu dhik teṣāṃ / yeṣāṃ na vasati hṛdaye kupathagativimokṣako rudraḥ //*; Dehejia and Davis 2010, 4; Francis 2014, 176). The holier the site, it would seem, the more bitter the conflicts over it, whatever the religion concerned.

This raises the inevitable question as to what authority or authorities it was that granted, or caused to be granted,[36] the *parigraha*, "possession," recorded in these inscriptions to the *ācāryas* of the Sarvāstivādin or Sāṃmitīya-Vātsīputrīya *nikāyas*. We are not told anything about this directly, but all that we know of such matters leads us to think of some secular authority, such as a king or his agent. In this connection, it is natural to think in particular of the mysterious King Aśvaghoṣa, of whom we really know nothing except the date, "the year forty" (*catariśe savachare*), attributed to him in inscription A-2 on the Aśokan pillar. Notwithstanding Venis's dating of this inscription to 151 CE, which has been rightly rejected, and although a regnal year of King Aśvaghoṣa cannot be completely ruled out, the typical Kuṣāṇa dating formula leaves little reason to doubt that the year in question refers to the era of Kaniṣka, to which "the name of the local ruler of the time was added . . . according to the established custom" (Vogel 1906, 172). Both the paleographic features of the inscription and the characteristic Kuṣāṇa dating formula by year (*catariśe savachare*), number of the fortnight of the current season (*hematapakhe prathame*), and day of the fortnight (*divase daśame*)[37] suggest this, and if so, the inscription would most likely correspond to about 167–168 CE.

But Kaniṣka era 40 ≈ 167–168 CE would have fallen during the reign of Kaniṣka's successor, Huviṣka, whose attested epigraphic dates range over the Kaniṣka era years 26 to 60 = ca. 153–154 to 187–188 CE. Thus we might have expected his name, rather than Aśvaghoṣa's, to be cited in the dating formula of this inscription. This makes us wonder whether King Aśvaghoṣa might have been an independent or at least semi-autonomous ruler in the area of Sārnāth in the second century CE, and such historical information as we have about this phase of Kuṣāṇa history makes this scenario plausible. For although donative inscriptions from the time of Huviṣka are very numerous (more than forty in all), they are heavily concentrated in Mathurā, with only a few outliers in the northwest and in western Uttar Pradesh. Thirty-seven years earlier, Kaniṣka's name had been cited in the dating formulae of three inscriptions on a particularly prominent set of images at Sārnāth from the third year of his reign,[38]

36. Note that the gerundive form *parigahetāvaṃ*, discussed above, is apparently causative, as indicated by the stem vowel *-e-*; that is to say, it is equivalent to Sanskrit *parigrāhayitavyam*.

37. See Salomon 1998, 174. The date of this inscription is, however, somewhat untypical of Kuṣāṇa dates in that the numbers are all expressed in words rather than in numerical figures as is the usual practice. There are, however, some examples of Kuṣāṇa-period inscriptions in which the numbers are at least partially expressed with figures, as in the Jamalpur (Mathurā) stone slab inscription dated as *savatsare 70 4 varṣam[ā]se prathame divase triś[e] 30* (Lüders 1961, 66).

38. These images are discussed in some detail in Schopen 1988–1989.

two of which also refer to local satraps, the *mahākṣatrapa* Kharapallāna and the *kṣatrapa* Vanaṣpara. But after this there are no other inscriptions mentioning Kaniṣka or his successors in the region around Sārnāth. Moreover, the year forty of inscription A-2 falls within a period during the first half of Huviṣka's reign in which inscriptions are very few; the total number between Kaniṣka years 36 and 44 (= ca. 163–172 CE) is only three. Skinner attributes this pattern to an economic downturn, perhaps even an "empire-wide recession" (2017, 102).[39] If this explanation is correct, it would not be surprising to find that in year 40, in the middle of this apparent crisis period in Huviṣka's reign, a local ruler in the Sārnāth area could have been enjoying a degree of independence—possibly even virtual or complete independence—from the contemporary Kuṣāṇa imperial ruler, such that he could presume to have dates of the imperial era recorded in his own name.

In this connection, the physical position of the two supplementary inscriptions vis-à-vis the original Aśokan inscription is also revealing. The inscription dated in Aśvaghoṣa's name (A-2) is, in Vogel's words, "incised partly beneath the Aśoka inscription, continuing, as it were, its short last line" (1906, 171). One gets the impression that Aśvaghoṣa, or his agent(s), was attempting to invoke the authority of Aśoka, perhaps even trying to associate it with his own authority, by continuing, as it were, Aśoka's inscription.

The other altered inscription on the Aśokan pillar (A-1) "is engraved to the proper left of the Aśoka inscription [i.e., after it] and above that of Aśvaghôsha's reign" (Vogel 1906, 172). Adding all of this up, a clear pattern emerges: the Aśokan pillar was granted to the Sarvāstivādins by, or under the auspices of, the otherwise unknown King Aśvaghoṣa at a relatively early date, in the second century CE. This act was recorded in an inscription that was presented as a sort of continuation of or coda to Aśoka's inscription. At some later time, the Sarvāstivādins' possession of the Aśokan pillar was confirmed by another inscription, adjoining the original one. Perhaps this additional inscription was recorded in response to some threat or challenge after the time of King Aśvaghoṣa.

As to the source of this challenge, there can be no doubt: it was the Sāṃmitīyas who were responsible for removing the name of their rivals in the old inscription and altering it to their own in the later inscription, in an act of *damnatio memoriae*. But we also know, from the forged inscription on the monolithic stone railing, that this was part of a wider competition and rivalry between the two schools. There, the Sarvāstivādins seem to be taking a sort of tit-for-tat revenge by claiming a monument that, following Falk's proposal

39. Compare also Falk 2015, 121–122 ("Huviṣka in trouble?").

that it was transferred from the birth shrine at Lumbini, may have been as prominent and numinous as the Aśokan pillar. After altering the text of the original inscription proclaiming the possession of the Sāṃmitīyas, they apparently added a second inscription confirming their own possession, just as the Sarvāstivādins had done on the Aśokan pillar.

The details of this sectarian conflict we will unfortunately never know, but it would seem that the Sāṃmitīyas were ultimately the victors, at least to judge by Xuanzang's report in his *Travels* (*Datang xiyuji* 大唐西域記) of "one thousand five hundred monks, all of whom study the teachings of the Hinayana Saṃmitīya school" at Sārnāth in the seventh century.[40] We cannot know exactly how this happened, and what we can deduce from the seven relevant inscriptions gives us only a vague hint as to the entire, no doubt complex story. But they do at least give us a rare insight into the turf wars between Buddhist *nikāya*s in antiquity, and they confirm, as expected, the central role of royal (or other elite) patronage in their outcome.

The Kura Inscription: Mahīśāsakas and Mahāsāṅghikas (?)

Another instance[41] of the alteration of the name of a *nikāya* in a donative inscription appears on the stone inscription from Kura in the Salt Range in the Pakistani Punjab, dated in an illegible year of the reign of the Hun king Toramāṇa—that is, around 500 CE. The purpose of the inscription is the dedication of a vihāra. Its conclusion (lines 11–12) reads, according to Bühler's edition and translation (1892, 240–241), *ayaṃ puna vihārasyopakaraṇa cāturdiśe bhikṣusaṃghe parigrahe ācāryamahīś[āsakānāṃ]*), "But this benefaction[42] by

40. 僧徒一千五百人。並學小乘正量部法。; Taishō 2087.51.905b16–17; translation by Li 1996, 196 ≈ Beal 1884, 2:45. Xuanzang also reports that the Sāṃmitīyas were dominant in neighboring Vārāṇasī: "There are over thirty monasteries with more than three thousand monks, all of whom study the teachings of the Hinayanist Saṃmitīya school" (伽藍三十餘所。僧徒三千餘人。並學小乘正量部法。; Taishō 2087.51.905b4–5; translation by Li 1996, 195 ≈ Beal 1884, 2:44). However, as was pointed out in Suenaga 1937, 112, Huili's biography of Xuanzang (*Datang daci'ensi sanzangfashi zhuan* 大唐大慈恩寺三藏法師傳, Taishō 2053) agrees that the Sāṃmitīyas prevailed at Sārnāth but reports that in Vārāṇasī it was the Sarvāstivādins who prevailed: ". . . more than thirty monasteries and over two thousand monks who were adherents of the Hinayana Sarvāstivāda school" (伽藍三十餘所。僧二千餘人。學小乘一切有部。; Taishō 2053.50.235c2, translation by Li 1995, 85). This contradiction might have arisen from a mere scribal error or textual corruption, but it could rather be an echo of a continuing struggle between the two schools in Sārnāth and neighboring places.

41. This case was discussed briefly in Salomon 2009b, 117–118.

42. This is Bühler's translation for *upakaraṇa*, which should probably rather be taken in the sense of "support" or "endowment."

a Vihâra (*is*) for the congregation of the monks of the four quarters, for the acceptance of the teachers, the Mahîśâsakas." But in a footnote (240n7) on the last word, he notes that "The *ma* of *mahīśāsakānāṃ* is abnormal and looks like *tma*. Nevertheless, the reading seems certain. The bracketed letters of the latter word and those following seem to have been written under a line of intentionally obliterated characters. It also looks as if the characters of line 13 [the last line] have been defaced intentionally." The area concerned is indeed virtually illegible in the rubbing accompanying Bühler's edition (see fig. 9), which as far as I have been able to determine is the only published facsimile of

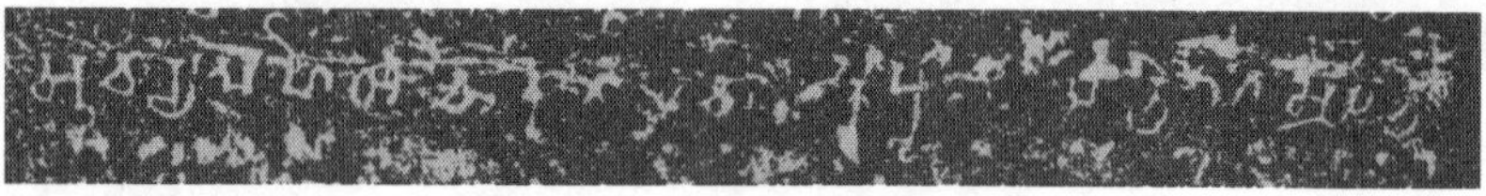

Figure 9. Detail of the defaced portion of the Kura stone inscription (line 12) (from *Epigraphia Indica* 1, plate facing p. 240).

the inscription, but his comments seem to be accurate.

As for the question of the original beneficiaries of the grant, our honoree (Schopen 2000, 15) has opined that "it is likely that the record originally read not Mahīśāsaka, but Mahāyāna." He based this suggestion on the fact that the inscription also contains—immediately before the passage quoted above—the "classical Mahāyāna donative formula" *sarvasattvānām anuttarajñānāvāptaye*, "for the attainment of supreme knowledge by all beings." But here I have to differ from our honoree, as I doubt that the original reading was *mahāyānānām* or the like, because (as far as I am aware) the middle term in the donative formula *ācāryānāṃ XX parigrahe* is always the name of one of the traditional *nikāya*s, and not "Mahāyāna" or one of its manifestations.

I therefore think it more likely that the original reading of the altered word was *mahāsāṃghikānāṃ* or the like.[43] Both of these schools, the Mahāsāṅghikas and the Mahīśāsakas, are well attested in Indian Buddhist inscriptions, including ones from the northwest,[44] and their names are similar so that it would have been a fairly easy matter to change the one into the other. Indeed, it seems possible to see some traces of the original syllables *-sāṃghi-* which were replaced by *-śāsa-*.

43. As has recently been suggested by Vincent Tournier (2018, 46n73).

44. See, e.g., Salomon 2012, 194.

With this, I conclude my brief exploration of the conflicts between *nikāyas* as revealed in Indian inscriptions. I hope that it will not seem inappropriate to end with a point on which I find myself respectfully differing from our honoree. However that may be, it is not the first time that we have disagreed on matters of detail, but the disagreements have always been stimulating, mutually respectful, and ultimately enlightening. I look forward to more of them in the future.

Works Cited

Abbreviations

CKI	Corpus of Kharoṣṭhī Inscriptions (part II of Baums and Glass 2002–).
Taishō	*Taishō shinshū daizōkyō* 大正新脩大藏經 (*The Buddhist Canon in Chinese, Newly Edited in the Taishō Era*). Edited by Takakusu Junjirō 高楠順次郎 and Watanabe Kaikyoku 渡邊海旭. 100 vols. Tokyo: Taishō issaikyō kankōkai 大正一切經刊行會, 1924–1935.

Alsdorf, L. 1959. "Aśokas Schismen-Edikt und das Dritte Konzil." *Indo-Iranian Journal* 3.3: 161–174.

Baums, Stefan. 2012. "Catalog and Revised Texts and Translations of Gandharan Reliquary Inscriptions." In Jongeward et al. 2012, 200–251.

Baums, Stefan, and Andrew Glass. 2002–. "Catalog of Gāndhārī Texts." https://gandhari.org/catalog.

Beal, Samuel, trans. 1884. *Si-yu-ki: Buddhist Records of the Western World. Translated from the Chinese of Hiuen Tsiang (A.D. 629)*. 2 vols. Trübner's Oriental Series. London: Trübner & Co.

Bloch, Jules. 1950. *Les inscriptions d'Asoka*. Collection Emile Senart 8. Paris: Société d'édition "Les belles lettres."

Bühler, G. 1892. "The New Inscription of Toramana Shaha." *Epigraphia Indica* 1: 238–241.

Dehejia, Vidya, and Richard Davis. 2010. "Addition, Erasure, and Adaptation: Interventions in the Rock-Cut Monuments of Māmallapuram." *Archives of Indian Art* 60: 1–13.

Falk, Harry. 2006. *Aśokan Sites and Artefacts: A Source-Book with Bibliography*. Monographien zur indischen Archäologie, Kunst und Philologie 18. Mainz am Rhein: Verlag Philipp von Zabern.

———. 2008a. "Another Reliquary Vase from Wardak and Consecrating Fire Rites in Gandhāra." In *Religion and Art: New Issues in Indian Iconography and Iconology*, edited by Claudine Bautze-Picron, 63–80. London: The British Association for South Asian Studies.

———. 2008b. "Kat.Nr. 177." In *Gandhara—Das buddhistische Erbe Pakistans: Legenden, Klöster und Paradiese*, edited by Christian Luczanits, 232. Mainz: Verlag Philipp von Zabern.

———. 2011. "Ten Thoughts on the Mathura Lion Capital Reliquary." In *Felicitas: Essays in Numismatics, Epigraphy and History in Honour of Joe Cribb*, edited by Shailendra Bhandare and Sanjay Garg, 121–141. Mumbai: Reesha.

———. 2012. "The Fate of Aśoka's Donations at Lumbinī." In *Reimagining Aśoka: Memory and History*, edited by Patrick Olivelle, Janice Leoshko, and Himanshu Prabha Ray, 204–216. New Delhi: Oxford University Press.

———, ed. 2015. *Kushan Histories: Literary Sources and Selected Papers from a Symposium at Berlin, December 5 to 7, 2013*. Monographien zur indischen Archäologie, Kunst und Philologie 23. Bremen: Hempen Verlag.

Fleet, J. F. 1912. "Remarks on Professor Venis' Note." *Journal of the Royal Asiatic Society of Great Britain and Ireland* 1912: 703–707.

Francis, Emmanuel. 2014. "'Woe to Them!' The Śaiva Curse Inscription at Mahābalipuram." In *The Archaeology of Bhakti I: Mathurā and Maturai, Back and Forth*, edited by Emmanuel Francis and Charlotte Schmid, 176–223. Pondicherry: Institut française de Pondichéry / École française d'Extrême-Orient.

Hargreaves, H. 1920. "Excavations at Sārnāth." *Archæological Survey of India. Annual Report 1914–15*: 97–131. Calcutta: Superintendent Government Printing, India.

Hultzsch, Eugen. 1925. *Inscriptions of Asoka: New Edition*. Corpus Inscriptionum Indicarum 1. Oxford: Clarendon Press, for the Government of India.

Jongeward, David, Elizabeth Errington, Richard Salomon, and Stefan Baums. 2012. *Gandharan Buddhist Reliquaries*. Gandharan Studies 1. Seattle: Early Buddhist Manuscripts Project.

Konow, Sten. 1929. *Kharoshṭhī Inscriptions with the Exception of Those of Aśoka*. Corpus Inscriptionum Indicarum 2.1. Calcutta: Government of India Central Publication Branch.

Li, Rongxi, trans. 1995. *A Biography of the Tripiṭaka Master of the Great Ci'en Monastery of the Great Tang Dynasty*. BDK English Tripiṭaka 77. Berkeley: Numata Center for Buddhist Translation and Research.

———. 1996. *The Great Tang Dynasty Record of the Western Regions*. BDK English Tripiṭaka 79. Berkeley: Numata Center for Buddhist Translation and Research.

Lüders, Heinrich. 1961. *Mathurā Inscriptions: Unpublished Papers Edited by Klaus L. Janert*. Abhandlungen der Akademie der Wissenschaften in Göttingen. Philologisch-historische Klasse, Dritte Folge 47. Göttingen: Vandenhoeck & Ruprecht.

Marshall, John, and Alfred Foucher. 1940. *The Monuments of Sāñchī*. 3 vols. Calcutta: Government of India.

Marshall, J. H., and S. Konow. 1909. "Sārnāth." *Archæological Survey of India. Annual Report 1906–7*: 68–101. Calcutta: Superintendent Government Printing, India.

———. 1911. "Excavations at Sārnāth." *Archæological Survey of India. Annual Report 1907–8*: 43–80. Calcutta: Superintendent Government Printing, India.

Norman, K. R. 1987. "Aśoka's 'Schism' Edict." *Bukkyōgaku seminā* 佛教學セミナー (*Buddhist Seminar, Otani University*) 46: 1–33. Reprinted in K. R. Norman, *Collected Papers* 3:191–218. Oxford: The Pali Text Society, 1992.

Oertel, F. O. 1908. "Excavations at Sārnāth." *Archæological Survey of India. Annual Report 1904–5*: 59–104. Calcutta: Superintendent Government Printing, India.

Oguibenine, Boris. 1983. "From a Vedic Ritual to the Buddhist Practice of Initiation into the Doctrine." In *Buddhist Studies: Ancient and Modern*, edited by Philip Denwood and Alexander Piatigorsky, 107–123. Collected Papers on South Asia 2. London: Curzon Press and Totowa, NJ: Barnes & Noble Books.

Sahni, Daya Ram. 1914. *Catalogue of the Museum of Archaeology at Sārnāth*. Calcutta: Superintendent Government Printing, India.

Salomon, Richard. 1998. *Indian Epigraphy: A Guide to the Study of Inscriptions in Sanskrit, Prakrit, and the Other Indo-Aryan Languages*. South Asia Research Series. New York: Oxford University Press.

———. 1999. *Ancient Buddhist Scrolls from Gandhāra: The British Library Kharoṣṭhī Fragments*. Seattle: University of Washington Press / London: British Library.

———. 2009a. "Aśoka and the 'Epigraphic Habit' in India." In *Aśoka in History and Historical Memory*, edited by Patrick Olivelle, 45–51. Delhi: Motilal Banarsidass.

———. 2009b. "The Fine Art of Forgery in India." In *Écrire et transmettre en Inde classique*, edited by Gérard Colas and Gerdi Gerschheimer, 107–134. Études thématiques 23. Paris: École française d'Extrême-Orient.

———. 2012. "Gandharan Reliquary Inscriptions." In Jongeward et al. 2012, 164–199.

Schopen, Gregory. 1988–1989. "On Monks, Nuns and 'Vulgar' Practices: The Introduction of the Image Cult into Indian Buddhism." *Artibus Asiae* 49.1–2: 153–168. Reprinted in Schopen 1997, 238–257.

———. 1994. "Doing Business for the Lord: Lending on Interest and Written Loan Contracts in the *Mūlasarvāstivāda-vinaya*." *Journal of the American Oriental Society* 114.4: 527–554. Reprinted in Schopen 2004, 45–90.

———. 1997. *Bones, Stones, and Buddhist Monks: Collected Papers on the Archaeology, Epigraphy, and Texts of Monastic Buddhism in India*. Studies in the Buddhist Traditions. Honolulu: University of Hawai'i Press.

———. 2000. "The Mahāyāna and the Middle Period in Indian Buddhism: Through a Chinese Looking-Glass." *The Eastern Buddhist*, n.s., 32.2: 1–25. Reprinted in Schopen 2005, 3–24.

———. 2004. *Buddhist Monks and Business Matters: Still More Papers on Monastic Buddhism in India*. Studies in the Buddhist Traditions. Honolulu: University of Hawai'i Press.

———. 2005. *Figments and Fragments of Mahāyāna Buddhism in India: More Collected Papers*. Studies in the Buddhist Traditions. Honolulu: University of Hawai'i Press.

Shizutani Masao 静谷正雄. 1965. *Indo bukkyō himei mokuroku: Guputa jidai izen no bukkyō himei* インド仏教碑銘目録：グプタ時代以前の仏教碑銘 (*Catalogue of Indian Buddhist Inscriptions: Pre-Gupta Dynasty Buddhist Inscriptions*). Kyoto: Heirakuji shoten 平楽寺書店.

Skilling, Peter. 2016. "Rehabilitating the *Pudgalavādins*: Monastic Culture of the Vātsīputrīya-Sāṃmitīya School." *Journal of Buddhist Studies* 13: 1–53.

Skinner, Michael C. 2017. "Marks of Empire: Extracting a Narrative from the Corpus of Kuṣāṇa Inscriptions." PhD thesis, University of Washington, Department of Asian Languages and Literature.

Suenaga Shinkai 末永眞海. 1937. "Rokuon ikuō sekichū tenka kokubun ni tsuite" 鹿苑育王石柱添加刻文に就て (Additional Inscriptions on the Aśoka Pillar at Sarnath). *Bukkyō kenkyū* 佛教研究 (*Journal of Buddhist Study*) 1.2: 108–112.

Tieken, Herman. 2000. "Aśoka and the Buddhist *Saṃgha*: A Study of Aśoka's Schism Edict and Minor Rock Edict I." *Bulletin of the School of Oriental and African Studies* 63.1: 1–30.

Tournier, Vincent. 2018. "A Tide of Merit: Royal Donors, Tāmraparṇīya Monks, and the Buddha's Awakening in 5th–6th-Century Āndhradeśa." *Indo-Iranian Journal* 61.1: 20–96.

Tsukamoto Keishō 塚本啓祥. 1996. *Indo bukkyō himei no kenkyū* インド仏教碑銘の研究 (*A Comprehensive Study of the Indian Buddhist Inscriptions*), vol. 1. Kyoto: Heirakuji shoten 平楽寺書店.

Venis, Arthur. 1912. "Note on the Sarnath Inscription of Asvaghosha." *Journal of the Royal Asiatic Society of Great Britain and Ireland* 1912: 701–703.

Vogel, J. Ph. 1906. "Epigraphical Discoveries at Sarnath." *Epigraphia Indica* 8: 166–179.

About the Contributors

Yael Bentor is a professor emerita in the departments of Comparative Religion and Asian Studies at the Hebrew University of Jerusalem. She enjoyed the good fortune of attending graduate school at Indiana University at the same time Gregory Schopen was teaching there. As a supervisor of both her master's thesis and PhD dissertation, Gregory Schopen was an enduring inspiration throughout her entire academic career. It began with an edition and translation of the *Adbhutadharmaparyāya*, a short text from Gilgit on tiny stūpas and images for the MA degree and continued with a study of Tibetan consecration rituals for stūpas and images as part of the PhD degree. These eventually led to her more recent studies, including the paper contained in this volume on the workings of Buddhist tantric practices. Among her publications are the recent *Ocean of Attainments: The Creation Stage of the Guhyasamāja Tantra according to Kedrup Jé* with Dr. Penpa Dorjee and *The Cosmos, the Person, and the Sādhana: A Treatise on Tibetan Tantric Meditation.*

Daniel Boucher is an associate professor of Sino-Indian Buddhism at Cornell University. He specializes in the study of early Mahāyāna traditions with particular interests in the use of early Chinese translations for the study of Indian Buddhism, Gandhāran Buddhism and the recent early manuscript discoveries from that region, and sociological and literary critical methods for understanding the emergence of Mahāyāna literature and the authorial communities that produced and circulated it. He has published articles in a variety of venues on discerning the underlying Indic source language of early Chinese translations of Mahāyāna sūtras and is the author of *Bodhisattvas of the Forest and the Formation of the Mahāyāna: A Study and Translation of the* Rāṣṭrapālaparipṛcchā-sūtra. He is also proud to count himself as one of Gregory Schopen's first students at Indiana University, an influence that has percolated through his academic career to the present.

Robert L. Brown is a professor emeritus at the University of California, Los Angeles, and curator emeritus at the Los Angeles County Museum of

Art. He studies the relationships among the art, cultures, and religions across South Asia and has published studies of regions from Afghanistan to Indonesia. His research is often object and monument focused, topics that he has pursued in his dual positions as curator of South and Southeast Asian art and as professor of Indian and Southeast Asian art history. His publications include *The Dvaravati Wheels of the Law and the Indianization of South East Asia*, *Southeast Asian Art at LACMA* (at seasian.catalog.lacma.org), and *Carrying Buddhism: The Roll of Metal Icons in the Spread and Development of Buddhism*. He has directed the PhD research of twenty-one students at UCLA, several of whom worked closely with Gregory Schopen.

SHAYNE CLARKE is an associate professor in McMaster University's Department of Religious Studies, where Gregory Schopen first formally embarked on his graduate training. He has taught courses on Indian and East Asian Buddhism and storytelling since completing his PhD under Gregory's caring and careful supervision at UCLA in 2006. He is a specialist in the study of Indian Buddhist monastic law (Vinaya), working primarily on legal texts—both canonical and commentarial—preserved in Sanskrit, Tibetan, and Chinese. The author of *Family Matters in Indian Buddhist Monasticisms* (2014), he aims to recover, among other things, lost voices and views from premodern sources, including those related to pregnant nuns and monastic mothers: Buddhist monasticism, but not as we have generally imagined it.

KATE CROSBY is the Numata Professor of Buddhist Studies at the University of Oxford. She previously held posts at King's College London and at the universities of Edinburgh, Lancaster, Cardiff, and SOAS. She studied Sanskrit, Pāli, Tibetan, Indian religions, and Buddhism at Oxford (MA and DPhil). She also studied at the universities of Hamburg and Kelaniya and with traditional teachers in Pune, Varanasi, and Kathmandu. She works on Sanskrit, Pāli and Pāli-vernacular literature, and Theravada practice in the premodern and modern periods, including on premodern meditation and its relationship to temporal technologies. She has conducted fieldwork in most countries with a substantial Theravada population. Her publications include a translation and study of Śāntideva's *Bodhicaryāvatāra* (with coauthor Andrew Skilton, 1994), *Mahābhārata: The Women and the Dead of Night* (2009), *Traditional Theravada and Its Modern-Era Suppression* (2013), *Theravada Buddhism: Continuity, Identity, Diversity* (2014), and *Esoteric Theravada: The Story of the Forgotten Meditation Tradition of Southeast Asia* (2020).

ROBERT DECAROLI is a professor of South and Southeast Asian art history at George Mason University. He is the author of *Haunting the Buddha: Indian Popular Religions and the Formation of Buddhism* and various articles and book chapters. Most of this work addresses early (third century BCE to fifth century CE) aspects of South Asian material culture and Buddhist interactions with devotion to terrestrial deities. His second book, *Image Problems: The Origin and Development of the Buddha's Image in Early South Asia*, explores the origin of the Buddha image and the social, political, and religious factors that led to its codification and spread. Recently, he co-curated *Encountering the Buddha: Art and Practice across Asia* at the Smithsonian Institution's National Museum of Asian Art. He has been awarded a Getty Research Institute Fellowship and the Robert H. N. Ho Family Foundation Research Fellowship.

JENS-UWE HARTMANN was first professor of Tibetology at Humboldt University in Berlin (1995–1999) and then professor of Indology at the University of Munich (1999–2018). He is a full member of the Bavarian Academy of Sciences and a corresponding member of the Austrian Academy of Sciences. His research focuses on the recovery and reconstruction of Indian Buddhist literature based on Indic manuscripts and Chinese and Tibetan translations. Within this field, he pays particular attention to poetic works and canonical sūtra literature. Among his publications are an edition of the *Varṇārhavarṇastotra* of Mātṛceṭa (1987), a study of the Dīrghāgama of the Sarvāstivādins (1991), the coauthored series Buddhist Manuscripts, devoted to the publication of ancient Indic manuscripts from Afghanistan (2000, 2002, 2006, 2016), and the coedited conference volume *From Birch Bark to Digital Data: Recent Advances in Buddhist Manuscript Research* (2014).

STEPHANIE W. JAMISON is Distinguished Professor of Asian Languages and Cultures and of Indo-European Studies at UCLA. She focuses primarily on ancient Indo-Iranian languages and texts, especially (Vedic) Sanskrit, Middle-Indo-Aryan, and Avestan. She works not only on language and linguistics but also on literature and poetics, religion and law, mythology and ritual, and gender studies in these languages, and comparative mythology and poetics, especially with Greek materials. Of her reasonably numerous articles and books, her most substantial publication is the English translation (with Joel P. Brereton) of the *Ṛg Veda*, the oldest Sanskrit text. She has enjoyed being Greg Schopen's colleague at UCLA for more than twenty years.

PETRA KIEFFER-PÜLZ is an independent scholar. Her primary fields of interest include the cultural history and literature of South and Southeast Asian Buddhism with a special focus on Pāli literature and Buddhist monastic traditions (Vinaya). Besides numerous articles and reviews, her authored and co-translated works include *Die Sīmā* (1992), *Verlorene Gaṇṭhipadas* (2013), *Overcoming Doubts (Kaṅkhāvitaraṇī)* (2018), and *A Manual of the Adornment of the Monastic Boundary* (2021).

RYŌJI KISHINO is a lecturer at Kyoto Pharmaceutical University. He received his BA (2004) and MA (2006) in Buddhist studies from Kyoto University in Japan and his PhD (2013) from UCLA under the supervision of Gregory Schopen. His research focuses on the daily lives and religious activities of Buddhist monks and nuns and primarily explores Buddhist monastic law codes (Vinaya) preserved in Chinese, Indic languages (Pāli and Sanskrit), and Tibetan. Currently he is investigating how the *Mūlasarvāstivāda-vinaya* and one of its major handbooks, the *Vinayasaṃgraha*, were transmitted and circulated in Japanese and Tibetan Buddhist traditions, as well as studying writings on those texts by Japanese Edo-period scholar-monks such as Gakunyo 學如 (1716–1773) and Mitsumon 密門 (1719–1788) and the Tibetan polymath Bu ston (1290–1364).

DIEGO LOUKOTA SANCLEMENTE† (1985–2024) was an assistant professor of Indian and Central Asian Buddhism at UCLA. He handled sources in a variety of languages (Sanskrit, Gāndhārī, Khotanese, Tocharian, Chinese), with a special interest in still-unedited documents, and his research attempted to integrate the insights gleaned from this corpus with archeology, epigraphy, art history, and premodern historiography in order to gain an image of the role of Buddhism in culture and society within the multicultural mosaic of the continental Silk Road. He completed his PhD in Buddhist studies under Gregory Schopen, with whom he learned oodles, agreed and disagreed in equal measure, and whom he came to love deeply.

JASON MCCOMBS is an associate professor of religious studies at Santa Fe College, where he teaches courses on Asian religions, American religions, challenges in contemporary religious communities, theory and methodology in religious studies, and Asian humanities. His research interests include Mahāyāna Buddhist history in India, Mahāyāna sūtra and śāstra literature, Indian epigraphy, religious and social identity, and religious giving. He studied under Gregory Schopen at UCLA.

NICOLAS MORRISSEY is an associate professor of Asian art history and religion in the Lamar Dodd School of Art at the University of Georgia. His research interests include the relationship between visual culture and religious change in ancient and medieval South Asia, the emergence of Mahāyāna Buddhism, and the dialectical interactions between Buddhist and non-Buddhist religious traditions in South Asia. He was a student of Gregory Schopen at both the University of Texas at Austin and the University of California, Los Angeles, though it should be noted that he almost certainly learned more from "the Boss" on the basketball court than in the classroom.

PATRICK OLIVELLE is a professor emeritus at the University of Texas at Austin and a past president of the American Oriental Society. He was awarded the honorary doctorate of Humane Letters by the University of Chicago in 2016 and elected to the American Academy of Arts and Sciences in 2020. His current research focuses on the Indian legal tradition and Emperor Aśoka. His recent publications include *A Dharma Reader: Classical Indian Law*, *Kauṭilya's* Arthaśāstra, *Viṣṇu's Code of Law: A Critical Edition and Translation of the Vaiṣṇava-Dharmaśāstra*, and *Yājñavalkya: A Treatise on Dharma*. His latest book, *Ashoka: Portrait of a Philosopher King*, is a biography of Aśoka based on his inscriptional corpus.

JUHYUNG RHI is a professor of art history at Seoul National University and specializes in Buddhist art focusing on the traditions of early India, Central Asia, and Korea. During his doctoral work in the 1980s, he was fascinated by Schopen's inspiring works, which he found very different from other writings in Buddhist studies of the period. Since then, he has been a great admirer of Schopen and profoundly affected by his scholarship. Although he may not agree with all of Schopen's interpretations, he shares a number of important ideas with him, one of which is presented in his contribution to this volume.

RICHARD SALOMON is a professor emeritus in the University of Washington, where he taught Sanskrit and related Indological subjects in the Department of Asian Languages and Literature between 1978 and 2022. His specializations include Indian epigraphy, Gāndhārī language and Gandhāran manuscripts and inscriptions, Buddhist literature in Sanskrit and Hybrid Sanskrit, and classical Sanskrit literature. Since 1974 he has published seven books and over 170 articles on these and other Indological subjects. These include two articles cowritten with Gregory Schopen, who has been a source of intellectual stimulation and illumination for many decades and continues to be so.

SHIZUKA SASAKI is a distinguished professor of Buddhism at Hanazono University specializing in the study of Vinaya and Abhidharma and the relationship between Buddhism and science. Currently, he is interested in the method of elucidating the process of the Vinaya's formation by examining the mistakes made by the compilers of the Vinaya. To show as many people as possible how interesting and important Buddhism is, he continues to distribute videos on Youtube, with over five hundred videos currently. He has published more than twenty books, including *What Is Buddhist Ordination?*, *The Transformations of Indian Buddhism: Why Has Buddhism Become so Diversified?*, and *The Rhinoceros Horns: The Basic Relation between Buddhism and Modern Science.*

ANDREW SKILTON is a Fellow of the Faculty of Asian and Middle Eastern Studies at Oxford University and teaches Pāli and Buddhist Sanskrit literature there. His current interests include the exegesis of Pāli and Sanskrit Buddhist texts, the character of premodern Theravāda meditation, and a lingering amour with the *Samādhirāja-sūtra*. His most recent writing includes a four-part study of the Vinaya rule prohibiting surgery, a vindication of Ciñcā, the vagrant girl, and an interpretation of the *Upāḷi-sutta* as psychodrama. When not watching Netflix, he studies the psychology of the Patterdale Terrier. He first met Gregory Schopen in Oxford in 1996 but also recalls even more vividly, some ten years before that, the very first time he read Gregory's formative 1975 article, "The Phrase '*sa pṛthivīpradeśaś caityabhūto bhavet*' in the *Vajracchedikā*: Notes on the Cult of the Book in the Mahāyāna," which planted the seed idea that research might be interesting.

Studies in Indian and Tibetan Buddhism
Titles Previously Published

Among Tibetan Texts
History and Literature of the Himalayan Plateau
E. Gene Smith

Approaching the Great Perfection
Simultaneous and Gradual Methods of Dzogchen Practice in the Longchen Nyingtig
Sam van Schaik

Authorized Lives
Biography and the Early Formation of Geluk Identity
Elijah S. Ary

The Buddha's Single Intention
Drigung Kyobpa Jikten Sumgön's Vajra Statements of the Early Kagyü Tradition
Jan-Ulrich Sobisch

Buddhism Between Tibet and China
Edited by Matthew T. Kapstein

The Buddhist Philosophy of the Middle
Essays on Indian and Tibetan Madhyamaka
David Seyfort Ruegg

Buddhist Teaching in India
Johannes Bronkhorst

A Direct Path to the Buddha Within
Gö Lotsāwa's Mahāmudrā Interpretation of the Ratnagotravibhāga
Klaus-Dieter Mathes

The Essence of the Ocean of Attainments
The Creation Stage of the Guhyasamāja Tantra according to Paṇchen Losang Chökyi Gyaltsen
Translated by Yael Bentor and Penpa Dorjee

Foundations of Dharmakīrti's Philosophy
John D. Dunne

Freedom from Extremes
Gorampa's "Distinguishing the Views" and the Polemics of Emptiness
José Ignacio Cabezón and Geshe Lobsang Dargyay

Himalayan Passages
Tibetan and Newar Studies in Honor of Hubert Decleer
Edited by Benjamin Bogin and Andrew Quintman

Histories of Tibet
Essays in Honor of Leonard W. J. van der Kuijp
Edited by Kurtis R. Schaeffer, Jue Liang, and William A. McGrath

How Do Mādhyamikas Think?
And Other Essays on the Buddhist Philosophy of the Middle
Tom J. F. Tillemans

Jewels of the Middle Way
The Madhyamaka Legacy of Atiśa and His Early Tibetan Followers
James B. Apple

Living Treasure
Tibetan and Buddhist Studies in Honor of Janet Gyatso
Edited by Holly Gayley and Andrew Quintman

Luminous Lives
The Story of the Early Masters of the Lam 'bras Tradition in Tibet
Cyrus Stearns

Mind Seeing Mind
Mahāmudrā and the Geluk Tradition of Tibetan Buddhism
Roger R. Jackson

Mipham's Beacon of Certainty
Illuminating the View of Dzogchen, the Great Perfection
John Whitney Pettit

Ocean of Attainments
The Creation Stage of the Guhyasamāja Tantra according to Khedrup Jé
Translated by Yael Bentor and Penpa Dorjee

Omniscience and the Rhetoric of Reason
Śāntarakṣita and Kamalaśīla on Rationality, Argumentation, and Religious Authority
Sara L. McClintock

Reason's Traces
Identity and Interpretation in Indian and Tibetan Buddhist Thought
Matthew T. Kapstein

Reasons and Lives in Buddhist Traditions
Studies in Honor of Matthew Kapstein
Edited by Dan Arnold, Cécile Ducher, and Pierre-Julien Harter

Remembering the Lotus-Born
Padmasambhava in the History of Tibet's Golden Age
Daniel A. Hirshberg

Resurrecting Candrakīrti
Disputes in the Tibetan Creation of Prāsaṅgika
Kevin A. Vose

Saraha's Spontaneous Songs
With the Commentaries by Advayavajra and Mokṣākaragupta
Klaus-Dieter Mathes and Péter-Dániel Szántó

Scripture, Logic, Language
Essays on Dharmakīrti and His Tibetan Successors
Tom J. F. Tillemans

Sexuality in Classical South Asian Buddhism
José I. Cabezón

The Svātantrika-Prāsaṅgika Distinction
What Difference Does a Difference Make?
Edited by Georges Dreyfus and Sara McClintock

Vajrayoginī
Her Visualizations, Rituals, and Forms
Elizabeth English

About Wisdom Publications

Wisdom Publications is the leading publisher of classic and contemporary Buddhist books and practical works on mindfulness. To learn more about us or to explore our other books, please visit our website at wisdom.org or contact us at the address below.

Wisdom Publications
132 Perry Street
New York, NY 10014

We are a 501(c)(3) organization, and donations in support of our mission are tax deductible.

Wisdom Publications is affiliated with the Foundation for the Preservation of the Mahayana Tradition (FPMT).